Lecture Notes in Computer Science 13314

More information about this series at https://link.springer.com/bookseries/558

Pei-Luen Patrick Rau (Ed.)

Cross-Cultural Design

Product and Service Design, Mobility and Automotive Design, Cities, Urban Areas, and Intelligent Environments Design

14th International Conference, CCD 2022
Held as Part of the 24th HCI International Conference, HCII 2022
Virtual Event, June 26 – July 1, 2022
Proceedings, Part IV

Springer

Editor
Pei-Luen Patrick Rau
Tsinghua University
Beijing, China

ISSN 0302-9743 ISSN 1611-3349 (electronic)
Lecture Notes in Computer Science
ISBN 978-3-031-06052-6 ISBN 978-3-031-06053-3 (eBook)
https://doi.org/10.1007/978-3-031-06053-3

This Springer imprint is published by the registered company Springer Nature Switzerland AG
The registered company address is: Gewerbestrasse 11, 6330 Cham, Switzerland

Foreword

Human-computer interaction (HCI) is acquiring an ever-increasing scientific and industrial importance, as well as having more impact on people's everyday life, as an ever-growing number of human activities are progressively moving from the physical to the digital world. This process, which has been ongoing for some time now, has been dramatically accelerated by the COVID-19 pandemic. The HCI International (HCII) conference series, held yearly, aims to respond to the compelling need to advance the exchange of knowledge and research and development efforts on the human aspects of design and use of computing systems.

The 24th International Conference on Human-Computer Interaction, HCI International 2022 (HCII 2022), was planned to be held at the Gothia Towers Hotel and Swedish Exhibition & Congress Centre, Göteborg, Sweden, during June 26 to July 1, 2022. Due to the COVID-19 pandemic and with everyone's health and safety in mind, HCII 2022 was organized and run as a virtual conference. It incorporated the 21 thematic areas and affiliated conferences listed on the following page.

A total of 5583 individuals from academia, research institutes, industry, and governmental agencies from 88 countries submitted contributions, and 1276 papers and 275 posters were included in the proceedings to appear just before the start of the conference. The contributions thoroughly cover the entire field of human-computer interaction, addressing major advances in knowledge and effective use of computers in a variety of application areas. These papers provide academics, researchers, engineers, scientists, practitioners, and students with state-of-the-art information on the most recent advances in HCI. The volumes constituting the set of proceedings to appear before the start of the conference are listed in the following pages.

The HCI International (HCII) conference also offers the option of 'Late Breaking Work' which applies both for papers and posters, and the corresponding volume(s) of the proceedings will appear after the conference. Full papers will be included in the 'HCII 2022 - Late Breaking Papers' volumes of the proceedings to be published in the Springer LNCS series, while 'Poster Extended Abstracts' will be included as short research papers in the 'HCII 2022 - Late Breaking Posters' volumes to be published in the Springer CCIS series.

I would like to thank the Program Board Chairs and the members of the Program Boards of all thematic areas and affiliated conferences for their contribution and support towards the highest scientific quality and overall success of the HCI International 2022 conference; they have helped in so many ways, including session organization, paper reviewing (single-blind review process, with a minimum of two reviews per submission) and, more generally, acting as goodwill ambassadors for the HCII conference.

This conference would not have been possible without the continuous and unwavering support and advice of Gavriel Salvendy, founder, General Chair Emeritus, and Scientific Advisor. For his outstanding efforts, I would like to express my appreciation to Abbas Moallem, Communications Chair and Editor of HCI International News.

June 2022 Constantine Stephanidis

HCI International 2022 Thematic Areas and Affiliated Conferences

Thematic Areas

- HCI: Human-Computer Interaction
- HIMI: Human Interface and the Management of Information

Affiliated Conferences

- EPCE: 19th International Conference on Engineering Psychology and Cognitive Ergonomics
- AC: 16th International Conference on Augmented Cognition
- UAHCI: 16th International Conference on Universal Access in Human-Computer Interaction
- CCD: 14th International Conference on Cross-Cultural Design
- SCSM: 14th International Conference on Social Computing and Social Media
- VAMR: 14th International Conference on Virtual, Augmented and Mixed Reality
- DHM: 13th International Conference on Digital Human Modeling and Applications in Health, Safety, Ergonomics and Risk Management
- DUXU: 11th International Conference on Design, User Experience and Usability
- C&C: 10th International Conference on Culture and Computing
- DAPI: 10th International Conference on Distributed, Ambient and Pervasive Interactions
- HCIBGO: 9th International Conference on HCI in Business, Government and Organizations
- LCT: 9th International Conference on Learning and Collaboration Technologies
- ITAP: 8th International Conference on Human Aspects of IT for the Aged Population
- AIS: 4th International Conference on Adaptive Instructional Systems
- HCI-CPT: 4th International Conference on HCI for Cybersecurity, Privacy and Trust
- HCI-Games: 4th International Conference on HCI in Games
- MobiTAS: 4th International Conference on HCI in Mobility, Transport and Automotive Systems
- AI-HCI: 3rd International Conference on Artificial Intelligence in HCI
- MOBILE: 3rd International Conference on Design, Operation and Evaluation of Mobile Communications

List of Conference Proceedings Volumes Appearing Before the Conference

1. LNCS 13302, Human-Computer Interaction: Theoretical Approaches and Design Methods (Part I), edited by Masaaki Kurosu
2. LNCS 13303, Human-Computer Interaction: Technological Innovation (Part II), edited by Masaaki Kurosu
3. LNCS 13304, Human-Computer Interaction: User Experience and Behavior (Part III), edited by Masaaki Kurosu
4. LNCS 13305, Human Interface and the Management of Information: Visual and Information Design (Part I), edited by Sakae Yamamoto and Hirohiko Mori
5. LNCS 13306, Human Interface and the Management of Information: Applications in Complex Technological Environments (Part II), edited by Sakae Yamamoto and Hirohiko Mori
6. LNAI 13307, Engineering Psychology and Cognitive Ergonomics, edited by Don Harris and Wen-Chin Li
7. LNCS 13308, Universal Access in Human-Computer Interaction: Novel Design Approaches and Technologies (Part I), edited by Margherita Antona and Constantine Stephanidis
8. LNCS 13309, Universal Access in Human-Computer Interaction: User and Context Diversity (Part II), edited by Margherita Antona and Constantine Stephanidis
9. LNAI 13310, Augmented Cognition, edited by Dylan D. Schmorrow and Cali M. Fidopiastis
10. LNCS 13311, Cross-Cultural Design: Interaction Design Across Cultures (Part I), edited by Pei-Luen Patrick Rau
11. LNCS 13312, Cross-Cultural Design: Applications in Learning, Arts, Cultural Heritage, Creative Industries, and Virtual Reality (Part II), edited by Pei-Luen Patrick Rau
12. LNCS 13313, Cross-Cultural Design: Applications in Business, Communication, Health, Well-being, and Inclusiveness (Part III), edited by Pei-Luen Patrick Rau
13. LNCS 13314, Cross-Cultural Design: Product and Service Design, Mobility and Automotive Design, Cities, Urban Areas, and Intelligent Environments Design (Part IV), edited by Pei-Luen Patrick Rau
14. LNCS 13315, Social Computing and Social Media: Design, User Experience and Impact (Part I), edited by Gabriele Meiselwitz
15. LNCS 13316, Social Computing and Social Media: Applications in Education and Commerce (Part II), edited by Gabriele Meiselwitz
16. LNCS 13317, Virtual, Augmented and Mixed Reality: Design and Development (Part I), edited by Jessie Y. C. Chen and Gino Fragomeni
17. LNCS 13318, Virtual, Augmented and Mixed Reality: Applications in Education, Aviation and Industry (Part II), edited by Jessie Y. C. Chen and Gino Fragomeni

18. LNCS 13319, Digital Human Modeling and Applications in Health, Safety, Ergonomics and Risk Management: Anthropometry, Human Behavior, and Communication (Part I), edited by Vincent G. Duffy
19. LNCS 13320, Digital Human Modeling and Applications in Health, Safety, Ergonomics and Risk Management: Health, Operations Management, and Design (Part II), edited by Vincent G. Duffy
20. LNCS 13321, Design, User Experience, and Usability: UX Research, Design, and Assessment (Part I), edited by Marcelo M. Soares, Elizabeth Rosenzweig and Aaron Marcus
21. LNCS 13322, Design, User Experience, and Usability: Design for Emotion, Well-being and Health, Learning, and Culture (Part II), edited by Marcelo M. Soares, Elizabeth Rosenzweig and Aaron Marcus
22. LNCS 13323, Design, User Experience, and Usability: Design Thinking and Practice in Contemporary and Emerging Technologies (Part III), edited by Marcelo M. Soares, Elizabeth Rosenzweig and Aaron Marcus
23. LNCS 13324, Culture and Computing, edited by Matthias Rauterberg
24. LNCS 13325, Distributed, Ambient and Pervasive Interactions: Smart Environments, Ecosystems, and Cities (Part I), edited by Norbert A. Streitz and Shin'ichi Konomi
25. LNCS 13326, Distributed, Ambient and Pervasive Interactions: Smart Living, Learning, Well-being and Health, Art and Creativity (Part II), edited by Norbert A. Streitz and Shin'ichi Konomi
26. LNCS 13327, HCI in Business, Government and Organizations, edited by Fiona Fui-Hoon Nah and Keng Siau
27. LNCS 13328, Learning and Collaboration Technologies: Designing the Learner and Teacher Experience (Part I), edited by Panayiotis Zaphiris and Andri Ioannou
28. LNCS 13329, Learning and Collaboration Technologies: Novel Technological Environments (Part II), edited by Panayiotis Zaphiris and Andri Ioannou
29. LNCS 13330, Human Aspects of IT for the Aged Population: Design, Interaction and Technology Acceptance (Part I), edited by Qin Gao and Jia Zhou
30. LNCS 13331, Human Aspects of IT for the Aged Population: Technology in Everyday Living (Part II), edited by Qin Gao and Jia Zhou
31. LNCS 13332, Adaptive Instructional Systems, edited by Robert A. Sottilare and Jessica Schwarz
32. LNCS 13333, HCI for Cybersecurity, Privacy and Trust, edited by Abbas Moallem
33. LNCS 13334, HCI in Games, edited by Xiaowen Fang
34. LNCS 13335, HCI in Mobility, Transport and Automotive Systems, edited by Heidi Krömker
35. LNAI 13336, Artificial Intelligence in HCI, edited by Helmut Degen and Stavroula Ntoa
36. LNCS 13337, Design, Operation and Evaluation of Mobile Communications, edited by Gavriel Salvendy and June Wei
37. CCIS 1580, HCI International 2022 Posters - Part I, edited by Constantine Stephanidis, Margherita Antona and Stavroula Ntoa
38. CCIS 1581, HCI International 2022 Posters - Part II, edited by Constantine Stephanidis, Margherita Antona and Stavroula Ntoa

http://2022.hci.international/proceedings

Preface

The increasing internationalization and globalization of communication, business and industry is leading to a wide cultural diversification of individuals and groups of users who access information, services and products. If interactive systems are to be usable, useful, and appealing to such a wide range of users, culture becomes an important HCI issue. Therefore, HCI practitioners and designers face the challenges of designing across different cultures, and need to elaborate and adopt design approaches which take into account cultural models, factors, expectations and preferences, and allow to develop cross-cultural user experiences that accommodate global users.

The 14th Cross-Cultural Design (CCD) Conference, an affiliated conference of the HCI International Conference, encouraged papers from academics, researchers, industry and professionals, on a broad range of theoretical and applied issues related to Cross-Cultural Design and its applications.

Cross-cultural design has come to be a lateral HCI subject that deals not only with the role of culture in HCI and across the amplitude of HCI application domains, but also in the context of the entire spectrum of HCI methods, processes, practices, and tools. In this respect, a considerable number of papers were accepted to this year's CCD Conference addressing diverse topics, which spanned a wide variety of domains. One of the most prominent topic categories was interaction design, as seen from a cross-cultural perspective, exploring cross-cultural differences and intercultural design. Application domains of social impact, such as learning, arts and cultural heritage have constituted popular topics this year, as well as work conducted in the context of creative industries and virtual reality. Health, well-being, and inclusiveness were emphasized, as was business and communication, which are fields that were all challenged during the ongoing pandemic. Furthermore, among the contributions, views on contemporary and near-future intelligent technologies were presented, including those addressing mobility and automotive design, as well as design in intelligent environments, cities, and urban areas.

Four volumes of the HCII2022 proceedings are dedicated to this year's edition of the CCD Conference:

- Cross-Cultural Design: Interaction Design Across Cultures (Part I), addressing topics related to cross-cultural interaction design, collaborative and participatory cross-cultural design, cross-cultural differences and HCI, as well as aspects of intercultural design.
- Cross-Cultural Design: Applications in Learning, Arts, Cultural Heritage, Creative Industries, and Virtual Reality (Part II), addressing topics related to cross-cultural learning, training, and education; cross-cultural design in arts and music; creative industries and Cultural Heritage under a cross-cultural perspective; and, cross-cultural virtual reality and games.
- Cross-Cultural Design: Applications in Business, Communication, Health, Well-being, and Inclusiveness (Part III), addressing topics related to intercultural business

communication, cross-cultural communication and collaboration, HCI and the global social change imposed by COVID-19, and intercultural design for well-being and inclusiveness.
- Cross-Cultural Design: Product and Service Design, Mobility and Automotive Design, Cities, Urban Areas, and Intelligent Environments Design (Part IV), addressing topics related to cross-cultural product and service design, cross-cultural mobility and automotive UX design, design and culture in social development and digital transformation of cities and urban areas, and cross-cultural design in intelligent environments.

Papers of these volumes are included for publication after a minimum of two single–blind reviews from the members of the CCD Program Board or, in some cases, from members of the Program Boards of other affiliated conferences. I would like to thank all of them for their invaluable contribution, support and efforts.

June 2022 Pei-Luen Patrick Rau

14th International Conference on Cross-Cultural Design (CCD 2022)

The full list with the Program Board Chairs and the members of the Program Boards of all thematic areas and affiliated conferences is available online at

http://www.hci.international/board-members-2022.php

HCI International 2023

The 25th International Conference on Human-Computer Interaction, HCI International 2023, will be held jointly with the affiliated conferences at the AC Bella Sky Hotel and Bella Center, Copenhagen, Denmark, 23–28 July 2023. It will cover a broad spectrum of themes related to human-computer interaction, including theoretical issues, methods, tools, processes, and case studies in HCI design, as well as novel interaction techniques, interfaces, and applications. The proceedings will be published by Springer. More information will be available on the conference website: http://2023.hci.international/.

General Chair
Constantine Stephanidis
University of Crete and ICS-FORTH
Heraklion, Crete, Greece
Email: general_chair@hcii2023.org

http://2023.hci.international/

Contents – Part IV

Cross-Cultural Mobility and Automotive UX Design

Cross-Cultural Product and Service Design

Cross-Cultural Design: A Discussion of Industrial Product Packaging Based on the Product Service System and Technological Evolution Principles

Xin Cao[1,2](✉), Yen Hsu[2], and Weilong Wu[2]

[1] Fuzhou University of International Studies and Trade, 28, Yuhuan Road, Shouzhan New District, Changle District, Fuzhou 350202, Fujian Province, China
caoxindesign@163.com

[2] The Graduate Institute of Design Science, Tatung University, No. 40, Sec. 3, Zhongshan N. Road, Taipei City 104 10461, Taiwan

Abstract. The problem of over-consumption and waste of product packaging has aroused public concern. This study introduces the concept of product service system design and the technological evolution principle to address this social problem. By analysing the current situation of product packaging, the necessity and feasibility of improving the design of product packaging is derived. As the effective implementation of product service system design requires certain theoretical and technical support, the TRIZ of technological evolution principle is introduced as a support tool for product service system, and the concept of sustainability is applied to the field of product packaging in a practical way. Through the combination of the principle of technological evolution and the concept of product service system, it effectively alleviates the problems of serious waste and difficulties in recycling of product packaging, and extends the scope of application of product service system design, and the application of the principle of technological evolution also brings a new development direction for product service system. This study validates an example of the application of product service system in combination with the principle of technological evolution, using the packaging of information and communication equipment as an example. The results demonstrate that combining product service systems with technological evolutionary principle leads to better sustainability goals for industrial product packaging.

Keywords: Industrial product packaging · Product service system · Technological evolution principle

1 Introduction

The problem of transporting industrial products in large quantities and many times has led to the over-consumption of product packaging and the problem of serious waste has raised concerns among companies and designers. As the business users faced by industrial products are relatively fixed and the transport of products in the same field has

P.-L. P. Rau (Ed.): HCII 2022, LNCS 13314, pp. 3–20, 2022.
https://doi.org/10.1007/978-3-031-06053-3_1

commonalities, it is feasible to achieve sustainable goals such as recycling and effective recovery of packaging.

China's Ministry of Industry and Information Technology and Ministry of Commerce issued the "Guidance on Accelerating the Transformation and Development of China's Packaging Industry" in 2016, stating that "around key technologies in the fields of green packaging, safe packaging and intelligent packaging, systemic technical solutions will be developed, and the incubation, application and promotion of major scientific and technological achievements will be promoted". The advent of big data and artificial intelligence has prompted the packaging industry to shift in the direction of intelligence. The Suning Group's floating box programme was launched in 2017, with thousands of courier boxes placed on the streets of Shenzhen in the name of "sharing", but ultimately ended badly due to low public awareness and the difficulty of recycling. Subsequently, Jingdong Group also launched a recycling bag with a drawstring design and a PP video box, which can be recycled nearly 20 times, but is difficult to operate due to costs and problems with recycling and recovery. A Shenzhen-based technology company, concerned about the problems of the packaging industry, has introduced a packaging 'rental' model instead of a 'purchase' model, which is the first manifestation of the servicification of the packaging industry.

At present, most of the research in the field of industrial product packaging stays in the areas of material selection, technology and how to improve the added value of the product. With the emergence of the concept of sustainability, designers and companies are gradually taking green and environmentally friendly ideas into account in the design process and promotion, but the end result is minimal and only meets the concept of sustainability at a relatively superficial level. The most effective method is the recycling of packaging as well as effective recycling. Improvements in packaging materials and processes can achieve recycling, but the infrequent use often goes unused, leading to another way of wasting resources. At present, for enterprises and individuals, it is often difficult to meet these two points at the same time. Some enterprises propose to transform logistics packaging into a sharing model and combine the Internet of Things with it, but this service model, or business model is not supported by systematic theories and methods, and is proposed purely from a packaging perspective, which lacks a certain degree of feasibility.

With the emergence of technologies such as big data and cloud computing, which have given rise to the information age, product service system cannot be applied without the product itself, and the development of technology has provided opportunities for new products to emerge. Product service system, as the third stage of sustainability, is a research method that integrates product and service as a system, which is effective for saving resources and reducing energy consumption. Product service system applied to industrial product packaging design process, not simply service instead of product, product to increase service, but through a systematic view of the entire design process, gradually from a single product tends to the design of service, intangible service instead of tangible product is the key element of product service system for sustainable design. In addition, the product service system is used as a new business model for companies to meet user needs while reducing costs and maximising benefits. If the product service system concept is applied directly to the packaging design process it will not achieve its original purpose. Technological advances lead to the emergence of new products, which provide direction for PSS, and the evolution of technological system follows a certain pattern. The TRIZ principle of technological evolution as a predictive tool for technological development can support the design of product service system. Through the analysis and study of the TRIZ principle of technological evolution, this study applies the principle of technological evolution to the design of product service system, which can lay the theoretical foundation for the development of a single product to a service-oriented design and give full play to the role of product service system in the design of industrial product packaging, so that packaging design can better achieve sustainable goal.

Faced with the wastefulness of industrial product packaging, this study applies product service system (PSS) to the design process, replacing tangible product with intangible service to the maximum extent possible, and supporting the effective implementation of PSS in the field of industrial product packaging through TRIZ technology evolution principle, which can achieve the recycling of resources, effective recovery, saving resources while reducing damage to the environment, embodies the concept of sustainability.

2 Literature Review

2.1 Product Service System

Product innovation design method can reduce the negative environmental impact of product and product production processes. However, product innovation alone is not sufficient to achieve the fundamental need for sustainability [1]. Indeed, even if these innovations may improve the sustainable performance of product, these improvements can be negatively countered by increased levels of consumption (Binswanger, 2001). For example, over the last 20 years, the environmental benefits gained through increased vehicle efficiency (10%) have been offset by a corresponding increase in the number of cars on the road and total distance travelled (30%) [2]. Product innovation methods can be the solution to sustainability problems, but they cannot address the root causes of sustainability problems. Therefore, there is a need to move from a product improvement orientation alone to a production and consumption system-led organisational structure.

For this reason, several researchers have started to look at Product Service System (PSS) as an effective method for sustainable development [3–5]. PSS can be defined as "a combination of tangible products and intangible services that can be designed to ultimately meet the needs of the customer" [6]. PSS aims to meet the needs of users by delivering functionality rather than the product itself (e.g. from selling heating systems to providing thermal comfort services; from selling cars to providing travel services, etc.). PSS therefore advocates a shift from ownership-based consumption to access-based and shared consumption.

From an environmental perspective, PSS can distinguish economic value from energy consumption [7]. As the manufacturer retains ownership of the product and provides a functional service to the customer, it economically enables the manufacturer to minimise the materials and energy required to provide that functional service [8]. In addition, PSS can provide companies with new strategic market opportunities, increase competitiveness and build strong and longer-term relationships with customers [9].

In addition to environmental concerns, some researchers have combined PSS with social ethics of sustainability [10]. Another area that has received much attention is the application of PSS to low-income populations, namely the Design for the Base of the Pyramid (BoP) PSS design.

2.2 Industrial Product Packaging

Product packaging in the logistics sector is divided into commercial product packaging and industrial product packaging according to the role of circulation, i.e. packaging for sales purposes and packaging for transportation purposes. This study refers to the classification of packaging in the field of logistics and the types of products, the packaging is broadly divided into industrial product packaging and commercial product packaging, commercial products are mostly a variety of household items, their shape is diverse, transport packaging is difficult to unify, often using larger boxes and filler for packaging, the uncertainty of the shape caused by the packaging is difficult to unify, the amount of fragmented, complex user groups, resulting in more difficult to recycle. Industrial products are often transported from company (or factory) to company (or factory), so the purpose of packaging is to ensure that transport products are not damaged, easy to transport, etc. And industrial product packaging has the characteristics of high demand, large transport scale, high transport efficiency requirements and more uniform product specifications. The packaging of commercial products, on the other hand, has multiple layers of significance, with its aesthetic value and increased added value of the product being key elements in preventing damage to the product. A comparative analysis of commercial product packaging and industrial product packaging shows that improved designs for industrial product packaging are easier to implement and more valuable to optimise, as shown in Table 1. Based on this, this study combines the PSS design concept with the TRIZ principle of technological evolution to propose a systematic improvement in the design of industrial product packaging.

Table 1. Contrasting analysis of commercial and industrial product packaging

	Commercial product packaging	Industrial product packaging
Target users	Single-user individual	Company or factory
Design elements	Function, appearance and shape	Functionality, transport efficiency
Purpose	For sales purposes, to prevent damage to the product, to increase its value, to match aesthetics and to promote consumption	For transport purposes, to prevent damage to the product and to facilitate storage and transport
Daily needs	Low usage and low uniformity	High usage and more uniformity
Scale of transport	More fragmented	More uniform
User experience	Focusing on the aesthetic needs of the user and providing spiritual enjoyment	Functionality oriented, easy to use, good user experience

At present, most of the research on industrial product packaging stays in the areas of material selection, technology and how to improve the added value of the product. With the emergence of the concept of sustainability, designers and companies are gradually taking green and environmental protection into account in the design process and promotion, but the final effect is minimal, and the concept of sustainability is only met at a relatively superficial level. The most effective method is the recycling of packaging as well as effective recycling. Improvements in packaging materials and processes can achieve recycling, but the infrequent use often goes unused, leading to another way of wasting resources. At present, it is often difficult for companies and individuals to meet these two points at the same time. Some companies have proposed the emergence of logistics packaging as a "sharing model" and the combination of the Internet of Things with it, but this service model or business model is not supported by systematic theories and methods, and is proposed purely from the perspective of packaging. The sustainability of industrial product packaging requires a joint effort between companies and designers, not only for the business model but also for the entire design process, including the product.

3 Integrated Application of PSS and Technological Evolution Theory

With the emergence of technologies such as big data and cloud computing, giving rise to the information age, the application of product service systems cannot be separated from the product itself, and the development of technology provides an opportunity for new products to emerge. Product service system applied to industrial product packaging design process, not simply service instead of product, product to increase service, but through a systematic perspective of the entire design process, gradually from a single product tends to the design of services, intangible services instead of tangible products is the product service system for sustainable design key elements. The original purpose cannot be achieved if the product service system concept is applied directly to the packaging design process. The design of the product service system focuses on the design of the product module and the service module. The necessary condition for the interconnection and interaction between the two is the existence of a support system. Advances in technology have led to the emergence of new products and product developments that can provide direction for PSS. The evolution of technological systems follows certain rules and the TRIZ principles of technological evolution can support the design of product and service system as a predictive tool for technological development. Through the analysis and study of the TRIZ principle of technological evolution, the application of the principle of technological evolution to the design of product service systems can lay the theoretical foundation for the development of a single product to a service-oriented design, giving full play to the role of product service systems in the design of industrial product packaging, so that packaging design can better achieve sustainable goal.

3.1 Overview and Application of TRIZ Principle of Technological Evolution

As one of the important results of TRIZ, Kauffman (1995) proposed that technological systems evolve according to certain objective laws, and that the principle of technological evolution is a general rule for the evolution of technological systems and an effective tool for predicting and developing new products [11]. As the principle of technological evolution is universal in characterising the evolution of product technology, it is feasible to apply it to the design of product service system to ensure the effective implementation of PSS, thereby achieving the sustainable goals of resource conservation and environmental protection.

The focus of past research as TRIZ theory continues to be applied in companies, more and more experts and scholars are applying the principle of technological evolution as a tool for technological forecasting or selecting technological routes to primarily solve product innovation design problems, etc. Yang (2018) applying principle of technological evolution to the innovative design of parking warning devices to provide a systematic design process with implications for the rapid development of products that meet user needs. Peng (2020) presented an analytical study of food waste treatment technologies, applying the principle of technological evolution to predict technological maturity and thus assess their development. Wang (2018) conducted an analytical study on the technological evolutionary route of rotary drilling rigs, which was applied to the innovative design of rotary drilling rigs through an analytical description of the principle of technological evolution. Zhang (2004) proposed a model for a goal-based decision-making process that combines the TRIZ principle of technological evolution with product innovation design, bridging the limitations in the design of new product development. Cai (2008) applied the principle of technological evolution and the modular fixture development model to predict the future direction and possible development trends and to classify the patents, demonstrating that the principle of technological evolution is an effective way to provide guidance for the development of the industry.

The current state of application of the principle of technological evolution around the world shows that the theory has a wide range of applications, but its application in product design is mostly in the area of innovation and optimisation of the design process, providing direction and reference for specific problem solving, but as a design method support tool to improve the design process is not yet mature. Therefore, the application of the theory of technological evolution to the design of PSS can greatly enhance its application and has good prospects for development.

The TRIZ principle of technological evolution are an effective tool for predicting and developing new products. The nine principles of technological evolution are mainly proposed to describe the regularity of the evolution of technological systems from nine aspects, and each principle has many evolutionary routes. The principles are relatively independent of each other, and it is possible to predict the direction of evolution from a particular principle; the principle are not completely independent of each other, and there are some links, as shown in Table 2.

Considering that the ultimate aim of the product service system is to improve the sustainability of industrial product packaging, as well as the research and analysis of the nine principles, it was found that principle 1, principle 3, principle 4 and principle 8 can be applied to the product service system design research as a technical support for

Table 2. Principles of technological evolution

No.	Description
Principle 1	Raising the level of idealisation
Principle 2	Uneven development of subsystems
Principle 3	Improving dynamics
Principle 4	Evolving to complex system
Principle 5	Evolving to microsystems
Principle 6	Making it complete
Principle 7	Shortening of energy flow path lengths
Principle 8	Improving controllability
Principle 9	Increasing coordination

product development, as shown in Fig. 4. Improving the sustainability of packaging is analysed in three ways. Firstly, the replacement of user ownership is typical of the design of product service systems, and forms such as sharing and leasing are effective ways of reducing costs and increasing utilization. And this type of approach means that packaged products face a rich group of users with different needs, and so need to be addressed with improving dynamics (Principle 3). Secondly, increased sustainability means reduced costs and resource consumption, and product service system save costs and reduce resources by replacing physical product with intangible service. So there is a need for greater servitization, and improving controllability (Principle 8) can address issues such as lower costs and greater servitization. Increased recyclability and serviceability requires smart packaging. Evolving to complex system (Principle 4) can enhance the intelligence of packaging through complex system such as information technology and big data. Finally, the principle of raising the level of idealisation is the general direction of system development and the ultimate aim of sustainable industrial product packaging (Fig. 1).

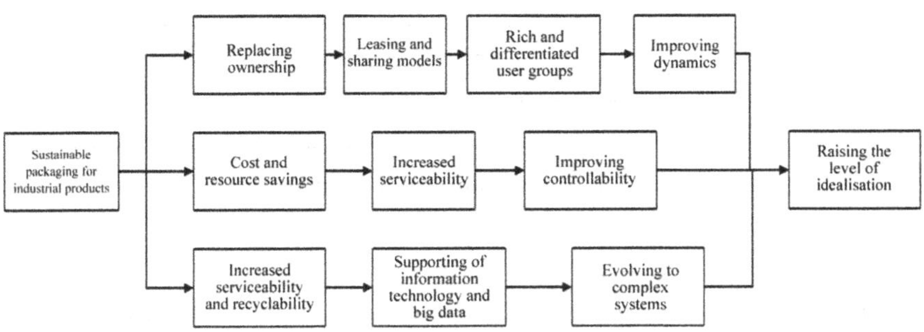

Fig. 1. Applying the principles of technological evolution to achieve sustainable goals

Raising the Level of Idealization. Raising the level of idealisation (Principle 1) is the general direction of system evolution, and the system evolves the other principles to raise the level of idealisation as well, as shown in the relationship between the nine principles in Fig. 2. The greater the proportion of services in a product-service system, the greater the degree of idealization. According to the classification of the proportion of products and services, it can be seen that product-oriented to use-oriented to result-oriented, in line with the trend of gradually increasing the proportion of services and decreasing the proportion of products. Therefore, a result-oriented approach is the ultimate ideal of a product service system. The system has always developed in the direction of the final ideal state, taking the car rental service system as an example, the general process is APP order, shop pick-up, shop return, etc. Travel is no longer the choice of those who have a car, the car rental method is increasingly popular among consumers. On the one hand, it can provide convenience to users who do not have the budget to buy a car; on the other hand, it improves the utilisation of cars while ensuring the economic efficiency of the company and reducing the problem of idle cars, which is also a typical expression of the concept of sustainability. The rental company provides a platform for the user, who enjoys the convenience of the car itself as well as the services that come with renting a car. Whereas the ideal outcome is the arrival of the user at a location, the trend in product service system design is towards a gradual and sustainable progression towards the ideal outcome.

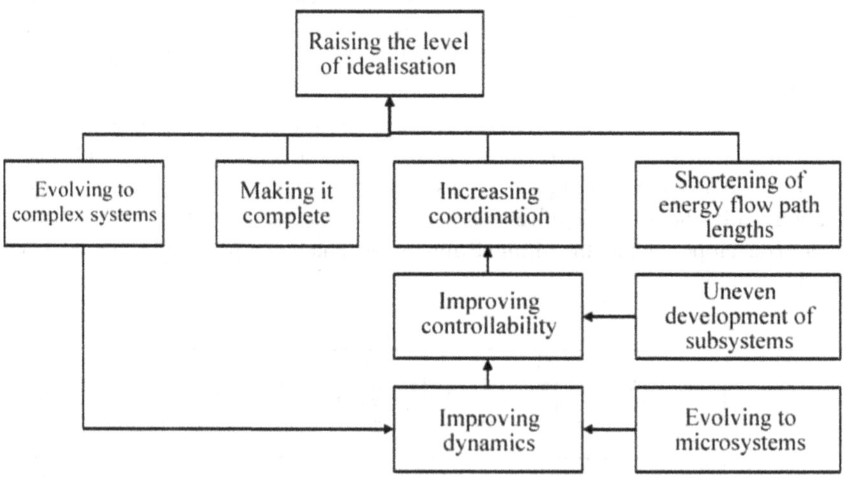

Fig. 2. Relationships among the nine principles

The principle of raising the level of idealisation is positively correlated with sustainability. Only by continuously raising the level of idealisation can the sustainability of the product service system be enhanced, and sustainability is the ultimate ideal state of the product service system. Therefore, raising the level of idealisation is the law that drives the general direction of development of product service system applications.

Improving Dynamics. Improving dynamics (Principle 3) means that a system has more than one state that interacts with the outside world, and the system needs to have the ability to change its operating state in response to changes in the environment and the system. The design of product in product service system is faced with a rich variety of user groups with different needs, and the application of the principle of dynamism in the design of product service system can be maximised to suit different users. Shared bicycles are a typical product service system, and their "shared nature" is a good indicator of the diversity and richness of the user community. The seat height of the shared bicycle is adjustable and its adjustment system is constantly changing, the principle of evolution enables predictions to be made early in the design process. The seat adjustment part of the shared bicycles differs from that of previous household bicycles, evolving from a swivel mechanism to the current easier-to-use opening and closing mechanism, which is completed in three steps by raising, adjusting to the right seat height and lowering the reinforcement. The seat height can be adjusted and fixed directly according to the user's needs, regardless of the strength of the user, avoiding the problem of the product not working well or not working due to differences in the user group, as in Fig. 3. Therefore, improving dynamism (Principle 3) can meet the multi-adaptability of product service systems. Product service systems in the form of sharing and leasing have a rich user base and increased dynamism can facilitate better implementation of product service systems.

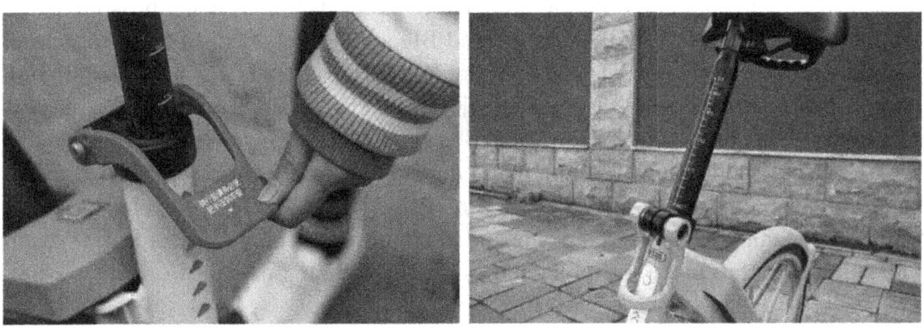

Fig. 3. The case for shared bicycles

Evolving to Complex System. Evolving to complex system (Principle 4) refers to the transition to complex systems when a system has reached maturity and has exhausted its own resources, with the technological system evolving from a single system to multiple dual systems and multiple systems. However, technical system will in some cases trim redundant resources to simplify into a new single system, as shown in Fig. 4. The process of designing product service system for industrial product packaging is no longer based on the traditional packaging of the past, but on the application of technologies such as cloud computing, big data and information technology to promote intelligent packaging development, increase management tools and improve utilisation and recycling rates. The shared printing system under the product service system, for example, provides self-printing and resource finding functions through online cloud and APP links, and uses cloud services to establish a resource library to facilitate the selection and integration of resources by users, and completes the interaction with users through offline printer settings.

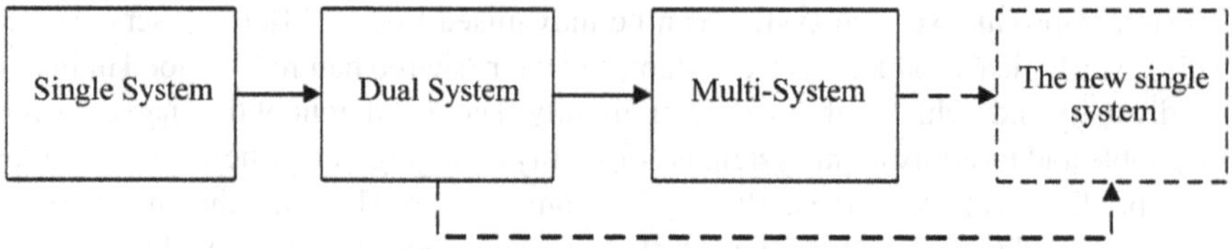

Fig. 4. The route of evolving to complex system

Principle 4 can provide the theoretical basis and technical support for product service system, and the emergence of smart devices is a manifestation of the gradual development of systems from single system to multi-system trends, with smart product system having intelligent interaction and intelligent sensing. In the past, printing required going to a print shop and communicating with professionals to print on your behalf, but the emergence of intelligent product service system has made self-service printing a reality, with the whole system changing from printing at a print shop to printing through the cloud services of the printing system and APP, as shown in Fig. 5. Nowadays, users can also use APPs for shopping, ordering food and other needs that were not possible in the past, and the emergence of GPS systems and Bluetooth are typical of the information society. Intelligence is a typical feature of product service system and a bridge and link between users, products and services. The development and application of the Internet and various APPs has led to the emergence of product service system design products such as sharing and leasing. The intelligent development of industrial product packaging can greatly improve its utilisation and recycling rate. Although the emergence of information technology such as big data and the Internet of Things has made the system more complex, it has made it simpler and easier for users to operate.

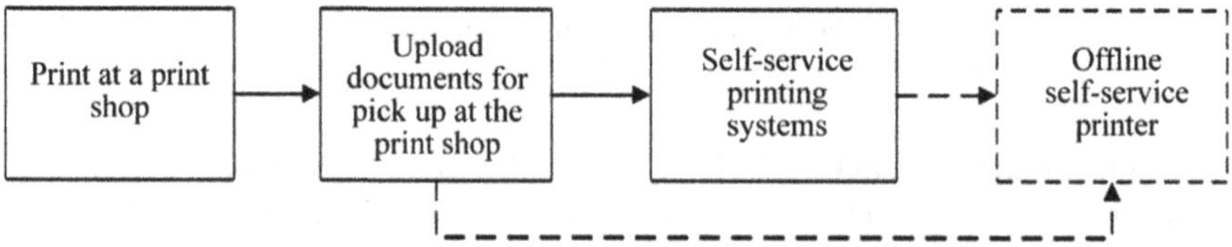

Fig. 5. Improvement route for printing systems

Improving Controllability. Improving controllability (Principle 8) refers to the extent to which a system state can be achieved within a specified time constraint; better controllability will result in a shorter time to achieve the intended state. The application of the principle of controllability to product service system can increase the level of automation of the product, increase the stability of the system and thus reduce service costs. Take the example of a solar panel in the basket of a shared bicycle, as shown in Fig. 6. The "shared" nature of shared bicycles means that they are used all the time. Users scan the code to unlock the bicycle and close the lock when they have finished using it, avoiding the loss and damage of the bicycle and ensuring the interests of the business to a certain extent. The lock requires electricity to operate, and the solar panel converts sunlight into electricity by absorbing it, keeping the bike fully charged at all times. This simplifies staff management, reduces service costs and enables the lock to be self-charging, a sign of increased controllability. Improving controllability is an important principle in improving the stability of a product service system. The higher the controllability of the system, the greater the user operability and the greater the stability of the PSS. By using solar panels to recharge themselves, shared bicycles greatly improve the stability of their use while reducing the cost of the service. The application of the principle of controllability in the design process of industrial product packaging improves the operability of the packaging itself. Increased operability means increased stability of the packaging and increased serviceability, which in turn makes the logistics packaging easier to manage and the whole system develops towards the highest idealised level. Therefore, successful product service system use cases can improve stability by improving controllability (Principle 8).

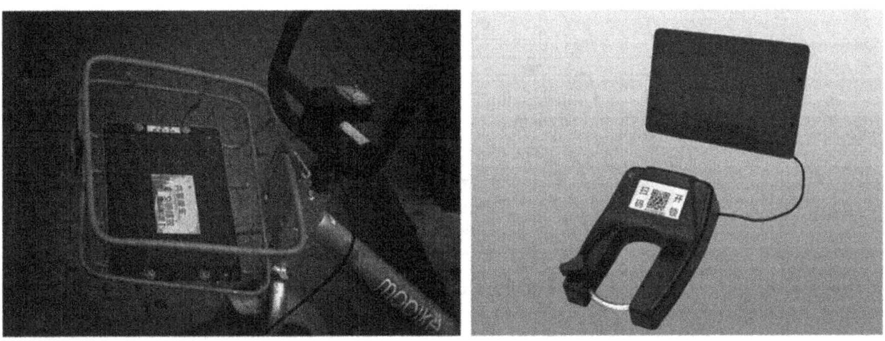

Fig. 6. Solar panel basket with lock

Integrated Application. Through the analysis of the principle of technological evolution, examples are given to illustrate the role of the principle of technological evolution in supporting the design of product service system, the development of technology can promote the smooth implementation of PSS, can lay the foundation for the gradual transformation of industrial product packaging to service. The design of packaging is no longer the design of a single product, but the design study of packaging as the provision of an entire packaging service can greatly improve the sustainability of this product design process, intangible services to maximise the replacement of tangible products, reduce resource consumption while increasing utilisation, and is a major innovation in the field of industrial product packaging.

Through the study of product service system application in the field of packaging design, it is found that the application process of PSS has certain drawbacks and needs to be supported by the application of TRIZ technology evolution theory tool, and according to the PSS design process and technology evolution principle, the industrial product packaging design process is summarised, as shown in Fig. 7.

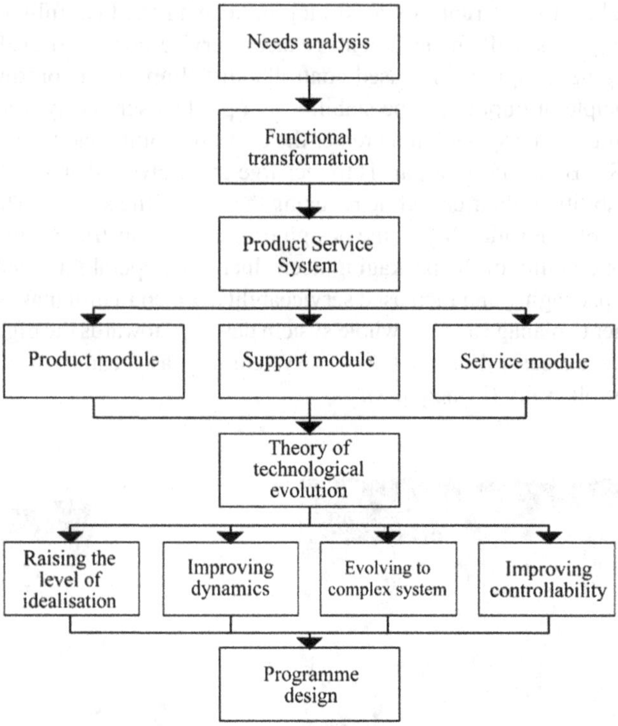

Fig. 7. Design process

3.2 Verification of Industrial Product Packaging Examples

Based on the current state of the industrial product packaging market, the product service system is designed to address the problems of fragile and wasteful boxes, and the " shared" model is used to improve the utilisation rate and thus solve the problems of recycling. Traditional boxes are disposable products, and although a number of experts have proposed solutions they have not yet been implemented or are more difficult to implement.

This study takes the case of a communications equipment company's packaging box design as an example of a solution design based on the design process from the perspective of a third party service provider for its packaging box products and services. Firstly, for third party companies, the entire process of developing, designing, applying and even recycling industrial product packaging boxes needs to take into account the characteristics, basic requirements and so on of the product service system. The product service system design process starts with a stakeholder requirements analysis, translates the requirements into functionality, and is supported by the application of PSS and technology evolution principles to arrive at a solution.

Needs Analysis. Stakeholders in the packaging of industrial products include: third party companies, users (communication equipment companies) and the environment. Third party enterprises are third party enterprises providing industrial product packaging and related services, whose greatest need is economic efficiency, so products and services need to meet the characteristics of low cost and high efficiency, in addition, easy management and high frequency of use are also important points of their needs. The users are employees of communication equipment companies (users of the boxes), whose needs are low cost, high utilisation, ease of operation, etc.. The greatest demands on the environment are low energy consumption, improved utilisation and zero environmental pollution, which are common to both third party companies and users, as shown in Table 3.

Table 3. Stakeholder needs analysis

Stakeholder	Needs analysis
Third party companies	Low cost: materials, processing techniques, etc. to meet functionality while minimising costs
	High yield: products and services with a good user experience and increased user demand
	Ease of management: dynamic tracking of packaging and products
	Easy to recycle: recyclable after a certain number of uses
Users	High durability: good quality product, made of resistant, hard-wearing and durable materials
	Low cost: ownership of the right to use without ownership
	Ease of operation: conforming to the human machine and adapting to different users as far as possible
	High level of serviceability: systematic and integrated service including products
	Recyclable: recycling service available
Environment	Low-carbon and environmentally friendly: degradable and non-polluting materials
	Sustainable: recyclable

Functional Transformation. Based on the requirements analysis, a categorisation study is carried out to determine the final functionality, which is then supported by the principle of technological evolution, as shown in Table 4.

Table 4. Functional transformation

Stakeholder	Needs	Principles of technological evolution	Functional transformation
Third party companies	High earnings	Improving dynamics	Ergonomic design of industrial product packaging
Users	Easy to operate		
Third party companies	Easy to manage	Evolving to complex system	Each industrial product is packaged with individual labels, with the addition of a GPS system and an operable app, etc
Users	Easy to operate		
Users	Easy to operate	Improving controllability	Real-time tracking via APP
Third party companies	Easy to recycle	Raising the level of idealisation	Providing industrial product packaging, logistics and recycling services
Users	High level of serviceability		
Environment	Sustainability		

Product Service System. According to the product service system design process, the PSS of industrial product packaging requires a simple division of product modules, service modules and support systems, as shown in Fig. 8.

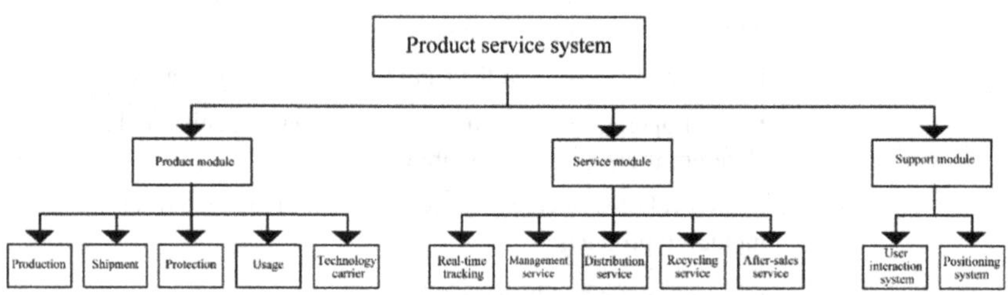

Fig. 8. Product service system module

Product Module. Through market research and analysis, after practical investigation found that PP material most meet the requirements, has the characteristics of anti-drop, anti-collision, low temperature and high temperature resistance, can guarantee the safety of products in various harsh conditions, packaging production using ultrasonic technology to seal the edge, strong and easy to achieve. The thickness of the box edge is about 1 cm and the box is used about 15–20 times. By placing the GPS chip in the RTP structure and process, the product and the box in transit can be tracked in real time through big data, cloud computing and other technologies for analysis. Through a survey of the product volume of communication equipment enterprises, mainly for wiring frames (including intelligent and non-intelligent), including ODF, EDF, VDF, DDF, and commonly used communication equipment, such as switches, integrated access equipment, PTN and other equipment, the packaging box specifications are set to 50.5 cm × 30 cm × 40.5 cm, which can meet the above communication products The shape is shown in Fig. 9.

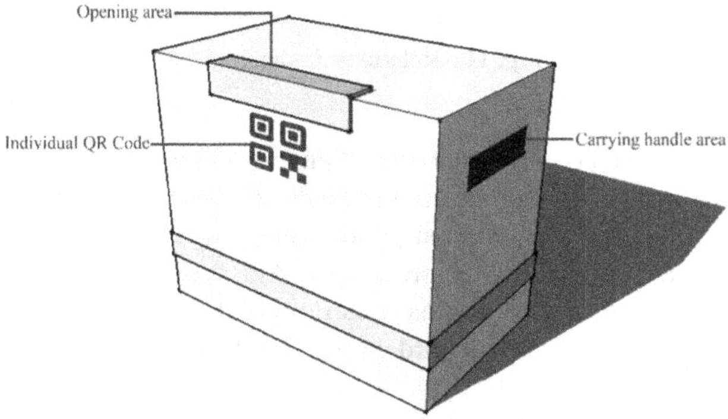

Fig. 9. Industrial product packaging concept diagram

Service Module. The application of the principle of technological evolution as a tool for the realisation of functions is now detailed according to the three phases of logistics before, during and after transport, as shown in Fig. 10, and the analysis of the relationship between the third party, the box user company (product issuing company) and the product receiving company, as shown in Fig. 11.

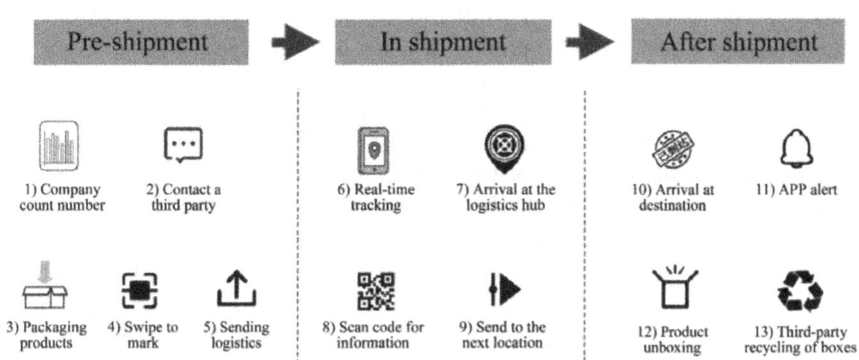

Fig. 10. Service design diagram

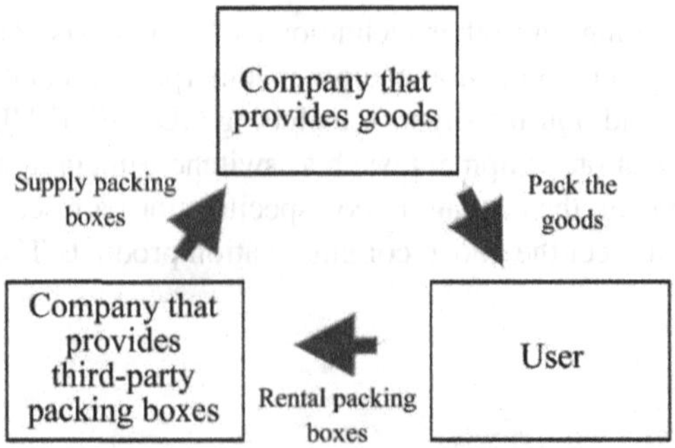

Fig. 11. Relationship diagram

Before shipping, the communications equipment company determines the number of boxes required by the type of industrial product to be shipped and the corresponding quantity, contacts the third party company and receives the boxes. Each box has its own individual label, and after loading the product the APP code is used to mark the box to be transported and the third party company carries out the logistics dispatch.

During shipping, companies and third parties can share the logistics situation in real time through the APP and track the dynamics of the transported products. In the case of long-distance transport, logistics staff can scan the code to obtain transport information and initiate the next transport dynamics once the product arrives at the hub.

After shipping, the APP will be updated automatically after the goods are received by the receiving enterprise or factory, and the shipping enterprise can obtain the information at the first time. The receiving company or factory will then dismantle the boxes, and the dismantled boxes can either be notified to the third party company for recycling or returned to the local management service of the third party company, while the deposit will be returned by the platform.

For the management of packaging boxes, each box is equipped with GPS positioning system, staff regularly through the background investigation, the location of abnormalities will have special management personnel to manage the investigation, a certain area of packaging boxes too much or too little, timely supplementation and coordination. The entire design ensures that the product function is realised and also requires a systematic design of the service process. The service module contains information network construction, logistics and transport services, recycling services and after-sales services.

According to the analysis of the whole system design process, from the third-party packaging box provider to the product enterprises that need packaging, and then to the product user enterprises, and finally back to the third-party packaging provider, is a closed-loop process, the third-party enterprises to provide packaging and services for profit, the goods to provide enterprises only need to rent packaging boxes to achieve logistics protection and thus reduce costs, and user enterprises by cooperating with the third-party packaging can be recycled. This model solves the problem of difficult recycling and recovery of packaging boxes. However, the existence of third-party companies is not only to provide users with boxes and corresponding logistics services, the recycling of boxes is equally important to ensure that the enterprises themselves benefit while improving resource utilisation and reducing the pressure on the environment caused by wasted resources, which is an important manifestation of sustainability.

The sustainable forms of product service systems such as sharing and leasing are undoubtedly the best form of sustainable development for society at present and the best choice to meet people's needs in life. The general trend from the past single product output, products and additional services to the current state where products and services are inseparable is a constant march towards the most idealised state.

4 Conclusion

With the emergence of technologies such as big data and cloud computing, giving rise to the information age, the application of product service systems cannot be separated from the product itself, and the development of technology provides an opportunity for new products to emerge. Product service system applied to the process of industrial product packaging design is not simply a service to replace the product, the product to increase the service, but through a systematic view of the entire design process, gradually from a single product tends to the design of services, intangible services instead of tangible products is the key element of the product service system for sustainable design. The initial purpose cannot be achieved if the product service system concept is imposed directly on the packaging design process. The focus of the PSS design is on the design of the product and service modules, the necessary condition for the interconnection and interaction between the two is the existence of a support system. The evolution of technological system follows a certain pattern, and the TRIZ principle of technological evolution, as a predictive tool for technological development, can provide support for the design of product service system.

This study indicates the necessity and feasibility of product service system design for industrial product packaging by analysing the current situation of product packaging. Product service systems are composed of product and service modules. The integrated and systematic design of industrial product packaging can, to a certain extent, reduce energy consumption and environmental pollution, and is another innovation in the application of product service systems in the field of design. In the process of product service system application, through the exploration of TRIZ technology evolution, the principle of technology evolution is applied to product service system design, which can lay the theoretical foundation for the development of a single product to a service-oriented design, and give full play to the role of product service system in industrial product packaging design. While providing technical support and direction for the development of PSS, it also improves the effectiveness of product service system in the field of industrial product packaging. With the high volume of industrial product packaging and the commonality of products, it is of some practical importance to improve the design and research of packaging in this field. Finally, this study has validated an example of the application of product service system in combination with the principle of technological evolution, using information and communication equipment packaging as an example. The results demonstrate that the combination of product service system and technological evolution principle leads to better sustainability goals for industrial product packaging.

References

1. Author, F.: Article title. Journal **2**(5), 99–110 (2016)
2. Ceschin, F., Gaziulusoy, I.: Evolution of design for sustainability: from product design to design for system innovations and transitions. Des. Stud. **47**, 118–163 (2016)
3. Ceschin, F., Vezzoli, C.: The role of public policy in stimulating radical environmental impact reduction in the automotive sector: the need to focus on product-service system innovation. Int. J. Automot. Technol. Manag. **10**(2–3), 321–341 (2010)
4. Evans, S., Gregory, M., Ryan, C.G., Bergendahl, M.N., Tan, A.: Towards a Sustainable Industrial System: With Recommendations for Education, Research, Industry and Policy. University of Cambridge, Institute for Manufacturing (2009)
5. Heiskanen, E., Jalas, M.: Dematerialization Through Services-A Review and Evaluation of the Debate. Edita Publishing OY, Helsinki (2000)
6. Mont, O.K.: Clarifying the concept of product–service system. J. Clean. Prod. **10**(3), 237–245 (2002)
7. Tukker, A., Tischner, U.: Product-services as a research field: past, present and future. Reflections from a decade of research. J. Clean. Prod. **14**(17), 1552–1556 (2006)
8. Stahel, W.R.: The functional economy: cultural and organizational change. In: The Industrial Green Game: Implications for Environmental Design and Management, pp. 91–100. National Academy Press, Washington, DC (1997)
9. Halme, M., Jasch, C., Scharp, M.: Sustainable homeservices? Toward household services that enhance ecological, social and economic sustainability. Ecol. Econ. **51**(1–2), 125–138 (2004)
10. Manzini, E., Vezzoli, C.A.: Product-Service Systems and Sustainability: Opportunities for Sustainable Solutions. UNEP-United Nations Environment Programme (2002)
11. Vezzoli, C., Ceschin, F., Diehl, J.C., Kohtala, C.: New design challenges to widely implement 'sustainable product–service systems.' J. Clean. Prod. **97**, 1–12 (2015)
12. Kauffman, S., Macready, W.: Technological evolution and adaptive organizations. Complexity **1**(2), 26–43 (1995)

A Pilot Study of LED Lighting Fixtures Suitable for Computer Monitor Working Spaces

Jen-Feng Chen(✉), Po-Hsien Lin, and Rungtai Lin

Graduate School of Creative Industry Design, National Taiwan University of Arts, New Taipei City, Taiwan

jenfeng0328@gmail.com, t0131@ntua.edu.tw, rtlin@mail.ntua.edu.tw

Abstract. Commercially available desk lamps are generally designed for reading books, and their traditional lighting designs are not suitable for working environments with computer monitors. However, the general public uses conventional desk lamps in their computer monitor working environment because they do not understand the difference, which may lead to eye fatigue and discomfort. In recent years, lights specially designed for a computer monitor working environment have appeared on the market to offer users more comfortable lighting. The objectives of this study are to define the main lighting elements via literature review and expert discussions, and to conduct experiments to investigate the design elements necessary to provide good lighting in a computer monitor working environment, thereby offering better lighting solutions in the future. This study organized the relevant industry guidelines and design principles, in which the BenQ Screenbar was used as the sample and different color temperature and illumination mode combinations were adopted as variables. A total of 22 subjects participated in the experiment. The goal was to investigate what lighting elements are required to optimize the computer monitor working environment, identify the most suitable lighting modes, and provide a reference for developing such products in the future.

Keywords: Computer monitor workspace lighting · Superior lighting · Color temperature · Il-luminance

1 Introduction

The eyes are critical sensory organs for human beings to receive information from the outside world. Approximately 90% of the external information is obtained through vision [13]. In the modern information age, people live highly digitized lives where they obtain information through the Internet, communicate with other people on social media, and play or work via the cloud. However, these ordinary activities all have to be conducted through an interface on a screen. According to a survey conducted by Acuvue on 2,000 employees [2], an average office worker spends approximately 6.5 h in front of a computer monitor every day. According to the latest survey by TrendForce, global computer monitor shipment statistics showed that 140 million units were shipped in 2020 [45]. These two statistics show that the number of computer monitor users is very

P.-L. P. Rau (Ed.): HCII 2022, LNCS 13314, pp. 21–35, 2022.
https://doi.org/10.1007/978-3-031-06053-3_2

large, and they use computer monitors for a long time every day. Long-term use of these visual display terminal (VDT) devices may gradually lead to various eye, physical, and mental health problems that can impact the users' health [51].

In the past few decades, there have also been many discoveries on how lighting affects eye fatigue for VDT users as well as the physiological and psychological effects [28]. For example, Bangor (2000) conducted a study on VDT visual fatigue-related problems and found that illuminance brighter or dimmer than certain levels may easily cause eye fatigue. JM Katabaro (2019) found that poorly designed office environments lighting can impact human health and work performance [1, 23, 48].

Numerous studies have found that low and medium illumination are suitable for VDT operations [6, 16]. Y. Akashi and P.R. Boyce proposed that many offices have higher illuminance than needed. Reducing the ambient illumination while maintaining the desktop's localized illumination can conserve energy without affecting visual comfort [50]. Office buildings are often listed as one of the most energy-intensive buildings compared to other facilities. Therefore, offices should adopt a lighting plan with lower ambient lighting and sufficient localized lighting on desktops to reduce the office building's overall energy consumption [37]. The ambient illuminance in most offices is approximately 600 lx. If lamps are installed on desktops, then the lights that need to be installed on the ceiling can be reduced to around 1/3, it would provide sufficient lighting while conserving energy [42].

The general public has used traditional reading lamps on their computer monitor work tables for a long time. The conventional desk lamp lighting design is unsuited for the computer monitor working environment. The symmetrical light source produced by traditional desk lamps may easily cause reflections and glare on computer monitors. It is difficult to place a desk lamp in a position that can evenly illuminate the whole environment. Therefore, lights specifically designed for the computer monitor working environment have appeared in the market recently. This special computer monitor lighting fixture pioneered by BenQ has adopted an asymmetric light source design to reduce eye strain caused by glare reflected from the monitor while providing uniform and comfortable lighting. The product has been well received by computer monitor users and has become quite popular in the market. Many other similar products have also appeared.. Special lamps for monitors can meet the key needs of consumers. This study has adopted literature review and experiment methods to investigate lighting elements that may affect users physiologically and psychologically, thereby providing better lighting for computer monitor workers.

2 Literature Review

2.1 Principles for Designing Superior Lighting

According to the International Commission on Illumination (CIE), adequate illumination can create an environment in which people can see clearly, move safely, and complete visual tasks effectively and precisely without causing inap-propriate visual fatigue or discomfort. In addition to improving users' visual acuity and physiological comfort at work, a good lighting environment can also affect people's sleep quality, alertness, happiness, and health [33, 44]. This highlights the importance of lighting for people. The design of lighting fixtures must comply with relevant international standards to make excellent products that satisfy users' needs.

In Accordance with National Standards, such as CNS12112 in Taiwan, EN 12464-1 standard in EU and regulations of the US Department of Energy [11], five criteria for evaluating high-quality lighting are summarized as below: 1. Illuminance: The illumination intensity is a fundamental factor for clear visibility. Average illuminance that is too low may cause eye fatigue and myopia, while high average illuminance may cause glare and eye discomfort. Illuminance intensity can affect reading speed, accuracy, and legibility [22, 41]. 2. Uniformity: If there are large differences in the illumination intensity between different surfaces within the user's line of sight in a working environment, the eye will need time to adjust as sight lines move from one surface to another. Having to frequently make such adjustments may lead to visual fatigue. Therefore, good lighting requires uniform illuminance distribution. The ratio between minimum and average illuminance intensities should be as close to 1.0 as possible, and it is generally recommended to be higher than 0.5 [3, 39]. 3. Glare: This refers to feelings of discomfort to the eyes caused by bright light sources or objects. Examples include LED light sources shining directly into the eyes or reflected from surfaces or objects, thus causing eye discomfort and difficulty seeing other things within the visual range [8, 9]. 4. Color Temperature: This refers to the color characteristics displayed by lighting products. The unit of measurement for color temperature is the kelvin (K). Different color temperatures have different color lights. Low color temperatures are associated with a reddish color light while high color temperatures are associated with a blueish color light. Color temperature can affect people's cognition and emotion [18, 40]. 5. Color Rendering Index: This refers to the degree of color rendering on an object after a light source illuminates it. The closer the lighting is to natural light, the higher the color rendering. CRI values closer to 100 indicate higher color rendering. Generally, indoor lighting usually has a standard of CRI $>$ 80. With the growing emphasis on lighting quality in recent years, many manufacturers have raised the standard to CRI $>$ 90 [35].

2.2 Key Points for the Design of Office Lighting

Both quality and quantity must be considered for ambient lighting, which can provide good visual clarity and a high degree of comfort, and meet the physical and psychological needs of users [43]. Various lighting conditions must be researched for different lighting scenarios to meet suitable ambient lighting requirements [17]. In recent years, numerous studies on office ambient lighting have shown that improving office lighting can positively impact employees, and good lighting can lead to better job performance, fewer errors, better safety, and lower absenteeism [46]. Good lighting can also improve comfort, health, and work productivity in a modern office environment [4, 27]. Among all lighting elements, illuminance and color temperature are the most frequently explored factors [29]. Many studies on illuminance have indicated that the higher the environmental illuminance, the greater the visibility. However, high illuminance may increase fatigue while not improving visibility [25]. Proper office illumination adjustments can improve employees' work performance and health [26]. Relevant studies have found that color temperature can impact people's physiology and emotions. The higher the color temperature, the more excited people become; contrariwise, the lower the color temperature, the more relaxed and relieved people are [24]. The color temperature in an office space significantly impacts the mood, happiness, and work performance of employees [21, 36]. Color temperature can also affect people's eyesight, and a higher color temperature can improve people's ability to recognize text [32]. A good office lighting environment must meet the user's psychological preferences and provide physical comfort [30]. Therefore, finding a suitable illuminance and color temperature combination to improve the psychological needs of users under different work scenarios is the primary focus of office lighting research [7, 12].

There is a trend in the lighting industry nowadays towards meeting office workers' physical and psychological needs. Therefore, many international lighting manufacturers' recent designs and developments have focused on improving comfort and work efficiency through light sources. For example, Interact, a company that produces smart lighting connection systems, mentioned that light could regulate the inherent functions of human beings. It can determine our internal body clock and strongly affect our mood. Therefore, a lighting design that mimics the changing sequence of natural light sources can help regulate employees' biological clocks and strengthen their vitality. For older employees, light brightness can also be adjusted to meet their need for a brighter light source and help them to see more details [19, 49]. In terms of improving work efficiency using high-quality lighting, Philips Lighting stated on its official website that according to research, improving light source conditions can increase comfort and have positive impacts on employee performances. Such influences include improving mental and memory functions by 25%, enhancing telephone processing efficiency by 12%, and increasing productivity by 23%.

2.3 Lighting for VDT Workspace

Under the European Union's "2030 climate & energy framework," there are two primary objectives for the planning of office buildings with higher energy consumption demands [34]: to meet the lighting needs while also achieving energy conservation in the office [15]. In response to the ongoing trend towards saving energy, the Task Ambient Lighting (TAL) design method aims to reduce energy consumption by decreasing open office environment lighting fixtures, ambient illuminance, and work desktop lighting. This method has proven quite popular in Europe, the US, and Japan [14]. TAL lighting design plans can save energy while increasing worker comfort and satisfaction [20, 38]. Computer monitors have become ubiquitous in recent years, and workers' visual work surfaces have gradually changed from horizontal desktops to vertical VDT devices. Many relevant studies have shown that ambient lighting considerably impacts VDT work performance and comfort. For example, well-lit areas may cause monitor reflection problems [31], the contrast between monitor brightness and ambient lighting illuminance for different work contents may call for differing illuminance recommendations [10, 47], and color temperature may lead to cognition problems for workers [52]. As the number of people working on VDT devices increases, various countries have formulated health and safety design specifications to serve as related guidelines for computer operation lighting methods and illuminance. Examples include the International Organization for Standardization's ISO 9241, the European Norm EN 12464-1, the US's MIL STD, Germany's DIN standard, the Japan International Center for Occupational Safety's (JICOSH) Kihatsu No.

0405001, and the UK's HSE. A list of such specifications is shown in Table 1, which indicates that optimal illuminances are between 300 lx and 500 lx.

Table 1. VDT illumination recommendations

National standards	Illumination recommendations
ISO 9241	500 lx
EN 12464-1	500 lx
MIL STD 1472B	≥540 lx
DIN 66234	300 lx–500 lx
JICOSH Kihatsu No. 0405001	300 lx–500 lx
British HSE	300 lx–500 lx

3 Research Methodology

The BenQ Screenbar is a lighting device specifically designed for the computer monitor working environment. Its asymmetric light source design can prevent monitor reflections from causing discomfort to the users' eyes. It can be clipped onto the center of the top of a computer monitor to ensure uniform brightness for the work area. The product's main features include allowing users to adjust the brightness and color temperature, automatically detecting the ambient illumination, and boosting the illuminance to 500 lx. These designs and features can improve lighting for the computer monitor work area and meet the basic needs of people working with monitors. However, there is still a dearth of research on the lighting elements in computer monitor work areas in professional settings. Therefore, this study used the BenQ Screenbar lighting device as the sample to investigate the degree to which lighting modes designed by professional lighting engineers with different illuminance and color temperature combinations may affect subjects' subjective psychological feelings and objective work efficiency. This study aims to find lighting modes suitable for computer monitor working environments and improve user satisfaction. The research method is described below.

3.1 Subject Recruitment Conditions

A total of 22 subjects were recruited to participate in this experiment. The subjects were office workers or interns aged 20 to 55. Each gender accounted for 50% of the subjects, and none of the subjects had eye diseases such as color blindness, cataracts, or macular degeneration. Subjects with myopia must wear ordinary glasses or contact lenses to participate in the experiment. A NT$500 subsidy was provided to each subject to increase the subjects' willingness to participate and concentration level, which was paid after the experiment was over.

3.2 Experimental Design

A "within-subjects design" was adopted for this experiment [5]. The experiment sequence was varied for each subject to prevent experimental errors caused by subjects' fatigue or the "practice effect" due to the repeated exposure to the experiment.

The experimental design involved consulting experts throughout the process to formulate the overall structure for this experiment. For the lighting mode settings and questionnaire design, the light sources were designed to simulate energy-conserving office environment lighting and were divided into ambient and computer monitor work lights. A remote control programmed by a professional lighting engineer was used to produce multiple levels of illumination and color temperature.

The questionnaire content was divided into three parts. The first part comprised key points to note and basic information. Before the experiment officially started, the subjects were asked to confirm the following precautionary items: They were asked to verify whether they have myopia and must wear glasses, whether they suffer from other eye diseases, and whether they are color blind. The subjects were instructed to adjust their seat to an appropriate height, keep the distance between the eyes and the computer monitor at 40 cm, adjust the brightness of the monitor and report the brightness value, and adjust the display ratio for on-screen contents while keeping texts on the left and right sides of the monitor in the same positions. The second part was sensory evaluation. Subjects were asked to experience different lighting modes and rate, on a five point scale, the clarity, comfort, color temperature and brightness preference, the degree of brightness felt, and other subjective perceptions. The third part was the objective work efficiency evaluation. The subjects were asked to compare two texts, A and B, which each had a thousand words of a similar level of reading difficulty, with ten words being different between the two texts. The subjects were asked to read the texts within three minutes and mark the different words between them. This test method investigated whether the 11 lighting modes would affect the subjects' reading speed and accuracy.

3.3 Lighting Mode Settings

The lighting of an office environment was simulated using a ceiling lamp, which was set to a general energy-conserving brightness of 250 lx and a medium color temperature of 4000 K. The lighting for the computer monitor work area was set to high, medium, and low illuminance at 750 lx, 500 lx, and 250 lx respectively; these were combined with the high, medium, and low color temperatures of 6500 K, 4000 K, and 2700 K to form nine lighting modes. There were two additional modes with the computer monitor turned off and the light illumination manually adjusted by the subjects themselves. Therefore, the experiment comprised 11 lighting modes in total, which are listed in Table 2.

Table 4. Sensory score ranking for various monitor lighting fixture modes

Rank	1	2	3	4	5	6	7	8	9	10
Clarity	M3 3.955	M2 3.886	M7 3.841	M6 3.795	M9 3.705	M10 3.705	M4 3.659	M5 3.659	M8 3.545	M1 3.455
Comfort	M2 3.773	M3 3.591	M4 3.545	M5 3.500	M6 3.386	M1 3.295	M8 3.295	M7 3.273	M9 3.136	M10 3.068
Fatigue	M9 3.023	M10 2.909	M1 2.864	M8 2.864	M7 2.864	M6 2.795	M4 2.795	M5 2.727	M3 2.636	M2 2.568
Brightness perception	M2 0.045	M3 −0.045	M5 −0.068	M4 −0.114	M8 −0.25	M6 −0.364	M7 −0.5	M1 0.568	M10 −0.568	M9 −0.659
Color temperature preference	M3 3.750	M2 3.705	M6 3.636	M5 3.455	M9 3.455	M4 3.273	M1 3.273	M7 3.091	M8 2.955	M10 2.932
Brightness preference	M2 3.636	M3 3.614	M4 3.341	M5 3.341	M6 3.295	M7 3.068	M9 3.045	M1 3.023	M8 2.955	M10 2.909

evaluation. Therefore, the color temperature of 2700 K and 4000 K with an illuminance of 500 lx was optimal for a computer monitor work environment.

The study divided illuminance level into A = 250 lx, B = 500 lx, C = 750 lx, and D = 1000 lx to explore their sensory feedback. The results are listed in Table 5 below. The illuminance with 500 lx had the best score in terms of sensory perception, followed by 750 lx. The 1000 lx illuminance had the worst scores in terms of comfort, fatigue, color temperature, and brightness preference. The 250 lx illuminance without the monitor light turned on had the worst scores in terms of clarity and brightness.

Table 5. Illumination perception ranking

Rank	1	2	3	4
Clarity	B 3.833	C 3.765	D 3.651	A 3.455
Comfort	B 3.636	C 3.386	A 3.295	D 3.166
Fatigue	D 2.931	A 2.864	C 2.795	B 2.666
Brightness perception	B 3.037	C 3.310	D 3.492	A 2.432
Color temperature preference	B 3.575	C 3.393	A 3.273	D 3.113
Brightness preference	B 3.530	C 3.234	A 3.023	D 2.969

The rankings for reading accuracy rate and reading speed scores are listed in Table 6 below. Although mode 1 had the highest reading accuracy rate and mode 4 had the highest reading speed score, there was no correlation between the test results and the lighting modes.

4.2 Two-Way ANOVA for Brightness and Color Temperature on Comfort

The two-way ANOVA method was used to analyze the impacts that the illumination modes and color temperatures have on comfort. The data outputted using SPASS indicated that the F value of the L variable (illumination) was 5.981, reaching the significance

Table 6. Comparison test ranking

Rank	1	2	3	4	5	6	7	8	9	10	11
Reading accuracy rate	M1 4.50	M3 4.27	M10 4.23	M5 4.18	M6 4.09	M2 4.00	M8 3.95	M7 3.91	M11 3.86	M4 3.77	M9 3.59
Reading speed	M4 840.77	M1 837.18	M9 832.91	M2 827.73	M10 826.05	M3 816.82	M5 802.05	M6 801.05	M7 787.45	M8 784.09	M11 780.09

threshold of 0.01. This means that the monitor viewing comfort varied significantly under different illumination levels. The F value of the K variable (color temperature) was 1.704, which did not reach the significance threshold of 0.05. This means that color temperature changes did not affect monitor viewing comfort. The F value of (L × K) interaction was 0.036, which did not reach the significance threshold of 0.05. This means that illuminance and color temperature had no interaction effect on computer monitor viewing comfort. The results are shown in Table 7 below. The one-way ANOVA method was used to analyze the illuminance's impacts on comfort. The F value of illuminance was 18.222, which reached the significance threshold of 0.001. This meant that monitor viewing comfort varied significantly under different illuminance levels, as shown in Table 8 below.

Table 7. Two-way ANOVA for comfortability by illumination and color temperature of computer monitor light

Source of variation	SS	df	MS	F
SSs	21.739	21	1.035	
SSl	7.290	2	3.645	5.981**
SSk	1.768	2	.884	1.704
SSlk (L × K)	.035	4	.009	0.036
SSsl	25.598	42	.609	
SSsk	21.788	42	.519	
SSslk	20.909	84	.249	

$^{**}p < 0.01$

Figure 2 shows no interaction between the two variables L and K, and the comfort level decreased with L1, L2, and L3. This means that the illuminance of 500 lx offered the best comfort, followed by 750 lx, and 1000 lx had the worst performance. Moreover, comfort levels from the three color temperatures of K1, K2, and K3 also deteriorated as the illuminance increased. Under the same illumination, K1 (2700 K) provided the highest comfort level, followed by K2 (4000 K), and K3 (6500 K) had the worst performance.

Table 8. One-way ANOVA for comfortability by illumination of computer monitor light

Source of variation	SS	df	MS	F
SSs	45.294	65	.697	
SSl	7.290	1	7.280	18.222***
SSsl	46.543	130	.317	

***p < 0.001

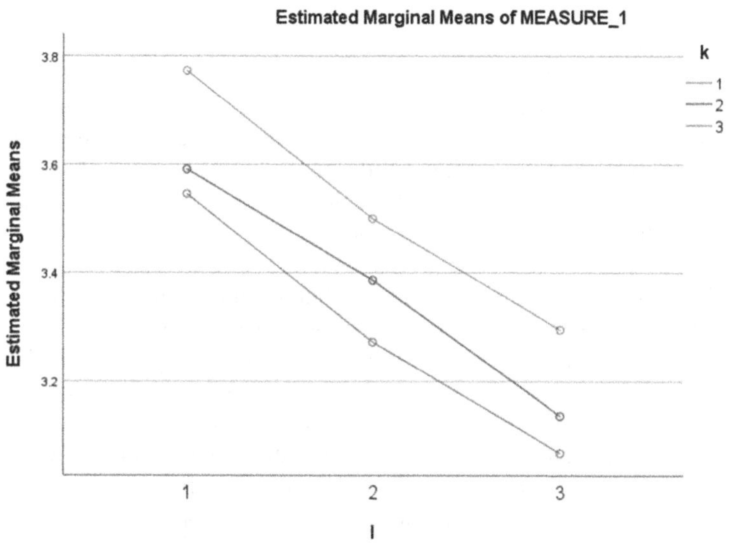

Fig. 2. Interaction diagram for the impacts that illuminance and color temperature have on comfort

4.3 Differences Perceived Under Different Lighting Modes Before and After the Test

The comfort, fatigue, and brightness preference sensory scores obtained before and after the reading tests using the Paired Sample t-test method indicated significant differences are as shown in Table 9 below. Fatigue showed a negative t value. This means that the post-test score was higher than the pre-test score, or the second fatigue score was higher than the first. For comfort and brightness preferences, both scored higher during the first sensory test than the second test. The results indicated that regardless of the lighting modes, the subjects' comfort, fatigue, and brightness preferences would deteriorate after the three-minute reading test.

5 Conclusions

This study aimed to discover which combination of illuminance and color temperature is most suitable for the office computer monitor working environment via literature

Table 9. Comfort, fatigue, and brightness preference differences before and after the test

Items	M	SD	t	
Comfort	Before	3.533	.304	2.99*
	After	3.330	.249	
Fatigue	Before	2.595	.189	−5.684***
	After	2.942	.212	
Brightness preference	Before	3.392	.356	4.375**
	After	3.185	.326	

*p < .05 **p < 0.01 ***p < 0.001

review and experiments. The goal was to improve the subjective perceptions and objective work efficiency for computer monitor users, provide practical and useful design recommendations for computer monitor dedicated lighting fixtures, and strengthen the people-oriented innovation value. Based on the preceding research and analysis, the relevant research recommendations are as follows:

(1) The literature review indicated that office lighting must consider both quality and quantity, and meet the physical and psychological needs of workers to improve their comfort, health, and productivity. The literature indicated that the modern office lighting trend uses a combination of public environment lighting and work area lighting. Lighting devices specifically designed for computer monitor users have rapidly become popular in recent years, illustrating the vast demand for dedicated lighting in computer monitor working scenarios. Therefore, this study conducted an in-depth lighting fixture study to explore the psychological needs of this user group.
(2) The results of this study indicated that the computer monitor lighting mode with the illuminance of 500 lx and color temperature of between 2700 K and 4000 K has the best perception scores, followed by 750 lx. The 1000 lx illuminance had the worst performance in terms of comfort, fatigue, and color temperature. Clarity and brightness perceptions were the worst before the computer monitor light was turned on.
(3) The study results indicated that computer monitor lighting illuminance is significantly correlated to comfort quality. The 500 lx illuminance provided the best comfort, followed by 750 lx, and 1000 lx was the worst. In terms of fatigue, the average fatigue level from the color temperature of 6500 K was higher than that of 2700 K and 4000 K, but the fatigue level from the color temperature of 4000 K was higher than that of 6500 K when the illuminance reached 1000 lx.
(4) The study results indicated significant sensory evaluation differences in terms of comfort, fatigue, and brightness preference before and after the reading test. In sum, the subjects' comfort, fatigue, and brightness preference have declined after the three-minute reading test.
(5) The following are recommended for future computer monitor working environment lighting fixture-related research. First, conduct more in-depth research on

illuminance by adding environmental illuminance factors into the experiment to investigate which office public environment illuminance combination and computer monitor working environment can best satisfy the workers' comfort and preference needs. Second, further improve the work efficiency test content designs to measure the impact of lighting on work efficiency. Third, study what equipment in a computer monitor working environment may affect lighting (table color, keyboard texture, monitor light height, etc.) to construct a comprehensive computer monitor working environment with high-quality lighting.

References

1. Aaron, W.B.: Display technology and ambient illumination influences on visual fatigue at VDT workstations. Published Ph. D thesis, Virginia Polytechnic Institute and State University, Virginia (2000)
2. Average: Office workers spend 1,700 hours a year in front of a computer screen. https://www.independent.co.uk/news/uk/home-news/office-workers-screen-headaches-a8459896.html (2018)
3. Anthony, I.S., Peter, R.B.: Illuminance uniformity on desks: where is the limit? Light. Res. Technol. **22**(4), 165–174 (1990)
4. Avery, D.H., Kizer, D., Bolte, M.A., Hellekson, C.: Bright light therapy of subsyndromal seasonal affective disorder in the workplace: morning vs. afternoon exposure. Acta Psychiatrica Scandinavica **103**(4), 267–274 (2001)
5. Benton, J.U., John, J.S.: Experimentation in Psychology, p. 113. Liou Publishing, Taipei (1989)
6. Benz, C., Grob, R., Haubner, P.: Designing VDU Workspace. Gestaltung von Bildschirm-Arbeitsplätzen, Deutsche Ausgabe. Verlag TÜV heinland Köln, Cologne (1983)
7. Chang, C.-Y., Shie, M.-Y., Feng, C.-C.: Psychological responses toward light and heat in interior lighting. J. Des. Sci. **12**(1), 103–127 (2009)
8. Chang, C.-F., Wang, T.-Y., Liu, C.-H.: Research and analysis of the unified glare rating (UGR) of indoor lighting. J. Technol. **28**(4), P243-249 (2013)
9. Sun, C.-C., Chen, C.-H.: Development of LED and its application in lighting. J. Adv. Technol. Manag. **2011**, 1–23 (2011)
10. Lin, C.-C., Huang, K.-C.: Effects of ambient illumination and screen luminance combination on character identification performance of desktop TFT-LCD monitors. Int. J. Ind. Ergon. **36**(3), 211–218 (2006)
11. Martinsons, C., Zissis, G.: Potential health issues of solid-state lighting. In: Report number: Energy Efficient End-Use Equipment (4E). International Energy Agency Solid State Lighting Annex (2014)
12. Dangol, R., Islam, M., Hyvärinen, M., Bhushal, P., Puolakka, M., Halonen, L.: User acceptance studies for LED office lighting: preference, naturalness and colourfulness. Light. Res. Technol. **47**(1), 36–53 (2015)
13. Zhou, D., Yang, Y., Yan, H.: A smart \"virtual eye\" mobile system for the visually impaired. IEEE Potentials **35**(6), 13–20 (2016)
14. Chou, D.-C., Chou, T.-Y., Lin, Y.-C., Hsieh, H.-Y.: Luminance evaluation model applied to office TAL lighting for space brightness evaluation and energy saving. J. Archit. **104**, 53–71 (2018)

15. Manolis, E., Doulos, L.T., Niavis, S., Canale, L.: The impact of energy efficiency indicators on the office lighting planning and its implications for office lighting market. In: 2019 IEEE International Conference on Environment and Electrical Engineering and 2019 IEEE Industrial and Commercial Power Systems Europe (EEEIC/I&CPS Europe), pp. 1–6 (2019)
16. Newsham, G.R., Veitch, J.A.: Lighting quality recommendations for VDT offices: a new method of derivation. Light. Res. Technol. **33**(2), 97–116 (2001)
17. Nakamura, H., Karasawa, Y.: Relationship between illuminance/color temperature and preference of atmosphere. J. Light. Vis. Env. **23**(1), 29–38 (1999)
18. Hartstein, L.E., LeBourgeois, M.K., Berthier, N.E.: Light correlated color temperature and task switching performance in preschool-age children: preliminary insights. PLoS ONE **13**(8), e0202973 (2018)
19. Heschong Mahone Group: Daylighting in Schools. An investigation into the Relationship between Daylight and Human Performance. Detailed Report, Fair Oaks, CA (1999)
20. Ishii, H., et al.: Intellectual productivity under task ambient lighting. Light. Res. Technol. **50**(2), 237–252 (2018)
21. Knez, I., Enmarker, I.: Effects of office lighting on mood and cognitive performance and a gender effect in work-xRelated judgment. Environ. Behav. **130**(4), 553–567 (1998)
22. Dobres, J., Chahine, N., Reimer, B.: Effects of ambient illumination, contrast polarity, and letter size on text legibility under glance-like reading. Appl. Ergon. **60**, 68–73 (2017)
23. Katabaro, J.M., Yan, Y.: Effects of lighting quality on working efficiency of workers in office building in Tanzania. J. Environ. Public Health **2019**, 1–12 (2019)
24. Katsuura, T.: Are human physiological responses affected by the quality of light? J. Illum. Eng. Inst. Japan **84**(6), 350–353 (2000)
25. Matsuura, K.: Architectural Lighting. Kyoritsu Shuppan, Tokyo (1971)
26. Vimalanathan, K., Ramesh, B.T.: The effect of indoor office environment on the work performance, health and well-being of office workers. J. Environ. Health Sci. Eng. **12**, 113 (2014)
27. Manav, B.: An experimental study on the appraisal of the visual environment at offices in relation to colour temperature and illuminance. Build. Environ. **42**(2), 979–983 (2007)
28. Öner, M.: Measure of visual fatigue as a link between visual environment and visual and non-visual functions of VDT users. EEEIC/I&CPS Europe (2018)
29. Hsieh, M.-Y.: Effects of illumination factors on task performance—using four situations as an example. J. Archit. **94**, 23–37 (2015)
30. Hsieh, M.-Y., Yeh, M.-H.: Research on the effects of illuminance level and color of light on subjective evaluation in reading. J. Archit. **72**, 117–128 (2010)
31. Kubo, M., Ochi, T., Narutaki, Y., Shinomiya, T., Ishii, Y.: Development of "Advanced TFT-LCD" with good legibility under any ambient light intensity. J. Soc. Inf. Display **8**(4), 299–304 (2000)
32. Navvab, M.: Visual acuity depends on the color temperature of the surround lighting. J. Illum. Eng. Soc. **31**(1), 70–84 (2002)
33. Aarts, M.P.J., Aries, M.B.C., Straathof, J., van Hoof, J.: Dynamic lighting systems in psychogeriatric care facilities in The Netherlands: a quantitative and qualitative analysis of stakeholders' responses and applied technology. Indoor Built Environ. **24**(5), 617–630 (2015)
34. Santamouris, M., Dascalaki, E.: Passive retrofitting of office buildings to improve their energy performance and Indoor Environment: the office project. Build. Environ. **37**(6), 575–578 (2002)
35. Pimputkar, S., Speck, J., DenBaars, S., et al.: Prospects for LED lighting. Nature Photon **3**, 180–182 (2009)
36. Mills, P.R., Tomkins, S.C., Schlangen, L.J.M.: The effect of high correlated colour temperature office lighting on employee wellbeing and work performance. J. Circadian Rhythms **5**, 2 (2007). https://doi.org/10.1186/1740-3391-5-2

37. Chen, R.-L., Chou D.-C.: A study of energy saving manual for office lighting. Architecture and Building Research Institute Ministry of the Interior Research Project Report (2007)
38. Chraibi, S., Lashina, T., Shrubsole, P., Aries, M., van Loenen, E., Rosemann, A.: Satisfying light conditions: a field study on perception of consensus. Build. Environ. **105**, 116–127 (2016)
39. Lin, S.-S., Ke, C.-T., Wu, C.-F.: A study of an optimizing LED light using on writing motion. Chin. Inst. Design **5**, 1249–1254 (2015)
40. Chen, S.-J., Lin, C.-L.: The effect of lighting models in coffee shop on the psychological responses of consumers. J. Ergon. Study **17**(2), 73–80 (2015)
41. Smith, S.W., Rea, M.S.: Performance of a reading test under different levels of illumination. J. Illum. Eng. Soc. **12**(1), 29–33 (1982)
42. The illuminating Engineering Institute of Japan: Lighting Handbook, 2nd ed. Chuan Hwa Book (2006)
43. Kruisselbrink, T., Dangol, R., Rosemann, A.: Photometric measurements of lighting quality: An overview. Build. Environ. **138**, 42–52 (2018)
44. Chung, T.M., Burnett, J.: Lighting quality surveys in office premises. Indoor Built Env. **9**(6), 335–341 (2000)
45. TrendForce: Monitor shipment for 2021 expected to reach 150 million units due to strong demand generated by COVID-19 pandemic, says trendforce https://www.trendforce.com/presscenter/news/20210512-10780.html (2021)
46. van Bommel, W., van den Beld, G.: Lighting for work: a review of visual and biological effects. Light. Res. Technol. **36**(4), 255–266 (2004)
47. Veitch, J.A., Newsham, G.R.: Preferred luminous conditions in open-plan offices: research and practice recommendations. Light. Res. Technol. **32**(4), 199–212 (2000)
48. Duffy, V.G., Chan, A.H.S.: Effects of virtual lighting on visual performance and eye fatigue. Hum. Factors Ergon. Manuf. **12**(2), 193–209 (2002)
49. Loftness, V., Hartkopf, V., Gurtekin, B.: Linking energy to health and productivity in the built environment. In: Greenbuild Conference, Center for Building Performance and Diagnostics. Carnegie Mellon University, USA (2003)
50. Akashi, Y., Boyce, P.R.: A field study of illuminance reduction. Energy Build. **38**(6), 588–599 (2006)
51. Yoko, T.: IT ophthalmopathy and VDT syndrome. Hist. Med. **214**(12), 1029–1032 (2005)
52. Zhigang, H., Yi, C., Hao, J., Qiao, X., Guo, X.: Comparative study on the effects of lighting on cognitive ergonomics in single and multi-working modes. NeuroQuantology **16**(5), 341–349 (2018)

Participatory Curation and the Construction of Its Application Models in Exhibitions of Traditional Furniture Industry: A Case Study of Daxi, Taoyuan, Taiwan

Tien-Li Chen[1] and Yung-Cheng Chen[2](✉)

[1] Department of Industrial Design, National Taipei University of Technology, Taipei City, Taiwan

[2] College of Design, National Taipei University of Technology, National Museum of History, Taipei City, Taiwan

audichen81@gmail.com

Abstract. Taoyuan Daxi, a city located on the border between the Xueshan mountain range and the plains in northern Taiwan and along the banks of the Dahan River, has been one of the major manufacturing towns of the traditional furniture industry in northern Taiwan for over a century. Given the gradually declining development of the Daxi wood art industry, the Daxi Wood Art Ecomuseum (hereinafter DWAEM) in Taoyuan City was renamed "Daxi Gallery of Wood Furniture" after the restoration of the historical building "Daxi Assembly Hall". The gallery has been established to serve as an exclusive platform for wood art craftsmen to present their creations and exchange dialogues, in the hope that through the exhibition, the public can reacquaint themselves with the past, present and future of the Daxi wood art industry.

This study aims to introduce the concept of "participatory curation" into the application of local museum exhibition curatorship through action research design. This enables each participating wood craftsman to engage deeply in the curatorial process and understand the concept of the theme so that the exhibitor can accurately deliver the creative concept of the craftsman and the brand as well as the design concept of the exhibited work.

Finally, through in-depth interviews with exhibitors, museum colleagues, and senior volunteers, the "Application of Participatory Curatorial Model" for traditional furniture exhibitions was gradually revised. Opinions were compiled through post-exhibition curatorial sharing meetings, resulting in six positive curatorial outcomes. At the same time, the DWAEM and most of the local wood craftsmen are willing to participate in the exhibitions operated in such a style, so that together we can carry out the vision of creating and sustaining the local industry with the concept of learning and wellbeing together.

Keywords: Participatory curation · Traditional furniture · Industrial revival · Local museum · Community development · Re-utilization of historic sites and buildings · Curation design

P.-L. P. Rau (Ed.): HCII 2022, LNCS 13314, pp. 36–53, 2022.
https://doi.org/10.1007/978-3-031-06053-3_3

1 Foreword

Daxi Taoyuan, a city located in the northern part of Taiwan at the border of the Xueshan Mountain Range and the plain beside the Dahan River, has been one of the major manufacturing centres of the traditional furniture industry in northern Taiwan for more than a century since the late Qing Dynasty in the 19th century, through the Japanese rule era to the 1970s and 1980s in the 20th century. Following the '80s when Chinese and Southeast Asian cheaper wooden furniture were increasingly dumped into Taiwan, Daxi's traditional furniture industry underwent a rapid decline after the '90s. At this time, the Council for Cultural Affairs of the Executive Yuan has been actively promoting the policy of "Community Development". Through years of participation and experience of scholars, experts, local residents and local governments, Daxi has managed to maintain the characteristics of traditional industries and community cultural development, becoming one of the few local communities that still have distinctive cultural industry characteristics and social creation energy.

In the spirit of community development, the Council of Cultural Affairs of the Executive Yuan (hereinafter referred to as the CCA) initiated the first phase of the "Local Culture Hall" project from 2001 to 2007, followed by the five-year "Local Culture Hall Second Phase Project" in 2008. The establishment of the local cultural centre has become the common vision of local residents.

1.1 Study Motives

In 2015, in response to the decline of the Daxi traditional furniture industry and the continuous promotion of the "Local Culture Hall" project throughout Taiwan, the Taoyuan City Government established the "Taoyuan Municipal Daxi Wood Art Ecomuseum DWAEM" (hereinafter referred to as DWAEM) with the expectation that the museum would lead local wood industry to re-gather consensus and take up the task of passing on and promoting the Daxi wood art culture. Through the restoration and reuse of the historic building, it was planned as an exhibition space and was positioned as the "Daxi Gallery of Wood Furniture," with long-term planning of in-depth study on Daxi wooden furniture-related subjects. The establishment of an exchange platform for wood art exhibitions and performances contributes to the inheritance and development of wood knowledge and the promotion of the public's understanding of wood life through exhibitions. DWAEM has transformed the historic building into an experience space for displaying and appreciating wood art, promoting museums' educational concepts and intellectual learning leisure activities, with the hope of bringing vitality to local development. Over the past five years, DWAEM has organized many exhibitions in various genres and themes of wood art and furniture. The challenge for DWAEM and the local staff was to figure out the know-how of revising and implementing the past experience in future exhibition planning.

1.2 Purpose of the Study

This study focuses on the experience of curation of DWAEM. Through new curation practices, we discussed and reviewed the curation process with the participants to construct a participatory curatorial model that can be applied to the future Daxi traditional wood furniture industry. The following objectives were expected to be achieved:

1. A closer integration and common understanding of the exhibition theme with the local wood furniture industry craftsmen;
2. Deepening the participation of local wood craftsmen and increasing the chance of the craftsmen to be witnessed by the public.
3. Allowing the public to better understand the traditional wood art culture of Daxi and to achieve the purpose of passing on and promoting wood knowledge.

1.3 Limitations of the Study

This study focuses primarily on the curatorial practices of the first two exhibitions after the opening of the "Daxi Gallery of Wood Furniture," and targets the woodworkers who participated in the first two exhibitions while giving comments and suggestions on the results of the participatory curatorial process from the perspective of the DWAEM workers and senior volunteers. The experimental model of the Wood Museum may not be universally applicable to all traditional industries in the curatorial application of local museums, but it should have a positive reference value for local museums similar to Daxi that still have local traditional industries and cultural ecologies such as employees.

2 Literature Review

2.1 Local Museums and Taoyuan City Daxi Wood Art Ecomuseum

The development of national cultural policy has been the most influential factor in shaping the cultural environment of citizens. Under the influence of a series of policies and programs initiated by the Executive Yuan in 1994, the Council of Cultural Affairs(CCA) initiated the first phase of the "Local Culture Hall" project from 2001 to 2007. In 2008, the second phase of the "Local Culture Hall" project was launched for five years, constructing the global trend of building the attitude and life of "cultural citizens" with local identity as the core. The project has combined the project concepts of historical buildings and the reuse of vacant space to improve software and hardware and integrate resources. Through the establishment and integration of local cultural sites, it is hoped that the cultural differences between urban and rural areas could be balanced, and the cultural construction and economic industries would be sustainably developed for the local community while expecting that it would have the spirit and nature of a community museum and that it would fully absorb the participation of the community people and exist for them [1, 2]. In the CCA "Local Culture Hall Project" guideline, the objective of this project was to focus on establishing a cultural center in rural areas to achieve balanced development of urban and rural areas as well as to create new cultural vitality by using vacant public space. This emphasizes the development of local cultural characteristics invigorating creativity and sustainable operation.

The Local Culture Hall has based on the features of regional humanities, arts, history, culture, folklore, crafts, landscape, ecology, industrial resources, etc., with the core content of promoting arts and cultural activities and nurturing arts and cultural talents and passing on traditional culture and arts [3].

The Daxi Wood Art Ecomuseum was established in 2015. With the promotion of the aforementioned background and the national cultural policy for many years, the Ecomuseum was the first museum in Taiwan which was established in the name of "wood art" and "ecology". DWAEM was given the task of passing on and promoting the culture of Daxi wood art, promoting the development of wood knowledge, and popularizing the public's understanding of wood life. The abundance of cultural values and assets in Daxi and the participation of the residents in cultural affairs are the basis for DWAEM to constantly promote various projects, and the full revitalization and reuse of monuments and historical buildings are also the key factors for the foundation of "Museum without Walls" in Daxi.

Ideally, the eco-museum brings all the efforts of the community together to maintain; the content of the museum should also be the physical culture and knowledge of the local area. However, the maintenance and operation of the eco-museum are often resident-oriented, resulting in difficulties in terms of funding, decision-making, and publicness. The tug-of-war and challenges of public-private collaboration have shown that such development does face barriers [4]; a similar challenge occurs in the case of the DWAEM as well.

For more than five years, the museum has engaged in community building and the promotion of the Local Culture Hall. It has been preserving the local culture and transforming it into cultural tourism and promotional area through the educational management of the museum. These engagements have transformed the historic building into a field for displaying and experiencing the wood art theme, injecting abundant vitality into the local development and linking more Tahitians to participate in it. This study and curatorial practice is based on such a spirit. With the participation of local craftsmen and through participatory curatorial guidance, it was expected that the spirit of "sustainability and heritage of the woodworking industry in Daxi" could be revived, demonstrating the energy of Daxi and reclaim the glory of the "Furniture Township".

2.2 Participatory Curation

Participatory curation derives from participative design. In this study, there are two levels of "participation" implied respectively. The first level is participatory observation, in which curators and wood craftsmen jointly engage in the process of curating and creating exhibits, and share the experience of the curatorial process. The second level is the participatory experience in experiential design, that is, participatory design, which is extended to as "participatory creation" (the creation refers to curatorial creation, not the work of the wood craftsman's participation).

Participatory Observation: Before the data collection in the field, though the researcher was able to obtain a preliminary understanding of the research field and the target population through the literature, there was no reliable way to understand the genuine opinions and requests of the local community from the external data. Therefore, it was necessary to adopt the method of participatory observation to fully understand the inside situation of the Daxi wood industry. Jorgensen (1989) and Bernard (1998) mentioned that participatory is suitable in "the limited knowledge of the researcher about the phenomenon under study so that the researcher can develop a preliminary understanding of the phenomenon under study through participatory observations" [5, 6].

Participatory curation has broad definitions and applications across a wide range. In each exhibition production process, many proposals need to be negotiated [7], and in every culture and community, there could be different negotiation mechanisms that can be discussed and applied [8]. When the wood craftsmen participate in exhibition curations, their role exceeds that of a participant, but serve as co-curators. At this point, the concern of the craftsmen is not only the presentation themes and creative ideas but also the experience of co-working with the curator in the process of completing a curatorial design. They have gradually sorted out the common ideals and concepts of the local wood art craftsmen, telling their own stories in the curatorial discourse and telling every visitor the vision of happiness of the craftsmen in Daxi.

As local museums seek to integrate and interact with their communities, N. Simon listed five most commonly questioned and criticized issues of cultural institutions:

1. Cultural institutions are disconnected from the life experience of people.
2. Cultural institutions rarely make changes in their exhibitions or other related matters, which makes people less likely to return to them.
3. Cultural Institutions' exhibitions rarely integrate the viewpoint of the audience or allow them to understand the content or context of the exhibition.
4. Cultural institutions are not creative places where the audience can express their personal history, science or art.
5. Cultural institutions are not a comfortable social space in which to interact with friends or strangers.

In response to the five issues, Simon suggested that "participatory strategies" could be implemented by the cultural institutions. Through actively responding to diversified ideas of the audience and facilitating a cultural platform for open opinions and participation, the cultural institute will link closer to the local real-life context and will be valued by the audiences for being an inclusive environment [9].

2.3 Curatorial Design

Exhibition design is a professional discipline in which the visual arts are transformed into expression and communication. Renee Sandell, professor at the Institute of Art Education at George Mason University, believes that humanity is facing a new visual literacy in the 21st century. Learning to see the ever-changing world in a new light is an inevitable issue for artists and art educators (including museums) [10]. In the past, art education was divided into two main subjects: form and content. This dual-oriented concept of art education can no longer face coping with the fast-changing and complex visual world of the 21st century. Therefore, Sandell proposed the FTC model in 2006, using "context" as the third dimension in the examination of art. The structure of Art =

Form + Theme + Context, helps us to explore the connotation and meaning of artworks from three perspectives: formal, thematic and contextual. Therefore, it is essential to learn and construct an exhibition of traditional furniture in three aspects: form, theme, and context through curatorial practice, sorting out and presenting to the public and promoting further understanding of traditional furniture culture.

In addition, Sandell believes that to enhance visual literacy, several corresponding skills are needed: the ability to interpret, use, appreciate, and create still and moving images through the use of traditional or new media to enhance people's understanding, thinking, decision-making, communication, and learning. In addition to art creation and art history, we should also help people to build a more comprehensive understanding of images, objects, and activities of past or present art so that art can be more closely related to everyone's life. This is the biggest difference between FTC and the traditional DBAE (Discipline-Based Art Education) theory of E.W. Eisner [11]. Given the above, this study attempts to lead traditional woodworkers to interpret their works during the curatorial process. In the process of practicing and interpreting their creative concepts, craftsmanship and technical characteristics, they grow.

The three elements of successful exhibition space, especially a design-related one, include at least three elements: 1. creating a Kansei space; 2. providing an affective experience; 3. presenting qualia products. A Kansei space is a contextual way of telling stories by attracting the audience and make them feel the function of the situation. The final goal is to create the affective experience of audience. The affective experience is created by arranging a Kansei Space and providing Qualia Products to satisfy the psychological needs of the audience. Therefore, sensual scene imagery and sensual merchandise design are the key factors that affect the audience's experience [12].

The current creative aspiration of design tends to be "simple and rich - simplifying hardware and enriching software". The purpose of design is to improve the quality of human life and enhance the cultural taste of society. After the global financial crisis in 2008, the purchasing behavior of consumers has changed radically; simplicity and abundance have become the core value of consumption. Therefore, curatorial design has become a topic worthy of our consideration [13, 14]. Based on the same concept, we hope to successfully convey the core value of "simplicity, clarity and richness" of the Daxi wood furniture industry through the curatorial practice and continuous revision of the "Wood Furniture Gallery" of the DWAEM.

3 Design of Study

Given the current situation of the promotion of the wood art industry in Daxi, it is necessary to approach the issue from different angles and methods. The core of the overall community development is "people" and only through the active participation and practice of people can the development of the community last [15]. Therefore, this study takes the curatorial practice of the "Wood Furniture Gallery" at DWAEM as an example, and through a participatory curatorial approach like action research, we hope to achieve the participation and concern of wood art workers. In the study process, we faced multiple complicated and unanswered questions. Therefore, we have adopted multiple ways to obtain multifaceted data, through action research, participatory observation, interviews, and questionnaires, to gain a deeper understanding of the research subjects and the field. We hope to find another possible way to revitalize the wood art industry in Daxi.

3.1 Action Research Method

The action research method emphasizes the integration of "action" and "research". According to Ching-Tian Tsai's book, "Action Research in Education," it has been fifty years since "action research" was advocated by American scholars such as Kurt Lewin and Stephen M. Corey during the 1940s [16]. As explained by Tzu-Chau Chang in the Encyclopedic Dictionary of Education in 2000, action research is a research method that combines the characteristics of a problem in a specific time, place and context based on relevant theories. The method can be evaluated according to the circumstances of individual implementation [17, 18].

The objective of the action research method consists of optimizing the process, improving quality, refining techniques, and strengthening professional skills. The design of the research method integrates an overall framework to solve the situations encountered in the experimental process and find of new directions for development. This method relies on authentic observations and behavioral data for analysis and improvement, and it has been regarded as empirical research. The process of action research is flexible and adaptive, which allows adaptive changes during the study while forgoing control measures to enable spontaneous responses and innovative field experimentation. The theory can be based on the framework of naturalism, and such research is inseparable from the subjectivity of the researcher's judgment of value and the context in which the research question exists. Therefore, reliability and validity can be assessed by a qualitative research approach. The curatorial process can be divided into the following steps of analysis and consolidation (Fig. 1).

1. Define the problem or establish the goal.
2. Inventory the contents of past exhibitions and identify relevant curatorial foundations.
3. Formulating a curatorial strategy that is practical and verifiable.
4. Design the curatorial environment and clearly establish the curatorial procedures and conditions.
5. Establish measurement techniques, methods and perform operations.
6. Analyzing and discussing the results and recommendations.

This study was based on the planning of the "Daxi Assembly Hall" themed as the "Wood Furniture Gallery" exhibition and the reopening of the historical building in June 2020. The author participated in the "Daxi Wood Furniture Living Hall Construction Planning and Implementation Project" in 2019 and the first expansion of the project in 2020. Through on-site curatorial opportunities, the participatory curatorial model was introduced in the process. A total of 12 groups of local wood craftsmen and those who have just settled in Daxi participated in the curatorial process of this exhibition.

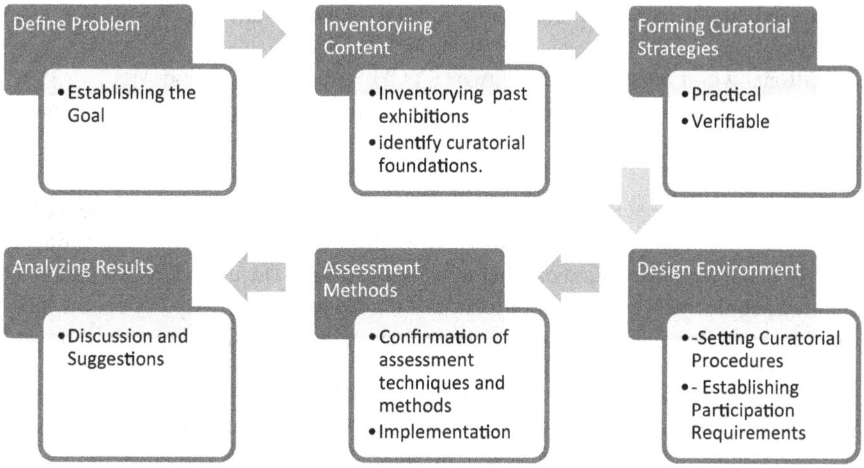

Fig. 1. Curatorial research procedure diagram

3.2 In-Depth Interviews

Interviewees. In this study, the participatory curatorial model was adopted for comparison with the traditional exhibition curatorial model. To ensure the reliability and validity of the interview content, the sampling of this in-depth interview was designed as follows: the main respondents were the wood craftsmen who participated a second time in the exhibition. The target of this study was the two exhibitions before the opening of the wood furniture gallery in DWAEM, and 12 craftsmen participated in each of these exhibitions; three craftsmen did not continue to participate in the second exhibition, so three additional wood crafts companies were invited to the exhibition. A total of nine members who participated in both exhibitions, and six of the wood craftsmen who participated in both exhibitions were selected as the main interviewees, and the Orange and White Studio, which is not from the traditional woodworking background of Daxi, was chosen as the main interviewees for comparison with the local traditional wood craftsmen in this study.

In addition to the exhibitors, this study interviewed three DWAEM staff and two senior volunteers to obtain diverse perspectives from non-exhibitors and post-exhibit interviews from outside visitors. In addition, the curatorial sharing sessions after the second exhibition were held to collect the audience opinion and finally summarize and analyze the results of the interviews. The target audience and background of this exhibition are as follows:

Exhibitors: A total of seven exhibitors. among the participants of the two exhibitions, we selected the three-generation old stores, young generations craftsmen, representatives of traditional artisans, and workers with different backgrounds, such as newcomers to Daxi from other places, as interviewees.

- Three-generations wood shop current operators: A total of two (Xie Sheng Wooden, Long Da Furniture)

- Younger generation wood craftsmen: A total of two (Tang He Wood, ZU Wood Industry)
- Traditional wood artists: A total of two (SYCH Wood, Sanhe Wood Art)
- Newly immigrated wood artists: One (Orange and White Workshop (now renamed moofoo)

Museum Curator: Three Staff Members It is designed to discuss the effectiveness of this curatorial approach and future suggestions from different perspective of the administration section and the observation of other museum sections. The interview was conducted with three people, including the coordinator of the Collection Display Group, the leader of the Education Promotion Division, and members of the Education Promotion Division.

Senior Museum Volunteers: A total of two (one each for holiday and weekday shifts) Apart from understanding the needs and opinions of the exhibitors themselves, we also added two volunteers to the interviewees in order to balance the similarity of the opinions of the people involved in the exhibition. In hope that through the experience and perspective of the volunteers, we can provide corresponding feedback to the curatorial model of the exhibition.

Interview Outline Design. To distinguish the differences between the results of traditional exhibitions and this participatory curatorship and to observe participants' sense of recognition and participation in local industries and local museums, the respondents were asked to express their opinions on the results of this curatorial practice in four different aspects. The results were then collected and consolidated as a reference for subsequent curatorship. Please refer to Chapter 4, Study Results for more details on the design and topics of the interview.

3.3 Preliminary Framework for Participatory Curation Operations

To establish a curatorial pre-operation mechanism for the initial operating period of the Wood Furniture Gallery, the first two exhibitions after the opening of the gallery, the museum and the curatorial team adopted the concept of participatory curation and introduced it into actual curatorial practice after discussions at the preliminary working meetings. The preliminary process and structure were set as follows:

Organizing a Curatorial Consensus Meeting to Promote the Exchange and Interaction of the Tahitian Wood Art Community. There was at least one curatorial consensus meeting, in which local woodworkers, wood sculptors, and paint specialists were invited to share their experiences, promote the concept of a wood furniture museum, and collect opinions from the woodworking community. The meeting was held to gather consensus on the following purposes: the curatorial theme; and to discuss the management strategy of the Wooden Furniture Living Hall; the vision of the industry development; the preliminary understanding of the current development of wood art in Daxi; the regular information collection; to co-plan the annual exhibition replacement project; and the proposal of the future exhibition plan of the Wooden Furniture Gallery.

Curatorial Workshops Held to Define the Theme and Content of the Exhibition. At least three curatorial workshops were held, in which wood art professionals who have participated in curatorial consensus meetings were invited to discuss, develop and implement the curatorial theme, the content of works, design concepts, copywriting and other curatorial substance. The content is as follows:

Theme Setting: Set the opening theme or design a new theme through workshops.

Display Content Planning: Including display copywriting, story line writing, and various display areas, display units, display methods, etc., and to show creativity and present new forms of design style.

Production of Exhibition Objects: Gathering wood craftsmen to run workshops for creative discussions and planning the production or selection of display works according to the curatorial direction, space characteristics and display needs of the exhibition venue.

Exhibition Design and Production. A professional display design and production team will participate in the exhibition, providing the main visual design (display layout, color scheme, warning and movement indicators), designing the "contextual display space", and designing the interactive display methods to enhance the audience's understanding of wooden furniture.

Organizing Curatorial Sharing and Exchange Meetings. After the opening and closing of the exhibition, a curatorial exchange meeting will be held to review and exchange the contents of the curatorial exhibition and the exhibition presentation, which will serve as a reference for the next curatorial execution and adjustment, and to gather the consensus and centripetal force of the participating wood art craftsmen again.

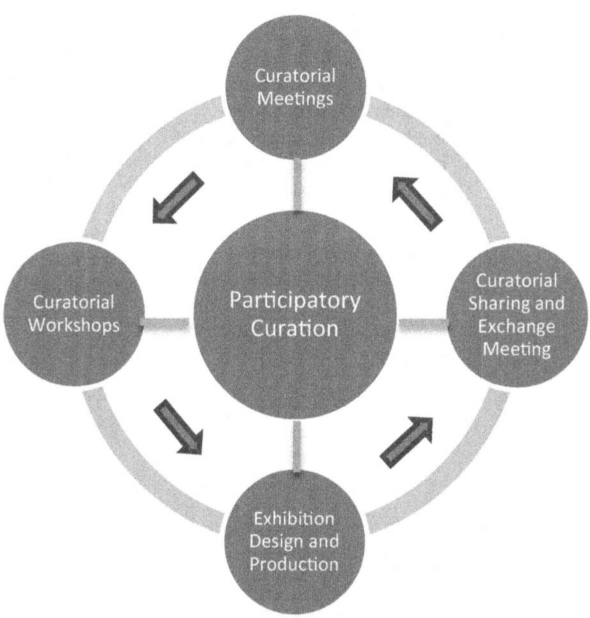

Fig. 2. The basic framework of participatory curation model

Through the process of actual curatorial practice, this study presents the basic model of "Participatory Curation" in Fig. 2.

4 Study Results

In the process of the two participatory curatorial practices during the exhibitions, the theme of these two exhibitions was developed through the curator's guidance and continuously discussed and revised with the museum staff and the participating wood craftsmen in numerous curatorial consensus meetings and workshops. Through this curatorial process, the exhibition also aims to build consensus and guide the future vision of local wood craftsmen.

In addition, to cultivate creative talents in wood art and enhance the innovative energy of the local industry, this curatorial project explored Daxi's culture and resources through the process of inventorying and researching cultural resources such as wood art and crafts, joint exchanges, and conducted an in-depth exploration of the industry as a background for the exhibition. The following discussion provides an overview of the core spiritual values of Daxi Furniture, the exhibition themes, and the framework of its operating model. We hope that this will serve as a basis and reference for future discussions on the spirit and values of the Daxi Furniture brand. The results of the interview are summarized as follows (Table 1).

Table 1. Summary of interview results.

Interview scope	Interview topics	Summary
About Exhibition Participation Experience	Participation in DWAEM Exhibitions (Exhibiting and Visiting)	1. In the past, participants of the exhibition could simply submit their works, but in this exhibition, we must not only discuss the theme of the exhibition together, but also think of the works that fit the theme 2. The exhibition process is long and requires someone to keep a close eye on everyone's progress 3. There is a certain impression of having made some contribution to Daxi furniture
	What are the differences between the curatorial model (participatory Curation Model) of the two exhibitions and the experience of previous exhibitions? What are the advantages and disadvantages?	
	Do you have any experience in other exhibitions outside of Daxi? Is there anything you can learn or suggest from that experience for Daxi?	

(continued)

Table 1. (*continued*)

Interview scope	Interview topics	Summary
Exhibition Preference and Theme Communication	Do you like the content of these two exhibitions?	1. The purpose of the exhibition has given people an imagination of a happy life in the future, and through the furniture display, the ideas of the woodworkers are expressed in a more concrete way 2. Through the discussion of the exhibition theme, although somewhat abstract, the spirit and value of Daxi furniture has been gradually shaped 3. Future exhibition themes can also be developed towards a single category or use of space, so that the works of wood craftsmen can highlight their creativity
	(Participatory Curation) Can the exhibition theme, developed through discussion, convey the core values of Daxi Furniture?	
	Regarding these two exhibitions, which one do you like the most, in terms of exhibition theme, artworks, design of exhibition space, visual design, etc.? Which part of the site feels more inadequate and can be corrected and adjusted again?	
Suggestions for Curatorial Model	Does this curatorial model bring positive benefits to the local craftsmen?	1. The participatory curatorial process allows wood craftsmen to rethink the relationship between their works and the lives of modern people 2. It is necessary to consider the current business conditions of the woodworkers in Daxi, who still must focus on their main career. It is hoped that the time to participate in curation and creation could avoid the peak season of the traditional furniture industry, so that they can have more time to devote to the exhibitions in DWAEM 3. Hopefully, the curatorial process can be accompanied by learning courses or visiting other woodworking furniture exhibitions to strengthen the creative motivation of woodworkers 4. The frequency of curatorial workshop discussions can be increased moderately by one or two times, so that the creative process can be corrected or break through the creative bottleneck through discussions
	What are the suggestions for revising the curatorial model (curatorial working meeting, consensus meeting, curatorial workshop, exhibition venue, installation, curatorial exchange meeting)?	
	Is the curatorial workshop sufficient? Too much or not enough?	
	Are you willing to continue to use this curatorial model (participatory curation) in the future, and further explore the construction of the core values that define the brand of Daxi Furniture?	

(*continued*)

Table 1. (*continued*)

Interview scope	Interview topics	Summary
Reflections on the future of Daxi Furniture	Reflections on the future of Daxi Furniture After this period of time, what do you think are the core values of Daxi Furniture?	1. Insisting on traditional woodworking techniques, using authentic materials and conveying traditional woodworking culture 2. Emphasizing the customization and customization features to serve the requirements of each customer 3. Hoping to learn more knowledge and skills about design, creation, and marketing 4. Integrating the characteristics of Daxi furniture, creating a common brand of Daxi furniture, and finding the past glory
	Can you tell us about your study and creative projects?	
	What is your vision and imagination for the future of Daxi furniture?	

4.1 Delivering the Core Value of "Simplicity and Clarity" of Daxi Furniture

To convey the core value of "Simplicity and Clarity" of the Daxi wood furniture industry, the participatory curatorial spirit of this study was to begin the curatorial phase of both exhibitions with a consensus meeting, followed by at least three curatorial workshops to discuss the theme of the exhibit. In the end, the curatorial main theme of the inaugural exhibition was "Wood Craftsman's Happiness Proposal," creating a common memory and emotional connection to the Daxi wood art industry. Each craftsmen were asked to create an exclusive piece of furniture for his or her beloved family members. This request was tend to encourage craftsmen and audiences to remember the original intention of art and bring about the core value of "Daxi Furniture" as the "furniture of happiness" (Fig. 3).

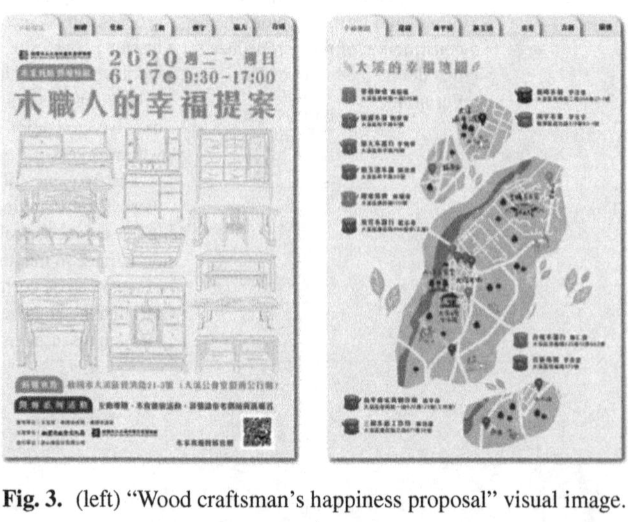

Fig. 3. (left) "Wood craftsman's happiness proposal" visual image.

Following the spirit of the "Wood Craftsman's Happiness Proposal," the second exhibition was developed under the theme of "A Gift from Daxi" after discussions at the consensus meeting and incorporated the connotations of traditional New Year gift culture into Daxi's woodwork and furniture, creating "Daxi woodwork and furniture" as the best choice to convey the owner's feelings in a custom-made way (Fig. 4). The operation of the two exhibits contributes to the stabilization of the Wood Furniture Gallery operation strategy but also gradually develops the operation mechanism of the Daxi Wood Art Exhibition and Exchange Platform. Moreover, it lays a solid foundation for future development towards shaping a regional shared brand for the Wood Furniture Gallery.

Fig. 4. (right) "A gift from Daxi" visual image.

A brief description of the exhibition themes and curatorial discussions of the two operational practices are as follows:

The First Exhibition Theme: "Wood Craftsman's Happiness Proposal." With each worker making a piece of furniture for the craftsmen's beloved family members, they may recall the original intention of learning the art. "Furniture" was taken as the carrier to reflect life history such as marriage, new born, growing up, family reunion, and finally personal faith and family succession, etc. Through the design, different levels of emotions such as "affection, sharing, reunion, and inheritance" are conveyed, bringing out the role and happy memories that wooden furniture has played in every period of life.

The Second Exhibition Theme: "Woodworkers' Happiness Proposal 2.0 - Gifts from Daxi." This exhibition continues the concept of "Woodworker's Happiness Proposal," showing the spirit of "gift etiquette" of human communication. By creating ritualistic wood artworks with special commemorative meaning, the wood art craftsmen emphasize traditional culture and humanistic feelings, integrating wood art creation into today's life and bringing surprise, fun and happiness to life.

"Gifts create a sense of ritual in daily life that makes one day different from other days and become a special memory moment." The wood has been the best gift from the mountains to mankind. Daxi wood craftsmen have inherited the traditional techniques and work together to transform the wood into warm gifts and send the sincere feelings to the people who want to be blessed.

Taiwan has been a courteous society, and gifts are always appreciated during New Year's Eve and special festivals. We have established a mutual connection between people, from gift-giving to mutual appreciation, to maintain the relationship and transmission of emotions, showing the warmth of human feelings everywhere.

The core values of the themes of the two exhibitions mentioned above, according to the feedback and results of the interviews and post-exhibition sharing sessions, the exhibition themes operated under this model were generally recognized by the museums and most of the local wood art craftsmen. At the same time, a consensus and cohesiveness were felt by all. According to the results of 552 questionnaires sent to the public during the exhibition, 65.2% of the public were very satisfied with the exhibition and 32.8% were satisfied with the exhibition results (Table 2). Therefore, the results of this curatorial model have been well-received by the staff and visitors, and both DWAEM and the participants are willing to plan and execute the next exhibition with this curatorial model.

Table 2. Exhibition visitors' level of satisfaction

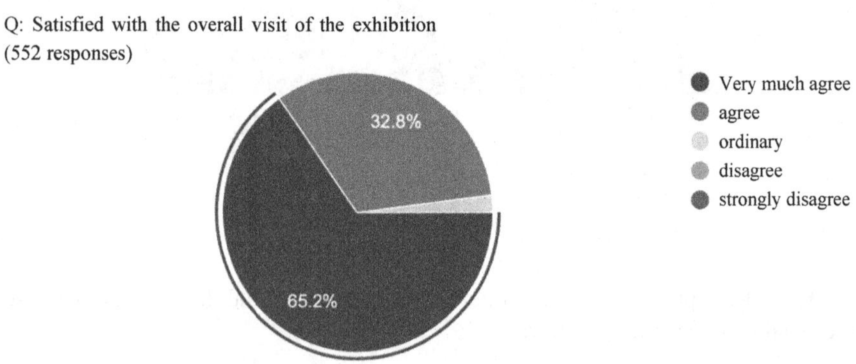

4.2 Suggestions for the Construction and Adjustment of the "Participatory Curation" Model

The results of the two exhibitions, after the post-exhibition sharing sessions and the in-depth interviews, have led to the following conclusions:

1. The operation of "participatory curation" in the two exhibitions has gained the recognition of the participating craftsmen and DWAEM, and the overall results are clear and the purpose has become clearer. Therefore, a continuous promotion is needed in the future, so that the craftsmen of Daxi wood furniture industry can grow together and enhance the energy of creativity.

2. Through the operation of the two exhibitions, DWAEM has further affirmed that the "Wood Furniture Gallery" will continue to be served as a platform for curating wood art exhibitions, which are closely related to local trade unions, and to reinforce the function of this exchange platform. It is expected, the Wood Furniture Gallery will become the best showcase for people to learn about wood art in Daxi. We also hope that through this model, the woodworkers will become more mature in their creations and work together to build the brand of Daxi woodcraft and shape the spirit and value of the Daxi woodcraft brand.
3. In the future, we hope to add training programs related to wood art creation and design in the participatory curatorial model, so that the participating staff can learn and work together in the process of co-curating, and enhance the staff's innovative creative ability.
4. The participatory curatorial process enables Daxi's wood craftsmen to come up with new ways of revitalizing the traditional furniture industry and overcoming the limitations of the current products. As it evolves to be more relevant to the daily lives of modern people and to pass on the traditional industry to sustainability.
5. This curatorial approach is progressive and steady, but it requires a longer period of time to lead the wood craftsmen to jointly develop each curatorial theme in order to shape and define the core values of the Daxi wood furniture industry. Therefore, lengthening the curatorial period should be one of the strategic suggestions that we can try to adjust in the next stage.

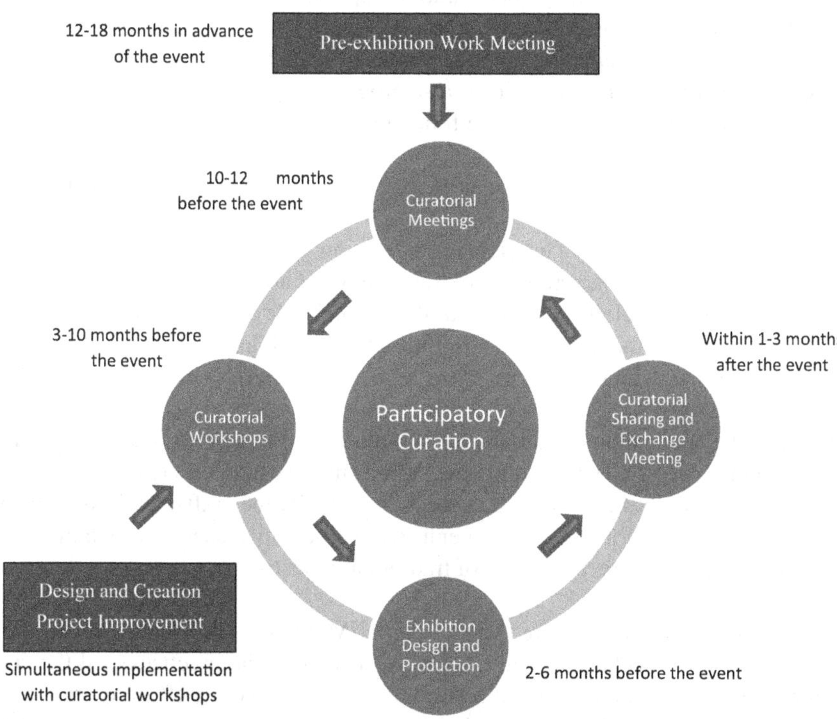

Fig. 5. (Revised) The basic framework of participatory curation model

6. Since participants are members of the traditional wood furniture industry, the exhibition schedule must be carefully coordinated and separated from the busy periods of the traditional furniture industry. Traditionally the peak periods take place after the Mid-Autumn Festival. This may reduce the willingness and creative energy of the woodworkers to participate in the exhibition.

Based on the above conclusions, the above original curatorial model and structure is proposed to be adjusted as follows Fig. 5.

5 Conclusion

Under the influence of "the transformation of Taiwan's traditional industries" and "the flourishing of cultural and creative industries", the Daxi wood furniture industry encounters new challenges. Since the traditional woodworking industry and personal workshops in Daxi lack modern marketing channels and solutions, they have tried to attract more customers by integrating and collaborating with several craftsmen through co-curation and creative strategies. These strategies have brought customers different feelings when they visit the exhibition, which in turn has generated interest and appreciation for Daxi's changes. The outcome of these changes has shown that participatory curatorial design research and practice has been invaluable to Daxi [19].

In 2020, as the only exhibition hall that presents furniture and woodware, the DWAEM introduced the participatory curation approach to its furniture themed exhibition "The Wood Furniture Gallery" as a curatorial experiment. Not only did Daxi initially construct a "participatory curation application model" for the traditional furniture industry, but over the past year, it has also progressively accomplished the expected objectives of this study and obtained the following positive curatorial results.

1. The exhibition theme is clear and can clearly convey the concept and expectation of the local wood art industry.
2. Through the application of participatory curation, the public can clearly feel the professionalism and characteristics of Tahitian wood art.
3. The theme of the exhibition is closer to the people's life and feelings.
4. The application of the participatory curatorial approach has reunited the local staff with the consensus and centripetal force for the future development of the wood art industry in Daxi.
5. Through the application of participatory curatorial models, traditional wood craftsmen gradually learn to understand how to find subjects for their creations.
6. By participating in this curatorial process intensively, the craftsmen have realized that through the exhibition, they can enhance their creative energy, which in turn is closely related to the revitalization of traditional industries.

In summary, based on the core spirit of DWAEM, the implementation of the "Participatory Curation" mechanism into local museums curatorial practices, and the construction of an applicable operational model, we have initiated the effort to bring back the local woodworking industry and gather the energy for the revitalization of the Daxi woodcraft industry. The vision for the creation and sustainability of local industry shall be realized together, to jointly build the "Daxi Furniture" style brand and establish a benchmark for fine woodcraft furniture in Taiwan.

References

1. Huang, J.-T., Guan, S.-S.: A Research of the developing process of the local museums in Taiwan. J. Design Res. **5**, 178–187 (2005)
2. Lin, H.-W.: Evaluation and analysis of the second phase project of the local cultural hall. Res. Eval. Bimonth. (研考雙月刊) **34**(3), 62–73 (2010)
3. Council for Cultural Affairs, Executive Yuan: Local Cultural Hall Planning Manual (added edition) (2004)
4. Huang, L.-Y.: A cultural governance perspective: preparation and birth of the Daxi Wood Art Ecomuseum. Museology Quarterly **30**(3), 81–97 (2016)
5. Neuman, L.W.: Social Research Methods. 7th ed. Pearson Education (2011)
6. Ko, C.-Y.: Welcome to My Home: Exploring Community-Based Art Education through Participatory Art Practice. Master's Thesis. Taipei National University of the Arts (2014)
7. Brown, A.K., Peers, L. (eds.): Museums and Source Communities: A Routledge Reader. Routledge, Routledge, London and New York (2005)
8. Lo, S.-M.: Anthropological practice of participatory curating: friction and trial of the collaborative exhibition "Kamaro'an i 'Atolan -land stories and life narratives of 'Atolan Amis." J. Eastern Taiwan Stud. **25**, 43–79 (2018)
9. Simon, N.: The participatory museum. Museum 2.0 (2010)
10. Sandell, R.: Using form+ theme+ context (FTC) for rebalancing 21st-century art education. Stud. Art Educ. **50**(3), 287–299 (2009)
11. Huang, C.-H., Chuang, M.-C.: A preliminary study of exploring FTCC model for curatorial decision making: a case study of "NCCU Very Fun Park" exhibition. Journal of Design **18**(4), 1–21 (2013)
12. Yen, H.Y., Lin, R.: A study of value-added from Qualia to business model of cultural and creative industries. J. National Taiwan Univ. Arts **91**, 127–152 (2012)
13. Segall, K.: Insanely simple: The obsession that drives Apple's success. Penguin Group, New York (2012)
14. Lin, R.: Prologue-From curatorial design to creative brokerage. Journal of Design **18**(4), 1–6 (2013)
15. Lin, J.-C.: Community-Building Educational Strategies(社區營造的教育策略). Lucky bookstore(師大書苑), Taipei (1998)
16. Hinchey, P.H.: Action research primer, vol. 24. Peter Lang (2008)
17. Hossni, M.: Action Research in Education. Theory and Practice (2019)
18. Tsai, C.-T.: Action research in education. Wu-Nan Book Inc., Taipei (2020)
19. Chen, T.-L., Fong, W.-C.: Curatorial design of a multi-brand joint exhibition. Journal of Design **22**(3), 21–44 (2017)

Research on the Development of High-Tech Imported Jewelry Composite Media Creation

Yen-Ju Chen[1,2], Rungtai Lin[2], and Chih-Long Lin[2(✉)]

[1] Visual Communication Design, Jinwen University of Science and Technology, New Taipei City 231307, Taiwan
[2] Graduate School of Creative Industry Design, National Taiwan University of Arts, New Taipei City 220307, Taiwan
rtlin@mail.ntua.edu.tw, cl.lin@ntua.edu.tw

Abstract. The 21st century belongs to the era of digital technology. Technology leads the development of craftsmanship, and innovative thinking is the world trend. With the help of technology, jewelry creation is different from traditional gold and silver craftsmanship and contemporary goldwork creation, spanning time and space. This study aims to explore: what are the possible contexts for the combination of metal jewelry and composite media. And how to use high-tech equipment to make creation more "freedom" and "imaginative". The above analysis is summarized as follows: (1) Creators can break through the previous limited framework when they conceive, let creative ideas not be restricted by the production process. (2) If the creator wants to weld extremely fine metal lines, Avoid time-consuming pro-duction engineering. (3) Relative position of welding hollow objects, more precises. (4) Complete repair function for metal repair. The continuous innovation of technology provides a strong guarantee for the development of jewelry craftsmanship, forming the so-called "Knowhow", but in the end, it is still the creator's concept that drives the progress. As far as the research samples are concerned, it is found that the creators make good use of modern technology to bring them into full play, and use the characteristics of equipment to make up for their own shortcomings. In addition, they also develop their own creative features.

Keywords: Jewelry craft · Multi-material · Craft design

1 Introduction

The 21st century belongs to the era of digital technology. It is a global trend that technology leads the development of craftsmanship and innovative thinking. With the help of technology, the performance of jewelry from traditional gold and silver craftsmanship to contemporary goldsmiths is also different across time and space. Jewelry represents a special carrier that satisfies people's pursuit of material and spirituality. In jewelry creation and design, the clever use of jewelry materials reflects the creator's own ideas. There are many factors that affect jewelry design, but in contrast, the most influential jewelry design is "material application.“ Traditional metalworking focuses on the development of precious metal materials in terms of material properties, while contemporary

P.-L. P. Rau (Ed.): HCII 2022, LNCS 13314, pp. 54–66, 2022.
https://doi.org/10.1007/978-3-031-06053-3_4

metalworking is more innovative in developing new works using composite media. In the past, traditional goldsmiths mostly referred to goldsmiths or diamond setting masters. Jewelry was priced based on materials, and most of them used precious metals, such as gold, silver and platinum group metals (ruthenium, rhodium, palladium, osmium, iridium, platinum). But in the creation of contemporary metalworking, precious metals are not the only option, on the contrary, the creation of composite media is more eye-catching, and the works will have more depth in art and narrative.

In recent years, Taiwan's metalworking industry has flourished. The outline of the development of metalworking and jewelry education and creation in the past 30 years. The input model of learning from abroad has developed into a trend of two-way equal exchanges with the international community. It has shown itself internationally and attracted attention [19]. The other part is the rise of contemporary metalworking, which is no longer limited to traditional forms, materials and construction methods in the past. New techniques or viewpoints are added to redefine the creation and use methods, making metalworking creations more innovative and composite media. The material experiment of 's plays a pivotal role in contemporary metalworking. However, due to the welding characteristics of gold and silver fine work materials, the temperature of metal reaches nearly 1,000 degrees when heated and welded. If composite media cannot withstand high temperature in creation, creativity will be hindered and it will be difficult to develop. At this time, if high-tech equipment can be used to assist jewelry creation and break through the limitations of metal bonding and welding techniques, it will help future creators to create performance. The use of high-tech equipment to introduce metalworking creations, whether in traditional or modern applications, is also worthy of discussion and research and development.

2 Literature Review

2.1 Jewelry and Metal Working

"Jewelry craftsmanship" refers to the craftsmanship and techniques used in making jewelry. The cultivation of early jewelry metalworkers mostly relies on the folk apprenticeship method to cultivate mature techniques through "3 years and 4 months", creating metalworking and diamond-setting masters. Wait. Gold and silver craftsmanship refers to metal craft creations that are mainly made of gold, silver and other precious metals, and have meticulous and beautiful workmanship, which is called "gold and silver craftsmanship". The craftsmanship of "gold and silver craftsmanship" was very developed in Taiwan in the early days. The gold and silver utensils that were made were based on folk rituals and religious activities, and played an extremely important role in all aspects of daily life. Tainan is the oldest ancient city in Taiwan. During the colonial period, there used to be many gold and silver craftsmanship shops, gathered in a street called "Platinum Town" [8]. After thousands of years of development, metalworking has accumulated many techniques [19], The range of metalworking technique is very wide. Depending on the era, its material, technique and processing process are very different. Modern metalworking technique can be said to include traditional and modern industrial technique [14]. "Technique" is like the basic structure of a building. Only on a solid foundation can a complete building be constructed. Using these operating methods to create "real" and aesthetic things is the spirit of metalworking [4, 9].

The field of metalworking was not included in the formal education system in Taiwan in the early days, and most of them were attached to other fields. The textbooks for jewelry and metalworking that can be used by colleges and universities or self-learners for reference, such as phoenix hair and scale claw, and domestic Chinese metalworking books are scarce. Fortunately, Taiwan Associate Professor Tan-Chi, Dandy Chao of the University of the Arts spent several years to complete the Chinese professional metalworking books "Metals Techniques Practices 1" and "Metals Techniques Practices 2", including: various important fields of metalworking, integrating Chinese and Western techniques and tools, with detailed explanations and pictures and texts. Recommended by Li-lun Zhou, associate professor of South China University and honorary chairman of Taiwan Jewelry Goldsmiths Association, those who want to learn metalworking can gain sufficient knowledge. Metalworking skills are as vast as the sea [6], so this study organizes the metalworking techniques according to "Metals Techniques Practices 1" and "Metals Techniques Practices 2" [4, 5].

Metals are classified according to the type of manufacturing method: 1. Forming method; 2. Mechanical cutting method; 3. Surface treatment method; 4. Joining method; 5. Method of changing physical properties. Among them, the joining method can be divided into welding, soldering, brazing, riveting, screwing, bonding and other methods [17]. However, the evolution of science and technology, in order to make welding more accurate and efficient, has also led to the introduction of electric welding machine equipment into the production of metal jewelry. There is no high temperature for local micro-welding, the combination of different materials is not limited, and the fine joints are precisely welded through a 10x microscope [16]. Jewelry brands begin to introduce technological 3D design and production. Import 3D printing into jewelry design and use parametric design. Jumping out of the existing design mode, the design and construction mode responds to parametric software and parametric digital manufacturing, so that components can present different forms and types, manage the variables of design conditions in an orderly manner, and also cause the design form and components to be in a complex relationship. It is more systematic in development, which is one of the values of parameterization, and it is also different from the thinking logic of drawing with drawings, rulers and rules or traditional computer drawing [3]. Traditional craftsmanship is facing the evolution of modern technology, and the jewelry and silver jewelry market is declining, which is enough to show that technology has the necessary influence in jewelry design.

2.2 Application of Composite Media in Jewelry Design

When the use of a certain material or medium reaches maturity, inertial creation also causes certain constraints and shackles in creation. Media can inspire designers to think about the possibilities of imagining a design [10]. The purpose of creating composite media is not only to increase the diversification of the design of the works, but also to take the advantages of various materials to increase their value, so as to form a variety of styles, (2) Welding, rivet, screw connection method: metal, (3) Nail connection method: wood, (4) Wrap connection method: use wire to wrap the outside, (5) Coupling connection:

leather, cloth, (6) Adhesive bonding: It is the most convenient material bonding today. (7) The joining method of hardware accessories: hinges and handles of movable door pieces [7]. If the creator wants to be free from the limitation of material characteristics, technology-assisted composite media creation can be further discussed.

2.3 Technology and Metalworking Evolution

Lampert exhibited the first micro welding machine PUK111 at the INHORGENTA MUNICH in 2002. The new welding technique significantly simplifies and speeds up the jewelry making process. The American jewelry industry selected the second-generation PUK2 as the AJM Product Design of the Year Award; the third-generation PUK3 won the iF Product Design Award in 2008 and the German Federal Design Award in 2009, which is also enough to show that German-made quality, function and design all meet Outstanding results. Lampert micro welding machine from Germany, evolved from the first generation of PUK111 in 2002, PUK2 in 2004, PUK3 in 2007, PUK3s in 2010, PUK04 in 2012, PUK4.1 in 2014, PUK5 in 2016, and PUK5.1 in 2021. The ninth generation PUK6(As shown in Table 1) [11]. During the more than 20 years of development of the micro welding machine, the equipment has been continuously updated and evolved, which is enough to show the needs of the jewelry industry.

Table 1. The evolution process of Lampert Welding Microscopes from 2001 to 2022

No:	1	2	3	4	5	6	7	8	9
years	2002	2004	2007	2010	2012	2014	2016	2021	2022
product									
model	Puk 111	Puk 2	Puk 3	Puk 3s	Puk 4	Puk 4.1	Puk 5	Puk 5.1	Puk 6

In the past 20 years of uninterrupted development and evolution, the meticulous and stable welding power has always been the key assistance to provide many professions around the world, especially metalworking jewelry production, maintenance, connection of precious metals and dissimilar materials, etc., tiny welding points, so that the quality of the work is more detailed and complete. The newly evolved electric welding machine has improved function and is more detailed: it can use precious metal wires and sheets less than 0.2 mm for welding; smoother: use precious metals with high thermal conductivity. For example: silver, red copper, bronze, smoother and smoother welding experience than in the past; more variety: on the precious metal materials used, there are more options for red copper and bronze, and more stable performance, allowing creative The possibilities are more diverse. Assist jewelry and metalwork creators through electric welding machines, improve the subtle welding of various metal and foreign media, enhance the creative energy, and cannot be limited by the metal material and thickness, and can perform the most accurate welding. By adjusting the fine welding parameters, and then control the welding of ultra-fine wire and thin plate, and put the wild and innovative ideas into reality. Many new-generation metal craft creators also gradually use industrial methods and digital processes in their creations, and retain the unique feel of metal craft production [2]. With advanced technology and equipment, creators need to have professional knowledge of their materials. Only when they can match each other can they inspire sparks to create unique works. For more detailed Lampert – PUK video, please refer to https://vimeo.com/showcase/4528259/video/374677443.

3 Evaluation Criteria

3.1 Study Scope and Sampling

The research scope of this study was shared by the German Lampert company's Welding Microscopes to Instagram users' pictures and text descriptions as the source of the research sample. Research limitations: Since the sample collection must be created by a microscopic electric welding machine, most of the creator's works are not clearly marked with what brand and model of electric welding machine were used to make or create. In order to ensure that the works are created by electric welding machines The source of the work is mainly the analysis of the pictures and text descriptions of Instagram users shared by Lampert Welding Microscopes in Germany.

3.2 Research Methods and Architecture

In the pre-operational stage of this research, the literature was compiled from the development of Taiwan's metal craft industry and the literature discussion of micro-electric welding machines, and the works shared by the Welding Microscope of the German Lambert company were selected from the ideas to share to the works of Instagram users, which is within the scope of this study research sample. In the field of social science research, Yin, RK [20]. divided research methods into Experiment, Survey, Archival Analysis, History and Case Study. and so on. This research chooses to use the following research methods according to the form of the research question and the research facts: (1) Literature analysis method: Based on the basic theoretical data as evidence, it discusses the development of Taiwan's metal craft industry and the application and analysis of the micro welding machine. (2) Interpretive content analysis method: This method is a kind of "case study method", which is a method of conveying intentions through intensive reading, understanding and interpretation of text content. The meaning of "interpretation" is not only at the level of simple explanation of facts, but at the overall and higher level to grasp the complex background and ideological structure of the text content, so as to discover the meaning of the product or the true meaning of the text content.

The research structure of this study is shown in Fig. 1, which are three steps: research question clarification, case study, and discussion of research findings. In the first step, the related literature on the evolution of jewelry gold and silver craftsmanship, innovative methods of different materials and technique metalworking was analyzed and integrated through literature. In the second step, this research is based on literature review, conducts case analysis and discussion, and analyzes the difference between the introduction of high-tech equipment and the optimization of works through the analysis of the works of the creators of the micro welding machine; The final third step summarizes the use of high-tech equipment to assist in the creation of works.

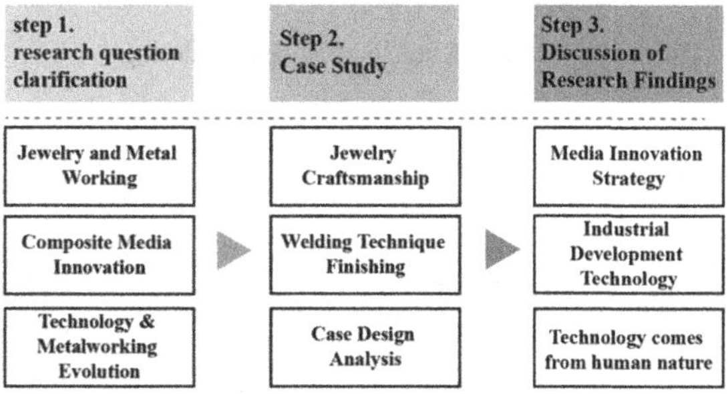

Fig. 1. Research structure

4 Analysis of the Introduction of Technology into the Creative Context of Jewelry Craftsmanship

4.1 Welding Techniques of Welding Microscopes

In traditional high temperature welding operations, accessories to assist high temperature welding include: pins 'heavy wire' binding wire 'soldering nest' ring stand & heating frame 'soldering turntables' soldering surfaces…, How to use solder: chip soldering 'stick feed soldering' probe soldering' sweat soldering [4]. In this study, Lampert-PUK video teaching was first used, and the arrangement is shown in Table 2 below. To understand the role of the Welding Microscopes in the metal joining process to evaluate its differences.

Table 2. German Lampert PUK Welding Microscopes metal welding teaching techniques

Case	Shape	Way	Micro Welding technique	Fire Welding Technique
	Brooch	Surface Pore Tonic	probe soldering	High temperature fire welding
	Watch	Strap Repair	probe soldering	unable to execute
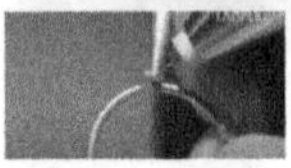	Ring	Broken Ring	sweat soldering	High temperature fire welding
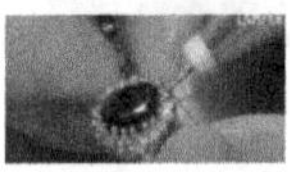	Ring	Restoring a prong setting	probe soldering	unable to execute
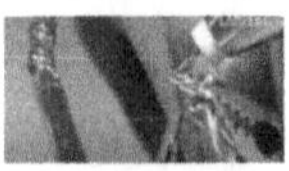	Chain	Repair bracelet loops	probe soldering	High temperature fire welding
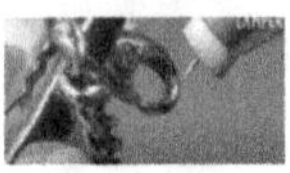	Chain	Repair chain buckle	probe soldering	unable to execute
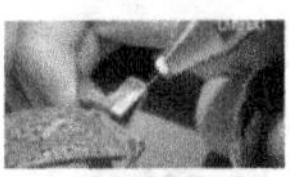	Bracelet	Repair bracelet shrapnel switch	sweat soldering	unable to execute
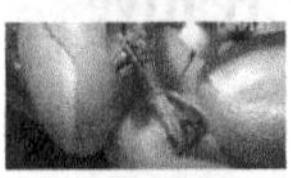	Earrings	ear pin welding	probe soldering	High temperature fire welding
	Shape Object	Object hollow butt welding	sweat soldering	High temperature fire welding
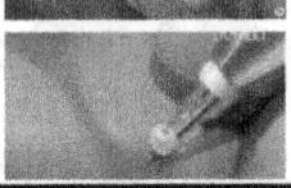	Accesso-ries	Pearl fixed	Welding of dissimilar materials	unable to execute

The differences between the electric welding technique and the fire welding technique of the micro electric welding machine are comprehensively sorted as follows: (1) The Welding Microscopes is more efficient in processing small welding objects with higher temperature and fire welding, and there is no need to re-pickling and polishing the welding objects to enhance the efficiency. (2) When there are dissimilar materials (such as gems, pearls, etc.) on the welding object, the Welding Microscopes only needs to be properly shielded, and the object can be directly welded without removing the object. (3) When the welding object needs to maintain the original metal elasticity or hardness, such as: ear pin welding, buckle fracture welding, repairing bracelet shrapnel switches, etc., the Welding Microscopes still performs better. (4) The relative position of the two hollow objects is welded, and it is more accurate to use Welding Microscopes to weld at a higher temperature. (5) For junior metal creators, the Welding Microscopes is easier to achieve the preset creation goals, and the degree of completion of the work is relatively complete.

4.2 Case Practice Design Analysis

Through the practical use of the above-mentioned creators who use the micro welding machine, the creation of works through PUK welding can extend unlimited creativity, thinking about changes in the production process of creation, without being limited by the sensitivity of inlaid gemstones, increasing the range of material selection, PUK welding machines allow small-scale precision work, concentrate heat in a specific area, allow welding close to gems and pearls, work accurately and efficiently, and avoid time-consuming manufacturing and repair processes, as sorted in Table 3 [18].

The above analysis is summarized as follows:

(1) The creator can break through the previous limited framework when conceiving, that is, limit the heat sensitivity when setting gemstones, so that the creative idea is not limited by the production process, glass, wood, etc.) Welding Microscopes only needs to be properly shielded, and it can be directly welded without removing the object. For example: Case 1, the claw setting method of the gemstone is welded by a micro electric welding machine, which is not limited by the heating of the gem. the gemstone is stably set by the metal ball, but still has the function of gemstone prong setting; In case 4, case 5 and case 8, the creators combined metal with a variety of different materials, and there are no restrictions on welding, and the creators are more open to the choice of media. In the past, if they wanted to make composite media works, it was necessary to consider the material and the joining method between materials, now using a micro welding machine, makes the choice of the medium of the work more open.

(2) If the creator wants to weld extremely thin metal lines, the micro welding machine can be used for accurate and efficient creation, avoiding time-consuming production engineering, and even welding of precious metal wires and sheets less than 0.2mm can be used. For example: Case 2 works in a linear shape, while Case 6 and Case 7 are composed of intricate metal wires. In the past, if there was overheating during welding, the metal wire would appear spherical or the whole work would melt and be damaged because it exceeded the melting point, resulting in the need for repeated production of works, through the micro welding machine, because of heating in a specific area, the production and processing are effectively carried out.

(3) For the relative position welding of hollow objects, it is more accurate to use Welding Microscopes to weld at a higher temperature, and even feature the solder joints. For example: case 9 is composed of sheet metal. During welding, the metal sheet and the metal sheet should achieve precise surface welding, and a more precise joint can be achieved through a micro welding machine; In case 3, the tiny solder joints were welded by a micro welding machine, and the solder joints were deliberately not hidden, and this was developed as a feature of the work.

(4) When the welding object needs to maintain the original metal elasticity or hardness, the Welding Microscopes can prevent the metal from softening or losing elasticity, maintain the metal characteristics, and perform complete repair functions for metal repair. For example: case 10 can still maintain a good condition when the watch is repaired.

Table 3. Inductive analysis of works by international creators using Welding Microscopes

Cases and Works			Shape	material	Micro Welding technique	Inductive analysis
1.		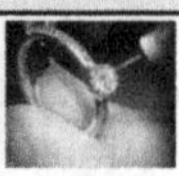	Ring	Metal. Diamond	Welding of dissimilar materials	Creators can break through the previous limited framework when they conceive, let creative ideas not be restricted by the production process
4.			Object	Glass. Metal	Welding of dissimilar materials	
5.	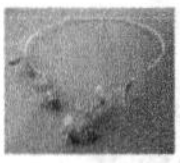		Necklace	Metal. Pigment. PET	Welding of dissimilar materials	
8.	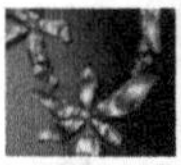		Necklace Brooch	Timascus Metal. Gem	Welding of dissimilar materials	
2.			Earrings	Titanium.	Sweat Soldering	If the creator wants to weld extremely fine metal lines, Avoid time-consuming production engineering
6.	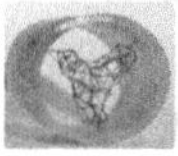	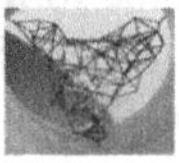	Object	Agate tube. Silver. Titanium	Welding of dissimilar materials	
7.			Object Brooch	Metal. Gem	Welding of dissimilar materials	
3.			Ring	Precious Metal	Sweat Soldering	Relative position of welding hollow objects, more precises.
9.			Object	Metal	Sweat Soldering	
10.	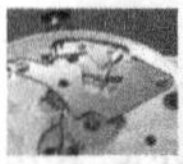		Watch	Metal. Spring	Welding of dissimilar materials	Complete repair function for metal repair.

5 First Section Conclusion and Follow-up Research

5.1 Innovative Strategies for Jewelry Craft Media

Today, jewelry metal craftsmanship has been introduced into the development of electric welding microscopes, and the concept of inspiration can be imagined. The evaluation of material color and processing techniques is the key to practical design ideas (see Fig. 2). In the process of creating jewelry metal craftsmanship, through inspiration and concept idea, material color evaluation, processing technique evaluation, prototype experiment trial, experimental sample correction, the creation of the work is completed. Imaginative concepts need to go through material color evaluation and processing techniques evaluation. In the past inspirational concepts, if the material cannot withstand high temperature, or the processing process is limited by different materials, the concept needs to be modified, resulting in a gap between the concept and the finished product. The metal fabrication technique is matched with the electric welding machine, showing the diversity of materials and the characteristics of the creation work itself. There are many advantages of using multimedia materials in product innovation [15]. It means that jewelry metal craftsmanship has developed designs and applications of different materials under the technical blessing of mature industries, and sparking sparks can become an innovative strategy for jewelry metal craft media.

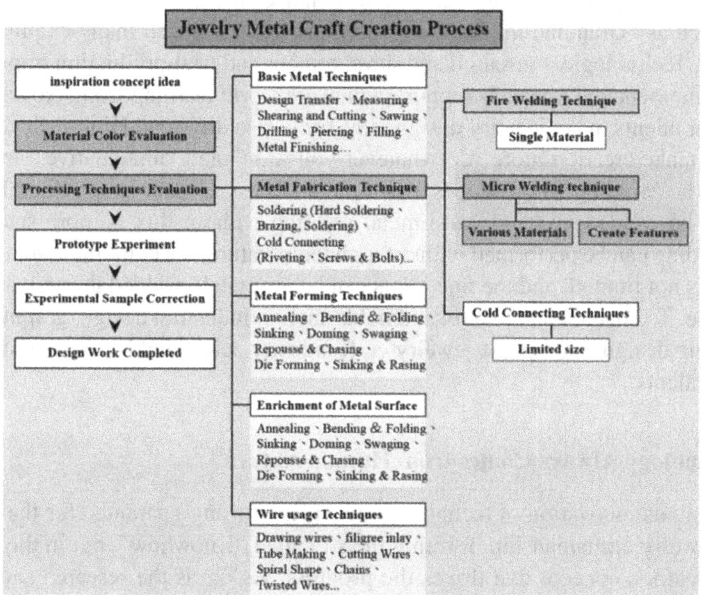

Fig. 2. Development context of Welding Microscope for Jewelry Metal Craft Creation

5.2 Improve Techniques to Continue Metalworking Industry

At the stage of learning jewelry craftsmanship, beginners are prone to restarting the entire object due to the failure of metal bonding and welding, reducing performance and losing confidence in the industry. In recent years, the development of Welding Microscopes has been stable, which can assist breakthroughs in metal fabrication technique, and has made breakthroughs in creative performance. According to the analysis of the teaching method of the research samples, the Welding Microscopes is more efficient when processing small welding parts with high temperature. If there is a composite medium, it can also be welded directly. When the welding object needs to maintain the original metal elasticity or hardness, such as: ear pin welding, buckle fracture welding, repairing bracelet shrapnel switches, etc., the Welding Microscopes machine still performs better. For the relative position welding of 2 pieces of hollow objects, it is more accurate to use a Welding Microscopes to weld with a higher temperature. In conclusion, for beginner jewelry metal craft creators, the Welding Microscopes is easier to achieve the preset creation goals, and the degree of completion of the work is relatively complete.

With the advancement of science and technology, more and more techniques tools have been introduced into the jewelry design industry, gradually bringing innovation and changes to the jewelry design industry. For example: Van Cleef & Arpels brand developed Mystery Setting with exquisite craftsmanship, and officially applied for an invention patent in 1934, becoming the brand's unique jewelry making technology. Cartier brand has continuously applied a number of traditional Chinese metal craftsmanship techniques, such as "Granulation, Enamel ", etc., and has produced many exquisite series of jewelry. Technological research and development and trial-production improvement require equipment and financial support, which are worth learning from. Nowadays, the demand for talents in the jewelry design industry is also different. High-tech equipment is used to make creation more "do whatever you want" and "imaginative." innovation strategy. The Welding Microscopes is simple and easy to use. It can directly fix the objects to be welded by hand, pure metal welding without flux is more stable, local micro-welding can be performed without high temperature, the combination of different materials is not limited, and the fine joints can be accurately welded through a 10 times microscope. To enable talents in related fields such as industrial design, graphic design, and clothing design to enter the jewelry craft industry across fields, and to enhance the ability of talents.

5.3 Technology Always Comes from Human Nature

The continuous innovation of technology provides a strong guarantee for the development of jewelry craftsmanship, forming the so-called "Knowhow", but in the end, it is still the creator's concept that drives the progress. As far as the research samples are concerned, it is found that the creators make good use of modern technology to bring them into full play, and use the characteristics of equipment to make up for their own shortcomings. In addition, they also develop their own creative features. For example: Case 3, deliberately not hiding the solder joints, and converting them into the characteristics of their own works, making them different from other creators. This is produced by the creator's reflection of human nature after being skilled in the operation of the equipment, which constitutes "Knowhow". In case 1, the combination of different materials is unrestricted by the use of Welding Microscopes, and then the traditional shape of the claw inlay is pointed, and then melted into a sphere, which has the function of claw inlay, and at the same time is converted into the characteristics of its own work. The above cases all show the ideological characteristics of "people". Explain that the biggest factor affecting the creation of jewelry craftsmanship is "people". With the different craft materials, the creative ideas given will also be different, and the products developed will be different. The craftsmanship is extremely related to people, and the materials It is the expression of human thought. For example, Rung-tai Lin [12] pointed out that with the development of science and technology, the development of design since the 20th century can be divided into five stages, each stage can be represented by an F: (1) Design for Function in the 1930s; (2) Design for Friendly in the 1950s; (3) Design for Fun in the 1970s; (4) Design for Fancy in the 1990s; (5) Design for Feeling in the 21st century. The core value of its design has evolved from functional and physiological needs to aesthetic and psychological needs. Pay attention to the complete presentation of "loyalty to materials", give full play to the characteristics of materials, and "shape at will". It can be seen that its functionality and practicality are also attached great importance, emphasizing that design is people-oriented, and the so-called "technology always comes from human nature".

The aesthetic intelligence of artificial intelligence connects and delights consumers, leading to inspiration [1]. That is to say, from functional satisfaction to experience needs, design is actually based on human values. The essence of craft creation for life will not change with the times, but the materials and techniques of craft creation will change with the progress of science and technology, and the type of creation will also be adjusted due to the change of concept [13]. It can be seen that "materials" and "technology" play an important role in the creation, and the value of "people" is the best driving force for the advancement of technology. Create a good story, use today's good technology and materials, and match good marketing tools to shape consumers' lifestyles and make products active in life. In the process of making products for life", the key to success lies in developing a brand, that is, how to make good use of technology to reflect human nature.

References

1. Brown, P.: Aesthetic Intelligence How to Boost It and Use It in Business and Beyond. New Taipei City (2020)
2. Chen, H.-C.: The Metal Product Creation of Emotional Symbol. Unpublished master's thesis. Chaoyang University of Technology (2011)
3. Chang, K.-L.: A study of parametric joint design with modeling logic. Jo. National Taiwan Coll. of Arts (106), 1–32 (2020)
4. Chao, T.-C., Wang, Y.-T.: Metals. Techniques. Practices -Advanced Metalsmithing. Forging Red Studio (2008)
5. Chao, T.-C.: Metals. Techniques. Practices -Fundamental Metalsmithing. Forging Red Studio (2014)
6. Chao, T.-C.: The Road Taken Silver Pots by Tan-Chi. Forging Red Studio, Dandy Chao (2017)
7. Chen, Q.-H.: Craft Design (Part 1). Zheng Wenshu Bureau, Taipei City (1994)

8. Fang, P.-H.: Su Chi Sung and Su Chien An's Religious Gold and Silver Fine Metalworking Craft. Unpublished master's thesis. National University of Tainan (2010)
9. Kang, J.-S.: An Overview of the Relationship among Craft Contests, Craft Creation, and Today's Economic and Technological Development, pp. 6–11. Taiwanese Craftsmanship (2008)
10. Laseau, P.: Graphic thinking for architects & designers, 3rd edn. John Wiley & Sons, New York, NY (2001)
11. Lampert: https://www.lampert.info/en/home. last accessed 10 Jan 2022
12. Lin, R.-T.: The combination of technology and humanity - cultural creativity. Sci. Develop. **396**, 68–75 (2005)
13. Lin, R.-T., Xiao, M.-T., Lin, P.-H., Li, Y.-F., Fang, B.-Q.: Humanity Achieved by Technology: Technological Development and Taiwan Craft. Taiwanese Craftsmanship (28), pp. 10–19. National Taiwan Craft Research Institute (2008)
14. Lai, T.-H.: Linking Metal Craft with Industrial Support. National Taiwan Craft Research Institute (2008)
15. Ma, J.-P.: The characters and meaning of contemporary bamboo multi-material products in Taiwan: the case of "Bamboo Traces: Contemporary International Bamboo Art & Craft Exhibition". J. Design **26**(4), 25–48 (2021)
16. Mano: http://www.manomanman.com/puk51. last accessed 6 Jan 2022
17. Ostwald, P.F., Begeman, M.L.: Manufacturing Processes. Wiley (1987)
18. Welding Microscopes: https://www.instagram.com/lampert_puk_precision_welding/. last accessed 15 Jan 2022
19. Xu, M.-Y.: Metalworking Topics - Interpretation of Metalworking Collections and an overview of the development of contemporary metalworking in Taiwan. New Taipei City Gold Museum (2016)
20. Yin, R.K.: Case Study Research: Design and Methods. Sage Publications Inc (1994)

A Study of Relationship Between Dharma Drum Mountain Website Design and Zen

Tze-Fei Huang(✉) and Chun-Liang Chen

Graduate School of Creative Industry Design, National Taiwan University of Arts, Taiwan
Daguan Rd., Banqiao Dist, New Taipei City 22058, Taiwan
s8820219@gmail.com.tw, jun@ntua.edu.tw

Abstract. Online marketing is not only a trend but a pioneering industry. Alongside the development of digital technology and all kinds of service websites, the internet has become a new media that is widely used in our daily lives. Through their online platform, Dharma Drum Mountain (DDM) presents their products and information more effectively, at the same time deliver 'Humanistic Buddhism'. This allows DDM to sprea their message and be accepted by the public more easily, which can also become more helpful for the social problems DDM has been trying to resolve. However, they face the questions of how to effectively use website to promote the business? Does internet platform help the public to understand DDM's business value? Can Zen be properly delivered through the visual design of DDM's website? How can a website successfully deliver business image? These are the questions this study intends to answer. At the start of this research, I used literature review and interviews with experts to pick out terms related to Zen. Semantic Differential was used to design the questionnaire for members of the general public in the middle of the study. At the end, I used Multidimensional Scaling to examine the questionnaire results. I hope this research could inform future website designers and cooperative bodies when setting up Zen themed websites.

Keywords: Internet platform · Semantic Differential · Zen

1 Introduction

1.1 Research Background

In order to be more accepted by the public, Dharma Drum Mountain (DDM) has been devoting themselves to public welfare activities. They have successfully delivered their ideas and values to people through modern media, such as written word, oral delivery, performance art, and a series of research projects, writings, editing, and publications. 'Humanistic Buddhism' has come more in trend these days: it can be more easily seen, heard and accepted by the publics, which at the same time makes it more helpful for the social problems DDM has tried to resolve. Through their online platform, DDM combines their products and information more effectively, extending their physical shop into the digital market and present themselves to a wider audience. In an era when the internet has developed quickly and information can be transmitted, websites have

P.-L. P. Rau (Ed.): HCII 2022, LNCS 13314, pp. 67–77, 2022.
https://doi.org/10.1007/978-3-031-06053-3_5

become an indispensable marketing tool. How to effectively use website to promote the business? Does the internet platform help the public to understand DDM's business values? Can Zen be properly delivered through the visual design on DDM's website? How can a website successfully deliver business image? These are the questions this study intends to answers.

1.2 Research Purpose

Based on the above section, it's not difficult to see online marketing is not only a trend but a pioneering industry and is an important method for business to convey their values and to approach to the public. Along with the development of digital technology and all kinds of service websites, the internet has become a new media that is being widely used in our daily lives. This study intends to understand the potential of Buddhism religion in the world of online marketing. Through general internet users' knowledge of Zen in Buddhism websites, I hope to provide future researchers and people in the relevant field a valuable input in visual design for websites.

Below are the three Research Purpose:

1. Understand and analysis the effectiveness of DDM's website as a media platform and its visual design Statistically analyze general internet users' differences in DDM's website's visual design's evaluation.
2. Suggestions for visual design on DDM's website.

1.3 Research Process

This research is to examine DDM's visual effect on its website, their online marketing items, and their general marketing outcome. The research process includes collecting and analysing second-hand information on their website, analysing their website features, and testing if their website can deliver Zen effectively to the users (Fig. 1).

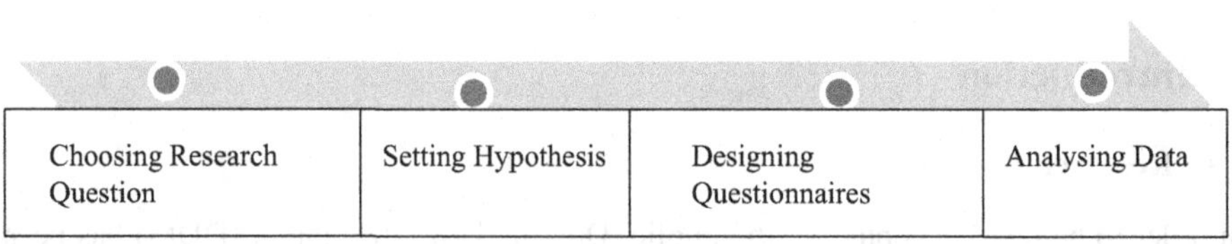

Fig. 1. Research process

2 Literature Review

2.1 Information Delivery

The method of information delivery is as followed: Source → Encoding → Medium → Decoding → Receiver → Feedback → Source. Marshall McLuhan once said "The medium is message" [1]. Under this definition, media is no longer medium as it used to be; not only delivering information to its receiver but delivering the medium itself though certain methods to allow meaningful information to reach their audiences. The new media is variable, in tune with our senses. Nowadays, we receive information so quickly and overwhelmingly, we are left with little opportunity to organize the inputs but barely have time to recognize them. Media medium has combined computers, TVs and telephone and has become a multi-way network. Through the internet, people can absorb new knowledge, exchange ideas, and create new information without limitation of time and space. The definition of information delivery is the activity of people using symbols and signal to deliver, receive and give feedback on the messages. It is a process of people exchanging ideas, thoughts and emotions in order to understand and at the same time influence each other. Information delivery saturates the world and every moment of our lives. Sheng Yan Master once mentioned the delivery of Buddhism should be popularized, globalized and more acceptable for younger generation. If Buddhism failed to popularize, it would diverge from society; if it failed to globalize, it wouldn't be visible to the world; if it can't be accepted by the youngsters, it would become an aging and elderly religion.

Buddhism has become more popular. In addition, economic development and the easing of political restrictions has made religious organizations willing to use a variety of platforms as their information delivery medium, all of which has encouraged Humanistic Buddhism to grow. Visual design on websites shouldn't be casually display creativity but must fit in to business' value, image, status and characteristic. In order to attract and impress the users, website developers should set the purpose, position, characteristic and the needs of their users as the principle at the start. Website developers need to reorganize visual image and function technology to help businesses create a new medium which contains 'visual image, 'function' and 'information' and to fulfil the purpose of delivering business image and creating its online brand value [2]. Websites' visual elements have become the main medium through which to communicate with our users. [3]. In general terms, visual design platforms 1. Deliver specific metaphors, images and ideas. 2. Decide general features in design and visual elements. 3. Define hyperlinks. These are not only to beautify the website but to become the foundation of increasingly positive user experiences [4]. Websites are a medium which combines texts, imagines and color. They deliver information to users, recall users'sensational feelings and feedback. Though users may come from different backgrounds, if the website can include several elements which are in tune with them it will appeal to the widest range of users [5].

2.2 Definition of Zen

There are many discussions regarding the definition of Zen. Based on Master Sheng Yan's publication 'Zen and Enlightenment' (2001), Zen can be defined as following four terms: 1. Dhyana, stability, inner peace; 2. Catvāri dhyānāni, different level in Zen; 3. Sitting Zen, practicing Zen in sitting position; 4. Zen Zong, Zen Zong originated from India, developed and matured in China, and reached Korea, Japan and Vietnam at the end [6]. Zen contains meanings deep in thought and observation, with the aim of retaining inner peace for people. Zen in arts is not merely aesthetic debates but an understanding of the core of human lives. The enlightenment in Zen shares similarity to inspiration in arts. We can see Zen in painting, poetry and calligraphy in Chinese arts. Chinese arts often use real and false as comparisons in order to represent the beauty of the ethereal and the natural, which is very similar to 'Kong' in Zen. Artworks which represent natural surrounding also at the same time express the artist's understanding of lives, society and their inner peace. Zen styles of arts often inspired their audiences with their multi-layered presentational skills. Zen emphasises instincts: therefore, if one wishes to realize Zen in daily life, one must understand the core values of Zen. D.T Suzuki said 'Artists should enter the items they wish to represent. They need to feel them from inside and live their lives.' To sum up, Zen focuses on the core of things which should be in tune with the rule of nature. It contains art features such as humility, innocence, simplicity, classical, quiet, lonely, distant, purposeless, combined and relaxing. D.T Suzuki also pointed out, Zen arts is unbalanced, asymmetric, single perspective, simplicity, lonely, distant and relaxing [7, 8].

3 Research Method

3.1 Procedure and Framework

In this research, a semantical differential scale was used to analyse visual features in websites. This chapter will explain and introduce the designing process and methodologies which were used in the research.

Semantical Differential (SD), designed by Osgood, Suci and Tannenbaum in 1957, is commonly used in product modelling studies. SD usually uses a 5, 7 or 9 scale along with a set of contradictory terms on either side of the scale, for instance: commonplace and unique, traditional and modern etc. It assumes subjects would choose a point on the scale and the result should be a normal distribution of the bell curve. The average scale point would be the point representing subjects' feelings about the products. The reason SD is commonly used stems from the idea of bipolarity, which is a rather instinctive expression from people [9]. Therefore, most studies assume people's feeling are bipolar, and people tend to use antonymic terms in describing part or all of the single scale. The bipolarity shows significant negative correlation [10].

In this research, I firstly select terms related to Zen or Buddhism through literature review; secondly, I picked out sentimental terms through questionnaires and decided which terms are most associated with Buddhism. Based on the analysis, I examined the websites to see if their visual design express specific models, imagines and ideas.

The method is listed below:

1. Collecting terms related to Buddhism websites.
2. Collecting sentimental terms and choosing representative terms through questionnaire.
3. Using questionnaires to analyze clients' websites.
4. Providing conclusions and suggestions based on the result.

3.2 Research Steps

There are 4 steps in this research. First, Data Collecting; Second, Website analysis; 3. Questionnaire subjects selection; 4. Visual analysis of Zen on the internet platforms (Fig. 2).

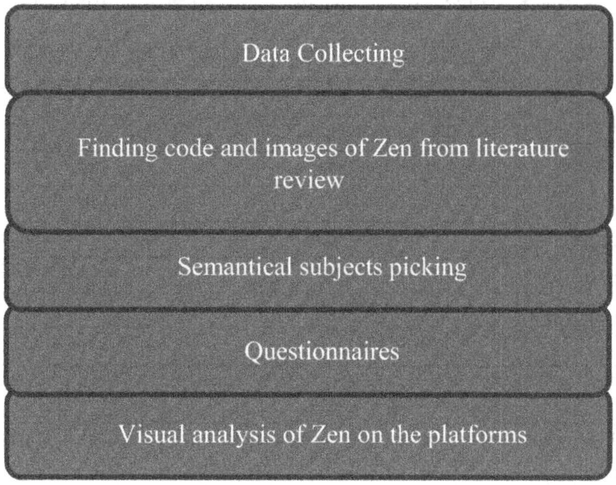

Fig. 2. Three levels of Zen product design (sorted out and drawn in this study)

3.3 Questionnaire Design

Firstly, I collected 30 Zen related terms from reviewed literature. Secondly, I invited Yi-Ying Jiang Professor from National Qing Hua University and Ms. Ren-Feng Chen from Qisda Cooperation to choose 8 representative terms (Tables 1 and 2).

Table 1. Zen terms

1. humble	2. flourish	3. ordinary	4. graceful	5. lively	6. stable	7. straight	8. obscure	9. secular	10. religious
11. simply	12. complex	13. kind	14. serious	15. happy	16. rational	17. casual	18. reserve	19. impressive	20. common
21. decorative	22. wise	23. tasteful	24. solemn	25. conservative	26. open	27. senstive	28. functional	29. glorial	30. peaceful

Table 2. Representative Zen terms

1. humble	2. obscure	3. religious	4. wise
5. impressive	6. relaxing	7. simple	8. stable

3.4 Questionnaire Design

In this survey, questionnaires with a 5-point scale are executed online, which are divided into two parts: the first part is the sub-item; the second part is the overall response to the tested sample. We also collect the basic information of the subjects. (Table 3).

Table 3. Content of the questionnaire (P1 as the instance)

	My feeling when I see this website?	
	1. humble or flourish	Low □1 □2 □3 □4 □5 High
	2. obscure or straight	Low □1 □2 □3 □4 □5 High
	3. religous or secular	Low □1 □2 □3 □4 □5 High
	4. wise or casual	Low □1 □2 □3 □4 □5 High
	5. impressiv or common	Low □1 □2 □3 □4 □5 High
	6. relaxing or serious	Low □1 □2 □3 □4 □5 High
	7. simple or complex	Low □1 □2 □3 □4 □5 High
	8. stable or lively	Low □1 □2 □3 □4 □5 High

9. You believe internet is the best platform to received Zen information ：	Low □1 □2 □3 □4 □5 High
10. When you have need, your first choice is looking up internet ：	Low □1 □2 □3 □4 □5 High
11.When someone asks for your advice, you would recommend this website ：	Low □1 □2 □3 □4 □5 High
12.You think the design of this website fit in the purpose of it ：	Low □1 □2 □3 □4 □5 High
13.Can you feel Zen in this website design ：	Low □1 □2 □3 □4 □5 High
14.The design of this website remind you of religions ：	Low □1 □2 □3 □4 □5 High
15.How much do you like this website ：	Low □1 □2 □3 □4 □5 High
16.Do you usually like Zen products ：	Low □1 □2 □3 □4 □5 High
17.Please choose the website you feel contain most Zen feeling (single selection)	
18.Please choose your favorite website (single selection)	

3.5 Questionnaire Design

According to the Cognitive analysis of the works by the respondents with different backgrounds:

(1) With design background(With or without religious belief)
(2) With art related background(With or without religious belief)
(3) General public(With or without religious belief)

In the Semantic Difference experiment, 10 participants with design education, 41 ones with art-related backgrounds, and 10 ones with no art or design education are used. It is also tested whether participants have a religious belief so as to help us detect cognitive differences between them. The data were collected from the questionnaires and analyzed by the SPSS software, Multidimensional Scaling(MDS) Discussion and analysis of product image and shape, Finally, the characteristic words were generalized and summarized.

3.6 Websites Chose to Be Used in the Questionnaire

This section lists down the pages we selected from Dharma Drum Mountain website and the reasons I chose them.

1. DDM home page is the initial page users encounter, therefore it can represent DDM.
2. Pages which can show the core DDM's value on its website

   (1) DDM's home page
   (2) DDM Chuan Deng Yuan
   (3) DDM Humanity Cooperation
   (4) DDM online chanting
   (5) DDM Sheng Yan online archive

Table 4. Tested Sample Web Page (after fixing)

(1)DDM's home page	(2)DDM Chuan Deng Yuan	(3)DDM Humanity Cooperation
	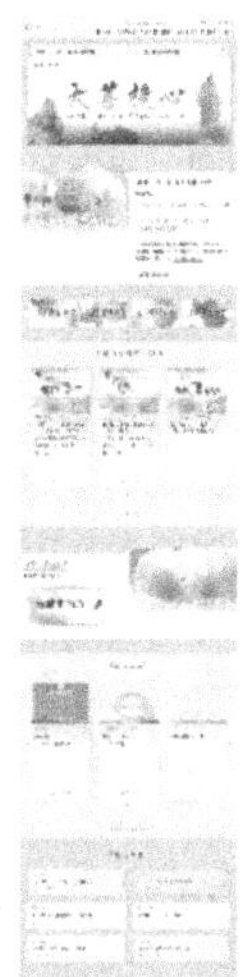	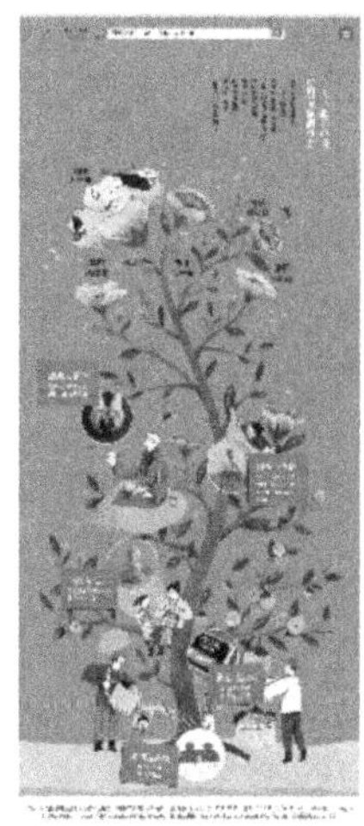
(4)DDM online chanting	(5)DDM Sheng Yan online archive	
	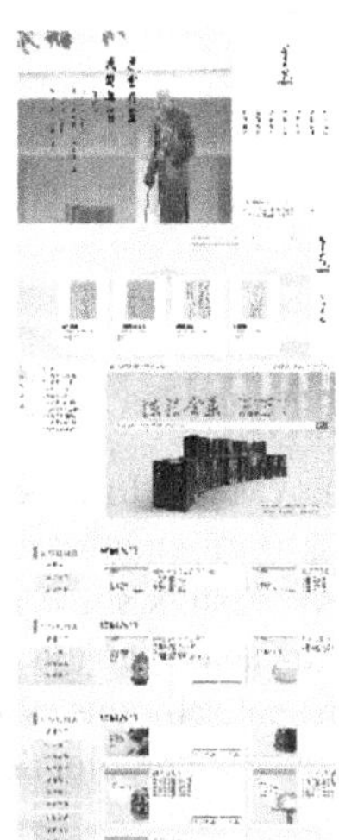	

4 Results

4.1 Overall Review

The composition of the subjects in this research are as follow: 34 people were from design field; 31 people were from arts field; 22 are from other fields. In total there were 87 subjects, 18 were male and 69 were female.

Table 4 displays subjects' average and standard deviation results. The results indicate (Table 5):

1. Web pages (P4 and P5) which include clear religious symbols provide subjects with strong links to religion. The terms humble, religious, stable, and serious stand out more.
2. Pages using religious illustrations (P1,P2 and P3) provided lively, secular, and relaxing feelings.

Table 5. Displays subjects' average and standard deviation result

	 p1	 p2	 p3	 p4	 p5
f1 humble -flourish	2.08	2.60	3.69	2.10	1.84
f2 obscure -straight	3.91	3.58	3.67	3.80	3.73
f3 religous -secular	2.41	2.22	3.48	1.61	1.52
f4 wise -casual	2.74	2.33	2.80	2.23	1.86
f5 impressive - common	3.77	2.78	3.10	2.97	2.72
f6 relaxing -serious	2.53	2.64	1.93	4.10	3.60
f7 simple -complex	2.01	2.41	3.07	2.56	2.10
f8 stable -lively	2.76	2.86	3.92	1.82	1.94

4.2 Product Attribute Factor Analysis

I used multidimensional scaling (MDS) to classify the product attribute factors and subjects' preferences. The stress coefficient used in this study was 0.06541 and RSQ was 0.98775. In other words, the results show a high level of consistency. In Image 4 we can see the eight attribute factors analysis and their represented products. P1 used adorable illustrations to present religious symbols, therefore most subjects gave it higher point in 'Common'; P2 used a watercolor design on the webpages, which drew the responses 'flourish' and 'lively'; P3 used a colorful illustration style which is different from previous pages and gave subjects 'lively' and 'secular' impressions; P4 and P5 directly used religious icons along with a portrait of DDM's fountain. They gave the subjects feeling such as 'religious' and 'stable' (Fig. 3).

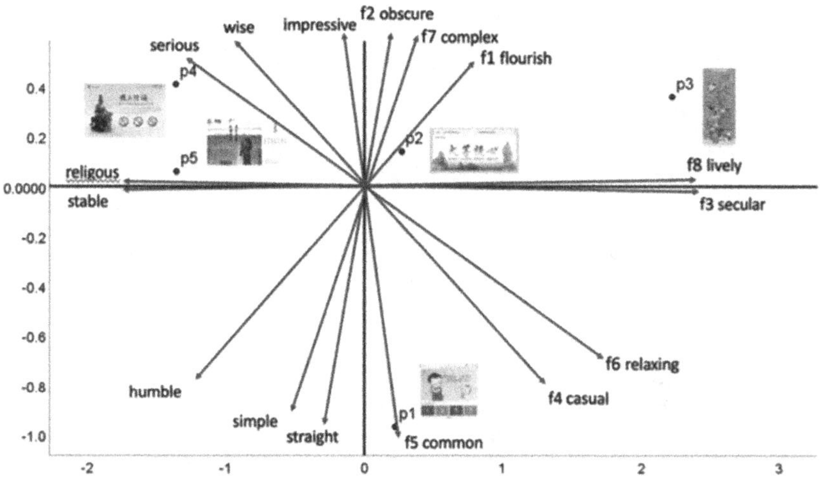

Fig. 3. Euclidean distance model

5 Conclusion

The results of this study show that people think DDM's website design contains high level of Zen, which also match the core value of DDM. Subjects showed higher preference towards web pages which use illustrations or stronger artistic features. This may result from the fact subjects were mostly from design or art fields. All the web pages achieve the passage of information they were designed to deliver. The best page to learn Zen is P5, Zheng Yan online archive, P4, online chanting. P3, DDM Humanity Cooperation, containing lively and secular terms, is most favoured by the subjects. In words, subjects like web pages which have obscure Zen aesthetic and artistic motifs more than web pages with strong religious messages. DDM Humanity Cooperation page tries to deliver their core value: 'mind purifying'. They wish to show more care to people and put it in to practice. Future researchers may want to analyse subjects from different education backgrounds and their attitude toward religious websites (Table 6).

Table 6. Average point of subjects' attitude toward different pages

Q1 You believe internet is the best platform to received Zen information					
Item	p5	p2	p3	p4	p1
Mean	3.91	3.90	3.87	3.70	3.39
Q2 When you have need, your first choice is looking up internet					
Item	p3	p5	p2	p4	p1
Mean	3.99	3.83	3.75	3.59	3.26
Q3 You think the design of this website fit in the purpose of it	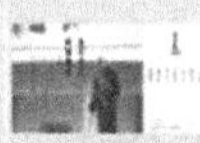				
Item	p5	p3	p2	p1	p4
Mean	4.01	4.07	3.92	3.78	3.77
Q4 Can you feel Zen in this website design					
Item	p2	p5	p4	p1	p3
Mean	4.05	4	3.87	3.49	3.17
Q5 The design of this website remind you of religions					
Item	p5	p4	p2	p1	p3
Mean	4.49	4.47	4.22	4	3.28
Q6 Please choose your favorite website					
Item	p3	p2	p1	p5	p4
Mean	49	17	13	4	4

References

1. Quan, J.: The influence of mobile platform digital image and information dissemination on visual culture. Int. J. New Develo. Eng. Soc. **1**(3), (2017)
2. Yi, F.T., Editing Department: Webpage Design of Corporate lmage. Yi Fong Tang Culture Publishing Co, Taipei (2004)
3. Wang, K.L.: The communicative lmplications of lmages in webpage design. In: Design and Management Conference, pp. 269–276 (2000)
4. Huang, C.-M., Zhao, M.-H.: Web Strategic Planning and Design. Shinning Culture Publishing Co., Taipei (2002)
5. Tsai, T.W.: The Relationship between Aesthetic Emotion and Visual Information of Webpages. Doctoral dissertation, National Chiao Tung University, Hsinchu, Taiwan (2009)
6. Shi, S.-Y.: Zen and Enlightenment. Dharma Drum Publications Corp, Taipei (2001)
7. Suzuki, D.T.: Zen and Japanese Culture (Lin Hui-jun, Trans.). Walkers Cultural Enterprises Ltd, New Taipei (1992)
8. Suzuki, D.T., Dabei, L.: Zen And Art. Heavenly Lotus Publication, Taipei (1988)
9. Russell, J.A., Carroll, J.M.: On the bipolarity of positive and negative affect. Psychol. Bull. **125**, 3–30 (1999)
10. Smith, C.A., Ellsworth, P.C.: Patterns of cognitive appraisal in emotion. J. Pers. Soc. Psychol. **48**, 813–838 (1985)

Research and Exploration of Future Intelligent Color-Changing Packaging Design for Fruits and Vegetables

Jiahong Jiang(✉)

Tsinghua University, Beijing, China
jiangjh19@mails.tsinghua.edu.cn

Abstract. Packaging is of great significance to the sales of fruits and vegetables. The future design for fruit and vegetable packaging is conducive to improving the circulation and sales of fruits and vegetables. As science and technology have developed, intelligent interactions are becoming popular. Meanwhile, the manufacturing of intelligent color-changing materials is also maturing. Combining intelligent interaction technology with new color-changing materials for the design of fruit and vegetable packaging is an attractive issue. Many researchers have focused on developing new color-changing packaging materials and technology, while few have studied intelligent color-changing packaging from the perspective of design. Therefore, our study took design as main perspective and discussed the current research about intelligent color-changing materials and technologies in fruit and vegetable packaging design. Speculative research and cluster analysis have been conducted based on relevant literature and practical cases. Finally, design strategies and suggestions have been proposed for intelligent color-changing packaging design of fruit and vegetable by combining plant properties and human emotional needs.

Keywords: Intelligent color-changing packaging · Fruit and vegetable packaging · Interactive experience · Packaging design · Green design

1 Introduction

As people's awareness of health is growing, growing attention has been paid to the functionality and safety of food packaging. The basic functions of traditional packaging are to protect product, facilitate transportation, promote sales and beautify product. A good food packaging could protect product from external intrusion and damage, thus increasing food safety [1]. The main role of traditional food packaging is to provide physical barrier to extend the shelf life and in-shelf life of food, protect them against microorganisms, physicochemical damage and unpredictable external conditions [2]. As packaging materials and technologies are updated constantly, new intelligent packaging is gradually developing and receiving increasing attention. Smart packaging is more preferred by young and middle-aged consumer groups, as it is capable to monitor and display the condition of food and provide consumers with information about product

P.-L. P. Rau (Ed.): HCII 2022, LNCS 13314, pp. 78–90, 2022.
https://doi.org/10.1007/978-3-031-06053-3_6

quality and safety [3, 4]. Smart packaging includes digital smart packaging, material smart packaging and structural smart packaging [5]. Among them, material smart packaging is more attractive as it is relatively cheap and attainable. Material smart packaging has many genres, such as color-changing smart materials, light-emitting smart materials, water-soluble smart materials, active smart materials, deformation memory materials, self-healing smart materials, etc. [6]. Color-changing smart materials are widely used in various packaging designs because of their low cost, convenience and feasibility. It can be applied in pharmaceuticals, cosmetics, cold fresh, fruits and vegetables. Through the feedback of color-changing materials, consumers can intuitively understand the quality of product. For example, consumers can identify the freshness of fruits and vegetables by referring to the color on packaging. This can greatly help consumers to make a judgement and improve their interaction experience with packaging [7].

Our study focuses mainly on intelligent color-changing packaging, which is an important branch of intelligent packaging. Intelligent color-changing packaging is usually composed by color-changing materials, sensors, indicators, microprocessors, and other components. They can provide feedback through color changes when the package is stimulated by light, electricity, gas, temperature, gravity, solvents, and other external stimuli. Their function is giving information like warning, reminding, or simply beautifying and entertaining [6, 8, 9]. For example, the sunscreen of Blue Lizard uses photochromic intelligent materials for its cap and body. The cap and body of the sunscreen can become darker when the outdoor UV intensity is high, and return to normal color when the UV is weak. Users can decide whether to use sunscreen based on the color change of the bottle. Such intelligent color-changing packaging design makes the product both interesting and practical, and can greatly enhance the competitiveness of product. Neretin Stas designed a cosmetic packaging according to the shape of woman body, and coated it with temperature and force responsive color-changing intelligent material. When the consumer touches the outer surface of the packaging, the packaging can change colors with pressure and temperature. This packaging design can not only reflect the characteristics of the product but also increases the interactivity between product and consumer. In addition to the interaction function, another merit of intelligent color-changing packaging is environmentally friendly. The indicators of smart color-changing packaging can be derived entirely from nature. For example, Tichoniuk et al. tested the feasibility of curcumin, grape skin extract and beet extract as indicators of cold freshness. In their experiments, they found that the color of these extracts could change in response to environmental pH value. Therefore, they can be used as indicators of smart color-changing packaging to detect specific gases produced during food storage. Consumers can judge the freshness of food based on the color change of package [10].

Though application of intelligent color-changing packaging has already existed for some time, its depth and breadth about packaging design is still in early stage. From the perspective of design, there is still room for improvement, such as visual language design, post-packaging functionality, packaging emotional interactivity and green design concepts. This paper takes intelligent color-changing packaging design for fruits and vegetables as starting point, systematically analyzed the relationship of packaging, product and consumer. Current status of intelligent packaging design was also discussed based on relative cases and literatures. Problems of intelligent color-changing packaging design was summarized from the perspective of graphics, color, form and material, cost and environmental protection based on consumers' physiological and psychological needs. An emotional design strategy about graphics and design suggestions for unified color feedback was proposed, as well as a closed-loop path to improve green design.

2 Intelligent Color-Changing Packaging Design for Fruits and Vegetables

The technology of intelligent color-changing packaging actually is not a new concept. It has been widely used in different fields due to the various stimuli can be applied, controllable cost, high sensitivity and stable performance. However, for the fruit and vegetable packaging, which has higher requirements for freshness and food safety, the application of intelligent color-changing packaging is still in the preliminary stage, and researchers are effortlessly exploiting its new area. In order to facilitate the development of intelligent color-changing packaging for fruits and vegetables, it is important to analyze the relationship of design, product and consumer. It is also of vital importance to study the graphics, colors, forms, and materials in intelligent color-change packaging of fruit and vegetable from the perspectives of practical use.

2.1 Relationship of Design, Product and Consumer in Intelligent Color-Changing Packaging

The main purpose of intelligent color-changing packaging design for fruits and vegetables is to show product freshness and safety. Fruits and vegetables are living organisms, which keep respiring during the whole process of collection, packaging, transportation, sale and storage. Intelligent color-changing packaging can monitor the oxygen, carbon dioxide and other gases produced in this process. It can also detect humidity, temperature, microbial bacteria inside the packaging and other variables. When changes of these variables reach the detection lower limit, packaging can change its color to remind people to eat or replace the product. Besides, when the packaging of fruits and vegetables is broken or damaged during transportation or storage, the intelligent color-changing packaging can give a reminder through corresponding changes, such as force-caused color change, electric color change, etc.

Apart from the main purpose, intelligent color-changing packaging design for fruits and vegetables should also meet the emotional needs of consumer. Donald Norman's emotional design proposes three levels: visceral, behavioral, and reflective. The visceral level of design is the law of nature, where physical characteristics such as gaze, feeling and sound play a dominant role. It corresponds to intuitive visual feelings such as the shape and color of product design. Behavioral level is related to product use, such as the functionality of product, easiness of understanding and use. This corresponds to the experience and utility of the product. The reflective level design is related to message, culture and meaning of the product. It corresponds to the reflection and reassessment the product brings [11]. Intelligent color-changing packaging design for fruits and vegetables can provide different forms of color feedback according to the internal and external environmental conditions. This color feedback can increase the pleasure of interaction between product and consumer. It can also promote the function of product, making it easier for consumers to understand and use at behavioral level. Another good thing is that most of the color-changing materials can come from fruits and vegetables themselves (e.g. anthocyanins, carotenoids, chlorophyll, etc.). This means we can extract raw materials from the product itself for color-change packaging. By doing so, a closed-loop green design concept of "from nature, back to nature" is established, which can create a sense of empathy and social responsibility at the level of emotional reflection.

In summary, intelligent color-changing packaging design for fruits and vegetables plays as the intermediate medium connecting fruits, vegetables and consumer. Thus, the packaging design needs to have the function of physical protection and the function of decoration. At the same time, intelligent color-changing packaging is supposed to play the role of reminding, indicating freshness and maturity, anti-counterfeiting and create a sense of empathy to consumer.

2.2 Graphics and Colors of Intelligent Color-Changing Packaging for Fruits and Vegetables

In intelligent color-change packaging design for fruits and vegetables, graphics and colors are the first visual feedback forms. The role of graphics and colors is important and special. Different graphics and color changes bring different visual senses to people. At present, graphics of existing intelligent color-changing packaging for fruits and vegetables can be divided into geometric graphics and figurative graphics. The color of these packaging can also be divided into two categories: colors based on natural pigments and colors based on human cognition.

Packaging Graphics.
Geometric Graphics. A large number of intelligent color-changing packaging design for fruits and vegetables using geometric expressions like circles, ovals, rectangles, squares and so on. Geometric graphics is simple, but it can indicate order and regularity and can also highlight information. The New Zealand RipeSense package is the world's first intelligent sensor label. This gas responsive color-change packaging using circle as its geometric graphics. Its sensor can respond to the gas released by the fruit. At the beginning, the sensor is red. And then it becomes orange as the fruit ripeness increases. When the fruit completely matures, the sensor turns into yellow (see Fig. 1) [12]. Consumers can decide which time to eat the fruits according to the label's color. They can also judge the storage time of fruits based on the label. This kind of intelligent color-changing packaging can greatly reduce the selection time for consumers. Besides, this packaging is environmental friendly and can be recycled. Another example is the 3 M™ MonitorMark™. This commercial smart label combines oval and circular as visual feedback graphics and can be placed inside shipping boxes for temperature-sensitive products. It can indicate both temperature change and the time exposed. The smart label has two types of windows: a large oval window to show ambient temperature to which the product is exposed and a small circular window to show the time of exposure at a given temperature. The oval area is large, so it is designed to show the degree. While the circular area is small, and is designed to show the evolution of time (see Fig. 2) [13]. These two types

of graphics represent different visual languages and meanings. And more information can be deduced when they were combined together.

Fig. 1. RipeSense fruit aerosol smart color change package

Fig. 2. 3 M™ MonitorMark™ time temperature indicator

Geometric graphics can be applied in different positions and scenes of the package to show different visual languages according to packaging area, arrangement and combination form. For example, the nodal expression of circles, the degree expression of ovals, the warning expression of triangles, etc.

Figurative Graphics. Figurative graphics are also a common method of visual expression in intelligent color-changing packaging for fruits and vegetables. The exact graphics can be selected according to the shape of product and what the design want to express. Because figurative graphics is similar to the shape of product, they are vivid, easy to understand and interesting. The Japanese To-Genkyo studio designed a gas responsive smart color-changing label in the shape of funnel. The smart label uses anthocyanin extract as natural dye. The color of the label can change with the amount of ammonia released when the food spoils. And when the food is inedible, the barcode of the funnel-shaped food label disappears, making it impossible to scan for purchase. The designer uses the funnel-shaped label to express time, which is intuitive and vivid. Such design can highlight the functionality of packaging and at the same time enhance the interactive behavior between consumers and products (see Fig. 3) [14]. Another case is the Apple Color Change Smart Indicator Label designed according to the shape of apple (see Fig. 4) [9]. The color of the label can change from red to blue as the apple changes from fresh to spoiled. By combing the shape of apple with the color, consumers can have a more real visual experience. This is also one of the unique and irreplaceable visual effect of figurative graphics.

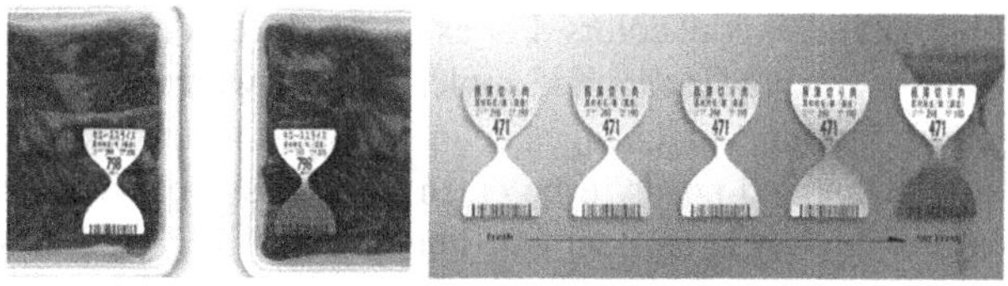

Fig. 3. Meat price tag based on gas responsive intelligent color-changing packaging

Fig. 4. Apple color change smart indicator label (red: fresh, blue: spoiled) (Color figure online)

Packaging Color. Art theorist Johannes Eaton says in The Art of Color, "The optical, electromagnetic and chemical effects that begin in the eye and mind often run parallel to those in the psychological realm. This repercussion of color experience can reach the deepest nerve centers and thus affect the major areas of mental and emotional experience." It is thus clear that the effect of color on human is the change of psychological perception, which results from physical properties [15, 16]. Color, as the main form of feedback for intelligent color-changing packaging, is of great importance in terms of visual and emotional aspects when interacting with people. Judging from interactive recognition relationships, it can be divided into colors that are based on natural pigmentation change patterns and colors that are based on human perception.

Colors Based on Natural Pigmentation Patterns. Most of the color-changing materials can be extracted from fruits and vegetables. For example, anthocyanins can be extracted from purple kale, eggplant, and blueberry, and most of them are red/blue/purple/pink. Betaine can be extracted from wolfberries, legumes, etc., most of them are red/purple. Chlorophyll, extracted from organisms that can conduct photosynthesis such as celery, chrysanthemum, and cabbage, is predominantly green. Carotenoids, extracted from carrots, tomatoes, and redwood seeds, are predominantly yellow/orange/red, etc. [17]. Anthocyanins are common smart color-changing packaging indicators. It can exhibit different colors in environments with different pH, usually red at acidic environment and blue at alkaline environment. And this property is perfect for detecting food spoilage [18]. Color changes like this are all based on the acidity and alkalinity of the environment. Thus, they are called colors based on natural pigmentation patterns.

Colors Based on Human Perception. Within the scope of human cognition, colors are divided into cool and warm colors according to the wavelength of visible light. Cool colors include blue, green, yellow-green, blue-violet, etc., which give people a natural, refreshing, calm and astringent emotional implication. Warm colors, such as red, yellow, orange, etc., have warmth, enthusiasm, exuberance, expansion and other emotional expression. The same can be applied to intelligent color-changing packaging for fruits and vegetables as a visual language. Normally, ripe and fresh fruits are mostly red, orange, yellow and other warm colors, while decaying and deteriorating fruits are brown, purple, blue and other cool colors. For example, the color change label of apples in Fig. 4 is red for fresh and blue for spoiled apples. The strawberry freshness monitoring indicator invented by Kukim et al. changes color from yellow to purple, indicating that the strawberry is overripe and needs to be eaten as soon as possible [19]. Such color change patterns as in Fig. 5 are consistent with human cognitive. According to consumer behavior studies, people rely heavily on the inherent concept of color and color in their cognitive system and such cognition can even dictate purchase behavior [16].

2.3 Forms and Materials of Intelligent Color-Changing Packaging for Fruit and Vegetable

Packaging, according to different properties, uses and scenarios, needs to be designed into a variety of forms. Such as heaven and earth cover packaging, tray packaging, tube packaging, open-window packaging, and fully transparent packaging. Form of intelligent color-changing packaging for fruits and vegetables are upgraded version of traditional packaging, which combines new function and technology. Commonly used forms are fully transparent type, open window type and transport type.

From

Fully Transparent. When people buy fruits and vegetables, the main criterion are freshness and appearance. Fully transparent packaging forms, whether traditional packaging or intelligent color-changing packaging are the best choice for fresh products such as fruits and vegetables. Such packaging is usually in the form of cling film and tray combinations or plastic boxes. They are relatively cheap and light, easy to pack and observe, thus, has become people's first choice while buying fruits (see Fig. 5). Most of the intelligent color-changing packaging for fruits and vegetables tend to place sensor and indicator on fully transparent packaging form (see Fig. 1 and Fig. 3). On one hand, the intelligent color-changing packaging for fruits and vegetables is still in the preliminary research stage, the fully transparent packaging can compare the contents status with the sensor feedback results, which is convenient for checking; On the other hand, the fully transparent packaging is convenient for consumers to do secondary confirmation, which can increase consumers' confidence in the use of intelligent packaging.

Fig. 5. Field research photos(Color figure online)

Open Window Type. This type of packaging provides a window on one side of the package, so that consumers can directly see the shape and quality of fruits and vegetables in a certain range. Such forms are often used in gift packaging, boutique packaging, etc. Intelligent color-changing packaging in this form usually utilize visualization graphic feedback. As only one side is used for opening window, other places can be designed graphically to highlighting the design atmosphere of the boutique packaging. However, there are only few intelligent color-changing packaging for fruits and vegetables using this form.

Transportation Style. As online consumption has become a common style of consumption, smart logistics is advancing the development of smart cities. Because fruits and vegetables are low-cost daily fast-moving consumer goods, most fruit and vegetable packaging are made by low-cost corrugated cartons, air pillows, pearl cotton and other materials, together with cushioning inside to absorb impact during transportation. The transport process of online purchased fruits and vegetables will encounter many uncontrollable factors, such as external impacts, weather changes. These uncontrollable factors are likely to cause irreversible damage to fruits and vegetables. Therefore, such forms of intelligent packaging need to be able to feedback the integrity of the product during transportation process. Currently, smart color-changing packaging usually uses sensors or indicators attached to the outside of the packaging to monitor and feedback. However, due to the low profitability and high cost of external sensors, the application of such smart color-changing packaging is still limited.

Materials

The color-changing materials, sensors and indicators in intelligent color-changing packaging for fruits and vegetables can be divided into biological and chemical categories. Biological types like natural polymers and natural pigments are more green options, as they were made from natural organisms and is recyclable and degradable. For example, purple corn cob waste is rich in anthocyanins and can be used to produce color-changing materials in food packaging coatings [20, 21]. Blueberry powder can be added to corn starch-based films to make color-changing materials whose color can change with pH value. [18]. The application of such biological materials can improve the recycling loop of packaging, and are truly green designs conform to "from nature, back to nature" concept. Chemical type color-change materials, sensors and indicators, due to the possible risk of direct contact with food, high cost, difficult recycling procedures, has a much stricter requirement for application.

2.4 Existing Problems of Intelligent Color-Changing Packaging Design for Fruits and Vegetables

Despite the rapid development of intelligent color-changing packaging for fruits and vegetables, it is still in the preliminary stage of the whole field. Based on current research of intelligent color-changing packaging design for fruits and vegetables, we found that there are still problems in the design of packaging, such as single design feedback graphics, lack of standardization of design color feedback, high material cost and incomplete recycling system.

Single Design of Feedback Graphics. Most of the intelligent color-changing packaging for fruits and vegetables only use single sensor or indicator, and feedback information is presented in small geometric or figurative graphics. Such expression form is not conducive to the development of intelligent color-changing packaging for fruits and vegetables, and will limit the scope of application. One reason is that the small-area color change may be difficult to read for some consumers. Another reason is that the single feedback graphic will limit the interactivity experience of consumer.

Lack of Standardization Color Feedback. Most of the color feedback of intelligent color-changing packaging for fruits and vegetables uses natural pigments or chemical dyes. The color change is mostly related to the properties of the extract. As a result, color feedback is diverse. Although there is classification rule between warm and cold color, the hue and trend are different, and the change properties are unstable. This leads to a relearning and identification process for consumers every time they buy a new product, which will increase the cost of time when purchase and use.

High Material Costs and Poor Recovery and Recycling System. Smart color-changing packaging uses color-changing materials, sensors and indicators as an important part for color feedback. As for fruit and vegetable packaging, chemical-based sensors or indicators cannot be used directly, as they may cause food safety problems. Some of the sensors require electronic components to become a complete smart color-change packaging. This will largely increase packaging cost and is not conducive to recovery and recycling.

3 Future Design Strategies and Suggestions for Intelligent Color-Changing Packaging for Fruits and Vegetables

Under different backgrounds, traditional fruit and vegetable packaging continues to adapt to the physiological and psychological needs of consumers. These needs include sumptuous visual effects, efficient function, various interactive experience, environmentalism and so on. With the development of science and technology, information technology continues to upgrade and constantly open up the boundaries of consumer needs. It has also become an important reference in fruit and vegetable packaging design. In general, the abovementioned visualization, experience, practicality, environmental protection and technology has constituted the new paradigm for fruit and vegetable packaging design in intelligent era. Their mutual influence and complement finally help to promote the development of intelligent packaging. Intelligent color-changing packaging for fruits and vegetables should not only meet the basic requirement of packaging, but also color-changing functions to further satisfy the dual needs of consumers' physiology and psychology. Designers are supposed to think deeply about the relationship between demand and attraction, expression of visual language and interactive experience. Finally, attention has to be paid to environmental issues such as recycling waste packaging (see Fig. 6). Based on above concepts, design strategies and suggestions are proposed for the existing problems of intelligent color-changing packaging for fruits and vegetables.

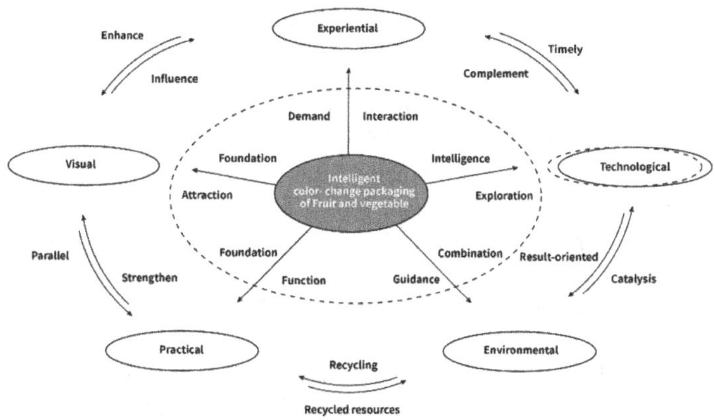

Fig. 6. New paradigm of fruit and vegetable packaging design

3.1 Enrich Packaging Graphic Form Based on Emotional Design

To enrich packaging graphic form, we need to design new intelligent packaging at the basis of current packaging and take advantage of emotional design. Meanwhile, it's a good idea to integrate the properties of color-changing materials into packaging. Although the main purpose of intelligent color-changing packaging is to monitor the freshness and safety of fruits and vegetables, good packaging design should have the basic function of packaging and also emotional visual language expression. Only such intelligent color-changing packaging can help people make the right decision while purchasing fruits and vegetables. And such packaging can also lead to good visual interaction and resulting comfortable emotional experience for consumers. This can not only promote sales, but also broadens the cognitive boundary of consumers. Using the three levels of Donald's emotional design and take it as initial logic, we have proposed several design ideas to enrich the graphics of intelligent packaging for fruits and vegetables.

First starting from the visceral level, plant properties can be used to highlight the visual performance of packaging. Design packaging according to the characteristics of fruit and vegetable by abstract visual elements from them and distillation. For example, intelligent color-changing packaging for blueberry, which is rich in anthocyanins, can be designed not only from the appearance of blueberries, but also from the feeling blueberries can bring about. We can transform these element and properties of blueberry into visual graphics, symbols, forms and then integrate them with packaging materials. Second, meet the needs of the behavior level and enhance practicality. The attributes and visual graphics of smart color-changing packaging are used to improve the recognition and practicality of distinguishing ripeness of fruits and vegetables, monitoring freshness, and providing real-time feedback on safety. Finally, provoking consumers' reflective level. By combining basic form of graphics or the visual language with other design elements, it can cause consumers to think further about environmental protection, recyclability, fun, retrospective memories, etc. The circular design thinking can help not only upgrade the intelligent color-changing packaging for fruits and vegetables, but also promote developments of other smart packaging.

3.2 Unify Color Feedback by Adopting Fruit and Vegetable's Color

The color feedback of intelligent color-changing packaging is attributed to different components of color-changing materials, sensors, and indicators. And because of the different component, colors can be varied from packaging to packaging. To reduce the learning process and time cost for consumers to use intelligent color-changing packaging, indicators can be matched with the plant properties of fruits and vegetables to unify the color feedback. For example, we can apply anthocyanins to the intelligent color-changing packaging of blueberries, purple kale, eggplant and other related plants as this color feedback overlaps with the cognitive path of consumers, and can reduce their learning cost.

Color of fruits and vegetables and color of packaging feedback can be unified into the same color system. The color of certain objects has become an inherent concept, such as blue sky and white clouds, red flowers and green leaves. Studies of consumer behavior show that inherent color can sometimes govern purchasing behavior, and consumers often connect the use of color based on their common knowledge and experience [16]. In this way, we can start from human's natural cognition, enhance the functional recognition of color-changing attributes, shorten the distance between consumers and increase the sense of identity.

3.3 Improve the Closed Loop of Green Design by Bio-Based Materials

As fruits and vegetables are all in high demand, it is necessary to consider the post-functional and recycling issue of packaging. In this paper, we advocate the design concept of "from nature, back to nature", and design intelligent color-changing packaging based on humans and environment (see Fig. 7). The whole ecological chain is composed by nature and human beings. The combination of nature and human then form a running society, in which fruits and vegetables are necessities. The intelligent color-changing packaging should be designed upon the combination of technology and design aesthetics to enhance the connection of people's psychological and physical demand. Meanwhile, a closed loop of green design is pursued based on the concept of "from nature, back to nature". Taking this loop as reference, the intelligent color-changing packaging for fruits and vegetables can be designed and produced with biological materials to improve the closed loop of green design while meeting various visual needs and functional requirements. For example, starch, extracted from plants like rice, corn, potatoes, and grains can be used for coating and film. Starch is easily attainable, inexpensive, biodegradable, and has good mechanical properties. It can be mixed with conventional polymers for fabricating packaging materials [21, 22]. Another example is natural dyes like anthocyanins, betaine, carotenoids, and chlorophylls, which can be extracted from various plants and animals, are nontoxic, harmless, and easily degradable, and can be used as indicators for intelligent color-changing packaging for fruits and vegetables or in color-changing films.

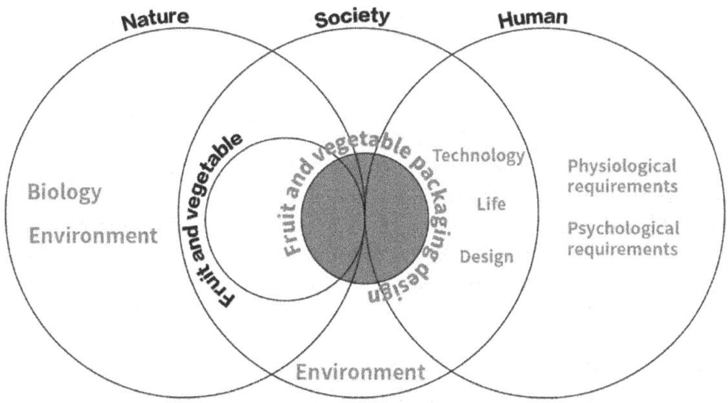

Fig. 7. Closed loop path for green design

4 Conclusion

In summary, the emergence of intelligent color-changing packaging design for fruits and vegetables has advanced the process of new packaging design to a certain extent. The intelligent color-changing packaging can not only help consumers shorten selection time, improve purchase rate and increase interactivity, but also reduce breakage ratio of fruit and vegetable during transportation, and extend the quality guarantee period of fruits and vegetables. Although there has been some progress in intelligent color-changing packaging for fruits and vegetables, it is still in its preliminary stage. This paper analyzes the existing problems in the development of intelligent color-changing packaging for fruits and vegetables from the perspective of design. The single feedback graphics, lack of standardization of feedback colors, low recycling efficiency of waste packaging are main problems need to be solved. Design strategies and suggestions to these problems are proposed, such as making design upon emotional design concept, adopting fruit and vegetable color in packaging and referring to closed green design loops etc. This current work may give some inspiration to researchers and designers in related fields, and facilitate their study on intelligent color-changing packaging for fruits and vegetables.

References

1. He, J.: Modern Packaging Design, 1st edn. Tsinghua University Press, Beijing (2018)
2. Khezrian, A., Shahbazi, Y.: Application of nanocompostie chitosan and carboxymethyl cellulose films containing natural preservative compounds in minced camel's meat. Int. J. Biol. Macromol. **106**, 1146–1158 (2017). https://doi.org/10.1016/j.ijbiomac.2017.08.117
3. European Commission: Commission Regulation (EC) No 1935/2004 of 27 October 2004 on materials and articles intended to come into contact with food and repealing Directives 80/590/EEC and 89/109/EEC. Official Journal of the European Union, OJ L 338, 4e17 (2004)
4. Loucanova, E., Kalamarova, M., Parobek, J.: The innovative approaches to packaging – comparison analysis of intelligent and active packaging perceptions in Slovakia. Studia Universitatis „Vasile Goldis" Arad – Economics Series **27**(2), 33–44 (2017). https://doi.org/10.1515/sues-2017-0007

5. Ke, S.H.: Intelligent Packaging Design Research, 1st edn. Jiangsu Phoenix Art Press, Hunan (2019)
6. Ke, S.H.: Material intelligent packaging classification and design applications. Packag. Eng. **39**(21), 6–10 (2018). https://doi.org/10.19554/j.cnki.1001-3563.2018.21.002
7. Sohail, M., Sun, D.W., Zhu, Z.W.: Recent developments in intelligent packaging for enhancing food quality and safety. Crit. Rev. Food Sci. Nutr. **58**, 2650–2662 (2018). https://doi.org/10.1080/10408398.2018.1449731
8. Sun, J., Ye, B., Xia, G., Zhao, X., Wang, H.: A colorimetric and fluorescent chemosensor for the highly sensitive detection of CO2 gas: experiment and DFT calculation. Sens. Actuators B: Chem. **233**, 76–82 (2016). https://doi.org/10.1016/j.snb.2016.04.052
9. Hu, Z.C., Ke, S.H.: Research on the application and design forms of intelligent color-changing materials on packaging. Packag. Eng. **41**(9), 117–123 (2020). https://doi.org/10.19554/j.cnki.1001-3563.2020.09.017
10. Latos-Brozio, M., Masek, A.: The application of natural food colorants as indicator substances in intelligent biodegradable packaging materials. Food Chem. Toxicol. **135**, 1–10 (2020). https://doi.org/10.1016/j.fct.2019.11097s
11. Donald, A.N.: Emotional Design: Why We Love (Or Hate) Everyday Things, 1st edn. Basic Books, New York (2007)
12. Nanotechnology Products Database Homepage: https://product.statnano.com/product/6730/ripesense. Accessed 27 Dec 2021
13. 3M Homepage: https://www.3m.com/3M/en_US/p/d/b00003869/#variation2. Accessed 27 Dec 2021
14. Packaging of the world: https://packagingoftheworld.com/2010/06/fresh-label.html. Accessed 27 Dec 2021
15. Johannes, I.: Art of Color, 1st edn. Dessain and Tolra, Paris (1961)
16. Liu, S.: Design Psychology, 1st edn. People's Fine Arts Press, Shanghai (2016)
17. Mohammadian, E., Alizadeh-Sani, M., Jafari, S.M.: Smart monitoring of gas/temperature changes within food packaging based on natural colorants. Compr. Rev. Food Sci. Food Saf. **19**(6), 2885–2931 (2020). https://doi.org/10.1111/1541-4337.12635
18. Luchese, C.L., Sperotto, N., Spada, J.C., Tessaro, I.C.: Effect of blueberry agro-industrial waste addition to corn starch-based films for the production of a pH-indicator film. Int. J. Biol. Macromol. **104**, 11–18 (2017). https://doi.org/10.1016/j.ijbiomac.2017.05.149
19. Kuswandi, B., Kinanti, D.P., Jayus, A.A., Heng, L.Y.: Simple and low-cost freshness indicator for strawberries packaging. Acta Manilana **61**, 147–159 (2013)
20. Pu Jing, M., Giusti, Mónica.: Characterization of anthocyanin-rich waste from purple corncobs (Zea mays L.) and its application to color milk. J. Agric. Food Chem. **53**(22), 8775–8781 (2005). https://doi.org/10.1021/jf051247o
21. Bayram, B., Ozkan, G., Kostka, T., Capanoglu, E., Esatbeyoglu, T.: Valorization and application of fruit and vegetable wastes and by-products for food packaging materials. Molecules **26**(13), 4031 (2021). https://doi.org/10.3390/molecules26134031
22. Yew, G.H., Yusof, A.M.M., Ishak, Z.A.M., Ishiaku, U.S.: Water absorption and enzymatic degradation of poly(lactic acid)/rice starch composites. Polym. Degrad. Stab. **90**(3), 488–500 (2005). https://doi.org/10.1016/j.polymdegradstab.2005.04.006

Research and Design of Future-oriented Smart Gas Station Service

Meiyu Lv[1,2](✉) and Xinyu Zhang[1](✉)

[1] School of Digital Media and Design Arts, Beijing University of Posts and Telecommunications, Beijing 100876, China
meiyulv@163.com, 820831958@qq.com

[2] Beijing Key Laboratory of Network Culture, Beijing University of Posts and Telecommunications, Beijing 100876, China

Abstract. In recent years, new energy vehicles represented by electric vehicles have rapidly occupied the automotive market in China, leading to a gradual decrease in the demand for automotive refined oil. At the same time, the single service content, outdated service models, and low level of informatization of China's gas stations lead to poor user experience. The operations of the gas station face challenges. This paper uses service design methods like field research, user interviews, user journey map and Kano model to discuss the problems existing in the current gas station and make design strategies for the future smart gas station. According to analysis, future smart gas stations should upgrade hardware facilities, innovate the service marketing model, and establish a smart operation management platform, and these strategies are realized by the design of the gas station space, the user app terminal and the staff pad terminal. From the perspective of service design, the innovative design of gas station service model is in line with the development direction of smart cities in the new era, which can meet the full-link service needs of multi-role stakeholders, and provide a reference for future gas station service design.

Keywords: Service design · Gas station design · User experience

1 Introduction

Since the 1990s, the rapid development of the national economy has led to a continuous increase in the number of cars per capita in China. The prosperity of fuel vehicles once led to an exponential increase in the number of gas stations. However, in recent years, with the widespread application of new energy technologies represented by electricity, new energy vehicles have rapidly occupied the automotive market share in China. According to data, in the first half of 2021, the production and sales of new energy vehicles in China reached 1.215 million and 1.206 million, a year-on-year increase of 200%. As of the end of June, the number of new energy vehicles in China was 6.03 million, accounting for about 50% of the world [1]. The rapid increase in the number of new energy vehicles has led to the adjustment of the vehicle energy structure, and the domestic demand for refined oil has gradually decreased. For a single gas station, its oil product sales have not

P.-L. P. Rau (Ed.): HCII 2022, LNCS 13314, pp. 91–105, 2022.
https://doi.org/10.1007/978-3-031-06053-3_7

increased significantly, and some have shown a downward trend [2]. At the same time, the single service content, the outdated service model, and the vacant online business cannot meet the consumer demand of customers in the new consumption era. Gas stations are facing difficulties in recruiting and retaining customers.

The market pattern of vehicle energy terminal consumption is gradually changing, and the wide application of new energy vehicles will be the general trend. In order to realize the transformation of gas stations from a traditional refined oil supplier to a comprehensive vehicle service provider, this paper proposes a future service design strategy for gas stations based on the actual needs of stakeholders and the future development trend of the industry from the perspective of smart service innovation, and applies Big data, artificial intelligence, self-service, new retail and other new technologies to build a future-oriented intelligent service system, aiming to revitalize gas station enterprises through service transformation.

2 Gas Station Service Analysis

2.1 Single Types of Energy Supply Facilities

In recent years, the promotion of new energy vehicles has been fully supported by China, driving the rapid development of the charging pile industry. From 2015 to 2020, the number of charging piles for electric vehicles in China has increased year by year, from 66,000 to 1.681 million [3]. Facing the transformation of power energy in the transportation field, petroleum companies not only need to systematically analyze the development trend of charging piles and continue to pay attention to energy reforms, but also need to combine their own advantages to seize the highlands of the charging pile industry in a timely manner [4]. At present, there is still a lack of experimentation and innovation in the combined operation of "oil" and "electricity" of gas stations in China.

2.2 Outdated Service Model

With the continuous development of science and technology, self-service applications are not uncommon in various fields, such as supermarket self-checkout machines and hospital self-service registration machines. At present, gas stations still use traditional manual services, with high labor costs and low service efficiency. At the same time, gas station convenience stores mainly operate under the light-asset model, that is, traditional snack department stores [5]. The single content of the items for sale and the outdated marketing model are difficult to meet the demand of consumers with diverse personalities, quality-oriented in the era of experience economy.

2.3 Unbalanced Development of Marketing Structure

Competition in the refined oil market has become increasingly fierce, and fuel sales profits have fallen, making it difficult for gas station companies to develop on oil product profits alone. At present, the profit of the non-oil business of European gas stations is continuing to rise, and its profit has accounted for 40%-50% of the total profit of gas stations. Compared with the turnover of developed countries, the non-oil business profits in China accounted for less than 1/3 of the international level, and only accounted for 10% of the total profit [6]. In the face of the slow growth of refined oil sales, the unilateral development of the marketing model of oil products will put gas stations in a hindered situation.

2.4 Low Degree of Informatization

In recent years, China has actively promoted the "Internet+" plan, through the Internet to promote the flattening of the energy system, and promote the revolution of energy production and consumption patterns. Under the current traditional operation mode of gas stations, customers' consumption records of different businesses belong to different management background systems, the data are independent of each other. It is difficult to provide complete and accurate data support for gas station operations. As a result, gas stations cannot use customers' real feedback and consumption data to perform cluster analysis, and can only blindly formulate sales plans.

In summary, there is optimization space for gas station facility construction, service mode, marketing structure, and operation mode. Industrial upgrading is inseparable from the assistance of new technologies and new concepts. Gas stations need to use smart service concepts to develop from a traditional energy supply station to a future-oriented "people-vehicle-life" station.

3 Study Basis

3.1 Service Design

The concept of service design was first proposed by G. Lynn Shostack in 1982. Service design is a user-centered, collaborative design activity with multiple stakeholders. System innovation is realized through the comprehensive integration of the innovation of personnel, environment, facilities, information and other elements. After years of development, the laws of service design are: human-centered, collaborative, iterative, sequential, real, and holistic [7]. In the process of service design, designers need to think from the perspective of users, build an overall collaborative service system framework according to the needs of stakeholders, and subdivide service points for design. The purpose is to let all stakeholders get better service experience and the overall service efficiency can be improved. As a new way of design thinking, service design breaks the boundaries between design and service with its co-creation, dynamic, and full-link characteristics, and establishes a new logic between innovative design and landing service.

3.2 Smart Design

In 2008, IBM put forward the concept of "Smart Earth" for the first time. Since then, many traditional service industries such as urban planning, traffic management, campus construction, and elderly care services have planned and developed under the concept of "wisdom ". In the context of design, "wisdom" can be understood as a combination of "intelligent technology" and "systematic thinking". Intelligent technology as a service provider, including organizations, institutions or individuals, uses emerging science and technology such as artificial intelligence, big data and cloud computing to interconnect and share data, information, and users. Systematic thinking is the use of cutting-edge business concepts to build a service system that serves various stakeholders, so that system functions can meet the needs of various roles, provide users with all-day, all-round services, and improve the synergy and sustainability of the system. Technology application and system design supplement each other to build an intelligent collaborative innovation system. The intelligent service system is an important way to transform the production paradigm into the service paradigm, which helps the public to realize the maximization of benefits together [8].

3.3 Design Method

In long-term practice, service design has formed a series of research-based design methods [9]. Common methods include user journey map, system map, service blueprints, persona, and KANO models. In practical applications, design methods need to be selected based on the different design goals. Based on the characteristics of multiple target users, rich service types, and complex information flow, this paper mainly uses two design tools, service blueprint and KANO model, to conduct research.

Service Blueprint. The service blueprint is an analysis model that is widely used in the service design. It decomposes activities into the foreground and the background, and accurately depicts the interaction between contacts, users, behaviors, and information. The service blueprint helps designers establish and improve the service system, helps all participants intuitively understand the business operation process, and clarify their personal responsibilities and the connections between their responsible parts and other parts of the system.

KANO Model. In the process of service innovation, balancing and resolving contradictions in various factors are the focus of research, and defining contradictory attributes is the key to solving contradictory problems [5] 06. The KANO model is a design tool invented by Noriaki Kano, a professor at Tokyo Institute of Technology. It can define the attributes of different needs through analyzing how the needs influence the user satisfaction [10]. In the design practice stage, the KANO model helps designers distinguish the authenticity of the user needs and do the development prioritization.

4 Research and Analysis of Smart Gas Station Service Design

4.1 Stakeholders

Compared with traditional product design, a very important difference is that service design not only needs to consider the needs of users, but also needs to consider the needs of all stakeholders involved in the implementation and completion of the service [11].

Through design, all stakeholders can complete the service process efficiently and happily. In the gas station service system, stakeholders are mainly divided into the following categories: service objects (drivers and passengers), service providers (gas station staff, gas station managers), suppliers (oil companies, convenience store suppliers), producers (facilities producers, designers, manufacturers) and regulators (government, public service departments). This paper starts the research from the service object and service provider.

4.2 User Research

In order to understanding of the needs of service object and service provider, we went to PetroChina and Sinopec in Tianjin and Beijing for field research. Questionnaire surveys and in-depth interviews were conducted on 100 drivers and passengers, 20 gas station staff, and 116 valid questionnaires were recovered, with an effective rate of 94.8%, and 20 in-depth interviews were conducted. On the basis of user research, we use the user journey map to find design opportunities by analyzing the user targets, touchpoints, experience,

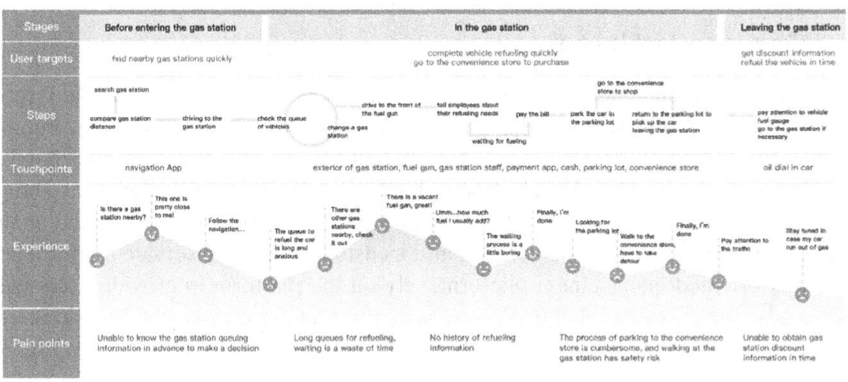

Fig. 1. User journey map of drivers

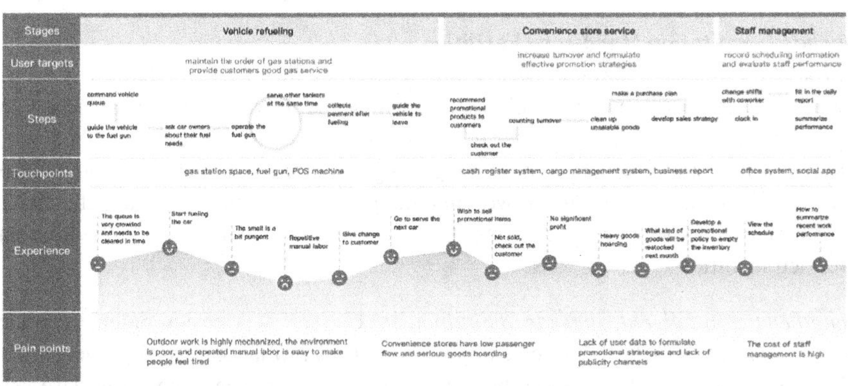

Fig. 2. User journey map of gas station staff

and pain points of the drivers (see Fig. 1) and the gas station staff (see Fig. 2) at different stages. The research found that: in terms of facility construction, the number of charging facilities is limited, and the drivers' time utilization rate is low during the charging process; drivers gather to refuel on holidays, which make the queue waiting time is long. In terms of service mode, employees' working environment is poor since they are exposed to volatile gases all day long, and the mechanized working content make the employees are lack enthusiasm for work. In terms of marketing structure, since most convenience stores are located in the innermost part of gas stations, their goods exposure rate and turnover ratio are low, and customers visit the store with low consumption frequency and small consumption amount. In terms of operation management, customer refueling data and convenience store consumption data are recorded in different databases, which make the employees hard to make correlation analysis between users and consumption behavior. Service providers and service objects have low satisfaction with the existing service mode, content and experience of gas stations, and there are many pain points in gas station services.

5 Design Strategy of Smart Gas Station

5.1 Information Architecture

The essence of the innovation of the smart service model of gas stations is the reform of the distribution and intercommunication model of resources, data, and users. Future-oriented gas station smart services, based on technology and data, use cutting-edge technologies such as artificial intelligence, cloud computing, and the Internet of Things to acquire, integrate and analyze data on users, equipment, and resources; based on the needs of stakeholders, use basic data to build a customer-oriented service platform and a manager-oriented management platform; rely on the platform to provide users with online and offline services, and finally use app, smart facilities, gas station spaces, and pad as terminal contacts for services to realize the landing of smart services (see Fig. 3).

5.2 Promoting Path of Smart Gas Station Service Model

Upgrade Gas Station Hardware Facilities

Incorporate Charging Piles into Gas Station. Driven by the rapid growth of new energy vehicles, the market demand for charging piles is bound to continue to increase. As an important source of vehicle energy supply, the future gas station will become a comprehensive energy service station integrating refueling and charging. The addition of charging piles in the station can well integrate existing resources, reduce the cost of charging piles, add new customer groups to gas stations, and increase the utilization rate of service facilities at gas stations.

Strengthen the Intelligent Upgrade of Equipment. Use self-service equipment to replace some manual services. Self-service equipment requires low labor costs for management and maintenance, which can effectively reduce gas station operating costs. Use self-service refueller and charging piles to replace manual tasks with high mechanical levels

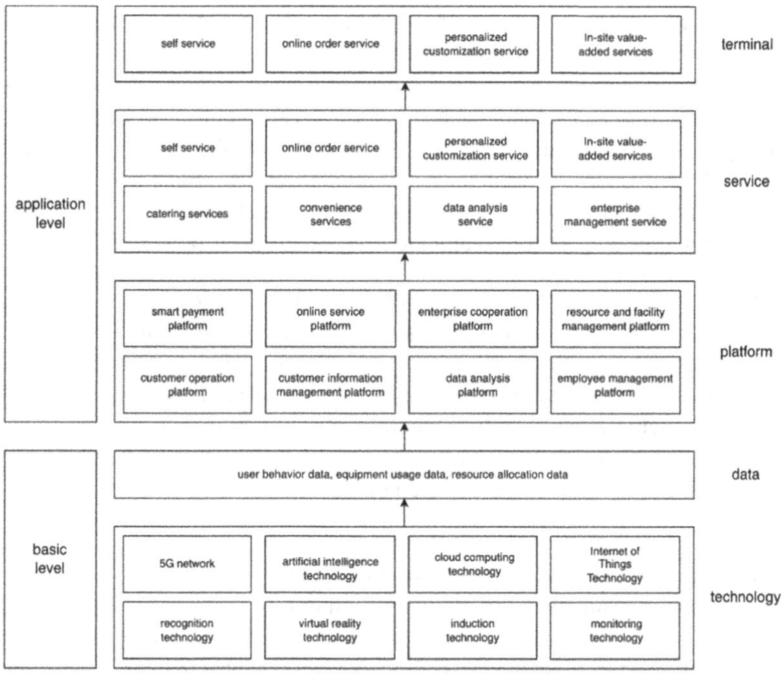

Fig. 3. Information architecture of smart gas station

and poor working environments, allowing employees to complete creative and decision-making tasks in a safe and comfortable environment. Install vehicle recognition and face recognition cameras on self-service equipment. After successful recognition, the user information pre-stored on the platform will be automatically synchronized to the machine, and a convenient self-service experience can be created through methods such as license plate payment and face payment. While promoting self-service, strengthen the guidance design of the self-service equipment use process, which can lower the using threshold of self-service equipment, simplify the self-service process, and make self-service the new normal at gas stations.

Innovate the Service Marketing Model of Gas Station

New Retailing Enhances Consumer Experience. Break through the barriers of online and offline retail services. Turn the gas station's current merchant-centric marketing strategy to consumer-centric, and make adjustments from the aspects of sales platforms, types of goods, shopping processes, and membership systems: set up an online platform to push preferential information for users and provide online shopping channels; expand product sales types, increase product categories to meet consumers' needs better; open a quick pick-up window in a convenience store, and users can place an order online then drive to the pick-up window to get their goods; establish a membership upgrade system, and different levels of members can enjoy different degrees of discounts, which is conducive to consolidating user loyalty and enhancing brand influence.

Provide Value-added Services. Create a diversified service experience for gas stations. Facing the dilemma of fuel sales, turning non-fuel business from accessories to necessities is the key to breaking the situation for future gas stations. Opening up value-added services such as auto care and maintenance, catering, rest and office space at gas stations, attracting car owners to consume by coupons, free membership for the first service, etc., to meet car owners' needs for vehicles in a one-stop service. It can not only provide a warm and comfortable waiting place for car owners while charging, but also help extend consumers' stay time at gas stations and increase the turnover of non-oil businesses.

Build a Cooperation Ecosystem Between Different Vehicles Industries. Provide integrated, full-process vehicle services. Gas stations can cooperate with platforms such as 4s stores, insurance companies, car maintenance companies, hotels, and ticket providers. Exchange customer resources through coupons sharing to enhance customer stickiness and maximize benefits. Establishing a cooperative ecology of vehicles in different industries will help gas stations break the commercial islands and complementary advantages", and build a community of interests centered on gas stations.

Establish a Smart Operation Management Platform

Big Data Operation. Establish a gas station customer information management system, collect various user consumption behavior data, and extend to realize precise marketing. Use the data collected from online and offline like station entry frequency, consumption preferences, consumption amount as a hand to draw user portraits and carry out customer hierarchical management, such as launching special promotion activities to attract specific groups of people to consume, targeted delivery of product discounts. Accurately meet the differentiated needs of users can improve service quality and customer satisfaction, and promote precise operations virtuous circle.

Build an Online Management Platform. Through the online management platform, integrate gas station facilities, resources, goods, orders, finances, employees, and other related information to realize integrated gas station management. The system connects all intelligent information equipment in the station, stores the data generated by the interaction between the user and the equipment, and synchronizes the oil and gas resource inventory in the station, equipment usage, transaction flow, and check on work attendance of the employees, forming a complete gas station logistics invoicing, funds streaming, and human resource data statistics system.

6 Design Practice

6.1 Service Framework

Service Blueprint. Draw the service blueprint of the future smart gas station according to the system design strategy. The service interaction process between the service object and the smart gas station is divided into three steps: before entering the station, during the station and after leaving the station. The service blueprint of smart gas stations sorts out how stakeholders interact at each stage (see Fig. 4).

It can be seen from the service blueprint that the service includes pre-setting of refueling information before entering the station, online convenience store shopping, rest at the station, car maintenance, coupons sharing in the station, and coupons exchange with partner companies, discount push after leaving the station. Smart gas stations provide full-link, multi-dimensional vehicle-related services for service targets through the cooperation of hardware and software facilities. The online and offline service model breaks the time and space constraints of interaction between customers and gas stations.

In the service process, gas stations collect personal information and consumption information of the customers through vehicle recognition cameras, self-service refueling machines, charging piles, apps and other terminal devices. The information includes refueling frequency, oil consumption, consumption preferences, consumption time, etc., which is uploaded to the central database, so that data acquisition and collection run through the entire service process, and provides real and effective data support for managers in data analysis and strategies-making. Information and data circulate between service objects and gas station systems, forming a closed loop of innovative and collaborative services.

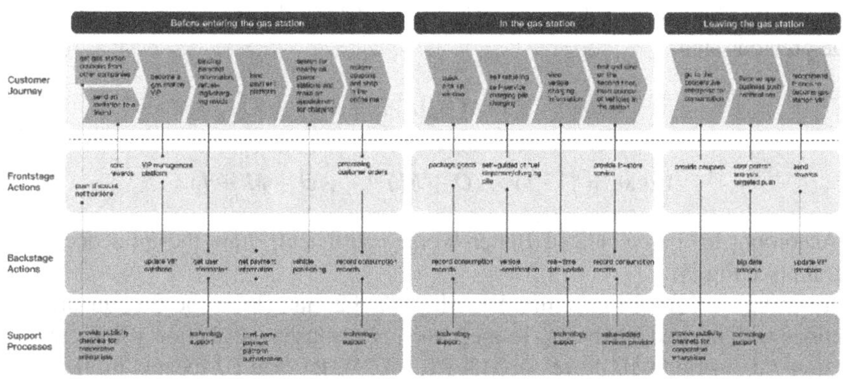

Fig. 4. Service blueprint

KANO Model Analysis. In the design practice stage, necessity judgment and prioritization of functions is an important part, which helps to make the design of the system more targeted and focused. The function points included in the system are obtained from the analysis of the service design strategy and the service blueprint, and the KANO model analysis is used to evaluate their importance and prioritize them. Distribute a two-dimensional service demand attribute scale to target users of the system, and select positive and negative evaluation options for each function. A total of 40 scales were issued and 36 effective scales were recovered. Then compare the KANO model analysis table, as shown in Table 1, count the number of samples that fall into each cell, compare the attributes represented by each cell in the figure below, calculate the proportion of each attribute of the function, and find the highest proportion as the functional attributes. Among them, M represents the required attribute, O represents the desired attribute, A represents the attractive attribute, I represents the indifferent attribute, R represents the reverse attribute, and Q represents the invalid result. The classification results are shown in Table 2.

Table 1. Kano model analysis table.

Dysfunctional						
Functional		Like it	Expect it	Don't'care	Live with	Dislike
	Like it	Q	A	A	A	O
	Expect it	R	I	I	I	M
	Don't care	R	I	I	I	M
	Live with	R	I	I	I	M
	Dislike	R	R	R	R	Q

Use formula (1) to calculate the Better coefficient and use formula (2) to calculate the Worse coefficient according to the statistical data in the requirement classification in the previous step:

$$Better = (A + O)/(A + O + M + I) \tag{1}$$

$$Worse = (-1) \times (O + M)/(A + O + M + I) \tag{2}$$

According to the calculated Better-Worse coefficient, draw the influence scatter diagram (see Fig. 5).

It can be seen from Fig. 5 that F1, M2, M7, F2, and B5 in the first quadrant are functions with desired attributes. To meet such needs, user satisfaction will increase; if not, user satisfaction will decrease. M3, P1, F4, P4, P5, and P7 located in the second quadrant belong to the charm attribute function. To meet such needs, user satisfaction will be greatly improved; if not, user satisfaction will not decline. F6, M6, P6, P2, F3, and M1 in the third quadrant belong to the indifferent attribute function. To meet such needs, user satisfaction does not change; if not, user satisfaction does not change. F5, M4, P3, and F7 located in the fourth quadrant are essential attribute functions. To meet such needs, and user satisfaction will not increase significantly; if not, user satisfaction will be greatly reduced. It can be carried out according to the priority order of functions generally adopted during system development, that is, necessary attribute > desired attribute > charm attribute > indifference attribute. For functions of the same type, priority is given to those with higher better coefficients and lower worst coefficients. The needs are prioritized as follows: F5 self-service guidance, M4 online order to store and pick up, P3 station equipment Resource management, P4 station marketing data statistics, F7 manual assistance, F1 additional charging pile, M2 appointment charging pile, M7 multi-enterprise point sharing, P5 member information management, F2 setting lounge and office area, B5 booking car beauty and catering services.

Table 2. Requirement attribute analysis table.

Number	Function	Q	A	O	M	I	R	Type
F1	Add charging pile	0.0%	34.5%	43.5%	15.0%	7.0%	0.0%	O
F2	Set up lounge and office area	0.0%	22.4%	35.6%	30.0%	12.0%	0.0%	O
F3	Set up a parking lot	0.0%	5.1%	8.4%	32.0%	54.5%	0.0%	I
F4	Convenience store quick pick-up window	0.0%	50.8%	32.5%	10.0%	6.7%	0.0%	A
F5	Self-service guidance	0.0%	16.0%	26.0%	48.0%	10.0%	0.0%	M
F6	Add a tanker stand	0.0%	14.5%	28.0%	20.0%	37.5%	0.0%	I
F7	Manual assistance	0.0%	2.5%	8.6%	68.5%	20.4%	0.0%	M
M1	GIS recommends nearby gas stations	0.0%	3.0%	10.8%	20.4%	65.8%	0.0%	I
M2	Reserve charging pile	5.0%	19.0%	42.0%	4.0%	12.0%	18.0%	O
M3	Real-time monitoring of vehicle charging status	2.5%	52.8%	30.5%	10.0%	4.2%	0.0%	A
M4	Order online and pick up in store	0.0%	12.0%	24.7%	48.3%	15.0%	0.0%	M
M5	Book car beauty and catering services	0.0%	16.0%	48.0%	26.0%	10.0%	0.0%	O
M6	In-site car maintenance	0.0%	14.4%	20.4%	24.4%	40.8%	14.5%	I
M7	Multi-enterprise points sharing	0.0%	24.5%	50.8%	12.0%	12.7%	0.0%	O
P1	Refueling/charging demand information preset	2.0%	44.5%	38.5%	3.0%	12.0%	0.0%	A
P2	Personalized preferential information push	0.0%	17.0%	3.0%	12.0%	68.0%	0.0%	I
P3	In-site equipment resource management	0.0%	12.3%	27.0%	55.0%	5.7%	0.0%	M
P4	In-site marketing data statistics	2.0%	10.0%	6.0%	47.5%	20.0%	0.0%	M
P5	Member information management	0.0%	23.6%	40.8%	15.5%	17.5%	2.6%	O
P6	Employee attendance management	0.0%	12.9%	10.6%	12.0%	64.5%	0.0%	I
P7	Cross-platform media promotion	0.0%	38.0%	22.0%	21.2%	18.8%	0.0%	A

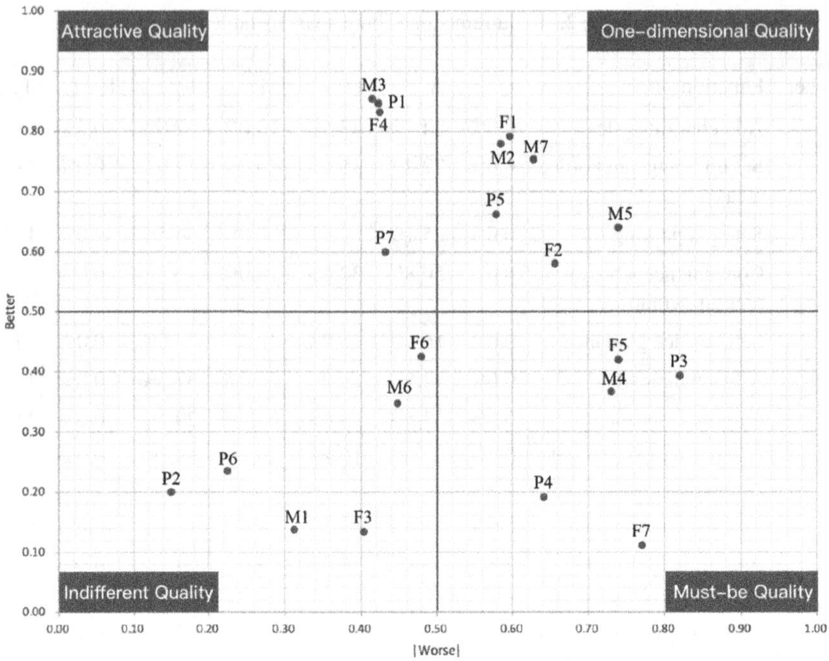

Fig. 5. Better-worse scatter plot

6.2 Touchpoint Design

Space Design of Gas Station. The space design of the smart gas station is the core touch point of the system, which carries all the offline interaction activities between the costumers and the gas station. Its main functions are to install charging piles, provide self-service facilities and guidance, set up venues for value-added services, and open convenience stores to quickly pick up goods. The space is mainly divided into seven areas: refueling area, charging area, convenience store, rest office area, dining area, car maintenance area, and parking lot (see Fig. 6).

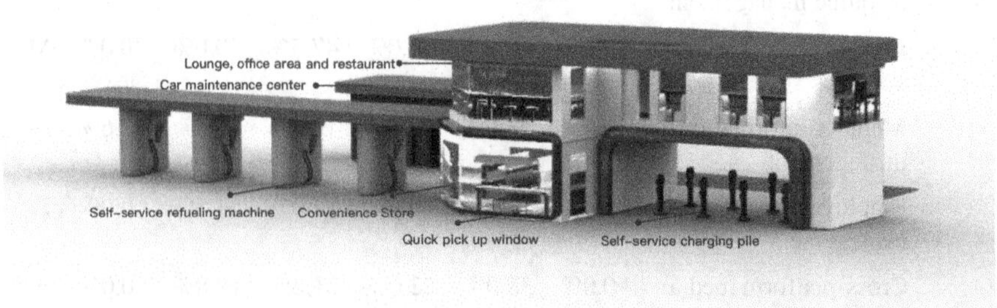

Fig. 6. Space design of gas station

The self-service refueling machine and charging pile in the station obtain the personal information reserved by the user on the app through license recognition. After the recognition is successful, the device screen automatically presents the vehicle information and the energy supply requirements preset by the user. The user can unlock the machine for self-service refueling or charging by pressing the anti-static metal button on the device. The self-service equipment provides a novice guidance mode, which helps users understand the self-service refueling process through page text and animation guidance, and assists users in completing refueling requirements acquisition, modification, machine unlocking, and facial payment operations (see Fig. 7). Set up a quick pick-up window in a convenience store, where users place an order online and then drive to the window to quickly pick up the goods. The charging time of the car is generally 30 min to 2 h. During this period, the drivers can go to the office or dining area in the station for rest. The car maintenance area provides preferential auto care and maintenance services. Car owners can get coupons by refueling, charging, shopping, catering, and car maintenance consumption in the station.

Fig. 7. Novice guidance mode design

App Design. Drivers and passengers use the app to set personal information, shop online, and reserve services. App consists of 5 main interfaces, which are homepage, mall, petrol station service, vehicle service and me. After successful registration, the user can bind the vehicle information and payment account for license plate recognition and self-service payment. Users can place orders in online shopping malls in advance or make reservations for in-site services. If users need to make an appointment for charging, they can check the usage of the charging pile, make an appointment during the time when the charging pile is not occupied, and check the vehicle charging progress and pickup reminders in real time through the app during the charging process. In addition, users can redeem coupons to enjoy preferential services from cooperative companies such as car maintenance, car after-sales service, and car insurance (see Fig. 8).

Pad Design. The gas station pad terminal is mainly used by gas station employees and managers, providing functions such as station resource equipment management, marketing data statistics, and member information management. The system conducts real-time statistics on the passenger flow in the station, the turnover of each business line, and the occupancy of charging piles. Tag and categorize member consumption data through different dimensions to help managers identify the needs of different types of customers, build accurate consumption profiles of costumers, predict consumption trends, and formulate differentiated marketing strategies (see Fig. 9).

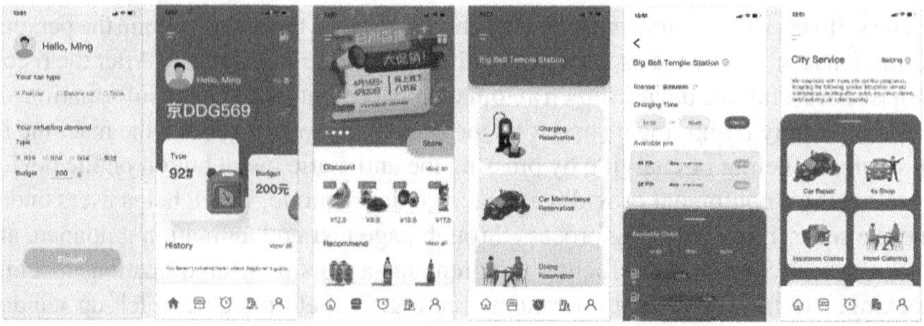

Fig. 8. App design

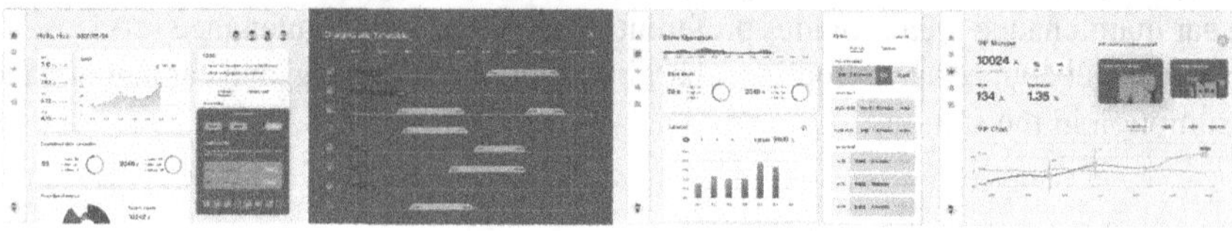

Fig. 9. Pad design

Design Evaluation. Questionnaires were issued to car owners and gas station employees at four gas stations in Beijing. Show the interviewees the interactive prototypes of the smart service system, let them score the existing service model and the designed smart gas station service model in four dimensions: innovation, practicality, convenience, and systemicity. The score uses the Likert 7-point scale. The larger the score, the higher the satisfaction. The score is shown in Table 3. It can be seen that the user satisfaction of the future-oriented gas station smart service system after the design has been improved.

Table 3. User satisfaction evaluation.

Service model	Innovative	Practicality	Convenience	Systematic
After	4.29	5.29	4.71	4.57
Before	5.57	5.43	5.29	5.00

7 Conclusion

This paper uses service design to realize the systematic innovation of service content, process, touch points, and environment, effectively creating a pleasant service experience for service participants, and realizing multi-party win-win business and social value. Smart services use new technologies and new concepts to influence every link from manufacturing to product delivery, helping traditional industries to complete future-oriented service innovations. This paper uses field research, user interviews and other research methods to analyze the needs of stakeholders, and formulates smart gas station service design strategies; build a system framework through service blueprints and KANO models. Therefore, applying the service design concept for smart gas station design helps to broaden the ideas and methods of smart gas station design, and provides a new reference for the intelligent and platform-based development of the industry. At present, there is still room for improvement in the service process perfection of smart gas stations facing the future. It is necessary to further strengthen service contact design and business model exploration to promote the construction of smart gas station smart service systems.

References

1. China Economic Net. https://baijiahao.baidu.com/s?id=1703314921603130163&wfr=spider&for=pc,last. Accessed 23 June 2021
2. Zhenhua, S.: Analysis of gas station management in refined oil retail industry. Chem. Manag. **26**(22), 16–17 (2019)
3. Jiangxue, C.: Development status of new energy vehicle charging infrastructure in China. Auto Time **17**(16), 97–98 (2021)
4. Yueqing, L.: Smart gas station + charging pile may become the mainstream development model. China Petroleum Enterprise **24**(04), 56–57 (2018)
5. Tao, Z., Hanxuan, Z.: Design of service system of gas station under "new retail" mode. Idea Design **13**(02), 4–8 (2021)
6. Mingkui, F.: Explore the transformation and upgrading of gas stations and build an integrated commercial value chain. Pet. Petrochem. Today **28**(03), 23–28 (2020)
7. Jiajia, C.: The focus of service design is to define the service itself - Chen Jiajia on service design. Design **33**(04), 42–48 (2020)
8. Peng, D.: Research on the construction of domestic government smart service model. Econ. Res. Guid. **16**(07), 174–177 (2020)
9. Juan, Z.: Analysis on the creative thinking and design methods of product service design——comment on "service design thinking." Journalism Lover **34**(10), 101–102 (2019)
10. Hong, Y., Lusheng, Z., Xing, X.: Thinking and methods of optimizing and innovative design of smart city shared products——Taking Qingdao tourism shared products as an example. J. Nanjing Arts Inst. (Fine Arts & Design) **42**(03), 189–193 (2019)
11. Xiong, D., Junlin, D.: The primary principle of service design: from user-centered to stakeholder-centered. Zhuangshi **63**(03), 62–65 (2020)

Marketing Cultural Jewelry Products: A Case Study on Egyptian Cultural Product Designs

Eman Ramadan[1,2] and Yu Wu[1](✉)

[1] School of Art and Design, Wuhan University of Technology, Wuhan, China
eman.salah@fsed.bu.edu.eg, wu.yu@whut.edu.cn
[2] Department of Art Education, College of Specific Education, Benha University, Benha, Egypt

Abstract. The word marketing seems closer to the world of economics and the world of commerce, industry, and business. However, this word can be associated with the world of culture and creativity, and creative cultural industries. Marketing and promoting commercial goods are close to culture marketing and transforming them into high-value products. This article discusses cultural products and their creation and cultural products related to marketing. The article deals with the following topics: the nature of cultural products and cultural production, the preservation of identity through cultural products and their marketing, the effects of cultural production processes for marketing aspects, and the study of how designs affect consumers' attitudes towards shopping for cultural products and the intention to buy, as it appears that individuals have particular drawings of cultural creativity, especially those related to the originality of the product and the origins of the product. This constitutes an important target market for the sale of cultural products, as the product characteristics and cultural features were one of the crucial factors affecting the positive attitude toward shopping for cultural products. This study places marketing as a context and framework for a system of cultural production. We chose jewelry products inspired by Egyptian patterns as a case study. On this basis, we have addressed the following central question, to what extent can cultural marketing save cultural products from the danger of demise?

Keywords: Marketing · Cultural products · Consumers · Ancient Egyptian culture · Jewelry

1 Introduction

1.1 Research Background

Cultural product and cultural industry are two terms defined by UNESCO. They are identity-bearing products imbued with values, full of connotations, and economic and social development factors. The first and second indications work together, often consciously and unconsciously. The state should preserve them for the good of cultural diversity by encouraging the establishment of cultural industries capable of stability

P.-L. P. Rau (Ed.): HCII 2022, LNCS 13314, pp. 106–124, 2022.
https://doi.org/10.1007/978-3-031-06053-3_8

locally and internationally [1]. The two terms are closely related to the overall challenges to our society at the social, political, economic, and cultural levels. Therefore, cultural creativity, initiative thought, and visions of change are needed. However, the cultural product, whatever its type, remains a product besieged by many problems, perhaps the most dangerous of which is the difficulty of marketing; in a changing world based on unequal competition, most governmental and private institutions and all cultural institutions suffer from marketing stagnation, which threatens the demise of some industries cultural [2]. In our Arab world, the cultural product of all kinds suffers from significant marketing problems. This is reflected in most governmental and private cultural institutions publishing and distribution houses, where cultural marketing products differ from marketing products for mass consumption. The industrial establishment must adapt to consumers' demands to obtain the largest market share [3].

The situation is different with many cultural institutions that have to search for consumers for their products without compromising the cultural nature of their products, where Cultural production concerns the creation, diffusion, and consumption of cultural products. Therefore, in light of the information boom, the tremendous technological progress, and the increased reliance on social media and search engines, attention is turning to the importance of activating the role of technology in the cultural field. The last three decades have witnessed tremendous development in the field of knowledge and the means of acquiring it thanks to the achievements of the information revolution and the tremendous progress achieved in communications [4]. The future possibilities regarding the creative industries are numerous. The two communications and information revolutions may firmly push the creative industries forward, with the great potential they offer in the production and dissemination of culture, and may lead to the emergence of new concepts of cultural production [5].

The development strategy (Egypt Vision 2030) has been paid attention to the cultural industries are clear, as the first goal in the culture axis stipulates: "Supporting cultural industries as a source of strength for the economy"; The definition of the goal stated that it is intended to "enable cultural industries to become a source of strength to achieve development and value-added for the Egyptian economy, making it a basis for Egypt's regional and international soft power, Studies and research have proven that the majority of people have ideas and culture, which makes this matter affect their decisions, and their thinking [6]. Each person thinks about the limits of his culture, standards, and cultural value. The designers implanted different cultural standards and values and used them well within the products. When the designer decides to design work For a cultural product, it must take into account the marketing problems facing cultural products, monitor the general atmosphere and what is happening in the culture in terms of developments, and see the market need in order to provide it with its need in order to achieve success from this product, where these products can be marketed via the internet, a large number of websites have sold cultural products from a wide range of countries around the world. However, the analysis of these researchers revealed that the scarcity of narrative information and images about products and cultures might hinder customer attraction to websites and buying behavior [7].

1.2 Research Purposes and Questions

The importance of marketing in culture management as an essential part of the process of promoting creativity and introducing it The importance of the role of marketing and its ability to highlight the cultural product and give it its proper dimension, and draw attention to the need to study the market and the interests of the target audience culturally, in an attempt to answer questions related to marketing [8]. This article aims to discuss the notion of cultural products within marketing. Also, to develop a framework for a new strategy for marketing cultural products and knowing consumers' expectations for purchase, aesthetic meanings associated with cultural practices are related to how individuals and organizations negotiate commerce and consumer culture [9]. The main contribution of the research is to enlarge our understanding of the cultural marketing processes as they pertain to the marketing and consumption of cultural products. In this context, we also examine how emerging developments in postmodern aesthetics and posthumanism have augmented new ways of thinking about related issues. The article's broad research question is: Is it possible to view a product's cultural marketing as providing both a context and an institutional framework for the cultural production system in the contemporary postmodern world? [10]. If so, what does it entail in terms of our conceptualization of the elements of the cultural production system and their specific relationship to the institution of marketing?

Specifically, the following research questions will be addressed:

1 What is cultural marketing, and who are the actors involved in it?
2 How can a cultural product be produced to compete in global markets?
3 How to create a new framework for marketing cultural products and encouraging cultural shopping?
4 What, finally, are the implications of the cultural production processes for individuals and consumer behavior?

2 Theoretical Framework and Hypotheses

2.1 Cultural Content and Cultural Production

Cultural and creative industries have become an essential engine of economic growth in many countries, strengthening gross national output and increasing trade balance. Cultural industries play an essential role in developing societies from inside trade speed. At the same time, it provides a platform that strengthens the bonds of identity and community dialogue and thus raises the level of the community's quality of life [11]. Creative industries are characterized by high degrees of creativity in their production and distribution processes. To grasp innovation in creative industries, we first must identify the distinguishing characteristics of their products. The goods and services derived from these industries have an aesthetic or semiotic content that sees creative industries as characterized by 'content creativity.' Cultural content can be created out of different resources and cultural assets [12]. Content may also be delivered via various media; some cultural content can be 'repurposed' for different media, while others are more tied to a specific medium or format. Some authors contend that content has been neglected as an area for study, possibly because it is viewed more as an issue of cultural creativity than one addressed in innovation processes. Therefore, the "knowledge-based creative economy" has become an essential part of the global economy in the past few years [13]. The intertwined nature of the creative economy is a driving force and a base on which to renew the economic fabric of society and strengthen the components of development strategies. Moreover, that contributes to the added value of many Local economic projects and the experiences of many countries of the European Union, the United States, China, Japan, South Korea, and Malaysia [14].

2.2 Cultural Product Marketing

People have cultural boundaries; their thinking and decisions are affected by their cultural values and norms. Marketers implant cultural values and standards in ads where consumers can relate to the characters in the ads. The importance of marketing in culture management is an integral part of promoting creativity and introducing it, as marketing is an essential issue for the actual creator [15]. The cultural product in the jewel means that there is a cultural message that we want to reach the public, so we resort to marketing as a means of conveying the message to the recipient, as marketing is also a way to promote the cultural good or service, as the cultural product becomes a cheap good unless it reaches the citizens, where the crisis It is not a crisis of a cultural product or service, but a crisis that product needs marketing, Perhaps the marketing means are the great hope with which the Egyptian culture expresses safety [16], to become the most influential in the conscience and mind of the Egyptian citizen, The role of websites, social networks and the media in marketing the cultural product calls for the necessity of studying the form and quality of the cultural product because of its importance in achieving successful marketing of the product, He dealt with the role of outlets for selling the cultural product and the extent of the spread and presence of sales outlets that attract customers for the cultural product in various governorates and the importance of opening new marketing outlets inside and outside Egypt, as the cultural product is the soft power that Egypt began to lose and retreat in during the last period, There are some concepts that must be corrected, including that creativity and marketing do not meet, and this is a big mistake, as both are complementary to the other, and there must be a marketing plan before producing cultural and creative work [17, 18], Fig. 1.

Fishbein's theory (1975) was used as a framework to explain the structural interrelationships between consumer psychology, cultural product, shopping attitude, and purchase intent. The situation is affected by behavioral beliefs, as cultural products are supposed to affect consumers' intention of buying and shopping through their impact on attitude beliefs. Cultural creators constitute a quarter of adults globally and have distinct opinions about lifestyle and consumers [20]. They share perspectives, values, and lifestyles, where cultural designs can build society and create a better society. Cultural creators are distinguished through the things they buy and the shopping experiences they choose. With a strong desire for product authenticity, cultural creators buy integrity and authenticity artifacts [21].

The interests of cultural creators in indigenous cultures, production origins, and the process of focusing on creativity is a personal style that matches the motives of consumers of cultural products to purchase cultural products, such as communication with artisans

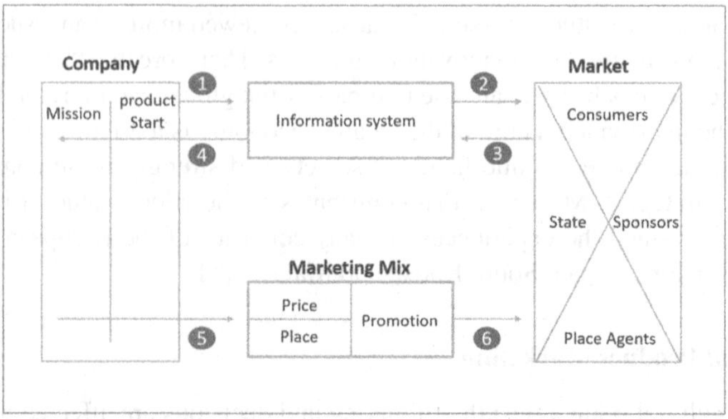

Fig. 1. Traditional marketing model Colbert believes that the traditional marketing model describes the reality of commercial and industrial enterprises, as it depends on a sequence of vehicles whose starting point is the market. Needs and then assesses their capabilities to respond to them, considering their resources [19].

and establishing identity. So, we assume H1 The method of marketing cultural products easily through which the consumer can know everything. The product quickly identified cultural designs, which are jewelry designs inspired by the eye of Horus pattern, which is one of the important symbols in ancient Egyptian civilization. The ancient Egyptian civilization left us [22], characterized by artistic accuracy and beauty formation. The ancient Egyptian realized the value of ornaments and adornment tools, fell in love with them, and knew their decorative value that shows the wearer's beauty and gives him attractiveness. The ancient Egyptian woman in particular, who is fond of sophistication and sophistication in all kinds of adornment, looking for what makes her charm, where here we can facilitate the way the consumer knows [23].

The product quickly lets him know the cultural features, patterns used, and materials so that the consumer can think about buying. It also helps to exchange cultures because it will be available to all countries. In all languages, H2 Consumers who show high cultural levels and positive attitudes about cultural products have been conducted to identify important attributes of cultural products [24]. Most of these studies were based on users' evaluative criteria and meanings associated with craft souvenirs they bought during travel or with consumers who had purchased products from alternative trade organizations through catalogs. Synthesizing previous research, identified essential attributes of cultural products. Craftsmanship and aesthetic properties were the most recognized criteria by consumers. The craftsmanship of cultural products was associated with high quality in production, fine attention to detail, and time involved in the handwork [25].

Aesthetic attributes of cultural products were related to uniqueness, creativity, appealing colors, or quality of designs. Several researchers reported that craftsmanship and aesthetic properties had significant relationships with attitude and intention to shop for cultural products. Kim and Littrell (1999) found that users' attitudes toward craft criteria such as design, color, and uniqueness significantly predicted their purchase intention [26]. Yu and Littrell (2003) also showed that users with stronger beliefs that a cute craft was associated with uniqueness, quality, and aesthetic pleasure had more positive attitudes toward shopping for cultural products. However, these cultural product attributes from previous studies should be verified in online purchase behavior [27]. We therefore hypothesize:

H3: Consumers who have positive beliefs about cultural products will have positive attitudes toward online shopping for cultural products. In addition to the goods' properties, there are various features related to the Web site store, such as the ease of use, privacy, and security that influence consumers' shopping attitudes. It was also necessary to provide an easy marketing experience in search and ordering processes as well as to prevent related problems of consumer privacy and transaction security and thus assume H4: consumers who have positive beliefs about the new product marketing strategy [17, 28], positive attitudes towards shopping for cultural purposes, however, beliefs may influence behavioral intentions Aside from influencing attitudes, attitudes are not just a product of information processing and belief structures so that beliefs may influence purchase intentions. So, we propose H5: Consumers who have positive beliefs about cultural products will demonstrate a high intention to shop for cultural products using the [29].

H6: Consumers who have positive beliefs about the website selling cultural products will demonstrate a high intention to shop for cultural products on the internet.

H7: Consumers who have a positive attitude toward shopping for cultural products on the internet will demonstrate a high intention to shop for cultural products; the seven hypotheses are depicted in Fig. 3.

2.3 Pattern Deconstruction and Description

The ancient Egyptians were bested in anatomy and medicine. This can be found in documenting papyrus, as well as the walls of many temples and tombs. In the creation of eye of Horus, ancient Egyptians combined their artistic abilities and knowledge of anatomy with their deep belief in mythology [30]. The eye of Horus has been used for many metaphors over the years, "Eye of the mind, third eye, the eye of the truth or insight, and the eye of God in the human mind". The ancient Egyptians, because they believed in the eye of Horus' mystic powers, gave all these names to the eye of Horus, this symbol has an astonishing connection between neuroanatomical structure and function. Artistically, the eye is comprised of six different parts [31]. From the mythological standpoint, each part of the Eye is an individual symbol. Additionally, parts of the Eye represent terms in the series 1/2, 1/4, 1/8, 1/16, and 1/32; when this image is superimposed upon a sagittal image of the human brain, it appears that each part corresponds to the anatomic location of a particular human sensorium. Is it mere coincidence that the eye of Horus seems almost identical to this cerebral component, also that it is divided into the five senses plus thought and the components included do this function in our brain. [32], Fig. 2.

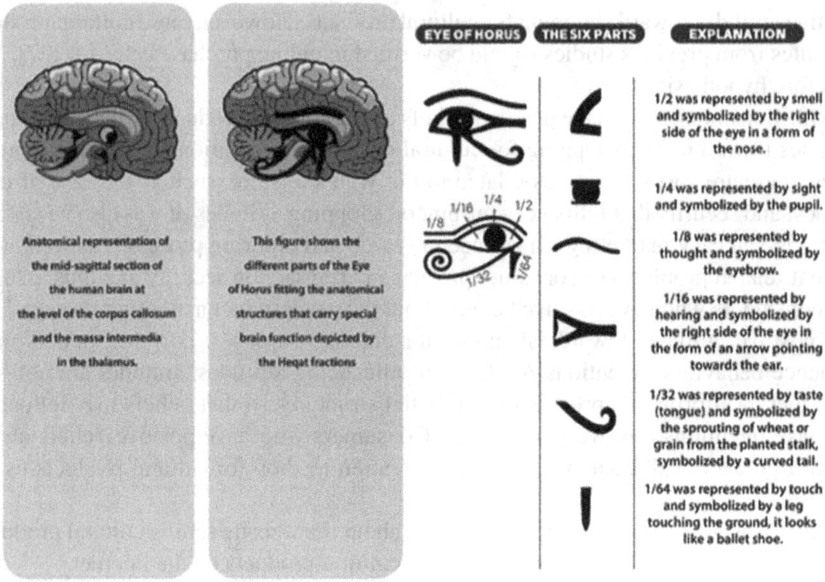

Fig. 2. Shows the symbol (eye of Horus) and the resemblance to the center of the brain and pineal gland.

3 Research method

This research was conducted using a questionnaire to survey the opinion of the Egyptian consumers and the intention to buy cultural products on the internet, where we designed cultural products represented in jewelry inspired by the eye of Horus pattern. We have made a simple shopping strategy for these products, as it makes it easier for the consumer to know the product from all sides and to know all the information about the product, especially if he is a non-Egyptian person and does not have enough information about the Egyptian culture [33]. With insights about the designers who designed the product, the site images and attached descriptions of the products using rich sensory language motivate consumers to create aesthetic experiences with cultural products as part of the shopping process. Consumers are encouraged to buy cultural products by dealing with designers and their culture [34], Fig. 3.

The appreciation of cultural activity on the part of individuals is based mainly on the dimensions of symbolism. The specificity of the formula for processing the information of cultural products is in the form of three steps of imagination, feeling, and pleasure, which compensate for the traditional sequence. Perception, feeling, behavior, and traditional marketing determine individuals' behavior based on rational decisions. In contrast, in the case of cultural marketing, determining the individual's behavior requires studying the sensory aspects of the experience of consuming the cultural product, which is an essential step for the consumer to determine the value of these products.

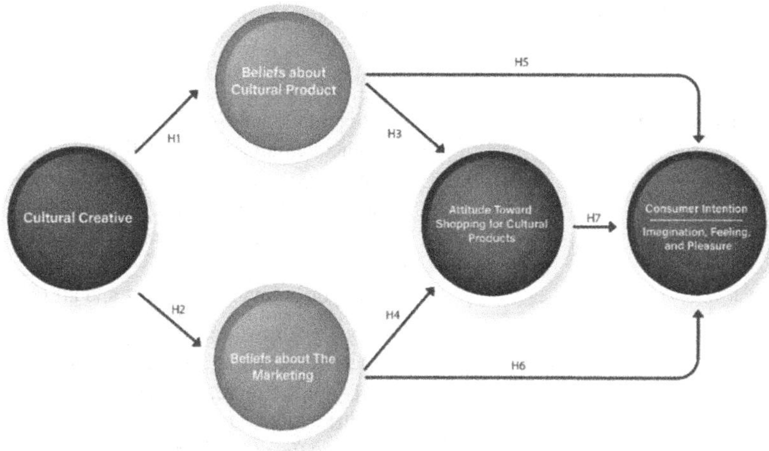

Fig. 3. Proposed model of marketing cultural products.

3.1 Marketing Strategy for Cultural Products

Creating a new strategy for cultural shopping to help the consumer know everything about the piece made. This strategy can be applied in the future to tourists, as we have created cultural products inspired by the ancient Egyptian culture in jewelry designs, as the jewelry is a favorite of most consumers and is presented in different forms on various occasions [35]. This strategy includes quick access to all information about the product. It can be promoted anywhere globally by using QR for each product to make it easier for consumers worldwide. The feature is to identify products inspired by the ancient Egyptian culture smoothly and simply.

3.2 The Questionnaire

We designed a questionnaire about the marketing of cultural products in the form of jewelry inspired by the ancient Egyptian civilization, especially the Eye of Horus pattern and cultural creativity, perceptions of the questionnaire design regarding four internal structures (product style/ personal style, beliefs about buying cultural products, global interest, and attitude towards shopping for cultural products. The questionnaire items were developed to reflect our scientific interests and consumers' opinions, the questionnaire was reviewed, and items were negotiated between researchers. The design of the questionnaire is shown in Table 1.

Table 1. Questionnaire design for Marketing cultural products.

Structures	Question
Product/ personal style	Q1. It is important to you that consumer goods are authentic rather than imitations Q2. When you shop, you want to know where a product came from and how it was made Q3. Do you like to have a unique cultural product? Q4. Do you enjoy having crafts and art objects?
Global concern	Q5. you think of issues that affect the cultural products of the world, such as the neglect of culture—furthermore, the lack of preparation to direct the new generation towards understanding culture and the cultural product Q6. Do you concerned with issues affecting culture in developing countries around the world? Q7. Do you like learning about ways of culture in different parts of the world?
Intention to purchase	Q8. do you have a passion for buying cultural products that bear the ancient Egyptian cultural character? Q9. Do cultural products touch your feelings and interest you? Q10. Do you find a good shopping strategy for cultural products through which the consumer can learn about the product and culture?
Attitude toward shopping for cultural products	Q11. Do you find cultural products unique and innovative? Q12. Have you tried buying cultural products specific to a particular culture before?

A sample was taken of the Egyptian consumer individuals that we conducted the questionnaire on, as 140 individuals responded with a response rate of 10.4%; 120 usable questionnaires were used to analyze the data, as the response rate for this study was acceptable.

3.3 Psychological Planning for Cultural Consumers

For measuring the psychographics of cultural consumers, ten statements were developed based on Ray (2000). These statements reflected consumers' perspectives, values, and lifestyles, for example (you like learning about ways of life in different parts of the world, you love learning about other people's culture, you enjoy owning unique pieces of art inspired by ancient cultures) all of this qualifies consumers to care and buy a cultural product, ranging from Strongly Disagree, to Strongly Agree [36].

3.4 Behavioral Beliefs

Behavioral beliefs are formed through the strength of the belief that a cultural object has certain traits that must be evident in cultural products, several researchers have pointed to the potential problem of measuring belief strength, as accurate weights exceed the average decision-maker and require an unrealistic level of accuracy, Beliefs about cultural products Cultural products are identified, craftsmanship, [37] quality, and cultural creativity are described e.g. Demonstrating attention to detail in their production, Demonstrating creativity of designers, Demonstrating some unique features Attributes were used as a measure of beliefs about cultural products where the alpha coefficient for this result was 0.88, to measure beliefs about a website about cultural products, where attributes reflect trade, quality of information, and ease of quick access to everything about the cultural product, for example information about the designers who designed the product Ease of browsing and searching, and security in transactions.

3.5 Attitudes Toward Shopping for Cultural Products

For the cultural products that we designed, we made a strategy to market them on the internet by housing a QR for each piece and knowing all the information about it. We asked consumers to rate their overall experience with shopping in this way for cultural products with four elements (bad/good, negative/positive, unpleasant (fun, hard/easy). The sum of the items for the measurement was calculated, and the Cronbach's alpha coefficient for this measurement is 0.93.

4 Results and Discussion

4.1 Egyptian Cultural Product Design

This study focuses on Egypt, especially the ancient Egyptian civilization, and a development is carried out across three layers, which are the cultural space, the cultural layers, and the characteristics of cultural products in terms of style, the pattern of Eye of Horus in the tombs (the afterlife) and the daily life of the ancient Egyptian. The external feature, the exterior design was implemented by reference. To the visceral level, to achieve the goal of a design based on the meaning, the Egyptian style that was used mainly in the daily life of the ancient Egyptian was translated in terms of rituals and worship and the decoration of jewels and temples due to its great importance in the ancient Egyptian civilization (Eye of Horus has been translated into a group of modern jewelry that is in line with the current era, besides that, is the great importance of the jewelry industry in the ancient Egyptian civilization and the great supremacy that the ancient Egyptian reached. In addition to that, jewelry is one of the things that the consumer tends to and wants to acquire on an ongoing basis, especially the youth group, Fig. 4.

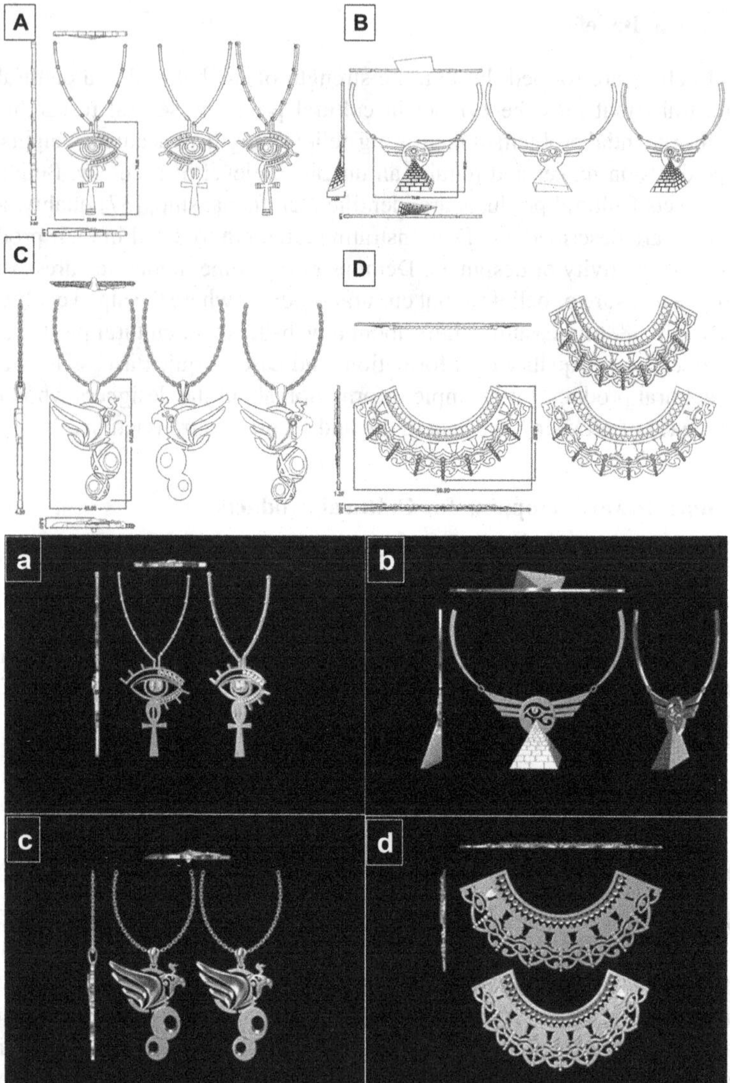

Fig. 4. Four cultural product designs inspired by Egyptian cultural pattern (Eye of Horus).

4.2 Marketing Strategy for Cultural Products

This study focuses on Egypt, especially the ancient Egyptian civilization, where cultural products are created from the ancient Egyptian patterns, especially the Eye of Horus pattern because of its great importance, where products were created in the form of jewelry inspired by the ancient Egyptian civilization, to achieve the goal of a design based on the meaning, the Egyptian style that was used mainly in the daily life of the ancient Egyptian was translated in terms of rituals and worship and the decoration of jewels and temples due to its great importance in the ancient Egyptian civilization (Eye of

Horus has been translated into a group of modern jewelry that is in line with The current era, besides that, is the great importance of the jewelry industry in the ancient Egyptian civilization and the great supremacy that the ancient Egyptian reached,In addition to that, jewelry is one of the things that the consumer tends to and wants to acquire on an ongoing basis, especially the youth group, with regard to the product, achieve the goal of design based on perception, which reached its, climax in the designs of eye of Horus necklaces, We have proposed a marketing strategy for cultural products that relies on a unique site for the products, and put a QR code on each product to make it easy to access all the information about the product and make it easy to purchase and identify it and what it symbolizes, Fig. 5.

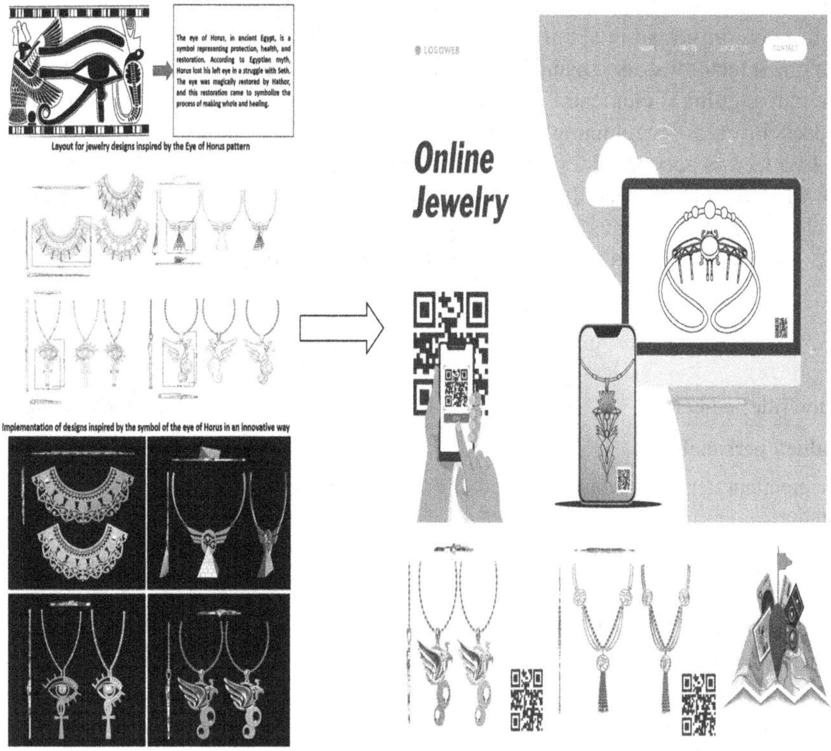

Fig. 5. Eye of Horus inspired designs with marketing strategy.

4.3 Sample Characteristics

Most of the respondents were female (72%) aged between 30–40 (61%); more than half of them reside in urban areas (60%). Respondents represent a well-educated group (65%) who hold a university degree of these; more than half also had graduate degrees (75%) and were (25%) working in teaching. Many respondents had traveled internationally at least once. It used the internet for 1 to 6 h (40%) or 7 to 10 h (25%) For many reasons other than work. The participants commented on the shopping strategy by placing a QR on each piece, which facilitates the purchase process and knowledge of the piece's details, which leads to the support of cultural products and the expansion of their marketing in international markets.

4.4 Psychographics Associated with Cultural Creatives

The respondents were like cultural creators. They enjoyed handicrafts (M = 2.49) and loved cultural patterns and design products inspired by these cultural patterns that express our identity as Egyptians (M = 2.41). It was also important to them that consumer goods be original and not imitation (M = 2.24), they loved learning the ways of life through culture (M = 2.31), they wanted to know the source of the product and how it was made, and to know information about the style used and who made it (M = 1.91), the base component factor was used using Varimax rotation to determine the dimensions between the creative cultural elements. The Eigenvalue, more significant than one, was one of the decision rules for retaining the cultural elements. The cultural pattern was created. The two factors accounted for 73% of the total variance. Loads of the workers ranged from 61 to 89. emphasized the customers' desire for the product's originality, which is closely related to their interest in creating a unique product of cultural patterns through crafts and artistic objects and knowledge of the product's origins, Table 2.

Table 2. Factor Analysis Results for Psychographics of Cultural Creative.

Factor Title and Items	Factor Loading
Product/ personal style	
It is important to you that consumer goods are authentic, rather than imitation.	78
When you shop, you want to know where a product came from, how it was made.	71
You like to have a unique cultural product.	68
You enjoy having crafts and art objects.	61
Cronbach's alpha = 0.81 **Global concern**	
you think of issues that affect the cultural products of the world, such as the neglect of culture.	80
Moreover, the lack of preparation to direct the new generation towards understanding culture and the cultural product.	77
you concerned with issues affecting culture in developing countries around the world.	70
you like learning about ways of culture in different parts of the world.	75

(continued)

Table 2. (*continued*)

Factor Title and Items	Factor Loading
Cronbach's alpha = 0.83 **Intention to purchase**	70
you have a passion for buying cultural products that bear the ancient Egyptian cultural character.	69
Do the cultural products touch your feelings and interest?	
Do you find a good shopping strategy for cultural products?	
through which the consumer can learn about the product and culture.	
Cronbach's alpha = 0.80	80
Attitude toward shopping for cultural products	78
you find cultural products unique and innovative.	
Have you tried buying cultural products specific to culture before?	
Cronbach's alpha = 0.85	

The global concern factor reflected consumers' integrated interests in world cultures; Cronbach's alpha coefficient values were .81 and .83 for "product/personal style" and "global concern," respectively. Beliefs about shopping for cultural products also reflected consumers' interest in the product, as Cronbach's alpha coefficient values were 85. To 80. For the intention to purchase, indicating acceptable levels of reliability.

4.5 A Model of Marketing Cultural Products on the Internet

The proposed model for hypothesis testing consists of two external structures (product pattern/global interest) and four internal structures (beliefs about cultural products, attitude toward shopping for cultural products online to purchase cultural products. The overall mean responses are summarized in Table 3, and the causal model analysis was conducted by performing a maximum likelihood estimation using (AMOD). Figure 6 presents the coefficients and t-values for each path; The results revealed a quality-of-fit

Table 3. Summary of research constructs.

Research constructs	Mean	Std. Dev
Product/personal style	2.01	0.65
Global concern	1.85	1.03
Beliefs about cultural products	2.11	0.61
Beliefs about the Web site selling cultural products	2.22	0.64
Attitude toward shopping for cultural products	2.42	0.71
Intention to shop for cultural products on the internet	2.13	0.90

index (GFI) of 0.98, a quality-of-fit ratio (AGFI) of 0.91, and a mean residual squared root (RMSR) of 0.03, which indicates that the conceptual model fits the data well, Fig. 6.

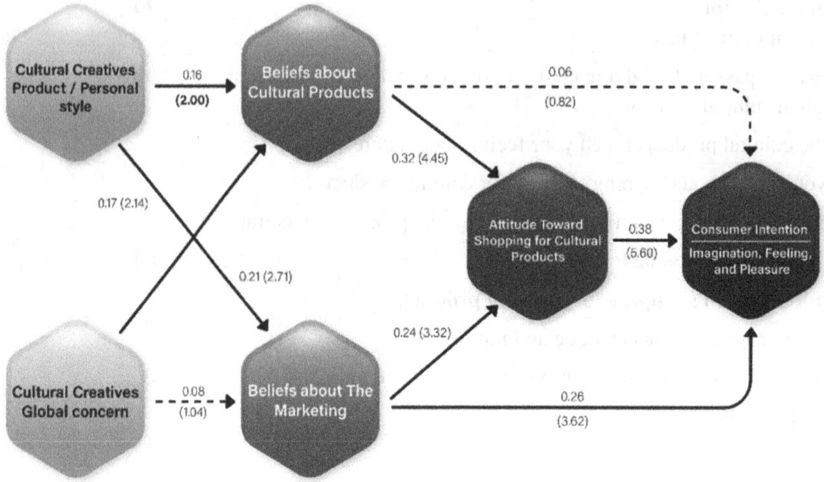

Fig. 6. The resulting model of marketing cultural products. t-values are in parentheses ($t > 2.00$). Dotted arrows indicate insignificant paths.

4.6 Hypothesis Tests

The first hypothesis suggested an easy marketing strategy for cultural products inspired by the ancient Egyptian civilization and great interest in cultural products ($t = 2.71$). Therefore, the hypothesis was supported 1- Consumers have high requirements in clarifying everything related to the product through this marketing strategy, which facilitates access to the products and information that the consumer wants, which must be available in the shopping feature of cultural products on the Web site ($t = 1.04$), as cultural products are unique and need clarification so that the consumer can purchase them.

The second hypothesis 2 suggested positive relationships between consumers' psychological planning and beliefs about cultural products. The dimensions of cultural designs, product, cultural style and global interest were significantly associated with beliefs about cultural products ($t = 2.14$, $t = 2.00$). Therefore, hypothesis 2 was supported. Consumers have high with the originality of the products and the strong desire to create a unique product. They had positive beliefs about cultural products. Likewise, they had a significant rise in interest in different cultures. They also had positive beliefs about cultural products.

Hypothesis 3 predicted the positive influence of consumers about cultural products about the website. There was a significant positive relationship between the product/cultural style and beliefs about the website ($t = 2.70$), indicating consumers who have a high interest in the original product and a solid desire to invent new cultural products Hypothesis 3 partially supported. Hypothesis 3.4 tested the effect of beliefs about cultural products and the website on attitudes towards shopping for cultural products, beliefs about cultural products (t = 4.45), and beliefs about the web (t = 3.32) expected attitudes towards shopping for cultural products. Therefore, hypotheses 3, 4, and 5.6 suggest these beliefs. Cultural products and beliefs about marketing may positively predict the intention to purchase cultural products on the internet. There was a significant positive relationship between beliefs about the website and the intention to purchase cultural products (t = 3.62); no statistically significant relationship was found between beliefs about cultural products and the intention to purchase cultural products (t = .80). Thus, hypothesis 6 was supported, but not Hypothesis 5. As suggested by Hypothesis 7, the marketing strategy towards cultural products significantly affected the intent to purchase cultural products on the internet (t = 5.60). The hypothesis is supported that consumers have positive attitudes towards shopping for cultural products, Table 4.

Table 4. Decomposition of total, effects for the model.

Dependent Variable Independent Variable	Total Effects
Intention to purchase	
Attitude toward shopping for cultural products.	0.38 (5.60)
Beliefs about cultural products.	0.18 (1.60)
Beliefs about the Website.	0.18 (1.60)
Product and Personal style.	0.10 (2.25)
Global concern.	0.06 (1.49)
R2	0.31
Attitude toward shopping for cultural products	
Beliefs about cultural products	0.32 (4.45)
Beliefs about the Website	0.24 (3.32)
Product and Personal style	0.10 (2.03)
Global concern	0.05 (1.81)
R2	0.24
Beliefs about cultural products	
Product and Personal style	0.16 (2.00)
Global concern	0.17 (2.14)
R2	0.08
Beliefs about the Website	
Product and personal style	0.21 (2.71)
Global concern	0.08 (1.04)
R2 0.07	

Note: *t*-values are in parentheses, and significant effects are in bold font ($t > 2.00$)

4.7 Decomposition of Effects

To further substantiate the effects of the proposed model, an analysis of the decomposition of effects was conducted (see Table 3). Attitude toward shopping for cultural products, beliefs about the Web site, and product/personal style significantly affected intention to purchase cultural products on the internet. Significant indirect effects of product/personal style on attitude and intention suggested cultural creatives, primarily related to their product/personal style attributes, as important target market psychographics. Beliefs about cultural products had the only indirect effect on consumers' intention to purchase cultural products on the internet. However, they had the most substantial total effect on attitude toward shopping for cultural products on the internet. Consumers' positive beliefs about the Web site were more critical in predicting their intention to purchase. This finding emphasized the importance of both products (e.g., craftsmanship, quality, and creativity) and Website design (e.g., information quality, security, products in stock) for marketing cultural products on the internet. However, it gave greater importance to the Web site in affecting intention to purchase cultural products on the internet.

5 Conclusions and Implications

Consumer and producer psychology are critical factors affecting consumers' intention to buy cultural products. These consumers shop for cultural purposes. The results are consistent with consumers who shop for cultural products, like cultural designs. These consumers were attracted to and were interested in indigenous cultures, product origins, production processes, and the artifacts used to create unique cultural products. Consumers of cultural products were interested in global issues and other cultures, but these views did not affect their beliefs about websites and the intent to purchase cultural products. Consumers' beliefs about cultural products significantly predict their attitude towards shopping for cultural products. Both product quality and site attributes affect attitudes when shopping for a cultural product, where only consumers' beliefs about the website significantly influence their intent to buy. The attributes of the website that determine a positive attitude towards shopping for cultural products are related to the quality of information, e.g., product information, country and culture, and promotion, for example, keeping products at competitive prices. The interface, for example, is easy browsing and the ordering process, with attention to all these details to attract shoppers of cultural products.

5.1 Recommendations for Future Research

Future research is needed to define further the psychographics related to shopping for cultural products. Our study suggested that consumers of cultural products differ from ordinary people because they have specific purchase intention preferences for cultural products. Not all psychographics of consumers were included. For example, the interest of consumers was not measured—consumers by nature, the environment, and distinct values and beliefs regarding gender and sustainability.

References

1. Schadewitz, N.: Design patterns for cross-cultural collaboration. Int J Des **3**, 37–53 (2009)
2. Moalosi, R., Popovic, V., Hickling-Hudson, A.: Culture-orientated product design. Int J Technol Des Educ **20**, 175–190 (2010). https://doi.org/10.1007/s10798-008-9069-1
3. Baucom, I.:Cultural Studies (2006)
4. Lin, R., Kreifeldt, J., Hung, P.: Cross-cultural design applications in mobile interaction. Education, Health, Transport and Cultural Heritage **9181**, 263–273 (2015). https://doi.org/10.1007/978-3-319-20934-0
5. Wang, W., Bryan-Kinns, N., Sheridan, J.G.: On the role of in-situ making and evaluation in designing across cultures. CoDesign **16**, 233–250 (2020). https://doi.org/10.1080/15710882.2019.1580296
6. Li, H., Yi, X., Chen, M. Symbolic Meanings of Pharaoh's False Beard in Ancient Egypt, pp. 352–359 (2017). https://doi.org/10.25236/ssah.2017.77
7. Design Council: Design for public good. Annu Rev Policy Des **1**, 1–50 (2013)
8. Siu, N.W.C., Dilnot, C.: The challenge of the codification of tacit knowledge in designing and making: a case study of CAD systems in the Hong Kong jewellery industry. Autom Constr **10**, 701–714 (2001). https://doi.org/10.1016/S0926-5805(00)00088-1
9. Ulusman, L., Bayburtlu, C.: Paradigm for art education; creation story of jewels, theme, design, artwork, 3D. Procedia - Soc Behav Sci **51**, 284–288 (2012). https://doi.org/10.1016/j.sbspro.2012.08.160
10. Banyte, J., Matulioniene, L.: The singularities of the cultural element in consumer behavior. Innov Mark 1 (2005)
11. Lee, S.E., Littrell, M.A.: Marketing cultural products on the internet: targeting cultural creatives. Cloth Text Res J **24**, 33–45 (2006). https://doi.org/10.1177/0887302X0602400103
12. Shavitt, S., Cho, H.: Culture and consumer behavior: the role of horizontal and vertical cultural factors. Curr Opin Psychol **8**, 149–154 (2016). https://doi.org/10.1016/j.copsyc.2015.11.007
13. Luna, D., Luna, D.: Cross-cultural consumer behavior 45 An integrative framework for cross-cultural consumer behavior An integrative framework for cross-cultural consumer behavior
14. Ser, S.: On culture-oriented product design: a study to transform cultural features to design elements. Int J Creat Futur Herit **6**, 163–197 (2018)
15. Osafo, J.: From cross-cultural to cultural thinking in psychological research and practice in Ghana. Int J Cult Ment Health **11**, 447–456 (2018). https://doi.org/10.1080/17542863.2017.1409780
16. Bohemia, E., Harman, K.: Globalization and product design education: the global studio. Des Manag J **3**, 53–68 (2010). https://doi.org/10.1111/j.1948-7177.2008.tb00014.x
17. Chang, T.-Y.: Developing cultural products to promote local culture : a marketing design for the former tainan state magistrate abstract, 1–12
18. Gautam, V., Blessing, L. Cultural influences on the design process. Proc ICED 2007, 16th Int Conf Eng Des DS **42**, 1–8 (2007)
19. Colbert, F.: Entrepreneurship and Leadership in Marketing the Arts. Int. J. Arts Manage. **6**, 30–39 (2003)
20. Ryan, M.J., Bonfield, E.H.: The Fishbein Extended Model and Consumer Behavior. J. Cons. **2**, 118–137 (1973)
21. Webb, V.: Three faience rosette discs in the museo egizio in turin: the early ramesside pharaohs in the eastern delta, and their glittering palaces. Riv. Del. Mus. Egizio. **1**, 1–21 (2017). https://doi.org/10.29353/rime.2017.1208
22. Leigh, M., Elwell, M., Cook, S.: Recreating Ancient Egyptian Culture in Second Life (2017). https://doi.org/10.1109/DIGITEL.2010.45

23. Bevan, A.: Ancient perspectives on Egypt. Choice Rev Online **41**, 41–6064h-41–6064h (2004). https://doi.org/10.5860/choice.41-6064h
24. Arnould, E., et al.: Market Oriented Ethnography Revisited Related papers Market-Oriented Ethnography Revisited. https://doi.org/10.2501/S0021849906060375
25. Ramadan, E.: A study of framework development and research of jewelry design. Based on Pattern Egyptian Culture (Lotus Flower) **2**, 630–645. https://doi.org/10.1007/978-3-030-90328-2
26. Grotevant, H.D.: Toward a process model of identity formation. J Adolesc Res **2**, 203–222 (1987). https://doi.org/10.1177/074355488723003
27. Yu, H., Littrell, M.A., Littrell, M.A.: Tourists 'Shopping Orientations for Handcrafts Tourists' Shopping Orientations for Handcrafts : What Are Key Influences ?, pp. 37–41 (2008). https://doi.org/10.1300/J073v18n04
28. Craig, C.S.: Creating cultural products: cities, context and technology. City, Cult Soc **4**, 195–202 (2013). https://doi.org/10.1016/j.ccs.2013.06.002
29. Berbel-pineda, J.M., Palacios-florencio, B., Santos-roldán, L., Hurtado, J.M.R.: Relation of Country-of-Origin Effect , Culture, and Type of Product with the Consumer's Shopping Intention : An Analysis for Small- and Medium-Sized Enterprises (2018)
30. Kathy, J.: Secrets of the Ancient Egyptian Sacred Blue Lotus, pp. 1–3 (2015)
31. Atherton-Woolham, S., McKnight, L., Price, C., Adams, J.: Imaging the gods: animal mummies from Tomb 3508, north saqqara, Egypt. Antiquity **93**, 128–143 (2019). https://doi.org/10.15184/aqy.2018.189
32. Hedegaard, S.B., Delbey, T., Brøns, C., Rasmussen, K.L.: Painting the palace of apries II: ancient pigments of the reliefs from the palace of apries, Lower Egypt. Heritage Science **7**(1), 1–32 (2019). https://doi.org/10.1186/s40494-019-0296-4
33. Ko, Y.-Y., Lin, P.-H., Lin, R.: A study of service innovation design in cultural and creative industry BT – internationalization. Design and Global Development, 376–385 (2009)
34. Soboci, M.: The Role of Marketing in Cultural Institutions in the Context of Assumptions of Sustainable Development Concept — A Polish Case Study, pp. 1–15 (2019)
35. Lee, Y., Kim, S., Seock, Y.K., Cho, Y.: Tourists' attitudes towards textiles and apparel-related cultural products: A cross-cultural marketing study. Tour Manag **30**, 724–732 (2009). https://doi.org/10.1016/j.tourman.2008.10.007
36. Johnson, C., Amaral, M.: The interaction of news and advocate frames : manipulating audience perceptions of a locae pubeic poeicyissue. Related papers
37. Shim, K.-S.: Culture management through vision and practical of jewelry design education. J. Korea Contents Assoc. **7**, 140–149 (2007)

Cultural and Creative Products with Macao Road Signs as Elements

Yu-Meng Xiao, Jin-Shan Shen, and Rungtai Lin(✉)

Graduate School of Creative Industry Design, National Taiwan University of Arts, New Taipei City 220307, Taiwan
rtlin@mail.ntua.edu.tw

Abstract. Macao has benefited from the integration of multi-culture. It has diversified cultural contexts and unique historical and cultural representations. This manifestation is the collision between Portuguese and Macao cultures, showing its cultural value. In addition to the well-known buildings such as the Archway of San Ba in Macao, some totems in Macao culture have also created its unique local visual elements, and their characteristics frequently appear in the public's field of vision, which is rich in Macao regional characteristics. However, Macao's cultural and creative products are limited in variety, and up to now can not clearly reflect the unique image and culture. Also the local cultural attributes of the products are relatively lacking. As a result, instead of having a good promotion effect on history and culture, it may have ignored consumers' demand for cultural experience, which makes it hard for consumers to buy satisfactory featured goods. In this study, ceramic road signs with blue characters on white background are selected as extraction elements to design and discuss cultural and creative products, so as to explore how to transform Macao culture into cultural and creative products, and whether the produced cultural and creative products can improve consumers' purchase intention and cultural identity.

Keywords: Cultural and creative products · Macao street signs · Purchase intention · Cultural identity

1 Introduction

Incorporated into the design of creative cultural products, culture plays a critical role in the addition of value in the products. The designers can add extra value to the products by utilizing cultural characteristics. This not only promotes social and economic growth but also presents the local unique culture on a global arena [1]. The previous studies have shown that the innovative products with value added by culture are able to make a change in the consumers' concept of culture and thus allow the products to be a cultural medium as well as help the consumers interact with each other through traditional culture and modern life [2, 3]. The consumers may have a further understanding of traditional culture and local features by means of creative cultural products which are not only both functional and distinct in modern life but also serve as cultural inheritance [4].

P.-L. P. Rau (Ed.): HCII 2022, LNCS 13314, pp. 125–138, 2022.
https://doi.org/10.1007/978-3-031-06053-3_9

Macao has benefited from the integration of multi-culture. Since the Portuguese brought western cultures to Macao, Macao's economic development and the integration of trade exchanges between the East and the West have made it a characteristic city with various civilizations in Haina. It has diversified cultural contexts and unique historical and cultural representations. This manifestation is the collision between Portuguese and Macao cultures, showing its cultural value. In addition to the well-known buildings such as the Archway of San Ba in Macao, some totems in Macao culture have also created its unique local visual elements, and their characteristics frequently appear in the public's field of vision, which is rich in Macao regional characteristics, such as Macao streets and ceramic street signs with blue characters on white background that can be seen everywhere in Macao.

In addition, Macao receives a large number of tourists from all over the world every year. According to the news published on DSEC's official website, the number of inbound tourists stood at 4.09 million [5]. Hence, a large number of products with local cultural characteristics are available to the tourists. However, Macao's creative cultural products not only are limited in variety but also currently can not deliver a clear reflection of the unique image and culture. There is also a lack of local cultural attributes of the products. As a result, instead of having a good promotion effect on history and culture, it may have ignored consumers' demand for cultural experience, which makes it hard for consumers to buy satisfactory featured goods.

Macao's cultural content is rich in variety and complexity. The combination of Macao's cultural content gives an embodiment of cultural uniqueness. However, creative cultural products are ultimately designed to artify and materialize a specific building, or a specific feature or culture so as to be present to the consumers.

This study's specific purposes are shown as follows based on the background information mentioned above:

(1) To explore into the procedure on how to transfer Macao's culture into creative cultural products.
(2) To explore into whether the creative cultural products delivered can improve consumers' purchase intention and cultural identity.

2 Literature Review

2.1 Creative Cultural Products

Culture represents an assembly of all the aspects of the previous life. How to originate from traditional culture and look for potential resources and creative ideas is part of design with culture incorporated [6]. To rethink or review the functions of products as well as to incorporate cultural elements into the design of products and make them cultural products allow for the products to be part of the society and meet the consumers' needs to deliver aesthetic value [7]. Incorporating cultural elements into design of products brings people closer to history than before, and deliver more possibilities and more fun [8]. Traditional cultures are integrated into modern life to improve the consumers' interest in the products and their reflection upon traditional cultures as cultural medium can be realized by design [2]. Most importantly, the innovation in and properties of the products allow for cultural inheritance and practical uniqueness and allow the consumers to have a new understanding of traditional cultures and local features [9]. In addition to promoting culture at a greater extent, the design of products allow the consumers to have a deep resonance with the products themselves through understanding of cultural implications and their concept [10].

Rung-Tai Lin manages to classify cultural elements by three layers of Norman culture [11]. The 1st layer (shape) refers to outer layer relevant to tangible and physical properties of cultural products. The properties of cultural products to be considered involve color, texture, shape, lines, grain on surface, detail processing and composition as well; the 2nd layer refers to the middle one (behavior), including the rituals and customs used in cultural products. The properties of products shall involve operation, safety, functionality, easy use, structure and combination. The 3rd layer (psychology) refers to inner layer, including the ideology and invisible spirit embedded into the cultural products. The properties of cultural products on this layer involve special meaning, story-based properties, sensation, cultural characteristics (see Fig. 1).

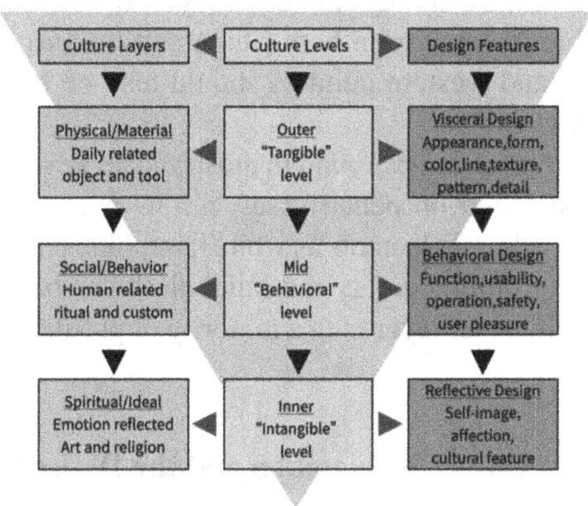

Fig. 1. Comparison of proportion error in imitation.

At present, cultural elements applied to the products are visual, with a focus on outer layer. Visual attributes are used to enrich cultural implication instead of using such elements as behavior, spirit and others behind culture [12]. Cultural elements can help the designers deliver products with cultural implications. But it is a challenge to mitigate consumers' misunderstanding with respect to conversion of cultural elements. Therefore, designers have to understand and know how to convert cultural subjects to cultural elements as well as how to apply them to new products [13].

2.2 Macao's Distinctive Culture and Existing Creative Cultural Products

Since cultural exchange between China and the West has been around for more than 400 years along with Macao's diversity and inclusiveness, historic essence of cultural exchange between China and the West can still be found in the Historic Centre of Macao which is the oldest, largest-in-size, the most completely preserved and most centralized historic town in China. It is mostly covered by western buildings with Chinese-western-style buildings speaking in a perfect dialogue. It represents a historically important witness of spreading of western religious culture in both China and Far East Area. It represents a witness of complement of cultural exchange between China and the West and co-existence of diversity in Macao [14].

Analysis of uniqueness of world cultural heritage in Macao has been made, with consideration of structure, size, history, exquisiteness and others of stand-alone buildings. Macao's western-style churches and the buildings for civil, administrative and military purposes find no chance to compare with those magnificent, exquisite buildings in Europe. The Chinese temples and residence in Macao are incomparable to those in Mainland which are rich in variety, long-standing and large in size. However, the features of Macao's cultural heritage lie in her acting as the witness of cultural exchange and collision between China and the West. These architectural legacy represents a comprehensive embodiment of art of the oldest western buildings and Chinese-western-style buildings, and serves as a extremely distinctive combination among China's historic cities. Such combination with a focus on western buildings and Chinese-western-style buildings speaking in a perfect dialogue, and endowed with European romanticism is unique and incomparable in any city in both China and the East. Therefore, the vivid combination of Chinese and western cultures should also be present in the design of creative cultural products.

The implication of 1st layer can be found in most Macao's creative cultural products. Such implication can be found on pencil cases, pillow bags, recycle bags and other souvenirs since such key cultural elements as white base, blue letters and border patterns are printed and dyed into clothes like flax and sailcloth. It can be seen that the design of existing products lies in the outer layer with a minority of products designed by spiritual consideration.

2.3 The Consumers' Degree of Recognition and the Desire to Buy Cultural Products

To understand the market trend and how to orient the design play a key role in the conversion of culture into cultural products [4]. The consumers' preference for traditional culture, local features and innovative fashion is studied based on the research into the consumers' recognition with and preference for culture, the investigation into aesthetic image, innovative materials, product's function, functionality, quality of design, unique creativity, innovative design, grain, emotion, fashion, environment, integrity of products "assessment of design", the use of special implication, cultural characteristics, evoking emotion, the implication of stories passed on by products, the fashion of appearance, local features and historical origin to explore into cultural elements (see Table 1) [2]. Today's young Chinese's attitude toward traditional culture is studied by their attitude toward products, their intention of purchase, novelty, nature of cultural growth and cultural elasticity i.e. this product is very attractive. I would like to buy this product.

Purchase intention is a strategy to study the consumers' cause of purchasing products [15]. Purchase intention can be considered as the consumers' subjective inclination toward the selection of specific products and also proven to be a important indicator to predict the consumers' behaviour [9]. To define purchase intention as the inclination toward purchasing a specific product under a specific condition is often associated with the consumers' behaviour, recognition and attitude as well. Purchase intention is critical in consumers' acquisition and assessment of products. It may be subject to change due to price, perception of quality and value of products. The influential factors for purchase intention include people, objects and scenes. People refer to demographic factors such as gender, age, level of education and others. Objects refer to value of use, appearance property, quality, price and others. Scenes refer to the surrounding environment, atmosphere of products and other factors.

Table 1. Assessment of level of preference for cultural products.

Scholar, Year	Assessment
Hsu, Fan, Lin, & Lin, 2014	Design evaluation, Cultural evaluation, Product preference, Desire to buy
Chai, Bao, Sun, & Cao, 2015	Tangible level, Behavioral level, Intangible level
Tu, Liu, & Cui, 2019	Consumer preferences, Design attributes, Ranking of cultural and creative products
Chang, Shieh, Chen, & Chen, 2019	Practical level, Sensory level, Spiritual level
Qin, Song, & Tian, 2019	Product attitude, Novelty, Sustainable development

This study is expected to assess the consumers' preference for product design and to understand whether the consumers like or recognize the cultural meaning contained in the creative products including the road signs in this study by considering the results from the previous studies and using Likert 5-point scale which involves appearance and functions like image, unique creativity, integrity and others.

3 The Methods of Study

3.1 The Architecture of Study

This study falls into development phase, experiment process as well as study and results (see Fig. 2).

Development phase: to explore into and understand the previous cases and suggestions by review of literature and to draw design samples.

Experiment process: to design creative cultural products and to investigate into purchase intention and cultural identity by the results.

Study and results: to conduct questionnaire survey and semi-structured interview upon completion of experiment, and to study if the design of the procedure will end up with acquiring consumers' purchase intention and allowing the consumers to recognize the culture contained in the products.

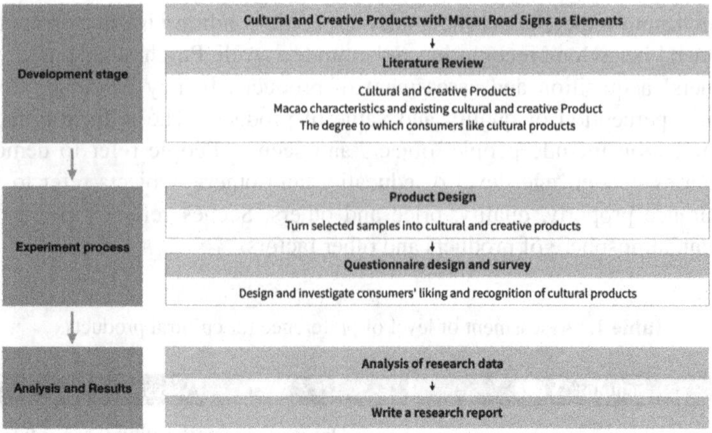

Fig. 2. The architecture of this study.

3.2 Product Design

The original Macao's creative cultural products mostly appear in forms of postcard, fridge magnet and pencil bags, represented by Macao's road signs. However, they all do not cause extensive resonance among the visitors. A recent study shows that the application of cultural elements at middle and internal layers is more likely to enhance consumers' satisfaction and purchase intention of products compared to those at outer layer. Hence, the consumers' preference can be understood using the three-layer theory that is to dig into the content at respective layers and then design the cultural products as well as to compare with the existing creative cultural products. The final products can be expected to trigger the consumers' preference for selection and to have a deep understanding of cultural traits through products that lie in Macao's street names.

The design philosophy as follows:

(1) The products are small in size and easy to carry with the tea set as a carrier. The top of tea cover is shaped like a road sign. The grain on Macao's road signs is used on the spout and handle. The grain on the cup is made blue like that on the road sign in order to shape the contour. The reason why tea set is chosen here is because tea culture boomed during the period of Tang and Song dynasties. Macao had already become a key port for China's foreign trade. Afterwords, Portugal opened up 3 international trade routes in Macao in a row, allowing Macao to be the first exporting port that transported tea to Europe by sea and play a key role in the history of exchange of tea culture between China and the West (see Fig. 3).

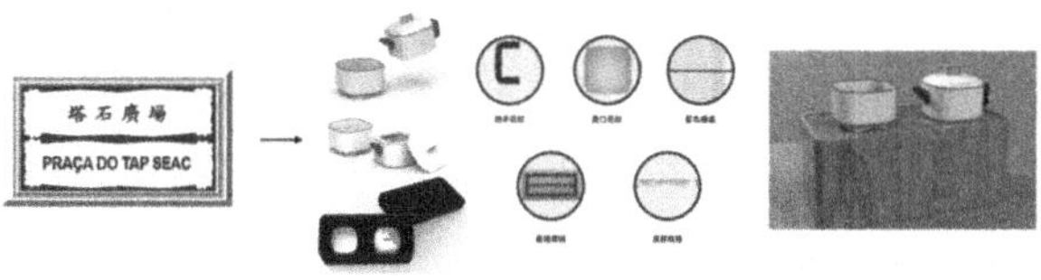

Fig. 3. The 1st product design concept.

(2) The road signs are directive for the visitors on the tour. And the lamps are directive too. The road signs are converted into a lamp, with their colors oscillating between blue and white (see Fig. 4).

Fig. 4. The 2nd product design concept. (Color figure online)

(3) Macao represents a city with coexistence of Chinese and western culture. The integration of Chinese and western culture gives birth to an unique Macao. The road signs are made of blue and white porcelain with distinct oriental characteristics. The name of road is written in both Chinese and Portuguese. Based on an integration of Chinese and western culture, the products of inner layer incorporates Tarot from the West into the Book of Changes from the East, with a set of the Book of Changes-based Tarots (see Fig. 5).

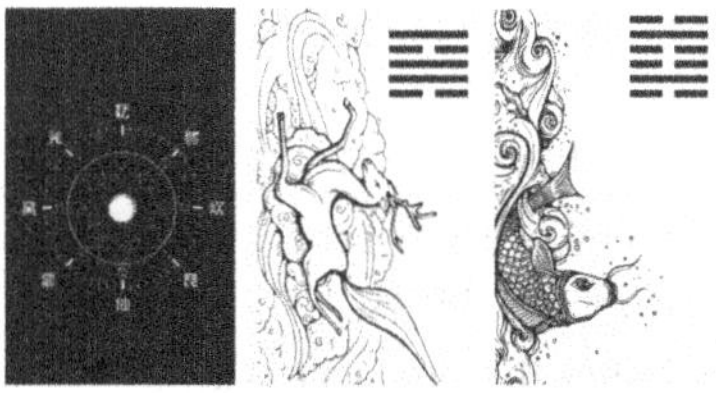

Fig. 5. The 3rd product design concept

By extracting special elements from Macao's road signs like traditional culture, regional traits, the collision of Chinese and western culture, the ideas are made into creative cultural products with cultural elements and cultural properties incorporated into design. The architecture of conversion mode is shown as follows (see Fig. 6).

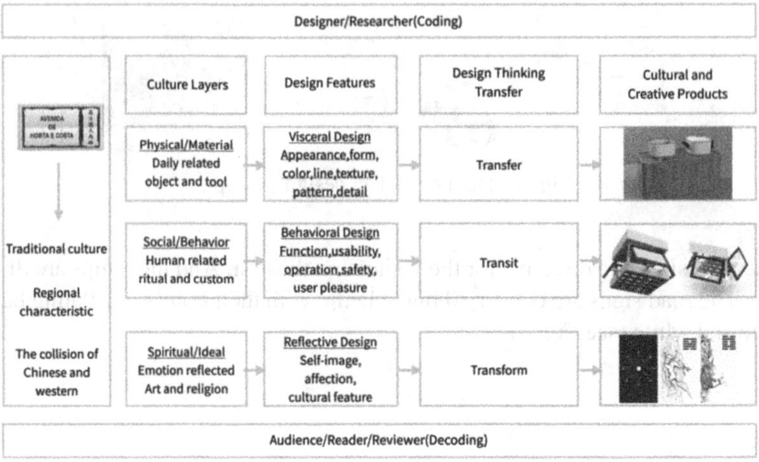

Fig. 6. The architecture of conversion mode

3.3 The Methods to Collect Information with Respect to Product Design

The questionnaire was internet-based. Macao's local people and the overseas students in Macao were enrolled into this study. Subsequently, 6 to 8 participants were interviewed by semi-structured interviews. The questionnaire falls into two parts. In the first part, there was the basic information. In the second part, there products designed by the authors, Macao's existing creative cultural products and other products from other places all over the world were compared. This study was expected to refer to the questionnaires used in the previous literature and explore through Likert 5-point scale into questionnaires with respect to the consumers' purchase intention for the cultural products and degree of cultural recognition (see Table 2). Scoring is based on Likert 5-point scale, namely 1 = Strongly Disagree, 2 = Disagree, 3 = Neutral,4 = Agree and 5 = Strongly Agree. As the total score added up from every single item gets higher, there is a greater purchase intention and higher degree of cultural recognition for the products.

Table 2. The questionnaire with respect to purchase intention and cultural recognition.

Dimensions	Question	Reference
Commodity aesthetic feeling	I think this product has an attractive appearance	Lin (2011)
	I think this product has a pleasing color	
	I think this product has a well-designed shape	
	I think this product has a pleasant texture	

(continued)

Table 2. (*continued*)

Dimensions	Question	Reference
	The appearance of this product is aesthetic	Chang, Shieh. Chen, & Chen (2019)
Cultural implications	This commodity conveys the spiritual meaning of this culture	
	This commodity conveys the historical significance of this culture	
Purchase intention	This product is highly attractive to me	Schiffman & Kanuk (2000)
	I will consider buying this product	
	I would like to recommend friends and relatives to buy this Wenchuang product	
	I have a high possibility of buying this product	

4 Result and Discussion

4.1 Questionnaire Results

Macao's local people and the overseas students in Macao were enrolled into this study. Some 125 questionnaires were released via internet, with 120 ones collected. There were 62 men, 58 women; one person aged between 0 and 18, 54 ones aged between 18 and 25, 24 ones aged between 26 and 30, 26 ones aged between 31 and 40, 15 ones aged between 41 and 50; there were 24 persons with an academic degree lower than high school, 31 ones with a high school degree, 44 ones with a bachelor degree, 17 ones with a master degree, 4 ones with a doctoral degree; there were 76 persons with a major in design, 44 ones from other majors (see Table 3).

Table 3. Demographics.

		Frequency	Percentage (%)
Sex	Male	62	51.7
	Female	58	48.3
Age	0–18	1	0.8
	18–25	54	45.0
	26–30	24	20.0

(*continued*)

Table 3. *(continued)*

		Frequency	Percentage (%)
	31–40	26	21.7
	41–50	15	12.5
Level of education	Lower than high school	24	20.0
	High school	31	25.8
	Bachelor degree	44	36.7
	Master degree	17	14.2
	Doctoral degree	4	3.3
Educational background	Design major	76	63.3
	Non-design major	44	36.7

Spss26.0 was used for statistical study and verification during this study. Reliability and validity of the questionnaire was studied (see Table 4). As the study results show, standardized 1st questionnaire's reliability coefficient was 0.966 and all the reliability coefficients were lower than 0.966 with items deleted accordingly. Thus, there was no need to adjust the 1st questionnaire (reliability coefficient ranges from 0 to 1. As the value is closer to 1, the reliability is higher); standardized 2nd questionnaire's reliability coefficient was 0.940 and all the reliability coefficients were lower than 0.940 with items deleted accordingly. (reliability coefficient ranges from 0 to 1. As the value is closer to 1, the reliability is higher); standardized 3rd questionnaire's reliability coefficient was 0.962 and all the reliability coefficients were lower than 0.962 with items deleted accordingly (reliability coefficient ranges from 0 to 1. As the value is closer to 1, the reliability is higher); KMO sampling appropriateness inspection and Bartlett sphericity test were used on the data from the 2nd group of samples. The test results show that KMO value was 0.947. X2 was 851.510, with statistical significance level achieved ($p = 0.000 < 0.05$); KMO sampling appropriateness inspection and Bartlett sphericity test were used on the data from the 3rd group of samples. The test results show that KMO value was 0.967. X2 was 1190.587, with statistical significance level achieved ($p = 0.000 < 0.05$); the results show that factor analysis is applicable to the data from this questionnaire. Based on the verification results mentioned above, this questionnaire with respect to purchase intention and cultural recognition delivered a relatively good reliability and validity.

Table 4. Study of reliability and validity of purchase intention and cultural recognition.

Group	Cronbach's α	KMO	X^2	sig.
Group1	.966	.965	1273.056	0.000
Group2	.940	.947	851.510	0.000
Group3	.962	.967	1190.587	0.000

The totaling of the score from every single group was studied (see Table 5). The total score of 1st group is 26.28, with standard deviation standing at 12.003. The minimum score is 14 and the maximum is 55; the total score of 2nd group averages at 36.17, with standard deviation standing at 9.357. The minimum score is 14 and the maximum is 53; the total score of 3rd group averages at 41.75, with standard deviation standing at 11.770. The minimum score is 16 and the maximum is 55.

Table 5. Study of total score among groups.

Group	Mean	Std.	Minimum	Maximum
Group1	26.28	12.003	14	55
Group2	36.17	9.357	14	53
Group3	41.75	11.770	16	55

The degree of recognition of creative cultural products was evaluated by Friedman inspection. X2 stands at 89.318 and P approximates 0 by comparison upon adjustment between every two groups, which shows that there is significant difference in the respondents' degree of recognition of creative cultural products among such three groups. Furthermore, multiple analysis method was used to make comparison between group 1 and group 2, or group 1 and group 3, or group 2 and group 3. The inspection results show that the level of significance approximates 0, which shows the respondents' degree of recognition of the products of the 3rd group is superior to that of the 2nd group. And that of the 2nd group is superior to that of 1st group (see Table 6).

Table 6. Friedman inspection results with respect to cultural implication of creative cultural products from three groups.

Group	Mean	Std.	Minimum	Maximum	Median	X^2
Group1	11.84	5.348	6	25	9	89.318
Group2	16.52	4.423	7	25	18	
Group3	19.08	5.401	6	25	21	

The cultural implication of creative cultural products was evaluated using Friedman inspection. X2 stands at 74.991 and P approximates 0 by comparison upon adjustment between every two groups, which shows that there is significant difference in the respondents' degree of recognition of creative cultural products among such three groups. Furthermore, multiple analysis method was used to make comparison between group 1 and group 2, or group 1 and group 3, or group 2 and group 3. The inspection results show that the level of significance approximates 0, which shows the respondents' understanding of cultural implication of the products of the 3rd group is superior to that of the 2nd group. And that of the 2nd group is superior to that of 1st group (see Table 7).

Table 7. Friedman inspection results with respect to cultural recognition of creative cultural products from three groups.

Group	Mean	Std.	Minimum	Maximum	Median	X^2
Group1	4.78	2.367	2	10	4	74.991
Group2	6.53	2.029	2	10	7	
Group3	7.58	2.270	2	10	8	

The purchase intention for creative cultural products was evaluated using Friedman inspection. X2 stands at 73.435 and P approximates 0 by comparison, which shows that there is significant difference in the respondents' purchase intention for creative cultural products among such three groups. Furthermore, multiple analysis method was used to make comparison between group 1 and group 2, or group 1 and group 3, or group 2 and group 3. The inspection results show that the level of significance approximates 0 upon adjustment between every two groups, which shows the respondents had a preference for the products from the 3rd group. Those from 2nd group ranks 2nd in such preference, followed by the 1st group (see Table 8).

Table 8. Friedman inspection results with respect to purchase intention of creative cultural products from such three groups.

Group	Mean	Std.	Minimum	Maximum	Median	X^2
Group1	9.66	4.592	4	20	8	73.435
Group2	13.12	3.465	4	18	14	
Group3	15.09	4.502	5	20	17	

4.2 Semi-structured Interview Results

This study summarized the highlights from the semi-structured interview and gave an analysis of the purchase intention and cultural recognition for creative cultural products like Macao's road signs, with results classified as follows:

(1) Strong cultural traits
"I prefer simple and creative cultural products. Mostly, I would like to buy the ones that connect package to local features or typical colors, and those with some traits incorporated into design to enrich cultural traits. Like such three groups of products, the 1st group is of a public taste, without any features. It is very hard to associate the texture and colors with creativity and Macao's local culture in the 2nd group. The color used in the 3rd group represents that of the road signs. The products are functional." (respondent, female, 20 years old).

"I often buy some products that can be used in daily life. It they bear historical and cultural meaning, I have a stronger feeling about the product concept. I would like to recommend them to my friends. The affordable ones are more popular. In addition, I feel the products should be more diversified. I feel the variety of such three groups is rich." (respondent, female, 24 years old).

(2) Reasonable price
"All creative cultural products available currently tend to be expensive like those existing ones (1st group) in Macao. I would probably feel a bookmark is not as much expensive as it should be. I would not buy a bookmark at a price of over 100 yuan. It would be a lot better if the price gets lower." (respondent, male, 26 years old).
"During the questionnaire, I tended to consider the creativity of such a product first, followed by price and quality. It is because I would like to measure its value when purchasing it. If it is much more expensive than it should be, I tend not to buy it. I feel creative cultural products tend to be small in size and exquisite." (respondent, male, 35 years old).

5 Conclusion and Suggestion

As homogenization is getting increasingly stronger in creative cultural products, the designers shall design and develop products with local culture incorporated. This study covers the design of creative cultural products represented by the road signs in Macao by considering the conversion mode of three cultural layers. The study results show that the products designed by such conversion mode tend to be higher in terms of purchase intention and cultural recognition than the existing Macao's cultural creative products and those from other cities. The current creative cultural products tend to lack in uniqueness of design. The designers are able to process and recreate by extracting cultural elements and by modernized means. Then, the cultural implication is conveyed to the consumers and users through the creative cultural products.

Due to a limited number of respondents under investigation, this study was conducted via internet. By doing so, a majority of respondents came from those who are active on internet. Those aged above 50 were not included. Although creative cultural products are mainly popular among the young, the young's perception of the creative cultural products does not completely reflect that of people of different ages.

References

1. Lin, R.T.: Transforming Taiwan aboriginal cultural features into modern product design: a case study of a cross-cultural product design model. Int. J. Des. **1**(2) (2007)
2. Qin, Z., Song, Y., Tian, Y.: The impact of product design with Traditional Cultural Properties (TCPs) on consumer behavior through cultural perceptions: evidence from the young Chinese generation. Sustainability **11**(2), 426 (2019)
3. Qin, Z., Ng, S.: Culture as inspiration: a metaphorical framework for designing products with traditional cultural properties (TCPs). Sustainability **12**(17), 7171 (2020)

4. Hsu, C.H., Fan, C.H., Lin, J.Y., Lin, R.: An investigation on consumer cognition of cultural design products. Bulletin Jpn. Soc. Sci. Des. **60**(5), 5_39–5_48 (2014)
5. Government of Macao Special Administrative RegionStatistics and Census Servic.: https://www.dsec.gov.mo/zh-MO/ (2021)
6. Xiao, M.Y.: Cultural creativity and design transformation case analysis (2011)
7. Luo, S.-J., Dong, Y.-N.: Role of cultural inspiration with different types in cultural product design activities. Int. J. Technol. Des. Educ. **27**(3), 499–515 (2016). https://doi.org/10.1007/s10798-016-9359-y
8. Chang, C.L., Hsieh, M.H.: Next step of cultural and creative products-embracing users creativity. In: International Conference on Human Interface and the Management of Information, pp. 409–419 (2015)
9. Herrmann, A., Xia, L., Monroe, K.B., Huber, F.: The influence of price fairness on customer satisfaction: an empirical test in the context of automobile purchases. J. Prod. Brand Manag. **16**, 49–58 (2007)
10. Chen, C.H., Lin, S.C.: Message delivery of cultural and creative products under cultural industries. In: International Conference on Human-Computer Interaction, pp. 15–23 (2016)
11. Lin, R.T.: Cultural creativity. Design bonus. Art Appreciation **1**(7),26–32 (2005)
12. Gharib, I.: An emotional design approach to develop new cultural products. Archit. Arts Human. Sci. Mag. **29**(5461), 1–8 (2017)
13. Cheng, W.T., Shanat, M.: The alternative of product creation: exploring innovation through cultural element. J. Appl. Arts **2**(1), 88–93 (2020)
14. Cultural Affairs Bureau of Macao.: Macao World Heritage Folder. http://www.3icm.gov.mo (2011)
15. Shah, H., et al.: The impact of brands on consumer purchase intentions. Asian J. Bus. Manag. **4**(2), 105–110 (2012)

Cross-Cultural Mobility and Automotive UX Design

Effects of Multi-sensory Channel Materials and Emotional Situations in Emotion Induction for Affective Driving Studies

Zeling Deng, Ruiying Lyu, Xin Yang, Xue Zhao, and Hao Tan(✉)

Hunan University, Changsha Hunan 410006, China
{dengzeling,htan}@hnu.edu.cn

Abstract. During the driving process, the emotional state of the driver affects their performance significantly. To keep the driver in the most suitable state, inducing the expected emotions effectively is the priority in the research of emotion-aware interfaces and the design of interactive systems. Multi-sensory channel materials and emotional situations are two categories of emotion induction methods with high effects and universality. However, their impact in the driving environment remains unclear. In this study, film clips were selected to represent multi-sensory channel materials, recollections were used to represent emotional situations, and their combinations were employed to investigate their emotion induction effects from the intensity, duration, and purity. Our results demonstrate that the effects of film + autobiographical recollection (F + AR) and autobiographical recollection (AR) are significantly stronger compared to film + non-autobiographical recollection (F + NAR) and film (F). Nevertheless, there are no significant differences between F + AR and AR, F + NAR and F. Thus, applying F + AR in design is suggested in this study. Hopefully, it can provide a reference for the affective issues in future automotive researches.

Keywords: Emotion induction · Affective driving · Multi-sensory channel materials · Emotional situations · Procedures · Emotion-aware interface

1 Introduction

Emotion detection research possesses a wide application in the automobile driving environment. Modern cars are equipped with some detection instruments for the driver's emotional state [1]. They can improve the comfort level by influencing sensors [2] or adjust the user interface in the car to handle the driver's anger issues [3], so as to enhance its safety. Emotions have effects on driving behavior. An individual's emotional state affects their cognitive processes [4]. The driver's cognitive load during driving affects their concentration. Drivers would be required to conduct driving behavior in many situations, though we are entering the autopilot era. Therefore, it is important to comprehend and guide the driver's emotional state [5, 6].

To evaluate these interactive interfaces for driver state detection designed in the field of automotive driving, researchers need to evoke the participants' specific emotions.

P.-L. P. Rau (Ed.): HCII 2022, LNCS 13314, pp. 141–153, 2022.
https://doi.org/10.1007/978-3-031-06053-3_10

Eliciting intense, long-lasting, and accurate emotions is the primary prerequisite for a smooth evaluation [7]. However, it is difficult to induce participants' specific emotions in the automotive environment because the effect of the induction task before driving will decline as the driving task dominates the mind. Moreover, the driving task during the driving process will compete directly with the emotional induction over the cognitive load, weakening the emotions.

Two sources of information (subjective data and self-report) were considered to explore the effect of four kinds of emotions induced by multi-channel materials and emotional situations on drivers from three aspects (emotion intensity, duration, and purity). The results of this experiment revealed the influence of different inducing methods on drivers' emotions. The research demonstrated that the combination of multi-sensory channel materials and emotional situations can effectively induce the emotion of drivers. Hopefully, comparing the effects of several emotion induction methods that are highly versatile in driving would contribute to a reference for affective driving studies.

2 Related Work

2.1 Two Dimensions of Emotion

Previous researchers have made numerous attempts to categorize emotions. The emotions that may be experienced in driving mainly include happiness, sadness, anger, fear, boredom, and stress. They can be represented in a circumplex model of emotion leveled in two dimensions: arousal and valence [8] (see Fig. 1).

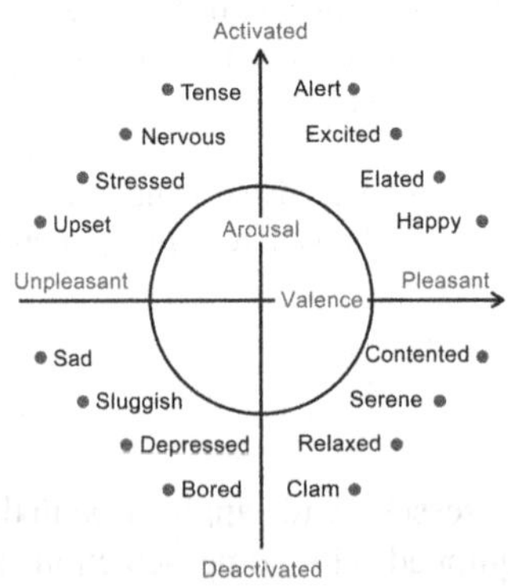

Fig. 1. The circumplex model of affect

How the specific combinations of these dimensions affect performance is instructive [9]. Negative valence combined with medium arousal leads to optimal performance [9] and helps focus on a higher priority driving task [10] while negative valence combined with high arousal results in the opposite. Positive valence affects the ability of visual attention [11] and is associated with enhancing cognitive flexibility [12], causing individual fixating on positive things in a peripheral environment [13].

An optimal state for driving would be a high valence with medium arousal. This state is related to a medium level of performance [9]. Specifically, the driver's state will deviate from what is required for driving performance when the emotion is in an extreme zone [4].

2.2 Types of Emotion Induction

There has been a lot of history in the current study of emotional arousal/induction methods [14]. These known ways of emotional induction can be divided into emotional material induction and emotional situational induction [15].

Emotional materials primarily include visual materials (pictures), auditory materials (music), olfactory materials, and multi-sensory channel materials (music video, film clip, VR scenes [16]). Among them, the multi-sensory channel emotional material induction has the advantages of cost, practicality, and flexibility. Since the way of stimulus presentation is simple and easy to conduct, it can meet the demanding requirements of fMRI, PET, and other brain mechanism research and be widely used in various studies. A typical representative of multi-sensory channel emotion material induction through film clips is a combination of dynamic visual images and sounds. The visual signal and audio are closely related to emotions [17]. Face expression plays a significant role in visual signals. The relationship between facial expressions and emotional arousal has been confirmed by a series of studies in the field of psychology [18, 19]. In auditory signals, speech conveys emotional information. Some basic emotions from non-linguistic vocalizations, such as laughing, crying, sighing, and yawning, can be accurately sensed by listeners. The basic prosodic features related to emotions extracted from audio signals are pitch, energy, and speech rate. Speeches also carry emotional information through words and content [18]. Emotional information can be derived from words with an emotional orientation, or be hidden in the semantic context of language [17]. Besides, the narrative script with the emotional tendency in the film is closely related to emotional induction. The emotion of the movie is predictable because the narrative lines tend to follow the usual principles, and the music is suitable for placing the viewer in the appropriate emotional channels. The viewer's emotion is influenced by the evaluation of the film event rather than itself [20].

The development of film emotion elicitation has been in sync with complex than elicitation of emotions by pictures [24]. Film is considered the most effective and popular method of emotion elicitation material [15].

Emotional situations include game scenes, expressions/postures, and recollections/imaginations [15]. Among them, the effects caused by facial expressions and postures are hardly convincing, making it difficult to exclude the influence of recollection [25]. Recollection includes autobiographical recollection and non-autobiographical recollection. The vital difference is that autobiographical recollection involves self-referencing [26]. Self-reference is a cognitive process, in which one can use self-related information in memory to understand incoming information.

Recollection was first used as an experimental method to elicit emotion in the 1980s [27]. In recent years, with the increasing research on brain mechanisms, recollection has regained the attention of sentiment researchers because of its advantages combining the simplicity of text-based materials, and high ecological validity of laboratory simulations

[28]. Autobiographical recollection is verified to be more effective than imagination [29]. It causes greater changes in arousal than in a combined procedure of music and guided imagery [30]. A recent study indicates that autobiographical recollection is more effective than videos when music is used to extend emotions [31]. However, there is little research on combined film and recollection. Previous studies have revealed that self-referencing can promote the immersive degree in narrative experiences, which may have a potential impact on shaping effects [32]. For example, in advertising, writing a self-focused story can signally enhance choice than an other-focused one [33].

Therefore, we assume that emotion elicitation by film clips contributes to altering the effect of autobiographical recollection though affecting the self-reference process.

3 Experiment

3.1 Experiment Design

To sum up the factors above, we first chose film clip, recollection, and their combinations as the representative of multi-sensory channel emotional materials and emotional situations to analyze their respective roles and mutual influences in the driving environment. Besides, 4 emotion induction methods include Film (F), Film + Non-autobiographical Recollection (F + NAR), Autobiographical Recollection (AR), and Film + Autobiographical Recollection (F + AR) (see Table 1).

Table 1. Induction methods.

Method	Content
F	Participants need to watch a film clip that contains target emotions
F + NAR	Participants need to watch the film clip first. After watching, they have 5 min to recall and write down the content of non-biographical recollection (which is the story and emotion based on the former video). When driving, they need to retell it to themselves
AR	Participants need to recall specific emotions as required from their own relevant experiences. They have 5 min to recall and write it down; then, they recollect it by themselves during driving
F + AR	A combination of F and AR. Participants need to first watch the film clip and then perform the AR process

Second, the emotional states used in the experiment are four extreme dimensions of high and low levels of pleasure and arousal according to Russell's circumplex model of affect (see Fig. 2).

Third, two indicators (intensity and duration), supplemented by purity, which is the most commonly used in emotion evaluation [7], are employed to test the effect of these methods comprehensively, so as to obtain more stable results.

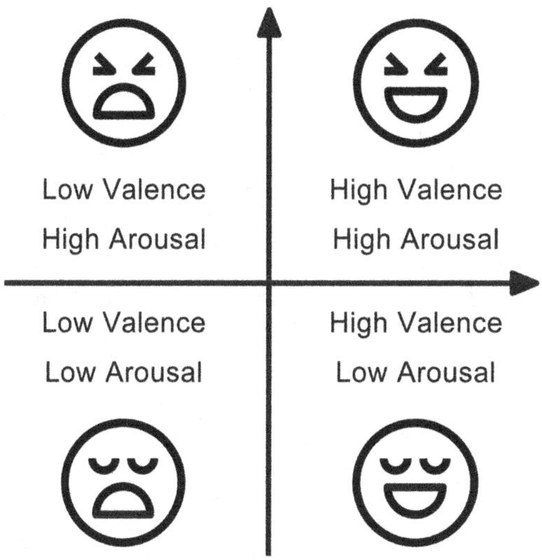

Fig. 2. The circumplex model of affect

3.2 Film Materials

Our hypotheses focus on the effects of different emotion elicitation materials. Due to the timeliness and cultural differences of the film clip materials, they are screened according to proven methods [34].

Our film clip materials come from two sources: previous papers and keyword search results on major video platforms. For 4 different emotional states, we collected 3 video clips for each, 12 in total. The length of the videos is about 3 min to ensure the stimulating effect while avoiding possible fatigue [35]. Then, these video clips were randomly sorted into a questionnaire and given to 30 people aged 18–25 to evaluate the emotional effects subjectively [7].

According to the results, one video is selected for each of the four states (Table 2).

Table 2. Induction methods.

Emotion	Title	Duration
Happiness	Tom and jerry	3′12″
Contentment	March of the penguins	3′10″
Anger	My first client	3′06″
Sadness	Dad's lie	3′04″

An H5 applet on a 10.5-inch iPad is used to sample the emotion level [31]. Pictures of expressions and body movements in it are also applied to visualize changes (see Fig. 3).

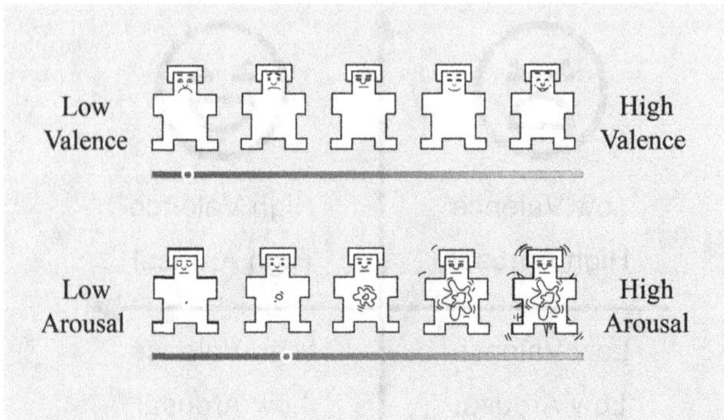

Fig. 3. Valence-arousal applet.

3.3 Apparatus and Scenario Design

The experiment has been held in a seminar room of the library in Hunan University in Changsha, Hunan province on a consumer-grade static driving simulator. The simulator platform is the G29 from the Logitech G Driving Force series, consisting of a steering wheel and a pedal to simulate real driving. The G29 is available for PC. Thus, a laptop of Acer Shadow Knight 3 Ruilong Advanced Version is used for the visual and sound rendering of the driving scene in our study.

The scenario was provided by RFactor v1.2.5.5 on the Steam platform. Participants were supposed to drive the same circle route in a suburb environment named Jonesville Speedway (see Fig. 4). Since there are no traffic lights, the vehicle could drive without stopping. Some stationary trucks were simulated in the middle of the route but no pedestrian. We chose this route because its simplicity ensures fewer additional attentional demands.

Fig. 4. Experiment environment and scenario circuit.

3.4 Participants

Specifically, 24 participants (12 females and 12 males) between 18 and 25 (MD = 23.5) years old joined the paid experiment. All participants have a driving license and driving experience. All participants signed up for informed consent for study participation.2.5 Experiment Procedure.

3.5 Experimental Tasks

Before the experiment, the participants would be introduced to the static driving simulator, the experiment procedure [36], and the terms involved (Pleasure-displeasure, Arousal-nonarousal) [1].

Each participant experienced 4 sessions with different induction methods and emotional states, which were combined into a 4*4 mixed distribution to avoid carry-over-effects; 4 sessions are illustrated in Fig. 5.

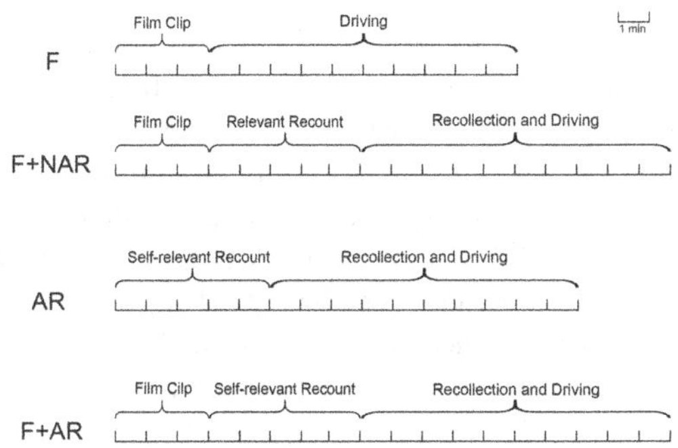

Fig. 5. This table summarizes the conducted trials in the experiment.

Each session consisted of emotion sampling before and after the induction, followed by simulated driving for 10 min and a short interview. During driving, the level of induced emotions was sampled every one minute.

The experimenters would not be presented when they were going through the recollection procedures to protect the participants' privacy and to reduce interference [31].

After the experiment, participants had a final interview and ranked the methods by the effect.

4 Results

IBM SPSS Statistics 25.0 was employed to analyze the experimental data, and covariance analysis was conducted to exclude the impact of confounding factors on emotion intensity and duration. The results obtained directly from the experiment are detailed as follows.

4.1 Intensity

Emotional intensity is reflected in the average score of each emotion on the self-rating scale. The higher the average score, the stronger the emotion. Participants' feedback tended to the same based on their self-report results. The Independent sample test indicated that the scores of F + AR and AR were different among the groups ($p < 0.05$), implying that the emotion intensity induced from F + AR (M = 4.86, SD = 1.19) and AR (M = 4.88, SD = 2.03) was significantly higher than that from F (M = 3.88, SD = 1.62) and F + NAR (M = 4.26, SD = 1.58) (see Fig. 6). Besides, 8/24 participants believed that the emotion induced by F + AR is the strongest; 6/24 participants insisted that the emotion induced by AR is the strongest.

No significant difference is observed neither between F + AR and AR ($p = 0.282 > 0.05$) nor between F and F + NAR ($p = 0.512 > 0.05$). Combined with the performance of AR, it can be confirmed that the participation of AR mainly affects the emotion intensity induced by F in F + AR.

4.2 Duration

Emotional duration is determined based on a subjective self-rating scale and subsequent interviews. The result suggests that the scores of F + AR and AR are different among groups ($P < 0.05$). In other words, the duration of emotion induced by F + AR (M = 5.73, SD = 3.00) is the longest and significantly longer compared to F + NAR (M = 3.25, SD = 2.61) and F (M = 2.5, SD = 1.59) (see Fig. 7). The average dwell time of emotion induced by F + AR or F can reach about 5′40″.

However, no significant difference is discovered neither between F + AR and AR (M = 5.7,SD = 2.38) ($p = 0.967 > 0.05$) nor between F + NAR and F ($p = 0.100 > 0.05$).

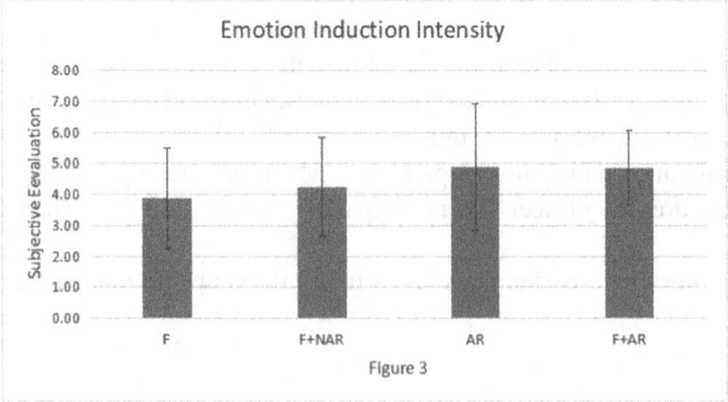

Fig. 6. Emotion induction intensity.

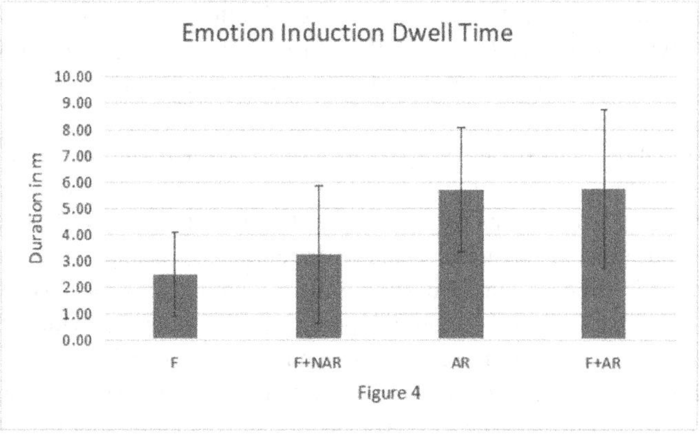

Fig. 7. Emotion induction duration.

4.3 Purity

The emotion is observed using subjective scores of arousal and pleasure. Most participates felt the target emotion during the inducing process. The deviation mainly occurred during F or F + AR session. One of the participants assessed that they felt other emotions (in addition to happiness) during a high-arousal and high-pleasure F + AR session. The emotion from both the film clip and the autobiographical recollection was consistent with the target. However, negative judgments of the content generated and reduced the pleasure in the process of recalling. Moreover, the scores demonstrated that they felt the target emotions. though a few participants were confused by the emotions expressed in the film when inducing low arousal and high pleasure.

4.4 Interaction

Most participants stated that the emotions brought about by videos can be suppressed by NAR but promoted by AR. F + AR is more likely to cause associations about one's own experience compared to only AR, suggesting that the combination of film content and AR resulted in the highest level of self-reported self-reference.

5 Discussion

5.1 Explication and Analysis

Results from participants' self-report anger revealed the successful induction combination procedure.

F has the weakest emotional intensity and the shortest duration. F, as a comprehensive material with multimodal afferent information in real-time, can cause a wide range of emotions. Nonetheless, its specificity is inferior. Thus, its effect is easy to be influenced by deviations due to subjective factors. Besides, whether F can arouse self-association highly depends on the person's self-experiences. F is only deficient in immersion and self-referencing. As the driving task occupies the people's attention and cognitive resources, the driver spontaneously detached from the last emotional scenario driving by moral principle and common sense. Therefore, it is easier to recover from the emotions induced by F.

The emotional intensity of the F + NAR is weak, and the duration is short. Recollections of the content can increase the degree of participation towards the materials while it is difficult to elicit associations with oneself. If the participants focus too much on the content, this method would be more likely to encourage participants to think logically away from the induced emotions, weakening the emotional influence. There is no significant difference between non-autobiographical recollections and videos. Combined with interviews, it can be speculated that F is dominant in F + NAR.

AR has a higher emotional intensity and longer duration. This can also be confirmed by other experiments [37]. F + AR has the highest emotional intensity and the longest duration. As illustrated from the overall results, AR has a major impact on F + AR. Involving F can guide participants' AR processes while it has a limited effect on emotional duration.

Participants also deemed that AR can promote the emotions caused by F. This supports our hypothesis about self-reference in F + AR. According to the data, there was no significant difference in emotional intensity or duration. This can be explained by the attribution of films. The emotion and content in combined emotion-inducing materials cannot be separated. F, as a multi-sensory channel and multi-dimensional stimulus source, is a complex external material. The emotion induced by F has a high intensity but can be induced from the content, storyline, ideas, or other dimensions, which are the basic appeal of emotional materials [38]. During the AR process, a person may be appealed by one of them depending on their self-experience and be immersed by a deviated emotion scenario. The stimulus source of AR is generated internally. It is a process of self-referencing, contributing to deepening the degree of deviation. Therefore, the emotions F + AR induces are more likely to be biased by subjective factors. Furthermore, the potential behind the feature of disorientation in F + AR can be exploited when the induction of specific emotions is not necessary.

Since it is an uncontrolled process for drivers to spontaneously regulate their emotions through recalling in the driving environment, multi-sensory channel materials inducing the recalling process may effectively improve the emotional state of drivers when the cognitive load is not occupied, such as before driving.

5.2 Limitation

Although the methods and procedures used in this experiment are universal, it still has some issues requiring better solutions in the future due to many constraints.

Though the method of selecting materials guaranteed a high target emotion hit rate, users' reaction still varies by the same video. Even under the same user intention level and similar demographic information, their responses may still be entirely different ascribed to variations in personal habits and characteristics. Therefore, personalization should be considered to achieve the best induction effect when there is a need to induce users' emotions in a driving environment.

Moreover, during the driving process, the subjective evaluation of the breakpoints has a fatigue effect, and the process of emotional sampling of participants may interfere with their feelings.

Simultaneously, this method cannot accurately reflect the continuous change curve, which may be affected by memory bias, defense mechanism, and interference of emotional expression rules [39].

The size of the display might have limitations during the film playing process and driving scenario. Since our study focuses on emotion materials, the medium of emotion presentation may influence the presence and immersion of the induced emotion [40]. However, it is feasible to present F in the 2D form given the economic efficiency of using F in a laboratory environment.

6 Conclusion

This study aims to explore the effects of multi-channel material and emotional situations in emotion induction methods in the driving environment.

Our results indicated that the effects of film + autobiographical recollection (F + AR) and autobiographical recollection (AR) are significantly stronger compared to film + non-autobiographical recollection (F + NAR) and film (F). Among the combination procedures of F + AR, the process of self-reference plays a major role. The emotions induced by F can be promoted by AR, demonstrating the disorientation attribution of F + AR.

According to the results of this study, two points should be considered when inducing drivers' emotions:

F + AR should be considered while inducing a series of emotions to examine the effectiveness of the vehicle's emotion-aware interfaces.

Multi-channel material related to the driver's experience could be presented to design an in-vehicle-multimodal interface for altering the driver's emotional state.

Considering that the method selected in this study is highly versatile, a reasonable combination of multi-channel sensory emotional materials and emotional situations can provide a possible tool to improve the motion-aware interface and user experience, and ensure safe driving in related designs.

References

1. Li, J., Braun, M., Butz, A., Alt, F.: Designing emotion-aware in-car interactions for unlike markets. In: Proceedings of the 11th International Conference on Automotive User Interfaces and Interactive Vehicular Applications, pp 352–357 (2019)
2. Eyben, F., et al.: Emotion on the road: necessity, acceptance, and feasibility of affective computing in the car. Adv. Hum. Comput. Interact. 1–17 (2010)
3. Hassib, M., Braun, M., Pfleging, B., Alt, F.: Detecting and influencing driver emotions using psycho-physiological sensors and ambient light. In: Lamas, D., Loizides, F., Nacke, L., Petrie, H., Winckler, M., Zaphiris, P. (eds.) INTERACT 2019. LNCS, vol. 11746, pp. 721–742. Springer, Cham (2019). https://doi.org/10.1007/978-3-030-29381-9_43
4. Yerkes, R.M., Dodson, J.D.: The relation of strength of stimulus to rapidity of habit-formation. J. Comp. Neurol. Psychol. **18**(5), 459–482 (1908)

5. Miller, D., et al.: Distraction becomes engagement in automated driving. Proc. Hum. Factors Ergon. Soc. Annu. Meet. **59**(1), 1676–1680 (2015)
6. Solovey, E.T., Zec, M., Perez, E.A.G., Reimer, B., Mehler, B.: Classifying driver workload using physiological and driving performance data: two field studies. In: Proceedings of the SIGCHI Conference on Human Factors in Computing Systems, pp 4057–4066 (2014)
7. Xie, Y., Yang, Z.: A comparative study on the validity of different mood induction procedures (MIPs). Studies Psychol. Behav. **14**(5), 591–599 (2016)
8. Posner, J., Russell, J.A., Peterson, B.S.: The circumplex model of affect: an integrative approach toaffective neuroscience, cognitive development, and psychopathology. Dev. Psychopathol. **17**(3), 715–734 (2005)
9. Kuhbandner, C., Zehetleitner, M.: Dissociable effects of valence and arousal in adaptive executive control. PLoS ONE **6**(12), e29287 (2011). https://doi.org/10.1371/journal.pone.0029287
10. Zwosta, K., Hommel, B., Goschke, T., Fischer, R.: Mood states determine the degree of task shielding in dual-task performance. Cogn. Emot. **27**(6), 1142–1152 (2013)
11. Wadlinger, H.A., Isaacowitz, D.M.: Positive mood broadens visual attention to positive stimuli. Motiv. Emot. **30**(1), 87–99 (2006)
12. Dreisbach, G., Goschke, T.: How positive affect modulates cognitive control: reduced perseveration at the cost of increased distractibility. J. Exp. Psychol. Learn. Mem. Cogn. **30**(2), 343–353 (2004)
13. Rowe, G., Hirsh, J.B., Anderson, A.K.: Positive affect increases the breadth of attentional selection. Proc. Natl. Acad. Sci. U.S.A. **104**(1), 383–388 (2007)
14. Fakhrhosseini, S.M., Jeon, M.: Chapter 10 – affect/emotion induction methods. In: Emotions and Affect in Human Factors and Human-Computer Interaction, pp. 235–253. Elsevier (2017). https://doi.org/10.1016/B978-0-12-801851-4.00010-0
15. Zheng, P., Liu, C., Yu, G.: An overview of mood-induction methods. Psychol. Sci. **20**(1), 14–55 (2011)
16. Gaggioli, A., Magoni, S., Chirico, A.: Effects of autobiographical self-referencing on presence and emotions in immersive storytelling: an exploratory study. In: CYPSY24: 24th Annual CyberPsychology, CyberTherapy & Social Networking Conference (2019)
17. Zeng, Z., Pantic, M., Roisman, G.I., Huang, T.S.: A survey of affect recognition methods: audio, visual, and spontaneous expressions. IEEE Trans. Pattern Anal. Mach. Intell. **31**(1), 39–58 (2009)
18. Russell, J.A., Bachorowski, J.A., Fernandez-Dols, J.M.: Facial and vocal expressions of emotion. Annu. Rev. Psychol. **54**, 329–349 (2003)
19. Goeleven, E., Raedt, R.D., Leyman, L., Verschuere, B.: The karolinska directed emotional faces: a validation study. Cogn. Emot. **22**(6), 1094–1118 (2008)
20. Baveye, Y., Chamaret, C., Dellandrea, E., Chen, L.: Affective video content analysis: a multidisciplinary insight. IEEE Trans. Affect. Comput. **9**(4), 396–409 (2018)
21. Philippot, P.: Inducing and assessing differentiated emotion-feeling states in the laboratory. Cogn. Emot. **7**(2), 171–193 (1993)
22. Gross, J.J., Levenson, R.W.: Emotion elicitation using films. Cogn. Emot. **9**(1), 87–108 (1995)
23. Hagemann, D., Naumann, E., Maier, S., Becker, G., Lurken, A., Bartussek, D.: The assessment of affective reactivity using films: validity, reliability and sex differences. Personality Individ. Differ. **26**(4), 627–639 (1999)
24. Uhrig, M., et al.: Emotion elicitation: a comparison of pictures and films. Front. Psychol. 180–180 (2016)
25. Matsumoto, D.: The role of facial response in the experience of emotion: more methodological problems and a meta-analysis. J. Pers. Soc. Psychol. **52**(4), 769–774 (1987)
26. Debevec, K., Romeo, J.B.: Self-referent processing in perceptions of verbal and visual commercial information. J. Consum. Psychol. **1**(1), 83–102 (1992)

27. Brewer, D.H., Doughtie, E.B., Lubin, B.: Induction of mood and mood shift. J. Clin. Psychol. **36**(1), 215–226 (1980)
28. Baker, R.C., Guttfreund, D.O.: The effects of written autobiographical recollection induction procedures on mood. J. Clin. Psychol. **49**(4), 563–568 (1993)
29. Wright, J.C., Mischel, W.: Influence of affect on cognitive social learning person variables. J. Pers. Soc. Psychol. **43**(5), 901–914 (1982)
30. Jallais, C., Gilet, A.: Inducing changes in arousal and valence: comparison of two mood induction procedures. Behav. Res. Methods **42**(1), 318–325 (2010)
31. Braun, M., Weiser, S., Pfleging, B., Alt, F.: A Comparison of Emotion Elicitation Methods for Affective Driving Studies. In Adjunct Proceedings of the 10th International Conference on Automotive User Interfaces and Interactive Vehicular Applications, 77–81 (2018)
32. Escalas, J.E.: Self-referencing and persuasion: narrative transportation versus analytical elaboration. J. Consum. Res. **33**(4), 421–429 (2007)
33. West, P.M., Huber, J., Min, K.S.: Altering experienced utility: the impact of story writing and self-referencing on preferences. J. Consum. Res. **31**(3), 623–630 (2004). https://doi.org/10.1086/425097
34. Jin, X., Deng, G., Jing, M., L, G.: The evaluation of emotion elicitation effect of videos. Psychol. Explor. **29**(6), 83–87 (2009)
35. Braun, M., Serres, K.: ASAM: an emotion sampling method for the automotive industry. In: Proceedings of the 9th International Conference on Automotive User Interfaces and Interactive Vehicular Applications Adjunct, pp 230–232 (2017)
36. Westermann, R., Spies, K., Stahl, G., Hesse, F.W.: Relative effectiveness and validity of mood induction procedures: a meta-analysis. Eur. J. Soc. Psychol. **26**(4), 557–580 (1996)
37. Janssen, J.H., et al.: Machines outperform laypersons in recognizing emotions elicited by autobiographical recollection. Hum. Comput. Interact. **28**(6), 479–517 (2013)
38. IJsselsteijn, W.A.: Presence in the past: what can we learn from media history?. In: Being There: Concepts, Effects and Measurements of User Presence in Synthetic Environments, pp. 17–40. Ios Press (2003)
39. Fredrickson, B.L., Kahneman, D.: Duration neglect in retrospective evaluations of affective episodes. J. Pers. Soc. Psychol. **65**(1), 45–55 (1993)
40. Baños, R.M., Botella, C., Alcañiz, M., Liaño, V., Guerrero, B., Rey, B.: Immersion and emotion: their impact on the sense of presence. Cyberpsychol. Behav. **7**(6), 734–741 (2004)

Comfort or Promise? Investigating the Effect of Trust Repair Strategies of Intelligent Vehicle System on Trust and Intention to Use from a Perspective of Social Cognition

Yushun Feng[1] and Hao Tan[2](✉)

[1] School of Design, Hunan University, Changsha, China
fengyushun@hnu.edu.cn

[2] State Key Laboratory of Advanced Design and Manufacturing for Vehicle Body, Hunan University, Changsha, China
htan@hnu.edu.cn

Abstract. The trust issue between intelligent system and humans is faced with more complex challenges. As the intelligent systems are gaining more autonomy, new modes and frameworks are required to investigate human-computer interaction in the days to come. This article aims to explore the trust repair strategies of intelligent vehicle system after a traffic accident from the perspective of social cognition, specifically, by comparing the impact of different trust repair strategies including admission and denial, comfort and promise, on the participants' perceived warmth, perceived competence, trust and intention to use. An online research based on video material with 432 participates in total was conducted. As indicated by the results, trust repair strategies had a significant impact on the perception and attitudes of users. Comforting and apologizing after the accident increased the perceived warmth of participants on the vehicle system. More importantly, their trust and intention to use were supported. Promising to avoid the accident in the future increased the perceived competence, which supported users' intention to use it indirectly. The trust repair strategy of intelligent vehicle system based on the social cognition theory has a significant influence on the cognition and attitudes of users, which provides not only a new perspective for the relevant practitioners in the field of human-computer interaction but also direct reference for the design of personified and anthropomorphic vehicle system agent.

Keywords: Trust repair · Social cognition theory · Human-computer interaction · Intelligent vehicle system

1 Introduction

With the advancement of AI technology and the popularization of intelligent vehicle market, the relationship between human and intelligent vehicle system is shifting from the interaction between humans and autonomous system to that between human and autonomy system. What's different from the traditional autonomous system is that autonomy

P.-L. P. Rau (Ed.): HCII 2022, LNCS 13314, pp. 154–166, 2022.
https://doi.org/10.1007/978-3-031-06053-3_11

performs tasks to achieve the goals set by humans without supervision. They have the ability to learn, reason and solve problems independently, in addition to changing themselves flexibly with the passage of time. Nonetheless, the consequence of their behaviour may be unknown [1]. It means that this technology may develop in a way that people can't predict, while the trust between people and autonomy systems will face more complex challenges. It is thus urgent to apply new design and research framework to solve some critical questions in relation to this field.

Although the Insurance Institute for Highway Safety released a research report suggesting that the promotion of autonomous driving technology can reduce traffic accidents by at least 1/3, the accidents associated with intelligent vehicle have led to widespread mistrust and concern. Therefore, the building of trust in humans and intelligent vehicle, especially the trust repair after trust violation, has become an urgent topic.

1.1 Trust Repair in HCI

Trust repair between humans and autonomy system needs to be explored by adopting the theory of social science. Trust is defined as the expectation or intention of an individual, which includes the expectation of performance or result achieved by others, as well as the willingness to act in a certain way or stay in a state of perceived vulnerability or risk [2]. Trust violation is a violation or consequence of the principal, which undermines the trust of the trustor. Trust repair refers to the behaviour that makes trust more positive after the violation occurs. When trust breaks down, it is often the responsibility for the trustee, one who broke the trust, to repair it by implementing some measures such as apology (attributing the violation to one's own responsibility and expressing apology), and denial (attributing the violation to external factors), etc. [3].

In the field of human-computer interaction, human beings tend to show social reactions to computer [4], which is because people tend to endow non-human entities with the personality and quality of humans. Accordingly, Kohn, S.C. et al. [5] believe that the paradigm of interaction between people and autonomy systems should imitate and adopt the model of interaction between humans. Therefore, it is suggested that the future design of autonomy systems behaviour, including trust repair, should draw on the knowledge and theory in relation to the field of social science.

In the research of social science, Kim et al. [3] are the first to conduct a systematic study on the issues related to trust repair. They categorized trust violation into competence-based trust violation and integrity-based trust violation, and then obtained the experimental results suggesting that apology can restore trust more effectively than denial after competence-based trust violation. However, there is also evidence collected from several studies that excuses are often beneficial to those making mistakes [6], because they reduced the responsibility burdened by violators [7]. It can be seen that apology is to admit the fault in the trust violation and to shift the responsibility to the trustee, thus damaging the trust-based relationship between the trustor and the trustee to a large extent. On the contrary, denying the mistakes in the trust violation and attributing the mistakes to external factors can make the trustor continue to believe the breaching party.

Therefore, it is still worth investigating the effect of different behaviors of trust repair, especially the aforementioned controversial behaviour implemented by vehicle system on the cognition of trustor. SC Kohn et al. [5] investigated different types of trust repair behaviour to determine which remediation is the most effective solution to mitigating the impact of trust violation, mainly including the adaptation of Kim as well as the apologies and denials of others, along with several kinds of repair options that the experimenter chooses subjectively. It was found out that apologies can be more effective in restoring trust than denial. However, there is still a research gap in this area and few follow-up researches have been conducted to explore the possibility of active trust repair by vehicle system after the violation of trust.

1.2 The Perspective of Social Cognition

In the field of social cognition, it is proved that individuals make evaluation of others from the perspectives of warmth and competence: over the past few years, the studies conducted through experimental social psychology experiments, election polls and cross-cultural comparisons have clearly shown that there are two universal dimensions of human social cognition: perceived warmth and perceived competence [8]. The former reflects the characteristics related to intention, including friendliness, the willingness to offer help, sincerity, trust and integrity, while the latter reflects the characteristics linked to ability, including intelligence, skills and efficiency.

The double dimensions of warmth - competence and the two types of integrity - competence trust violation proposed by Kim et al. laid a foundation for applying the social cognitive theory to the research on trust repair. For example, David Cameron et al. [9] studied the different trust repair strategies applied by guided robots after making mistakes in the paradigm of social cognitive theory. The results show that the robots with high warmth can arouse people's likeness more than those with high competence after making mistakes. Most importantly, this kind of likeness increased the intention of people to use robots.

1.3 Human Reaction in Emergency Situation

In an emergency, trust repair will face more complex factors. The trust violation of vehicle in human-computer interaction can include emergency traffic accidents, operation failure, and the user privacy disclosure caused by the failure of vehicle system, among which traffic accidents are common in reality and on social media. In case of emergency, autonomy system needs to deal with the physiological and psychological reactions of people as well [10].

Stress will have a direct impact on the cognitive ability of people. Negative emotional state is related to the emergency situations involving stress. Fear, anxiety, irritability, embarrassment, depression, helplessness, excitement, depression and hostility are the most common feelings related to emergencies.

In addition, people's trust in agents may show deviation in an emergency. In the research of P Robinette et al. [11], it was found out that the participants would be overly trust of the robot in an emergency, and follow the wrong instructions of the robot. It can be seen that in an emergency, people may also place excessive trust on the autonomy system. As a result, despite the possibility for intelligent agents to save lives in an emergency, it may also cause disastrous consequences for the improper trust of humans.

Thus, the trust repair in an emergency situation may be different than in a non-critical situation, which is worthy of further investigation.

To sum up, it is essential to investigate the critical issue with trust repair in a critical situation for the vehicle system. The of social cognition is to be applied in this study for adaptation to the new relationship between humans and the intelligent system.

2 Modeling and Hypothesis

2.1 Trust Repair Model Based on Social Cognition Framework

In the causal attribution model of trust repair proposed by Edward C. Tomlinson et al. [12], the perception of trust breach involves two main processes. The first one is the judgment of causal ascription, which includes competence-based trust violation and integrity-based trust violation. According to the social cognitive theory, after the occurrence of trust violation, the implementation of warmth-centred response or competence-centred response will have a positive impact on the perceived warmth and perceived competence of the trustor respectively. The other is responsibility attribution judgment. In the study of Kim [13], the attribution of trust breach is classified into internal attribution and external attribution [14]. That is to say, the reason for the mistake stems from the personal factors of the principal or external environment factors. According to the above model and the features of human-computer interaction, a trust repair model based on social cognition is established, as shown in Fig. 1.

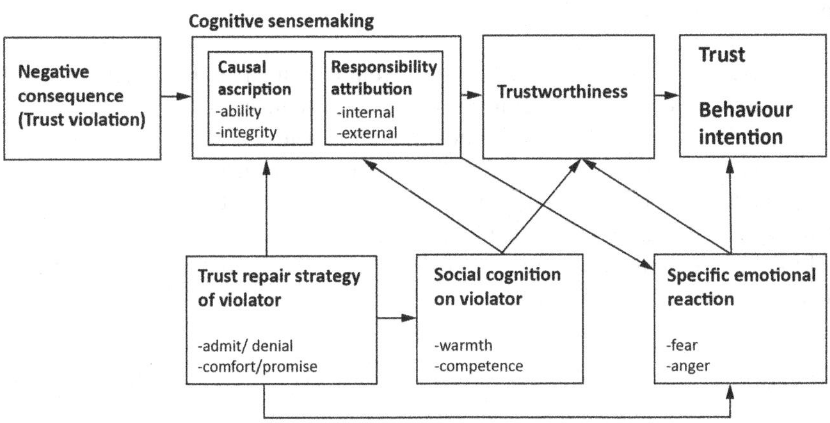

Fig. 1. Trust repair model based on social cognition theory

Based on the attribution of trust breach and the social cognitive response, the trust repair strategy of intelligent vehicle system in this research can be defined and classified into four categories as shown in Fig. 2. According to this Classification of trust repair, the apology in previous studies actually includes two elements: the recognition behaviour of internal attribution and emotional comfort, while the denial in previous studies explains only the effect of external attribution. Therefore, it is necessary to further investigate both responsibility attribution and social cognitive response.

The causal attribution / The social cognitive response	Warmth-centred response	Competence-centred response
Internal attribution	admit to cause the consequence and offer emotional comfort	admit to cause the consequence and promise to avoid it in future
External attribution	denial to cause the consequence and offer emotional comfort	denial to cause the consequence and promise to avoid it in future

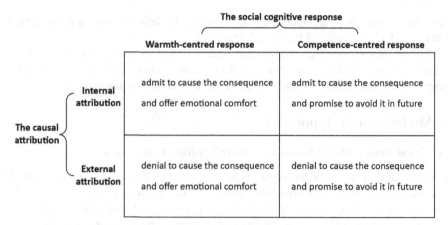

Fig. 2. Classification of trust repair strategies based on social cognition theory

2.2 Hypothesis

This study focuses on comparing the impact of trust repair strategies, including admission (internal attribution) or denial (external attribution) and emotional comfort (warmth-centred response) or promising to avoid possible accident (competence-centred response), on the participants for their perceived warmth, perceived competence, trust and intention to use the vehicle after a traffic accident. The specific research hypotheses are presented as follows:

- H1a: Admitting to causing the accident will reinforce trust on the vehicle.
- H1b: Emotional comfort will reinforce trust on the vehicle.
- H1c: Promise will increase the intention to use the vehicle.
- H2a: Promise will increase perceived competence on the vehicle.
- H2b: Emotional comfort will increase perceived warmth on the vehicle.
- H3a: Perceived warmth plays a mediating role in the impact of comfort on trust
- H3b: Perceived competence plays a mediating role in the impact of promise on the intention to use

3 Method

3.1 HCI Videos

The experiment is conducted as an online questionnaire, with scenario simulation videos used to describe the interaction scene in the vehicle. It is very common to use indirect methods such as video in human-computer interaction research [15], and it has been empirically verified [16]. The video clip describes the behaviour of an intelligent vehicle system. It collides with the front vehicle during rear-end collision. Then, the vehicle system explains it in different ways. The detailed description of explanation made by the vehicle system includes the following four cases.

1. The collision was due to the vehicle system failure. I'm very sorry for this incident. Please keep calm and handle the accident carefully. (Fig. 3 a)
2. The collision was due to the vehicle system failure. The event data has been archived for vehicle optimization to ensure that such events will not happen again.
3. The collision was due to the wet and slippery pavement. I'm very sorry for this incident. Please keep calm and handle the accident calmly.
4. The collision was due to the wet and slippery pavement. The event data has been archived for vehicle optimization to ensure that such events will not happen again. (Fig. 3 b)

Fig. 3. Snapshot of video material

3.2 Measurement

The experiment was conducted in a 2 × 2 design, with the attribution of responsibility as the first independent variable, including internal attribution and external attribution. The second independent variable is the type of social cognitive response, including warmth-centred response and competency-centred response.

The dependent variables as measured in the experiment include trust, the intention to use the vehicle, perceived competence and perceived warmth. The measurement of trust was selected from the trust scale developed by Jian et al. [18], for the description of the participants' trust on computer. The measurement of intention to use the vehicle was adapted from the study of Ilias panagiotopoulos et al. [14], including one item to measure the willingness of participants to use vehicles in the future. The measurement of perceived competence and perceived warmth was selected from the Godspeed questionnaire [17].

3.3 Participant

A total of 432 Chinese participants were recruited through social media, e-mail and Sojump sample collection services. Some of the participants completing the questionnaire were excluded by the following criteria:

1. 42 participants were excluded because they did not pass the attention test randomly set in the questionnaire (for example, to verify whether you have read the question carefully, please choose a city locate in southern China: A. Qingdao B. Beijing C. Shenzhen D. Harbin);
2. Three participants aged under 18 were also excluded;

The remaining sample consisted of 387 participants (including 262 males and 125 females), of whom 45.5% had been driving for less than 3 years, 42.6% had been driving for 3–20 years, and 11.9% had been driving for more than 20 years.

3.4 Procedure

The participants were given a brief introduction on the experiment before filling in the questionnaire, and were required to watch one of the four videos. Then, the participants were asked to assess the competency, warmth with five points scale, trust and intention to use the vehicle using a seven-point scale. Finally, the participants completed a basic demographic survey, including gender and driving age. In order to eliminate participant bias [19], the introductory part of the questionnaire only explained that the purpose of this study was to investigate the participants' attitude towards the vehicle system, further details were not mentioned.

4 Result

4.1 Manipulation Check

With the reliability analysis method and the cloned Bach coefficient (α coefficient) used, the scale's Clonal Bach reliability coefficient of the total scale was obtained as $\alpha = 0.857$. The reliability of the scale is high.

Based on the principle of exploratory factor analysis, KMO and Bartlett's test of sphericity was conducted. The results are shown as follows. The observed values $\chi 2 = 2856.217$, $df = 190$, $Sig. = 0.000 < 0.001$, so that the data of this sample can be analyzed by factors. The KMO value of the sample is $0.898 > 0.7$, indicating the excellent validity of the questionnaire.

The results of statistical analysis of trust, the intention to use the vehicle, perceived competence and warmth under different responsibility attribution and social cognitive responses are shown in Table 1.

Table 1. Descriptive statistics of dependent variable tests

Types	Trust		ITU		PW		PC	
	Mean	SD	Mean	SD	Mean	SD	Mean	SD
RA								
Internal	20.485	5.469	4.300	1.693	10.359	2.490	10.354	2.682
External	21.392	4.660	4.660	1.439	9.651	2.839	10.702	2.494
SCR								
Comfort	21.708	4.853	4.770	1.460	9.733	2.816	11.032	2.27
Promise	20.178	5.556	4.190	1.649	10.254	2.551	10.045	2.788

Note. Acronyms are denoted as follows: responsibility attribution (RA), social cognitive response (SCR), intention to use (ITU), perceived warmth (PW), perceived competence (PC)

4.2 The Effect of Trust Repair Strategies on Trust and Intention to Use

According to the trust of the participants and their intention to use the vehicle, the data was analyzed using the two-way ANOVA method. The results are listed in Table 2.

Table 2. Results of Two-way ANOVA on trust and intention to use

Types	Trust		Intention to use	
	F	Sig	F	Sig
RA	3.272	0.071	5.757*	0.017
SCR	8.487*	0.004	14.169**	0.000
CA × SCR	0.384	0.536	0.270	0.604

Note. Acronyms are defined as follows: responsibility attribution (RA), social cognitive response (SCR). $^{*}p < .05$; $^{**}p < .01$

It can be seen from Table 1 that the casual attribution has no significant effect on the trust of the participants, so that H1a is rejected;

The results show that the social cognitive response has a significant impact on the trust and intention to use of the participant, while the trust and intention to use are significantly different among different social cognitive responses;

The interaction between accident responsibility attribution and social cognitive response is not less than 0.05 in trust (Sig. = 0.536) and the intention to use (Sig. = 0.604), while the interaction effect is insignificant.

According to the above results and the data shown in Table 1, there is no significant difference in trust between recognition and denial, so that H1a is rejected. As for social cognitive response, the trust and intention to use under comfort offering are significantly higher than those under promising, so that H1b is supported while H1c is rejected.

4.3 The Effect of Trust Repair Strategies on Perceived Warmth and Competence

According to the perceived competence and perceived warmth of the participants, the data was analyzed using two-way ANOVA method. The results are shown in Table 3.

Table 3. Results of Two-way ANOVA on perceived warmth and competence

Types	PC		PW	
	F	Sig.	F	Sig.
RA	7.252**	0.007	2.561	0.110
SCR	4.156*	0.042	15.882**	0.000
RA × SCR	0.002	0.962	2.662	0.104

Note. Acronyms are denoted as follows: responsibility attribution (RA), social cognitive response (SCR), intention to use (ITU), perceived warmth (PW), perceived competence (PC). * $p < .05$; ** $p < .01$

It can be seen from Table 3 that the main effect of accident responsibility attribution on perceived competence ($F = 7.252$, Sig. $= 0.007 < 0.05$) is significant, which indicates that accident responsibility attribution has a significant impact on the perception of participants about the competence of vehicle system;

The results show that the social cognitive response has significant influence on the participants for their perception of competence and warmth of vehicle system, and sig. is less than 0.05 on perceived competence ($F = 4.156$, Sig. $= 0.042 < 0.05$) and perceived warmth ($F = 15.882$, Sig. $= 0.000 < 0.05$). There are significant differences in perceived competence and perceived warmth among different social cognitive responses;

The interaction between accident responsibility attribution and social cognitive response is not less than 0.05 in the sense of trust (Sig. $= 0.962$) and intention to use (Sig. $= 0.104$), so that the interaction is insignificant.

The above significant results and the data shown in Table 1 suggest that for the social cognitive response of comfort, perceived warmth is significantly higher than the perceived competence, so that the hypothesis H2a holds. For the repair behaviour of commitment, perceived competence is higher than perceived warmth, so that H2b is supported.

4.4 Mediating Effect of Perceived Warmth and Competence

Through the bias-corrected bootstrapping test of mediating effect analysis method, this paper analyses the indirect relationship between perceived warmth and trust, as well as the indirect relationship between perceived competence and intention to use. If the confidence interval (CI) excludes zero from the analytical results, the significance of mediating effect ($P < 0.05$) will be treated as statistically significant [20].

Mediating analysis showed that perceived warmth (boot SE $= 0.2911$, CT $= [-1.6484, -0.5093]$) had a significant indirect effect on the trust of participants. At the same time, perceived competency (boot SE $= 0.0906$, CT $= [-0.3692, -0.0143]$)

had a significant mediating effect on trust repair behaviour and the intention to use, so that both H3a and H3B are supported.

5 Discussion and Conclusion

Considering the importance of trust issue to the interaction between intelligent vehicle and passengers, and the relative lack of research on trust repair in emergency, this study attempts to have a better understand on not only how people perceive the trust repair strategy through vehicle system after a traffic accident, but also the impact of trust repair on their perception about the vehicle. To this end, we conducted an online survey using video materials to determine how humans perceive vehicle systems and to establish their trust and the intention to use vehicle based on trust repair strategy.

The results show that the trust repair strategy based on social cognition affects the perception of users about warmth and competency on the vehicle system. More importantly, it enhances their trust and intention to use the vehicle.

5.1 Conclusion

Through experiments and data analysis, the following conclusions are drawn:

1. The trust repair strategies based on social cognition has a significant impact on people's perceived warmth and competence on the vehicle system. A short and targeted description of vehicle system can significantly affect the individual's social cognition on the vehicle system. More specifically, the system apologizes for the accident and offers emotional comfort, which can promote the individual's perception about its warmth. Making a promise to avoid possible accidents can increase individual's perception about its competency. This supports the research result of David Cameron et al. [9], that is, the social cognitive response centred around warmth (or competence) can significantly affect people's social cognition of agents. At the same time, it also proves that the experimental method using video materials has a stimulating effect on the perception of participants.
2. The results also show that social cognitive response affects the user's trust and intention to use the vehicle system. It can be found out that offering emotional comfort is generally more effective than non-comfort in promoting people's trust in vehicle after accidents, which suggests that the results are consistent with the findings of Kim et al. [3]. In addition to our prediction, offering emotional comfort is also more effective than avoiding verbal commitments in encouraging people to continue the use of autopilot. According to Robinette et al. [21], the potential sense of danger may increase the significance of robot ability, thus affecting people's intention to use it. People feel more concerned about the psychological characteristics of personal safety [22] when in the context of automatic driving. However, in this study, the trust and intention to use the vehicle as induced by comforting behaviour are significantly higher than those of the promise behaviour. The possible reason for this is that in video materials, impact accidents do not cause serious life-threatening consequences. However, it is of great challenge to fully simulate the sense of danger posed by taking a real car.

3. Perceived warmth and competency have significant mediating effects on trust and intention to use the vehicle. That is to say, users' perceived warmth on vehicle system drives their trust and competence perception, thus driving their future intention to use autopilot. Therefore, users' different social cognition of vehicle system can be used to explain their different attitudes towards vehicle system after the accident.
4. There is no significant difference in trust caused by different responsibility attributions in the scenario of accident involving automatic driving vehicle. This is different from the previous study of Kim [3] that when it comes to competence related matters, trust can be more successfully repaired by using internal rather than external attribution to apologize. The possible reasons include the cognitive deviation in the emergency situation, which leads to the influence of the emotion in the emergency and the interpretation of the vehicle system.

Personified and anthropomorphic agents are being widely applied in the emerging intelligent vehicle system, while it needs to be determined through the knowledge and theory in the field of social science and HCI what kind of impression and image should be set up by the vehicle system, and how influential its behaviour is on user's perception.

By referring to social cognition, a classification of trust repair strategies is developed, which provides a clearer and well-understood perspective for the definition of trust repair strategies.

A trust repair model is also built for the autonomy system and the result indicated that trust repair strategy based on the social cognition theory indeed has a significant influence. This model can be a reference in other human-computer interaction research.

The findings of this study provide a direct reference for the field of human-computer interaction in intelligent vehicle. Especially, it offers inspiration for how the vehicle agent and trust repair strategy affect the user's perception and provides reference for intelligent vehicle designers, engineers and manufacturers to formulate human-computer interaction strategies in case of emergency.

5.2 Limitation and Future Work

The limitations of this research are detailed as follows. First of all, thi s study was conducted in the form of online questionnaire, in which the participants responded to the video clips of the vehicle system, rather than studying live human–autonomy interaction. Although the effect may be more significant when the participants are arranged in front of a real vehicle environment and vehicle system, the current research shows that even video clips can produce statistically significant effects. Secondly, in this study, people's trust in the vehicle system is modeled as the initial trust, while the effect and influence of trust repair in the long-term human-computer relationship were not discussed.

In the future research, the impact of human emotion on human-computer trust restoration in emergency should be further explored. It is known that human emotion has an important impact on trust restoration. Especially in the case of car accident, human emotion will have greater fluctuations and reactions, such as fear, anger, and uneasiness, etc. Future research can focus on these emotions. In addition, this study ignored the combined influence of warmth and competence. In the theory of inclined dimensions of social cognition, the perception of warmth will weaken the perception of competence

[23], and vice versa. Therefore, future research can also involve the related combination strategies and other types of trust repair strategies, such as defence, compensation and so on.

References

1. Xu, W.: From automation to autonomy and autonomous vehicles: challenges and opportunities for human-computer interaction. Interactions **28**(1), 48–53 (2020)
2. Lee, J.D., See, K.A.: Trust in automation: designing for appropriate reliance. Hum. Factors **46**(1), 50–80 (2004)
3. Kim, P.H., Donald, L.F., Cecily, D., Kurt, T.D.: Removing the shadow of suspicion: the effects of apology versus denial for repairing competence-versus integrity-based trust violations. J. Appl. Psychol. **89**(1), 104 (2004)
4. Edwards, C., Edwards, A., Stoll, B., Lin, X., Massey, N.: Evaluations of an artificial intelligence instructor's voice: social identity theory in human-robot interactions. Comput. Hum. Behav. **90**, 357–362 (2019)
5. Kohn, S.C., Quinn, D., Pak, R., de Visser, E.J., Shaw, T.H.: Trust repair strategies with self-driving vehicles: an exploratory study. In: Proceedings of the Human Factors and Ergonomics Society Annual Meeting, pp. 1108–1112. SAGE Publications, Los Angeles (2018)
6. Snyder, C.R., Higgins, R.L.: Excuses: their effective role in the negotiation of reality. Psychol. Bull. **104**(1), 23 (1988)
7. Riordan, C.A., Marlin, N.A., Kellogg, R.T.: The effectiveness of accounts following transgression. Soc. Psychol. Q. 213–219 (1983)
8. Fiske, S.T., Cuddy, A.J., Glick, P.: Universal dimensions of social cognition: warmth and competence. Trends Cogn. Sci. **11**(2), 77–83 (2007)
9. Cameron, D., et al.: The effect of social-cognitive recovery strategies on likability, capability and trust in social robots. Comput. Hum. Behav. **114**, 106561 (2021)
10. Tan, H., Hao, Y., Sun, A., Guo, X., Guo, D.: A bibliometric analysis and social network analysis on ergonomics studies of emergency equipment. In: Stephanidis, C., Duffy, V.G., Streitz, N., Konomi, S., Krömker, H. (eds.) HCII 2020. LNCS, vol. 12429, pp. 568–583. Springer, Cham (2020). https://doi.org/10.1007/978-3-030-59987-4_40
11. Robinette, P., Li, W., Allen, R., Howard, A.M., Wagner, A.R.: Overtrust of robots in emergency evacuation scenarios. In: 11th ACM/IEEE International Conference on Human-Robot Interaction, pp. 101–108. IEEE, New York (2016)
12. Tomlinson, E.C., Mryer, R.C.: The role of causal attribution dimensions in trust repair. Acad. Manag. Rev. **34**(1), 85–104 (2009)
13. Kim, P.H., Dirks, K.T., Cooper, C.D., Ferrin, D.L.: When more blame is better than less: the implications of internal vs. external attributions for the repair of trust after a competence-vs. integrity-based trust violation. Organ. Behav. Hum. Decis. Process. **99**(1), 49–65 (2006)
14. Panagiotopoulos, I., Dimitrakopoulos, G.: An empirical investigation on consumers' intentions towards autonomous driving. Transp. Res. Part C Emerg. Technol. **95**, 773–784 (2018)
15. Piçarra, N., Giger, J.C.: Predicting intention to work with social robots at anticipation stage: assessing the role of behavioral desire and anticipated emotions. Comput. Hum. Behav. **86**, 129–146 (2018)
16. Dautenhahn, K., et al.: How may I serve you? A robot companion approaching a seated person in a helping context. In: Proceedings of the 1st ACM SIGCHI/SIGART Conference on Human-Robot Interaction, pp. 172–179. ACM, New York (2006)

17. Bartneck, C., Croft, E., Kulic, D.: Measuring the anthropomorphism, animacy, likeability, perceived intelligence and perceived safety of robots. In: Proceedings of the 3rd ACM/IEEE International Conference on Human-Robot Interaction, pp. 37–44. ACM, New York (2008)
18. Jian, J.-Y., Bisantz, M., Colin, G.D.: Foundations for an empirically determined scale of trust in automated systems. Int. J. Cogn. Ergon. **4**(1), 53–71 (2000)
19. Mubin, O., D'Arcy, T., Murtaza, G., Simoff, S., Stanton, C., Stevens, C.: Active or passive?: Investigating the impact of robot role in meetings. In: The 23rd IEEE International Symposium on Robot and Human Interactive Communication, pp. 580–585. IEEE, New York, August 2014
20. Złotowski, J., Yogeeswaran, K., Bartneck, C.: Can we control it? Autonomous robots threaten human identity, uniqueness, safety, and resources. Int. J. Hum. Comput. Stud. **100**, 48–54 (2017)
21. Robinette, P., Howard, A.M., Wagner, A.R.: Timing is key for robot trust repair. In: Tapus, A., André, E., Martin, JC., Ferland, F., Ammi, M. (eds.) ICSR 2015. LNCS, vol. 9388, pp. 574–583. Springer, Cham (2015). https://doi.org/10.1007/978-3-319-25554-5_57
22. Adubor, O., St. John, R., Steinfeld, A.: Personal safety is more important than cost of damage during robot failure. In: Proceedings of the Companion of the 2017 ACM/IEEE International Conference on Human-Robot Interaction, p. 403. ACM, New York (2017)
23. Rosenberg, S., Nelson, C., Vivekananthan, P.S.: A multidimensional approach to the structure of personality impressions. J. Pers. Soc. Psychol. **9**(4), 283 (1968)

Investigation on the Spatio-Temporal Mobility and Smartphone Usage of College Students

Xiaojun Lai[1], Jingyu Zhao[1], Lili Dong[1], Bin Li[2], and Pei-Luen Patrick Rau[1(✉)]

[1] Department of Industrial Engineering, Tsinghua University, Beijing, China
rpl@mail.tsinghua.edu.cn

[2] Service Laboratory, Huawei Technologies CO., LTD, Shenzhen, China

Abstract. User attributes, such as gender, age, and education background, affect users' spatio-temporal mobility and smartphone usage. A two-week diary study was conducted among thirteen participants to investigate the spatio-temporal behavior and smartphone usage of college students. Data including the mobility trajectory, the overall smartphone usage, and the mobile application usage were collected three times per day, and the participants reported the travel distance from their residence every day. The results showed the impact of temporal characteristics on spatial mobility and smartphone usage. For example, participants visited traffic areas the least on weekdays and the most on holidays, and they used the communication applications most often and for the longest time in all parts of the day and on all types of days. Besides, the different movement patterns presented by participants during the study can be coded as higher regularity and higher mobility. An 87.30% prediction accuracy was achieved using the classification model of the support vector machine, suggesting that the features of spatio-temporal behavior and corresponding smartphone usage can reflect and predict participants' daily patterns. Information and communication technology providers can provide college students with personalized services such as cellular data support in different parts of the day and different types of days. Future research can extend to other user groups for their information communication requirements.

Keywords: Spatio-temporal mobility · Smartphone usage · College students

1 Introduction

With the intelligence and richness of various mobile applications, smartphones have become a tool that accompanies people's daily life. People's behavior patterns with smartphones are becoming more and more diverse, and the smartphone usage might have a high correlation with the attributes and the spatio-temporal mobility of users [1]. User attributes include gender, age, occupation, education background, permanent residence, socioeconomic status, personality traits, etc. Spatio-temporal mobility represents daily behavior characteristics, spatial characteristics, and temporal characteristics [2, 3]. Daily behavior characteristics include daily work, life patterns, and travel patterns. Spatial and temporal characteristics include movement scope, frequent residence points

P.-L. P. Rau (Ed.): HCII 2022, LNCS 13314, pp. 167–179, 2022.
https://doi.org/10.1007/978-3-031-06053-3_12

with the timestamp, and time type [1, 4]. Considering the influence of user attribute factors, information and communication technology (ICT) service providers could provide personalized support to different user groups based on their ICT requirements by investigating their spatio-temporal mobility and smartphone usage.

Previous studies regarding mobility patterns usually require high-density and massive amounts of data to achieve accurate classification or prediction results [5]. These data typically come from smartphone usage records provided by communication operators [6], network perception information provided by network service operators [7], or personal detailed data voluntarily provided by users in high authorized mode [2, 8]. Based on big data, researchers use methods such as machine learning to conduct data-driven research. With the global emphasis on personal privacy information, such high-density data access faces increasingly strict licensing requirements. Therefore, this study considered the combination of demographic information and tried to achieve the determination of movement patterns through low-density data acquisition.

To investigate the spatiotemporal behavior and smartphone usage using low-density data, this study focused on college students with special user attributes. The purpose of the study includes: 1) describing spatiotemporal mobility, overall smartphone usage, and mobile application usage of college students; 2) exploring the correlations of user attributes, mobility, and smartphone usage; 3) achieving a classification of daily movement patterns of college students supported by low-density data. The study conducted a two-week diary study among thirteen college students and collected detailed data on mobility trajectory information, overall smartphone usage, and mobile application usage. In the subsequent sections of this paper, literature on user attributes, spatiotemporal mobility, and smartphone application usages was reviewed. Specific methodology and results were introduced. Conclusion and limitations were discussed in the end.

2 Literature Review

2.1 User Attributes and Smartphone Usage

User attributes have a significant impact on smartphone usage. First, for gender, Van Deursen et al. [9] categorized user behaviors of smartphone use and explored the effect of gender on smartphone addictive behaviors. The findings suggested that women were more likely to use smartphones to maintain social relationships and engage in more conversations on their phones than men. Similar results were found in a study by Montag et al. [10]. Second, for age, the study of Van Deursen et al. [9] also found that as people aged, they spent less time on their smartphones for process and social usage [11], and experienced less social stress. Glasscock and Wogalter [12] conducted a study on individual differences in smartphone feature preferences, such as Alarm Clock, Camera, and Web/Internet Browser. The results indicated that as age increased, the reported possibility of using these features decreased, as did the number of features reported as likely to be used. Third, educational and socioeconomic status also influence user acceptance and availability of smartphones. Blumenstock and Eagle [13] combined field survey data with smartphone carrier transaction log data, and found that smartphone owners were generally wealthier and better educated in Rwanda.

Conversely, smartphone usage can predict user personality attributes, such as age, gender, and socioeconomic status. First, in terms of gender and age, Sarraute et al. [14] conducted an observational study of smartphone use across gender and age groups and detected significant differences in phone usage across populations. Similarly, Felbo et al. [15] developed a method that could achieve state-of-the-art age and gender prediction accuracy using only the temporal modality in mobile metadata. Al-Zuabi et al. [16] proposed a method to predict user gender and age based on user behavior, service, and contract information as well. Second, smartphone user data can also be used to predict the socioeconomic status of a population. Using phone survey data, corresponding call detailed records, and Demographic and Health Survey data, Blumenstock et al. [17] found that an individual's socioeconomic status can be inferred from his or her past history of mobile phone use.

2.2 Spatio-temporal Mobility

Each individual develops his or her own spatio-temporal mobility through spatio-temporal semantics. The behavior and purpose of users could endow specific time, location, and space with personalized or general semantics. First, time could be interpretable such as holidays, weekdays, weekends, or peak travel hours. Time coding is consistent and periodic, typically with weeks as the cycle, hours as the granularity of time division, and minutes as the unit of duration. Duration, working days, and rest days are important features in time semantics [18]. The semantic construction of moments related to the individual user can be in units of hours, and visual presentation can be considered [19]. The sequence of active moments in temporal semantics can also be referred to as rhythm, which is also an important semantic and is closely related to user attributes [20]. Second, spatial semantics include features such as location, distance, and motion, which are complex to encode and are commonly added by massive data-driven computational methods. The location classification in spatial semantics can include residential, business, traffic, and entertainment areas [21]. And important residency points, called spatial anchor points, are mainly residential and office locations. Place labels could be inferred from demographic (age and gender) and temporal features using a machine learning approach [22]. Das et al. [23] proposed the concept of contextual location and selected four different categories of locations including residence, college campuses, cafeterias/restaurants, and airports/travel. Third, among the various collection methods of human mobility data, GPS traces are mostly preferred, Call Detailed Records are coarse, and user privacy should be taken into account when collecting [4].

2.3 Spatio-temporal Mobility and Smartphone Usage

Smartphone usage behaviors associated with user spatio-temporal mobility include overall usage, such as use duration and data usage, and mobile application usage. Trestian et al. [24] used the association rule-mining approach to reveal the impact of user mobility and location on application preference from the perspectives of users and locations. For example, In the "comfort zone," especially at home, music apps were prevalent. Similarly, Böhmer et al. [25] found that people were more likely to use multimedia apps while traveling and less likely to use travel apps. Lu et al. [26] found that users with high mobility were more likely to use smartphones frequently and generate more traffic on mobile data networks. Furthermore, H. Wang et al. [27] proposed a Bayesian mixture model to predict future application usage based on time, location, and current application usage, and they noted a clear correlation between the distribution of points of interest (POI) and the class of apps being used. Similarly, Zhao et al. [28] used a random forest model to predict user application usage behavior from geospatial data, and verified that user movement patterns are highly correlated with their application usage behavior.

Analyzing and predicting human mobility based on smartphone usage patterns is possible. Early studies have looked at people's travel behavior based on users' e-travel and travel balances [29]. In addition to classifying users by their e-travel and business travel balances, there were also studies comparing the accuracy of different location prediction models [5]. Qiao et al. [21] proposed a Latent Dirichlet Allocation model based solution to correlate data traffic, user behavior, and urban ecology, and found that the functions of locations had different influences on the data usage patterns of heavy and normal users. For example, in entertainment areas, for online browsing behavior, heavy users were interested in richer information, such as inns, clothing, and massages, while normal users only search for information about dining.

3 Methodology

3.1 Participants

Thirteen students were recruited from Tsinghua University in Beijing to participate in the experiment, including five males and eight females. The participants included ten undergraduate students, one master's student, and two Ph.D. students, aging from 19 to 27 years ($M = 21.83$, $SD = 2.43$). Basic information about the participants was collected according to the general situation in the past six months. First, in terms of spatio-temporal mobility, twelve participants' daily travel range was basically within 2 km from their residence, and one participant's daily travel range was 3–5 km away from the residence. Their average wake-up time is 07:09–09:28, and their average sleep time is 23:28–01:46. The locations where participants performed their basic daily activities included dormitories ($N = 13$), canteens ($N = 11$), academic buildings ($N = 11$), libraries ($N = 8$), supermarkets ($N = 5$) and laboratories ($N = 4$), and their main daily travel methods were cycling ($N = 13$) and walking ($N = 10$). Second, in terms of smartphone usage, ten participants used Huawei smartphones ($N = 10$) and three participants used Apple smartphones. The daily use duration of smartphones was distributed between 2–4 h ($N = 6$), 4–6 h ($N = 5$), and 6–8 h ($N = 2$). Moreover, applications about communication (55.70%; 46.85%) and entertainment (17.40%; 24.20%) had the highest percentage of use frequency and use duration in all types of applications. Last, other electronic devices frequently used by the participants included laptops ($N = 13$) and tablets ($N = 9$).

3.2 Data Collection

The diary study collected detailed information about the participants' daily mobility trajectory, overall smartphone, and application usage during the three parts of the day.

Part 1 was from 0:00 until lunch, Part 2 from lunch until dinner, and Part 3 from dinner until 11:59 p.m. First, screen-on time, unlocking times, overall and per-app mobile data usage, and WLAN data usage were collected using the built-in statistics functions of the smartphones; second, the movement method, location name, arrival time, and departure time of each location visited by participants were collected in chronological order; third, at each location, the names of the mobile applications used were also collected, as well as the use times, the use duration and the use purpose. In addition to the statistics three times a day, participants were asked to report whether their daily travel range was within 2 km, or a distance of 3–5 km, 5–10 km, or more than 10 km from the place of residence every day.

A two-week diary study was carried out from April 30, 2021 to May 13, 2021 on the thirteen recruited students, covering 5 days of holidays (May Day), 7 days of weekdays, and 2 days of weekends. In the end, a total of 390 valid data were collected, including 3 parts per day for 10 days per person.

3.3 Data Process

Smartphone applications used in different locations at different moments of the day were coded into corresponding application types based on their use purposes, including communication, media, shopping, navigation, tools, reading, beautification, games, travel, health, office, and other. In addition, the reported names of travel locations were coded into different types, including residential, business, traffic, and entertainment areas. Therefore, for each participant's three parts of the day, first, the spatio-temporal mobility of each part can be obtained, including the visit number and stay duration in different types of places; second, the smartphone usage of the corresponding part of the day can be obtained, including the screen-on time, unlock number, mobile data usage, and WLAN data usage; third, the mobile application usage of each part of the day can be obtained, including the use times, use duration, mobile data usage, and WLAN data usage of different types of mobile applications.

4 Results

4.1 Descriptive Statistics

Spatio-temporal Mobility. As shown in Fig. 1, during holidays, participants spent the shortest amount of time in business areas, the longest amount of time in traffic and entertainment areas, and the least number of visits in residential and business areas. During weekdays, participants spent the longest time and appeared the most in business areas, the shortest time in residential and entertainment areas, and appeared the least in traffic areas. On weekends, participants spent the longest time and appeared the most in residential areas and spent the shortest time in traffic areas.

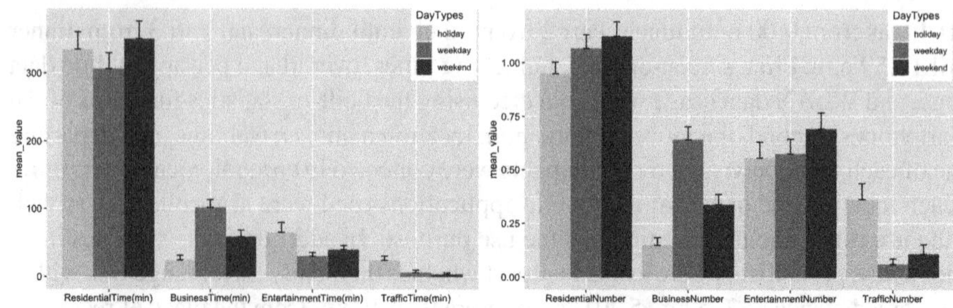

Fig. 1. Stay duration (left) and visit number (right) of locations on different types of days

Overall Smartphone Usage. As shown in Fig. 2, participants had more screen-on time of smartphones and used more WLAN data during Part 1 of the day, which might be due to the fact that participants used their smartphones after 0:00 before sleeping and the data was accounted into Part 1. In addition, participants unlocked their smartphones more often and used more mobile data during Part 2 of the day. For the different types of days, participants had the most screen-on time and used the least amount of mobile data on holidays, while on the weekends the opposite was true and meanwhile participants used the least amount of WLAN data.

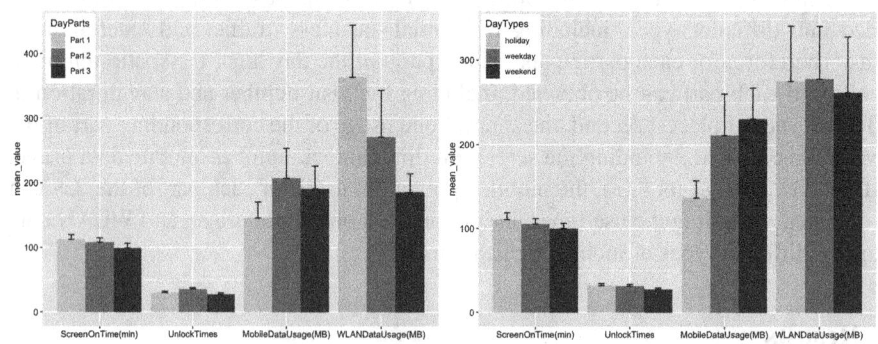

Fig. 2. Smartphone usage in three parts of the day (left) and on different types of days (right)

Mobile Application Usage. *Application usage in different parts of the day.* As shown in Fig. 3(a) and (c), participants used the communication apps most often and for the longest time in all parts of the day with no significant differences. Figure 3(b) and (d) amplified the differences between three parts of the day for other types of applications by removing the apps with larger values such as communication apps (subsequent radar figures used a similar method). Comparing the usage of each type of apps in different parts of the day, we can see that media applications were used the least in Part 2 but the longest Part 1. Shopping applications were used the most in Part 2 and the longest in Part 2 and Part 3. Reading applications were used the least in Part 3, while office applications were used the shortest in Part 1.

As shown in Fig. 4(a) and (c), during a day, communication applications had higher mobile data usage than other types of applications in all parts of the day, with the highest mobile data usage in Part 3 and the highest WLAN data usage in Part 2. Media applications had the highest mobile data usage in Part 3 and WLAN data usage in Part 1 compared to other applications. In addition, as shown in Fig. 4(b) and (d), shopping applications had the lowest mobile data usage in Part 1, while game applications had the highest mobile data usage in Part 2 of the day.

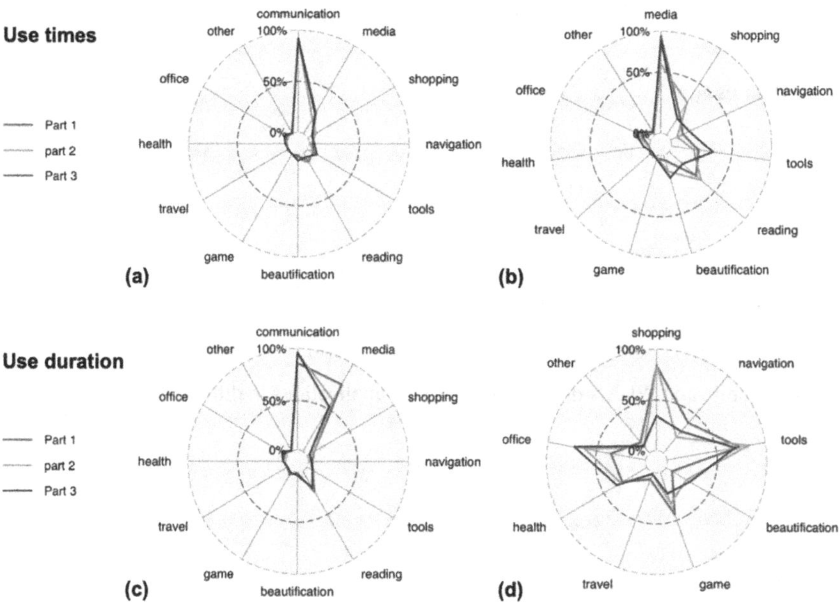

Fig. 3. Use times and use duration of mobile applications in different parts of the day

Application Usage on Different Types of Days. As shown in Fig. 5, participants used the communication applications most often and for the longest time on all types of days. In addition, comparing the usage of each type of apps on the three types of days, we can see that media applications were used the most and the longest on holidays, the least on weekdays, and the shortest on weekends; shopping applications were used the most frequently but the shortest on weekends; navigation applications were used the longest on holidays; game applications were used the longest on weekdays; and office applications were used the least and the shortest on holidays.

As shown in Fig. 6, communication applications had higher mobile data usage than other types of applications on different types of days, with the highest mobile and WLAN data usage on weekends. Besides, media applications had the highest mobile data usage and the lowest WLAN data usage on weekends, while they had the lowest mobile data usage and the highest WLAN data usage on holidays. Shopping applications had the lowest mobile data usage on holidays; reading applications had the lowest WLAN data usage on weekends; game applications had the highest mobile data usage on weekdays

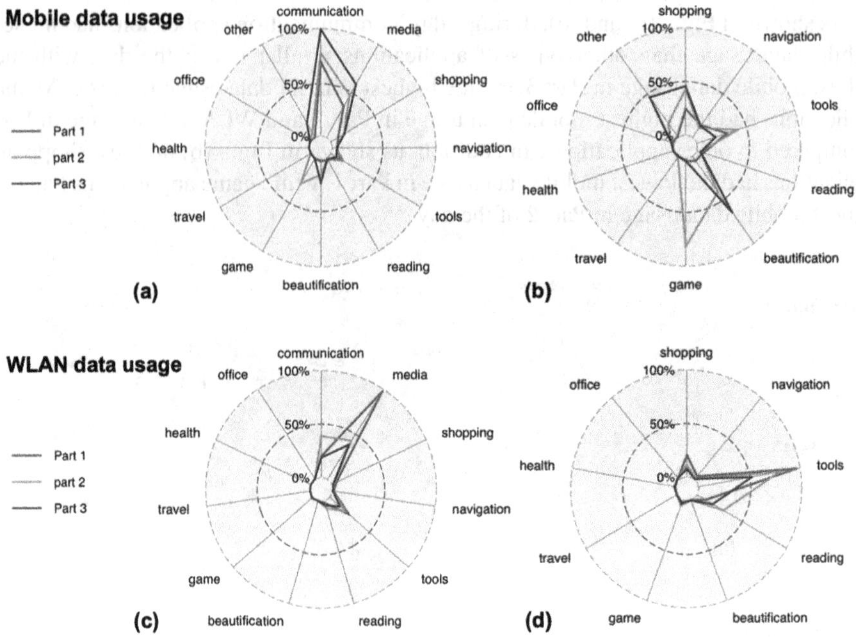

Fig. 4. Mobile and WLAN data usage of mobile applications in different parts of the day

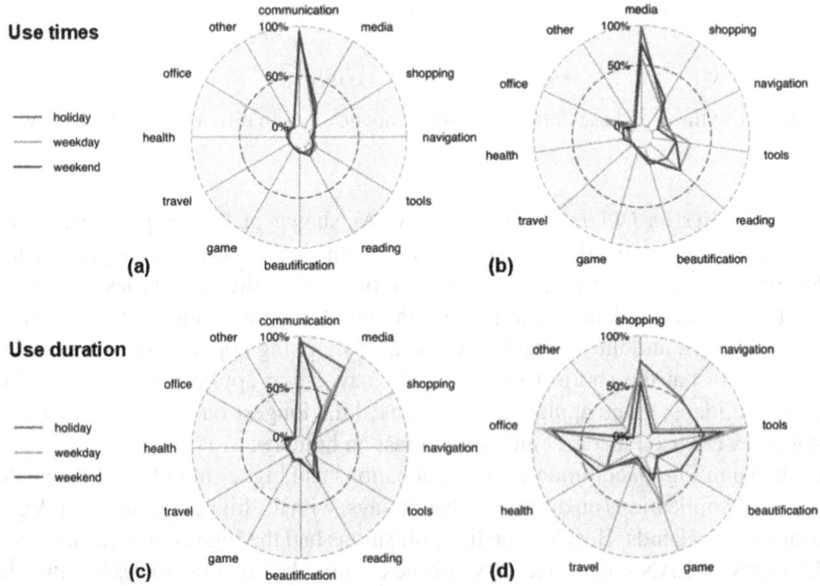

Fig. 5. Use times and use duration of mobile applications on different types of days

and the highest WLAN data usage on weekends; the beatification applications had the lowest mobile data usage and the highest WLAN data usage on holidays.

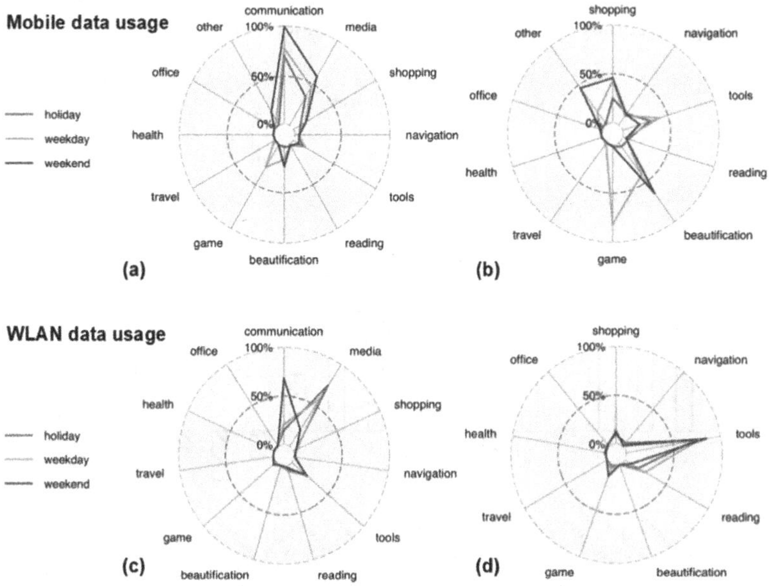

Fig. 6. Mobile and WLAN data usage of mobile applications on different types of days

4.2 Movement Pattern Classification

The daily travel range of the participants was distributed within 2 km (62.5%), 3–5 km (14.06%), 5–10 km (4.09%), and more than 10 km away (18.75%) from their residence. Considering that in the past six months the participants' daily travel range was basically within 2 km from their residence (N = 12), we can say that the participants experienced diverse mobility during the study covering three types of days.

Support vector machines (SVM) was used to verify whether the features of spatio-temporal mobility and smartphone usage can reflect the movement pattern of the participants. First, mobility type was adopted as the predictor: the days that the participants traveled within 2 km from their residence and visited no more than 9 locations were coded as higher regularity, while the rest of the days were coded as higher mobility. A total of 65 data of higher regularity and 61 data of high mobility were obtained (the data for two days of two participants was deleted because the travel range of the days was not reported). Second, the feature set included the day types, the visit number and stay time of different types of locations, the screen-on time, unlock times, mobile and WLAN data usage of smartphone, the use times, use duration, mobile and WLAN data usage of different types of mobile applications in the three parts of the days (181 features in total). The features were centralized and normalized to remove the dimension influence.

Third, the L1 regularization penalty term was used in the SVM model to verify the feature selection and determine the important features that play roles in classification. As shown in Fig. 7, 21 features with non-zero coefficients were screened out by setting C = 0. 035. Last, a 10-fold cross-validation was selected for the SVM model, and an 87.30% average accuracy of classification was obtained (in Table 1).

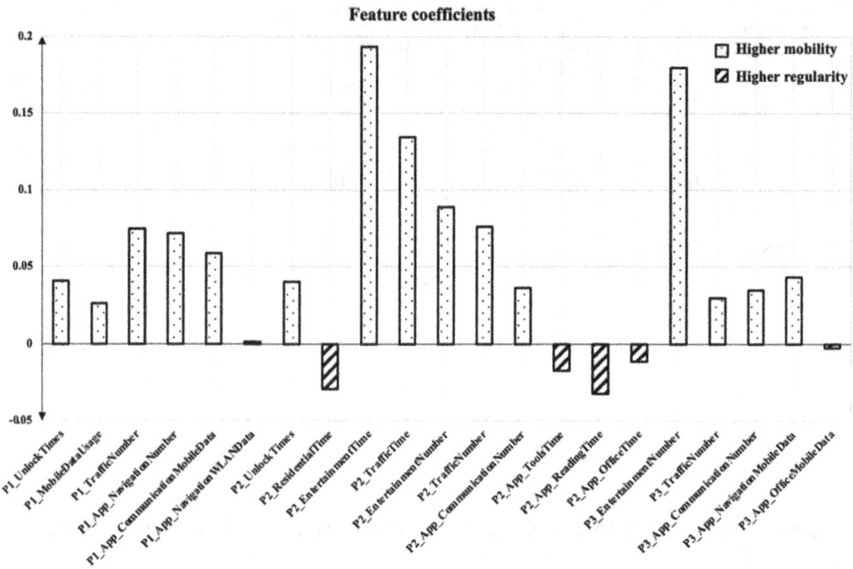

Fig. 7. Feature selection results of SVM (according to coef_)

Table 1. Classification confusion matrix

True\predicted	Higher regularity	Higher mobility
Higher regularity	60	5
Higher mobility	11	50

Combining the descriptive results in Sect. 4.1 with the feature coefficients in Fig. 7, we can see that features with positive coefficients corresponded to higher mobility, while features with negative coefficients corresponded to higher regularity. Therefore, we can conclude that:

1. Features corresponding to higher mobility included:

   - Higher number of visits in traffic areas in all parts of the day (P1_TrafficNumber, P2_TrafficNumber, P3_TrafficNumber).
   - Higher number of visits in entertainment areas in Part 2 and Part 3 of the day (P2_EntertainmentNumber and P3_EntertainmentNumber).

- Longer stay time in entertainment areas in Part 2 of the day (P2_EntertainmentTime).
- Higher unlock times of smartphones in Part 1 and Part 2 of the day (P1_UnlocksTimes and P2_UnlockTimes).
- Higher mobile data usage of communication applications in Part 1 of the day (P1_App_CommunicationMobileData).
- Higher use times of communication applications in Part 2 and Part 3 of the day (P2_App_CommunicationNumber and P3_App_CommunicationNumber).
- Higher use times of navigation applications in Part 1 of the day (P1_App_NavigationNumber).
- Higher mobile data usage of navigation applications in Part 3 of the day (P3_App_NavigationMobileData).

2. Features reflecting higher regularity included:

- Longer stay time in residence areas in Part 2 of the day (P2_ResidentialTime).
- Longer use duration of reading and office applications in Part 2 of the day (P2_App_ReadingTime; P2_App_OfficeTime)
- Lower mobile data usage of office applications in Part 3 of the day (P3_App_OfficeMobileData)

5 Discussion and Conclusion

This study proposed a method to explore the spatio-temporal mobility and smartphone usage of college students using low-density data collected three times a day. Results from a two-week diary study of thirteen college students showed that temporal characteristics affected users' spatial mobility and smartphone usage. For example, participants used the communication applications most often and for the longest time in all parts of the day and on all types of days. Office applications were used the shortest in Part 1 of the day and used the least and the shortest on holidays. Traffic areas were visited the least on weekdays and the most on holidays. In addition, the data of each participant per day was coded with a higher regularity or higher mobility pattern based on their daily travel distance and the number of locations visited. The classification results showed that the features about spatial-temporal mobility and the corresponding smartphone usage can reflect and predict the user's diverse movement pattern. ICT providers can provide college students with personalized services in different parts of the day and different types of days based on the research results. For example, social communication applications can be supported with more stable and consistent cellular data in all parts of the day and on all types of days. Besides, more cellular data support can be provided in the traffic and entertainment areas during holidays, especially for media applications.

There are a few limitations in our research. First, this study covered a short period of time, with only two weekends, five holidays, and seven weekdays, and the sample size of students was also small. Further research can incorporate the current low-density data collection methods to further extend the study duration and expand the sample size. Second, data on ICT requirements for different types of user groups can be collected and verified. For example, postgraduates have more regular movement patterns than undergraduates studying in classrooms and libraries because are usually required to conduct scientific research such as experiments in laboratories. In addition, users who are significantly more mobile than students, such as office workers and taxi drivers, will present different patterns of spatio-temporal mobility and smartphone usage. For example, we can say that office workers may have a higher number of visits in traffic areas on weekdays rather than holidays due to the need to commute. Future research based on high- or low-density data can combine user attributes to explore ICT requirements of different types of smartphone users.

References

1. Alessandretti, L., Aslak, U., Lehmann, S.: The scales of human mobility. Nature **587**(7834), 402–407 (2020). https://doi.org/10.1038/s41586-020-2909-1
2. Li, M., Wang, H., Guo, B., Yu, Z.: Extraction of human social behavior from mobile phone sensing. In: Huang, R., Ghorbani, A.A., Pasi, G., Yamaguchi, T., Yen, N.Y., Jin, B. (eds.) AMT 2012. LNCS, vol. 7669, pp. 63–72. Springer, Heidelberg (2012). https://doi.org/10.1007/978-3-642-35236-2_7
3. Papanikolaou, G.: Spatial and individual influence on commuting behaviour in Germany (2006). https://www.econstor.eu/handle/10419/118378. Accessed 03 June 2021
4. Solmaz, G., Turgut, D.: A survey of human mobility models. IEEE Access **7**, 125711–125731 (2019). https://doi.org/10.1109/ACCESS.2019.2939203
5. Lv, Q., Qiao, Y., Ansari, N., Liu, J., Yang, J.: Big data driven hidden markov model based individual mobility prediction at points of interest. IEEE Trans. Veh. Technol. **66**(6), 5204–5216 (2017). https://doi.org/10.1109/TVT.2016.2611654
6. Dong, Y., Yang, Y., Tang, J., Yang, Y., Chawla, N.V.: Inferring user demographics and social strategies in mobile social networks. In: Proceedings of the 20th ACM SIGKDD International Conference on Knowledge Discovery and Data Mining, New York New York USA, August 2014, pp. 15–24 (2014). https://doi.org/10.1145/2623330.2623703
7. Yang, J., Qiao, Y., Zhang, X., He, H., Liu, F., Cheng, G.: Characterizing user behavior in mobile internet, vol. 3, no. 1, p. 12 (2015)
8. Yan, J., Qiao, Y., Yang, J., Gao, S.: Mining individual mobile user behavior on location and interests. In: 2015 IEEE International Conference on Data Mining Workshop (ICDMW), Atlantic City, NJ, USA, November 2015, pp. 1262–1269 (2015). https://doi.org/10.1109/ICDMW.2015.122
9. van Deursen, A.J.A.M., Bolle, C.L., Hegner, S.M., Kommers, P.A.M.: Modeling habitual and addictive smartphone behavior. Comput. Hum. Behav. **45**, 411–420 (2015). https://doi.org/10.1016/j.chb.2014.12.039
10. Montag, C., et al.: Smartphone usage in the 21st century: who is active on WhatsApp? BMC Res. Notes **8**(1), 331 (2015). https://doi.org/10.1186/s13104-015-1280-z
11. Pearson, J.C., Carmon, A., Tobola, C., Fowler, M.: Motives for communication: why the millennial generation uses electronic devices. J. Commun. Speech Theatre Assoc. North Dakota **22**(1), 45–55 (2010)
12. Glasscock, N.F., Wogalter, M.S.: Evaluating preferences for smartphone features. In: Proceedings of the Human Factors and Ergonomics Society Annual Meeting, vol. 50, no. 12, pp. 1259–1263, October 2006. https://doi.org/10.1177/154193120605001211
13. Blumenstock, J., Eagle, N.: Mobile divides: gender, socioeconomic status, and smartphone use in Rwanda. In: Proceedings of the 4th ACM/IEEE International Conference on Information and Communication Technologies and Development - ICTD 2010, London, United Kingdom, pp. 1–10 (2010). https://doi.org/10.1145/2369220.2369225

14. Sarraute, C., Blanc, P., Burroni, J.: A study of age and gender seen through smartphone usage patterns in Mexico. In: 2014 IEEE/ACM International Conference on Advances in Social Networks Analysis and Mining (ASONAM 2014), pp. 836–843, August 2014. https://doi.org/10.1109/ASONAM.2014.6921683
15. Felbo, B., Sundsøy, P., "Sandy" Pentland, A., Lehmann, S., de Montjoye, Y.-A.: Modeling the temporal nature of human behavior for demographics prediction. arXiv:1511.06660 [cs], November 2017. http://arxiv.org/abs/1511.06660. Accessed 03 June 2021
16. Al-Zuabi, I.M., Jafar, A., Aljoumaa, K.: Predicting customer's gender and age depending on mobile phone data. J. Big Data **6**(1), 1–16 (2019). https://doi.org/10.1186/s40537-019-0180-9
17. Blumenstock, J., Cadamuro, G., On, R.: Predicting poverty and wealth from smartphone metadata. Science **350**(6264), 1073–1076 (2015). https://doi.org/10.1126/science.aac4420
18. National Bureau of Statistics: National Time Use Survey Bulletin (2018). http://www.stats.gov.cn/tjsj/zxfb/201901/t20190125_1646796.html. Accessed 23 June 2021
19. Yishan, X., Zhou, D., Liu, K.: Research on the elderly space-time behavior visualization and community healthy livable environment. J. Arch. **S1**, 90–95 (2019)
20. Duanmu, Y.., Chai, Y.: Time use research of workers' daily activities in Beijing: a comparison between 2007 and 2017. J. Hum. Geogr. **36**(02), 136–145 (2021)
21. Qiao, Y., Yu, J., Lin, W., Yang, J.: A human-in-the-loop architecture for mobile network: from the view of large scale mobile data traffic. Wirel. Pers. Commun. **102**(3), 2233–2259 (2017). https://doi.org/10.1007/s11277-017-5049-7
22. Krumm, J., Rouhana, D.: Placer: semantic place labels from diary data. In: Proceedings of the 2013 ACM International Joint Conference on Pervasive and Ubiquitous Computing, Zurich Switzerland, September 2013, pp. 163–172 (2013). https://doi.org/10.1145/2493432.2493504
23. Das, A.K., Pathak, P.H., Chuah, C.-N., Mohapatra, P.: Contextual localization through network traffic analysis. In: IEEE INFOCOM 2014 - IEEE Conference on Computer Communications, Toronto, ON, Canada, April 2014, pp. 925–933 (2014). https://doi.org/10.1109/INFOCOM.2014.6848021
24. Trestian, I., Ranjan, S., Kuzmanovic, A., Nucci, A.: Measuring serendipity: connecting people, locations and interests in a mobile 3G network. In: Proceedings of the 9th ACM SIGCOMM Conference on Internet Measurement Conference - IMC 2009, Chicago, Illinois, USA, p. 267 (2009). https://doi.org/10.1145/1644893.1644926
25. Böhmer, M., Hecht, B., Schöning, J., Krüger, A., Bauer, G.: Falling asleep with Angry Birds, Facebook and Kindle: a large scale study on mobile application usage. In: Proceedings of the 13th International Conference on Human Computer Interaction with Mobile Devices and Services - MobileHCI 2011, Stockholm, Sweden, p. 47 (2011). https://doi.org/10.1145/2037373.2037383
26. Lu, Z., Feng, Y., Zhou, W., Li, X., Cao, Q.: Inferring correlation between user mobility and app usage in massive coarse-grained data traces. Proc. ACM Interact. Mob. Wearable Ubiquitous Technol. **1**(4), 1–21 (2018). https://doi.org/10.1145/3161171
27. Wang, H., et al.: Modeling spatio-temporal app usage for a large user population. Proc. ACM Interact. Mob. Wearable Ubiquitous Technol. **3**(1), 1–23 (2019). https://doi.org/10.1145/3314414
28. Zhao, X., Qiao, Y., Si, Z., Yang, J., Lindgren, A.: Prediction of user app usage behavior from geo-spatial data. In: Proceedings of the Third International ACM SIGMOD Workshop on Managing and Mining Enriched Geo-Spatial Data, San Francisco California, June 2016, pp. 1–6 (2016). https://doi.org/10.1145/2948649.2948656
29. Roy, P., Martínez, A.J., Miscione, G., Zuidgeest, M.H.P., van Maarseveen, M.F.A.M.: Using social network analysis to profile people based on their e-communication and travel balance. J. Transp. Geogr. **24**, 111–122 (2012). https://doi.org/10.1016/j.jtrangeo.2011.09.005

Research on the Trend of Automotive User Experience

Aiqi Liu[1(✉)] and Hao Tan[2]

[1] State Key Laboratory of Advanced Design and Manufacturing for Vehicle Body, Hunan University, Changsha, China
3316647479@qq.com

[2] School of Design, Hunan University, Changsha, China

Abstract. In the development direction of automobiles, "smart" is undoubtedly the most important trend. From the perspective of transportation systems and travel tools, smart cars will profoundly change the way humans travel and drive. In particular, the interaction of intelligent vehicles as an intelligent subject and human society and the impact on human emotions and user experience have great theoretical and practical significance for the development and progress of human society. This research focuses on "intelligence", "interaction" and "experience". It is based on the "Automotive Intelligent and Interactive Experience Research" jointly carried out by the School of Design, Hunan University, the State Key Laboratory of Advanced Design and Manufacturing of Automobile Body, and the UCD Department of Huawei 2012 Laboratory. Based on the project, the research adopts bibliometrics, qualitative literature research combined with case study to obtain basic data. Then data analysis is carried out through clustering induction and case analysis so as to form design insights into automotive user experience design, and finally summarize the eight major trends in automotive user experience design.

Keywords: Smart cars · User experience · Interaction · Trend research

1 Introduction

Driving is the most complex human-computer interaction for many individuals. And the popularization of smart cars is bound to bring about an innovative revolution in the driving experience. Since 2018, with the auto market entering a period of stock competition, the auto industry has begun to enter the new auto era of "experience-driven change", and auto products are urgently moving from homogenization to differentiation. In terms of research on automotive user experience or human-computer interaction trends, Gao Han [1] and others have built a "human-vehicle" life cycle model. By studying the brand and consumer market, the design positioning and framework of the in-car HMI of Roewe Motors in 2025 are obtained. Based on the projects of Baidu and Hunan University, Hao Tan [2] and others discussed the future trend of human-computer interaction design of smart cars. From this point of view, automotive user experience will become an important research direction in the automotive field in the future.

P.-L. P. Rau (Ed.): HCII 2022, LNCS 13314, pp. 180–201, 2022.
https://doi.org/10.1007/978-3-031-06053-3_13

2 Research Methods

2.1 Forecasting and Trend Research

The study of design trends essentially belongs to forecasting. For any discipline, scientific and reasonable forecasting is the prerequisite and guarantee for scientific decision-making [3]. The root of the word "forecasting" is a term derived from ancient Greece. Forecasting is to analyze, judge, estimate, assume and infer the future development of objective things [4]. In summary, forecasting is a discipline to study the future development trend of things and the regularity in the development process.

2.2 Methods of Research of Automotive User Experience Trends

Although the research on automotive human-computer interaction design started late in our country, it has developed rapidly. The current research methods in the industry are mainly divided into quantitative and qualitative research methods (see Fig. 1).

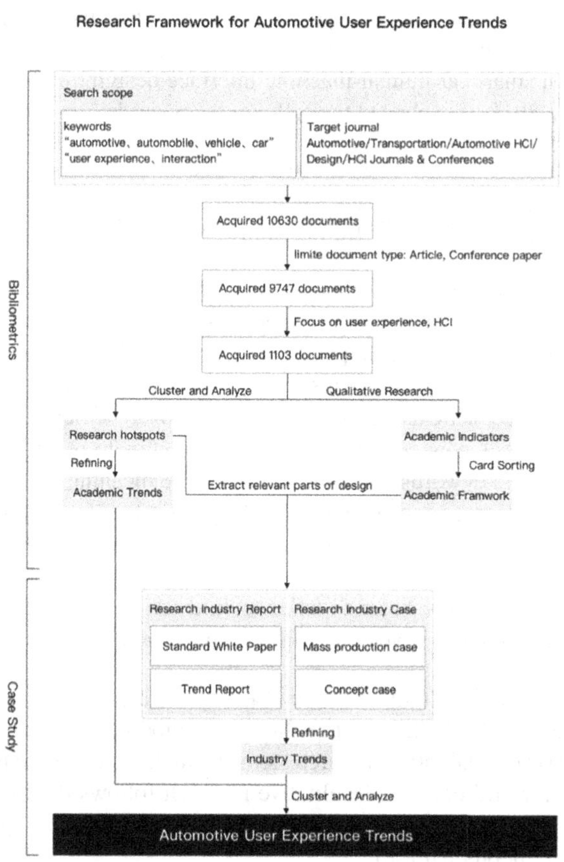

Fig. 1. Research framework for automotive user experience

Bibliometrics Research. Bibliometrics is a multifaceted discipline, structural, dynamic, evaluative, and predictive scientometrics is included in it [5]. It has continuously evolved and has been used to analyze patterns of academic communication and evaluate output of research widely [6]. The advantages of bibliometrics have been demonstrated by many studies. Firstly, compared with peer review and expert judgments, bibliometrics can provide quantitative indicators to ensure the objectivity of academic outputs through statistical analysis. For example, ZG. Liu et al. [7]. studied the structure and evolution of innovation system research with CiteSpace. Additionally, bibliometric analysis enables us to monitor and outline research content and trends on specific topics, which can assist young researchers in seeking future research directions [8]. Zhang Lie and Pan Husheng [9] of the Academy of Fine Arts of Tsinghua University used bibliometrics to select relevant documents from 5 commonly used citation index databases such as SSCI from 1985 to 2018 as the data basis. From the perspective of quantitative analysis of knowledge graphs, they focused on describing the current status, progress and trends of foreign interaction design disciplines, providing valuable reference and enlightenment for related researchers.

For the bibliometrics design of automotive user experience, the most important thing is to discover and determine the keywords of bibliometrics methods. According to the research project on smart car human-machine interface design trends jointly launched by us and Baidu in 2018, we selected the following keywords:

"vehicle" or "car" or "automotive" or "automobile"

And "user experience" or "UX" or "interaction" or "HCI" or "HMI".

Co-occurrence Word Analysis. Co-occurrence word analysis is to count the number of times a pair of words appear in the same paper. It is generally believed that if two keywords frequently appear in the same paper, it means that there is a close relationship between the two keywords. Based on this theory, we limited the time of literature data to 2010–2020, and then searched the core journals of Web of Science with the above keywords to find 11,821 papers and exported their complete records. After that, we cleaned the data of the keywords, cleaning out the same meaning and different expressions such as abbreviations, mixed Chinese and English, singular and plural, synonyms, synonyms, etc. Then the VOSviewer software was used to analyze these co-occurring words to obtain the co-occurring word clumps as shown in the figure below (see Fig. 2). It includes seven research topics: user experience, interaction outside the car, co-driving, simulation experiments, electric vehicles, disease, material & structure.

Qualitative Research. Qualitative research belongs to a paradigm of social science research, and some scholars believe that qualitative methodology belongs to pure theory. The theoretical basis of qualitative research stems from the interpretive methodology of knowledge and the world outlook. Qualitative research follows the inductive method, mainly collecting text and social information, and then transforming the obtained text and social data into theoretical forms.

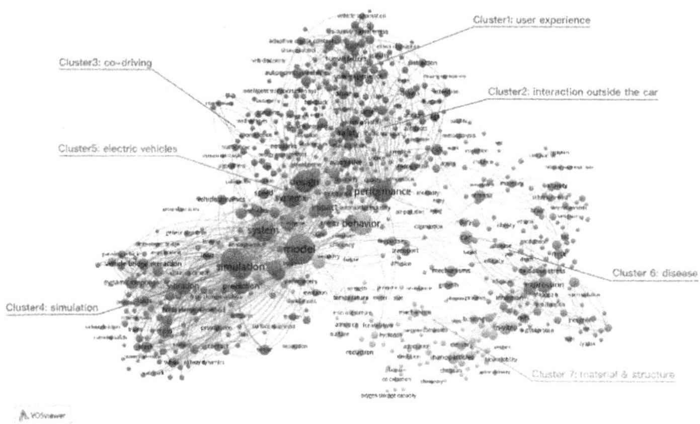

Fig. 2. Keyword co-occurrence analysis results

In terms of human-computer interface interaction, Tijana uses qualitative literature research to conduct a qualitative analysis of 148 interactive gesture-related research literature, and summarizes the main framework and development trend of current gesture interaction research. This article uses the method of literature qualitative research to analyze the literature of automobile user experience design. The following Table 1 gives a summary of the sources. On the basis of these papers, qualitative research on the design of automotive user experience is carried out.

Table 1. Origins of data for literature qualitative research

Field	Type	Data source
Car-related	Periodical/conference	Transportation PartA/C/F
Automotive HCI related		AutoUI (Automotive User Interfaces and Interactive Vehicular Applications)
HCI related		IUI (ACM International Conference on Intelligent User Interfaces). CHI (ACM Conference on Human Factors in Computing Systems). TOCHI (ACM Transactions on Computer-Human Interaction). IJHCI (International Journal of Human-computer Interaction) HCI (Human Computer Interaction)
Design related		Design Studies. Design Issue

Based on the results of above methods, we have organized the following research points and trend points as shown in the Table 2 below.

Table 2. Summary of research points and trend points

Level 1	Level 2	Level 3	Level 4
Human	Cognition	Workload	Haptic feedback can improve takeover efficiency and reduce load HMI learning cost for autonomous driving is high (control and display)
		Situation awareness	Providing relevant information prior to takeover can increase takeover awareness
		Personification	Uncanny valley theory Kindness & warmth
		Active interaction	Automated systems understand driver status Predict driver intent
	Behavior	Distraction	Degraded driving skills, participation in non-driving repeat (NDR) tasks, and "out-of-the-loop" situations with reduced driver awareness Gestures + HUD reduce distraction Multimodal feedback can reduce driver distraction, mental load and reaction time
		Driving performance	Visual and audible warnings are used in pedestrian warning systems to reduce collision risk and improve overall driver acceptance All multimodal combinations of audio, visual and haptic modes to alert drivers to events of varying urgency, more ways mean faster, more accurate responses, and a higher sense of urgency
	Emotions & experiences	Build trust between driver & vehicle	Driving assistance (requests based on human output) can derive model parameters to a greater extent to accurately determine user trust values Cultural background factors, situational environmental factors, and risk factors are also important research trends in the future

(*continued*)

Table 2. (*continued*)

Level 1	Level 2	Level 3	Level 4
		Driver emotion	Entertainment information can change driver's negative emotions Music is an important means of mediating driver's emotions
		Others	Manual driving turns into a horse-riding hobby Build emotional relationships Gamification design
Human-vehicle	Control	Voice	Compared with vision, voice interaction can increase driver's situational awareness Voice increases primary driving task performance and recall secondary tasks Voice interaction has a higher sense of security experience Personalized voice reminder systems are not only significant, but also enhance the monitoring of traffic conditions and decision-making about entering intersections
		Touch	Ensuring the usability of touch screen interaction is a necessary attribute of touch screen interaction Ultrasonic haptic feedback
		Somatosensory	Lots of auto companies invest in and research and develop in-car aerial gestures In-air gesture interaction has many advantages over other interaction methods Ultrasound feedback technology offers new opportunities for in-air gesture interaction

(*continued*)

Table 2. (*continued*)

Level 1	Level 2	Level 3	Level 4
		Multimodal	Multimodal feedback can reduce driver distraction, mental load and reaction time All multimodal combinations of audio, visual and haptic modes to alert drivers to events of varying urgency, more ways mean faster, more accurate responses, and a higher sense of urgency Visual and audible warnings are used in pedestrian warning systems to reduce collision risk and improve overall driver acceptance
	Display	Visual	Visual interaction forms can still cause users to reduce situational awareness Peripheral visual reminders can be used to improve reliability and increase synergy efficiency
		Light interaction	Peripheral light interaction is a good display method for driving speed perception The ambient light concept may also be applied to self-driving cars to enhance the driving experience while driving
	Feedback	Content	Uncertain information Explainable AI Convey context situation
		Carrier & Medium	The development of vehicle touch screen from resistive screen to capacitive screen and infrared screen with better control experience Multi-screen display Multi-device interconnection
Human-vehicle-environment	Physical environment	Interior space	Cab is a private space
		Outside space	Many institutions and enterprises use lights, LEDs and other displays to communicate with pedestrians Certain types of eHMIs (smiley faces, front brake lights, LED strips) need to be learned, while the text display is straightforward to understand

(*continued*)

Table 2. *(continued)*

Level 1	Level 2	Level 3	Level 4
	Social environment	User sociodemographic attributes	Social context is critical to designing self-driving car technology Demonstration and competitive awareness of young drivers
	Task environment	Change of task	The promise of autonomous driving is to engage drivers in tasks unrelated to driving Driving behavior is often not the most important thing in the car Human-machine cooperative driving New technology trends create a different dimension for driver-vehicle-environment relationship - restoration of situational awareness
		Change of identity	Degraded driving skills, participation in non-driving repeat (NDR) tasks, and "out-of-the-loop" situations with reduced driver awareness Interaction research in smart cars must be holistic extreme case

Case Study. Case study is a common method in the field of product design, and it is also one of the ways to quickly understand the classification of product characteristics and main trends. Robert K. Yin believes that the case study method is an empirical research method in the field of social sciences that parallels experimental methods, survey methods, and historical analysis methods. He believes that this method is suitable for studying events that occurred in the contemporary era but cannot be controlled by related factors.

The case analysis is very extensive. In terms of design science, a large number of entity companies and Internet companies have provided a large number of product samples, and certain mechanisms and specifications have been formed under the screening and iteration of the market. Well-known design competitions at home and abroad, such as The Red Dot Award, IF Award, and Golden Dot Award also provide a wealth of research samples for case studies in the design field.

For the "Automotive Intelligent and Interactive Experience Research", the scope of the survey focuses on the actions of traditional automobiles, new forces, related suppliers and technology-driven enterprises. A total of 51 automobile companies, 28 suppliers, 93 automobiles, and 151 automobile human-computer interaction related cases are investigated. The case research data is as follows (Table 3).

Table 3. Origins of data for case study

Traditional car				
EXEED BMW AIWAYS Chery Cadillac Chevrolet Acura Nissan	Geely Weimar Audi Pioneer Haval Dongfeng Buick Porsche	Leapmotor Ford Hyundai WEY Benz Jaguar Peugeot Lexus	Alfa Romeo Range Rover Junma Mitsubishi Daimler Toyota Volkswagen BYD	RINSPEED Renault Honda GAC BAIC JAC Skyrim Pentium
New forces	Supplies		Technology-driven enterprises	
Roewe Byton Xiaopeng Tesla Lixiang Volvo Nio	Cerence Cocoa Zejing Electronics Border WayRay Carrot Future black technology	Bosch Desay SV American Garmin Zebra Nuance Faure UNTOUCH	Tencent Uber Waymo Tmall Amazon IFlytek Alibaba Sogou	SenseTime Affectiva Synaptics Google mainland Baidu Semcon Gaode Map

Trends Cluster and Analyze. Facing a large amount of research text and network data, traditional content research methods are no longer applicable. Cluster analysis methods based on text data mining are increasingly used in data extraction and analysis. Text Data Mining, also known as text knowledge discovery, is a process of obtaining implicit and latent patterns from text. Cluster analysis is widely used in text mining research, and is often used in the analysis of the hotspots and development trends of future research. This study uses cluster analysis to analyze the research trends of automotive user experience. Initially, 115 trend points were formed. Through clustering induction, they were refined to 8 trend directions.

3 Eight Trends in Automotive User Experience

In this research, data visualization of 8 trends in automotive user experience was carried out. Additionally, trend framework chart and a summary chart of the 8 trends were formed (see Fig. 3).

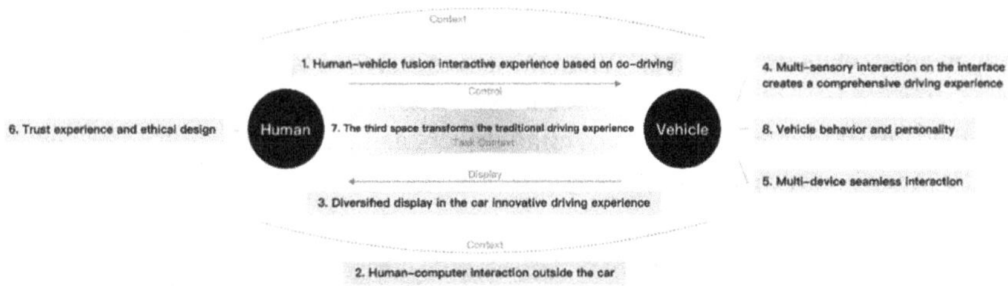

Fig. 3. Schematic diagram of the relationship between the eight trends

3.1 Human-Vehicle Fusion Interactive Experience Based on Co-driving

Before the realization of fully automated driving, cars will be in the L3–L4 automation level for a long time, and co-driving will become the mainstream of automotive human-computer interaction for a long time. Deepening the degree of human-vehicle integration and interaction through the use of flexible control rights, natural takeover and handover, and biometrics and perception based on emotional computing will become the trend of future development. The trend diagram is as follows (see Fig. 4).

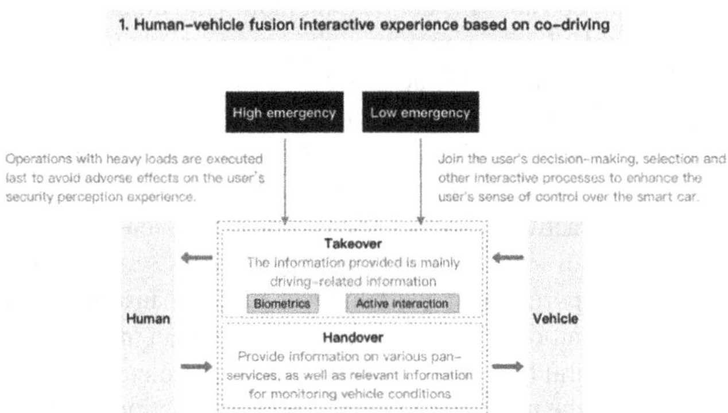

Fig. 4. Human-vehicle fusion interactive experience based on co-driving

Differentiated User Experience Design with Different Control Rights. Control is the core element of smart car user experience, and it is also a core element to enhance the user's sense of trust in the smart car. In the case of co-driving, the control will be switched between the driver and the self-driving vehicle. In the case of different control rights, the car user experience design should also be different: when the driver has the control right, the information provided by the user interface is mainly driving-related information. When the control is transferred to the self-driving vehicle, the roles of people and vehicles have changed. The role of the driver is transformed into a supervisor, and the nature of the driving task is changed from "action" to "monitoring" or "performing other tasks." The interface design will provide various types of general-service information, while providing relevant information for monitoring the condition of the vehicle. For example, in manual driving mode, the Peugeot E-Legend's display will show what is usually needed when driving a car. When the driver wants to take a break, he switches to the autopilot mode, and the display screen also switches from driving-related information to the "entertainment mode", providing drivers and passengers with entertainment information such as movies and scenery (see Fig. 5).

Fig. 5. Peugeot E-Legend

Context-Based Interactive Design of the Handover Process. The takeover and handover of smart car control rights is the main task of car interaction and experience design. It is necessary to consider the context, including the urgency, the human factor and other related elements. For example, in a high emergency situation, the intelligent system will assume more control. In the process of takeover and handover, the operations with greater operational load and cognitive load can be executed at the end of the task, avoiding too many operations at the same time that will adversely affect the user's safety perception experience. In low-emergency situations, users are not affected by urgent tasks, and interactive processes such as user decision-making and selection can be added to the handover process to enhance the user's sense of control over the smart car. Due to the importance of the handover process, instinctive, intuitive, and minimally conscious human-computer interaction is having an important impact on the handover [10] such a natural takeover handover can be completed with less awareness of the driver. At present, the natural human-computer interaction technology based on contextual metaphor is gradually mature, and the natural takeover handover design will become one of the main directions in the future.

Affective Computing-Based Biometrics and Perceptual Flexible Human-Vehicle Relationship. In terms of technology, the car monitors various biological characteristics of the user through the biometric technology based on contextual computing, so as to actively analyze the interactive context, make active interaction behaviors, and build a flexible human-vehicle relationship. In the field of smart cars, when the biometric system detects that the driver's physical state is not suitable for driving, it needs to be reminded. In this way, the "car-to-person" active interaction is constructed, which automatically reduces the driver's burden of "person-to-car" interaction during driving. And when necessary, it gradually controls the driving rights of the vehicle through the background to realize the conversion of flexible control rights.

3.2 Human-Computer Interaction Outside the Car

Self-driving cars, especially driverless cars, will inevitably have relationships with pedestrians, people in other vehicles, and people in infrastructure during road operation. For example, when a driverless car is driving to a crosswalk, because there is no driver in the car, its driving intention needs to be transmitted to people outside the car to ensure traffic safety and pedestrian experience. In this case, human-computer interaction outside the car has become an inevitable and important trend (see Fig. 6).

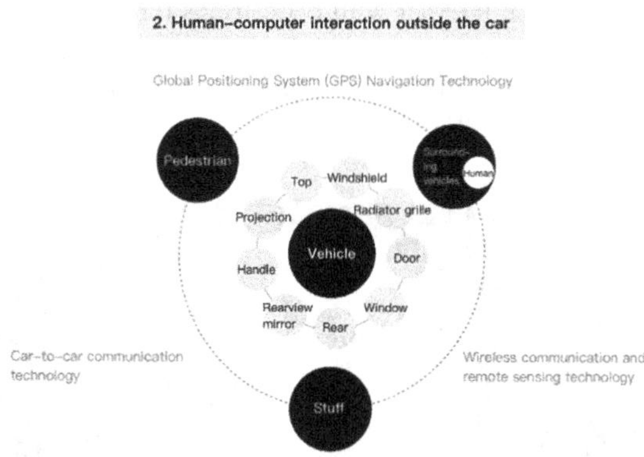

Fig. 6. Human-computer interaction outside the car

Diversified Positions of Human-Computer Interaction Interfaces Outside the Car. The screen is the main medium for human-computer interaction outside the car. With the rapid development of display technology, especially the development of special-shaped screens, curved screens, and flexible screens, as well as the development of projection technology outside the car, it has become technically possible to project on the car body and the ground. At present, there are many different positions of human-computer interaction interface outside the car, mainly located on the top of the car, windshield, radiator grille, door and road surface [11], including car windows, the rear of the car, and some special parts, such as Rearview mirrors, handles and other areas. For different areas, there will be some changes in the design, especially the outside information display will be relatively affected by the environment. Therefore, it is necessary to fully consider the impact of external factors such as different times and climates. The information displayed on the top of the car, radiator grille and other areas that are more affected by the weather has higher purity and brightness, while the information displayed on the windows and doors of the areas less affected by the weather has relatively low purity and brightness.

Peripheral Interaction. Driverless cars can communicate with other surrounding cars, people, and things by integrating global positioning system (GPS) navigation technology, car-to-car communication technology, wireless communication, and remote sensing technology to form peripheral interactions. Peripheral interaction allows the vehicle to transmit basic information such as speed, position, and direction. It also allows the vehicle to communicate with all possible "connections" nearby, including cyclists, traffic lights, etc., so as to help the vehicle really "see" (turns and corners). Peripheral interaction can expand the content and scope of information transmission outside the car, so that the surrounding pedestrians, cars, etc. can obtain richer surrounding scene information, not just the information inside the car. At the level of human-computer interaction design, the complexity of information dimensions makes the information design of peripheral interaction in the future may undergo tremendous changes. Information architecture and information hierarchy design will be the core of peripheral interaction design. For example, it is necessary to consider the multi-level use of text information and pattern information, dynamic information and static information, and different color information. For example, Arrival can interact with pedestrians through voice recognition and the glass surface on the display screen around the car. Pedestrians can query related line information, surrounding traffic information, and obtain information about the station surrounding the next station (see Fig. 7).

Fig. 7. Arrival bus

3.3 Diversified Display in the Car Innovative Driving Experience

The rapid development of display technology in the car is that its display position and display methods are all diversified, which reduces the driver's cognitive load, improves the driver's driving efficiency, and significantly improves the user's driving experience (see Fig. 8).

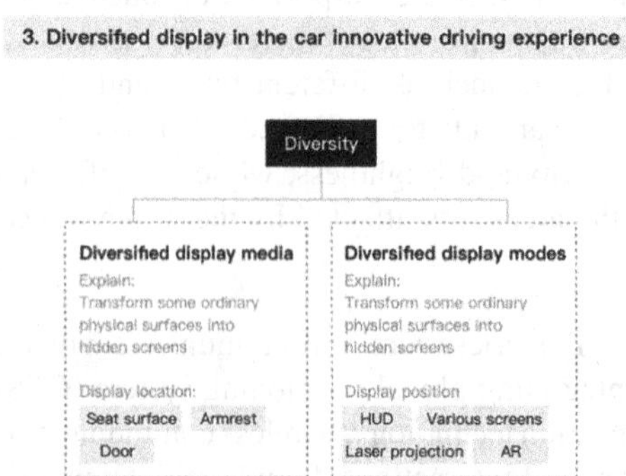

Fig. 8. Diversified display in the car innovative driving experience

Ubiquitous Smart Surface Display Design. Smart surfaces transform some ordinary physical surfaces into hidden screens. The advantage is that these surfaces can exist anywhere: seat surfaces, armrests, doors, etc. Passengers can use the screen in any place in the car, which greatly improves the rear passengers. It saves space in the car while experiencing it. The design of the smart surface is closely related to the choice of interior materials. For example, the surface material of the fabric is difficult to display with high accuracy, but it can create different interactive effects. The hard surface material is ordinary in physical appearance but can be displayed with high precision. For example, BMW VISION INEXT uses smart fabric interior materials (see Fig. 9).

Fig. 9. BMW VISION INEXT

Integrated Design of Multiple Visual Display. Different display devices and display methods such as head-up display, augmented reality, laser projection, and various screen displays (LCD screen, flexible screen, special-shaped screen, curved screen, etc.) continue to enter the interior space of smart cars. These display forms are very different, which easily causes the complexity and conflict of the internal space display. Thereby affecting the corresponding design. Therefore, it is necessary to integrate different display methods so as to reduce the interference to the driver while the information transmission efficiency is high. At the same time, it is necessary to consider related issues such as interconnection of multiple display devices, consistent experience, and vision.

3.4 Multi-sensory Interaction on the Interface Creates a Comprehensive Driving Experience

From the perspective of smart cars, multi-sensory interaction based on a multi-channel user interface can provide a rich perceptual experience for the driving space, and has become an important factor in creating a comprehensive driving experience (see Fig. 10).

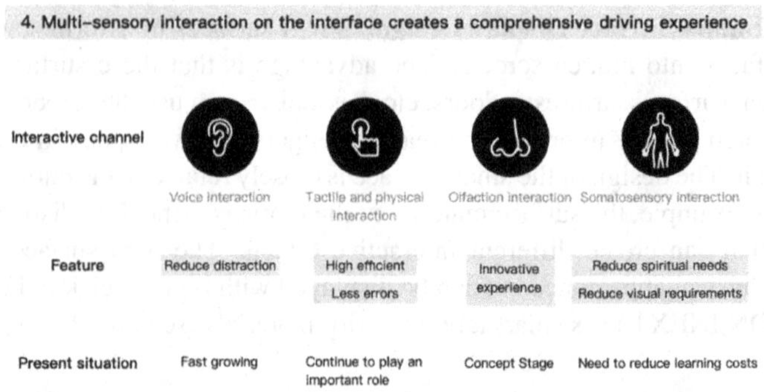

Fig. 10. Multi-sensory interaction on the interface creates a comprehensive driving experience

Fast-Growing Voice Interaction. In-vehicle voice interaction is intuitive, fast and personalized [12]. Compared with the human-computer interaction method based on "touch screen control", the human-computer interaction method based on "listening-speaking" can reduce distraction and sight deviation in the context of car driving, thereby effectively improving the level of driving safety. With the continuous improvement of voice technology, intelligent voice systems are becoming the mainstream way of human-computer interaction in automobiles, providing users with a safe, convenient and pleasant experience. Compared with the interaction between touch screens and buttons, voice is the interaction method that takes the least attention and operation of the user. Based on the design principles of reducing distraction and focusing on driving, the voice interactive experience is encouraged. The sound interaction design in the car must first consider the influence and interference of the complex noise environment in the car on the sound interaction. simultaneously simulate the real dialogue scene, and compose the dialogue and establish the interaction logic and flow according to the scene, so as to achieve a more natural and reasonable sound interaction experience. Due to the characteristics of the information dissemination of voice interaction, it may affect other occupants in the car and cause privacy concerns, and different sounds will produce masking and differential perception effects, so avoiding the interference of voice interaction becomes its human-computer interaction design. Since voice interaction has the characteristics of information dissemination, it may affect other occupants in the car and cause privacy concerns. In addition, different sounds will produce masking and differential perception effects, so avoiding sound interactions from interfering with other passengers has become the core issue of human-computer interaction design. In addition, sound information has a strong time characteristic. The response time of humans to sound will lag between 0.2–0.5 s, which poses a certain risk to the car driving situation. Therefore, when designing in-vehicle sound interaction, it is necessary to design the time compensation for the sound information, such as increasing the duration of the information.

Tactile and Physical Interaction will Continue to Play an Important Role. Haptics and physical interaction are the main methods of human-computer interaction in traditional automobiles. Although the rapid development of digital technology has produced a large number of new interaction channels, traditional tactile and physical interaction will still play an important role in the future automotive human-computer interaction interface due to its high operating efficiency and relatively low error rate. On the one hand, the feedback is enhanced in the existing touch screen control. Traditional touch screen system interface elements can only be seen, but not felt. The loss of tactile feedback weakens the user's experience of virtual elements on the screen [13]. On the other hand, innovate ways to enhance tactile perception, such as steering wheel vibration, waist tactile vibration, etc. Shadan Sadeghian Borojeni [14] and others designed a steering wheel with a vibration signal to test its reminder function in the takeover request. The results show that due to the deterministic effect of the vibration signal, the overall workload rating of the driver is reduced.

Olfaction and Somatosensory Interaction Design. Compared with traditional touch-based interaction, gesture interaction based on somatic perception reduces the mental and visual requirements of the driver [15]. Just by making a general gesture in the air, the driver can adjust the temperature in the car, choose the next song or decline the call. However, due to the novelty of aerial movement technology, people's understanding of the influence of aerial movement on driving performance, visual attention and psychological load is still incomplete. For example, being unfamiliar with the gesture system will have a negative impact on the driver's lane keeping ability and mental load [16]. At the same time, due to the separation of the user's hand from the interface, the user will lack a sense of control over the interface. These are additional factors that reduce user satisfaction, safety, and gesture usability. Therefore, the gesture design needs to conform to the general public's understanding of the meaning expressed by a certain gesture, so as to reduce the user's learning cost. Compared with other interaction methods, olfactory interaction is currently mainly in the conceptual design of related enterprises.

3.5 Seamless Interaction Between Multiple Devices

Mobile devices and wearable devices as carry-on items are the basic needs of human travel. Therefore, a large number of mobile devices (such as mobile phones, Pads, laptops, etc.) will enter smart cars. How to achieve seamless interaction between multi-device systems and cars has become an important issue in automotive user experience design (see Fig. 11).

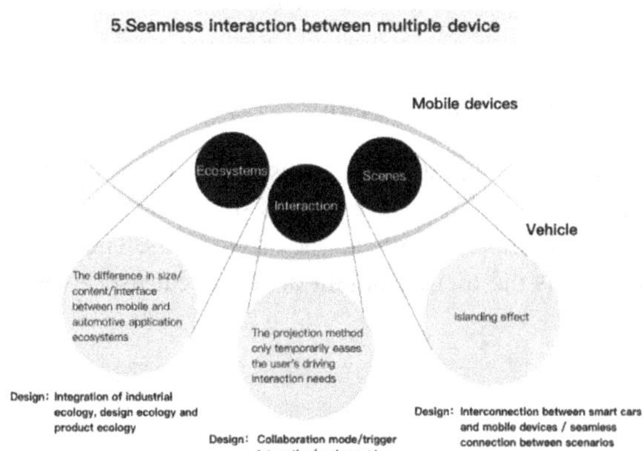

Fig. 11. Multi-device seamless interaction

New Ecological Integration of Mobile Terminals and Vehicles. In terms of design ecology, the application ecosystems of mobile terminals and automobiles are very different in size, content, and interface. The migration cost is also relatively high. How to achieve the integration of the industrial ecology, design ecology and product ecology of mobile phones and car machines is a key issue in automotive user experience design in this field. The concept of "people-car-home" smart interconnection scene was proposed by BMW, Volkswagen and other car companies as early as 2016. Since then, Skyrim, Toyota & Panasonic, Geeke, Geely and others have also proposed smart ecosystems.

Interactive Integration of Mobile Devices and Cars. Currently, mobile devices such as mobile phones and smart cars are interconnected by screen projection, which only temporarily eases the user's driving interaction needs. The relationship between mobile terminals and cars is undergoing tremendous changes. At the same time, the mobile phone is the user's personal belongings, which can be online 24 h a day and fully control the car. Therefore, the future integration of mobile phones and cars at the interactive level should fully consider the human-computer interaction between cross-devices. In the triggering interaction mechanism, it is necessary to fully consider the active and passive factors that are triggered by the interaction between the car and the mobile device. In addition to this, we must also consider the interaction of the device in the spatial relationship, such as considering the placement of the device, people's habits of using mobile phones in the car, and so on. For example, Ideal one's new car WeChat supports voice announcements and voice responses, and the car owner can also wake up WeChat through the buttons on the steering wheel or voice. There is no need to look down at the phone information during driving, which is more convenient and safer for the driver (see Fig. 12).

Fig. 12. Lixiang one

3.6 Trust Experience and Ethical Design

At present, people still have a great sense of distrust in the perception of autonomous vehicles. A large number of studies have proved that people's trust in smart cars has significant shortcomings compared with people driving cars. Therefore, how to improve the design of smart cars is the main problem of future car user experience design (see Fig. 13).

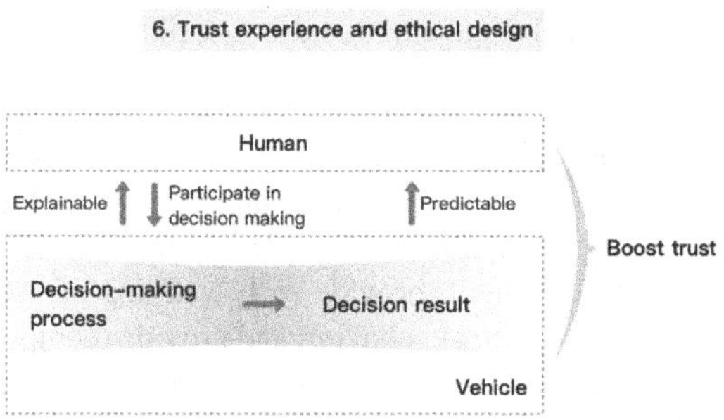

Fig. 13. Trust experience and ethical design

Explainable AI. A large number of user experience studies have shown that the transparency of autonomous driving systems [17] has a direct and positive impact on trust. Therefore, it is necessary to explain the intention behind these behaviors to users in a correct way in the design of automobile human-computer interaction interface [18]. In the behavior design of autonomous driving, it is necessary to explain the behavior of autonomous driving so that users can understand the intention of the car behavior. For example, as a private car, Waymo one tends to convey the car's understanding of road conditions to users in a concise and hierarchical form of information visualization, so as to arouse users' sense of trust (see Fig. 14).

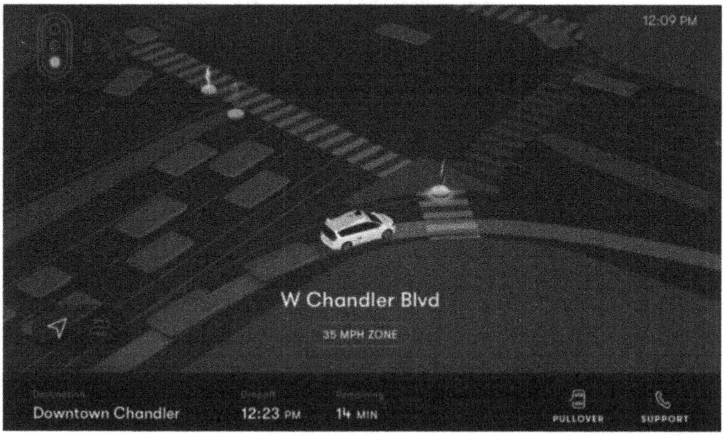

Fig. 14. Waymo one

Human Participation in the Interactive Decision-Making Process. The human-computer interaction of future self-driving cars may not be completely divorced from human automatic decision-making and fully automatic driving processes. People should still maintain the main body and core position in the operation mechanism of the intelligent system of the intelligent car. Therefore, the participation of humans in the training of the intelligent system and the guidance and correction of the system is of great significance for autonomous vehicles.

Predictable Interaction and Ethics. In addition to being understandable, the future behavior design of smart cars needs to conform to human's psychological expectations, especially the prediction of potential future risks has become a very core content. For example, smart cars should be able to provide early warning of possible failures and the consequences of driving equipment behavior, and provide prompts for traffic service information. In the prediction of car behavior, the prediction of ethical decision-making results is the key to the design of future driverless cars. For example, the Moral Machine Experiment completed by the Massachusetts Institute of Technology in the United States is typical research on ethical decision-making algorithms.

3.7 The Third Space Transforms the Traditional Driving Experience

The car is no longer just a tool for travel, but a relatively independent third space that cannot be obtained in homes and offices. During the unmanned driving of the car, the driver can complete other tasks, which reflects the inevitable transformation of the car as the third personal space. Therefore, the space of future smart cars is essentially a space beyond travel (see Fig. 15).

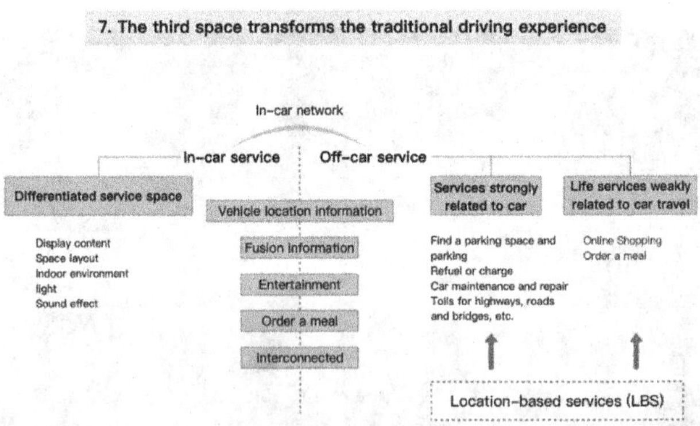

Fig. 15. The third space transforms the traditional driving experience

In-car Scene Beyond Travel. The concept of service space is the biggest difference between smart cars and traditional mobile devices (such as mobile phones). Smart cars can provide users with differentiated service spaces through changes in display content, space layout, interior environment, lighting, and sound effects. Scenarios will drive smart cars and interactive design to a specific combination of functions based on usage orientation [19]. Design needs to consider how to flexibly define the function of each module for different scenarios, and appropriately migrate the characteristic elements in the scene to form a new interior scene, like the same display area is given different functions in different modes. For example, the interior design of the Volvo 360c concept is derived from the bedroom and includes four driving modes: sleeping environment, mobile office, living room and entertainment space. In office mode, the window can be used as a projection screen. In entertainment mode, the window can be used as a home theater (see Fig. 16).

Fig. 16. Volvo. 360c concept

Socialization and Personalization. In the future, users will connect with the outside world through the in-vehicle network on the one hand, and provide consumers with a personalized experience based on functions such as vehicle location information, fusion information, entertainment, meal ordering, and interconnection. On the other hand, more people enter the car, and the space inside the car will provide users with a socialized experience because of the integration of more intimate social relationships. Under this trend, how to meet the different needs of different users according to the characteristics of autonomous vehicles has become the key. For example, adjust the direction of the seat arrangement to promote/isolate communication between passengers.

3.8 Vehicle Behavior and Personality

The so-called "personality" refers to a consistent role image inferred from the comprehensive characteristics of the user during the interaction with the agent. In the future, the expression and design dimensions of intelligent humanoids will be more comprehensive, and drivers and pedestrians can feel more vivid intelligent car humanoids (see Fig. 17).

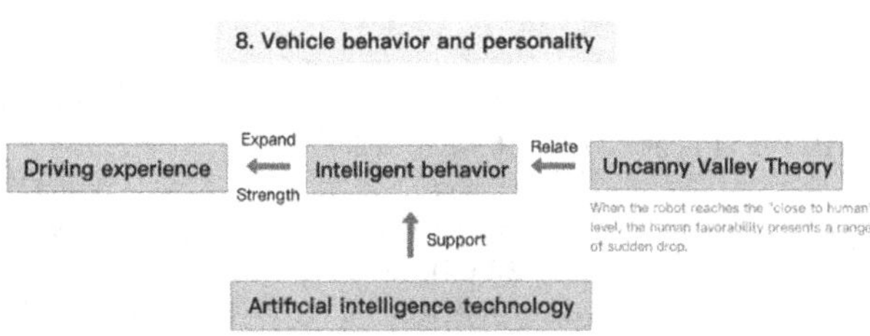

Fig. 17. Vehicle behavior and personality

Intelligent Behavior and Experience. In recent years, artificial intelligence-driven machines have increasingly integrated into our society [20], bringing new experiences and feelings to users. For smart cars, how to expand and enhance the driving experience through artificial intelligence technology so that the car becomes the object of emotion again is a problem that needs to be considered in the design of smart behavior. For example, how the smart car communicates with the driver and how to learn the behavior of the driver and even form a specific driving style.

Personification. Artificial intelligence can provide accurate user demand information. In the interactive communication with users, how to improve the user experience is an urgent problem that artificial intelligence needs to solve. Anthropomorphic artificial intelligence has become an important breakthrough in solving user experience, and therefore will become an inevitable trend of future development. Research in the context of human-computer interaction has shown that the use of human features such as language, eye contact or gestures can increase the persuasive power of agents [21]. In addition, anthropomorphic information can promote people's perception of self-driving cars as social subjects and enhance their trust in these cars [22].

4 Conclusion

The continuous development of automobiles has brought about huge changes in driving behavior, so the research on automotive user experience has become more and more important. This research derives eight major trends in the field of automotive user experience through the analysis of practical cases in the industry and combined with literature measurement. The research results can provide directional opinions for the research and development of academia and industry, help relevant researchers grasp the latest trends in driving, and determine or change the direction of future research. The innovation of this research lies in: Although the prediction of the future is full of uncertainty, this research innovatively uses bibliometric methods to collect and cluster research hotspots in the field of automotive user experience on the basis of literature and case studies. In this way, future trends in this field are put forward to ensure that the research results are more objective and convincing.

References

1. 高晗, 李博, 韩挺.: 未来汽车人机交互系统发展趋势研究. 包装工程 **39**(22), 22–28 (2018). https://doi.org/10.19554/j.cnki.1001-3563.2018.22.005
2. 谭浩, 孙家豪, 关岱松, 周茉莉, 齐健平, 赵颖.: 智能汽车人机交互发展趋势研究. 包装工程 **40**(20), 32–42 (2019). https://doi.org/10.19554/j.cnki.1001-3563.2019.20.005
3. 张亮: 图书馆预测学论纲. 现代情报 **30**(05), 18–20 (2010)
4. 蒋建华: 预测学在图书馆藏书建设中的应用初探. 江苏图书馆学报 **988**(02), 15–18+10. https://doi.org/10.16810/j.cnki.1672-514x.1988.02.004
5. Mao, G., Liu, X., Du, H., Zuo, J., Wang, L.: Way forward for alternative energy research: a bibliometric analysis during 1994–2013. Renew. Sustain. Energy Rev. **48**, 276–286 (2015)

6. Hammarfelt, B., Rushforth, A.D.: Indicators as judgment devices: an empirical study of citizen bibliometrics in research evaluation. Res. Eval. **26**(3), 169–180 (2017)
7. Liu, Z.G., Yin, Y., Liu, W.D., Dunford, M.: Visualizing the intellectual structure and evolution of innovation systems research: a bibliometric analysis. Scientometrics**103**(1), 135–158 (2015). https://doi.org/10.1007/s11192-014-1517-y
8. Wang, J.J., Chen, H., Rogers, D.S., Ellram, L.M., Grawe, S.J.: A bibliometric analysis of reverse logistics research (1992–2015) and opportunities for future research. Int. J. Phys. Distrib. Logist. Manag. 47(8), 666–687 (2017)
9. 张烈, 潘沪生.: 国外交互设计学科的研究进展与趋势—基于SSCI等引文索引的文献图谱分析. 装饰 (05), 96–99 (2019). https://doi.org/10.16272/j.cnki.cn11-1392/j.2019.05.020
10. Ramm, S., Giacomin, J., Robertson, D., Malizia, A.: A first approach to understanding and measuring naturalness in driver-car interaction. In: Proceedings of the 6th International Conference on Automotive User Interfaces and Interactive Vehicular Applications, pp. 1–10 (2014)
11. Fridman, L., Mehler, B., Xia, L., Yang, Y., Facusse, L.Y., Reimer, B.: To walk or not to walk: crowdsourced assessment of external vehicle-to-pedestrian displays. arXiv preprint arXiv: 1707.02698 (2017)
12. Dasgupta, R.: Voice User Interface Design: Moving from GUI to Mixed Modal Interaction (2018)
13. Richter, H., Ecker, R., Deisler, C., Butz, A.: HapTouch and the 2+1 state model: potentials of haptic feedback on touch based in-vehicle information systems. In: Proceedings of the 2nd International Conference on Automotive User Interfaces and Interactive Vehicular Applications, pp. 72–79 (2010)
14. Borojeni, S.S., Wallbaum, T., Heuten, W., Boll, S.: Comparing shape-changing and vibrotactile steering wheels for take-over requests in highly automated driving. In: Proceedings of the 9th International Conference on Automotive User Interfaces and Interactive Vehicular Applications, pp. 221–225, September 2017
15. Kajastila, R., Lokki, T.: Eyes-free interaction with free-hand gestures and auditory menus. Int. J. Hum. Comput. Stud. **71**(5), 627–640 (2013)
16. Choi, J.K., Ji, Y.G.: Investigating the importance of trust on adopting an autonomous vehicle. Int. J. Hum.-Comput. Interact. **31**(10), 692–702 (2015)
17. Reimer, B., Mehler, B., Dobres, J., Coughlin, J.F.: The effects of a production level "voice-command" interface on driver behavior: summary findings on reported workload, physiology, visual attention, and driving performance. Technical report, p. 17. Massachusetts Institute of Technology, Cambridge, MA (2013)
18. Koo, J., Kwac, J., Ju, W., Steinert, M., Leifer, L., Nass, C.: Why did my car just do that? Explaining semi-autonomous driving actions to improve driver understanding, trust, and performance. Int. J. Interact. Des. Manuf. (IJIDeM) **9**(4), 269–275 (2014). https://doi.org/10.1007/s12008-014-0227-2
19. Trautmann, L., Piros, A., Hámornik, B.: Handling human factors in car interior design. Hum. Behav. Des. 113–124 (2019)
20. Rahwan, I., et al.: Machine behaviour. Nature **568**(7753), 477–486 (2019)
21. Ham, J., Midden, C.J.: A persuasive robot to stimulate energy conservation: the influence of positive and negative social feedback and task similarity on energy-consumption behavior. Int. J. Soc. Robot. **6**(2), 163–171 (2014)
22. Niu, D., Terken, J., Eggen, B.: Anthropomorphizing information to enhance trust in autonomous vehicles. Hum. Factors Ergon. Manuf. Serv. Ind. **28**(6), 352–359 (2018)

Research on the Similarity Design of Rail Vehicles Based on the Perspective of Regional Culture

Honglei Lu(✉)

Product Design, Department of Design, School of Art, Anhui University, No. 111, Jiulong Road, Hefei 230601, Anhui Province, China
luhongleidesign@gmail.com

Abstract. Background Along with the rapid development of economy, the cultural boundaries of different places are slowly broken down, making different cultures in the trend of integration. At the same time, the design based on local culture is also changing, and the phenomenon of design style convergence is becoming more and more serious, and the study of regional design has gradually become one of the main trends in the development of industrial design today. This study is mainly intended to use a combination of literature, comprehensive analysis, questionnaire, experimental research, shape grammar and other methods to carry out research. (1) Literature research method: to search and collect relevant standards, research reports, books and academic papers related to urban rail vehicles, train modeling design, design genes, product modeling design, etc., to obtain as much relevant literature as possible, so as to provide the basis and supporting materials for the research of Hefei rail vehicle design genes. (2) Comprehensive analysis method: The domestic and foreign rail vehicles with distinctive features are used as cases, and the innovation and importance of design genes in the appearance design of urban rail vehicles is clarified by analyzing the connection between their styling characteristics and brand image. (3) Experimental research method: select designers and the general public as experimental samples, obtain important modeling features of existing rail vehicles through eye-tracking experiments, and extract features as modeling design genes by line analysis method. (4) Shape grammar: The shape grammar is used to deduce the shape design genes to obtain new shapes, and finally the design practice of Hefei rail vehicles is carried out by combining the shape design theory with the relevant specifications of vehicle design. This study expects to explore the regional culture through systematic and scientific research. In particular, it highlights the expression of the inner cultural heritage of the traditional regional cultural symbols of Huizhou. Firstly, the background, significance, research method and proposed innovation of the study are elaborated, and then the regional culture is taken as the starting point to dig deeper into its extension and connotation, which is taken as the theoretical framework of the whole text to ensure its unity, regularity and logicality in the research process. Secondly, we introduce typical rail transportation design cases and analyze the design concepts and cultural characteristics of German and French rail transportation systems as well as Chinese rail transportation in a horizontal way, and conclude that cultural connotation has become an important means to enhance the added value of products, and that cultural appeal is feasible for rail transportation

P.-L. P. Rau (Ed.): HCII 2022, LNCS 13314, pp. 202–211, 2022.
https://doi.org/10.1007/978-3-031-06053-3_14

design and is the direction of rail transportation design development. Summarize the method of rail transportation design oriented to regional culture. Prepare the technical pavement for the subsequent design of itself. Again, while presenting and analyzing the typical Chongqing regional cultural elements, this paper introduces the design concept of regional design, which is also an important research method cited and applied in this paper. Then, we analyze the cultural demands, social influences and application prospects of Hefei rail transportation design, and summarize the main entry points of the design, so as to provide theoretical references and methodological guidelines for the subsequent design.

Keywords: Regional culture · Rail transportation · Design strategy · Modeling design

1 Introduction

Since the 19th Party Congress, the construction of socialism with Chinese characteristics has entered a new era, and the report of the 19th Congress mentioned that "without a high degree of cultural self-confidence, without cultural prosperity, there is no great rejuvenation of the Chinese nation". General Secretary Xi also said "four self-confidence" Chinese cultural self-confidence is a more basic, broader and deeper self-confidence, cultural self-confidence is the most fundamental self-confidence. In recent years, with the expansion of urban scale, the rapid development of urban rail transit, the huge volume of urban rail transit vehicles has become an important part of the urban landscape. However, at present, China's urban public transportation system generally lacks overall image planning, connection and integration with urban humanistic environment, and systemic, cultural and regional characteristics. Therefore, how to build and disseminate the regional culture of urban rail transit vehicles becomes a problem that requires designers and engineers to think together.

As the first city in the world to build a subway line, London has a history of 150 years of rail transit design and construction since 1863. Foreign rail transit design has made tremendous progress, both in terms of the exterior shape, color matching, and functional combination of transportation, as well as in terms of its cultural connotations given. Many cities have chosen station architectural designs from the unique and charming works of masters, not only making rail transit a symbol of the city and making it an example of a structure to beautify the urban landscape, but also paying more attention to reflecting the rich local cultural connotation and better integrating with the regional environment. The rapid development of society and the rapid advancement of the times have created rail transit. Looking at the transformation of rail transit stations around the world, whether combined with existing buildings or built independently, each classic design has its own unique architectural style in different countries in the world and in different time periods, showing the construction of a city and the development of architectural technology, and also recording the architectural and cultural trends in It also records the embodiment of architectural and cultural trends in different historical stages, presenting the unique humanities of different cities and the unique views of architects on urban culture, and playing a role in driving the design of future generations.

The development of society and the progress of the times have led to the rapid development of rail transit. From the evolution of the architectural forms of rail transit stations in the world, whether the design of individual buildings or the design combined with existing buildings, the design of rail transit stations in different periods and countries have shown unique architectural styles, and these different styles and characteristics have witnessed the development of cities and the progress of architectural technology, and also recorded the cultural trends in the field of architecture at different stages, including the humanistic style of cities and the understanding of architects for urban culture, which have deeply influenced the design styles of later generations [1].

The purpose of this study is to inject cultural elements into the design of rail transportation, so that it can invariably fit the regional characteristics of Hefei, and to integrate the elements extracted from the regional symbols into the design, so that the rail transportation of Hefei can become a typical symbol of the city and build an identity in the spiritual level of people's life. At the same time, this paper pays special attention to the overall matching of the color and shape of the rail transportation, and will have in-depth consideration and generalization on the coordination, wholeness and matching of the design.

In the field of rail vehicle design, due to the extremely strict technical requirements of high-speed trains, some similar "international" style features will appear in their styling design, and at the same time, because high-speed trains often run in regions with large spatial distance, Lijun [2] and Wang Zhiquan (2016) believe that the distinctive The distinctive regional culture is not obviously reflected [1, 3]. In contrast, urban rail vehicles run as a flowing landscape in a specific city space, which should be free from the phenomenon of "pan-culture". It is believed that regional culture can only be applied if it is perceived. Therefore, according to the regional cultural characteristics of different cities, a unique, specific and clear modeling language is used to design and organically integrate with the existing human environment of the city. For example, the Chengdu suspended monorail takes giant pandas as the main design element, imitating the shape and color scheme of pandas in a lifelike way [4, 5]. Harbin, on the other hand, uses the color of ice and snow as the base, embellished with snowflake patterns, and integrates the local climate elements for the train according to the local climate characteristics [6, 7]. Hefei is a key city in the central part of the country, because in the current form of cultural convergence, the rail vehicle design that incorporates regional culture shows its preciousness.

2 Literature Review

At present, domestic experts and scholars have different emphasis and expressions on the study of regional culture, and combined with specific research directions, this topic believes that urban regional culture refers to the cultural carrier of urban characteristic areas with distinctive characteristics within a certain time frame, and with the process of urban modernization, the connotation of urban regional culture is being extended outward, which includes language characteristics, leisure and entertainment, in addition to clothing, food, housing and transportation [8, 9]. The scope of regional culture is expanding, it is necessary to systematically analyze and study the composition of regional culture, and find out the most representative regional culture carrier to be used in the design of rail vehicles [10, 11]. It is necessary to maximize the cultural experience of regional culture to users.

Foreign Research Status

Not only in China, foreign research on the theory of regional culture and its application is also very extensive, and foreign scholars often use the combination of regional culture and other aspects such as economy and consciousness for the study and application of specific characteristics of a region [12]. For example, the French TVG high-speed train design focuses on luxury and fashion, and the whole design focuses on interior decoration, which is full of French national romanticism; the design of the tram shape in Lyon, France, combines regional industrial culture with vehicle design, and the silkworm baby shape is deeply popular, and the Melbourne, Australia, tram design integrates urban sculpture culture into the train design. Claudio, through the study of the culture and strict attention to the link between ideological production to analyze political and economic regional cultural differentiation and homogenization [13]; Brons proposes culture as a behavioral map that can be indirectly measured through silver analysis and in this way explores five dimensions of Dutch regional culture [14]; Monnion designs clothing from the perspective of regional tourism culture, which not only satisfies user needs, but also highlights the role of cultural souvenirs [15] (Fig. 1).

Fig. 1. Rail vehicle design, Lyon, France, TVG, Melbourne, Australia

After the above theoretical research can be concluded, most of them are based on the basic characteristics of regional culture, the connotation of regional culture, the cultural elements of regional culture, the essence of regional culture and other perspectives on regional culture research application, but the relevant research from the perspective of Hefei rail vehicle design that combines Anhui regional culture still seems relatively scarce. Hefei is located in east China, central Anhui, between Jiangsu and Huaihua, surrounded by Chaohu Lake, is the deputy center of the Yangtze River Delta city group, one of the most modern multifunctional cities, with more than 2,000 years of cultural accumulation, known as "the hometown of the Three Kingdoms, the hometown of Bao Zheng" and so on constitute the unique cultural connotation of Hefei, its rich regional characteristics, with Its rich regional characteristics have irreplaceable regional characteristics. As an important symbol of the modernization of the city, Hefei rail transit vehicle plays the role of a new generation of means of transportation in the city, which is closely related to the development of the city and people's life [16]. Therefore, it is of great importance to reflect the typical regional character of Huizhou in the design of rail transit vehicles (Fig. 2).

Fig. 2. Summary analysis of existing rail vehicles

3 Design and Culture

Design has numerous attributes, such as functional attributes, aesthetic attributes, ethical attributes and cultural attributes, which are all elaborated with human beings at the core. As we all know, design is a spontaneous creation activity of human beings based on survival needs, so its subjectivity is necessarily emphasized, while human beings are the products of society, and society produces culture. Generally speaking, culture is a social phenomenon, a product formed by people's long-term creation, and at the same time culture is a historical phenomenon, a precipitate of social history. To be precise, culture refers to a country or nation's history and geography, customs and people, traditional customs, lifestyle, literature and art, behavioral norms, ways of thinking, values, etc. Thus, culture is the breeding ground for design, and design activities and their processes must have cultural attributes [17]. Design is the visible, audible, and textured external form of man-made objects in the cultural sense, so design is the "skin of culture" [2, 18]. In the history of human development, all activities for survival can be called culture [19].

With the acceleration of global economic integration, people's material needs have been greatly satisfied. According to Maslow's hierarchy of needs theory, human needs are from lower to higher levels, and when the material level reaches a certain height, human beings begin to pursue higher levels of spiritual and cultural needs. Products are the products of creative activities carried out by human beings to meet their needs. In the environment of changing social needs, the pursuit of cultural value of products has become the trend, and cultural connotation has become an important means to enhance the added value of products.

Today, in the era of consumer culture, the cultural attributes of products have more symbolic significance, and if one ignores the level of product symbolism, one simply cannot grasp the basic nature of today's industrial product design profession. Further, ignoring the cultural attributes of a product and being paranoid about the basic needs of consumers and the design considerations of good, usable, and use will often ignore the needs, desires, and identity of consumers on a higher psychological level, which will eventually lead to the shrinking of the product market or even affect the development of an enterprise or even a country. The design of product cultural connotation is the flag of an enterprise's production products, and is also the soul of an enterprise's existence.

Therefore, in the face of today's business war, the design of the cultural connotation of products is particularly important for enterprises and countries. So culture has become one of the factors that designers must consider when designing products.

3.1 Cultural Expression of General Industrial Products

The expression of cultural attributes in product design is more reflected in the application of cultural symbols in product design. Cultural symbols are the abstract embodiment of the unique culture of an enterprise, a region, a nation or a country, and are an important carrier and form of cultural connotation. Symbols are composed of energy and reference. The energy refers to the form used by the symbol, which is the concrete material image used in design. In product design, it refers to the external form of the product, including shape, structure, color, material, layout and other elements. The meaning and purpose of the design symbols is the meaning of the energy symbols, which is the connotation semantics of the product, such as the way the product is used, emotional meaning, cultural value, etc. Product has material function and non-material function, material function is the use value of the product, while non-material function is the additional value of the product, that is, cultural value, spiritual value. Therefore, product symbols can be divided into functional symbols and cultural symbols. Functional symbols are symbolic languages that convey the use of functions, while cultural symbols are symbolic languages that can cause psychological feelings and convey the spirit of culture. The design is to combine the ideas and emotions to be conveyed into the creation of the product in the form of symbols, and to express the abstract spiritual connotation in the form of figurative language. The use value of the product is the material basis of its existence, while the cultural value of the product is the soul of its existence. The cultural symbols of products reflect the living habits and customs of people in various regions in various times, which means that products are also a cultural symbol. The product itself is a cultural symbol.

Design and culture are paved together, culture influences design, design reacts to culture and plays a certain counter role to culture. Through the analysis and integration of rail transportation systems in Germany and France, it is verified that cultural connotation has become an important means to enhance the added value of products to a certain extent, and culture is one of the factors that designers must consider. And, for the design of rail transportation, cultural appeal is feasible and is the trend of rail transportation design development. And regional culture is the source form that the cultural expression of design often takes and can be easily utilized in the design. Based on the analysis and summary lesson of the above case, the basic method of rail transportation design by regional culture design is shown in Fig. 2.17. Firstly, the local regional cultural characteristics are outlined, and typical cultural elements are extracted from their typical cultural categories, which can be cut from traditional folk handicrafts or from local cultural forms such as natural landscape, flora and fauna, totems, and humanistic character. Secondly, find the symbols with higher identity from these typical cultural symbols, such as shapes, colors, descriptive words, etc., and abstract, simplify and transplant them. Finally, these refined design symbols are applied to the design of rail transportation, and the linear and dynamic relationships of their shapes are evolved to finally create a rail transportation form with typical regional culture.

4 Methodology

The content of this study includes, taking the regional humanistic landscape as the research entry point and the existing rail transportation design as the case study, exploring how to integrate the typical elements of the historical cultural corridor into the modern rail transportation design, and how to use the regional cultural factors to enrich the diversity of the design research with the existing technical support, creating more humanistic and intuitive regional characteristic symbols for the rail transportation design to create active sensual factors [20]. The specific contents are as follows.

① Analyze the extension and connotation of regional culture, classify regional culture, and clarify the role and significance of regional culture in this study. Following that, we analyze the cultural types of Anhui's regional culture at the levels of natural environment, social environment and human environment, select the typical cultural landscape and cultural phenomenon in Huizhou as the object of analysis, analyze its current application status, and find the breakthrough of design.

② Analyze the demand, innovation point and entry point of the design, provide methodological guidance for the subsequent design, and introduce the typical cases of foreign advanced countries' rail transportation design at the operation level, improve the design method by studying the matching of color and shape, and propose the principles to be grasped for the series of this design. We also study how to transform such intangible ideas of regional culture into unique regional symbols.

③ Explore the specific application of cultural elements in rail transportation design, propose a series development strategy, put forward the preliminary idea of cultural symbol implantation design, and start the design practice to summarize the design scheme (Fig. 3).

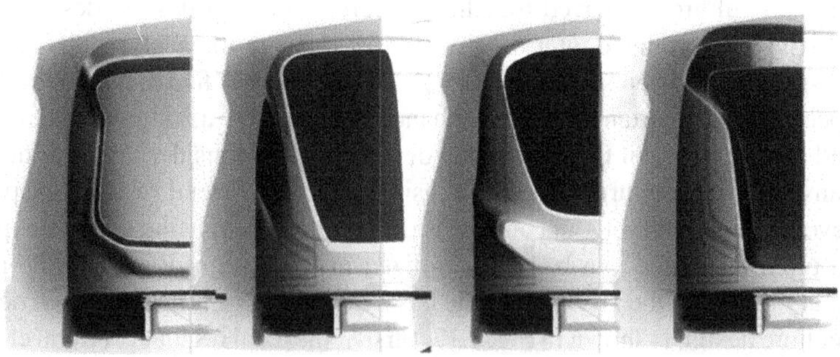

Fig. 3. Geographical rail vehicle design extrapolation process

Research Method. This can research content mainly intends to use literature method, comprehensive analysis method, questionnaire survey method, experimental research method, shape grammar and other combination of methods to carry out research. Specifically as follows.

1. Literature research method: search and collect relevant standards, research reports, books and academic papers involving urban rail vehicles, train modeling design, design genes, product modeling design and other issues to obtain as much relevant literature as possible to provide basis and supporting materials for the study of Hefei rail vehicle design genes.
2. Comprehensive analysis method: Take rail vehicles with distinctive features at home and abroad as cases, and clarify the innovation and importance of design genes in the appearance design of urban rail vehicles by analyzing the connection between their styling features and brand image.
3. Experimental research method: select designers and general public as experimental samples, obtain important modeling features of existing rail vehicles through eye-tracking instrument experiments, and extract features as modeling design genes with line analysis method.
4. Shape grammar: use shape grammar to deduce shape design genes to obtain new shapes, and finally combine shape design theories within the relevant specifications of vehicle design for Hefei rail vehicle design practice.

5 Conclusions

The design of rail transportation studied in this paper is not only the optimization and renewal of culture at the level of artifacts, but also a process of constructing a new regional culture. Traditional cultural symbols and traditional regional elements are important carriers of historical and cultural heritage, as well as important ways of regional cultural expression, they are symbols of the development of local people and epitomize the diligence and wisdom of working people. To sum up and summarize this paper, the following conclusions are drawn.

First, the current status of rail transit design at home and abroad is collected and summarized, and the regional representative examples of modern rail transit systems such as Lyon, France, TVG, Melbourne, Australia, and China's rail transit systems are reviewed and summarized, making it clear that cultural connotation has become an important means to enhance the added value of products, and that culture is one of the factors that designers must consider.

Secondly, from the existing typical rail transit cases, combined with the general principles of rail transit design, we discuss and summarize the regional characteristics that should be reflected in the design of rail transit system, and verify that the cultural appeal is feasible for the design of rail transit and one of the main trends in the development of rail transit design, and propose a set of design methods on the design of rail transit for regional cultural characteristics.

Thirdly, according to the design method of rail transportation for regional culture, this paper conducts a comprehensive research and summarizes the local regional culture of Hefei. The typical symbols that fit the local characteristics are extracted from them to make them more regional.

Fourth, by extracting typical regional elements such as Huizhou culture and natural landscape, and then finding the key modeling symbols (mainly lines, blocks and colors) from these typical cultural symbols, and simplifying and deforming them; finally, these elements are applied to the design of Chongqing rail transportation. The lines of the car body shape are continuously refined to create the unique regional cultural characteristics of Anhui regional light rail form. Based on these elements, the author developed two sets of exterior design and two sets of interior design to make it a part of the rail transit system with Chongqing's regional cultural characteristics.

Regional design is a design based on cultural lineage, place and ecology, and the design of regional culture based on Huizhou is to build cultural ecology and improve human living environment. At the same time, rail transportation is a typical urban landscape, and its design and construction are greatly enriching to Chongqing's nature, humanity and society. Therefore, it is especially important to grasp the essence of regional culture-based design at a high level in the design process, which is the conclusion of this study and a necessary concept for all regional designs.

Finally, after the completion of the theoretical framework, research method specification, typical case analysis and design techniques, the author proposes the design procedure and development strategy of rail transportation for the regional culture of Hefei, and completes the final design scheme, which is a certain guiding significance for the regional characteristics of Hefei rail.

Acknowledgements. The authors are very grateful for the support of this study in Anhui Province Social Science Innovation and Development Research Project 2021CX144 and Anhui University Humanities and Social Science Research Project SK2021A0055, and the authors are also very grateful to those who contributed to the study.

Anhui Province Social Science Innovation Development Research Project, Project Approval Number: 2021CX144.

Research Project on Humanities and Social Sciences in Anhui Universities, Project Approval Number: SK2021A0055.

References

1. Jiwu, W., Liliu, W.: Research on spatial planning and design based on regional cultural vocabulary. Huazhong Arch. **25**(8), 86–88 (2007)
2. Lijun, C.: Analysis of locality in station architectural design. China Railway **9**, 37–41 (2017)
3. Forman, E.H., Gass, S.I.: The analytic hierarchy process—an exposition. Oper. Res. **49**(4), 469–486 (2001)
4. Jun, C.: The interpretation of traditional cultural symbols in Chinese contemporary art. East China Normal University (2007)
5. Zerui, X., et al.: Review of industrial design research of urban rail trains in China. J. Southwest Jiaotong Univ. **56**(6), 1319–1328 (2021)
6. Xinrui, L., Shiyu, D.: The design application of regional cultural symbols in rail vehicle painting–Chengdu Metro as an example. Design (2020)
7. Sijun, H., et al.: Cultural transmission and construction in the appearance design of urban rail trains. Packag. Eng. **41**(2), 142–147 (2020)
8. Weiming, Z., Songhua, W., Weibo, X.: Regional culture is the soul of design art. Art Des. **10**, 75–77 (2008)
9. Hai, Y., Ye, J., Junqi, Y.: Qualitative and quantitative analysis of product functional requirements. J. Mech. Eng. **5**, 191–198 (2010)

10. Ling, C.B., et al.: Research on the design of subway vehicle shape combining regional culture and bionic imagery. Urban Rail Transit. Res. (2020)
11. Yuanqing, Z.: Exploring the integration design of regional culture and metro architecture. Collection **4** (2020)
12. Jianping, Z., Xiang, L.: Exploring the application of aesthetic laws in the appearance design of rail vehicles. In: Proceedings of the Academic Exchange Conference on Dynamic Vehicles and Passenger Cars (Dynamic Vehicles Book) (2012)
13. Wei, W., Zhe, W.: Foreign modern tram appearance design analysis. Metro Express Transp. **6**, 140–142 (2013)
14. Xiang, Z.: Wuhan regional culture in the visual design of metro traffic. Great Stage **9**, 99–100 (2013)
15. Bochu, X., Chao, W., Zerui, X.: Study on the image of urban public transportation system considering regional culture. Art Observ. **8**, 130–131 (2014)
16. Jun, X., Qinglong, G., Wei, L.: Rail transportation modeling design based on regional culture. Technol. Mark. **21**(4), 14–15 (2014)
17. Ling, Y., Yang, L., Jining, L.: Creative design of series of products for regional culture. Packag. Eng. **36**(22), 100–103 (2015)
18. Yang, L.: Regional cultural semantic design of urban rail vehicles. Railroad Technol. Innov. **5** (2019)
19. Lujun, R.: Research on the application of Huizhou regional culture in the design of rail transportation modeling. Ind. Des. **8** (2019)
20. Rongxin, D.S., Jianghao, X.: Subway vehicle exterior design based on shape grammar and regional culture. Packag. Eng. **41**(16), 230–235 (2020)

Study on Drivers' Situation Awareness in a Glance During Automated Driving

Hua Qin[1,2], Ning Chen[1], and Yue Wang[1](✉)

[1] Department of Industrial Engineering,
Beijing University of Civil Engineering and Architecture, Beijing 102616, China
yueaivae@163.com

[2] Beijing Engineering Research Center of Monitoring for Construction Safety, Beijing 102600, China

Abstract. Driving automation leads to meaningful changes in the role of the driver, from the primary party responsible for executing all dynamic driving tasks to the supervision of selective tasks in automated driving systems with varying levels of automation. In partially automated systems, drivers are required to resume control occasionally, either voluntarily or involuntarily. This paper aims at exploring human factors influencing the course of the takeover. Through a review of a large body of literature and a summary of observations, some particularly influential driver-related issues are identified. These issues include mental workload and distraction, situation awareness, and trust. Based on the consideration of these issues, the timing and the efficiency of driver's takeover are analyzed.

Keywords: Situation awareness · Secondary tasks · Automated driving

1 Introduction

The aims of automated driving systems are to reduce traffic accidents and improve road safety (Meng and Spence 2015; Wan and Wu 2018a), as some research implies that most car accidents can be attributed to human error (Dingus et al. 2006). These systems function as supportive automation to complete partial driving tasks. So, reducing a driver's workload allows the driver to be out-of-the-loop to some degree. However, present partial automated systems expect the driver to stay in the loop, to monitor the whole driving process, and to be prepared to take control of the driving task at any moment (Lu et al. 2016). Therefore, when out-of-the-loop drivers suddenly need to take over control from an automated driving system, accidents are more likely to occur if the time of takeover required is more than the available time (Jamson et al. 2013; Merat et al. 2014; Zeeb et al. 2015). To reduce the time that drivers' attention returning to the driving, it is necessary to understand the instantaneous situational awareness of the driver returning to the traffic scene from the secondary tasks.

Therefore, the aim of this study is the driver's instantaneous traffic situation awareness when their attention leaves the traffic scene for a period of time. In order to examine

P.-L. P. Rau (Ed.): HCII 2022, LNCS 13314, pp. 212–227, 2022.
https://doi.org/10.1007/978-3-031-06053-3_15

the instantaneous traffic situation awareness, this study would measure spatial perception, including object position and spatial relationship of the objects, the risk classification of the traffic scene and predicting the driving decision of the vehicle ahead, etc. And the purpose is to study the influence of the driver immersed in the second-task on situation awareness in a glance. The research results provide the basis for the design of driver assistance information in the future.

2 Secondary Tasks and Situation Awareness in a Glance

In partially automated systems, the driver's task changes from actively operating to passively supervising the system. Clearly, the difficulty associated with the driver's interaction during partial automation, similar to in a Level 2 or 3 vehicles, is that it assumes the driver is always available. However, it is more likely that drivers will shift their attention to non-driving related tasks because of a low workload. Drivers may seek to engage in other activities, such as entertainment instead of monitoring and supervising the autonomous driving system (Carsten et al. 2012; Merat et al. 2012). The number and duration of off-road glances and other secondary tasks all increase under some forms of automated driving (Jamson et al. 2011; Cho et al. 2006). Another study found that participants will reduce horizontal gaze dispersion and side mirror checks (He et al. 2011). As this underload occurs, delayed reactionary performance can occur (Merat and Jamson 2009; Young and Stanton 2001). Tests on the performance on secondary tasks show improvement under automated driving, which demonstrates the additional attention allocated to them (Rudin-Brown et al. 2003). The results apparently indicated that the more driving automation involved, the more drivers are willing to rely on automation to permit them to perform non-driving related tasks. Therefore, these research studies have illustrated that drivers may be more vulnerable to distractions during periods of driving automation, which leads to a safety issue when suddenly regaining control of the vehicle is required (Merat et al. 2012).

Endsley (1995) considered situation awareness (SA) to be "the perception of the elements in the environment within a volume of time and space, the comprehension of their meaning, and the projection of their status in the near future." The three levels of SA are defined by perception, comprehension, and projection. Higher levels of SA depend on the success of lower levels (Endsley 1995). The first level of SA is to perceive the status, attributes, and dynamics of relevant elements in the environment. Based on a synthesis of disjointed Level 1 elements, the second level of SA is to comprehend the situation. Achieved through knowledge of the status and dynamics of the elements and comprehension of the situation (both Level 1 and Level 2), the third and highest level of SA is formed to project the future actions of the elements in the environment (Endsley 1995; Endsley and Kaber 1999). Therefore, SA is considered to provide a basis for decision-making and performance.

For automated driving, researchers have found that the impacts on a driver's situation awareness are direct. The results indicate that drivers are willing to rely on automation to permit them to perform secondary tasks. Because working memory plays a critical role in the driver's situation awareness and secondary tasks place demands on working memory, the secondary tasks degrade the driver's SA (Johannsdottir and Herdman 2010;

Heenan et al. 2014). Once an emergency occurs, such as an unexpected conflict or automation system malfunction, the situation requires quick reactions, which are based on the SA level. However, secondary non-driving-related tasks could decrease the SA level, and consequently, driving performance is decreased (Matthews et al. 2001; Merat et al. 2010). In addition, Endsley (1996) thinks that lower level of drivers' SA in the automated conditions is attributed to more passive decision making, in which the drivers rely on the automated expert system's recommendations.

Several empirical studies clearly demonstrate that SA is reduced with the aid of automation. For example, drivers utilizing ACC (Adaptive Cruise Control) have much higher braking-reaction-times than those manually controlling the vehicle, even when the braking event is expected (Young and Stanton 2007; Merat and Jamson 2009; Rudin-Brown et al. 2003). Deceleration rates with ACC were twice that of CCC (Conventional cruise control) and the ACC is significantly less safe when compared to manual driving (Fancher et al. 1998; Rudin-Brown et al. 2003). Moreover, when regaining vehicle's driving control from the automated system is needed, the driver also demonstrates a worse performance (Merat et al. 2010).

3 Method

In order to know drivers' situation awareness in glance, this study investigated characters of spatial perception, risk classification and tendency of driving decision of drivers on condition that different attention state while receiving warning information.

3.1 Experimental Design

The three independent variables were drivers' attentional state, risk degree of traffic situation, and presenting time of the situation. (The drivers' attentional state referred to degree of focusing on the driving situation while the vehicle is controlled by automated driving systems, which was presented by the participants performing the secondary tasks.) This variable had three levels, which were concentrating on the driving all the time, chatting with other persons and playing games. The risk degree of traffic situation also had three levels, which were low, middle and high. Since the understanding of the driving situation during driving is a repetitive cycle of perceiving environment, remembering gist of environment and searching objects actively and according to other research applied in the field of visual search (Henderson and Hollingworth 1999; Adams et al. 1995), the presenting time with two levels referred to 750 ms and 1500 ms.

The dependent variables were spatial perception, risk perception and prediction of driving decision. The spatial perception included object perception in the different position and perception of space-relationship of objects. The risk perception was consisted of risk-degree judgement, time of risk-degree judgement and risk factors perception of the situation. The prediction of driving decision included prediction of the vehicle ahead and controlled by drivers. This study used a mixed-model experimental design with one between-groups factor of attention states and two within-groups factors of risk degree of the situation and presenting time. Each participant under a certain attentive state completed tasks involving 12 traffic situations. Every four situations presented one level of risk degree. And for the four situations, two of them were presented for 750 ms and the other two were 1500 ms. In addition, the 12 situations for each participant were presented randomly in the course of experiments.

3.2 Participants

In the experiment, 36 participants were divided equally and randomly into three groups. And the participants of each group completed tasks under one of three attention states. Their average age is 25.89 and the standard deviation is 3.41. All of them were required to have 20/20 vision or to wear corrective glasses or lenses. Moreover, they should hold a driver's license at least two years and driving distances were not less than 10 thousand kilometers. In addition, the three groups had no significant difference in participants' background information or driving experience.

3.3 Materials

Identification of Risk Traffic Situation. Firstly, the risk traffic situations were defined. Then 60 pictures presenting the situations were determined. And the risk degrees of these pictures were also assessed. Finally, 12 pictures of them were chosen according to risk degrees, which represented high, medium and low level respectively.

In China, overspeed, grabbing ways, fatigue driving, people and vehicles mixed at a crossroad, and other traffic violation were the main reasons of accidents caused by drivers. Among them, overspeed and grabbing ways were a major part (Li et al. 2016; Zhang et al. 2016). As a result, the risk situations for this study were selected from the following six kinds of scenarios.

(1) The vehicle ahead changes the lane arbitrarily or suddenly.
(2) The vehicle ahead brakes suddenly.
(3) The vehicle ahead doesn't make a light when turning on or turning around.
(4) When the vehicle drives forward at crossroad, an electric bicycle crosses the road suddenly.
(5) When the vehicle drives forward on the straight road, pedestrians cross the road without on the zebra crossing.
(6) When the vehicle drives forward on the straight road, an electric bicycle changes into the motorway suddenly.

According to the scenarios, more than 30 related videos were selected from the website of videos recorded by driving recorder (https://v.autohome.com.cn/general). And 60 pictures representing traffic situations were intercepted from the videos. Then 10 drivers with 15-year driving experience evaluated the risk degree of the 60 pictures. It was supposed that the vehicle was running at the speed of 50 km/h to the position presented in the picture. According to their experience and criteria, drivers measured the risk degree of the situations. The evaluation criteria for the three levels of the risk are as follows:

- High level
- Even if measures are taken as quickly as possible, accidents will inevitably occur.
- Medium level
- If measures are taken in time, accidents can be avoided.
- Low level

There is no possibility of an accident.

The drivers didn't have to consider elements that were not presented in the pictures when determining traffic conditions. After the end of the risk assessment, four pictures were selected respectively for each risk level (Figs. 1, 2 and 3).

Fig. 1. Traffic situation with low level risk.

Fig. 2. Traffic situation with medium level risk.

Fig. 3. Traffic situation with high level risk.

Questionnaire. In order to explore drivers' situation awareness in glance while they returning back to the traffic situation, this study also adopted a subjective questionnaire in addition to the objective data. The questionnaire included five types of questions, which were objects, perception at different position based on a driver's perspective, perception of spatial relations between some objects, discrimination of risk factors, driving prediction of vehicles ahead, and driving decision controlled by participants. The questions only involved the objects near the head of the cars. In addition, spatial relations between some objects referred to the relationship between an object and another, which the objects near the head of the cars, for example, the motorbike is on the left side of the black car.

Because different pictures presented different traffic situations, twelve questionnaires were designed for the twelve situations. After each picture was presented in a certain short period of time, the participants chose the answers based on their memories.

3.4 Task and Procedure

This experiment took each participant approximately one hour. Before formal experiments, participants completed a demographic survey and informed consent. Also, they received instruction and explanations of the tasks and backgrounds.

In order to simulate the driver's attention, converting from a different attention state into the traffic situations, each of the participants were in one state of attention before a picture was presented, which were completely focused on the screen or chatting with the experimenter or playing a Snakey game with experimental cellphone.

Take the experimental procedure of playing the Snakey game as an example. At the beginning of the screen was blank, at this time the participant began to play the snake game. After a period of time, a warning sound indicated that there was an emergency situation needed to be noticed. Then a picture was presented on the screen for 750 ms or

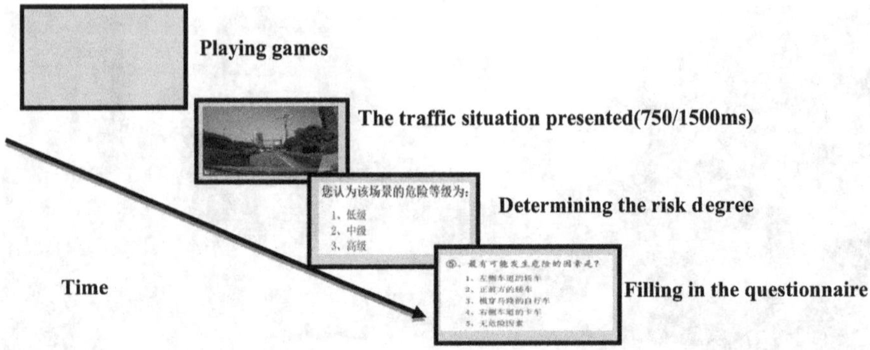

Fig. 4. Procedure of a participant performing the experiment (the secondary task is playing game).

1500 ms. Once the picture disappeared, the participants were asked to quickly discriminate the risk degree of the situation. Then a questionnaire corresponding to the situation was immediately presented. So far, the tasks for one traffic situation were completed (Fig. 4).

Based on E-prime program, each participant completed the tasks of the 12 traffic situations and participates performances were recorded. The differences of the other two attention state were at the beginning of the procedure. For chatting, at the beginning the participants talked with the experimenter, which the topics were about the latest TV plays or film. After a period of time, a warning sound also was sent out. The rest of the procedures were similar. For focusing on the screen, at the beginning the center of the screen was presented with a "+". The participants stared at the center. For a while, a picture was presented on the screen. Also, the rest of the procedures were similar to the playing Snakey game.

4 Results and Discussion

In order to analyze drivers' situation awareness in a glance, spatial perception, risk perception and tendency of driving decision of the drivers were investigated respectively. For the spatial perception, perception of objects in a space and spatial relationship of the objects were analyzed. For the risk perception, this study computed judgement of risk degree and identification of potential risk factors. For the tendency of driving decision of drivers, prediction of a vehicle ahead and driving decision on the vehicle controlled by participants were analyzed.

4.1 Spatial Perception in a Glance

Table 1 presented number and percent of correct answers for spatial perception corresponding to each attention state.

Table 1. Number and percent of correct answer for traffic situation awareness corresponding to each attention state (spatial perception).

Variables		Concentrating		Chatting		Playing		Total	
		N	%	N	%	N	%	N	%
Objects position	Upper-left	52	36.1	43	29.9	44	30.6	139	27.4
	Upper-right	37	25.7	23	16.0	24	16.7	84	16.6
	Lower-left	**59**	**41.0**	**63**	**43.8**	**49**	**34.0**	**171**	**33.7**
	Lower-right	39	27.1	45	31.3	29	20.1	113	22.3
Total		**187**	**36.9**	174	34.3	146	28.8	507	100.0
Spatial relationship		**47**	**32.6**	32	22.2	35	24.3	114	100.0

Note: The pictures of traffic situation were nearly divided into four regions, which were Upper-left, Upper-right, Lower-left and Lower-right. And the objects near the head of the cars were belonged to each region

36 participants were divided equally and randomly into three groups. Based on E-prime program, each participant completed the tasks of the 12 traffic situations and participates performances were recorded.

For perception of objects in a space, there are four positions that objects appeared possibly, which were upper-left, upper-right, lower-left, and lower-right related to the participant. The results indicated that the accuracy of spatial perception in all attention status except for chatting has the highest correct answers when the observed object appeared in the lower-left position, and the second highest number of correct answers was the upper-left position, followed by lower-right and upper-right. The possible reason that participants perceiving more objects in the lower-right was due to the experimenter sitting on the right side of them. Therefore, in general the objects located on the left of the drivers were easy to perceive. For perception of the spatial relationship between objects in a glance, the accuracy is not high. And the most accurate percentage of the concentrating participants was only 32.6%.

Table 2. ANOVA for spatial perception in glance.

Independent variables		Perception of objects			Spatial relationship between objects	
		F	Sig.	Multiple comparisons	F	Sig.
Drivers' attention state	Concentrating	3.79	.023*	Concentrating > Playing	2.25	0.11
	Chatting					
	Playing					
Presenting time	750 ms	6.36	.012*		1.19	0.28
	1500 ms					

(continued)

Table 2. *(continued)*

Independent variables		Perception of objects			Spatial relationship between objects	
		F	Sig.	Multiple comparisons	F	Sig.
Objects position	Upper-left	15.82	.000*	Upper-left > Upper-right; Upper-left > Lower-left; Upper-left > Lower-right; Upper-right > Lower-left; Upper-right > Lower-right; Lower-left > Lower-right		
	Upper-right					
	Lower-left					
	Lower-right					

Table 2 showed the results of Analysis of Variance (ANOVA). The results of driver perceiving objects indicated that there was a significant effect ($p = 0.012$) on condition concentrating on driving than playing games. But the difference between concentrating on driving and chatting or between chatting and playing games were not significant. For the object's position, ANOVA results revealed significant effects. Participants demonstrated significantly greater perception while objects appeared on upper-left than the other positions. Then the better position was upper-right. And participants demonstrated worst perception while objects appeared on the lower-right. With regards to presenting time, ANOVA results also revealed significant effects, which drivers demonstrated significantly greater perception while the objects presenting 1500 ms. And the less presenting time indeed degraded drivers' perception. As for spatial relationship between objects, no matter drivers' attentional state or presenting time, ANOVA results didn't reveal significant effects.

The results of spatial perception in glance showed that people can quickly perceive the objects in a short time. However, they behaved differently in different situation: For distraction, people behaved significantly better in concentration than playing the game; for object position, they had the highest perception in the lower-left position, followed by the upper-right and the lowest was lower-right; for presenting time, people behaved significantly better in 1500 ms than 750 ms.

Besides, it should be noted that participants' judgments of spatial position were not accurate enough, and had no significant variation for different distraction and presenting time. Thus, it may take more time for people to discern spatial relationships.

4.2 Potential Risk Identification

Table 3 presented number and percent of correct answers for risk perception corresponding to each attention state.

For identification of potential risk factors, the accuracy of identification was higher than 55% for participants in different attention states, with a high accuracy of 61.8% of participants in concentrating status. For the judgment of risk degree, however, the accuracy of participants in the different attentional state were all less than 50%. Especially,

Table 3. Number and percent of correct answer for traffic situation awareness corresponding to each attention state (risk perception).

Variables	Concentrating		Chatting		Playing	
	N	%	N	%	N	%
Identification of potential risk factors	**89**	**61.8**	80	55.6	81	56.3
Judgement of risk degree	47	32.6	**66**	**45.8**	58	40.3

Table 4. Means and standard deviations for time needed of risk-degree judgment.

Variables		Mean (ms)	SD
Attention states	Concentrating	**2457.9**	1497.2
	Chatting	1810.4	1310.4
	Playing	1852.9	1233.5
Presenting time	750 ms	**2180.2**	1328.8
	1500 ms	1900.7	1419.7

the participants in concentrating was the least, only 32.6%. This percentage was even lower than the other two states which were higher than 40%.

Two reasons may explain this phenomenon which participates in concentrating did better in identification of potential risk factors than judgment of risk degree: (1) it took them more effort into searching risk factors; (2) they were more likely to be overstressed, as a result, it reduced judgment in emergency situations.

Table 4 presented means and standard deviations for time of risk-degree judgment. The results shown how fast the participants judged risk degree of the traffic situations. For different attention states, the participants in concentrating needed the longest time, which was 2457.9 ms. But the participants in chatting and playing only needed 1810.4 ms and 1852.9 ms, respectively. For the judgment of risk degree in the Table 3, the accuracy of the participants in concentrating was also the least.

Why participates in concentrating took the longest and had the least accurate to judge risk-degree? We could explain this in terms of the stress response: it was possible to be confident about how long a task will take while you are focused on driving. Meanwhile, it took them more time to make a relatively precise judgment so that the likelihood of making a mistake increased. However, this state was not bad at perceiving risk factors and making driving predictions and decisions of the vehicle. For the presenting time of each traffic situation, the shorter the presenting time, the longer the participants needed to determine the risk level.

Table 5. ANOVA for accuracy of Drivers' attention state and presenting time.

Independent variables		Judgement of risk degree		Identification of potential risk factors	
		F	Sig.	F	Sig.
Drivers' attention state	Concentrating	2.67	0.070	0.78	0.461
	Chatting				
	Playing				
Presenting time	750 ms	9.41	0.002*	24.47	0.000*
	1500 ms				

Table 5 showed the results of Analysis of Variance (ANOVA). The results of driver's judging risk-degree and identifying potential risk factors indicated that there weren't significant effects ($p = 0.070$, $p = 0.461$) among different attention states. But there were significant effects ($p = 0.002$, $p = 0.000$) between different presenting time.

Risk- judgment and recognition are deep-seated decisions, so in a flash, whether to concentrate or not, there is no significant difference in the accuracy of judgment while people do not need to make a deep decision to judge; the perceptions of whether there are objects ahead are based on sensation and memory that don't require deep-seated decision making, therefore, the difference of drivers' attention state has significant effects on it.

4.3 Driving Decision

Driving decisions included predicting for a vehicle ahead and determining for a vehicle controlled by a participant. And the driving decisions included changes of speed and lane on condition the traffic situation.

Table 6. Number and percent of answer for traffic situation awareness corresponding to each attention state (driving decision).

			Concentrating		Chatting		Playing	
			N	%	N	%	N	%
Driving prediction of a vehicle ahead	Lane changing	Stay the lane	**79**	**55.9**	**78**	**54.2**	**82**	**56.9**
		Right lane	29	20.1	32	22.2	27	18.8
		Left lane	36	25.0	34	23.6	35	24.3
	Speed changing	Maintain	**63**	**43.8**	41	28.5	**62**	**43.1**
		Increase	32	22.2	36	25.0	25	17.4
		Decrease	49	34.0	**67**	**46.5**	57	39.6

(continued)

Table 6. *(continued)*

			Concentrating		Chatting		Playing	
			N	%	N	%	N	%
Driving decision of the vehicle controlled by participants	Lane changing	Stay the lane	**109**	**75.7**	**93**	**64.6**	**103**	**71.5**
		Right lane	19	13.2	32	22.2	18	12.5
		Left lane	16	11.1	19	13.2	23	16.0
	Speed changing	Maintain	23	16.0	18	12.5	32	22.2
		Increase	6	4.2	3	2.1	3	2.1
		Decrease	**115**	**79.8**	**123**	**85.4**	**109**	**75.7**

Table 6 presented number and percent of answer for prediction of driving decision corresponding to each attention state. For driving prediction of a vehicle ahead, more than 50% of the participants believed the vehicle ahead would stay the lane. For speed changing, 43.8% of the participants in concentrating on the driving and 43.1% of the participants in playing the games predicted the vehicle would maintain the original speed. And 46.5% of the participants in chatting with experimenters believed the vehicle ahead would slow down. For driving decisions on the vehicle controlled by participants, more than 60% of the participants would stay the lane. For speed changing, even more than 75% of the participants would slow down.

Table 7. Summary.

Relation	Dim	Singular value	Inertia	Chi square	Sig.	Proportion of inertia		Confidence singular value	
						Accounted for	Cumulative	SD	Correlation
									2
The vehicle ahead and participant's driving decision (lane changing)	1	.174	.030			.934	.934	.047	−.004
	2	.046	.002			.066	1.000	.048	
	Total		.032	13.954	.007	1.000	1.000		
The vehicle ahead and participant's driving decision (speed changing)	1	.388	.151			.994	.994	.043	.001
	2	.030	.001			.006	1.000	.047	
	Total		.152	65.503	.000	1.000	1.000		

The results of Analysis of Variance (ANOVA) on driving decision indicated that there was no significant effect among driver attention states. Whether the driving strategy of the vehicle ahead or the driving decision on the vehicle controlled by a participant, none of them had a significant relationship with the driver's state. However, there was a significant connection between the driving decision of the participants' and the driving strategy of the vehicle ahead (Table 7).

The results of Correspondence Analysis indicated that decision for staying the lane had a strong correlation with a prediction for staying the lane of vehicle ahead, while other correlations were less obvious; decision for maintaining speed had a strong correlation with a prediction for maintaining speed of the vehicle ahead, meanwhile, decision for decreasing speed had a strong correlation with prediction for both increasing and decreasing of the vehicle ahead (Fig. 5).

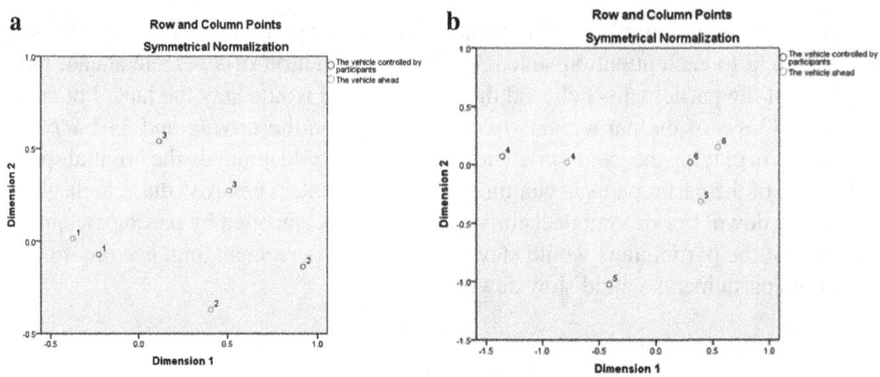

Fig. 5. a. Lane changing. b. Speed changing. (Lane changing: 1-Stay; 2-Right; 3-Left; speed changing: 4-Maintain; 5-Increase; 6-Decrease).

4.4 General Discussion: Traffic Situation Awareness in Glance

Fisher and Strayer (2014) consider that driving is dependent on several cognitive processes, including visual scanning of the driving environment for, predicting and anticipating potential threats, identifying threats and objects in the driving environment, deciding an action and executing appropriate responses (SPIDER). When drivers engage in secondary tasks unrelated to the driving, attention is often diverted from driving and the performance on these SPIDER-related processes are impaired (Regan and Strayer 2014). Consequently, activities that diverting driver's attention from the tasks degrade their situation awareness.

SA includes spatial content perception, spatial object interrelation location perception, and decision-making, which are the different stages of SA: In the early stage, the content perception of drivers in different states was significantly different, and their perception of objects in different positions was also significantly different. Meanwhile, there were significant differences in perception of risk-objects; in the middle stage, for different distraction, there were no significant difference of judgment in position relation or risk degree; in the later stage, there was no significant difference in the decision of drivers in different states. The results showed that during the instantaneous takeover, the different states of drivers only had a significant impact on the perception in the early stage of SA, but had little impact on the decision-making in the later stage. It Indicated that no matter what state the driver was in, the instantaneous decision depends on the reflex rather than the rational decision. As a consequence, in case of an emergency, the automated system should either not relinquishing control, or providing auxiliary decision to the driver.

In another perspective, the construction of drivers' situation awareness in glance is a process, in which the driver abstracts the gist of the scene and makes driving decisions based on the gist. This experiment was based on real traffic scenes that contained more complex situations, and the extraction of the gist in such scenes was hierarchical: The driver could perceive the spatial perception quickly in glance and then made deeper judgments. In these judgments, the observation of one or several objects was more prominent, and thus abstracted the gist of the scene at the moment.

When abstracting the gist of traffic scenes, objects with danger were normally sudden and uncommon. Therefore, dangerous objects were novelties. It has been noticed that objects with novelty were more likely to generate the extraction of the gist, and the longer the scene was presented, the more easily objects with novelty were perceived (Hao 2010). As a result, drivers could identify the potential risk in glance and were more likely to focus on the risky object when they had more time, and taking them as the new gist of the scene. This could also explain that in the early stage of establishing situation awareness, drivers' attention status did not affect their identification accuracy of risk factors significantly, while presenting time of the scene had a significant effect on their accuracy.

5 Conclusion

This paper experimentally explored the staged characteristics and influencing factors of driver's establishment of situation awareness in glance and the reasons of why these factors had an effect on the establishment of awareness in a glance. It was found that in the early stage of establishing context awareness, driver's spatial perception and identification of dangerous objects were significantly in different situations. The difference of attentional state, the position of the scene being processed and presenting time of the scene could affect the driver's spatial perception of objects; the difference of processing time could affect driver's identification of dangerous objects. In the middle stage when deeply processing information was needed, the driver's judgment of the spatial relationship of objects was not affected by the attention state or the presenting time; drivers' accuracy in judging the risk level of a scene is mainly affected by the length of time spent in processing information, and the effect of attention state on the judgment result is not significant. In the later stages, drivers were more likely to make driving decisions according to the condition of the car ahead, especially for the speed and lane changing of the car ahead.

It can be concluded that the situation awareness established by the driver in glance had limited relevance to whether they were performing a second task or not, and that drivers' extraction and understanding of the situation was not reliable. Therefore, it is difficult for the driver to make a rational driving decision in the moment of an emergency. Based on the analyses, it was concluded that in an emergency situation, the automated system should either not handing over control to the driver or offering driver auxiliary decisions.

References

Adams, M.J., Tenney, Y.J., Pew, R.W.: Situation awareness and the cognitive management of complex systems. Hum. Factors **37**(1), 85–104 (1995)

Carsten, O., Lai, F., Barnard, Y., Jamson, A.H., Merat, N.: Control task substitution in semi-automated driving: does it matter what aspects are automated? Hum. Factors **54**, 747–761 (2012)

Cho, J.H., Nam, H.K., Lee, W.S.: Driver behaviour with adaptive cruise control. Int. J. Autom. Technol. **7**(5), 603–608 (2006). Korean Society of Automotive Engineers, Seoul, Korea

Dingus, T.A., Klauer, S.G., Neale, V.L., Petersen, A., Lee, S.E., et al.: The 100-car naturalistic driving study, phase II-results of the 100-car field experiment (Report No. HS-810 593). National Highway Traffic Safety Administration, Washington, DC (2006)

Endsley, M.R.: Toward a theory of situation awareness in dynamic systems. Hum. Factors **37**(1), 32–64 (1995). Human Factors and Ergonomics Society, Santa Monica, CA

Endsley, M.R.: Automation and situation awareness. In: Parasuraman, R., Mouloua, M. (eds.) Automation and Human Performance: Theory and Applications, pp. 163–181. Lawrence Erlbaum, Mahwah (1996)

Endsley, M.R., Kaber, D.: Level of automation effects on performance, situation awareness and workload in a dynamic control task. Ergonomics **42**(3), 462–492 (1999)

Fancher, P., Ervin, R., Sayer, J., Hagan, M., Bogard, S., et al.: Intelligent cruise control field operational test, Report No. DOT-HS-808-849. National Highway Traffic Safety Administration, Washington, DC (1998)

Hao, C.: Gist abstraction mechanism of natural scenes. Zhejiang University (2010). (in Chinese)

He, J., Becic, E., Lee, Y-C., McCarley, J.S.: Mind wandering behind the wheel: performance and oculomotor correlates. Hum. Factors **53**(1), 13–21 (2011). Human Factors and Ergonomics Society, Santa Monica, CA

Heenan, A., Herdman, C.M., Brown, M.S., Robert, N.: Effects of conversation on situation awareness and working memory in simulated driving. Hum. Factors **56**, 1077–1092 (2014)

Henderson, J.M., Hollingworth, A.: High-level scene perception. Annu. Rev. Psychol. **50**(1), 243–271 (1999)

Jamson, H., Merat, N., Carsten, O., Lai, F.: Fully-automated driving: the road to future vehicles. In: Proceedings of the Sixth International Driving Symposium on Human Factors in Driver Assessment, Training, and Vehicle Design, University of Iowa, Iowa City, IA (2011)

Jamson, H., Merat, N., Carsten, O., Lai, F.: Behavioral changes in drivers experiencing highly-automated vehicle control in varying traffic conditions. Transp. Res. Part F Traffic Psychol. Behav. **30**, 116–125 (2013)

Johannsdottir, K.R., Herdman, C.M.: The role of working memory in supporting drivers' situation awareness for surrounding traffic. Hum. Factors **52**, 663–673 (2010)

Li, Y.B., Sun, Y.T., Xu, C.L.: Developing trends of automotive safety technology: an analysis based on traffic accident data. Autom. Saf. Energy **7**(3), 241–253 (2016)

Lu, Z., Happee, R., Cabrall, C.D., Kyriakidis, M., de Winter, J.C.: Human factors of transitions in automated driving: a general framework and literature survey. Transp. Res. Part F Traffic Psychol. Behav. **43**, 183–198 (2016)

Matthews, M.L., Bryant, D.J., Webb, R.D.G., Harbluk, J.L.: Model for situation awareness and driving: application to analysis and research for intelligent transportation systems. Transp. Res. Rec. **1779**, 26–32 (2001). Transportation Research Board, Washington, DC

Merat, N., Jamson, A.H.: How do drivers behave in a highly automated car? In: Proceedings of the Fifth International Driving Symposium on Human Factors in Driver Assessment, Training, and Vehicle Design. University of Iowa, Iowa City, IA (2009)

Merat, N., Jamson, H., Lai, F., Carsten, O.: Automated driving, secondary task performance and situation awareness. In: Human Factors: A System View of Human, Technology and Organization, pp. 41–53, Shaker Publishing, Maastricht (2010)

Merat, N., Jamson, A.H., Lai, F., Carsten, O.: Highly automated driving, secondary task performance and driver state. Hum. Factors **54**, 762–771 (2012)

Merat, N., Jamson, A.H., Lai, F., Daly, M., Carsten, O.: Transition to manual: driver behavior when resuming control from a highly automated vehicle. Transp. Res. Part F Traffic Psychol. Behav. **27**(Part B), 274–282 (2014)

Rudin-Brown, C., Parker, H.A., Malisia, A.R.: Behavioral adaptation to adaptive cruise control. In: Proceedings of the Human Factors and Ergonomics Society Annual Meeting, vol. 47, no. 16, pp. 1850–1854. Human Factors and Ergonomics Society, Santa Monica (2003)

Young, M.S., Stanton. N.A.: Size matters: the role of attentional capacity in explaining the effects of mental underload in performance. In: Harris, D. (ed.) Engineering Psychology and Cognitive Ergonomics, Volume 5: Aerospace and Transportation Systems. Ashgate Publishing, Surrey (2001)

Young, M.S., Stanton, N.A.: Back to the future: brake reaction times for manual and automated vehicles. Ergonomics **50**(1), 46–58 (2007). Taylor & Francis, New York

Zeeb, K., Buchner, A., Schrauf, M.: What determines the take-over time? An integrated model approach of driver take-over after automated driving. Accid. Anal. Prev. **78**, 212–221 (2015)

Zhang, Q., Yang, P.Z., Yan, C.L., Fan, Q.F.: Human factors analysis of road traffic accidents in China. Automob. Appl. Technol. **2016**(6), 7–8 (2016). Author, F.: Article title. Journal **2**(5), 99–110 (2016)

Smart Product-Service System Design Based on Human Mobility with the Medium Autonomous Vehicles

Bei Ran[1] and Jingyan Qin[2(✉)]

[1] South China University of Technology, Guangzhou 510006, China
ranbei@scut.edu.com
[2] University of Science and Technology Beijing, Beijing 100083, China
20443530@qq.com

Abstract. With the approaching digital age, technologies have become the core driver for human society. Technologies including the Internet of Things, Big Data, Deep Learning and intelligent networks have accelerated the social digital transformation. To follow this trend, the key is building Smart Product-Service System, which integrates smart products and e-services into a single solution. As a typical intelligent product, Autonomous Vehicles enable to collect human mobile data and connect to the intelligent cloud system. The explosive growth in the amount of intelligent mobility knowledge is the source driver for the construction of sustainable intelligent ecosystem based on the interconnection of products and services of heterogeneous intelligence. The hierarchical structure model of human mobility knowledge shows the trans-formation process of human mobility knowledge from data, information and knowledge to wisdom from the bottom up at the technical level. The mapped design methods belong to a top-down process from service system architecture design and information relationship architecture design to product function specification design.

Keywords: Smart product-service system design · Intelligent mobility · Intelligent mobility ecosystem

1 Research Background

The technology has become the core driver of human society with the approaching of the digital age. Technologies including Internet of Things (IoT), big data, deep learning and intelligent network have accelerated the digital transformation of society. The most important step to follow this trend lies in the construction of the cyber-physical system (CPS) based on services and smart products interconnected by heterogeneous devices, which is an ecosystem that integrates physical and digital objects. The concept of Smart Product Service System (Smart PSS) is emerging in the design field. Smart PSS integrates smart products and e-services into social service scenarios that covers singe solutions of physical, information and cognitive spaces. Smart products depend on information and communication technologies (ICT) to collect and produce data and information,

P.-L. P. Rau (Ed.): HCII 2022, LNCS 13314, pp. 228–247, 2022.
https://doi.org/10.1007/978-3-031-06053-3_16

while services are based on the application and implementation of data and information. The Smart PSS has become an indispensable area of research with advances in Internet implementation, computational intelligence and Web technologies. Compared to the traditional design methods for physical design objects, the design objects and design methods of Smart PSS have changed significantly.

On the one hand, Autonomous Vehicles (AVs), as the smart product that changes productivity in social service scenarios, is a typical representative of driving the construction of Smart PSS. On the other hand, autonomous vehicles enrich the connotation of human mobility. The emergence of cars has expanded the time and space for individual and human group to move freely, enabled them to break through the limits of physical ability without the restrictions of rail and route transportation, and provided human mobility with the attributes of flexibility and convenience. The emergence of autonomous vehicles has completely released human drivers from the traditional human-vehicle interaction relationship. The autonomous vehicles are used as autonomous mobile space in various scenarios of people's social life, so that the context of human-vehicle interaction is extended from driving scenarios to scenes of life. Therefore, the SPSS design with autonomous vehicles as medium should focus not only on the concept and phenomenon of objectization of autonomous vehicles, but also on the mobile relationship network of service recipients and providers constructed by autonomous vehicles in the system.

2 Smart Product-Service System

2.1 A Subsection from Product-Service Systems to Smart Product-Service Systems

The concept of Product-Service System (PSS) was firstly proposed by four scholars including Goedkoop [1] in 1999 who defined PSS as the collection of products and services that satisfy customer needs. The composition of products and services in PSS could be diverse with the purpose of achieving functional or economic value. The concept of PSS highlights three key words, namely product, service and the combined relationship between them. The product refers to the materialized tangible goods produced for sale, the service to the valuable activities offered to the customer, and the relationship to the combination of product and service in the system. Maussang [2] argued that PSS consists of architecture design and product specification. PSS is composed of physical objects being entities that perform the basic functions of system and service units being virtual bodies that ensure the operation of system. Designers need to detailedly analyze the intricate relationship between physical objects and service units in the early stages of PSS design, and finally implement the output of PSS design into design characterization.

With advances in Internet implementation, computational intelligence and networking technologies, a new generation of product systems has emerged that are equipped with sensors and intensive communication between cyberspace and physical devices. Ana Valencia et al. defined Smart PSSs as the integration of smart products and e-services into single solutions delivered to the market to satisfy the needs of consumers [3]. The concept of Smart PSSs focuses on the opportunities Smart PSSs offer to create new interaction between service receiver and provider. Ana Valencia et al. also outlined six defining characteristics of Smart PSS [4], namely consumer empowerment, individualization of services, community feeling, service involvement, product ownership and individual/shared experience. The Smart PSSs combine smart products with e-services to meet the needs of service receivers. ICT embedded in products play an important role in Smart PSSs because it facilitates the generation and transmission of relevant information and guides the creation of e-services based on the products. Thus, the integration of smart products and e-services provides designers with a range of innovative opportunities to implement new interaction activities or touch spots that enhance the interaction between the service receiver and provider.

2.2 Design Methods of Smart PSS

User-Centric Design Methods of Smart PSS. Danni Chang et al. proposed the innovative design methods and strategies for User-centric SPSS (UC-SPSS) [5]. The designers establish the SPSS from physical space to cloud platform based on the user-centric perspective to realize product development and service implementation in physical space, as well as data synchronization and innovation value generated on the basis of data accumulation in cloud platform. The user-centric design methods of Smart PSS construct the multimodal user analysis module including society-economy-technology analysis with user needs and provider capability taken into consideration, so as to establish the service provider identification and integration network in material, data and value flows dimensions.

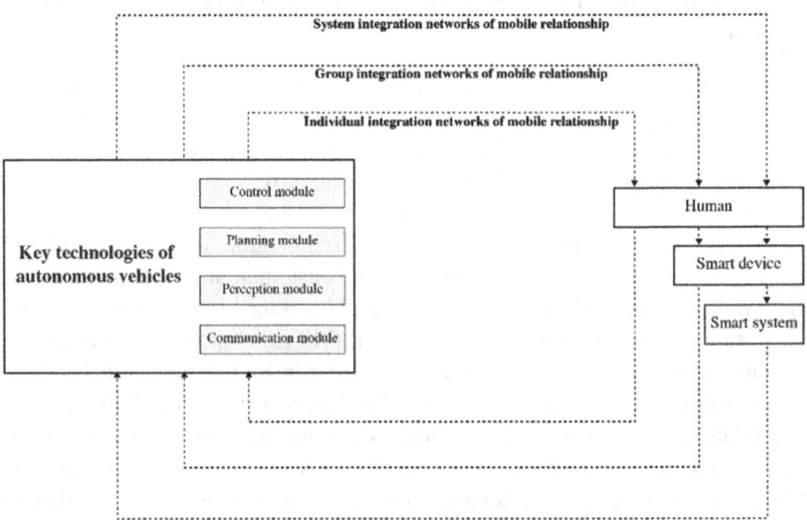

Fig. 1. Three integration networks of mobile relationship.

The four module technologies are the key technologies of autonomous vehicles, including perception module, planning module, control module and communication module, because of which the autonomous vehicles have data, learning, behavior and communication capabilities and the characteristics of context perception, intelligent decision making, active interaction and group intelligent innovation. The autonomous vehicles are the mediums of data production and collection, data calculation and analysis, and data application and execution in the smart logistics product-service system. The autonomous vehicles acquire environmental data through radar, ultrasonic, GPS and other sensor technologies in the service process. It acquires data related to autonomous driving and logistics services in multiple spaces in the past, present and future, and calculates and analyzes data information through on-board CPU algorithms for making autonomous driving decisions and logistics service decisions in the service process. The autonomous vehicles participate in the construction of three integration networks of mobile relationship between service receiver and provider, involving the product design, interaction design and service design of autonomous vehicles (see Fig. 1).

Service/Product Engineering. Japanese scholars Sakao and Shimomura proposed the concept of Service/Product Engineering (SPE) based on service engineering [6]. The product in SPE is regarded as a component of service, while the service system as a product-service system containing product. The service in SPE is defined as the activity that the service provider transforms the service receiver from one state to another, whose content and channel are the means to achieve the service [7]. The desired state change of the service receiver by the service provider is expressed in terms of Receiver State Parameters (RSPs) driven by the value demands of the service receiver, and a series of RSPs constitute the purpose, value and meaning of the product-service system design. In the whole process of service implementation, the state change of the receiver reflects the essence of human mobility and can be expressed by a series of RSPs, which is also the value demands of the product-service system design.

The tools of the service/product engineering could be applied to the product-service system design with autonomous vehicles as medium, including the flow model, scope model, scenario model and view model. As the expression of value demands for product-service system design, the Receiver State Parameters drive the construction of flow model, scope model, scenario model, view model and extended service blueprint. The flow model identifies the service relationships among service providers, intermediate agents and service receivers in the system, while the scope model expressed by RSPs analyzes the state changes among service providers, intermediate agents and service receivers in the system as a result of service implementation. The scenario model depends on the abstraction-detail to analyze different levels of RSPs in all state change processes, and selects the most adaptive and important RSPs from them. The view model investigates the function, content and channel that support the realization of the RPSs and conducts the structured expression. The extended service blueprint tool integrates the research outcomes of the above four modeling tools to model the entire product-service system.

3 Human Mobility

3.1 Research significance of Human Mobility

Human mobility is a common subject of interest in sociology, geography, physics, urban planning, epidemiology and other disciplines that study the movement of human individuals or groups in space and time. Human mobility represents the movement of human individuals or groups in space and time that implies social system elements, spatio-temporal distribution and evolution laws [8]. Human mobility, which reflects human spatio-temporal behavior, has been a long-standing focus of scholars in various fields. The human mobility data were mostly obtained by observation, interviews, questionnaires and travel logs in previous studies, which were costly, small in sample size and limited by time and space span so that it was difficult to observe and record the movement of human individuals and groups in space and time for a long time and on a large scale. With the widespread application of mobile computing devices with positioning capabilities, the user's behavior of uploading the current location via mobile terminal is called check-in in the location-based social networking services, and the resultant data with geo-tag is the check-in data. The check-in data is widely used in the analysis of human mobile behavior. Under normal circumstances, check-in data covers both geographic location information and semantic information about the point of interest (POI) carried at the location. Therefore, location or trajectory semanticization operation can be omitted in behavioral analysis [9, 10]. The generation of large amounts of spatio-temporally tagged human mobility big data with individual granularity provides the possibility for tracking individual spatial movements with high accuracy and efficiency over long periods of time. The application of ICT allows for more accurate access to large amounts of individual and group human mobility data, which can lead to information about group movement relationship and movement laws. The study of human mobility is of significant importance for urban planning, traffic forecasting, epidemic control and emergency management, and essential for the application of emerging information and network technologies in human social scenarios. Human mobility is considered to be a critical element in the design and management of intelligent transportation and smart cities.

3.2 Intelligent Mobility

In the period of big data, people could resort to big data technology to obtain massive individual and group movement trajectory data more precisely, and further obtain group movement relationship and movement law information. The intelligent mobility has become a new trend of human mobility in the information age, which refers to the process of applying emerging technologies to move people and things more intelligently and efficiently. The development of IoT technology has driven human mobility to intelligent mobility. The Internet of Things (IoT) depends on the perceptual system to collect information about objects and complete the information interaction between objects through transmission and intelligent processing systems, ultimately realizing the interconnection and management between objects and objects, and people and objects. As the application of IoT technology in the automotive field, the Internet of Vehicles (IoV) depends on on-board electronic sensing device to realize the real-time networking between vehicles and vehicles, vehicles and objects, vehicles and people, vehicles and roads, vehicles and systems through mobile communication technology, car navigation system, intelligent terminal devices and information network platform. IoV connects human mobile data through the integration of information system and physical system, and acquires human mobile information through the application of technologies including group intelligent computing, crowd sensing, social computing, crowdsourcing and cloud computing, Meanwhile, it reconstructs and organizes human mobile information effectively in scene of human life to acquire human mobile knowledge, and forms human mobile wisdom in the application of knowledge so as to provide people with well-experienced services.

3.3 Intelligent Mobility Ecosystem

Electrifcation of Vehicles (EVs), Connected and Autonomous Vehicles (CAVs) and Mobility-as-a-Service (MaaS) are three major trends in the future of intelligent transportation system that will fundamentally reshape the value and modal of human mobility. The automotive, transportation and broader mobility market are being influenced by cultural, social, technological and economic transformations that are disrupting the way people and objects move. Many industries associated with them are being impacted. The new business models emerge one after another while the convergence of emerging and old market models come into existence, so that traditional industries are facing a make-or-break situation. Under the background of continuing population growth, urbanization and environmental protection issues, new ways of human mobility are critical to support future population centers and economic activities.

The current human mobility systems are plagued by congestion, inefficiency, high accident rates and high prices. In the future, new forms of human mobility that are convenient, safe and economical will have a positive impact on human society and the environment. The current vehicle-centric human mobility landscape will change, with electrification of vehicles, connected and autonomous vehicles, and mobility-as-a-service facilitating a more efficient, data-enabled, multi-user-centric, multi-channel and multi-modal mobility ecosystem. Users will be able to shift between public, private, on-demand and scheduled mobility modes at will, and dynamic mobility and service information will be available for feedback or change at any time during the journey.

Autonomous vehicles drive the construction of intelligent mobility ecosystem and the huge new human mobility system. The intelligent mobility ecosystem possesses information perception, intelligent conduction and intelligent computing capabilities. Hence the traditional product design methods are no longer applicable to the design of intelligent ecosystem, and designers need to explore the design methods and tools integrating the empowerment of substantialization, motility and interaction for intelligent terminal design, intelligent network design and intelligent cloud design. The paper would explore the changes of human mobility due to the intelligent ecosystem driven by autonomous vehicles in human social scenarios, and propose the design methods and design evaluation criteria for the intelligent ecosystem driven by autonomous vehicles through taking human intelligence and artificial intelligence as the main subjects and the evolution process of human mobile data, information and knowledge to intelligence as the research scope.

4 Design Methods of Intelligent Mobility Ecosystem

The explosive growth in the amount of intelligent mobility knowledge is the source driver for the construction of sustainable intelligent ecosystem based on the interconnection of products and services of heterogeneous intelligence [11]. The intelligent mobility ecosystem is the upgrade and optimization of the information ecosystem and physical ecosystem in the AI era, consisting of the terminal (sensing layer), the pipeline (network layer) and the cloud (application layer). The terminal is responsible for information perception and action control, the pipeline for information transmission and exchange, and the cloud for memory, perception, recognition, learning, etc. As a typical closed-loop control system, the intelligent ecosystem includes four links, namely acquisition and integration, interaction and transmission, storage and processing, and mining and regeneration, mapping to the transformation process of human mobile data, information, knowledge and wisdom. The transformation of human mobile knowledge is circular and sustainable in the intelligent ecosystem.

4.1 A Hierarchical Structure Model of Human Mobility Knowledge

Knowledge is about the movement reflecting the particular position, perspective and purpose. The human being is the subject of knowledge, while knowledge is the internalization of information by the human being in a particular context in relation to his or her own situation. The author constructs a hierarchical structure model of human mobility knowledge (see Fig. 2) based on the Data-Information-Knowledge-Wisdom (DIKW) model. The scattered human mobile data is at the most basic level, which records the changes of human individual or group activities in space and time. The human mobile information is at the upper level of human mobile data that is linked to form human mobile information. The human mobile knowledge is at the upper level of human mobile information that is organized in a regular manner to form human mobile knowledge. The human mobile wisdom is at the top layer, and human mobile knowledge is applied to the scenes of human life to form human mobile wisdom.

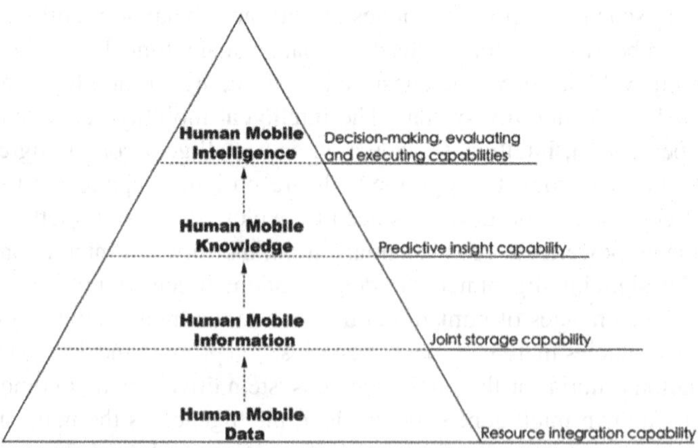

Fig. 2. A hierarchical structure model of knowledge of human mobility

4.2 Design Procedures and Methods of Intelligent Mobility Ecosystem Based on a Hierarchical Structure Model of Human Mobility Knowledge

The hierarchical structure model of human mobility knowledge shows the transformation process of human mobility knowledge from data, information and knowledge to wisdom from the bottom up at the technical level. The mapped design methods belong to a top-down process from service system architecture design and information relationship architecture design to product function specification design.

The system calculation of the edge and central control cloud system realizes the transformation of human mobile knowledge into human mobile intelligence. Autonomous vehicles are gradually applied to the urban security, urban transportation, service for the aged, municipal services, health care and other social service systems. Autonomous vehicles are involved in the construction of the autonomous vehicles system innovation model which requires the design of occupationally generated contents (OGC) for autonomous vehicles products and services, namely the architecture design of service system with the autonomous vehicles as the medium.

Autonomous vehicles possess network connectivity. The mobile internet, IoT and AIoT contribute to the connected autonomous vehicles, intelligent devices and central control cloud system and linked human mobile information in multiple time and space. Through the calculation and analysis of human mobile information by the central control cloud system, the human mobile information is transformed into human mobile knowledge such as material flow, information flow and capital flow and used for decision making and prediction in the process of autonomous vehicles service implementation. Autonomous vehicles are involved in the construction of autonomous vehicles group innovation model which requires the design of professionally generated contents (PGC) generated for autonomous vehicles groups, namely the architecture design of information relationship with the autonomous vehicles as the medium.

Autonomous vehicles perceive the occurred human mobile data through sensor technologies including radar, ultrasound and GPS. The human mobile data is computed and analyzed by on-board CPU algorithms for decision making and prediction in the process of service implementation. The autonomous vehicles with data, computation and decision-making capabilities actively interact with the external environment as an independent individual, and constructs the autonomous vehicles individual innovation mode which requires user generated contents (UGC) generated for autonomous vehicles, namely the product function specification design for autonomous vehicles.

Architecture Design of Service System. The service value demand is put forward to provide efficient and well-experienced smart logistics services from the perspective of design. It is supposed to determine the service participants of the smart logistics product-service system, identify the service demands of the service participants, and construct the service activity relationship between the system elements with the purpose of realizing the service demands of service participants. The flow model in the service/product engineering is a tool for modeling and expressing the service relationships among service providers, intermediate agents and service receivers in the sequential chain of time and space. In the flow model (see Fig. 3), the direct service relationship exists between the service provider and the service receiver, and so does the indirect service relationship where intermediate agents exist between the service provider and the service receiver. Autonomous vehicles and central control system are intelligent devices and system with the application of artificial intelligence technology, which can simulate human intelligence to carry out service activities, interactive actions and functional manipulation independently. Therefore, autonomous vehicles and central control system can act as service providers, intermediate agents and service receivers. The service participants are explored through the flow model which identifies the composition of the service participants of service system. The scope (see Fig. 4) model is used to define the service demands of service participants to the system.

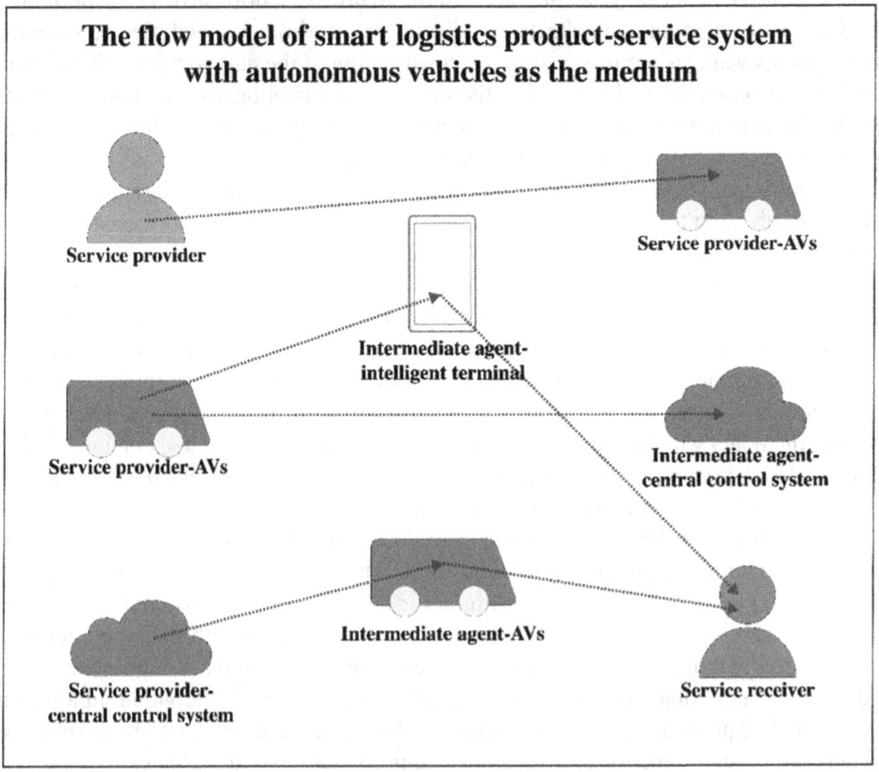

Fig. 3. Flow model

Architecture Design of Information Relationship. The scenario model (see Fig. 5) is used to explore the state change processes of service receiver in the service architecture model with a set of service receiver state change processes constituting the receiver's service journey. The target receiver state parameters of each process is analyzed which express the requirements for information interaction during the service journey. A series of target receiver state parameters constitute the information relationship architecture, which can be integrated through the customer journey diagram tool to build an information relationship architecture model. The scenario model expresses the information

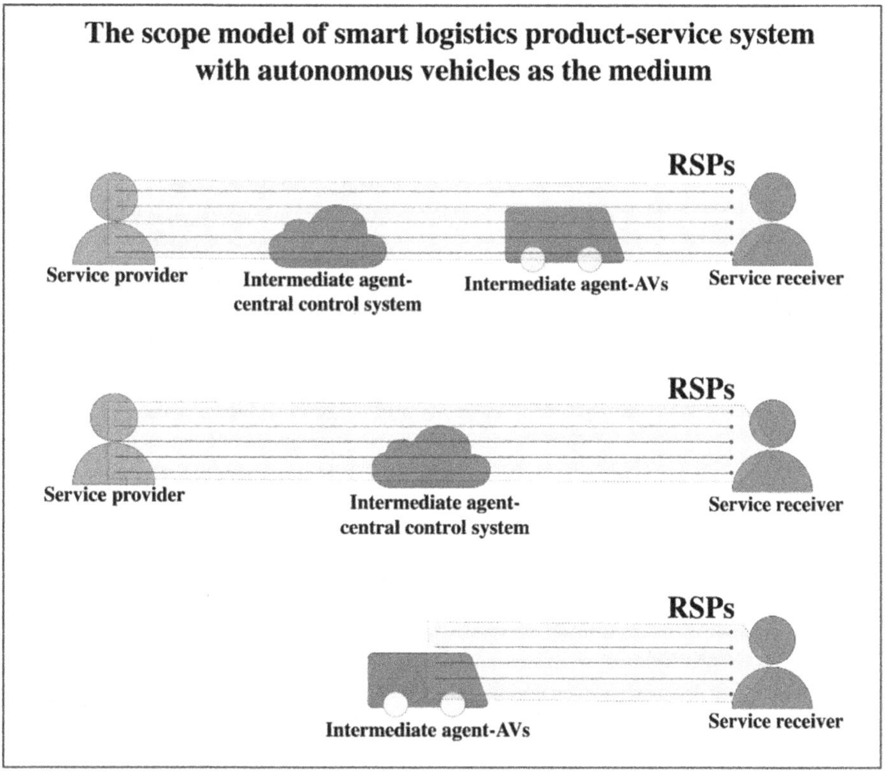

Fig. 4. Scope model

needs of the service receiver identified in the scope model, namely receiver state parameters, at different levels from abstraction to details. The scenario model is a method of modeling the information needs of the service receiver, whose elements include the state change process of the service receiver, receiver state parameters, significant receiver state parameters and target recipient state parameters. The analysis method of significant state parameters abstraction hierarchy is used in the multi-level recipient state parameters so as to select the significant receiver state parameters and the most important and adaptive target receiver state parameters. The target receiver state parameters express the information needs of the service receiver during the service implementation process.

Product Function Specification Design. The product design should analyze CMF product color schemes, product materials and product processing methods, and integrate IP brand strategy factors including PI product identification into design elements. The product design needs to conduct basic design analysis of functional specifications. Moreover, it is also necessary to analyze the service content endowed by the product, and to realize mass customization (MC) of the product in terms of functional specifications and content features through lean design and rapid agile interaction prototyping. The target receiver state parameters in the service receiver journey map are regarded as the touch spots of functional interactions in the message flow, supporting the realization

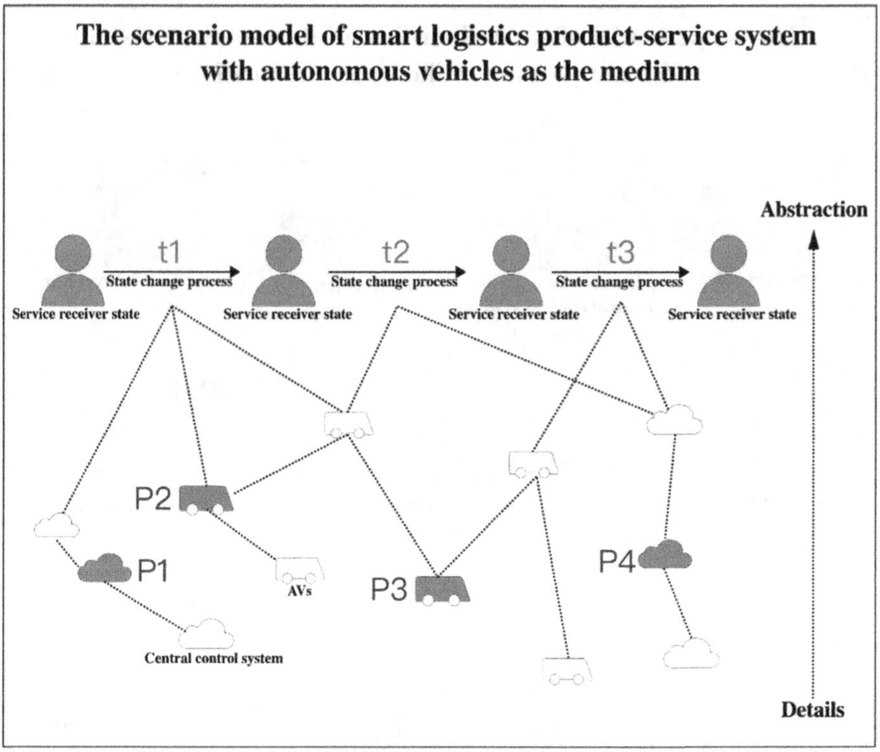

Fig. 5. Scenario model

of information requirements and support mediums of each target recipient state change parameter. In the product functional specification design, the view model (see Fig. 6) is applied to define the functions, contents and channels that the autonomous vehicles should have as the medium to support the message flow, and the functions, contents and channels of autonomous vehicles are characterized and designed to construct the product function prototype.

5 Product-Service System Design of Intelligent Logistics Autonomous Vehicles

In the scenario of last mile delivery in the park, the logistics company transports the goods to the distribution point in the park and then delivers the goods to the terminal customers through certain means or methods of transportation. The last mile delivery is the last link of logistics service where the logistics service directly faces the demands of terminal customers. Hence the user experience of the last mile delivery link determines the quality of logistics service. The last mile delivery of traditional logistics was mainly based on manual delivery, which shows the trend of diverse ways with the development of artificial intelligence technology. Nowadays, logistics service providers such as SF

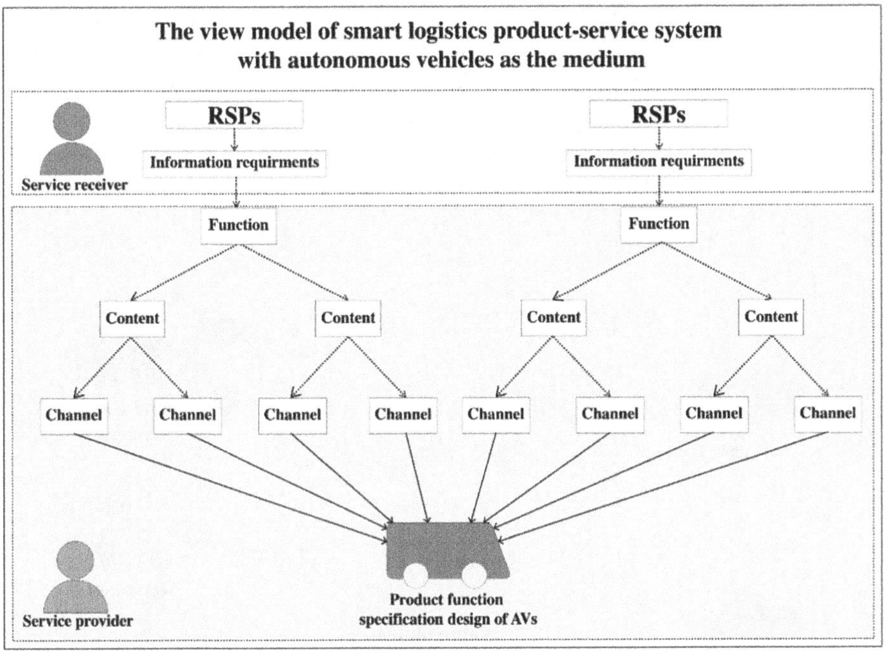

Fig. 6. View model

Express and ZTO Express, e-commerce platforms including Jingdong and Tmall, and Internet companies such as Tencent and Baidu focus on the research and development of autonomous vehicles in the scenario of last mile delivery. With the upgrading of residents' consumption capacity and the booming development of e-commerce in China, online shopping has become a fairly common form of daily consumption for residents. The last mile delivery is the last and most important link to reach terminal customers in the process of online shopping. Therefore, creating the satisfactory experience of last mile delivery is the final step to support the development of intelligent logistics based on network economy, platform economy and sharing economy.

5.1 Architecture Design of Service System

Service Participants Identification. In the last mile delivery scenario, autonomous vehicles and central control system of intelligent logistics have capabilities of individual intelligence and group intelligence. Autonomous vehicles and central control system can exist in the form of intermediate agents as well as the service receiver and provider in the service system. In the analysis of service relationship elements in the service system, the flow model is used to analyze the components of the service relationship, including the service provider, intermediate agent and service receiver, and the service relationship between the components is modeled and expressed through a sequential chain in time and space. Considering that the last mile delivery in the park consists of four stages including loading stage, driving stage, delivery stage and receiving stage, the elements constructing the service relationship with autonomous vehicles as the medium in each stage are explained and analyzed. The flow model (see Fig. 7) expresses the interaction between the service receiver and the service provider in the distribution stage.

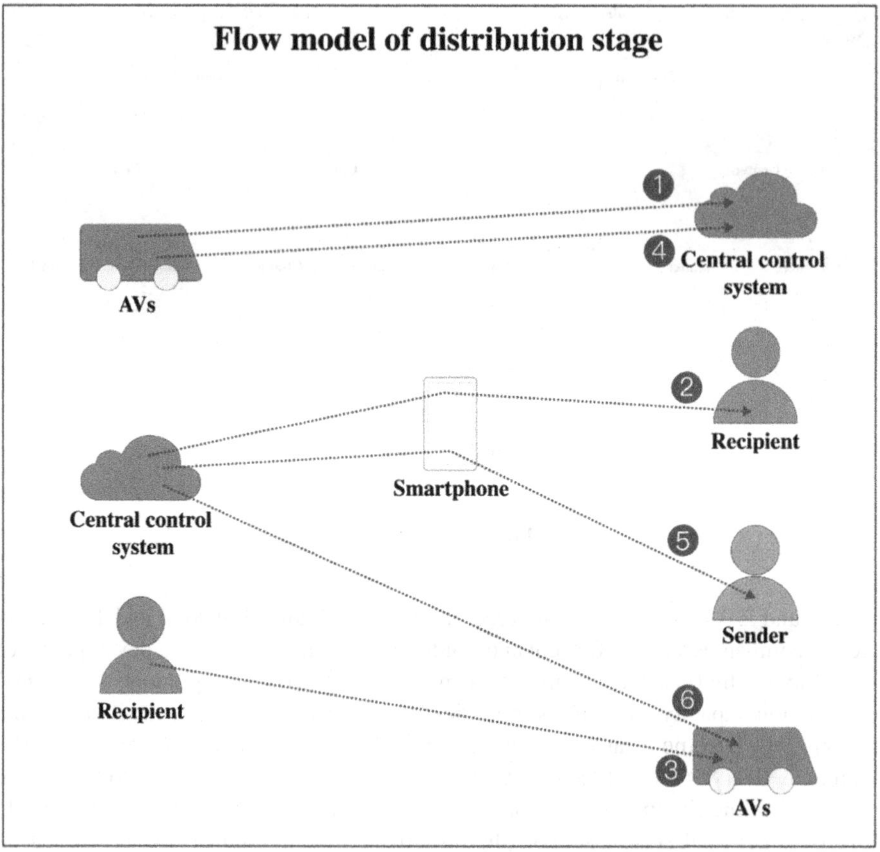

Fig. 7. Flow model of distribution stage

Service Needs Analysis. The service needs between the service provider, intermediate agent and service receiver in the service relationship are analyzed with the service needs expressed by receiver state parameters. The scope model (see Fig. 8) analyzes the service needs of service receiver in the distribution stage. (1) The central control system is informed that the autonomous vehicles have arrived at the delivery location; (2) The receiver is reminded of the package and goes to the designated location to pick it up; (3) The autonomous vehicles are informed that the package has been picked up and confirms the successful delivery; (4) The central control system is informed that the package has been successfully delivered; (5) The provider is informed that the package has been successfully delivered; (6) The autonomous vehicles receive the real-time updated optimal routes from the central control system and depart for the next destination. The above is expressed in the scope model of distribution stage.

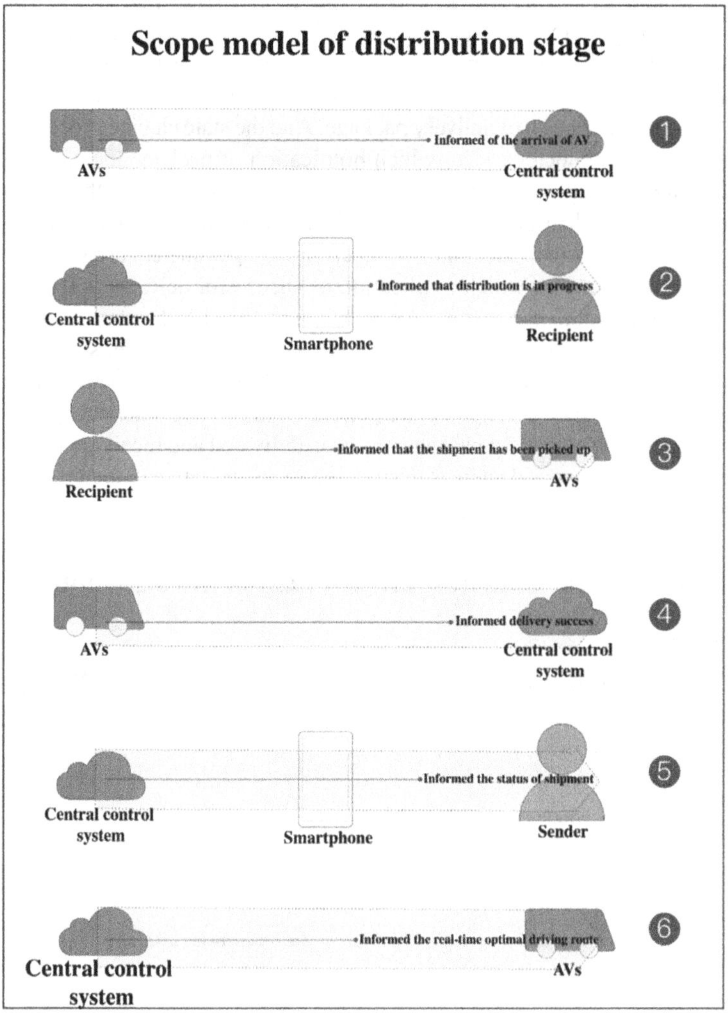

Fig. 8. Scope model of distribution stage

5.2 Architecture Design of Information Interaction

Information Requirements Analysis. The scenario model is applied to analyze the receiver state parameters of the receiver state change process in four stages including the loading, driving, distribution and receiving stages, and the target receiver state parameters are filtered out to express the information requirements that support the realization of the service demands. As is shown in Fig. 9, the state change process of the central control system in the distribution stage involves two receiver state change processes, namely notification of autonomous vehicles arrival and notification of successful delivery. The two state change processes generate four receiver state parameters from which location information of receiving package and information of receiving successful delivery are selected as the destination receiver state parameters. As is shown in Fig. 10, the recipient's state change process in the distribution stage involves a receiver state change process, namely notification of delivery package. And the state change process generates two receiver state parameters, from which notification of package location is selected as the destination receiver state parameters. As is shown in Fig. 11, the sender's state change process in the distribution stage involves a receiver state change process, namely notification of the package state, and two receiver state parameters are generated in the state change process, from which notification of successful delivery is selected as the destination receiver state parameters. As is shown in Fig. 12, the state change process of autonomous vehicles in the distribution stage involves two receiver state change processes, namely notification of successful package pick-up and notification of the driven routes. Five receiver state parameters are generated in the two state change processes, from which notification that the package has been delivered and receiving the route plan to the next destination are selected as destination receiver state parameters.

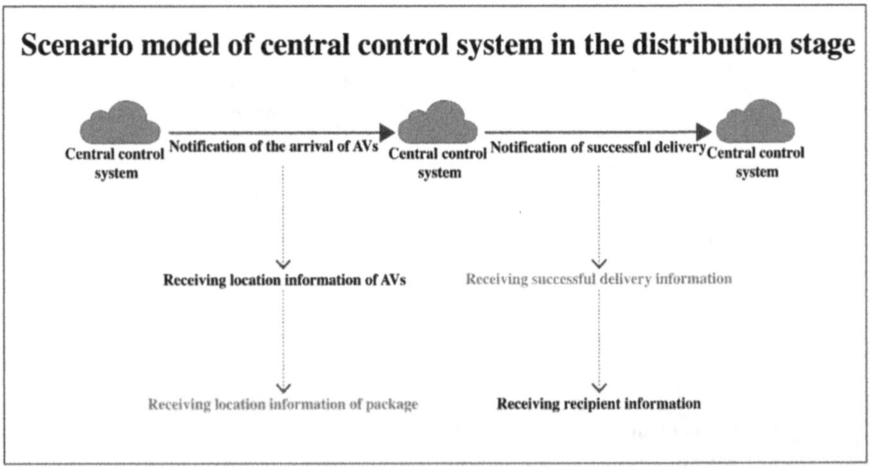

Fig. 9. Scenario model of central control system in the distribution stage

Information Requirements Analysis. The scenario model is applied to explore and analyze the information requirements that support the construction of service supply-demand relationship and the realization of purpose of service needs in the four stages of loading, driving, distribution and receiving. Based on the above, the information relationship architecture design model of loading stage, information relationship architecture

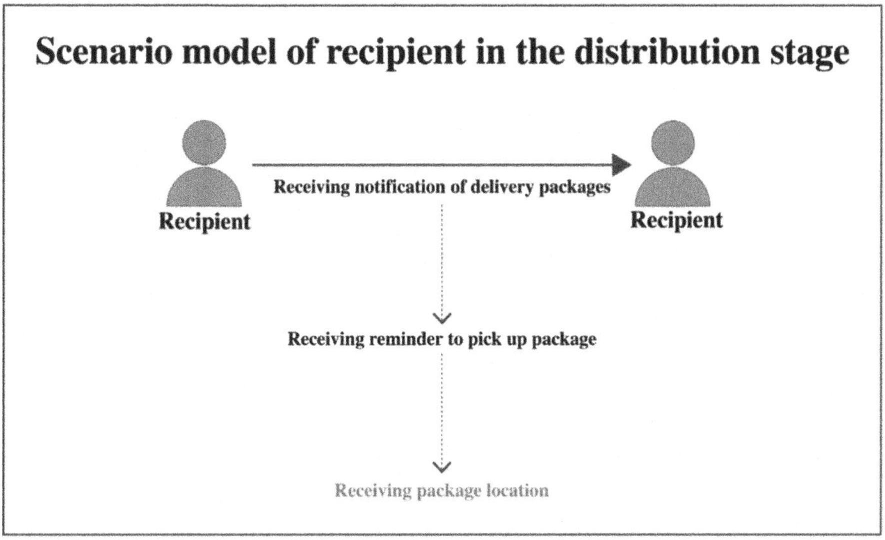

Fig. 10. Scenario model of recipient in the distribution stage

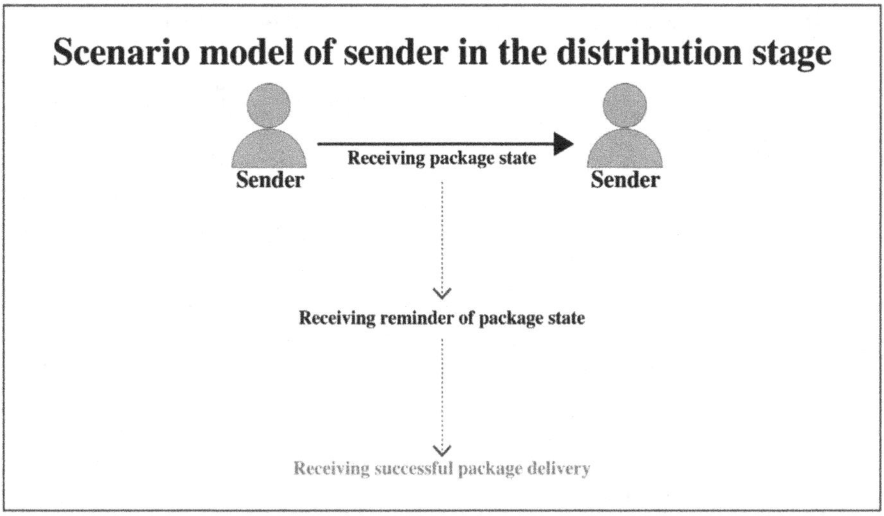

Fig. 11. Scenario model of sender in the distribution stage

design model of driving stage, information relationship architecture design model of distribution stage (see Fig. 13), and information relationship architecture design model of receiving stage are constructed. The above four information relationship architecture models represent the information requirements and information media in the system.

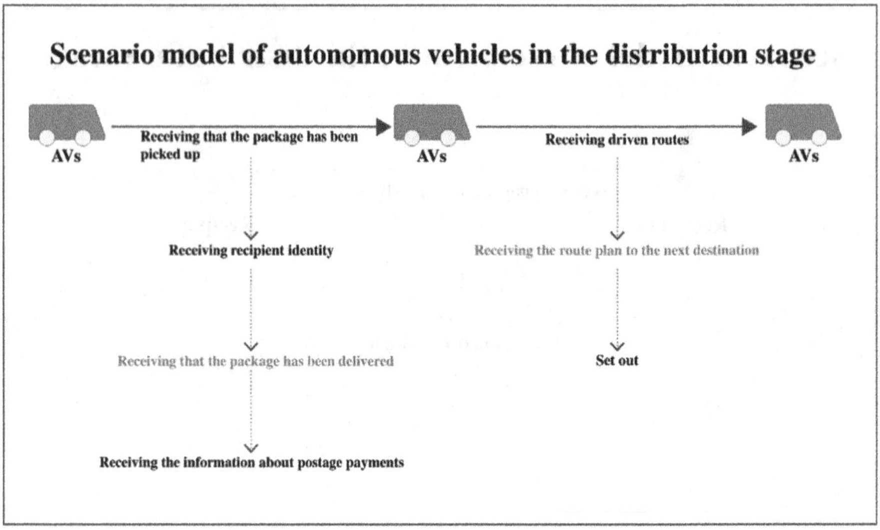

Fig. 12. Scenario model of autonomous vehicles in the distribution stage

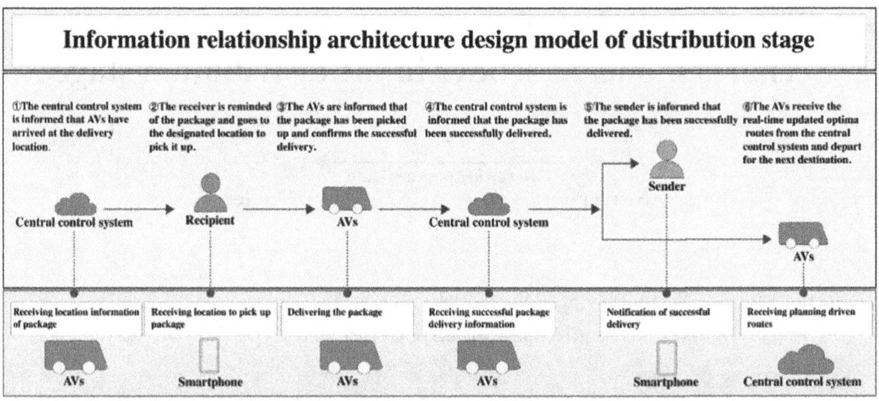

Fig. 13. Information relationship architecture design model of distribution stage

5.3 Product Function Specification Design

Functional Requirements Analysis. Take the distribution stage as an example, the service relationship, purpose of service needs and purpose of information requirements are analyzed to acquire the information requirements for autonomous vehicles that support the realization of system service needs and purpose, namely the central control system receiving the location information from autonomous vehicles, package delivery by autonomous vehicles and the central control system being informed that the package has been successfully signed. As is shown in Fig. 14, the view model of autonomous vehicles in the distribution stage is applied to analyze the functional specifications of autonomous vehicles product that support the realization of purpose of information requirements, including autonomous vehicles informing the location, autonomous vehicles delivering the package to the recipient and autonomous vehicles informing the central control system that the shipment has been signed. The content includes autonomous vehicles informing the arrival, autonomous vehicles informing the location information, identifying the recipient, delivering the package, the recipient information and sign time. The channel includes vehicle-mounted communication module, vehicle-mounted positioning system, face recognition, entering the pickup code, Alipay code scanning, opening cargo storage cabinet and vehicle-mounted communication module.

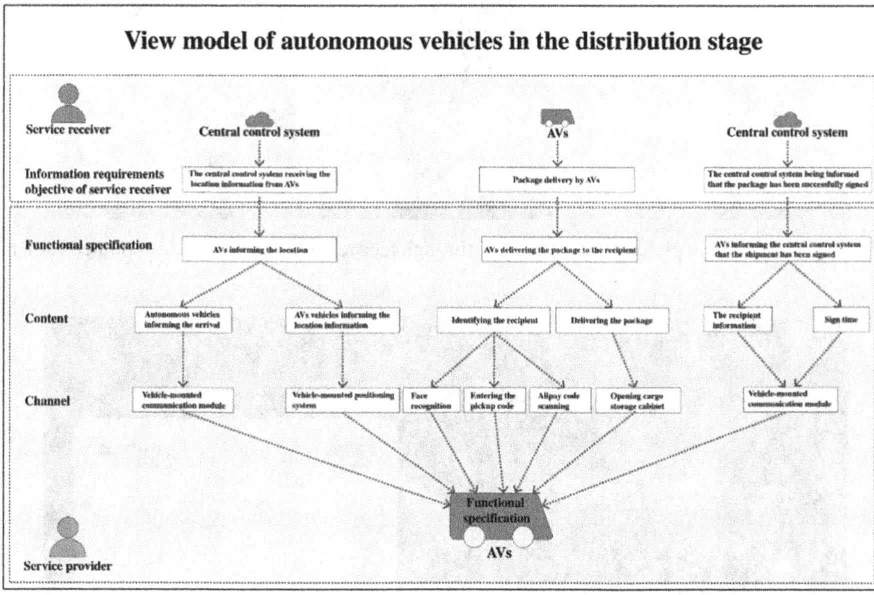

Fig. 14. View model of autonomous vehicles in the distribution stage

Product Prototype Design. The product functional parameters of autonomous vehicles are defined through product functional specification analysis. The parameters of the loading, driving, distribution and receiving stages in the autonomous vehicles view model are applied to the product characterization design of autonomous vehicles. Figure 15 shows the recipient picking up the package through face recognition of vehicle-mounted camera. Figure 16 shows the product characterization design of autonomous vehicles in the scenario of the vehicle-mounted onscreen interface when the recipient picks up the package.

Fig. 15. The recipient picking up the package through face recognition of vehicle-mounted camera

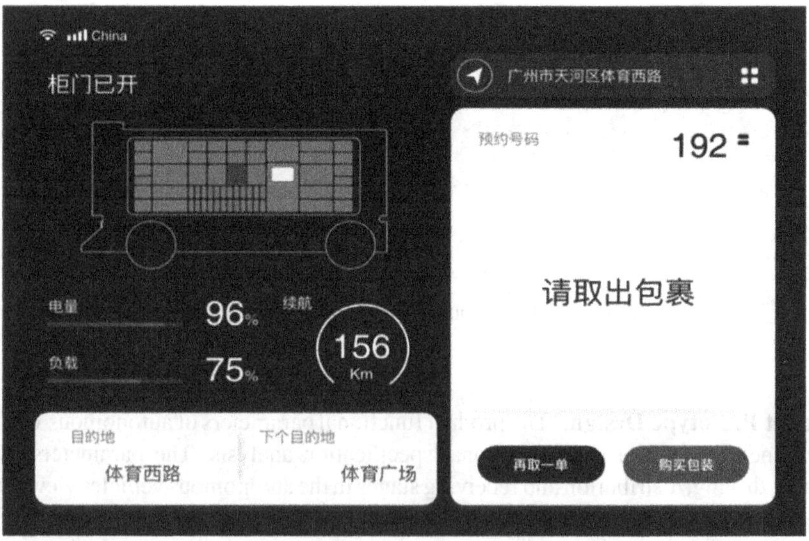

Fig. 16. Vehicle-mounted interface when the recipient picks up the package

6 Conclusion

With the empowerment of 5G technology, autonomous vehicles will have more room to be widely used in various social service scenarios. The content of autonomous vehicles design is gradually shifting from the interaction design of a monolithic task mode that focuses on driving performance to the product-service system design of a multichannel task mode that attaches importance to satisfy logistics service demands. The smart product-service system with autonomous vehicles as the medium resorts to the identification of user needs and service provider capabilities so as to construct the human mobility knowledge map, help users autonomously complete driving and transportation tasks under automation control, assist users in completing vehicle-mounted basic information interaction tasks, and collaborate with the whole system to meet social service needs.

References

1. Goedkoop, M., Haler, C.V., Te Riele, H., Rommens, P.J.: Product service systems, ecological and economic basics. Report for Dutch Ministries of Environment (VROM) and Economic Affairs (EZ) **36**(1), 1–122 (1999)
2. Maussang, N., Zwolinski, P., Brissaud, D.: Product-Service System design methodology: from the PSS architecture design to the products specifications. J. Eng. Des. **20**(4), 349–366 (2009)
3. Valencia, A., Mugge, R., Schoormans, J.P.L., et al.: The design of smart product-service systems (PSSs): an exploration of design characteristics. Int. J. Des. **9**(1), 13–28 (2015)
4. Valencia Cardona, A.M., Mugge, R., Schoormans, J.P.L., Schifferstein, H.N.J.: Characteristics of smart PSSs: design considerations for value creation. In: CADMC 2013: 2nd Cambridge Academic Design Management Conference, pp. 1–14. Delft University of Technology, Cambridge (2013)
5. Chang, D., Gu, Z., Li, F., Jiang, R.: A user-centric smart product-service system development approach: A case study on medication management for the elderly. Advanced Engineering Informatics (42), 100979 (2019)
6. Sakao, T., Shimomura, Y., Sundin E., et al.: Modeling design objects in CAD system for Service /Product Engineering. Computer-Aided Design (413), 197–213 (2009)
7. Komoto, H., Tomiyama, T.: Integration of a service CAD and a life cycle simulator. CIRP Ann. Manuf. Technol. **57**(1), 9–12 (2008)
8. Feng, L.U., Liu, K., Chen, J.: Research on human mobility in big data era. J. Geo-Inform. Sci. **16**(5), 665–672 (2014)
9. Noulas, A., Scellato, S., Mascolo, C., et al. An empirical study of geographic user activity patterns in Foursquare. In: ICWSM11, pp. 70–573 (2011)
10. Liu, Y., Sui, Z., Kang, C., et al.: Uncovering patterns of interurban trip and spatial interaction from social media check-In data. PloS ONE **9**(1), e86026 (2014)
11. Aquilani, B., Piccarozzi, M., Abbate, T., et al.: The role of open innovation and value co-creation in the challenging transition from industry 4.0 to society 5.0: toward a theoretical framework. Sustainability **12**(21), 8943 (2020)

Recognition Research and Innovative Design of Icons in In-Vehicle Infotainment System

Sizhuo Tang(✉)

Zhongnan University of Economics and Law, Wuhan, HB, China
1621249029@qq.com

Abstract. The icons and their recognition are of great significance to the development of electrification, intelligence, networking and sharing of vehicles all over the world. The intelligence of vehicles also puts forward higher requirements for the icon design of the in-vehicle display screens. Based on relevant research results at home and abroad, based on user experience and user needs, this paper adopted the case study method, used 24 icons for different purposes in three different systems such as Carplay, Android Auto, and CarLife to carry out paired tests, carried out a questionnaire survey, and discussed the usability of icon design, as well as the characteristics for recognition and the reasons for confusion or misunderstanding. The experimental results showed that the correct recognition rate of 4 icons was more than 90%, and the correct recognition rate of 13 icons was less than 60%. 73.6% of the subjects thought that the quality of the icons was very important and would affect the use of the car. At the beginning of using the car, 68% of the subjects often or occasionally misunderstood the icons of the in-vehicle system. The subjects held that the current in-vehicle system had some problems, such as low accuracy, single color, poor human-computer interaction experience and insufficient usability optimization in the driving environment. Finally, the paper has put forward the influence of six key elements for discussion, such as interface, color, icon recognition rate, icon features, icon shape, research and sorting, in order to make efforts in usability and innovation.

Keywords: Icon · Icon design · In-vehicle infotainment system · Usability · User experience

1 Introduction

With the rapid development of China's economy, people's practical demand for cars is becoming ever stronger. Many families already have more than one car. In this era of the interconnection of all things, the functions carried by in-vehicle systems are soaring. How to clearly present the rich and diverse content functions to users and make their operation more convenient and safe is a problem to be considered. How to balance the complexity of the functions of in-vehicle systems and the convenience of users also puts forward new requirements for icon design.

P.-L. P. Rau (Ed.): HCII 2022, LNCS 13314, pp. 248–259, 2022.
https://doi.org/10.1007/978-3-031-06053-3_17

The rapid development of urban transportation and the automobile industry all over the world provides a good opportunity for the popularization of in-vehicle systems. With the development of intelligence, the central control large screen has been widely used in cars. The in-vehicle display screens are now developing towards large screens, which has greatly changed the design style of icons in the in-vehicle infotainment system compared with the previous in-vehicle icons. Many in-vehicle icons have also changed from black-and-white icons or monochrome buttons to intelligent colorful icons. Therefore, in order to accurately recognize the meaning of icons, there are new and higher requirements for designers. At the same time, the larger the screen, the greater the probability that the driver's attention will be distracted. During driving, most of the driver's visual attention should be used to control the vehicle, maintain the driving state and deal with emergencies. The design of the in-vehicle information system must enable the driver to recognize and operate quickly and efficiently, so as to improve the use efficiency [5].

From the current icon design of the in-vehicle infotainment system, the designs of some icons were based on the visual design method of traditional media. The generation of these icons was mostly based on the designer's own understanding of the icons, ignoring the user's thinking mode and cognitive habits, so it was difficult to establish an effective connection between design and practical operation [25]. While exploring the icon design, we should also introduce the concept of user experience, understand and explore the needs of users, and take this as a reference for design, so as to design icons more in line with the thinking of users.

2 Literature Review

The icons and their recognition are of great significance to the development of electrification, intelligence, networking, and sharing of vehicles all over the world. The research on icon design abroad commenced relatively early, and the representative achievements are as follows: T*he Icon Book: Visual Symbols for Computer Systems and Documentation* compiled by William Horton (1994) [15]. It studies the origin of icon design, the function of icon language, the experience, and suggestions of icon design, icon design cases, etc. It also expounds on the theory of icons and provides guidance for design practice. Edited by Gregory Thomas, *How to Design Logos, Symbols & Icons: 24 Internationally Renowned Studios Reveal How They Develop Trademarks for Print and New Media* [14] mainly studies the combination of practice and theory from a wide range of design elements, strategies, and creative processes. Most of the papers on icon design are from the perspective of the experiment, such as Everett, Sarah P.'s, which mainly analyzes the change of icon spacing and its impact on users' visual search according to the data obtained from the eye tracker experiment [25].

There is little research on the theory of icon design in China, mostly involved in the study of digital interface. For example, the definition, type, relationship with semiotics, ways of conveying information, and other contents of icons are described in *The Art Design of Digital Graphical Interface* compiled by Lu Xiaobo and Zhan Binghong [10], which provides some theoretical support for subsequent researchers. With the advent of the era of the internet economy, experience economy, and metaverse, the internet industry has continuously promoted the continuous upgrading and optimization of user experience. The research on user experience in domestic academic circles has also begun to take effect, and a number of works and papers have emerged.

As an important factor of human-computer communication, icons can convey interface information figuratively and directly, shorten interaction steps, improve recognition efficiency and improve user experience. The traditional icon design concept and form can not meet the increasingly diversified needs of users, so it puts forward newer and higher requirements for icon design. In order to improve the usability of the in-vehicle infotainment system, this study selects icons for different purposes for pairing experiments to explore the usability of icon design, the characteristics for recognition, and the reasons for confusion or misunderstanding. It also discusses how to make choices on icon design, in order to make efforts in usability and innovation.

3 Research Methods and Analyses of the Experiment

This study adopted the method of case study, used 24 icons for different purposes in three different systems, and discussed the characteristics of icon communication significance from the perspective of user recognition, to provide designers with a full understanding and mastery of user needs and guide the direction of icon design in the future.

3.1 Specific Icons

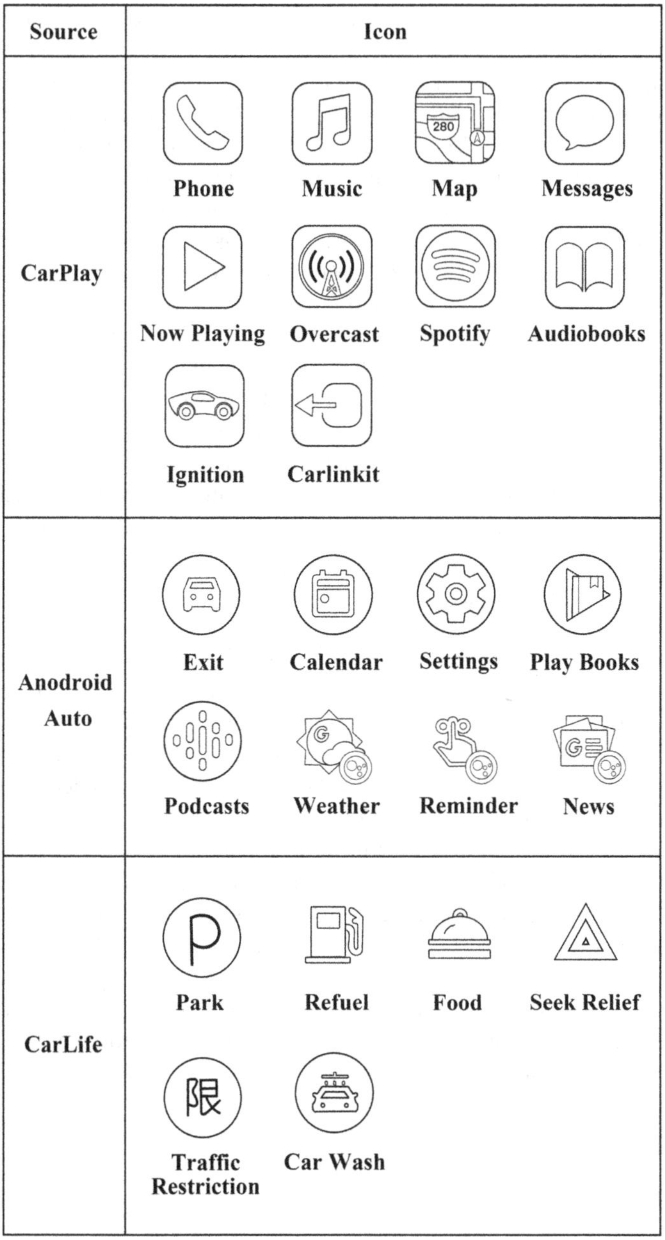

Source
Icon
CarPlay
280
Phone
Music
Map
Messages
Now Playing
Overcast
Spotify
Audiobooks
Ignition
Carlinkit
Anodroid Auto
Exit
Calendar
Settings
Play Books
Podcasts
Weather
Reminder
News
CarLife
Park
Refuel
Food
Seek Relief
限
Traffic Restriction
Car Wash

Fig. 1. 24 Icons for different uses

3.2 Survey by Questionnaire

3.3 Experiment

The in-vehicle systems have complex functions. In order to effectively convey all kinds of information, study the style of individual icons and fully understand the needs of users, the experiment selected 24 icons and text annotations for different purposes in three common systems on the market (see Fig. 1), and asked the participants to finish the pairing test and questionnaire (see Fig. 2). The three chosen systems were respectively Carplay system, Android auto system, and Carlife system. Among them, 10 icons of the Carplay system, 8 icons of the Android auto system, and 6 icons of the Carlife system were selected. There were 19 questionnaire questions. According to the audience of the in-vehicle infotainment system, 125 people with driving licenses in all walks of life of different ages were selected as participants and they were required to select the corresponding text meaning for the icons in the questionnaire. In order to ensure the influence of age difference on the understanding ability of icons, the number of subjects of all ages selected in this experiment was basically the same. 125 valid questionnaires were received. The experimental results of the paired test has been shown in Table 1. The horizontal axis in the table represents icons, the vertical axis represents the text meaning they represent, the middle column represents the matching accuracy of subjects, and the numbers in the table represent the matching times of icons and their text meanings.

3.4 Analyses of the Experiment

According to statistics, the correct recognition rate of 4 icons was more than 90%: Phone (99.2%), Refuel (95.2%), Parking (93.6%), and Music (92%). These four are called highly-recognized groups. The correct recognition rate of 13 icons was less than 60%: Overcast (32%), Spotify (6.4%), Ignition (8%), Carlinkit (3.2%), Exit (4%), Calendar (28.8), Play Books (9.6%), Podcasts (4%), Weather (36%), Reminder (13.6%), News (16%), Food (45.6%), and Seek Relief (22.4%).

There are some icons with similar meanings that can be calculated together. For example, Overcast and Podcasts are both podcast software. In Overcast icons, 32% of the people chose Overcast and 23.2% of the people chose Podcasts; Calculated by being recognized as podcast software, the recognition rate will reach 55.2%. For another example, both Audio books and Play Books contain the meaning of Audio books. In the Audio books icon, 62.4% of the people chose Audio books and 24% of the people chose Play Books. As calculated by being podcast software or not, the recognition rate will reach 86.4%. See Table 2 for details.

-What's your age?
-18-28, 29-39, 40-50, over 50

-What's your gender?
-Male, Female

-How long have you been driving?
-Within 1 year, 1-3 years, 3-10 years, over 10 years

-What's your occupation?

-What is the in-vehicle system you are using?
-CarPlay, Carlife, Android Auto or others.

-Have you used more than one in-vehicle system before?
-No; Yes: 2, 3, more than 3

-Is the in-vehicle system used by your car mainly electronic screen adjusted or button adjusted ?

-Do you often misunderstand the in-vehicle system icon in the early stage of vehicle use?
-Often, occasionally, once or twice, never

-Do you think the quality of icons is important in in-vehicle system? Does it affect your use of the car?
-Important and influential, unimportant but influential, important but not influential, unimportant and not influential

What do you think are the advantages and disadvantages of the in-vehicle system now used?

-Which color do you prefer among the in-vehicle system icons? (multiple choices)
-Black and white, warm, cool, colorful, monochrome, gradient, strong contrast

-How many colors do you prefer in in-vehicle system icon color matching?
-1-3, 3-5, 5 or more

-Do you think the size of the current in-vehicle system icon is appropriate ?
-Too big, too small, moderate

-What kind of icon design do you prefer?
-Background color + pure white silhouette, pure color silhouette, colorful figurative pattern, combination of letters and images, single line, don't care

-Which shape do you prefer?
-Circle, rectangle, rounded rectangle, don't care

-In the process of recognizing icons during daily driving, which one do you prefer to pay attention to? (Are you highly dependent on icons?)
-Icons, text annotations under icons, both, the in-vehicle system is rarely used

-Do you want the icon to attract your attention by flashing or other means when needed?
-I intensely don't hope, I don't hope, general, I hope, I intensely hope, I don't care

-Do you want the icon form in the in-vehicle system to be customized or have multiple theme modes?
-I intensely don't hope, I don't hope, general, I hope, I intensely hope, I don't care

-Do you want the position of the icon in the in-vehicle system to be customized?
-I intensely don't hope, I don't hope, general, I hope, I intensely hope, I don't care

Fig. 2. Questionnaire.

Table 1. Paired test results.

Accuracy / Order	Icon / %																								
Phone	99.2	**124**							2					1	2	1	3	2		3	2	2	1	2	3
Music	92		**115**	2	2	7		1					1		2	2	2	2	2			2	3	2	
Map	76			**95**					1		1	2		2	1		5	4	6						1
Messages	88.8				**111**		4	4			1				2	2	5		10				2		
NowPlaying	70.4		8			**88**	5	3				1	3	1	13	1	2	3	2		1	1			
Overcast	32			1	3	6	**40**	16	2	1	2		14		14	11	7	6	12			2	1		
Spotify	6.4					3		**8**				1	3		5	7	2	3	2			2	1		
Audiobooks	62.4						5	7	**78**		1		5		4	5	1	3	10			2			2
Ignition	8		1	1	1	1	1	3		**10**	6		17	1	3	4	3	24	2	2	1	5	9		2
Carlinkit	3.2			1		1	15		1	53	**4**	18	1	5	5	7	3	6	6			4	2		10
Exit	5			6	1			2			77	**5**	1		6			2				3	4		2
Calendar	28.8							1	2				**36**		3	7	4	4	7			3	1		2
Settings	82.4							3	1	2	2		2	**103**	3	5		5				2	3	1	1
Play Books	9.6					7	3	7	30		2		2	1	**12**	6	5	11	6	1		1	1	1	
Podcasts	4				4	3	29	15	3	2	1		3	1	6	**5**	7	5	10	1		2		1	
Weather	36							4				1	1	1	2	4	**45**		2			9	1		3
Reminder	13.6			1	2	3	6	16		2	11	5	12	5	13	22	10	**17**	13		1	16	37	4	
News	16						3	3	3		2		4	1	8	12	5	4	**20**		1		1		1
Park	93.6			4		1	1	1		29	1	41	1		2					**117**			3	1	3
Refuel	95.2			2	1			1		3	3	4	7		3	1	1	4	3		**119**	1			
Food	45.6		1	4				1	1	1		1	2	1	6	10	8	6	8			**57**	3	2	1
Seek Relief	22.4	1					11	3			2	4	4		2	2	4	11	1			3	**28**	2	3
Traffic Restriction	87.2			8		2	2		1	5	4	31	4	1	7	5	2	2	1			3	23	**109**	3
Car Wash	70.4									17	3	11	2	1	1	4	1	1	2			2		1	**88**

Table 2. Comparison of experimental recognition results of icons.

Icon	Recognized as 1	Recognized as 2	Icon	Recognized as 1	Recognized as 2
 Overcast	 Overcast 32%	 Podcasts 8.8%	 Audio Books	 Audio Books 62.4%	 Play Books 3.2%
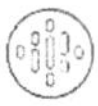 Podcasts	 Overcast 23.2%	 Podcasts 4%	 Play Books	 Audio Books 24%	 Play Books 9.6%

In the analyses of the questionnaire, it is found that 52% of the participants did not know the name of the in-vehicle system they were using. In the other half of the participants, the most frequently used in-vehicle systems were mainly Carplay (15.2%) and Android auto (16.8%), and the usage of Carlife system was 8%. 59.2% of the participants have only used one in-vehicle system, 28.8% have used two, and 12% have used three or more.

It is worth mentioning that 73.6% of the participants told that the quality of icons was significant and would affect the use of cars. In the early stage of using the car, 68% of the participants often or occasionally misunderstood the icons of the in-vehicle system.

At the same time, the participants held that the current in-vehicle system had some problems, such as low accuracy, difficulty in finding, too many texts with one single color, poor human-computer interaction experience, poor interface friendliness, insufficient usability optimization in the driving environment, etc.

In the color matching of icons, 35.2% of participants preferred the color matching of warm colors, and the proportion of people who chose strong contrast colors, colorful colors, and black and white colors is 29.6%, 22.4% and 20%. In terms of color selection, more than half (59.2%) preferred simple color matching of 1–3 colors. As for the form of icon design, 33.6% of participants preferred the combination of letters and images, while 29.6% thought that colorful figurative patterns were more pleasant.

For the discussion of icon shape, there was no obvious preference as a whole. 28% of the participants chose the circle, 13.6% chose the rectangle, 27.2% chose the rounded rectangle, and 31.2% said they didn't care.

In daily icon recognition, 43.4% of the participants paid more attention to the texts annotations, 30.4% paid more attention to the icons themselves, and 15.2% paid more attention to both.

4 Discussion

In the process of icon design based on user experience, we need to realize that although the method of case study can effectively break down user barriers and meet the market demand under the new situation, it is not difficult to see that the needs of users are extensive and difficult to be comprehensive in the sampling analysis of user needs. The target user group can be divided into expert users, casual users, and mainstream users. The sampled users are a random combination of three user groups, so the results of the experiment may be different. When analyzing the experimental results, we should take the main types of user needs as the main reference objects.

Through the study of icons, we have found the influence of the following key elements.

4.1 Interface

The simple and intuitive interface information can make the driver clear at a glance. While driving, drivers can't spend too much energy on the information interface, otherwise, there will be safety problems. This requires that the font size of icons and texts annotations should be moderate, and the proportion and position arrangement of the font size of icons and text annotations need to be further studied. Because the recognition of icons is faster than that of text annotations, the main consideration in the design is to give priority to icons, supplemented by texts, so as to enhance the visual recognition rate. At the same time, the interface layout shall be reasonable, and the frequently used and important icons shall be placed at the position of the visual center for easy viewing. The icons and their arrangement of them should be regular and logical.

4.2 Color

Color is often stronger and more direct than the visual sense of shape elements, thus it can enrich the form and content of digital interface, and is most easily attracted in recognition. As everyone's growth environment is different and their education and lifestyle are also different, different color matching will bring different psychological feelings to everyone. However, most people have a similar understanding of colors. While designing a complete set of in-vehicle system icons, we should be aware of the overall situation, and consider the design style and warm and cold color matching between icons and between icons and the overall application system consistently, so as to make the interface harmonious and unified and present the outstanding effect of icons. When designing a set of icons, the icon patterns and texts annotations should be clearly visible. Whether the important information can be presented clearly or not is directly related to the user's experience.

When emphasizing elements with colors, there should be obvious differences between colors. Through the color matching with different colors, special color effects can be produced. The main contrast methods are hue contrast, chroma contrast, lightness contrast, complementary color contrast, and area contrast. At the same time, in the use of the overall color, try to use no more than three colors as the main colors of the picture.

For the interface color, the two modes of day and night can be taken into consideration, because high saturation and high brightness are needed to make the recognition stronger during the day. However, the color and brightness at night will make the interface flash and affect driving safety. In the questionnaire survey, we found that most participants wanted the icons to attract people's attention by flashing or other ways when needed. We can also use some specific general colors, such as red for warning and green for safety. When a red icon flashes in the system, it will quickly attract the driver's attention. Moreover, appropriately enhancing the lightness difference on important icons can make them clearly visible.

4.3 Icon Recognition Rate

The metaphor and complexity of icons are important factors affecting the recognition rate of icons.

Designers can use figurative icons and adopt familiar styles in people's daily life. For example, Phone (99.2%) uses the shape of the landline microphone as the icon, and Music (92%) uses the shape of notes as the icon. As everyone is very familiar with these common icons, the correct recognition rates of them are very high.

The use of metaphorical icons. Utilizing common things in life or the visual image of things, abstracting and refining their basic characteristics to refer to the function of icons should be considered. From the cognitive point of view, people will unconsciously associate the icon they see with other known icons. When designing icons, we should grasp people's thinking and select appropriate icons to reduce the error rate and burden of memory.

There are many icons designed in the form of customization, which will lead to difficulty for users to understand their intention and cognitive impairment after these icons leave the text annotation. For example, Spotify (6.4%) and Podcasts (4%) use some special icon designs. Even looking at the text annotations below the icon, it is sometimes difficult to match them. If this icon is already a very well-known one, it will be easier to be recognized, but most of these irregular icons need users to memorize repeatedly. In particular, there is a large age gap among people driving cars. The elder may not understand what the young people know. Therefore, in the design of in-vehicle system icons, we should try to avoid and use fewer such icons, and design more icons that suit all.

4.4 Icon Features

When the two icons have similar meanings, highlight their features, strengthen key information to avoid confusion. Because there are too many functions of the in-vehicle system, and it is inevitable that some functions with similar meanings will appear. As they have similar icon design, if the driver does not observe carefully, it is easy to make icon recognition errors. For example, Now Playing and Play Books represent different meanings, but the Play Books icon only adds a small book logo compared to that of Now Playing, which is easy to be confused, and it will be difficult to find the required functions. In addition, as reflected in the survey, when the participants chose the meaning of the icon Play Books, they often understood it as the meaning of other similar functions. It has been shown that the icon recognition rate of Play Books selected in this case was very low and could not correctly represent its correct meaning. As shown in Table 3.

Table 3. Experimental recognition results of "Play Book" Icon.

Icon	Accuracy	Icon	Accuracy
 Audio books	24%	 Now Playing	10.4%
 Overcast	11.2%	 Play Books	9.6%

The composition of icons is mainly the arrangement of simple geometric figures of the basic structure, such as points, lines, and faces. Compared with other elements, the elements of point are easier to attract people's attention. In terms of the features of icons, frequent uses of elements of point will help express the icon's content, which will draw the user's attention to the features of icons, so as to improve the recognition rate of icons.

4.5 Icon Shape

Although in the questionnaire survey, participants did not have a clear preference for the shape of the outer contour of the icon, and even ignored its influence in the icon the shape of the icon is still of great importance. The screen style of the circular automobile display screen is mostly rectangular and irregular rectangle. Adding an appropriate amount of circular icons to many rectangular icons can quickly lead out of the rectangular interface. The ingenious combination of circle and square can also increase the interest and vividness of the picture and better guide users to find the needed functions.

4.6 Research and Sorting

There are also some icons, although in figurative expressions, representing meanings not the same as that understood by most people. It may be due to that the designer has not done sufficient preliminary research before the design. For example, the icon of Exit and the icon of Carlinkit. Many people thought they mean something else. 77% of the participants assumed Carlinkit's icons mean exit, 32.8% thought Exit's icons mean Park, and 24.8% took Carlinkit's icons as Traffic Restriction.

In short, the preliminary research work is very important for the design of any industry. Effective early preparation can provide more convenience and more possibilities for follow-up work. By summarizing and analyzing the obtained information, we can discover the essence of things, find new ideas, and see things deep under the surface, so as to broaden our vision and make the source of problems clearer, and thus to find design inspiration.

References

1. Chen, Z.: On graphic creativity and the form of thinking. Aesthetics **5**(4), 42–44 (2006)

2. Dong, J.M.: Human Computer Interaction: User Centered Design and Evaluation, 3rd edn. Tsinghua University Press, Beijing (2010)
3. Jesse, G., Translated by Fan, X.Y.: The Elements of User Experience: User-Centered Design for the Web and Beyond. 2nd edn. China Machine Press, Beijing (2007)
4. Kraft, C., Translated by Wang, J.F., Xie, L., Guo, W.: User Experience Innovation: User Centered Design that Works, 1st edn. Posts and Telecommunications Press, Beijing (2013)
5. Li, H.F., Li, Y.F.: In-vehicle information systems interface design. Chinese J. Ergon. **20**(5), 43–46 (2014)
6. Li, S.D.: General Introduction of Interaction Design, 1st edn. Tsinghua University Press, Beijing (2009)
7. Liang, N.J.: Contemporary Cognitive Psychology, 1st edn. Shanghai Education Publishing House, Shanghai (2014)
8. Liu, G.Z.: Design Methodology, 1st edn. Higher Education Press, Beijing (2011)
9. Liu, Y.: On the status of the user experience design in China market. Packag. Eng. **32**(4), 70–73 (2011)
10. Lu, X.B., Zhan, B.H.: The Art Design of Digital Graphical Interface, 1st edn. Tsinghua University Press, Beijing (2006)
11. Su, H.: On the application of graphic semantics in graphic design. Charming China **19**(2), 156–157 (2010)
12. Tan, H., Zhang, W.Q., Zhao, J.H., Wang, W.: Automobile user interface visual information display design research. Decoration **54**(9), 106–108 (2012)
13. Tan, H., Zhao, H.J., Wang, W.: Vehicle human machine interface design research. Chinese J. Autom. Eng. **2**(5), 315–321 (2012)
14. Thomas, G.: How to Design Logos, Symbols & Icons: 24 Internationally Renowned Studios Reveal How They Develop Trademarks for Print and New Media, 1st edn. Adams Media, Hong Kong (2000)
15. Winn, W.D.: The Icon Book: Visual Symbols for Computer Systems and Documentation, 1st edn. Wiley, New Jersey (1994)
16. Wu, Y.: The study of graphic design based on the visual perception understanding. Diss. Xi'an Polytechnic University, Xi'an (2012)
17. Xi, J.: The Usability Design Research of Interface ICONS in In-vehicle Infotainment System. Diss. Jiangsu University, Zhenjiang (2017)
18. Yang, B.: Research on Interface Design of Vehicle Navigation System. Diss. Tongji University, Shanghai (2009)
19. Yu, L., Zhang, X.L.: Interaction design in-vehicle digital entertainment products. Software **34**(2), 153–154 (2013)
20. Zeng, Y.: The Design Research of Visual-Friendliness on Digital Interface Icon. Diss. Hunan University of Technology, Xiangtan (2011)
21. Zhu, L.P., Li, Y.F.: Identification of washing machine interface icons for the elderly with different cultural levels. Packaging Eng. **38**(14), 140–144 (2017)
22. Zhu, Y.M.: Analysis of Visual Language: The form and Meaning of Symbolic Image, 1st edn. Nanjing University Press, Nanjing (2011)
23. Zhou, R.: On the ideology of aesthetics in graphics creation. Art Horizon **9**(4), 37–39 (2008)
24. Zhang, Y., Pang, Y.J., Wang, L.: Research on user experience and preference of in-vehicle infotainment system. Auto Time **17**(21), 179–180 (2020)
25. Zou, J.: Research on user experience-based icon design of digital interface. Diss. Suzhou University, Suzhou (2014)

Sound Design of Forward Collision Warning Scene in Automotive Intelligent Cockpit

Yu Wang[1,2](✉), Jie Wu[1], and Hanfu He[1]

[1] College of Design and Innovation, Tongji University, Shanghai, China
asterwangyu@126.com

[2] School of Pop Music and Dance, Shanghai Institute of Visual Arts, Shanghai, China

Abstract. With the continuous progress and development of science and technology, cars are getting popular in people's daily life, and the car cabin is becoming more and more intelligent. With the development of various intelligent interactive interfaces in the car cabin and the iteration of automatic driving assistance technology, how to design an audible, understandable and effective voice in the audio-visual design of multi-interface in the car cabin to enable driving safety and improve the driving experience has become a new design problem under the background of intelligent travel in the future. Through comprehensive literature investigation and audio analysis, this study firstly summarized the human factor parameters and design strategies of automobile warning sound design, which helps for the design of interactive sound in the forward collision warning scene, and then demonstrated the sound design through the case analysis of early warning sound of five mainstream brands of cars in this scene. Collectively, the study performed in this study provide useful guidance of the sound design under the forward collision warning scene towards an intelligence and safe driving.

Keywords: Sound design · Automotive intelligent cockpit · Forward collision warning

1 Introduction

With the continuous progress and development of science and technology, cars are getting popular in people's daily life, and the car cabin is becoming more and more intelligent. The intelligent development of car cockpit brings users different experience compared with the previous in terms of car interactive experience. With the development of various intelligent interactive interfaces in the car cabin and the iteration of automatic driving assistance technology, users often need multimodal sensory channel information to realize the reasonable distribution of attention in the context of man-machine driving, so as to improve driving performance and safety.

Relevant literature in the field shows that the auditory system can supplement the visual system's inability to detect occluded objects, objects outside the field of vision and objects in the dark. In the time domain, auditory sensitivity is higher than vision, so it has an advantage in the integration of audio-visual information [1]. The dual channel of audio-visual combination can allow people to selectively ignore the information

P.-L. P. Rau (Ed.): HCII 2022, LNCS 13314, pp. 260–275, 2022.
https://doi.org/10.1007/978-3-031-06053-3_18

brought through the visual sensory channel. It can also transmit necessary information through auditory channels when needed [2]. Therefore, according to the characteristics of human information integration and processing, adding auditory interaction elements to the early warning scene of automobile intelligent cockpit and assisting the information transmission of visual channel through the information design of sound channel can enable the driver to reduce the perceived load of visual channel and enhance the user's trust in the system. At the same time, the interactive information of visual and auditory channels is added, which is more effective for the warning of danger. When the degree of danger is high, it can be prompted at the same time through the visual and auditory channels.

Zaki, Ni, Mohd, et al. Conducted a comprehensive study on the auditory warning of in vehicle safety technology. The study found that the auditory warning signal affects the driver's behavior and response in unforeseen events. Auditory alarm with a high sense of urgency is effective [3]. Good interior warning tone design can quickly and accurately remind drivers of road conditions and vehicle information, reduce the probability of accidents and improve safety [4, 5]. However, poor interior warning tone design may scare the driver or have other negative effects on the driver's response. According to the sound characteristics provided by the audible alarm system in the vehicle, the driver's behavior and ability to avoid collision will also be different [3]. How to design an audible, intelligible and effective voice in the audio-visual design of multi-interface in the car cabin to enable driving safety and experience has become a new design problem under the background of intelligent travel in the future.

In the application scenarios of automatic driving assistance technology, the forward collision warning scenario is a scenario with high urgency and frequent application. Different brands of cars have also designed different warning tones in this scene to assist drivers to make safe driving judgments and actions, but this also brings new user pain points. How to make users perceive and understand the semantics of early warning sound in this scene faster and more effectively, improve users' driving safety performance, and summarize and summarize the design principles of early warning sound in this scene are the problems that need to be solved at present.

This paper defines the sound problem in automobile intelligent cockpit, and studies the sound information processing principle in attention distribution and multimodal interaction. The auditory design strategy in audio-visual dual sensory information fusion is explored. Based on the forward collision warning scene, the human factor parameters and related cases of sound are analyzed, and a set of sound design principles and methods of forward collision warning scene in automobile intelligent cockpit are designed and summarized.

2 Materials and Methods

2.1 Terminology Descriptions Related to Sound Design in Forward Collision Warning

There are three main types of interactive sound in the intelligent cockpit, which are **sound**, **music** and **voice.** Sound is mainly used to transmit information, including UI interactive sound (such as switch on/off; delete, etc.) and driving related feedback sound (such as driving danger tone), etc. Music is mainly used for entertainment and emotional resonance. Voice can be used to convey complex information, dialogue and interaction.

Forward collision warning (FCW) scenario refers to a scenario in which the vehicle system monitors the driving environment in front of the vehicle in real time and sends a warning message when a forward collision hazard may occur, so as to warn the driver. When the vehicle speed is greater than 30 km /h, the FCW function is activated. In the forward collision warning (FCW) scenario, we use sound to transmit early warning information.

We presented Fig. 1 and Fig. 2 to show the model of sound information processing and the perception process of interactive sound.

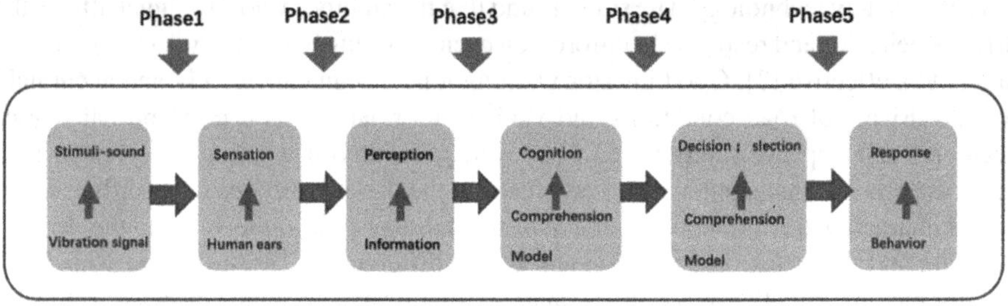

Fig. 1. Sound information processing model (From [6] p. 50)

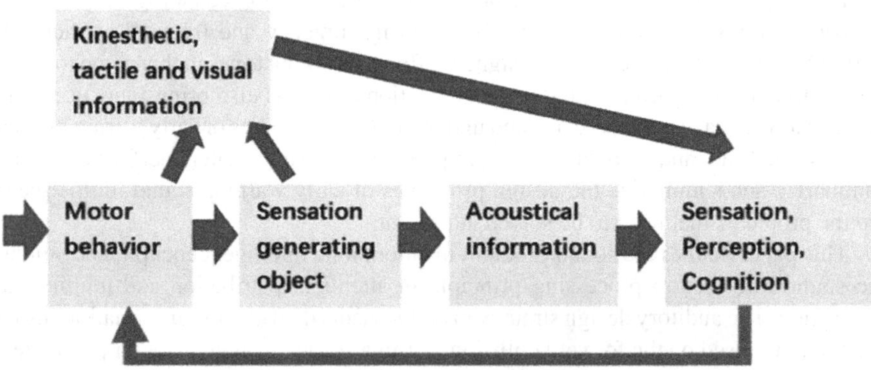

Fig. 2. Chain of events and processing stages involved in the perception and production of interactive sonic events. Arrows symbolize causal connections (From [7] p. 164)

2.2 Methods Designing

Research shows that there is an obvious interaction between auditory perception processing, attention mechanism and working memory. The timbre characteristics, loudness and delivery mechanism of poorly designed interactive sounds may lead to cognitive overload, perceived frustration and loss of main attention [8]. In the process of auditory perception processing, individuals can not consciously perceive and understand all sensory stimuli at the same time. Therefore, individuals have developed the ability to separate information flow, that is, audio-visual asynchronous processing. Attention mechanism triggered by hearing: alertness, orientation and executive control. When people hear sound, the behavior of performing control depends on the available cognitive resources, previous experience and prospective memory [8].

Therefore, combined with the five stages of sound information processing and the process of sound perception, we set the goal of automotive interactive sound design as: audibility, intelligibility and efficiency. In different scenarios of automobile intelligent cockpit, we need to design a sound that can be perceived by users and heard clearly (that is, the audibility of sound). At the same time, users should be able to quickly understand the information conveyed by the sound, reduce the user's learning cost (remember the intelligibility and efficiency of the sound), and consider the listening comfort of the sound on this basis.

ISO16352-2005 points out that the three constituent activities of driving task should be included: vehicle control; navigation; collision avoidance. In the scene of forward collision warning (FCW) in the car intelligent cockpit, we use the sound of warning category to prompt [9]. The four stages of warning include: A. target detection, sensor data reading, detection; B. Scene recognition; C. Scene evaluation; D. Output of warning.

We divide the sound design of the forward collision warning scene of the intelligent cockpit into the following levels:

(1) The first level is the sound physical attribute level. The human factor parameters of this level mainly include: frequency; Sound intensity; Sound panning. (2) The second level is the level of sound interaction mode. The design factors of this level mainly include the trigger mode of sound in the collision warning scene and the design of sound urgency. The trigger mode of sound mainly includes the design of trigger time and trigger conditions. (3) The third level is the sound design method level. The design factors at this level mainly include the design of the morphological characteristics of the sound signal, the time value of the sound, the number of cycles and the degree of urgency.

We have studied the relevant international standards published by National Highway Traffic Safety Administration (NHTSA), international organization for Standardization (ISO) and other organizations, and summarized the methods design standards of sound design in vehicle collision warning scene from the physical and psychological aspects. Relevant international standards mainly include:

(1) NHTSA DOT HS 808 535: In-Vehicle Crash Avoidance Warning Systems: Human Factors Considerations [10]
(2) ISO 11429-1996: Ergonomics System of auditory and visual danger and information signals [11]
(3) ISO 15006-2011: Road vehicles - Ergonomic aspects of transport information and control systems -Specifications for in-vehicle auditory presentation [12]
(4) ISO TR 16352-2005: Road vehicles - Ergonomic aspects of in-vehicle presentation for transport information and control systems - Warning systems [9]

Based on these summarized design standards, we will present the detailed sound design strategies as listed in the following section.

3 Sound Design Strategies of Forward Collision Warning Scene in Automotive Intelligent Cockpit

3.1 Physical Attribute Design of Sound

Frequency. The recommended frequency range for in-vehicle auditory signals is 200 Hz to 8 000 Hz. For tone signals, the main audible frequency component should be between 400 Hz and 2000 Hz, avoiding exceeding 2000 Hz, so as to include the elderly or hearing impaired. The fundamental frequency of audible alarm shall be at least in the range of 500–1500 Hz (iso15006-2011; iso16352-2005). When frequency is used as the code to distinguish the warning level, the selected fundamental frequency shall be widely distributed in the range of 200 Hz–3000 Hz rather than only concentrated in a small range. (For example, 200 Hz and 1600 Hz are selected as the main frequency points instead of 200 Hz, 300 Hz and 400 Hz) the frequencies selected should be those least affected by ambient noise. If frequency is used to encode the warning level, the impending collision avoidance warning will have the highest basic frequency (NHTSA dot HS 808 535).

From the perspective of spectral characteristics, if a single sound is used for collision avoidance warning, composite sound should be used instead of pure sinusoidal waveform. Changes in spectral characteristics can be used to encode warning levels. Complex sounds are easier to recognize than pure tones. Pure tone is also annoying for listeners. Because complex sounds contain various perceptual cues, it is easy to produce many signals that are easy to distinguish and absolutely recognize. On the contrary, the 'richness' of pure tone is low, it can only be identified according to its frequency (NHTSA dot HS 808 535). The mixing of broadband signals or narrowband signals with significantly separated center frequencies should be used to improve signal position detection and driver attention direction (iso15006-2011). For example, for the mixing of two narrowband signals, the main audible component is concentrated at about 600 Hz and the other component is concentrated at about 2000 Hz.

Sound Intensity. The recommended auditory sound pressure level range under all driving conditions is 50–90 db (a), and the ideal minimum sound signal is 75 db (A) At the driver's ear, the default intensity value of the audible warning shall be at least 20 dB, but no more than 30 dB, higher than the shielding threshold based on ambient noise under relative noise operating conditions (NHTSA dot HS 808 535).

The starting speed of the sound or tone used in the collision prevention warning shall be fast enough to remind the driver. However, the starting speed should not be too fast, otherwise it will cause serious startling effect. It is recommended that the initial speed of sound be greater than 1 dB/MS but less than 10 dB/MS. In order to avoid starling caused by sound, the sudden increase of sound should be less than 30 dB within 0.5 s. The time of warning sound, from onset to full loudness for key critical shall be less than 30ms. This is mainly because the sound head of the sound is blurred, resulting in weak warning in the sense of hearing (ISO 15006-2011). In addition, sound intensity should not be used to distinguish the urgency level of warning, because people have poor perception and judgment of sound intensity (NHTSA dot HS 808 535).

Sound Panning. Sound panning is a human factor parameter that reflects the physical properties of sound space, that is, the direction and distance information of sound. According to Simon effect, when the stimulus and response are spatially integrated (on the same side), the response speed of the subject is faster than that in the incompatible case. Therefore, the auditory stimulus should be consistent with the indicated spatial hazard information. If there is danger on the right, the orientation information of the sound points to the right, and the driver will respond faster.

Where appropriate, the warning shall cause an orienting response to make the driver look in a dangerous direction. The source of audible warning shall be consistent with the direction of danger.

3.2 Design of Sound Interaction Mode

Trigger Time. In the collision warning scene of automobile intelligent cockpit, when danger occurs, the central control instrument panel and HUD in the cockpit will give the driver corresponding prompt information on the visual channel, and the sound warning will often blend with the information of the visual channel. When to trigger sound warning is also a problem that designers need to consider.

In the brain's integration of stimuli, due to the electrochemical sensing system adopted by the retina of the visual system, vision is delayed by about 30–50 ms compared with the rapid auditory conduction system [13]. The sound appears before the image and responds quickly to the target stimulus; The sound appears synchronously with the image or the sound is delayed from the image, and the response time to the target stimulus is prolonged [14]. In order to synchronize the integration of audio-visual information and speed up the response to the target stimulus, the sound information needs to be more than 50 ms ahead of the visual information. Under the condition of close distance of hazard sources, the propagation time difference of audio-visual signals can be ignored. With the increase of distance, the sound collision warning signal needs to be presented prior to the visual signal to form audio-visual integration [15].

Trigger Condition. Minderhou and Bovy put forward the concept of time to collision (TTC). At present, the National Highway Traffic Safety Administration (NHTSA) is responsible for forward collision warning.

The test is mainly based on "TTC collision time" (distance between two vehicles/relative speed). Combining the sound trigger conditions of collision warning with the visual prompt in the intelligent cockpit or designing the trigger mode related to TTC level can improve the driver's driving performance in the collision warning scene to a certain extent.

3.3 Sound Design Method

Urgency. ISO 16352-2005 makes the following signal words standard for communicating hazard intensities, namely 'danger', 'warning' and 'caution'. This can be used as a general classification of interior signals, trying to attract the driver's attention to any dangerous state inside or outside the vehicle 'danger 'usually corresponds to the case of TTC = 1,' warning 'corresponds to the case of TTC = 2, both of which are high emergency, while' caution 'generally corresponds to the case of TTC = 3, which is low emergency. In the forward collision warning scenario, the urgency of the warning sound is generally "danger" high. Very urgent collision warning must be presented through at least two modes: visual + auditory or visual + tactile mode; The auditory channel is the recommended channel for emergency collision warning (ISO 16352:2005).

Sound Format Design. ISO 11429-1996 classifies the characteristics of auditory signals, as shown in Fig. 3:

Sound	Light	Meaning	Remarks
SWEEPING Sliding increase or decrease in frequency at a rate of 5 Hz/s to 5 Hz/ms (variation permitted during cycle)	RED	Danger, act urgently	Highest sweeping rate principally for high tone frequencies, and vice versa. Lowest rate not to be used for sound segments shorter than 5 s, and not for tone frequencies above 400 Hz
BURSTS, quick-pulses When grouped, at least five pulses in each group. Pulse frequency 4 Hz to 8 Hz (pulse length 60 ms to 100 ms)	RED	Danger, act urgently	Reverberation can cause perceptual difficulty at pulse frequencies above 5 Hz. See ISO 7731
ALTERNATING Stepwise sequence of two or three distinct pitches, each segment 0,15 s to 1,5 s	RED	Danger, act urgently	Intensity as well as duration of the ON phase of sound segments equal
SHORT sound Constant spectrum, minimum duration 0,3 s	YELLOW	Caution, be alert	When different sound segment lengths are used, a ratio of 1:3 is recommended
SEQUENCE Two or three different sounds, each with constant spectrum	BLUE	Command, mandatory action	
PROLONGED sound Constant spectrum	GREEN	Normal condition All clear	Signal given after PUBLIC ALARM shall not be interrupted within 30 s

Fig. 3. Scheme for character of auditory signals

The information in Fig. 3 shows that Sweeping (sliding frequency sound), Bursts (quick-pulses sound), Alternating (stepwise sequency sound) and short sound are the four types of sound that express dangerous situations morphology. Of these, 'Sweeping', 'Bursts' and 'Alternating' express a higher degree of urgency, while 'Short sound' expresses a relatively low level of urgency. Therefore, in a collision warning scenario, 'Sweeping', 'Bursts' and 'Alternating' are more likely to convey a higher level of urgency and these three sound patterns are more appropriate.

Pulse format and time between pulses influence the perceived urgency significantly. Urgent warnings should have a higher signal repetition rate, a higher intensity and a higher fundamental frequency than cautionary warnings (ISO 16352-2005).

Figure 4 and Fig. 5 summarize the sound format design:

High urgency	Urgency	Sound Character
	Danger	1. Sweeping (sliding frequency sound) 2. Bursts (quick-pulses sound) 3. Alternating (stepwise sequency sound)
	Caution	Short sound
Low urgency	Normal condition	Prolonged sound

Fig. 4. Corresponding table of emergency degree and sound form of sound

Sound Format	Design constraints	remarks
Sweeping	1.Continuously or discretely varying frequency signal. 2.The frequency increases or decreases smoothly in the proportion of 5Hz /s ~ 5Hz /ms	1.The highest sweep frequency is mainly used for treble frequency. 2.The lowest sweep frequency is used for bass frequency. 3.The minimum sweep frequency is not applicable to sound segments shorter than 5S and sound tones higher than 400Hz.
Bursts	1.The pulse sound group with short and obvious interruption occurs periodically, and the pulse period including interruption is 0.125-0.25s. 2.Each group shall have at least 5 sound pulses (monosyllabic), with pulse frequency of 4Hz-8Hz and pulse length of 60-80ms.	When the pulse frequency is higher than 5Hz, it may cause difficulty in perception.
Alternating	1.Continuously switch between 2 or 3 sound spectra, and the duration of each segment is equal, at least 0.15s. 2. 2 or 3 step sequences of different tones, each segment 0.15s-1.5s.	
Short sound	The minimum duration is 0.3s.	When using sound clips of different lengths, the recommended length ratio is 1:3

Fig. 5. Table of sound form and design constraints

Sound Duration. Time attribute is one of the most important characteristics of tone signal. They can attract attention and can also be used as discrimination factors and emergency tips. It is recommended to repeat intermittent beeps or beeps at a frequency of 1 to 8 sounds per second (i.e. the time value of single tone is between 125 ms–1000 ms) for warning and alarm in the vehicle (ISO 16352-2005).

Cycle Times. Tonal signals that are repeated intermittently or continuously for a long time can only be used under special circumstances (until appropriate measures are taken by the driver or passenger). These situations include: conveying very important information affecting the safety of vehicle occupants or the ability to drive the vehicle (iso15006-2011).

4 Case Study

In this study, we collected the early warning tone under the forward collision warning scene of intelligent cockpit of five mainstream automobile brands: Mercedes Benz, BMW, Tesla, XPeng and NIO, analyzed it from the aspects of sound signal characteristics and spectrum, and analyzed the characteristics of FCW sound design of these five brands. By comparing the sound design principles of vehicle intelligent cockpit forward collision warning scene summarized in the previous section, we summarize the commonalities of the warning tone of the five brands of vehicles in the forward collision warning scene, and discuss their shortcomings.

After denoising the recorded audio, we conduct sound analysis through Adobe audit software. The parameters analyzed mainly include the time value, sound format, frequency and cycle times of the sound. We use T_1 to represent monosyllabic time value, T_2 to represent syllable interval time value, T_3 to represent cyclic interval time value, and T_d to represent the total time length of warning tone.

Figure 6 is the sound signal waveform diagram (top) and sound spectrum diagram (bottom) of Tesla FCW, and Fig. 7 is the sound design parameter table of Tesla FCW.

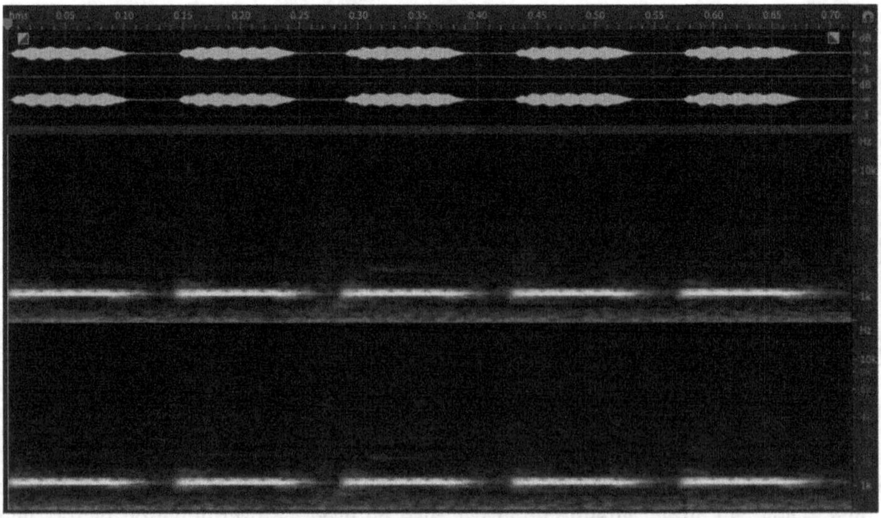

Fig. 6. Tesla FCW sound signal waveform (top) and spectrogram (bottom)

Frequency	Duration	Cycle Times	Sound Panning
Fundamental frequency range : 1033-1119Hz	T1 : 130ms T2 : 25ms Monosyllable number : 5 Td : 750ms	1 time	Not designed
Urgency	**Urgency Design**	**Sound Format**	
Danger : Vision (central control) + sound	Only one kind of warning tone	**Bursts sound** A group of 5 sound pulses (monosyllabic) Pulse period: 130ms + 25ms = 155ms (0.155s) Pulse frequency: 6.4Hz	

Fig. 7. Tesla FCW sound design parameter table

As can be seen from Fig. 6 and Fig. 7, Tesla FCW sound adopts short single pitch compound sound, and the sound format is' Burts'. Tesla FCW sound presents non changeable pitch, uniform repetitive rhythm, and no change in strength. Tesla FCW sound only circulates once in the design of cycle times, and there is no design direction of sound. In addition, in terms of emergency design, the early warning of Tesla FCW scene is realized through visual and auditory channels. In general, Tesla FCW sound is highly consistent with the designer's data summarized in the previous section.

Figure 8 is the sound signal waveform diagram (upper) and sound spectrum diagram (lower) of Benz FCW, and Fig. 9 is the sound design parameter table of Benz FCW.

As can be seen from Fig. 8 and Fig. 9 Benz FCW sound adopts short single tone compound tone. Benz FCW sound presents a non-variable pitch, uniform repetitive rhythm, no change in strength, and the sound format is 'short sound'. The fundamental frequency of Benz FCW sound is more than the recommended range, which sounds slightly harsh. In terms of cycle times design, Benz FCW sound adopts the method of cycle playback until measures are taken. Benz also did not design the spatial orientation information of sound. In addition, in terms of emergency design, the early warning of Benz FCW scene is realized through visual and auditory channels. Overall, the Benz FCW sound is generally consistent with the designer's performance data summarized in the previous section.

Figure 10 is the sound signal waveform diagram (upper) and sound spectrum diagram (lower) of NIO FCW, and Fig. 11 is the sound design parameter table of NIO FCW.

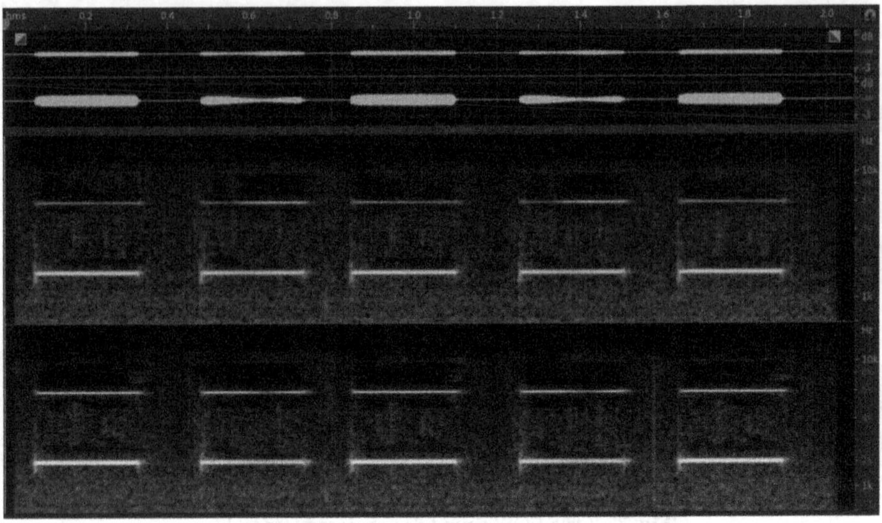

Fig. 8. Benz FCW sound signal waveform (top) and spectrogram (bottom)

Frequency	Duration	Cycle Times	Sound Panning
Fundamental frequency range：1893-5900Hz	T1：281ms T3：128ms Monosyllable number：1 Td：281ms	Cycle until action is taken	Not designed

Urgency	Urgency Design	Sound Format
Danger： Vision (central control) + sound	Only one kind of warning tone	**Short sound** Pulse period:281ms+128ms=409ms(0.409s) Pulse frequency: 6.4hz

Fig. 9. Benz FCW sound design parameter table

It can be seen from Fig. 10 and Fig. 11 that NIO FCW sound adopts short single pitch compound tone, and the sound format is 'Burts', but the number of sound pulses is only 3, which is lower than the recommended minimum value of 5. NIO FCW sound presents non changeable pitch, uniform repetitive rhythm, and no change in strength. In the design of cycle times, NIO FCW sound adopts the way of cycle playback until measures are taken. NIO did not design the spatial orientation information of sound. In terms of emergency design, NIO FCW scene early warning is realized through visual

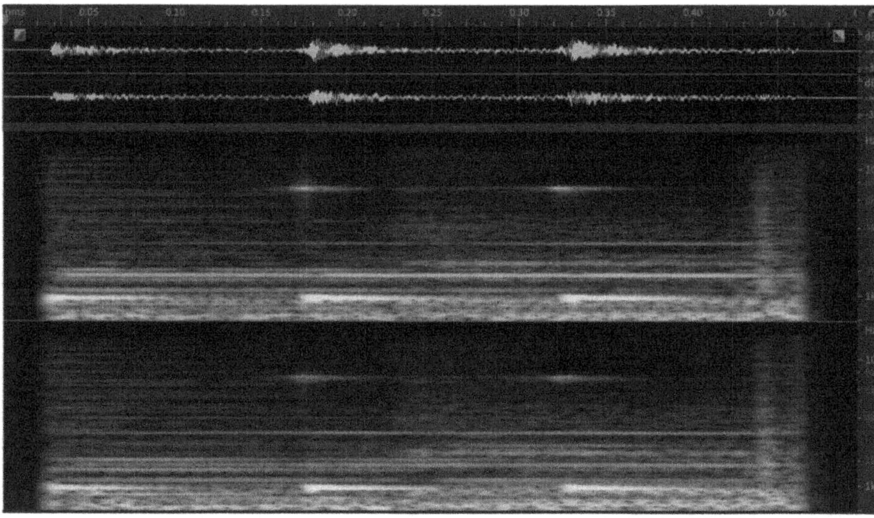

Fig. 10. NIO FCW sound signal waveform (top) and spectrogram (bottom)

Frequency	Duration	Cycle Times	Sound Panning
Fundamental frequency range : 861-1808Hz	T1 : 61ms T2 : 81ms T3 : 125ms Monosyllable number : 3 Td : 345ms	Cycle until action is taken	Not designed
Urgency	**Urgency Design**	**Sound Format**	
Danger : Vision (central control) + sound	Only one kind of warning tone	**Bursts sound** A group of 3 sound pulses (monosyllabic) Pulse period: 61ms+ 81ms= 142ms (0.142s) Pulse frequency: 7Hz	

Fig. 11. NIO FCW sound design parameter table

and auditory channels. Generally speaking, NIO FCW sound is generally consistent with the designer's performance data summarized in the previous section.

Figure 12 is the sound signal waveform diagram (upper) and sound spectrum diagram (lower) of Xpeng FCW, and Fig. 13 is the sound design parameter table of Xpeng FCW.

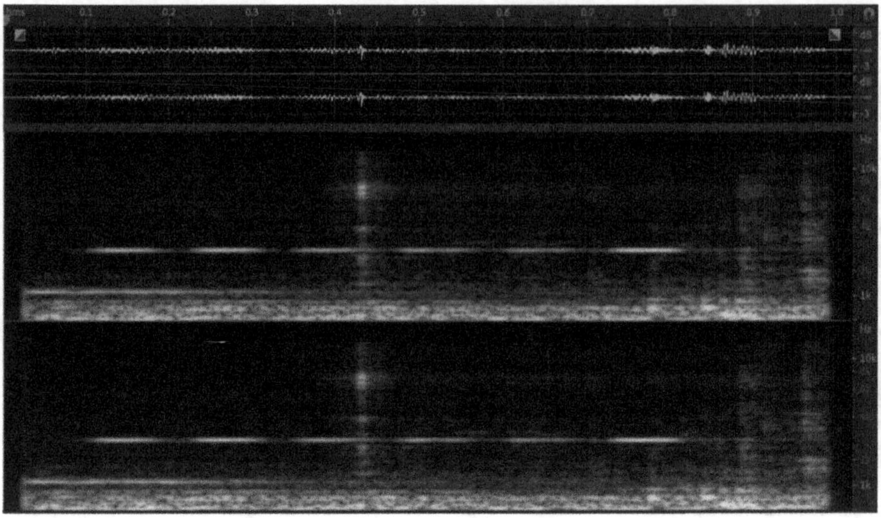

Fig. 12. XPeng FCW sound signal waveform (top) and spectrogram (bottom)

Frequency	Duration	Cycle Times	Sound Panning
Fundamental frequency range：2700-2900Hz	T1：95ms T2：30ms T3：900ms Monosyllable number：6 Td：850ms	Cycle until action is taken	Not designed
Urgency	**Urgency Design**	**Sound Format**	
Danger： Vision (central control) + sound	Only one kind of warning tone	**Bursts sound** A group of 6 sound pulses (monosyllabic) Pulse period: 95ms+ 30ms= 125ms (0.125s) Pulse frequency: 8Hz	

Fig. 13. XPeng FCW sound design parameter table

As can be seen from Fig. 12 and Fig. 13, Xpeng FCW sound adopts short single pitch compound sound, and the sound format is 'Burts'. Xpeng FCW sound presents non changeable pitch, uniform repetitive rhythm, no change in strength, and the sound format is 'short sound'. The fundamental frequency of Benz FCW sound is not within the recommended range, higher than the recommended range, and it is slightly thin in listening sense. In the design of cycle times, Xpeng FCW sound adopts the way of cycle playback until measures are taken. Xpeng does not design the spatial orientation information of sound. In addition, in terms of emergency design, the early warning of

Xpeng FCW scene is realized through visual and auditory channels. Overall, the Benz FCW sound is generally consistent with the designer's performance data summarized in the previous section.

Figure 14 is the sound signal waveform diagram (top) and sound spectrum diagram (bottom) of BMW FCW, and Fig. 15 is the sound design parameter table of BMW FCW.

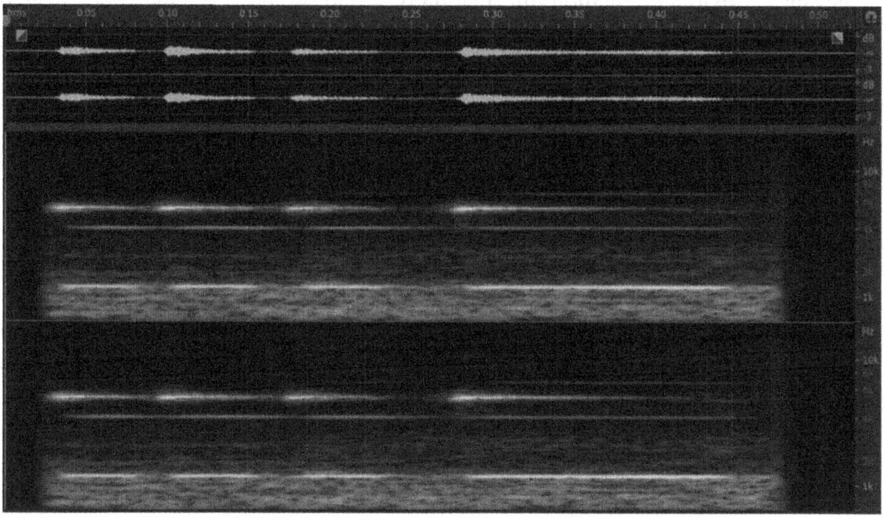

Fig. 14. BMW FCW sound signal waveform (top) and spectrogram (bottom)

Frequency	Duration	Cycle Times	Sound Panning
Fundamental frequency range : 1250-5400Hz	T1 : 60ms T2 : 15ms Monosyllable number : 4 Td : 430ms	1time	Not designed
Urgency	**Urgency Design**	**Sound Format**	
Danger : Vision (central control) + sound	Only one kind of warning tone	**Bursts sound** A group of 4 sound pulses (monosyllabic) , including 3 short monotones and 1 long monotone (2 times the time value of the short monotone) Pulse period: 60ms+ 15ms= 75ms (0.075s) Pulse frequency: 13Hz	

Fig. 15. BMW FCW sound design parameter table

As can be seen from Fig. 14 and Fig. 15, BMW FCW sound adopts short single pitch compound tone, and the sound format is 'Burts', but the number of sound pulses is only

4, lower than the recommended value of 5. The pulse frequency of BMW FCW sound is 13 Hz, which is more than the recommended value. It is too urgent to listen, which may cause the problem of reduced definition. The fundamental frequency of Benz FCW sound slightly exceeds the recommended range, which is slightly harsh to the ear. BMW FCW sound presents non-varying pitch, non-uniform repetitive rhythm, and strength changes. In the design of cycle times, BMW FCW sound only plays once. BMW did not design the spatial orientation information of sound. In terms of emergency degree design, the early warning of BMW FCW scene is realized through visual and auditory channels. In general, BMW FCW sound is less consistent with the designer factor data summarized in the previous section.

5 Discussion and Conclusion

Through the case study of five mainstream automobile brands, we found that most of the brands of cars does not fully comply with the provisions of relevant international standards in the design of early warning sound, and some sounds may be designed by designers with their own subjective consciousness. Although the design of FCW sound of five automobile brands (Tesla, Benz, NIO, XPeng, BMW) does not correspond to the ergonomic constraints of collision warning sound design, on the whole, the design of FCW sound of these five automobile brands is in high compliance with the ergonomic parameters recommended by relevant international standards.

In terms of sound format, four brands of cars have chosen 'burns sound', and only Benz has adopted 'short sound'. Benz's early warning sound format does not belong to the same type as other brand vehicles, which may cause cognitive impairment when users use cross brand vehicles, and users need to spend some time to adapt and learn it. In terms of the number of sound cycles of FCW, the number of sound cycles of BMW and Tesla is designed to be 1, which does not comply with the provisions of relevant international standards and may cause weak warning results.

In terms of sound panning, none of the five automobile brands has designed the orientation of early warning sound. When the auditory collision prompt sound stimulation is consistent with the indicated spatial hazard information (if there is danger on the right, the orientation of the warning sound comes from the right), the driver's risk avoidance response speed will be accelerated. Therefore, the orientation information of the warning sound can be added to the forward collision warning scene of the vehicle intelligent cockpit.

During the case study, due to the limited equipment for collecting sound materials, it is temporarily impossible to accurately judge the trigger time (audio-visual synchronization or audio-visual asynchrony) and trigger conditions (whether related to TTC) of the five FCW early warning sounds. We will make a more in-depth analysis in the follow-up research.

References

1. Ge, S.L., et al.: Current status of research on audiovisual cross-modal interactions. Beijing Biomed. Eng. **30**(4), 431–434 (2011)

2. Niu, D., et al.: A study on trust enhancement of unmanned vehicles based on multi-channel information. Packaging Eng. Art Edition **41**(6), 81–85 (2020)
3. Zaki, N.I.M., et al.: Auditory alert for in-vehicle safety technologies: a review. J. Soc. Automotive Eng. Malaysia **5**(1), 88–102 (2021)
4. Delle Monache, S., Rocchesso, D.: Bauhaus legacy in research through design: the case of basic sonic interaction design. Int. J. Design **8**(3) (2014)
5. Rocchesso, D., Polotti, P., Monache, S.D.: Designing continuous sonic interaction. Int. J. Des. **3**(3), 13–25 (2009)
6. Sanders, M., McCormick, E.J.: Human Factors in Engineering and Design, 7th edn. Tsinghua University Press (2009)
7. Franinovic, K., Serafin, S., (eds.): Sonic Interaction Design. MIT Press (2013)
8. O'Dea, R., Jedir, R.: Neff F. Auditory distraction in HCI: towards a framework for the design of hierarchically-graded auditory notifications. In: The 14th International Audio Mostly Conference: A Journey in Sound (2019)
9. ISO TR 16352-2005: Road vehicles - Ergonomic aspects of in-vehicle presentation for transport information and control systems - Warning systems
10. NHTSA DOT HS 808 535: In-Vehicle Crash Avoidance Warning Systems: Human Factors Considerations
11. ISO 11429-1996: Ergonomics System of auditory and visual danger and information signals
12. ISO 15006-2011: Road vehicles - Ergonomic aspects of transport information and control systems -Specifications for in-vehicle auditory presentation
13. King, A.J., Palmer, A.R.: Integration of visual and auditory information in bimodal neurones in the guinea-pig superior colliculus. Exp. Brain Res. **60**(3), 492–500 (1985)
14. Yiyang, L.: Properties and eye-movement cues of audiovisual information integration response. East China Normal University (2013)
15. Heron, J., et al.: Adaptation minimizes distance-related audiovisual delays. J. Vis. **7**(13), 5 (2007)

Research on Man-Machine Interface Design Based on Intelligent Vehicle

Zijiang Yang(✉), Jie Zeng, Xicheng Huang, and Yang Lu

Desay SV, Huizhou, China
{Zijiang.Yang,Jie.Zeng,Yang.Lu}@desay-svautomotive.com

Abstract. With the rapid development of smart car technology and the rapid rise of automotive human-machine interface design, it is necessary to explore the direction of smart car human-machine interface design. The purpose of this paper is to propose reference principles for the design of human-machine interface for smart cars, so as to improve the user experience of smart cars. The research method takes the design of Desay SV G6 intelligent cockpit system as an example, and the research adopts the methods of desktop research, expert interview and innovation workshop. At the same time, the basic data used in the design of intelligent vehicle man-machine interface is obtained by observing the user's driving behavior and driving experience map. Then, combined with the development trend and current situation of intelligent vehicle interaction design, the relevant cases are summarized, This paper discusses the design direction of man-machine interface for intelligent vehicle. It is concluded that the human-machine interface design direction of smart cars is mainly reflected in three aspects: gentle intelligence, efficient human-machine interaction and emotion. Let users feel mild intelligence before use. In combination with the future human-computer interaction design trend, multi-channel integrated interaction and intelligent emotional interaction mode are used to enable users to complete in vehicle interaction efficiently, Finally, based on emotional interactive experience, link the travel partnership between smart car and users.

Keywords: Keywords · Intelligent vehicle · Interface · Interaction design · User experience

1 Introduction

With the continuous advancement of the "New Four Modernizations" in the automotive field (sharing, networking, intelligence and electrification of automobiles), advanced technology has been rapidly applied and developed in the automotive field, and the interior space shape, interaction mode and human-machine interface function of automobiles have also undergone profound changes. According to the previous function-oriented product research and development mode, the man-machine interface is designed, it is easy to ignore the user experience. On the other hand, the design of human-machine interface of Intelligent Vehicle has become the focus of the industry and the key factor to attract users and provide differentiated services. Based on this, this paper discusses

P.-L. P. Rau (Ed.): HCII 2022, LNCS 13314, pp. 276–285, 2022.
https://doi.org/10.1007/978-3-031-06053-3_19

the design direction of human-machine interface of smart cars from the perspective of interactive interface.

2 Intelligent Vehicle and Man-Machine Interface

2.1 Definition of Intelligent Car and Man-Machine Interface

Quoted from the National Development and Reform Commission's "Intelligent Car Innovation and Development Strategy" definition of intelligent car: intelligent car refers to a new generation of cars with automatic driving function, which is equipped with advanced sensors and other devices and uses new technologies such as artificial intelligence, and gradually becomes an intelligent mobile space and application terminal. Smart cars are often called intelligent networked cars, self-driving cars and so on. International Association of Automotive Engineers (SAE) newly revised J3016(TM) "Classification and Definition of Standard Road Motor Vehicle Driving Automation System": driverless cars belong to smart cars, and SAE automatic driving classification is shown in Fig. 1.

SAE Autopilot classification			0	1	2	3	4	5
Name			No Driving Automation	Driver Assistance	Partial Driving Automation	Conditional Driving Automation	High Driving Automation	Full Driving Automation
Define			The performance by the driver of the entire DDT,even when enhanced by active safety systems.	The sustained and ODD-specific execution by a driving automation system of either the lateral or the longitudinal vehicle motion control subtask of the DDT (but not both simultaneously) with the expectation that the driver performs the remainder of the DDT.	The sustained and ODD-specific execution by a driving automation system of both the lateral and longitudinal vehicle motion control subtasks of the DDT with the expectation that the driver completes the OEDR subtask and supervises the driving automation system.	The sustained and ODD-specific perfomance by an ADS of the entire DDT with the expectation that the DDT fallback-ready user is receptive to ADS-issued requests to intervene, as well as to DDT performance-relevant system failures in other vehicle systems,and will respond appropriately.	The sustained and ODD-specific perfomance by an ADS of the entire DDTand DDT fal/lback without any expectation that a user will respond to a request to intervene.	The sustained and unconditinal (i.e. not ODD-specific)perfomance by an ADS of the entire DDT and DDT fallback without any expectation that a user will respond to a request to intervene.
Subject	Dynamic driving task	Driving performance	Driver	Driver and system	System	System	System	System
		Around the monitoring	Driver	Driver	Driver	System	System	System
	Dynamic Driving Mission Support		Driver	Driver	Driver	Driver	System	System
	System scope		There is no	Part				All

Fig. 1. Classification of SAE autonomous vehicles

Human Machine Interaction (HMI), also called user interface or user interface, is the medium and dialogue interface for information transmission and exchange between people and intelligent vehicle, and is an important part of smart cars. In the era of rapid development of technology, design does not create technology, but on the basis of technology, it creates better products and experiences for human beings through design Innovation. This is also the connotation of intelligent car human-computer interaction design [1].

2.2 The Development Status of Human-Machine Interface of Smart Cars

Nowadays, cars are more than just personal vehicles. Many consumers regard cars as intelligent mobile spaces, and have higher requirements for the activities in the cars. With the continuous development of computer technology, users begin to favor more efficient, fast and humanized automobile HMI design [2]. According to the subdivision of interior components, Including main HUD, lighting unit, central control panel, steering wheel, etc. [3]. With the continuous development of technology, the automotive electronics are updated, and the large-size central control LCD screen has almost become the standard, and the full LCD instrument has gradually replaced the traditional instrument. The integrated design of central control and instrument began to appear, and the driving information display system and multimedia entertainment system began to merge. As early as 2017 CES Asia Exhibition, Desay SV released the intelligent cockpit design integrating central control and instrumentation, as shown in Fig. 2.

Fig. 2. CES Asia 2017 Desay SV appeared in the smart cockpit

Future forms of interaction will no longer rely too much on visual information, but will emphasize the combination of multi-sensory channels [4]. Multi-channel fusion interaction is one of the important features of intelligent car man-machine interface design. Multi-channel fusion interaction is the integration of multiple sensory channels (vision, hearing, smell, touch, taste, body feeling, etc.) of people, and the interaction with products or systems. People can perceive, operate and experience products in an all-round, three-dimensional and comprehensive way, and then form a comprehensive cognition and emotional experience of products. Multi-channel integration can reduce driver's cognitive load and improve driving safety [5].

2.3 Research Introduction and Significance Innovation

Under the guidance of the international environment, China's self-owned brand automobile enterprises and suppliers have joined in the design reform of automobile HMI. After years of continuous development and independent research and development, Huizhou

Desay SV Automotive Electronics Co., Ltd. launched the first domestic concept of intelligent cockpit based on user use scene design in CES Asia in 2017, and its highlight is that it gives soul to automobile hardware. The intelligent cockpit design builds an intelligent car HMI system based on three concepts: reshaping the product design with the user experience as the core, taking the mobile phone operation design interaction prototype that users are accustomed to, and building the interaction principle with driving safety. With Desay SV introduction of the concept of intelligent cockpit, Domestic auto companies and suppliers also began to shift the design focus to the HMI.

In this paper, Desay SV relies on the intelligent cockpit to explore the development direction of Desay SV future automobile HMI through user experience research, grasp the user's demand, empower automobile enterprises and enhance the product competitiveness in the future.

3 Design Practice of Human-Machine Interface of Smart Car

By means of expert interviews combined with innovative workshops, the basic data of the questionnaire about the design of human-computer interface of smart cars were obtained. A total of 368 words related to future cars were obtained, and 188 words with obscure, unclear and incomplete contents were excluded. The remaining 180 words with the same lyrics and the same type of words were clustered and summarized to form a framework of 8 factors. Through the innovation workshop, five first-level factors of the questionnaire were identified, corresponding to 40 s-level factors respectively, and 30 questionnaire questions were formed through optimization. Finally, 297 questionnaires were collected, including 293 valid questionnaires, including novice drivers with driving experience of 0–1 month, as shown in Fig. 3.

The respondents of this questionnaire are employees of Desay sv Company, mostly expert users due to their professional background. According to the collection and statistics of the questionnaire, we make the following summary: 1. The main functions used in the car: music, navigation and radio are the most commonly used functions; 2. On the selection of navigation and mobile navigation in intelligent vehicle-mounted system, To a large extent, it is determined by the convenience of map updating and upgrading; 3. In the application and integration of new technologies, we should try boldly. The coexistence of various interactions on the vehicle is an inevitable stage. How to achieve better integration of audio, video and touch is a problem that should be broken through at the present stage. 4. For an individual, a small point can determine his judgment on a thing, If the radio receiver is not ideal (radio signal or sound quality problem), he thinks the receiver is of poor quality. Actually, let's change our thinking. For example, when the radio signal is not good, how can we deal with the noise caused by the bad signal? (Example: direct gradual silencing, sound source switching, beautiful melody substitution, etc.) In this way, the problem is turned into a bright spot to impress users.

Through the investigation and analysis of the user questionnaire, three usage scenarios that users pay attention to are refined, which are used to support the observation record of the owner's daily driving. The experience process is recorded with videos, images and Wen Zi, as shown in Fig. 4. On this basis, through observation and analysis of user behavior, case analysis, etc., three main design problems are refined and formed:

1. How do commuter car owners feel the smart care of our products? 2. How can the interaction and operation during driving not affect driving safety? 3. How to make drivers feel happy. So as to support the research and development of human-machine interface design of intelligent vehicle.

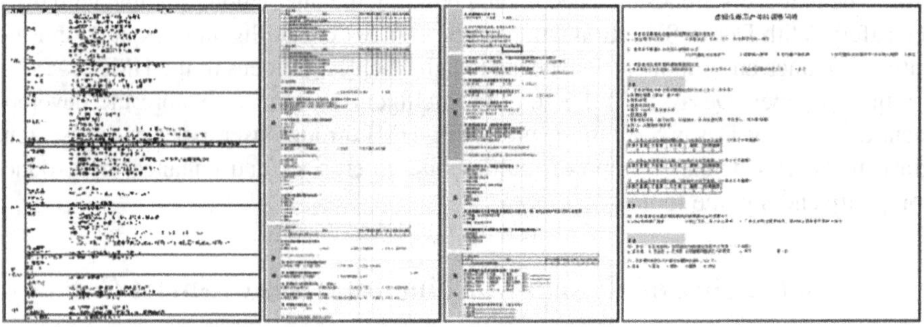

Fig. 3. Record of user questionnaire survey process

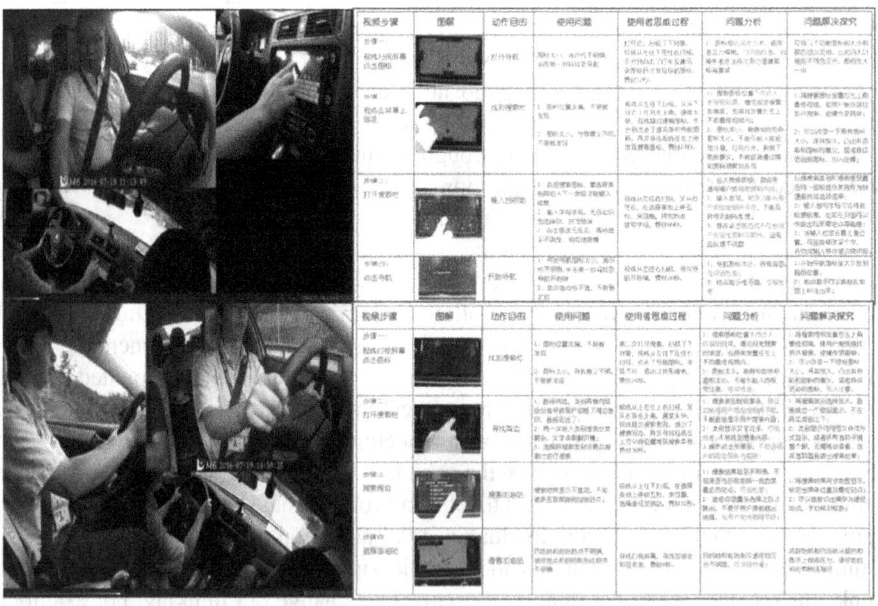

Fig. 4. Observation and research record of user's driving behavior

4 Key Points of Human-Machine Interface Design of Intelligent Vehicle

Based on user research and driving behavior analysis, this paper starts from three HMI design problems of intelligent vehicle, analyzes the scene embodiment under each problem, focuses on the interface design of instrument and central control, and makes prototype design from three dimensions: light function, efficient human-computer interaction and emotionalization. See Fig. 5.

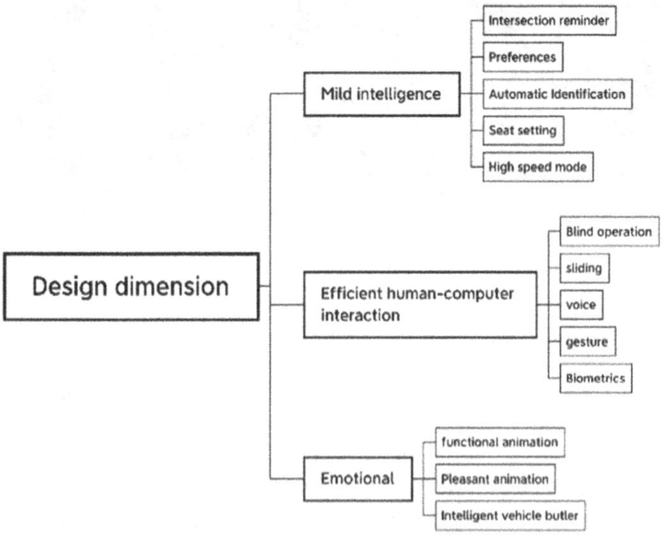

Fig. 5. Design dimension division based on user scenarios

4.1 Mild Intelligence

Intelligent product design under strong emotional integration can't be completely led by technology, but also should consider the emotional cognition and ethical constraints of people as free bodies and social bodies. Intelligent product design should focus on sustainable development, social ethics, emotional alienation and over-dependence. According to the use environment, users and use time, we adopt the design strategy of "moderate intelligence" for intelligent products, and gradually form "intellectual aesthetics" [6] in the era of artificial intelligence.

Through the study of user behavior, it is found that users usually have two habits in the commuter car scene: the first is to check the road information before getting on the bus; The second is to tell the family by phone that they are ready to leave and the estimated time of arrival at home. Based on the strategy of "moderate intelligence", according to the user's usage situation, we will send the traffic information on a regular basis, Push road condition information to users in real time. Before returning from work, it will also provide a telephone entrance to quickly inform family members according to the settings of common contacts, so as to be slightly intelligent. See Fig. 6 for the prototype interface design.

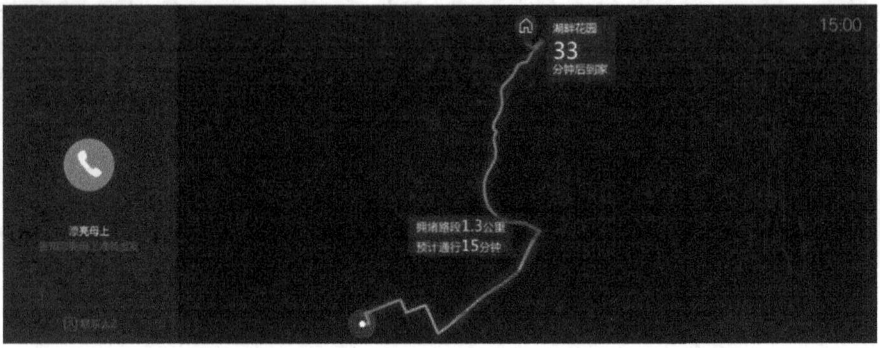

Fig. 6. Prototype effect of mild intelligent interface design.

4.2 Efficient Human-Computer Interaction

Natural human-computer interaction paradigm [1] makes full use of various information channels of human body, such as vision, hearing, touch, etc., and combines various natural information output modes of human body, such as voice, behavior, posture, EEG, body temperature, force, etc., to carry out diversified human-computer interaction. This interaction paradigm can make full use of the characteristics of human body. Multi-channel simultaneous input of multiple information makes interaction more stereoscopic, wider interaction bandwidth and more natural interaction process [2]; And natural and instinctive behaviors and postures are often more efficient in the process of interaction.

Through the study of user behavior, it is found that users will have dangerous driving habits of answering phones and switching music while driving. Therefore, without changing the original design, we have increased the interaction channel of behaviors and gestures, and used the gesture of distance to complete the interaction. Under any interface, answering/hanging up the phone and switching music, The user can complete the left and right gestures through gestures, reducing the sight of the user from the direction of vehicle travel and improving driving safety. See Fig. 7 for the prototype interface design.

4.3 Emotional

With the development of information technology, various high-tech means are integrated into the field of intelligent vehicle, which brings new innovation space to the design. Under this realistic background, product design should not only focus on the improvement of performance and function, but also on the use and safety to meet the actual needs of consumers from the emotional level [7]. Therefore, In the design of human-computer

Fig. 7. Interface effect of switching music tracks by gesture from a distance

interface of intelligent vehicle, we introduce emotional design to solve the problem of how to make drivers feel happy. The center of emotional design is people, which is a key point for products to be popular in the market forever. Especially with the improvement of material living level, people's pursuit of products is no longer just practical. But inner emotional and spiritual needs [7]. Then, in the design of human-computer interface for smart cars, how can users get such cognitive and emotional satisfaction during use? We have designed from two aspects, the first is interesting dynamic design, and the other is humanized voice assistant image design. Interest can be the appearance attribute of the product or the interest in the use of the product, which brings the users not only their own fun, but also the fun of life [8]. As a designer, we must start from this level and design some interesting and emotional products to increase the added value of products. Let users enjoy pleasant, positive and positive emotions during use, and relieve the pressure of users' life to a certain extent [9]. Based on the analysis of the characteristics of the human-computer interface dynamic effect of intelligent vehicle, the interesting dynamic effect establishes emotional connection with users, so that users can get unexpected surprises. See Fig. 8, There are corresponding different animation effects in three different states: incoming call, telephone access and calling.

Humanization is an important component of emotional design, which has far-reaching influence on product design [10]. To some extent, humanized design is an expression of emotional care and a practical way for products to meet users' emotional needs to the maximum extent. Through the design of cute pet image, relying on virtual 3D presentation, we integrate voice and give humanized design. At the same time, the interactive action of Meng Chong's image can be based on the user's action and habit learning, give feedback to various situations of users, actively interact during driving, ensure the driving safety of users, and obtain the optimal driving interactive experience. See Fig. 9.

Fig. 8. Interface effect of three States of incoming call, access and dialing

Fig. 9. Virtual 3D intelligent vehicle Assistant Image

5 Conclusion

The purpose of this paper is to discuss the design of human-machine interface for intelligent vehicle, and get the direction of Desay sv's human-machine interface design for intelligent vehicle. With the continuous maturity and perfection of information technology development, the development of human-computer interface design for intelligent vehicle is accelerating, and it has become the core competitive field in the field of automobiles. Through design practice, Desay sv puts forward that the design of human-computer interface for intelligent vehicle should be considered from three aspects: light intelligence, high-efficiency human-computer interaction and emotion, aiming at providing reference for future car designers, playing a certain role in attracting valuable attention, and bringing more perfect car experience to users.

References

1. Tan, H., Sun, J., Guan, D.: Research on the development trend of human-computer interaction in smart cars. Packaging Eng. **40**(20), 32–42 (2019)
2. Tan, H., Sun, J., Guan, D.: Development trend of human: computer interaction in intelligent vehicles. Packaging Eng. **40**(20), 32–42 (2019)
3. Gao, H., Li, B., Han, T.: Research on the future development trend of automobile human-computer interaction system. Packaging Eng. **39**(22), 22–28 (2018)
4. Gao, H., Li, B., Han, T.: Development trend of future automotive HMI system. Packaging Eng. **40**(20), 32–42 (2019)
5. Pitts, M.J., Burnett, G., Skrypchuk, L., et al.: Visual Haptic feedback interaction in automotive touch- screens. Displays **33**(1), 7–16 (2012)
6. Chai, M., Li, S.W., Sun, W.C., et al.: Drowsiness monitoring based on steering wheel status. Transp. Res. Part D: Transp. Environ. (2018)
7. Li, J., Yuan, P., Zhang, Y.: From industrial aesthetics to intelligent aesthetics. Packaging Eng. **43**(2), 29–34 (2022)
8. Shi, W., Li, C., Yang, M., Chen, R.: User interface based on natural interaction design for seniors. Comput. Hum. Behav. **75**, 147–159 (2017)
9. Yang, M., Tao, J., Hao, L., et al.: Multi-channel man-machine dialogue system for natural interaction. Comput. Sci. **41**(10), 12–18 (2014)
10. Liu, G., Li, S.: The future development trend of product design based on emotional design. Art Technol. **32**(2), 195 (2019)
11. Zhou, X.: Research on the design of interesting products based on emotion. Sci. Technol. Wind **377**(9), 218 (2019)
12. Fu, Y., Peng, J., Li, S.: Product design direction and practice based on emotional design. Packaging Eng. **42**(12), 228–231 (2021)
13. Mi, L.: Research on product design requirements under the concept of green design. Arts Life **3**, 42 (2019)
14. Zhang, Z., Zhu, L., Fu, G.: Research on the application of emotional design in product design. Sci. Herald **22**, 53 (2015)

Research on Applicability of Automobile Instruments Character Size

Zijiang Yang(✉), Peng Liu, Li Liang, Cuiyan Ji, Ruitang Liao, and Tao Wang

Desay SV, Huizhou, China

{Zijiang.Yang,PengCT_ITCMale.Liu,Liang.Li,Cuiyan.ji,
Ruitang.Liao,TaoCT.Wang}@desay-svautomotive.com

Abstract. The purpose of study the influence of automobile instrument character size on the driver's information recognition efficiency and recognition load, explore the best applicable range of instrument characters, and provide guidelines and suggestions for instrument interface design. The method is to use the literature desk analysis and ergonomics research methods to establish the instrument character recognition efficiency and character recognition load experimental scheme, conduct experiments based on the driving simulation system and eye tracker and other equipment, and collect the information acquisition efficiency and recognition load subjective of different character sizes. Reviews to explore the best user experience range for character size.

The result is that the character size was positively correlated with the information recognition efficiency within a certain range, but negatively correlated with the recognition load. When the character increases to a certain range, the recognition efficiency and recognition load are no longer affected by it, and the experience of character information recognition will decrease.

The result is that the character size is positively correlated with the information recognition efficiency within a certain range and is negatively correlated with the recognition load. When the character increases to a certain range, the recognition efficiency and recognition load are no longer affected by it, and the experience of character information recognition will decrease.

The conclusion is that the minimum value of the instrument character should be greater than 2.65 mm. This value is a statically recognizable character size value, but the recognition load is high. It is suitable for interface description information of instrument-independent driving, such as units and labels. Under driving conditions, the character size of driving-related information should be greater than 4.94 mm, and the optimal value for subjective reading experience is 6.58 mm. When it is larger than 8.23 mm, both the character recognition efficiency and the recognition load reach the optimum point. It can provide character size design reference suggestions for instrument information importance priority.

Keywords: Automobile instruments · Character size · Recognition load

1 Subject Background

With the development of science and technology, automobiles are also rapidly evolving towards intelligence and networking. They are no longer simply means of transportation

P.-L. P. Rau (Ed.): HCII 2022, LNCS 13314, pp. 286–296, 2022.
https://doi.org/10.1007/978-3-031-06053-3_20

instead of walking but have become the third space for people's lives. In the current era of data and information, the display screen in the car has become the main medium for human-vehicle interaction, and the instrument is the main carrier for displaying vehicle driving information and safety information. The efficiency and accuracy of information transmission are closely related to driving safety. This research will conduct experimental evaluation on users through simulated driving state and explore the optimal range of instrument character (Chinese characters) size combined with subjective questionnaires.

2 Research Status

More than 100 years ago, the automobile instrument was born to this day, and it has experienced four leaps and bounds, namely, the first generation of steam-mechanical instruments, the second generation of electrical instruments, the third generation of electronic instruments, and up to now the fourth generation of progressive motor-type all-digital automobile instruments. With the development of science and technology, more and more automobile instrument panels choose electronic liquid crystal display technology. This technology allows the instrument to display graphics, characters, symbols, and live simulation [1]. It makes the display of the instrument more flexible and more consistent with the user experience of the driver. Among them, character is one of the main information transmission modes in current instrument design, which is often used for alarm prompt, vehicle state description, road information prompt and so on. Reasonable visual coding of displayed characters can greatly improve the accuracy and efficiency of information recognition [2].

In the international standard ISO15008, the word height H is calculated by multiplying the visual distance by the minimum viewing angle/3600, and it is considered that 12 angles are the minimum value, and the recommended value is 20 angle minutes. Wang Qun found in the experimental study of ergonomics of cockpit display interface character coding that the recommended critical font size height in English is: $H = 0.0035 \times \text{Stadia} + 1.5548$; Height $H = 0.0026 \times \text{Stadia} + 1.407$; The height of Chinese characters is $H = 0.005 \times \text{Stadia} + 2.06$ (unit: mm) [3].

At present, there is not much research on instrument characters, but it can be found that this kind of ergonomic data is getting more and more attention, which is helpful to improve the safety and rationality of automobile HMI design.

3 Experimental Design

3.1 Research Ideas

This experiment was carried out on the automobile driving simulation platform, and a flat highway was selected as the experimental scene. The experiment will start after the subjects are familiar with the driving simulation cockpit. During the normal driving process, the instrument will display experimental character samples of different sizes, and the subjects will recognize the character information according to the experimental requirements. When the recognition is successful, The retelling of the recognized character object by the subject means that the recognition is successful. During the whole experiment, the eye tracker will be used to collect the visual behavior data of the subjects in the normal driving stage and the sub-task operation stage, and the audio-visual recording equipment will be used to record the experiment process. Collect the visual behavior data of the subjects under normal driving conditions through experiments, The instrument area box is selected as the target area AOI, and after the data recording is completed, the scanning times and scanning time of the target area are counted, and then the driver identification efficiency is studied and analyzed. The experimental observer will also record the recognition success rate. After the experiment is completed, the user will be interviewed with subjective feedback, and a subjective survey questionnaire will be filled in (Fig. 1).

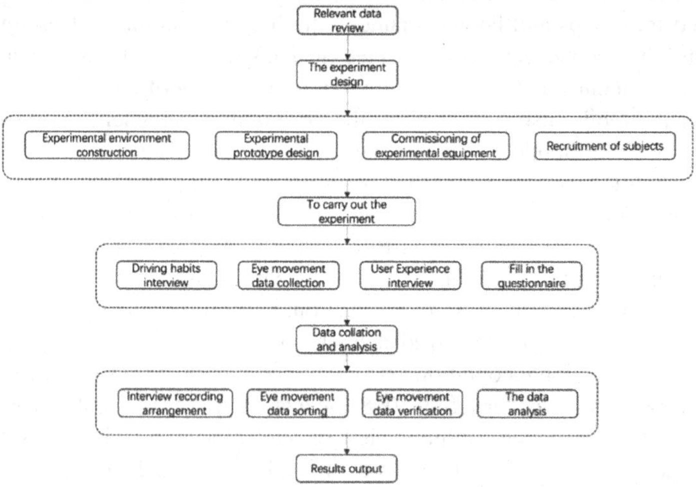

Fig. 1. Experimental research ideas

3.2 Experimental Indicators

This experiment is mainly to explore the influence of automobile instrument character size on driver information recognition efficiency and recognition load, and to explore the best applicable range of instrument characters. Therefore, when designing the experimental indicators, the experimental results will be verified and explained with subjective and objective data. The current evaluation methods of automobile man-machine interface can be developed from four aspects: safety, operation efficiency, operation load and user satisfaction [4]. After integrating the data ISO9241 and the evaluation method of automobile HMI, the following indexes are finally selected as the evaluation standard of the experiment: Task success rate, task completion time, stay time in AOI area, attention consumption (workload), subjective visual score and satisfaction (Tables 1).

Table 1. Description of experimental indicators

Evaluation indicators	Instructions
Mission success rate	The probability of completing a task at one time
Task completion time	The amount of time a user takes to complete a task
Residence time of AOI area	Total time spent in the AOI area
Scanning number of AOI area	Number of eye saccades to AOI area
Attention drain	Attention required to perform a task, scale: 1–7; 1 very low; 4 generally; 7 is very high
Subjective visual rating	Rating range: 1 to 7; 1 very low; 4 generally; 7 is very high

4 Experiment Development

4.1 Experimental Equipment and Instructions

See Table 2.

Table 2. Experimental equipment and instructions

Laboratory equipment	Instructions
Two-seater driving simulator	It includes vehicle cockpit, direction plate system, INPUT and output subsystem, CAN card, projection screen (3 sets), core driving simulation suite, scene control suite, supporting workstation, etc. It is mainly used to restore real driving experience and driving data collection records
12.3-inch meter screen	The resolution is 1920*720. According to the current mainstream instrument size research results, the final selection of 12.3 inch LCD instrument screen as the experimental standard object
Eyeglasses eye tracker	Model: Dikablis Glass 3. The eye movement device is binocular acquisition with a sampling rate of 60 Hz and an accuracy of 0.1–0.3° (maximum line-of-sight error)
Scene camera	The resolution is 1920*1080P. The view Angle of the scene camera is 90° (horizontal). Combined with the D-Lab human factor synchronization analysis system, the movement behavior of visual focus in AOI region was statistically analyzed
External camera	The resolution is 1920*1080 for recording the experimental process

4.2 Experimental Scenario

In order to reduce the interference of the external environment on the driver's attention, the experimental scene is selected as a four-lane high-speed closed-loop road section of 10 km, and there is no complicated road condition such as congestion and heavy traffic.

4.3 Experimental Prototype

In the character information of automobile instrument, in the same stadia level, numbers are the easiest to identify, followed by English, Chinese characters are the hardest to identify, and Chinese character identification is most affected by font size. However, in other reading studies, it is shown that the font of characters has little influence on reading efficiency, and too large or too small English fonts will reduce reading efficiency [5, 6]. However, there are two different views in the study of Chinese reading. One side thinks that the number of strokes will affect the accuracy and recognition time of Chinese characters [7], while the other side thinks that the complexity of Chinese strokes has no significant effect on Chinese characters recognition [8]. Therefore, in this experiment, according to the demand, the font, size and number of words of mainstream automobile instrument characters at home and abroad are comprehensively investigated. Based on the investigation results, the experimental prototype standard is determined.

Table 3. Investigation of 12.3-inch instrument character size

Proportion of font size					
Font size: 14–18	14	16	18		
Number	4	2	3		
Proportion	2.56%	1.28%	1.92%		
Font size: 20–28	20	22	24	26	28
Number	7	7	25	10	16
Proportion	4.49%	4.49%	16.03%	6.41%	10.26%
Font size: 30–36	30	32	34	36	
Number	14	7	12	3	
Proportion	8.97%	4.49%	7.69%	1.92%	
Font size: 40–48	40	42	44	46	48
Number	12	4	2	3	2
Proportion	7.69%	2.56%	1.28%	1.92%	1.28%
Font size: 50–54	50	52	54		
Number	4	1	2		
Proportion	2.56%	0.64%	1.28%		

(continued)

Table 3. *(continued)*

Proportion of font size					
Font size: 64–80	64	68	80		
Number	2	2	1		
Proportion	1.28%	1.28%	0.64%		
Font size: 110–152	110	112	120	152	
Number	1	1	2	1	
Proportion	0.64%	0.64%	1.28%	0.64%	

Proportion of character number		
Character number	Occurrences	Proportion
1	3	1.67%
2	9	5.00%
3	5	2.78%
4	30	16.67%
5	20	11.11%
6	24	13.33%
7	11	6.11%
8	18	10.00%
9	13	7.22%
10	20	11.11%
11	9	5.00%
12	8	4.44%
14	3	1.67%
16	2	1.11%
17	1	0.56%
18	1	0.56%
21	2	1.11%

The characters are Siyuan bold regular, which is set by the character size data of automobile instruments combined with ISO15008 international standard, and the font size is set to 12/18/24/36/48/60/72/96. There are eight groups of control experiments. The number of words in the character is 2/6/14, and the character selection is common character tips of automobiles and common words in daily life, and the stroke complexity is close to the same. In order to ensure good visibility of characters, Meet the barrier-free reading standard, and the strong contrast between the character and the background will not cause attention disturbance to the driver. After screening, the instrument background color value #393939, the character color value #FFFFFF, and the contrast ratio is 11.54:1 (Fig. 2).

Fig. 2. Experimental prototype design

4.4 Site Standard

Adjust the position of the instrument according to the results of ergonomics of automobile design and real vehicle investigation, and select the 90th percentile body size to ensure that the instrument is in a reasonable visual range [9]. In the experiment, the visual distance design of instrument panel mainly refers to American Henrry Dreffns standard, and the best visual distance of instrument panel is 550 mm. And that character content is locate in the center of the dashboard, When the driver's most natural eye rotation range is 15° left and right in the horizontal direction and 15° up and down in the vertical direction [10] (Fig. 3).

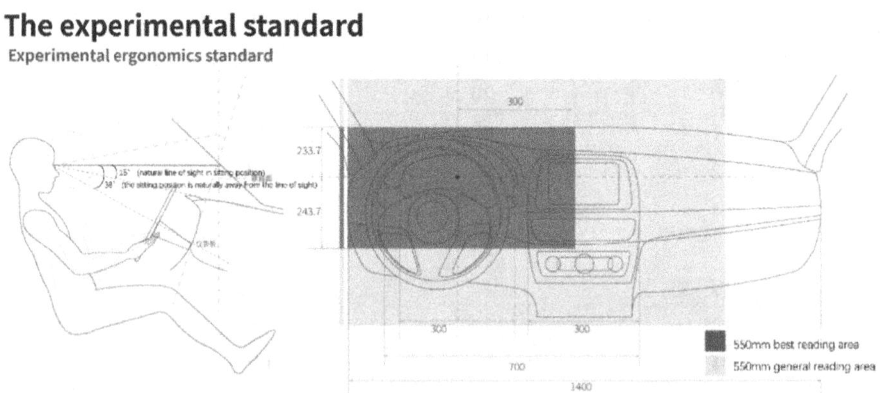

Fig. 3. Illustration of instrument ergonomics position

4.5 Subject Selection

In this experiment, 20 subjects were recruited, including 14 males and 6 females, aged between 25 and 45, with an average age of 32 years. And meet the following test selection conditions:

1. Because this experiment is directly related to visual perception, the subjects' visual requirements are strictly selected. According to the "Regulations on Application and

Use of Motor Vehicle Driving License", the naked or corrected visual acuity of both eyes reaches 4.9 or above, and there are no other physical reasons (color blindness, weak color or other reasons, including staying up late or overusing eyes before the test) that affect visual recognition.

2. Have 2 years or more driving experience, and the total mileage is more than 10,000 km.

4.6 Experimental Process

Equipment debugging, arrange the subjects to fill in basic information and conduct driving habit interviews, mainly to confirm the user's habit of using instruments; Read out the experimental statement and ask the subjects to sign the informed consent form. Then, the subjects were asked to adapt to the driving simulation cockpit for ten minutes. On the premise of ensuring that users are familiar with the use of the driving simulation cockpit, and there are no adverse reactions and questions, The staff told them to start the test. When the vehicle speed reaches 50 km/h and the driving is stable, the pilot will switch the instrument information, and the computer prompt "di" will tell the subject to start the experiment. When the subject completes the information capture and successfully retells the instrument character content, the pilot will switch the instrument character information. With the prompt "di". If the user fails to identify the retelling, the experiment guide will manually trigger the error prompt tone and switch the instrument information until all test tasks are completed. Each subject needs three groups of tests, each with eight groups of information switching and 24 groups of information identification tasks. Subjects can give subjective feedback during the experiment. Each person's experimental time is about 40 min. During the whole experiment, the experimental observer will record the feedback of the subjects. After the experiment, the subjects will be interviewed and asked to complete the questionnaire.

5 Analysis of Experimental Results

5.1 Data Processing

A total of 480 cases of data were exported in this experiment, among which the data of unfinished tasks are not included in the statistical category, and the statistical results of data average are shown in Table 3. Spearman coefficient was used to analyze the data, and the relationship between character size and other experimental indexes was studied. It can be seen that there is a significant relationship between the character size and the four indicators of task success rate, task completion time, stay time in AOI area and attention consumption (workload) (Tables 4 and 5).

5.2 Objective Data Analysis

Overall, in the range of 12–36 font size, the task success rate increases with the font size increasing. When the font size is 12, most of the subjects can't finish the task at one time, because the character is too small, and the subjects can't see clearly and misread it. When

Table 4. Statistical table of subjective and objective data of text size

Font size	12 (1.65 mm)	18 (2.65 mm)	24 (3.29 mm)	36 (4.94 mm)	48 (6.58 mm)	60 (8.23 mm)	72 (9.87 mm)	96 (13.16 mm)
Mission success rate/%	45.42	80.83	85	94.58	97.08	96.66	95.42	95.00
Task completion time/s	8.42	5.35	4.36	4.54	3.96	3.68	4.02	3.84
Residence time of AOI area/s	1.38	0.98	0.97	0.83	0.83	0.78	0.81	0.74
Scanning number of AOI area/times	3.46	2.55	2.26	2.04	2.05	1.99	2.08	2.13
Attention drain score	6.55	5.80	4.65	3.45	2.25	2.10	3.05	3.25
Subjective visual rating score	1.35	2.85	3.60	5.85	6.25	5.95	4.75	3.85

Table 5. Correlation between font size and subjective and objective data.

Correlations									
			Font size	Mission success rate	Task completion time	Residence time of AOI area	Scanning number of AOI area	Attention drain	Subjective visual rating
Spearman's rho	Font size	Correlation Coefficient	1.000	.762*	-.857**	-.970**	-.595	-.786*	.595
		Sig. (2-tailed)	.	.028	.007	.000	.120	.021	.120

the font size reaches 18, the success rate of the task has been significantly improved, but this font size will still make some users recognize mistakes. When the font size is greater than 36, the recognition success rate is relatively stable, and the success rate of the 48-word task is the highest.

The task completion time decreases with the increase of character. When the font size is 60, the task completion time is the least. Combined with the stay time in AOI area and the number of AOI glances, the character size has obvious influence on the recognition efficiency of the subjects. When the character is larger than 36, the efficiency of the subjects in performing tasks reaches the best (Table 6).

5.3 Analysis of Subjective Questionnaire Results

The subjective questionnaire data of this experiment includes attention loss and subjective visual score. The data results show that attention loss decreases with the increase of characters in a certain range. When the font size is 60, the score of attention loss is the lowest 2.10. Then, with the increase of character, attention loss increases. Feedback of subjective questionnaire survey results, because the character is too large, It influenced the reading habits and cognition of the subjects themselves. This also has an impact on

Table 6. Objective data analysis.

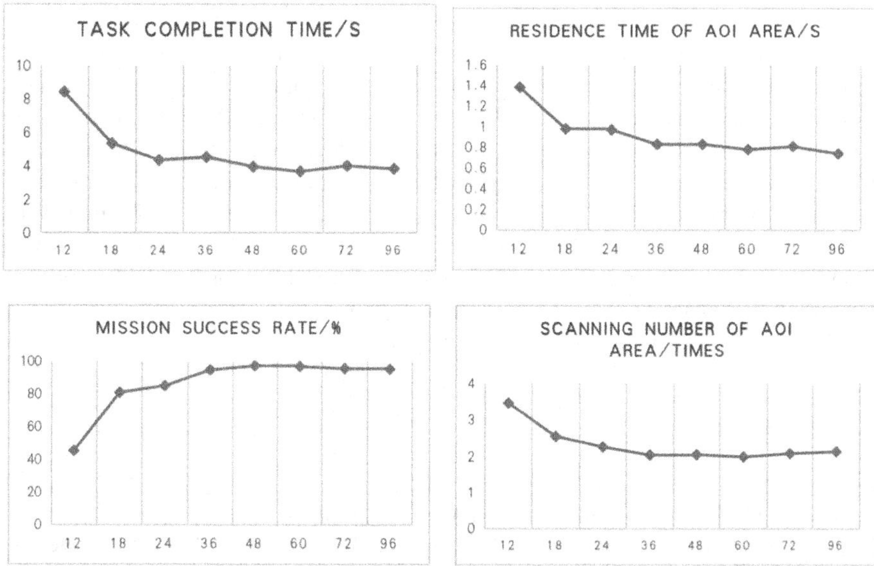

the subjective visual score. The font size below 18 is basically not accepted by users, and the best feedback result of font size is 6.25 of No.48. With the increase of font size, the subjective visual score also decreases. On the whole, the subjective evaluation results show that the results of No. 48 and No. 60 are the best (Table 7).

Table 7. Analysis of subjective questionnaire results.

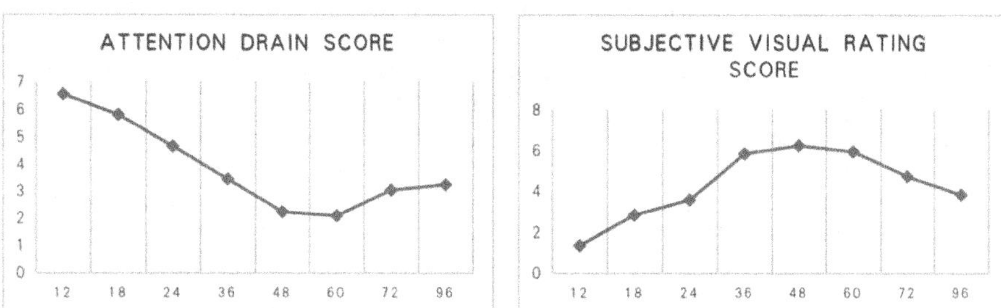

5.4 Conclusion

Character size is positively correlated with information recognition efficiency in a certain range, but inversely correlated with recognition load. When the character increases to a certain range, the recognition efficiency and recognition load will no longer be affected by it, and the experience of character information recognition will be reduced. It is suggested that the instrument character should be no less than 2.65 mm, which is a statically identifiable character size value. However, the identification load is high, which is suitable for the interface description information of instrument-independent driving, such as unit, label, etc. Under driving conditions, the character size of driving-related information should be greater than 4.94 mm, which can be used as the character size of instrument secondary information, and used for the prompt of interface secondary information unrelated to driving safety, such as temperature, time, etc. The b value of subjective reading experience is 6.58 mm, It is suggested to be the main information size of the general interface of the instrument, such as navigation information and driving tips. When the character is larger than 8.23 mm, the character recognition efficiency and recognition load reach the best, which can be used as the size of character information related to driving safety, such as early warning tips.

References

1. Ruozi, S.: Analysis and Research on Visual Display Design of Automobile Instrument. Shenyang University of Aeronautics and Astronautics, Shenyang (2015)
2. Lei, Z.: Research on Coding Mode of Flight Cockpit Information Display Interface. Beihang University, Beijing (2010)
3. Qun, W.: Experimental study on ergonomics of character coding in cockpit display interface. Vehicle and Power Technology, January 2015
4. Jiajie, H.: Comparative Study on User Experience Evaluation of Different Types of Automobile HMI Interfaces Based on Multiple Indicators. Zhejiang Sci-Tech University, Zhejiang (2018)
5. Legge, G.E., Rubin, G.S., Luebker, A.: Psychophysics of reading. V: the role of contrast in normal vision. Vision Res. **27**(7), 1165–1177 (1987)
6. Legge, G.E., Pelli, D.G., Rubin, G.S., et al.: Psychophysics of reading. I: normal vision. Vision Res. **25**(2), 239–252 (1985)
7. Xiaochao, G.: Influence of spatial frequency, stroke number and word frequency on Chinese character recognition. Ergonomics **5**(4), 5–11 (1999)
8. Jijia, Z., Huiping, W., Zhang, A., et al.: Influence of stroke complexity and repetition on stroke and Chinese character cognition. J. Psychol. **34**(5), 449–453 (2002)
9. Bhise, V.D.: Ergonomics in Automobile Design. China Machinery Industry Press, Beijing (2014)
10. Yin, M.: Research on the design method of man-machine interface of automobile cab. Xihua University (2014)

The Effects of Subjective Knowledge on the Acceptance of Fully Autonomous Vehicles Depend on Individual Levels of Trust

Xue Zhao[1](✉), Jialuo Yang[1], and Hao Tan[2]

[1] School of Design, Hunan University, Changsha, China
xuezhao9602@foxmail.com

[2] State Key Laboratory of Advanced Design and Manufacturing for Vehicle Body, Hunan University, Changsha, China

Abstract. The rapid development of autonomous driving technology has attracted great attention from society nowadays. However, the lack of consumer acceptance might be a prominent barrier to the large-scale adoption of fully autonomous vehicles (FAVs). This study argues that it is critical to predicting FAV acceptance before it is fully popularised. To investigate the relationship between the public FAV subjective knowledge and general acceptance, we conducted an online questionnaire. The results showed that respondents with higher levels of FAV subjective knowledge were more likely to accept FAV. In addition, a significant moderating effect of trust was found. Specifically, in groups with higher level of trust, the same level of subjective knowledge evoked higher level of acceptance. In conclusion, the insights from this study could greatly facilitate ongoing research related to FAV acceptance. And policymakers should consider consumer characteristics, such as subjective knowledge and trust, when formulating AV promotion strategies, so as to effectively improve consumer acceptance of FAV.

Keywords: Fully autonomous vehicles · Subjective knowledge · Trust · Acceptance · Moderation

1 Introduction

The automotive industry is facing a new turning point. In recent years, autonomous vehicle (AV) technology has received more and more attention from the public, whose interest and investment continue to increase. A Self-driving car is a vehicle that can drive to the destination on its own without drivers' operation. SAE International [1] divides autonomous driving into 6 categories according to different degrees of automation, ranging from level 0 (human drivers complete all driving tasks without automation) to level 5 (automatic driving). In level 5, the technical system can perform all under any circumstances, and in terms of driving tasks, humans are just passengers and never need to participate in driving. Safety is an urgent issue in the road transportation system. However, according to data from the World Health Organization [2], more than 1.2 million people die in road traffic accidents worldwide each year, which has a huge

P.-L. P. Rau (Ed.): HCII 2022, LNCS 13314, pp. 297–308, 2022.
https://doi.org/10.1007/978-3-031-06053-3_21

impact on health and development. In response to the aforementioned road safety issues, autonomous vehicle technology is considered to be able to play a significant role [3]. In addition, AV can also increase the mobility of vulnerable traffic groups. For example, it can expand the opportunities for socially vulnerable groups such as elderly drivers and the disabled to participate in society [4, 5]. Furthermore, The AV is also considered to improve traffic efficiency, reduce emissions, save fuel, and thereby reduce social costs. And the new business model brought about by the development of AVs will also create immeasurable market value. In summary, autonomous driving will have a profound impact on society, the environment, and transportation.

Although the benefits of AV are obvious, all these potential social benefits will not be realized if the public does not accept and use this technology. For companies and governments, it is urgent to comprehend the psychological mechanism behind consumers' acceptance of AV, and then formulate corporate strategies and policies. In particular, level 4–5 AVs are expected to account for 49% of the market by 2030, so it is crucial to understand public potential acceptance and its influencing factors before FAV fully enters the market [6]. An increasing number of studies were conducted to examine users' acceptance of AVs and their determining factors [7–9]. In addition, we had tried to explore the relationship between these influencing factors by establishing acceptance models [6, 10, 11], to better understand their direct and indirect influence on acceptance. However, most of these studies focus on the AV rather than the fully autonomous vehicle (FAV). It is believed that similar researches on FAV are also extremely urgent, especially at the moment when it is about to be realized. In addition, although the relationship between consumers' knowledge about the AV and acceptance has attracted the attention of researchers in recent years [12–14], the more detailed relationship between the two has not been explored. Therefore, this research aims to explore the relationship between the public's subjective knowledge and acceptance of FAV. More importantly, this research considers the moderating effect of trust on the relationship between subjective knowledge and acceptance (see Fig. 1), to understand more comprehensively and scientifically the mechanism of the public subjective knowledge on acceptance.

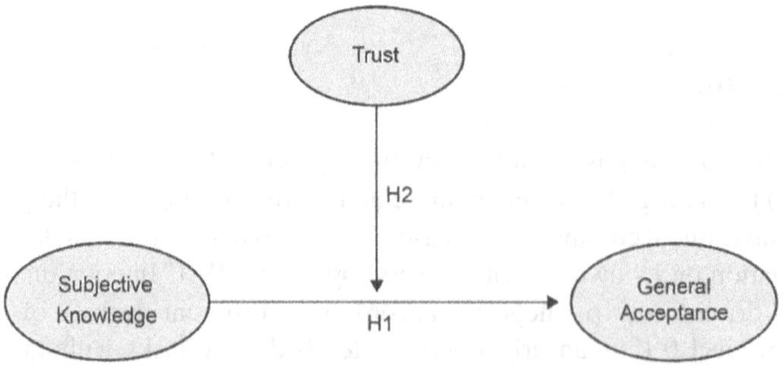

Fig. 1. Conceptual diagram of the moderation model

Our research finds that consumers' subjective knowledge will significantly positively promote general acceptance of FAV, and at the same time, this relationship could be moderated by the level of trust. Specifically, for people with the same subjective knowledge, the increase in trust could help inspire higher acceptance of FAV. Our research will contribute to the theory and practice in many ways. First of all, our research analyzed the influence of subjective knowledge on FAV acceptance through quantitative investigation and contributed to the AV acceptance literature. Second, we also made contributions by providing insights on how trust regulates the impact of subjective knowledge on acceptance. Finally, we contributed to the policymakers and AV promoters in their public communication by identifying the key factors affecting AV acceptance.

The main purpose of this research is to study the relationship between public subjective knowledge and general acceptance, and to investigate the moderating effect of FAV trust on this relationship. To the end, we suggest a research model and influencing factors based on theoretical background. The organization of this study is as follows: Sect. 2 provides the research model, hypothesis, and literature review, and Sect. 3 introduces our research methods. Section 4 explains the data analysis and results, and Sect. 5 discusses the results. We then continue with the conclusions and limitations in Sect. 6.

2 Related Works

2.1 General Acceptance

The subject of this article is the autonomous vehicle in Level 5, which is called the FAV that may not have a steering wheel, brake, or driver. Looking at the previous studies on the AV acceptance, researchers investigated public acceptance of AVs from different perspectives [15–18]. In recent years, the influencing factors of acceptance have attracted the attention of researchers, and numerous factors have been recognized. Among them, many researchers emphasized the influence of sociodemographic factors on AV acceptance [19–20], such as education, age, and gender. In addition, psychosocial factors are thought to affect general acceptance of FAV [7–8, 21], such as trust, perceived benefit/risk, perceived usefulness/ease. Furthermore, other researchers believe that mobility behavior is also the main factor affecting acceptance [22–24], such as vehicle ownership, driving license, and in-vehicle time. Among these factors, subjective knowledge and trust sparked our interest. The following subsections provide the theoretical foundation and empirical evidence for their relationships with acceptance (see Fig. 1).

2.2 Subjective Knowledge

Public negative attitude to science is often attributed to a lack of knowledge. The influences of knowledge on the acceptance of consumers have been measured in many studies in the growing body of literature. A large-scale survey across countries found that the improvement of the subjective knowledge of genetically modified foods significantly increased consumers' willingness to accept [25]. Among the respondents with a higher extremity of opposition to genetically modified food, the higher level of subjective knowledge, the lower extremity of opposition they held [26]. In the AV domain, it has attracted the attention of researchers that how much consumers know about AVs [14, 27, 28]. These papers focus on subjective knowledge of FAVs, which is how much knowledge of FAVs a person thinks he/she has. The subjective knowledge of AVs has been instrumental in the prediction of acceptance. Those having previously heard of AVs were more likely to be interested in having this technology on their vehicles [14]. It was found that consumers with higher levels of self-assessed knowledge showed a greater tendency and positive belief towards FAVs over private vehicles [12, 13, 29]. Overall, in the context of FAVs, consumers' acceptance of FAVs may be enhanced with the improvement of subjective knowledge of this technology. Thus, we will continue to verify the relationship between FAV's subjective knowledge and acceptance in this study:

H1. Subjective knowledge of FAV will positively affect general acceptance of FAV.

2.3 Trust

In 1998, trust was regarded as a state of mind, including the intention to accept vulnerability based on positive expectations of the intentions or behavior of others [30]. Later, Pavlou & Fygenson [31] proposed that trust was the belief that it would cooperate to fulfill the expectations of the client without taking advantage of its weaknesses. In summary, trust is the confidence of one party in the specific actions of the other party [32]. In the AV field, trust is particularly important for understanding the relationship between public and AVs. Researchers emphasized its importance for creating a willingness to use and rely on the technology of interest in its early stages [33]. The study found that the introduction of knowledge about automated systems would increase trust [34]. However, according to Hengstler et al. [33], trust is a psychological mechanism that enables us to reduce the awareness of uncertainty and thus is more willing to rely on FAVs to perform tasks. In addition, the trust provides a way to subjective assurance that can ensure that the trust achieves satisfactory results [35]. Therefore, we speculate that the effect of subjective knowledge on general acceptance may change due to changes in the trust level. For example, at a high trust level, subjective knowledge may stimulate higher acceptance and vice versa. In summary, we assume that trust will significantly moderate the impact of subjective knowledge on general acceptance:

H2. Trust will significantly moderate the relationship between subjective knowledge and general acceptance of FAV.

3 Methods

3.1 Participants

1609 participants completed the survey, 29 among them who failed an attention check were excluded from further analyses. This resulted in 1582 qualified completes used for analysis, with 51.5% (N = 814) male and 48.5% (N = 768) female. The ages of the participants were as follows: 661 were 18–29 years old, 673 were 30–39 years old, 190 were 40–49 years old, and 58 were 50 or older. Among these participants, 81.9% of them had driving experience.

3.2 Procedure

The online survey was administered on Baidu's Data Crowdsourcing Platform, with more than 17,000,000 respondents in its sample database and covering 300 cities in China. At the beginning of the questionnaire, they were told: "This questionnaire will ask you about your understanding and attitude towards Fully Autonomous Vehicles. The questionnaire will be conducted anonymously. All information is guaranteed not to be used for any commercial or personal purposes other than academic research". In addition, we showed them a concise description of the FAV. Subsequently, variable-related items and demographic questions needed to be answered. Participants were allowed to skip questions. However, they were not allowed to return to questions in a previous block after moving to a new block. Afterward, they were thanked for their participation and debriefed.

3.3 Measures

All measures in this survey were adapted and modified from previous literature to fit this research. And, all items are measured using a 5-point Likert scale. The details are as follows.

Subjective Knowledge. The respondents were first instructed to evaluate the subjective knowledge of FAVs adopted from Aertsens et al. [36]. They indicated their agreement with statements such as "I know FAV very well", "Among the people I know, I can be regarded as an 'expert' in the field of FAV", and "I know how to choose and judge FAV".

Trust. Participants were asked to indicate their agreement with the following statements about their trust: "I think FAV is dependable", "I think FAV is reliable", and "Overall, I can trust FAV", which were adapted from Choi and Ji [37].

General Acceptance. In the next section of the survey, participants were asked to assess the agreement of 5 statements about their general acceptance toward FAV, which were adopted from Liu et al. [35] and Xu et al. [15] as well as Yoon and Cho [38]. These items were measured using a 5-point Likert scale as follows: "Please rate your overall attitude toward the FAV" (1 = very negative and 5 = very positive), "Please indicate the acceptability level of the FAV" (1 = very unacceptable and 5 = very acceptable), and 3 items related behavioral intention such as "I intend to ride/buy/recommend the FAV in the future" (1 = strongly disagree and 5 = strongly agree).

4 Data Analysis and Results

Data analyses were performed using SPSS, and we further tested the moderation effect of trust using the plugin PROCESS based on SPSS and SAS developed by Andrew F. Hayes, which is directly able to calculate mediation effects in our proposed model. We first analyzed the measurement model and then tested the hypothesis we proposed.

4.1 Measurement Model

The reliability and validity of our measurement model were tested by SPSS. Cronbach's alpha value of all constructs was higher than 0.7, which indicated that reliability was of good quality. As for discriminant validity, the value of KOM was 0.899, higher than the suggested value of 0.8 (more details see Table 1). In addition, the correlations between variables were also calculated, and the results showed that all variables were significantly correlated (see Table 2). In conclusion, all of these results show that our measurement model has good psychometric performance.

Table 1. Scales for reliability and validity of measurement model.

Construct	Item	M	SD	Range	α
Subjective knowledge (SK)	SK1	3.11	1.048	1–5	0.790
	SK2	2.63	1.164		
	SK3	2.90	1.171		
Trust (TR)	TR1	3.35	0.975	1–5	0.748
	TR2	3.46	1.011		
	TR3	3.41	1.007		
General Acceptance (GA)	GA1	3.80	0.965	1–5	0.807
	GA2	3.62	1.028		
	GA3	3.63	0.973		
	GA4	3.68	0.886		
	GA5	3.66	0.911		
KOM = 0.899					

Note: M = mean, SD = standard deviation, α = Cronbach's alpha

Table 2. Correlation between variables.

Construct	SK	TR	GA
Subjective knowledge (SK)	/	0.486**	0.401**
Trust (TR)	0.486**	/	0.648**
General Acceptance (GA)	0.401**	0.648**	/

Note: Correlation is represented by Wilson coefficient. * $p < 0.05$; ** $p < 0.01$

4.2 Hypothesis Test

Main Effects. To test hypothesis H1, we first performed a regression-based analysis where subjective knowledge served as predictor variable, and general acceptance as outcome variable. As expected, the results showed that higher level of subjective knowledge led to greater general acceptance toward FAVs ($\beta = 0.303$, $p < 0.001$), which supported H1. For more details see Table 3.

Table 3. Regression model predicting the general acceptance.

	β	SE	t	P
Subjective knowledge (SK)	0.303***	0.017	17.381	0.0000
Constant	2.804***	0.053	58.038	0.0000
R-square = 0.161				

Note: * $p < 0.05$; ** $p < 0.01$; *** $p < 0.001$

Moderating Effect of Trust on Subjective Knowledge and General Acceptance. To examine whether trust moderates the effect of subjective knowledge on general acceptance, we performed moderation analysis using the PROCESS by Hayes (model 1), and further calculated the R-square change to the magnitude of the adjustment effect. See Table 4 and Fig. 2 for results. Subjective knowledge served as the independent variable, trust as the moderating variable, and general acceptance as the dependent variable for model analysis. As expected, this model is statistically significant ($P < 0.01$), the regression coefficients of subjective knowledge and trust are statistically significant ($P < 0.05$), and the product term subjective knowledge * trust is statistically significant ($P < 0.05$). Therefore, we believe that the relationship between subjective knowledge and general acceptance is significantly negatively moderated by trust, which supports H2.

Table 4. Regression model predicting the general acceptance – main effect.

	β	SE	t	P
Subjective knowledge (SK)	0.0937***	0.0167	5.5933	0.0000
Trust (TR)	0.5150***	0.0194	26.5846	0.0000
TR * SK	–0.427*	0.0166	–2.5712	0.0102
Constant	3.6932***	0.0150	246.9896	0.0000
R-square = 0.4314				

Note: * $p < 0.05$; ** $p < 0.01$; *** $p < 0.001$

Specifically, at different trust levels, including high, medium, and low level, subjective knowledge has a significant effect on the general acceptance of FAVs (see Table 5 and Fig. 3 for more details). In addition, concerning the size of the adjustment effect, we use the product term to estimate the change in the R side of the regression model. Process directly gives the R-square change of 0.0024, that is, the contribution of the adjustment effect to the variation is close to 0.24%.

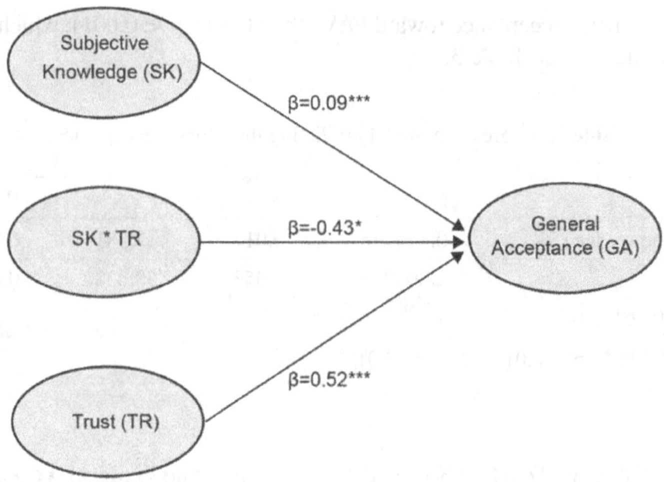

Fig. 2. Statistical plots for moderation model. **Note:** *p < 0.05; **p < 0.01; ***p < 0.001.

Table 5. Conditional effect of subjective knowledge on FAV general acceptance at values of trust.

	Trust (TR)	β	SE	t	P
Low	– 0.8132	0.1284***	0.0234	5.4740	0.0000
Medium	0.0000	0.0937***	0.0167	5.5933	0.0000
High	0.8132	0.0590**	0.0194	3.0456	0.0024

Note: Values for trust are the mean and plus/minus one SD from mean. * p < 0.05; ** p < 0.01; *** p < 0.001

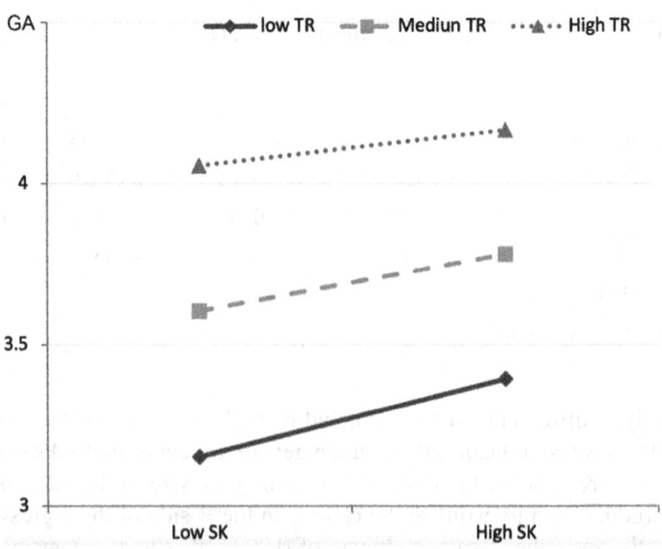

Fig. 3. Statistical diagram of the moderation model. **Note:** GA = general acceptance, SK = subjective knowledge, TR = trust.

5 Discussion and Implication

5.1 Discussion of the Results

The main purpose of this study is to comprehensively analyze the impact of the public subjective knowledge on FAV general acceptance through analyzing direct influence and moderating effect. Overall, the empirical results show that all of our hypotheses hold true.

Our results show that the subjective knowledge of FAVs significantly positively predicts its general acceptance. Specifically, higher level of subjective knowledge means higher level of general acceptance, which is consistent with previous findings [12]. Furthermore, with moderation, we tested whether the relationship between subjective knowledge and FAV general acceptance depended on the individual's level of trust in FAV. The findings show that the significant effect of subjective knowledge on general acceptance applies to groups of all trust levels (low, medium, high). Building on this, we also found that trust does increase the level of subjective knowledge that positively affects general acceptance of FAVs. Specifically, the same level of subjective knowledge inspires higher level of FAV acceptance as trust increases. Therefore, we can say that trust can further enhance the positive effect of subjective knowledge on the acceptance of FAVs. We speculate that this may be due to the role of the psychological mechanism of trust, which helps the public to overcome uncertainty and provides a subjective assurance to the public to a certain extent (Liu et al., 2019), thus people having the same with subjective knowledge, the higher trust level, the more willing to accept the FAV.

5.2 Contributions

Our findings have profound theoretical and practical implications. First, about theoretical contributions, our study partly fills the literature gap on FAV acceptance. We took the subjective knowledge as an independent variable, trust as a moderator variable, and general acceptance as an outcome variable, and obtained the statistical relationship between the three through data analysis, which is helpful for a more detailed and comprehensive understanding of public FAV acceptance mechanism. Secondly, concerning the practical significance, our research explores the moderating role of trust in the process of subjective knowledge-acceptance influence, which means that in the future when FAV popularization is conducted to the public, in addition to improving public subjective knowledge through educational exchanges, it is also necessary to develop appropriate strategies to increase public trust and thus more effectively improve FAV acceptance.

5.3 Limitations and Future Works

First, the generalizability of the study is limited by the distribution and size of the survey sample, and these users generally have high computer performance, but we believe they are largely representative of the user population of future technologies. Second, the experiment was done through an online questionnaire, whose form might lead to distraction thereby leading to experimental bias. In the future, a real car environment can be created for respondents to provide a more realistic experience. Finally, FAV has yet to gain real popularity, as our respondents can only make judgments by imagining the future, which inevitably leads to bias to some extent. Therefore, after the popularization of FAVs in the future, further updated investigations need to be obtained more accurate results.

6 Conclusion

In this study, we investigated the combined effect of an important factor (subjective knowledge) and its moderator (trust) on FAV general acceptance, which is the most discussed. In this paper, we verify that subjective knowledge has a significant effect on the general acceptance of FAVs. In addition, the study found that trust could significantly moderate the relationship between the two. Specifically, in people with higher level of trust, subjective knowledge stimulates FAV acceptance to a greater extent. We urge FAV practitioners and researchers to build on our findings to develop appropriate outreach and communication strategies to improve FAV acceptance by future users. Furthermore, we also hope that this work will advance research on FAV acceptance to help the public better understand the psychological mechanisms behind FAV acceptance.

References

1. SAE International: Taxonomy and Definitions for Terms Related to On-Road Motor Vehicle Automated Driving Systems, Report SAE J3016 (2016)
2. WHO.: Global Status Report on Road Safety 2015. World Health Organization, Geneva, Switzerland (2015)
3. Piao, J., Mcdonald, M., Hounsell, N., Graindorge, M., Graindorge, T., Malhene, N.: Public views towards implementation of automated vehicles in urban areas. Transp. Res. Procedia **14**, 2168–2177 (2016)
4. Sparrow, R., Howard, M.: When human beings are like drunk robots: driverless vehicles, ethics, and the future of transport. Transp. Res. Part C **80**, 206–215 (2017)
5. Meyer, J., Becker, H., Bsch, P.M., Axhausen, K.W.: Autonomous vehicles: the next jump in accessibilities. Res. Transp. Econ. **62** 80–91 (2017)
6. Park, M.H., Kwon, M.W., Kim, C.Y., Nah, K.: A Study on the influencing factors on the acceptance intention of autonomous vehicles level 4–5. J. Korea Multi. Soc. **23**(9), 1219–1228 (2020)
7. Zhang, T., Zeng, W., Zhang, Y., Tao, D., Li, G., Qu, X.: What drives people to use automated vehicles? a meta-analytic review. Accid. Anal. Prev. **159**, 106270 (2021)
8. Jing, P., Xu, G., Chen, Y., Shi, Y., Zhan, F.: The determinants behind the acceptance of autonomous vehicles: a systematic review. Sustainability **12**(5), 1719 (2020)
9. Golbabaei, F., Yigitcanlar, T., Paz, A., Bunker, J.: Individual predictors of autonomous vehicle public acceptance and intention to use: a systematic review of the literature. J. Open Innov. Technol. Mark. Complex. **6**(4), 106 (2020)
10. Yuen, K.F., Wong, Y.D., Ma, F., Wang, X.: The determinants of public acceptance of autonomous vehicles: an innovation diffusion perspective. J. Clean. Prod. **270**, 121904 (2020)
11. McLeay, F., Olya, H., Liu, H., Jayawardhena, C., Dennis, C.: A multi-analytical approach to studying customers motivations to use innovative totally autonomous vehicles. Technol. Forecast. Soc. Chang. **174**, 121252 (2022)

12. Sanbonmatsu, D.M., Strayer, D.L., Yu, Z., Biondi, F., Cooper, J.M.: Cognitive underpinnings of beliefs and confidence in beliefs about fully automated vehicles. Transport. Res. F: Traffic Psychol. Behav. **55**, 114–122 (2018)
13. Fernbach, P.M., Light, N., Scott, S.E., Inbar, Y., Rozin, P.: Extreme opponents of genetically modified foods know the least but think they know the most. Nat. Hum. Behav. **3**(3), 251–256 (2019)
14. König, M., Neumayr, L.: Users' resistance towards radical innovations: the case of the self-driving car. Transport. Res. F: Traffic Psychol. Behav. **44**, 42–52 (2017)
15. Xu, Z., Zhang, K., Min, H., Zhen, W., Zhao, X., Liu, P.: What drives people to accept automated vehicles? findings from a field experiment. Transp. Res. Part Emerg. Tech. **95**, 320–334 (2018)
16. Haboucha, C.J., Ishaq, R., Shiftan, Y.: User preferences regarding autonomous vehicles. Transp. Res. Part Emerg. Tech. **78**, 37–49 (2017)
17. Hulse, L.M., Hui, X., Galea, E.R.: Perceptions of autonomous vehicles: relationships with road users, risk, gender and age. Saf. Sci. **102**, 1–13 (2018)
18. Liljamo, T., Liimatainen, H., Pöllänen, M.: Attitudes and concerns on automated vehicles. Transport. Res. Traffic Psychol. Behav. **59**, 24–44 (2018)
19. Acheampong, R.A., Cugurullo, F.: Capturing the behavioural determinants behind the adoption of autonomous vehicles: conceptual frameworks and measurement models to predict public transport, sharing and ownership trends of self-driving cars. Transport. Res. Traffic Psychol. Behav. **62**, 349–375 (2019)
20. Ruggeri, K., et al.: In with the new? Generational differences shape population technology adoption patterns in the age of self-driving vehicles. J. Eng. Technol. Manag **50**, 39–44 (2018)
21. Wu, J., Liao, H., Wang, J. W., Chen, T.: The role of environmental concern in the public acceptance of autonomous electric vehicles: a survey from china. Transp. Res. 60F(JAN.), 37–46 (2019)
22. Adnan, N., Nordin, S.M., Bahruddin, M.B., Ali, M.: How trust can drive forward the user acceptance to the technology? in-vehicle technology for autonomous vehicle. Trans. Res. Part Policy Pract. **118**, 819–836 (2018)
23. Charness, N., Yoon, J. S., Souders, D., Stothart, C., Yehnert, C.: Predictors of attitudes toward autonomous vehicles: the roles of age, gender, prior knowledge, and personality other, **9** (2018)
24. Cunningham, M.L., Regan, M.A., Horberry, T., Weeratunga, K., Dixit, V.: Public opinion about automated vehicles in Australia: results from a large-scale national survey. Trans. Res. Part Policy Pract. **129**, 1–18 (2019)
25. Park, C.W., Lessig, V.P.: Familiarity and its impacts on consumer decision biases and heuristics. J. Consum. Res. **8**, 223–230 (1981)
26. House, L., Lusk, J. L., Jaeger, S., Traill, W. B., Moore, M., Valli, C., et al.: Objective and Subjective Knowledge: Impacts on Consumer Demand for Genetically Modified Foods in the United States and The European Union. 2004 Annual meeting, August 1–4, Denver, CO. American Agricultural Economics Association (New Name 2008: Agricultural and Applied Economics Association) (2004)
27. Sina, N., Joost, D.W., Miltos, K., Bart, V.A., Riender, H.: Acceptance of driverless vehicles: results from a large cross-national questionnaire study. J. Adv. Transp. 1–22 (2018)
28. Council, N. R.: A survey about public opinion about autonomous and self-driving vehicles in the U.S. the U.K. and Australia (2014)
29. Mielby, H., Sandee, P., Lassen, J.: The role of scientific knowledge in shaping public attitudes to gm technologies. Public Underst. **22**(2), 155–168 (2013)
30. Rousseau, D.M., Sitkin, S.B., Burt, R.S., Camerer, C.: Not so different after all: a cross-discipline view of trust. Acad. Manag. Rev. **23**, 393–404 (1998)
31. Pavlou, P., Fygenson, M.: Understanding and predicting electronic commerce adoption: an extension of the theory of planned behavior. MIS Q. **30**(1), 115–143 (2006)

32. Gefen, D.: E-commerce. The role of familiarity and trust. Omega **28**(6), 725–737 (2000)
33. Hengstler, M., Enkel, E., Duelli, S.: Applied artificial intelligence and trust—the case of autonomous vehicles and medical assistance devices. Technol. Forecast. Soc. Chang. **105**, 105–120 (2016)
34. Khastgir, S., Birrell, S., Dhadyalla, G., Jennings, P.: Calibrating trust through knowledge: introducing the concept of informed safety for automation in vehicles. Transp. Res. **96**, 290–303 (2018)
35. Liu, H., Yang, R., Wang, L., Liu, P.: Evaluating initial public acceptance of highly and fully autonomous vehicles. Int. J. Hum.-Comput. Interact. **35**(11), 919–931 (2019)
36. Aertsens, J., Mondelaers, K., Verbeke, W., Buysse, J., Van Huylenbroeck, G.: The influence of subjective and objective knowledge on attitude, motivations and consumption of organic food. Br. Food J. (2011)
37. Choi, J.K., Ji, Y.G.: Investigating the Importance of trust on adopting an autonomous vehicle. Int. J. Hum.-Comput. Interact. **31**(10), 692–702 (2015)
38. Yoon, S.B., Cho, E.: Convergence adoption model (CAM) in the context of a smart car service. Comput. Hum. Behav. **60**, 500–507 (2016)

Design and Culture in Social Development and Digital Transformation of Cities and Urban Areas

The Study of City Color Imagery, Affective Appraisal and Place Attachment

Jun-Liang Chen[1], Yu-Ju Lin[2(✉)], I.-Hsiu Huang[3], and Mo-Li Yeh[4]

[1] Department of Crafts and Design, National Taiwan University of Arts, New Taipei City 220307, Taiwan

[2] Department of Commercial Design and Management, National Taipei University of Business, Taoyuan 324022, Taiwan

naralin@ntub.edu.tw

[3] Freeimage Design, Taipei 106092, Taiwan

[4] College of Humanities and Design, Lunghwa University of Science and Technology, Taoyuan 333326, Taiwan

Abstract. Color is deeply related to people's living and plays extremely important role in visual communication. Color also makes important meanings of visual communication, and its configuration endues people with feelings. The city could straightly build "City color Imagery" and artistic conception by making good use of colors, and cities would highlight and construct unique goals through self-color identify. Given that most cities around the world are competing for their own characteristics, the "City color Imagery" has become the basic elements which shape the city's appearance and the carrier of culture and history. The purpose of this essay is based on the color analysis of New Taipei City and the Questionnaire Survey of the citizens, respectively discussing the color influence of 12 districts of New Taipei City. Our conclusions were as follows: 1. the color imagery can also form a high impact of strong evaluation, 2. According to the Edge element of The Image of the City, with substantial characteristics, such as rivers, mountains or buildings, can form a consensus on emotional evaluation with citizens., 3. When planning city color image, factors such as "significant significance," "generating a strong sense of belonging," "very special," and "representing regional personality" can be taken into consideration, making it easier for citizens to meet their psychological needs and identify. The consequence can also create the basis of "City color Imagery" in the future.

Keywords: City color imagery · Affective appraisal · Place attachment

1 Introduction

Color is one of the intuitive links of human emotion that could make things easier to memorize. As an important of visual communication, color matching has stimulating effect on vision and determines the accuracy of message transmission, which can easily engender people's emotional reactions. Appropriate color combination can improve the charm of marketing, and the match color should consider visual aesthetics and

P.-L. P. Rau (Ed.): HCII 2022, LNCS 13314, pp. 311–325, 2022.
https://doi.org/10.1007/978-3-031-06053-3_22

the color image as well [1]. The visual sense has profound impact on environmental experience and perception human beings rely on, and color is regarded as an important factor in strengthening shape and creating atmosphere. Through the transmission of environmental color, people can have alternative feelings and indirectly affect their behavior patterns [2]. The city color Imagery is the concept of urban color from the perspective of psychology, showing the psychological impression formed by people by observing the style of the city. It concluded a generalization of color characteristics even a representative symbol of city [3]. City color Imagery is mostly generated by the public through scenery, architecture, food, culture, products and things in daily life. Moreover, the color image can express uniqueness and connotation of the city through learning and experience, which also bring lots of important influence [4–6]. That different geographical environments directly affect the formation and development of human beings, customs, cultures, etc., and these factors all lead to different color expressions [7]. As was pointed out to the city color Imagery reflects the historical context and overall style of the city, which help people sort out the strong impression of the city [8]. Every citizen has had long associations with some part of his city, and his image is soaked in memories and meanings, a good environmental image gives its possessor an important sense of emotional security, He can establish an harmonious relationship between himself and the outside world [9].

With the advent of globalization, the homogenization of city communication became more and more obvious. In order to distinguish the unique characteristics of different cities, the established city image motivated people's cognition of the city environment, forming the memories and meanings. People recall the city image through imagination demonstrate a two-way interaction between the observer and the environment [10]. The discussion of city color covers with culture, humanities, beliefs, living style and regional atmosphere of a city, simultaneously reflecting the personality of city and civilization development as well [11]. In recent year, major cities around the world have created their own city image and characteristics by analyzing the representative color and promoted it to related applications. In the case of Kyoto, which is rich in culture and well-preserved ancient traditions in Japan, Kyoto has introduced Kyoto Landscape guidelines, which established strict specifications for the height, color, design of buildings and even outdoor advertisements so as to avoid modern architectural affairs destroying the original image of Kyoto. The provision emphasized all the corporate logos and signboard must be integrated into the original landscape. French colorists J. P. Lenclos and D. Lenclos proposed the concept of "color geography" showing the result of color surveys on cities that created a new environmental color chart [12]. Taiwan started with thinking about city color when it was nominated as 2016 World Design Capital. The whole city establish the management of Taipei Urban Living landscape Reconstruction Project, thinking about building the awareness of city color and improving the visual experience, which can enhance the aesthetics of the urban environment [13]. At present, most studies on city color Imagery mainly focus on the color association and emotion, while the research is rarely discussing the construction methods of color image. When it comes to the operation of using color, there is no construction to follow. This purpose of this research is to discuss the city color Imagery in 12 different districts of New Taipei City. It begins by conducting a questionnaire survey on the city color Imagery of New Taipei City citizens, and plotted the two results to analyze the differences. This study explores the city color Imagery of various districts and discuss the effect including citizens' place attachment and emotional evaluation.

2 Literature Review

2.1 Attachment Theory of City Imagery

One of the most important characteristic of a city is identity. Imagery refers to individuals receiving the simulation of environment, and perceived things after screening by cognitive assessment beget intangible representation or abstract environment. The imagery can be a basic understanding in design and reform unique features because it present not only visual image but multiple sense of feeling [14]. City image contains the meanings of various life styles such as food, clothing, housing, transportation, recreation, etc., and it implies the living intention constructed by citizens [15]. That cities are important heritages of the development of human civilization [16]. Through the accumulation of experience in development of city, people expressed values for real life. Kevin Lynch considered that the generation of imagery is a two-way process between the observer and the object. If the city image can be shaped more vividly, and integrated into the design of city, it will motivate unforgettable memories and images. The consist of the city image include five elements, path, edge, district, node, and landmark, which construct the space of a city. It is an important reference for residents to perceive the environment and represents the basic design principles that must be followed [9].

Place attachment refers to the functional dependence of people on the environment, as well as the spiritual connection and emotional identification. The Place attachment results in a sense of belongingness and becomes the degree of integration between individuals and the place [17, 18]. That local attachment can also have positive impact on environmentally responsible behavior [19]. Building the emotional connection between people and place usually takes a period of time, and this kind of emotion relationship is called "place attachment [20]." The formation of local attachment can promote people's expectations and local development [21]. In many studies, local attachment is considered to be a process of constructing emotional belief form a place. When places carry personal emotions and interpersonal relationships, it gives citizens special meanings and value and develops "place identity" and belongingness [22–24]. As discussed above, if citizens feel attached to the city, they may also have more environmentally responsible behavior and show higher loyalty to the city. This study is based on the scale measurement made by Williams and Vaske, dividing place attachment into two dimensions, "place dependence" and "place identity," which can be effectively measured and verified [25–27].

2.2 The Meaning of City Color in Planning and Designing

The aesthetics of a city is reflected in every corner from urban planning to color imagery, leaving citizens and visitors deep impression [28]. As pointed out in the study of Nippon Color & Design Research Institute, NCD, the psychological feelings engendered by color have commonality. Colors can be transformed into a practical scale to construct the equivalence of color and textual imagery [29]. Image of city color is about the psychological situation formed by perceiving the urban color, which can reflect the expectation and vision of citizens. The purpose of city color Imagery is to provide a new opinion of color planning and design research. The more prominent the color personality of the city is, the more profound the color image will be [30].

The relationship between the residents and their living lives will have emotional connections with some parts of the city. The city image is gradually collected in the memories which have its own significance [31]. That the differences between the color research with others when the city becomes the carrier of color are about the way of showing the environ mentality of city colors. From the previous discussion, there are two key points. First is large scale, which means different areas and colors will create different feelings, and the other is the sense of space, which means eyes' perception of city color comes from the spatial composition of structures and natural elements. The composition demonstrates different feelings about space. Therefore, we generate images and associations from the forms and colors we received thorough vision, so we can skillfully use the colors in design, and more importantly, the city color planning. This study is based on the research proposed by color expert Shigenobu Kobayashi in 1990, which discussed the landscape color and imagery and has listed 180 groups of image adjectives in relative color semantic samples. This study will search the keywords of different districts in New Taipei City through Google picture and screen 10 groups of suitable relative adjectives, studying them by semantic analysis.

2.3 Affective Appraisal and Related Theories

Affection is viewed as mental processes made up of feelings and emotions [32]. The measurement of emotion involves measurement theory and methods in psychology. Affective responses can be interpreted as the emotional responses that individuals give to environmental irritation, that is, emotional evaluations [33]. The most classic research method in measuring emotion is the PAD scale proposed by Mehrabian and Russell (1974; 1977), using the semantic scale which can detect individual's emotional response to the environment. P stands for pleasure-displeasure, which represents the positive and negative characteristics of emotional state. A stands for Arousal-no arousal, indicating the levels of neurophysiologic activation. D represents dominance-submissiveness, suggesting the individual's state of control over the situation and others and able to detect the emotional response to the environment [34]. Russell and Steiger proposed that "arousal" and "leasure" are the main dimensions of emotional response, and third dimension, "dominant", is required to fully describe the emotions of the subject and others [35]. However, there are no further discussions about the three emotions, pleasure, arousal and dominance variables in the PAD scale based on the place attachment of city color Imagery. This study follows on from the previous research, which laid out citizens' local attachment to city color Imagery and validated the positive impact on citizens' emotional evaluations. The study assumes that the dependence and identification of city color Imagery is positively related to three emotional factors.

3 Research Methods

This study explores the current status of the color image proposed by 12 districts in New Taipei City. This thesis discusses the finding which emerged from the analysis presented in the literature review. The following section will examine the questionnaire design that is used to screen and test the research objects. At this stage, the public's perception of city color Imagery is discussed. The color image of 12 districts in 2021 is obtained as the research sample, and the results and discussions will be formed in final.

3.1 Conceptual Framework and Research Hypothesis

Most related researches in the past mainly discussed the evaluation of overall city color Imagery and local attachment, but there was little intersection between emotional evaluations. When it comes to the vision and emotion of color, researches are mostly based on the psychological level, which mainly refers to the impact of emotions and the stimulation of vision. The impact will directly change people's psychology, feelings and emotions. Therefore, people will engender different reactions to color because of the inconsistency of the environment and background [36]. This study analyzes the established city color Imagery and explores the place attachment and affective appraisal of New Taipei citizens. As explained earlier, color image evaluation has its own measurement dimension, and affective appraisal also possess its own measurement standards. Nevertheless, in order to clarify the relationship between citizens' evaluation of color imagery and emotional assess of New Taipei City's 12 districts, this study will observe how affective appraisal factors related to place attachment.

3.2 Participant Selection and Testing

For the purpose of research, the current designation of city colors proposed by government in Taiwan are only the "Taiwan Red", "Taiwan Chic" and "Taiwan Gene," which were promoted by the Council for Cultural Affairs and Development in 2003. "Taiwan Red" shows the culture of Taiwan, "Taiwan Chic" stands for the beauty of natural scene in Taiwan while "Taiwan Gene" represents every Taiwanese story. In 2019, the exhibition "COLOR PROJECT" announced the cooperation with Pantone Color Institute to select representative colors or each city. Taipei as the first stop of activity, defined Timeless Gray, Vibrant Pink and Revitalizing Green as the symbolized color of Taipei. While most cities around the world make an effort to shape the city image with colors, there are few related plans discussed in Taiwan. Moreover, the government only informs the policy to public instead of making opportunity to let citizens participate in decision-making and express opinions. In view of the establishment of the Environmental Aesthetics General Advisory Group by the Local Departments of Urban Development of New Taipei City in 2021, composed of scholars, industry representatives and the head of the government, the representative color planning of 29 administrative districts will be launched. The representative color will be used as references for the design of new buildings and reconstruction of public facilities in the future. Thus, the selection of the research object takes the city color Imagery of 12 districts in New Taipei City as the main sample, hoping to reveal the public's cognition and evaluation of the current city color Imagery through questionnaires (Table 1).

Table 1. Case study the district/representative color as research samples.

	District/ Representative Color	Photo	The Image of the City
1	Banqiao/ Grey		Landmark/ Lin Family Mansionand Garden
2	Xinzhuang/ Brown		Landmark/ Xinzhuang Temple Street Business Circle
3	Xizhi/ Purple		District/ Technopole
4	Yingge/ Red		District/ Ceramics
5	Tamsui/ Cyan		Path/ Tamsui River
6	Wugu/ Blue		Edge/ Wetlands
7	Linkou/ Silver		District/ International Hi-Tech Media Park Development
8	Shenkeng/ White		Node/ Boiled Stinky Tofu
9	Pinglin/ Green		Node/ Pouchong Tea

(*continued*)

Table 1. (*continued*)

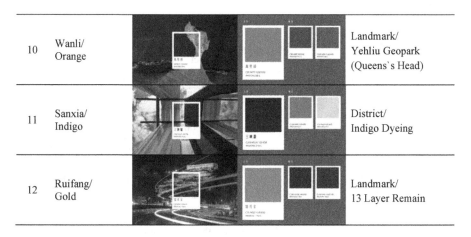

10	Wanli/ Orange		Landmark/ Yehliu Geopark (Queens`s Head)
11	Sanxia/ Indigo		District/ Indigo Dyeing
12	Ruifang/ Gold		Landmark/ 13 Layer Remain

3.3 Research Instruments

The following is a brief report on the instrument of the study. Through questionnaire design, based on the evaluation of color image, this paper explores the place attachment and affective appraisal of color imagery in 12 districts in New Taipei City. The questionnaire collects and defines sub-question elements such as assessment dimensions and assessment topics, developing an evaluation scale suitable for detecting the impact of color image on citizens' place attachment and emotional evaluation. The questionnaire is comprised of 6 dimensions and tests 21 evaluation questions. In order to obtain the feasibility of questionnaire design, the first step is to analyze after the measurement. The questionnaire evaluation scale is shown in Table 2.

Table 2. City color imagery/affective appraisal/place attachment and assessment scale.

Facets	Variable
Color image assessment ◦A1-J1. Impression of the district ◦A2-J2. Feelings of the color combination	A. Traditional-morden
	B. Cold-warm
	C. Artificial-natural
	D. Messy-tidy
	E. Energetic-gentle
	F. Pure-luxurious
	G. Steady-light
	H. Dark-bright
	I. Mature-young
	J. Vulgar-noble

(*continued*)

Table 2. (*continued*)

Facets		Variable
Place attachment	Place dependence	I am satisfied with the color matching of the district
		The color combination of the district is irreplaceable
		I would like to spend time understanding the color imagery of the district
		I reason color matching in the district is necessary
	Place identity	The color matching in the district has special meaning to me
		The color matching of the district gives me a strong belongingness
		The color matching of the district is special to me
		I agree that the color matching of the district can fully express the personality of region
Affective appraisal	Pleasure-displeasure	The color matching in the district will please me
	Arousal-nonarousal	The color matching in the district will awaken the understanding of the place
	Dominance-submissiveness	The color matching in the district impresses me

3.4 Experiment Design

The sample subjects selected included 48 males and 58 females, with a total of 106 subjects, ranging in age from 21 to 75 years old. The subjects were mainly citizens living in New Taipei City, and the questionnaires were distributed online. The researchers invited citizens to participate in the survey in advance and asked for the consent. This study adopts SD semantics, which will be divided into seven levels, and two opposite adjectives will be placed at the two ends of a ruler to evaluate the districts. The scale of the items is a Likert-type 7-point scale. For items, 1 point means "very disagree", 2 points means "disagree", and 3 points means "Slightly disagree", 4 for "average", 5 for "slightly agree", 6 for "meet", and 7 for "very agree". There are 11 assessment questions in total, and 101 valid questionnaires are recovered. The number of people tested is 9 times the number of questions in the questionnaire, which meets the needs of the number of samples. In the statistical part, the research is based on the structural equation model, and the data obtained from the questionnaire is analyzed by statistical software SPSS22.0.

4 Research Results and Discussion

4.1 Reliability Analysis

The result of reliability analysis, PAD Emotion Model and Place Attachment, is shown in Table 3, and the reliability coefficient of PAD Emotion Model is 0.582, the reliability coefficient of Place Dependence of Place Attachment is 0.630, and the reliability coefficient of Place Identity of Place Attachment is 0.746. The overall scale was 0.804, indicating the questionnaire in this study has the reliability of common standards.

Table 3. Reliability analysis summary sheet.

Facets	Variable	Amount	Cronbach's α
Affective appraisal (PAD emotion model)	Pleasure-displeasure	1	0.582
	Arousal-nonarousal	1	
	Dominance-submissiveness	1	
Place attachment	Place dependence	4	0.630
	Place identity	4	0.746
Overall attributes		11	0.804

4.2 Results of Color Imagery and Affective Appraisal

Scale between 2 to 3, and 5 to 6 is "obvious," and the number above 6 or below 2 means "strong." The basic image and affective appraisal scale analysis of each sample is arranged in Tables 4 and 5. With respect to the result, it is generally believed that the regional impressions of Xinzhuang, Pinglin, Wanli, Sanxia, and Ruifang are consistent with the color matching sensory imagery. The result also presents that the affective appraisal can form a stronger agreement of pleasant, understanding, and deep impression. The regional impressions of Banqiao, Xizhi, Yingge, Tamsui, Linkou, and Shenkeng are partially in line with the color matching sensory image presentation. Affective appraisal can form a high and strong evaluation for "awakening the understanding of the place" and "feeling impressed." Wugu's regional impression does not match the imagery of color matching, and it only forms an obvious evaluation on the feeling of pleasure.

Table 4. Analysis of color imagery and affective appraisal.

	Mean	SD	Mean	SD	Mean	SD	Mean	SD	Mean	SD	Mean	SD
	A				B				C			
	A1		A2		B1		B2		C1		C2	
1	5.86	1.50	4.87	1.01	4.69	0.95	4.70	1.05	2.77	1.04	2.71	0.89
2	3.00	0.97	2.87	0.97	4.17	0.51	4.13	0.46	4.04	0.37	3.98	0.37
3	6.29	0.68	6.44	0.62	3.94	0.60	4.01	0.64	1.59	0.78	1.90	0.84
4	1.59	0.67	1.97	0.81	4.12	0.52	2.25	0.93	4.12	0.52	4.25	0.54
5	2.38	0.89	1.97	0.71	1.94	0.98	3.80	0.71	6.63	0.61	4.56	0.59
6	3.94	0.49	4.05	0.33	3.79	0.48	3.70	0.53	2.52	1.36	5.94	0.80
7	6.43	0.71	6.50	0.72	3.89	0.81	2.67	0.88	1.78	0.81	1.69	0.80
8	2.37	0.87	2.50	0.81	3.60	0.72	5.05	0.83	3.73	0.60	3.86	0.68
9	3.40	0.78	3.14	0.74	3.01	0.85	3.08	0.83	6.91	0.29	6.84	0.37
10	3.89	0.79	3.88	0.82	4.00	0.85	5.02	0.87	6.73	0.51	6.52	0.74
11	1.98	0.66	2.07	0.70	4.22	0.56	4.07	0.57	4.22	0.56	4.31	0.56
12	3.59	0.71	3.22	0.84	3.98	0.49	3.46	0.87	5.09	0.84	5.15	0.85
	D				E				F			
	D1		D2		E1		E2		F1		F2	
1	4.30	1.40	4.09	1.31	2.15	0.98	5.06	0.96	5.95	0.83	4.76	0.85
2	3.67	0.80	3.77	0.85	3.87	0.59	3.94	0.65	3.83	0.38	3.89	0.44
3	4.57	0.73	4.37	0.86	5.45	0.73	6.04	0.86	4.18	0.54	4.82	1.06
4	3.12	0.85	3.18	0.85	3.93	0.70	3.46	0.88	1.54	0.69	2.80	0.87
5	5.39	1.37	5.01	0.88	5.50	0.78	5.01	0.66	2.16	0.78	2.41	0.75
6	4.18	0.46	4.29	0.50	4.63	0.99	4.72	0.97	3.20	0.75	3.01	0.82
7	6.54	0.66	6.28	0.81	2.62	0.69	3.27	0.88	5.95	0.83	5.60	0.79
8	3.93	0.78	3.87	0.56	3.88	0.59	3.76	0.68	2.16	0.78	2.04	0.79
9	5.82	0.48	5.80	0.62	5.29	0.95	5.54	0.85	1.99	0.83	1.99	0.77
10	4.08	0.52	3.06	1.27	4.51	0.78	4.61	0.75	1.53	0.73	2.39	0.97
11	3.25	0.85	3.64	0.72	3.87	0.69	3.98	0.51	1.70	0.66	2.97	0.83
12	3.21	0.82	3.45	0.99	4.02	0.53	4.11	0.58	1.55	0.62	2.35	0.94
	G				H				I			
	G1		G2		H1		H2		I1		I2	
1	5.29	1.32	4.45	0.97	5.67	0.98	5.09	0.69	5.40	1.36	4.96	0.81
2	3.57	0.68	3.72	0.76	3.60	0.72	3.54	0.73	3.96	0.60	3.82	0.61
3	4.82	0.78	4.98	0.71	4.08	0.34	0.45	0.71	4.55	0.97	4.66	0.94
4	3.57	0.68	3.70	0.77	3.50	0.74	3.59	0.71	3.41	0.72	3.04	0.82
5	5.68	0.77	5.77	0.72	5.97	0.73	5.74	0.69	2.45	0.92	2.99	0.78
6	4.01	0.67	4.29	0.71	4.60	0.91	4.81	0.91	4.08	0.54	4.21	0.61
7	5.73	0.68	5.68	0.62	6.30	0.83	6.43	0.80	6.34	0.75	6.57	0.59
8	4.06	0.66	3.88	0.70	5.27	1.17	4.13	0.88	3.09	0.93	3.66	0.79
9	5.55	0.75	5.59	0.72	5.76	0.75	6.04	0.82	3.20	0.81	3.49	0.83
10	4.21	0.59	4.29	0.62	4.56	0.97	4.49	0.88	3.91	0.35	3.52	0.81
11	3.45	0.73	3.64	0.76	3.48	0.67	3.66	0.74	3.53	0.72	3.72	0.85
12	3.62	0.66	3.73	0.68	3.57	0.67	3.73	0.71	3.38	0.71	3.17	0.83

(*continued*)

Table 4. (*continued*)

	J				Affective appraisal (pleasure -displeasure)		Affective appraisal (arousal -nonarousal)		Affective appraisal (dominance -submissiveness)	
	J1		J2							
	Mean	SD	Mean	SD	Mean	SD	Mean	SD	Mean	SD
1	6.17	0.71	5.63	0.72	5.71	0.80	5.72	0.85	5.93	0.83
2	3.88	0.41	3.94	0.44	5.86	0.85	6.01	0.83	6.07	0.79
3	4.03	0.39	4.50	0.86	5.76	0.80	5.75	0.85	5.95	0.78
4	3.88	0.41	4.06	0.54	5.86	0.86	5.95	0.83	5.97	0.73
5	4.40	0.57	4.37	0.66	5.84	0.86	5,93	0.85	5.91	0.60
6	4.51	0.74	4.58	0.72	5.49	0.80	4.69	0.77	4.71	0.79
7	6.31	0.69	6.41	0.68	5.76	0.80	5.76	0.86	5.98	0.80
8	3.58	0.82	3.53	0.82	5.07	1.09	5.05	0.93	5.62	0.87
9	3.94	0.68	3.97	0.61	6.05	0.93	6.12	0.82	6.05	0.83
10	4.31	0.54	4.46	0.74	5.80	0.82	6.01	0.73	6.09	0.83
11	3.98	0.51	4.11	0.55	6.17	0.94	6.20	0.81	6.23	0.79
12	4.03	0.41	4.21	0.50	6.11	0.77	6.17	0.75	6.13	0.77

Table 5. Analysis of differences in color imagery evaluation.

		Impression of the district	Feelings of the color combination	Degree of compliance
1	Banqiao	■Modern □Artificial □Energetic □Luxurious □Light □Bright □Young ■Noble	□Artificial □Gentle □Bright □Noble	Partly
2	Xinzhuang	□Traditional	□Traditional	Conform
3	Xizhi	■Modern ■Artificial □Gentle	■Modern ■Artificial □Gentle	Partly
4	Yingge	■Traditional ■Pure	■Traditional □Warm □Pure	Partly
5	Tamsui	□Traditional ■Cold ■Natural □Tidy □Gentle □Pure □Light □Bright □Mature	■Traditional □Tidy □Gentle □Pure □Light □Bright □Mature	Partly
6	Wugu	□Artificial	■Natural	Incompatible
7	Linkou	■Modern ■Artificial ■Tidy □Energetic □Luxurious □Light ■Bright ■Young ■Noble	■Modern □Cold ■Artificial ■Tidy □Luxurious □Light ■Bright ■Young ■Noble	partly

(*continued*)

Table 5. (*continued*)

		Impression of the district	Feelings of the color combination	Degree of compliance
8	Shenkeng	□Traditional □Pure □Bright	□Traditional □Warm □Pure	partly
9	Pinglin	■Natural □Tidy □Gentle ■Pure □Light □Bright	■Natural □Tidy □Gentle ■Pure □Light ■Bright	Conform
10	Wanli	■Natural ■Pure	□Warm ■Natural □Pure	Conform
11	Sanxia	■Traditional ■Pure	□Traditional □Pure	Conform
12	Ruifang	□Natural ■Pure	□Natural □Pure	Conform

■Strong □Obvious

4.3 Canonical Correlation Analysis

This section has analyzed the causes of the three dimensions of affective appraisal "Pleasure-Displeasure", "Arousal-Nonarousal", "Dominance-Submissiveness" as control variables and the Canonical Correlation Analysis between two variable of "Place Dependence" and "Place Identity." From the path diagram of the Canonical Correlation Analysis in Fig. 1, the coefficient value of the first group is 0.239, which is the highest, and the explanatory power reaches 0.057(0.2392). Among the Control Variable (X Variable) affective appraisal, the one with a higher correlation with the first canonical Variate (x_1) is "Dominance-Submissiveness", and the one with a higher correlation with the first canonical Variate (η_1) among the Criterion Variable (Y Variable) place attachments is "Place Identity". Therefore, the higher the satisfaction level of "Dominance-Submissiveness" in the affective appraisal, the higher the "Place Identity" in the place attachment (Table 6).

Table 6. Canonical correlation analysis results for first and second canonical variates. (N = 101)

Control variable (X variable)	First canonical variate		Criterion variable (Y variable)	Second canonical variate	
	x_1	x_2		η_1	η_2
Pleasure-displeasure	0.021[a]	0.977	Place dependence	−0.094[b]	−0.996
Arousal-nonarousal	0.062	−0.003	Place identity	0.932	−0.362
Dominance-submissiveness	0.972	−0.094			
Explained variance (%)	31.6	32.1	Explained variance (%)	43.9	56.1
Index of redundancy (%)	1.8	0.3	Index of redundancy (%)	2.5	0.5
			ρ^2	0.057	0.009
*$p < 0.05$			ρ	0.239* [c]	0.095

[a]: Canonical Loadings for Set-1
[b]: Canonical Loadings for Set-2
[c]: Canonical Between Set-1 and Set-2

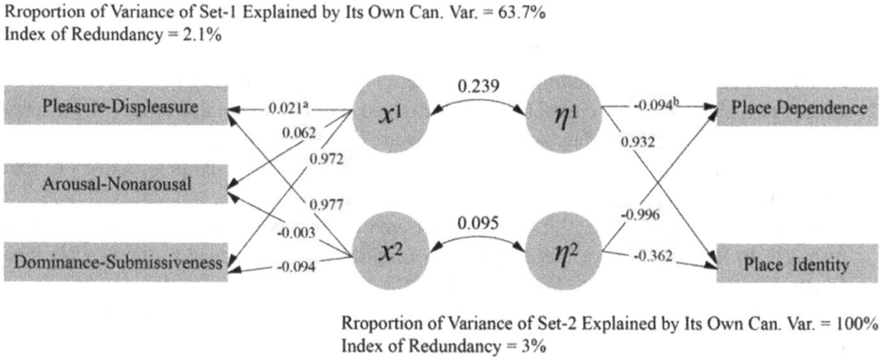

Fig. 1. Affective appraisal and place attachment for canonical correlation analysis.

5 Conclusion

This study was based on relevant literature researches, theoretical construction and analysis, formulating a scale through inference and verifying citizens' views on the achievement of color imagery in the 12 districts in New Taipei City. The results of this study can be used as a reference for city color layout in the future. The conclusions are as follows:

1. By investigating color image and emotional correlations, Color image matching color assessment and emotion will make citizens feel joyful, awaken their understanding, and feel deeply impressed. The color imagery can also form a high impact of strong evaluation.
2. According to the Edge element of The Image of the City, when constructing a color image, the boundary means a limited space. The communication of the elements are abstract, so it is necessary to strengthen the place attachment through objects with substantial characteristics, such as rivers, mountains or buildings. Those elements can easily form a consensus on emotional evaluation with citizens.
3. Canonical correlation analysis confirmed that the correlation between "Dominance-Submissiveness" and "Place Identity" of place attachment. When planning city color image, factors such as "significant significance," "generating a strong sense of belonging," "very special," and "representing regional personality" can be taken into consideration, making it easier for citizens to meet their psychological needs and identify.

As expected, the city color image is lacking in urban planning in Taiwan. The city planning needs to find features and unique styles to shape differentiated position. This study explores the color of city environment, which can increase the visibility of the city image and enhance the awareness of citizens. In addition, the results can be used as the basis for the construction city color image in the future.

References

1. Lin, Y.T.: Image of color combination in different types of objects (2013)
2. Chang, H.L.: Rational and sensual beauty intertwined: a brief introduction to the color scheme of cultural facilities. Bull. Mag. Arch. Inst. Taiwan **70**, 21–25 (2013)
3. Liu, Y., Zhang, M., Li, X.J.: Strategies of urban color planning in the perspective of urban color image. Art Des. **2**(12), 61–63 (2015)
4. Lee, S.L., Chien, C.C., Lee, C.Y.: The harbor environment color assessment and planning research. In: Proceedings of the 34th Ocean Engineering Conference in Taiwan National Cheng Kung University,pp. 625–630 (2012)
5. Chiu, Y.H., Zhang, Z.M.: The influence of environmental colors on city images: the case of Dasi in Taoyuan. City Plan. **40**(1), 81–102 (2013)
6. Su, Y.W.: Analyzing the color image of taiwan cities using data mining (2019)
7. Chang, H.F.: Regional color: a study of painting art in Macao (2018)
8. Kuo, C.Y.: Can cities be "designed"? On the contradiction and transformation between "urban design" policy and urban development. Arch. Inst. Taiwan **66**, 11–23 (2012)
9. Kevin, L.: The Image of the City. MIT Press, Cambridge (1964)
10. An Analysis of Urban Television's Remodeling of the City Image. http://media.people.com.cn/n1/2019/0319/c425665-30983955.html. Accessed 10 Dec 2021
11. Taipei color rules let the world know the city through the colors brewing in the daily life. Taipei Pictorial**626**, 12–15 (2020)
12. Lenclos, D., Lenclos, J.P.: Colors of the World: The Geography of Color. W. W. Norton & Co., New York (2004)
13. Transforming substations from the perspective of urban color. https://www.gvm.com.tw/article/31944. Accessed 10 Dec 2021
14. Lai, Y.M.: Exploring Residents' Rural Image of Fuhsing Community. Tungshiau, Miaoli (2007)
15. Chen, L.Y., Hsieh, W.Z., Wu, Y., Yang, W.X.: Interpretation of the city image illustrated by Zi Hui Taiwan: from the perspective of semiotics. J. Des. Sci. **22**(2), 93–120 (2019)
16. Wu, G.T.:Urban style and architectural. Artist Mag. Taipei (1994)
17. Yeh, S.C., Lee, M.T.: Effect of place attachment on users' perception of social and environmental conditions in the trail of Nature Park of Tzaishan. In: The 5th Symposium on Service Industry Management and Innovation, Tainan (2008)
18. Tsaur, S.H., Sun, C.Y.: Antecedents and consequences of place attachment. J. Geograph. Sci. **55**, 43–63 (2009)
19. Vaske, J.J., Kobrin, K.C.: Place attachment and environmentally responsible behavior. J. Environ. Educ. **32**(4), 16–21 (2001)
20. Liu, C.W.: Examining the relationships between place attachment and experience use history(2016)
21. Lu, Y.R.: On sense of place: a case study of Taipei urban forest (2001)
22. Giuliani, M.V., Feldman, R.: Place attachment in a developmental and cultural context. J. Environ. Psychol. **13**, 267–274 (1993)
23. Lin, Y.C.: Meanings of place attachment to ecotourism sites management: a case study of Yangmingshan national park. Natl. Park J. **16**(2), 41–59 (2006)
24. Pan, S.L., Wu, H.C., Chou, J.: Research on the relationships among volunteer interpreters' activity involvement, place attachment and satisfaction: a case study from the national museum of natural science. J. Outdoor Recreat. Study **21**(3), 23–47 (2008)
25. Williams, D.R., Vaske, J.J.: The measurement of place attachment: validity and generalizability of a psychometric approach. For. Sci. **49**(6), 830–840 (2003)

26. Lin, C.Y.: Establishing and verifying place attachment scale of national parks in Taiwan (2008)
27. Wang, P.C., Chen, Y.T.: The relationship among aesthetic experience, environmental attitude and environmental behavior. J. Agric. For. **15**(2), 17–34 (2018)
28. Reflection and Voice: Creating Urban Aesthetics for Taipei. https://www.biosmonthly.com/article/6106. Accessed 10 Dec 2021
29. Shang, K.C.Y.: Can color empower your energy? A study to assess the training effect of color energy(2017)
30. Chen, J.M., Li, Y.: Capital city color planning path based on urban color image. Packg. Eng. **37**(20), 189–193 (2016)
31. Hung, Y.J.: Study and application of urban visual color in Tamsui (2018)
32. Éthier, J., Hadaya, P., Talbot, J., Cadieux, J.: B2C web site quality and emotions during online shopping episodes: an empirical study. Inf. Manag. **43**(5), 627–639 (2006)
33. Nasar, J.L.: Urban design aesthetics the evaluative qualities of building exteriors. Environ. Behav. **26**, 377–401 (1994)
34. Mehrabian, A., Russel, J. A.: An Approach to Environmental Psychology. MIT Press, Cambridge (2974)
35. Russell, J.A., Steiger, J.H.: The structure in persons' implicit taxonomy of emotions. J. Res. Pers. **16**(4), 447–469 (1982)
36. Hsu,Y.C.: A study of image data categorization and query based on subjective feelings (2003)

Characteristics of the Power Load Profile and Renewable Energy Generation Variation in China

Yongbin Ding(✉), Mingquan Li, and Guozhu Jia

School of Economics and Management, Beihang University, Beijing 100191, People's Republic of China
dyb0628@buaa.edu.cn

Abstract. The reliable operation of the electric power system requires the real-time balance of the electric power supply and demand. With the rapid increase of the grid-connected capacity of renewable energy, the reverse output characteristics of wind power and "hump-type" output characteristics of solar power lead to the increase of the net load fluctuation of the power system, and increase the flexibility requirement of the electric power system. In order to carefully understand the challenges faced by the real-time balance of the supply and demand of the power system, it is urgent to study the temporal fluctuation of Chinese power demand, the time fluctuation characteristics of renewable energy output, the difference between the fluctuation characteristics of the two, and the specific challenges faced by each region. Based on the data of hourly power demand and wind/solar energy output in 2018, this study analyzed the seasonal characteristics, hourly variation and regional differences of power demand, as well as the temporal fluctuation characteristics and spatial disparity of wind power and solar energy output. The results show that there are obvious temporal variation and significant regional differences in seasonal, monthly and daily power demand, and there is a mismatch between the fluctuation characteristics of renewable energy power generation and power demand. The results of this paper can provide essential insights for ensuring the safe and reliable operation of the renewable-dominated power system and the power system flexibility design in the process of transition to deep-decarbonized energy system in China.

Keywords: Power load · Renewable energy · Temporal variation

1 Introduction

It is widely believed that developing renewable energy sources, especially wind and solar energy, is one of the important measures to mitigate global climate change. China's commitment to achieve a carbon peak by 2030 and to achieve carbon neutrality by 2060 will inevitably depend on the large-scale development of renewable energy [1, 2]. China's power system is mainly coal power. These coal power units have large installed capacity, new installed age, advanced technology and efficient operation, which plays an

P.-L. P. Rau (Ed.): HCII 2022, LNCS 13314, pp. 326–344, 2022.
https://doi.org/10.1007/978-3-031-06053-3_23

important role in realizing economic, stable and reliable power supply. However, with the continuous development of renewable energy sources such as wind and solar energy, as well as natural gas and nuclear power generation forms, China's power system is facing a profound transformation from traditional fossil fuels to clean and renewable energy sources, and gradually changing the current situation of excessive reliance on thermal power generation.

The stable and reliable operation of the power system must meet the real-time balance of supply and demand. With the continuous improvement of the proportion of renewable energy in the power system, the stability and reliability of China's power supply system have been severely challenged. The reasons include: first, the power generation of renewable energy is affected by natural resource conditions, with large fluctuations, seasonal periodic fluctuations and instantaneous random fluctuations; second, the prediction of renewable energy generation is greatly affected by the predicted advance time and requires higher flexibility of the power generation system; third, the geographical mismatch of renewable energy and power load and the limited transmission capacity of long-distance transmission grid bring serious power grid reception and consumption problems.

In order to explore the adjustment of supply and demand balance of power system under the large-scale development of renewable energy, a detailed analysis of the temporal fluctuation characteristics of the power system demand load and renewable energy output is required. The present researches lack the analysis of the fluctuation characteristics based on the power demand and renewable energy output, and it is difficult to provide effective support for the power system flexibility mechanism design under the development of a high proportion of renewable energy in China. To solve the above problems, this study aims to explore the fluctuation characteristics and fluctuation differences of power demand and renewable energy in China. Specifically, this paper analyzes the Northeast power grid, North China power grid, East China power grid, Central China power grid, Northwest power grid, Southwest power grid and China Southern power grid and the power demand load curve and wind/solar energy output curve of 8060 h, analyzes the seasonal characteristics of high wind/small wind, sufficient light/light scarcity, analyzes the typical daily power demand load and wind/solar energy output curve, and analyzes the flexible resource demand of different power grids.

2 Method and Data

2.1 Data and Description

Hourly Power Demand. This paper analyzes the power demand in each provinces in 2018. The set of data is based on the hourly level power demand in 2010 combined with the annual power demand growth in the same proportion to the hour level power demand in 2018 [3]. The data was compared with the typical power load fluctuation shape of various provinces released by the National Development and Reform Commission in 2019 to ensure the reliability of the data.

Hourly solar and wind energy resources. This paper uses solar and wind information from 2015 to estimate the solar and wind output of each geographic grid and summarizes the above geographic grid level information to the provincial level.

In 2015, the hourly wind speed and solar radiation information of each geographic grid of 0.5 latitude * 0.625 longitude in China was obtained from the data set of MERRA-2 (Modern-Era Retrospective analysis for Research and Applications-2) from NASA [4]. This data was calibrated in this study. Based on these data, hourly wind generation was estimated assuming that all wind fields had a 1.5 MW General Electric (GE) wind turbine (rotor diameter of 77m). This study extended the wind speed at 50 m in the MERRA-2 data set to 80 m.

Solar power generation per hour was calculated using PVwatts method, while assuming tilted photovoltaic panels, and solar radiation data are proofreading-adjusted based on MERRA-2. Feng et al. [5] proposed that the data in the MERRA-2 data set overestimate the solar radiance due to the imperfect parameters of the cloud and aerosol, and proposed the data set adjustment method used in this paper.

2.2 Method

Using statistical methods, the statistical analysis of power demand, solar power utilization and wind energy utilization in national and related provinces was conducted by calculating the mean value and standard deviation.

mean value

$$E(x) = \frac{\sum_{k=1}^{n} x_k}{n}, \tag{1}$$

standard deviation

$$\sigma(x) = \sqrt{\frac{\sum_{k=1}^{n} (x_k - E(x))^2}{n}} \tag{2}$$

3 Results and Discussion

3.1 Temporal Fluctuation and Spatial Differences of Power Demand

Aggregate Power Demand. According to Table 1, the average hourly power demand is 784,914 megawatt hours. Among the seven national power grids, East China power grid has the largest power demand, followed by North China power grid and South China power grid, while Southwest power grid is the least, and the power demand of East China power grid is about 4.5 times that of Southwest power grid.

Table 1. The hourly average of power demand in 2018.

power grid	North China power grid	Northeast power grid	East China power grid	Central China power grid	Northwest power grid	Southwest power grid	China Southern power grid	Nationwide
Electricity demand	185903	56682	190919	99182	78723	41697	131809	784914

Unit: megawatt hour

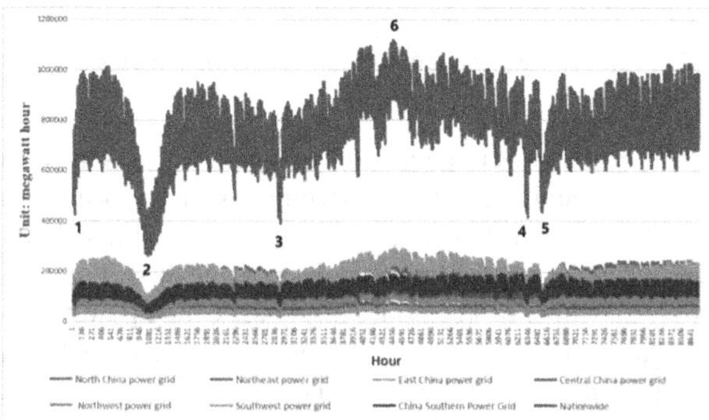

Fig. 1. The hourly power demand for the whole year

Figure 1 shows the 8,760-h power demand load curve for 2018, and point 2 (1,060 h, at 4:00 on February 14th) is the minimum annual power demand hour (2,66,334 megawatt hours), Point 1 (at 4:00 on January 2nd), 3 (at 4:00 on May 2nd), 4 (at 5:00 on September 22th) and 5 (at 5:00 on October 1st) are also relatively low values for the whole year. Point 6 (4476 h, at 12:00 July 6th) is the highest annual power demand hour (1117869 megawatt hours).

Analysis of the Fluctuation Characteristics of Power Demand

(a) *Changes of season and month.* According to Fig. 2, the power demand of each power grid is the highest in summer and the lowest in winter. In summer, the power demand increase trend of East China power grid is the most obvious, followed by central China power grid and North China power grid. In winter, China Southern power grid declines the most significantly, followed by North China and East China power grids. The variation of northwest power grid, southwest power grid and northeast power grid are relatively small.

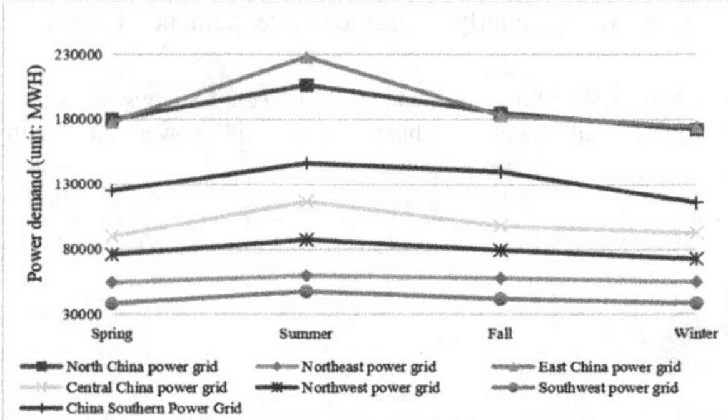

Fig. 2. Seasonal changes in power demand for different power grids

According to Fig. 3, the power demand of each power grid is the lowest in February and rebounds rapidly in March. In addition to China Southern power grid, the electricity consumption of each power grid decreases slightly in April and May. From June to October, all power grids experience a process of rising firstly and then falling. The highest values of North China power grid, Northwest China power grid and Northeast China power grid appear in June, East China power grid, Central China power grid and South China power grid in July, and China Southern power grid in August. From October to December, all power grids are gradually improved.

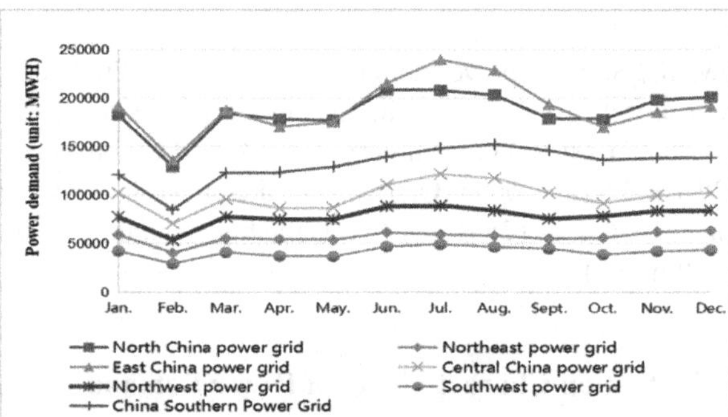

Fig. 3. Monthly changes in power demand for different power grids.

(b) *Hourly change.* Figure 4 shows the changes in national electricity demand throughout the day during the typical month. In terms of the hourly trend change, the electricity demand gradually decreases from 1:00, and reaches the lowest level at 5:00, raises gradually from 6 h, and reaches the first peak at 11:00 (or 12:00), then gradually decreases until 13:00, after it rebounds at 14:00, remains the high value level until 18:00 (or 19:00), and has a rebound at 21:00 and 20:00, respectively. Compared with different months, the average hourly electricity consumption in July is much higher than that in other months, followed by October and April. The situation is special in January, with low values at 7:00,8:00,9:00 and 14:00, and the rest of the periods are higher than April and October.

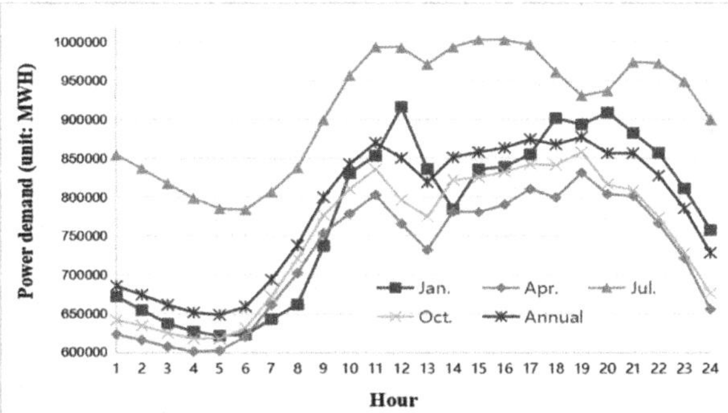

Fig. 4. The hourly variation in national power demand

The hourly change in demand is directly related to the enterprise production, heating (cooling) and other domestic and commercial electricity consumption. In July, due to the hot weather, air conditioning and other refrigeration equipment use much electricity. In January, affected by the enterprise holiday shutdown in Spring Festival holiday, the daytime electricity consumption is relatively low.

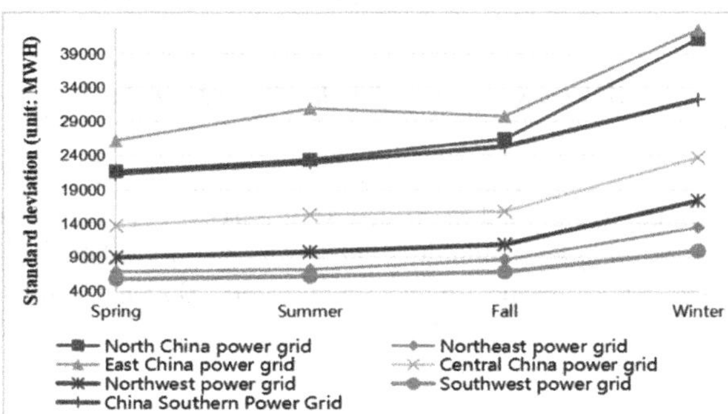

Fig. 5. Seasonal variation of the hourly standard deviation of power demand

According to Fig. 5, from the seasonal point of view, except for the East China power grid, which decreases in autumn, the hourly standard deviation of the power demand of each power grid shows a gradually increasing trend, and the increase is especially obvious in winter.

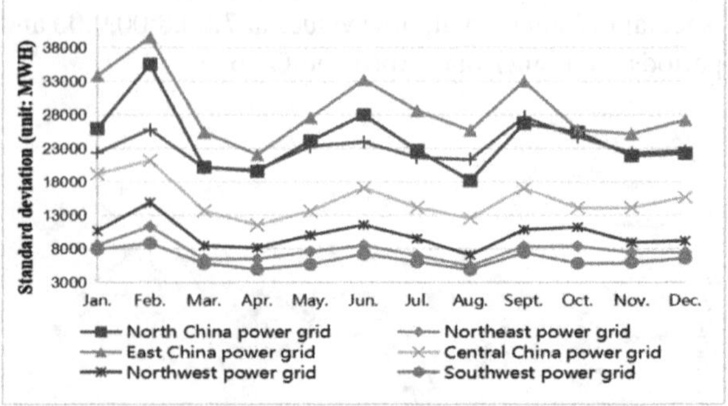

Fig. 6. Monthly variation in hourly standard deviation for power demand

The hourly standard deviation of power demand can reflect the fierce degree of the change of power grid demand to a certain extent. The greater the standard deviation, the greater the drastic the change in power demand, and the more difficult it is to regulate the power system. According to Fig. 6, the largest hour standard deviation of East China power grid is found, followed by North China power grid, China Southern power grid. From the perspective of month, the hourly standard deviation in February, in June and in September is relatively high, and the East China power grid, North China power grid and Central China power power grid are more obvious. The Northwest power grid and Northeast power grid also have relatively high hourly standard deviations in October.

3.2 Temporal Fluctuation and Spatial Disparity of Solar Energy Output

Distribution and Installation Capacity of Solar Energy in Various Regions

(a) *Annual hours of solar energy available in various regions.* The number of available solar annual hours varies widely in different parts of China. In western Qinghai and Tibet, the number of available solar energy is more than 2,500 h, Xinjiang, Gansu, and western Mongolia are located between 2,000 and 2,500 h, eastern Inner Mongolia, western part of central China, Yunnan are around 1500 h, Sichuan Basin, Chongqing and other places are less than 1000 h.

(b) *Installed situation of photovoltaic power generation capacity.* According to Table 2, Shandong has the largest installed capacity of photovoltaic power generation, followed by Hebei, Jiangsu and Zhejiang. The installed capacity of Qinghai, Ningxia, Xinjiang and other western regions are basically more than 10 million kilowatts, and the installed capacity of Hainan, Xizang, Chongqing and Beijing are less than 1.5 million kilowatts.

Table 2. Photovoltaic power generation installed capacity of each province (top 20).

Region	Installed capacity	Region	Installed capacity	Region	Installed capacity
Shandong	2606	Inner Mongolia	1309.3	Guangdong	860
Hebei	2365.6	Henan	1271.1	Jiangxi	820.1
Jiangsu	1764.6	Ningxia	1240	Hubei	735.2
Zhejiang	1621.6	Xinjiang	1233.5	Liaoning	412.1
Qinghai	1590.7	Shaanxi	1143.5	Hunan	407
Anhui	1459.5	Guizhou	1056.6	Yunnan	393.3
Shanxi	1337.2	Gansu	977.8	Heilongjiang	338.9

Unit: ten thousand kilowatts
Data source: By the first half of 2021, The National Energy Administration of China

Solar Power Generation in Typical Provinces

(a) *Selection of typical provinces.* Considering solar and wind energy distribution, installed capacity and regional distribution, this study selects Shandong province of North China power grid, Liaoning and Inner Mongolia east of Northeast power grid, Zhejiang and Jiangsu of East China power grid, Jiangxi of Central China power grid, Gansu and Xinjiang of Northwest power grid,Guangdong and Yunnan of China Southern power grid as typical provinces (Southwest power grid is mainly hydroelectric generation, not selected provinces) to analyze the situation of renewable energy power generation.

(b) *Analysis of the maximum hourly utilization rate of each day.* The maximum daily utilization rate can reflect solar utilization, and the highest hourly utilization rate in everyday is selected as the analysis data. According to Table 3, Xinjiang's solar energy utilization rate is the highest, with the annual mean of maximum daily hourly utilization rate reaching 72%. The value in Inner Mongolia east, Shandong and

Table 3. Annual mean and standard deviation of maximum daily hourly utilization rate of solar energy

province/numerical value	Liao ning	Inner Mongolia east	Xin jiang	Gan su	Guang dong	Yun nan	Zhe jiang	Jiang su	Jiang xi	Shan dong
Annual mean of the daily hourly utilization maximum rate(%)	59.38	65.54	72.83	69.32	45.68	59.24	43.88	48.34	40.48	65.4
Annual standard deviation of the maximum daily hourly utilization rate(%)	17.81	15.05	9.3	10.3	11.56	11.76	15.61	14.97	13.61	14.71

Gansu are more than 65%, and in Liaoning and Yunnan are about 59%. The value of Zhejiang, Jiangsu and Guangdong are only about 45%, so the three provinces have obvious light abandonment. From the standard deviation analysis throughout the year, Liaoning is the highest, followed by Inner Mongolia east, Zhejiang, Jiangsu and Shandong, and Xinjiang and Gansu are the lowest. Therefore, solar energy utilization rate in Xinjiang and Gansu fluctuate less and are more stable.

According to Fig. 7, the monthly mean of solar energy utilization rate in various provinces remains high in summer and drops sharply in winter. Liaoning, Inner Mongolia east and Shandong remain a high level until October, while in winter utilization rate are low, with a sharp drop in November. Xinjiang and Gansu change little throughout the year, are relatively low in June, and have an obvious growth trend in July and August. Jiangsu and Zhejiang remain a high level from March to May, and in September and October. Jiangxi remains high from August to October. Yunnan and Guangdong show a trend of "high level" throughout the year, and Yunnan is the lowest in August, Guangdong experiences a relatively significant decline in December. These phenomena are mainly related to two main factors: first, the solar lighting resource is sufficient in summer and insufficient in winter; second, in summer, cooling demand is high across the country, and in winter, cogeneration thermal units start in some areas.

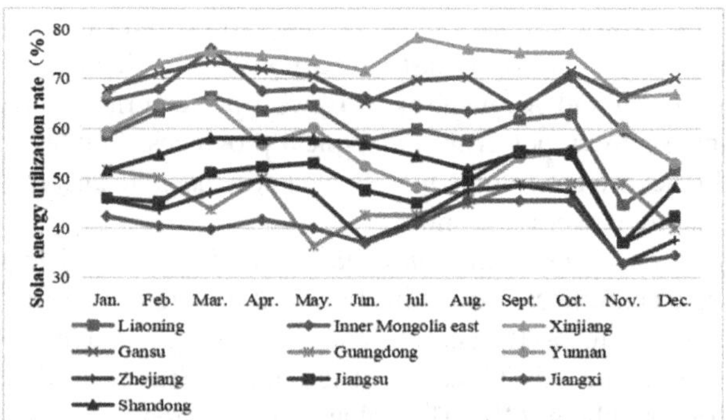

Fig. 7. Monthly mean of maximum daily hourly utilization rate of solar energy

(c) *Annual hourly distribution of solar energy utilization rates.* According to Table 4, during the 8,760 h throughout the year, Inner Mongolia east has four hours of solar energy utilization rate for more than 90%, and Xinjiang has one hour. Xinjiang has the most hours of utilization rate more than 80% (213 h), followed by Inner Mongolia east, Gansu and Liaoning.About the number of hours of utilization rate over 50%, the top five provinces are Xinjiang (2,277 h), Gansu, Inner Mongolia east, Liaoning and Yunnan, which have high solar energy utilization rates. Therefore, Jiangsu, Guangdong and Zhejiang have a lot of solar energy being abandoned.

Table 4. Annual hourly distribution of solar energy utilization rates.

Utilization/ province	Liao ning	Inner Mongolia east	Xin jiang	Gan su	Guang dong	Yun nan	Zhe jiang	Jiang su	Jiang xi	Shan dong
More than 90%	0	4	1	0	0	0	0	0	0	0
More than 80%	19	175	213	90	0	0	0	0	0	0
More than 50%	1512	1797	2277	2078	439	1137	563	747	334	1084

Unit: hour

(d) *monthly distribution of hourly solar energy utilization rates.* According to Fig. 8, the hourly distribution of solar energy utilization rates varies greatly among the provinces. Provinces of more than 20 h (the hourly utilization rate is above 80%) include Xinjiang (4 months) and Inner Mongolia east (2 months). Provinces of more than 100 h (the hourly utilization rate is between 60% and 80%) include Xinjiang (9 months), Gansu (6 months), Liaoning (3 months) and Inner Mongolia east(3 months). In addition, Shandong, Yunnan, Jiangsu and Zhejiang have more hourly utilization rate of more than 60% in spring and autumn. In general, high solar utilization mainly rate appears in spring, followed by autumn, and there is an overall trend of reduced utilization rate in summer.

Solar Power Generation in Typical Days. Select the representative July 6 (the day of the highest national annual power demand hour, the point 6 in Fig. 1) and February 14 (the day of the lowest national annual power demand hour, the point 2 in Fig. 1) to analyze the solar power situation in typical provinces.

(a) *Overall situation.* According to Fig. 9, the solar energy utilization rate shows the "parabolic" form of rising first and then falling all day, reaching the maximum value at noon. Compared with February 14, solar energy starts earlier and ends later on July 6, and the use time distribution is wider (about 4 h more). The utilization rate of Gansu, Inner Mongolia east and Liaoning increase significantly, and Jiangxi and Guangdong increase slightly. In stark contrast, Jiangsu, Zhejiang, Yunnan and Shandong decrease.
(b) *Match degree between solar energy utilization and power demand.* According to Fig. 10, on February 14, the demand for electricity in various provinces was low, solar energy utilization rates in Zhejiang, Jiangsu, Guangdong and Jiangxi are low, though other provinces, especially Inner Mongolia east, Xinjiang and Gansu have high utilization rates. On July 16, the utilization curve of Liaoning, Inner Mongolia east, Xinjiang, Gansu and Jiangxi increase significantly. In contrast, Jiangsu, Zhejiang, Yunnan and Shandong declined, indicating that the four provinces don't make full use of solar power in the summer.

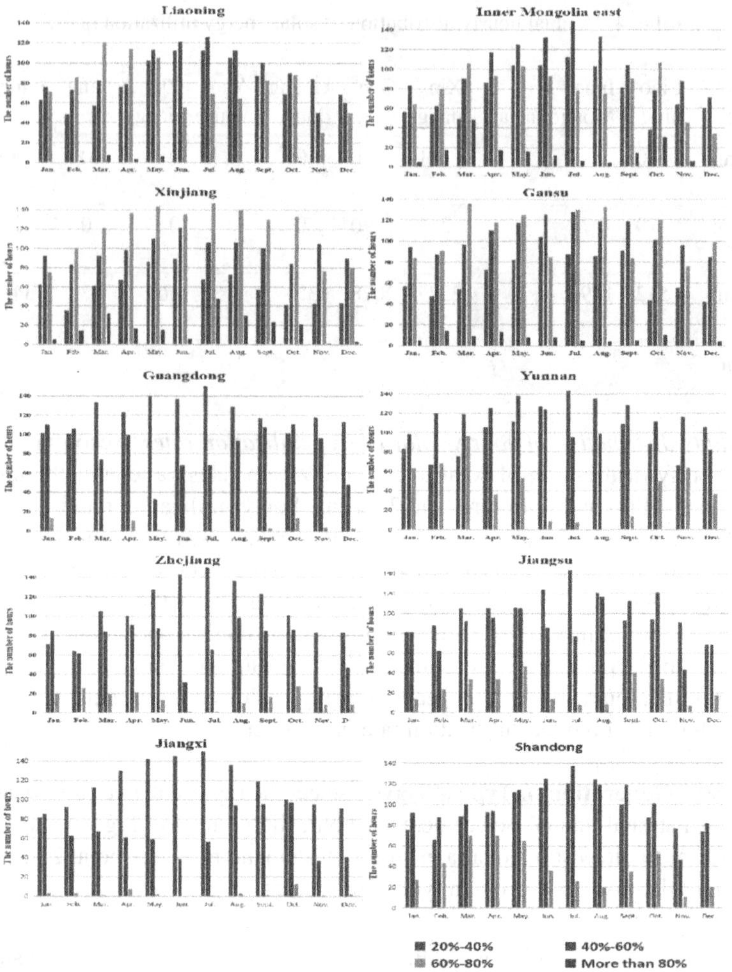

Fig. 8. The hourly distribution of solar energy utilization rates in different months

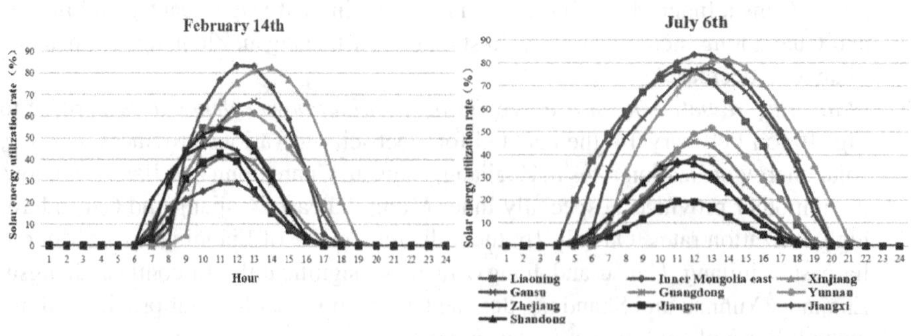

Fig. 9. Changes in solar energy utilization rate on typical days

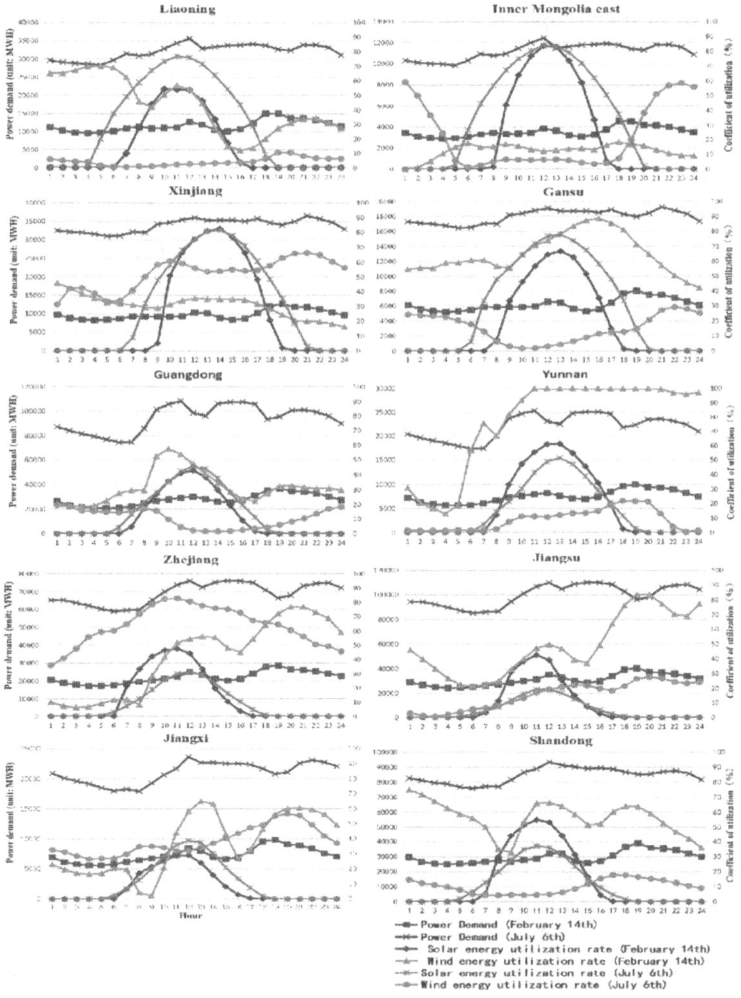

Fig. 10. Comparison chart of power demand and solar energy and wind energy utilization rate in typical provinces

On July 6, except for Yunnan and Guangdong, the maximum daytime demand in other provinces basically matches the maximum utilization time of solar energy, and the use of solar energy makes an important contribution to meeting the maximum power demand at noon. By comparison, the highest utilization rate of Jiangsu, Zhejiang, Jiangxi and Shandong are all below 50%, with the phenomenon of solar abandonment. More attention is needed to be paid to Guangdong and Yunnan, the overall utilization rate of solar energy is very low, and the phenomenon of solar abandonment is even more serious. When improving the utilization rate, the related provinces should reasonably solve the contradiction between the decline of power demand at noon and the maximum value of solar energy resources.

3.3 Analysis of the Temporal Fluctuation and Spatial Disparity of Wind Energy Output

Wind Energy Distribution and Installed Capacity

(a) *Distribution of wind energy resources.* As shown in Table 5, the inland rich wind energy resources in China are mainly in the wind energy rich zones: the" three north regions" (northeast, north China and northwest), such as Inner Mongolia, Xinjiang and three northeastern provinces.

Table 5. Provinces rich in wind energy resources in China.

Region	Wind energy resources	Region	Wind energy resources
Inner Mongolia	6178	Shandong	394
Xinjiang	3433	Jiangxi	293
Heilongjiang	1723	Jiangsu	238
Gansu	1143	Guangdong	195
Jilin	638	Zhejiang	164
Hebei	612	Fujian	137
Liaoning	606	Hainan	64

unit: ten thousand kilowatts
Data source: China Meteorological Administration

(b) *Wind power installed capacity.* As shown in Fig. 11, Inner Mongolia, Xinjiang and Hebei are among the top ten provinces with more than installed wind power are over 20 million kilowatts. In addition, Yunnan has an installed capacity of about 9 million kilowatts, and Guangdong has about 6 million kilowatts (on land). By comparison, Xizang, Chongqing, Hainan, Beijing and Tianjin have very little installed wind power capacity.

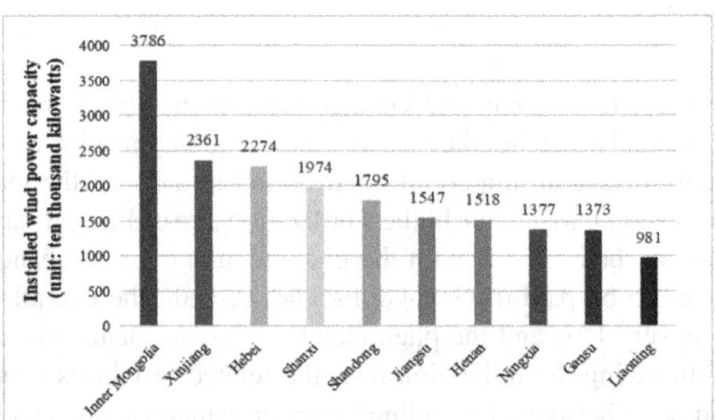

Fig. 11. Installation of wind power in each province (top 10). Data source: By the end of 2020, China Electric Power Enterprise Federation.

Wind Power Generation in Typical Provinces

(a) *Analysis of the maximum daily hourly utilization rate of wind energy.* According to Table 6, The annual mean of maximum daily hourly utilization rate of wind energy in Yunnan, Inner Mongolia east, Liaoning and Jiangsu are nearly 50%. Guangdong's wind energy utilization rate is the lowest, and the annual mean of maximum daily hourly utilization rate is 39.6%. Therefore,Yunnan, Inner Mongolia east, Liaoning and Jiangsu have a high wind energy utilization rate. Compared with solar energy, the overall utilization rate of wind energy is lower, and wind abandonment is more serious than solar abandonment, especially in Gansu, Xinjiang, Zhejiang, Jiangxi, Shandong and Guangdong. From the standard deviation, the wind energy utilization rate in Yunnan fluctuates greatly, though the Xinjiang and Gansu wind energy utilization rate fluctuates less, which is more stable.

Table 6. Annual mean and standard deviation of maximum daily hourly utilization rate of wind energy

Province/numerical value	Liaoning	Inner Mongolia east	Xin jiang	Gan su	Guang dong	Yunnan	Zhe jiang	Jiang su	Jiang xi	Shan dong
Annual mean of the daily hourly utilization maximum rate(%)	48.78	51.83	43.59	42.65	39.60	59.07	43.25	49.49	44.44	42.95
Annual standard deviation of the maximum daily hourly utilization rate(%)	27.07	27.84	16.03	17.73	21.93	37.95	24.27	27.91	30.87	26.74

According to Fig. 12, in terms of the monthly average, compared with solar energy, except for Xinjiang, Gansu and Zhejiang, most provinces have more obvious seasonal wind energy changes, with the highest in spring and the lowest in summer, and the sub-peak in winter around November. By comparison, the monthly mean in Xinjiang, Gansu and Zhejiang change little, maintaining a range of 35%–50%. The trend of Inner Mongolia east, Liaoning and Shandong are basically the same and change greatly: reaching the annual maximum in April, falling to the lowest value in August, and rebounding to get a relatively high value in October. Jiangsu reach its highest value in April and continue to fall later, but is abnormally relatively high in August before rebounding to November. The situation varies in Guangdong, with a sharp drop in August and gradually rebounding to its peak in December. Most particularly, Yunnan has the most dramatic monthly change in the year, reaching a high value of 98.85% in March and a low value of 26.67% in August.

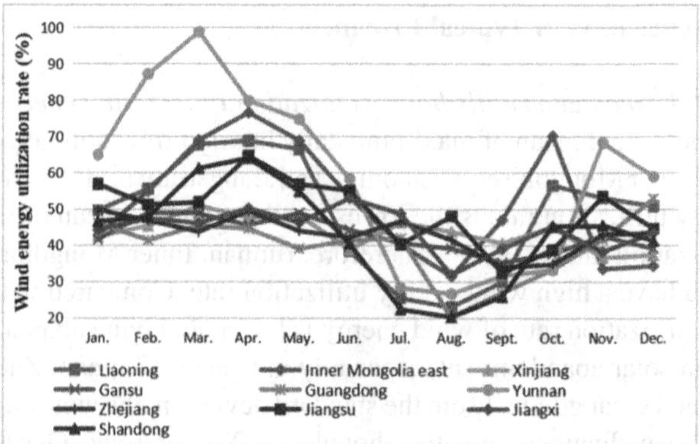

Fig. 12. Monthly mean of maximum daily hourly utilization rate of wind energy

(b) *Annual hourly distribution of wind energy utilization rates.* According to Table 7, during the 8,760 h throughout the year, in addition to the Xinjiang and Gansu provinces, other provinces have solar utilization rate above 90% in some hours, Yunnan has the largest number of hours (992 h), and Inner Mongolia east, Jiangsu and Jiangxi province all have more than 200 h. About the number of hours of utilization over 50%, the top five provinces are Yunnan (2,320 h), Inner Mongolia east, Liaoning, Jiangsu and Shandong,which have high wind energy utilization rates. In a sharp contrast, Gansu, Xinjiang and Guangdong have a lot of wind energy being abandoned.

Table 7. Annual hourly distribution of wind energy utilization rates.

Utilization/province	Liao ning	Inner Mongolia east	Xin jiang	Gan su	Guang dong	Yun nan	Zhe jiang	Jiang su	Jiang xi	Shan dong
More than 90%	177	284	0	0	21	992	149	251	217	122
More than 80%	422	550	8	73	126	1335	307	502	345	288
More than 50%	1813	2093	1102	812	1004	2320	1228	1664	1254	1386

(c) *monthly distribution of hourly wind energy utilization rates.* Figure 13 shows the hourly distribution of wind energy utilization rates in different months. Provinces of more than 100 h (the hourly utilization rate is above 80%) include Yunnan (7 months), Inner Mongolia east (2 months) and Jiangsu (1 month). Provinces of more than 100 h (the hourly utilization rate is between60% and 80%) include Liaoning (4 months), Inner Mongolia east (4 months), Jiangsu (1 month) and Shandong (1 month). In general, northern provinces and Yunnan show the phenomenon of high utilization rate in spring and winter, and low utilization rate in summer. In particular, Xinjiang, Gansu and Guangdong has low wind energy utilization rate throughout the year, with a relatively insignificant decline in the summer. It should also be noted that, Zhejiang, Jiangsu and Jiangxi generally increase slightly in July and August.

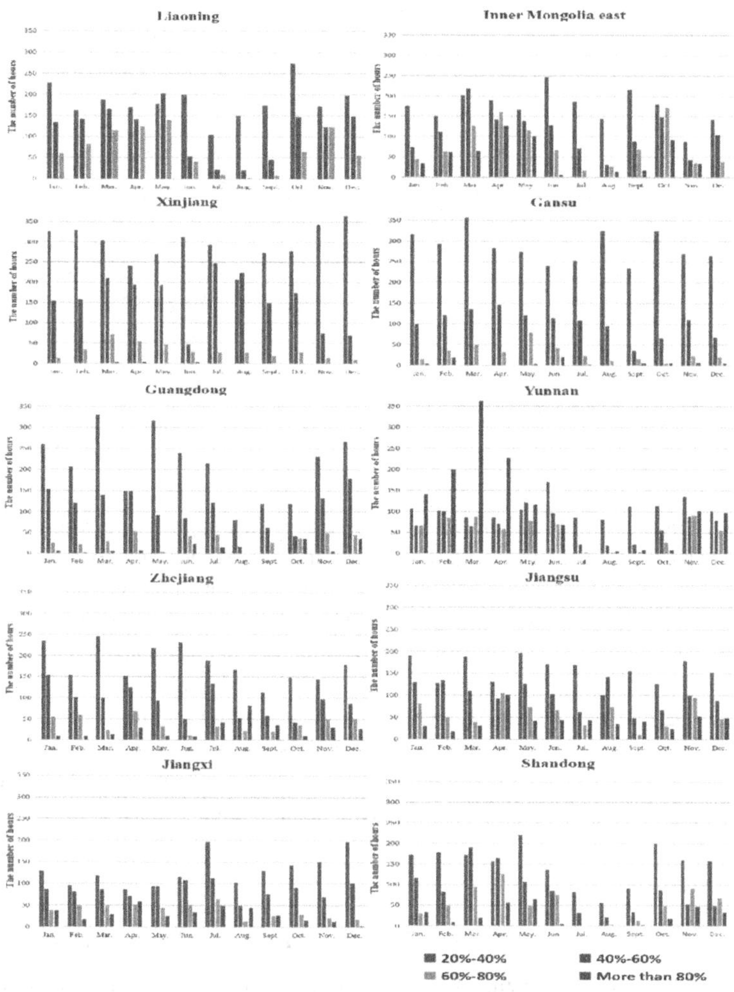

Fig. 13. The hourly distribution of wind energy utilization rates in different months

Wind Power Generation in Typical Days

(a) *Overall situation.* According to Fig. 14, wind energy utilization varies greatly at the hourly level on February 14 and July 6. Overall, most provinces have very low utilization rate from 6:00 to 19:00 (below 30%) on July 6. Compared with February

24, the following significant changes occur on July 6th: The wind energy utilization rate only in Zhejiang and Xinjiang increased significantly; It is worth noting that the utilization rate of other provinces (represented by Yunnan and Gansu) decrease significantly; From the perspective of the day change, the range of change during the daytime became smaller for most provinces, and only Inner Mongolia east has a significant increase after 19:00.

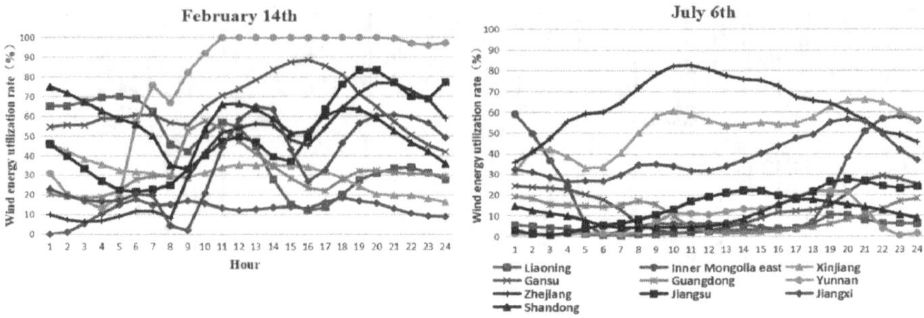

Fig. 14. Changes in wind energy utilization rate on typical days

(b) *Matching situation between wind energy utilization and power demand.* According to Fig. 10, the wind energy output curve in most provinces is not consistent with the power demand curve, especially at peak electricity consumption. On February 14, Inner Mongolia east and Xinjiang, which are rich in wind energy resources, have a very low wind energy utilization rate throughout the day. On July 16, excluding Inner Mongolia east, Xinjiang, Zhejiang and Jiangxi sometimes reach more than 50% in part of the time, and the wind energy utilization rate in other provinces are less than 30%. In particular, in Shandong, Jiangsu, Yunnan, Guangdong, Gansu and Liaoning, the above six provinces have a very low wind energy utilization rate in the summer, and the phenomenon of wind abandonment is serious.

4 Conclusion

4.1 There Are Obvious Seasonal and Daily Variations in Power Demand

In terms of the mean power demand, it is the highest in summer and the lowest in winter. Power demand in most areas is the lowest in February, and after a "rise and then fall" process, the average hourly electricity consumption in July is much higher than that in other months. At the daytime hourly level, power demand decreases from 1:00, the lowest value at 5, the first peak at 11:00, and remains a high level from 14:00 to 19:00. In terms of fluctuation, with the changes of the four seasons, the fluctuation of power demand shows a gradually increasing trend, with the largest fluctuation in winter. In February, June and September, the fluctuation of power demand show the strongest, even more pronounced with East China power grid, North China power grid and Central China power grid.

4.2 There Are Significant Geographical Disparity in the Fluctuation of Power Demand

The volatility of demand varies significantly in different regions. At the seasonal level, the power demand of East China power grid is the most obvious in summer, and the China Southern power grid is the most obvious in winter. At the monthly level, the highest power demand for North China power grid, Northwest power grid and Northeast power grid appeared in June, East China power grid, Central China power grid and Southwest power grid in July, and China Southern power grid in August. In terms of fluctuation, East China power grid fluctuates the most, followed by North China power grid, China Southern power grid and Central China power grid, the volatility of the Northwest power grid, Southwest power grid, and Northeast power grid are relatively small with the seasons.

4.3 Seasonal and Daily Fluctuations of Renewable Energy Power Output Are Obvious

Solar power generation: High solar energy utilization rate mainly appears in the spring, and the autumn utilization rate is also relatively high, and there is an overall trend of reduced utilization rate in the summer. Solar energy resources in Northeast China and North China linear decrease in late autumn and early winter. The Northwest power grid has higher resources in the summer months. China Southern power grid shows a trend of "high-low-highl" throughout the year. As for the daily fluctuations, each power grid experiences the process of "lift-down", and reaches the highest point at 12:00, contributing about 4 h output time more in summer than in winter. In terms of fluctuation, solar energy resources in the northeast region fluctuate greatly, and less resources in the northwest region.

Wind power generation: Northern provinces and Yunnan have high utilization rate in spring and winter, and low utilization rate in summer. At the monthly level, utilization rates peak in March to April in spring and in November in winter. Regarding the daily changes, there are three utilization peaks throughout the spring day. During the summer days, of the ten provinces studied in this paper, only Xinjiang and Zhejiang have large number of wind energy resources. As for the fluctuations, Yunnan and Jiangxi fluctuate the most, but less in Xinjiang and Gansu.

4.4 The Power Demand Profile and Power Output Fluctuation of Renewable Energy Are not Matched

On the summer peak electricity consumption day, there is an obvious mismatch between the solar energy output curve and the power demand load curve, which may lead to an obvious light abandonment phenomenon around noon. In terms of wind energy, the wind power capacity factors in Xinjiang, Zhejiang and Jiangxi also tend to be high during the peak power consumption period, while the wind energy utilization rate in Shandong, Jiangsu, Yunnan, Guangdong, Gansu and Liaoning are generally low throughout the day, and there is no increase in output in the peak power consumption, which may lead to obvious wind abandonment problems. In winter, the wind energy utilization rate in

Inner Mongolia east and Xinjiang is low. At the hourly level, during peak power hours such as 12:00,14:00 to 18:00 and 21:00, affected by the resource time distribution, the wind and solar energy output and the highest demand value are not matched enough, and the phenomenon of wind and solar abandonment is obvious.

5 Summary and Suggestions

Overall, there is a lot of room for improvement in renewable energy utilization rates, based on the above analysis. We present the following policy recommendations:

First, we should optimize the scheduling and operation of the power system, and give full play to the flexibility of the power system and the overall coordination role of the power grid. In particular, we should accelerate the construction of peak-regulating power supply, promote the flexible transformation of coal-power units in northeast China, and further create space for the consumption and utilization of renewable energy.

Second, we should establish a complete energy storage system as soon as possible to effectively improve the utilization rate of renewable energy. For example, the establishment of energy storage systems such as lithium batteries can effectively adjust the balance between power supply and demand, and can solve the problem of time mismatch between daytime renewable energy power generation and electricity demand; the establishment of large pumped storage, chemical energy storage and other systems, which can store electric energy across seasons; the establishment of heat storage systems, such as latent heat and thermal chemistry, can solve the problem of renewable energy waste in northern China regions during the winter heating period.

Third, we should speed up the construction of ultra-high voltage remote power transmission and electrolytic hydrogen production facilities, and deliver more energy from major renewable energy power generation provinces such as Inner Mongolia, Xinjiang and Gansu to developed areas in the central and eastern regions.

References

1. Li, Y., Pizer, W.A., Wu, L.: Climate change and residential electricity consumption in the Yangtze River Delta, China. Proc. Natl. Acad. Sci. **116**(2), 472–477 (2019)
2. Li, M., Patiño-Echeverri, D.: Estimating benefits and costs of policies proposed in the 13th FYP to improve energy efficiency and reduce air emissions of China's electric power sector. Energy Policy **111**, 222–234 (2017)
3. Price, L., Khanna, N., Fridley, D., Hasanbeigi, A., Lu, H., Wei, F., et al.: Reinventing fire: China–the role of energy efficiency in China's roadmap to 2050. Euro. Counc. Energy Effic. Econ. Summ. Study **2017**, 113–120 (2017)
4. Gelaro, R., McCarty, W., Suárez, M.J., Todling, R., Molod, A., Takacs, L., et al.: The modern-era retrospective analysis for research and applications, version 2 (MERRA-2). J. Clim. **30**, 5419–5454 (2017)
5. Feng, F., Wang, K.: Does the modern-era retrospective analysis for research and applications-2 aerosol reanalysis introduce an improvement in the simulation of surface solar radiation over China? Int. J. Climatol. **39**, 1305–1318 (2019)

The Dilemma of Authenticity: Spatial Redesign and Reconstruction of Tianjin Old City Hall in Multi-cultural Contexts

Yongkang Guan(✉)

School of Literature, Nankai University, 94 Weijin Road, Tianjin, China
yongkang.guan@mail.nankai.edu.cn

Abstract. In multi-cultural contexts, tourism and cultural industries have been involved in historic urban quarters, creating a multitude of cultural symbols that cater to consumers, the authenticity of recreated heritages is in doubt. In order to reveal the roots of the spatial evolution, the author takes Tianjin Old City Hall as an example to study the logic of spatial redesign and reconstruction, concentrating on the characteristics of spatial evolution in both the humanities and applied science with the method of comparative study. The results showed that governments, invaders, and capitalists dominated the three spatial reconstructions of Tianjin Old City Hall respectively. The original spatial texture has disappeared from the site and transformed into an "archaized commercial urban quarter" redesigned by planners guided by modern urban concepts. The author summarizes the spatial problems as follows: gentrification, superficiality, and capitalization. The paper proposes to value the field of cultural production theory and puts forward the authenticity of historic urban quarters redesign. In order to explore the cultural roots of cities and the spirits of social space in the multi-cultural context, it encourages multiple sectors to carry out high-quality design and creative policy intervention.

Keywords: Historic urban quarters · Spatial redesign · Spatial reconstruction · Authenticity · Multi-cultural contexts

1 Introduction

Authenticity has become a central academic theme among scholars in the field of urban planning and heritage. The word "authenticity" is derived from Greek and Latin, referring to "authoritative" and "originality" [1]. The traditional meaning of authenticity emphasizes uniqueness, based on professional techniques and scientific knowledge [2]. The Oxford Dictionary explains "authenticity" with terms such as "trustworthy", "original" and "undisputed origin". A recent definition is "authentic as original" or "truth as a trustworthy statement of fact". In medieval Europe, authenticity was used to justify political and religious authority. During the twentieth century, under the advocacy of international heritage institutions such as ICOMOS and UNESCO, authenticity gained a significant position as a fundamental principle of heritage conservation. The *Venice Charter* (1964) was considered the foundational framework for modern conservation,

P.-L. P. Rau (Ed.): HCII 2022, LNCS 13314, pp. 345–359, 2022.
https://doi.org/10.1007/978-3-031-06053-3_24

stating "our responsibility" to protect ancient heritage as our common value "in the full richness of their authenticity". Through the 1972 UNESCO World Heritage Convention, authenticity became a fundamental criterion for evaluating the World Heritage List. Meanwhile, the discussion of authenticity was begun in the heritage discipline. in 1973, MacCannell proposed the theory of "staged authenticity" laid the foundation for an extension of authenticity theory [3]. Since then, the main discussions have focused on the relationship between authenticity and commodification, with some scholars such as Greenwood, Berger, Price and MacCannell, and Boorstin, arguing that socio-economic commodification, through tourism, affects cultural authenticity and ultimately renders cultural products meaningless to residents [4–9]. Taylor points that this concept of authenticity is built on the fallacy that cultural and ethnic identity previously had a stable and "natural" state [9]. Benjamin believes that mass mechanized production has impacted authenticity, describing this phenomenon as "the loss of aura" [10]. The fundamental aspects of the culture being commodified are taken out of context, distorting the authenticity of identities [11].

There is a close relationship between authenticity, the identity of space, and a sense of spatial belonging [12–17]. The concept of authenticity emphasizes origins and continuity, not only in relation to local social, economic, and cultural characteristics but also with daily life and ideas of residents [12, 16, 17]. Wesner associates authenticity with the identity of space, pointing out that authenticity is an intrinsic value of places. Meanwhile, authenticity is a social concept of space, reflecting people's desires, interpretations, and identities [16]. Zukin links authenticity to a sense of place, defining it as "living local both in the local neighborhood and on the land" [12].

In the field of urban heritage conservation, although experts have reached some consensus on the relationship between authenticity and architectural heritage [18], the complexity of the historic city makes it difficult for the principle of authenticity to guide all aspects of urban development, which leads to the destruction of landscape and context through thematization and gentrification. In China, the superficial understanding of "authenticity" by local governments has led to inappropriate principles and standards for the conservation and reuse of historic quarters, with the space impacted by capitalism and multiculturalism, which has been criticized by experts and scholars in various fields. In order to facilitate advertising and public understanding, the culture reconstructed by the developers is often simplified symbolically. Some scholars called the phenomenon "constructed authenticity" [19].

The paper takes Tianjin Old City Hall as an example to study the role of authenticity in heritage conservation from the perspective of spatial redesign and reconstruction, as well as the current problems and inherent production mechanisms. Firstly, the paper reviews the evolution process of Tianjin Old City Hall, including the iconic building named Tianjin Drum Tower in the quarter, describing its historical status, value, and current condition. Secondly, from the perspective of spatial morphology, the author analyses the three spatial morphological evolutions and functional adjustments in the history of Tianjin Old City Hall, analyzing the external representation and internal motivations. Thirdly, the author summarizes the logic of spatial evolution, and the role of authenticity in space, considering the reasons for the decline of Tianjin Old City Hall and the problems that exist in the spatial reconstruction. Simultaneously, proposing feasible practical strategies for the redesign of historic quarters under the multi-cultural context in China.

2 Methods and Case Backgrounds

2.1 Research Methods

In this paper, the author uses the method of comparative study to study the spatial morphological redesign and reconstruction of Tianjin Old City Hall. Using maps and archives as the main materials for analysis, the article presents a comparative analysis of the spatial pattern and morphology of the quarter through fieldwork.

The maps of Tianjin Old City Hall from different periods were obtained from (1) *The illustration of Baojia in Tianjin* published during the Daoguang period of the Qing Dynasty, (2) *The Complete Map of the Tianjin City Concession* drawn by the Japanese in 1902 (now in the Tianjin Museum), (3) *The Latest Street Map of Tianjin* compiled by Shao Yuecheng and published by Times Book Company in 1946, (4) *The Planning Atlas of Tianjin Old City Hall* published on the government tender website in 2003. The study uses the most detailed and accurate maps that can be found, which can clearly present the spatial texture, buildings, and streets.

In addition, map superposition was used in the comparative analysis of spatial patterns. The spatial texture of Tianjin Old City Hall in different periods is redrawn and overlaid on top of each other to obtain the derived and dissolved spaces. Firstly, the spatial patterns of different periods are studied to find the differences and correlations between them, to study the design logic behind the spatial evolution of the historic quarter. Secondly, analyzing the position of residents and power relations and in the changing spatial forms, based on the historical archives. Thirdly, rethinking how the authenticity of space should be reflected in a city wrapped in cultural symbols, attempting to demonstrate the importance of the link between urban space and local culture from theory to practice.

Some Chinese scholars have already studied Tianjin Old City Hall from the perspectives of tourism, heritage, history, and architecture. Xie Qi focuses on the renewal and transformation of Tianjin Old City Hall in 2003 and proposes a more reasonable operational model at both the macro (relevant concepts and policy mechanisms) and micro (specific planning and design tools) levels [20]. Wang Yan suggests a sustainable and humanistic approach to the future development of Tianjin Old City Hall, based on a questionnaire survey on the evaluation of existing renovation projects by different types of people [21]. Hou Tianying selected three novels by Feng Jicai from the late Qing and early Ming dynasties, combined them with GIS to visualize the textual and emotional mapping of landscape elements, compared the differences between the literary landscape and the present condition, and summarized the characteristics of Tianjin's urban landscape [22]. However, there are few comparative studies on the spatial morphology of this quarter in the existing literature, and the discussion on the authenticity of heritage on this basis is even fever.

2.2 The History and Present Condition of Tianjin Old City Hall

Tianjin Old City Hall is an old urban area developed based on the Acropolis, with Tianjin Drum Tower as its spatial center, enclosed by the East, West, South, and North Streets. During the Ming and Qing dynasties, Tianjin Old City Hall was divided into four main quarters, with the south-west and south-east quarters focusing on residential functions, and the north-west and north-east blocks on administrative offices. The rectangular, symmetrical spatial form and the interlocking road network system reflect the traditional layout of the quarters in the northern plain cities of China. Historically, Tianjin Old City Hall has always been at a high density. During the Qing dynasty, Tianjin was a nationally famous commercial center, and the prosperity of trade attracted many southern merchants to settle in Tianjin, with a recorded population of nearly 200,000 during the Daoguang period of the Qing dynasty. Tianjin Old City Hall had a complex structure of inhabitants, with not only residents but also many aristocrats and litterateurs in the Qing dynasty [23]. The prosperity of commerce also led to the promotion of folk art, and the commercial streets in Tianjin Old City Hall were not only had traditional restaurants and gold shops but also had local specialties such as stone and wood carving workshops, which nurtured many masters of art such as Zhu Xinglian. Tianjin Old City Hall is one of the birthplaces of Chinese folk art with rich folklore and traditional culture.

On the 18th of October 2003, the front page of Tonight Newspaper entitled "Tianjin Old City Hall was demolished this morning", announced the start of the third spatial reconstruction. Only a few historical buildings were preserved in the quarter, the traditional texture was almost demolished. The intellectuals, represented by Feng Jicai, had launched a "Protecting Street Campaign" to protect Tianjin Old City Hall, but it did not succeed in stopping the developers, who are keen to pursue financial interests. Ultimately, the campaign failed and the quarter was rebuilt into a completely new spatial form guided by the commercial concept. In order to preserve the only memories of Tianjin Old City Hall, the newly appointed governments, at the initiative of Feng Jicai, have built the Old City Museum, with exhibits selflessly donated by people from all walks of life, bringing together the citizens' acute homesickness for Tianjin Old City Hall.

2.3 Two Reconstructions of Tianjin Drum Tower in the Quarter

Tianjin Drum Tower, an iconic landmark of Tianjin Old City Hall, has undergone two reconstructions in its history. According to the Old Stories of Tianjin Old City Hall edited by Jia Changhua, Tianjin Drum Tower was first built during the Hongzhi period of the Ming Dynasty [24]. The photographs taken in the late Qing dynasty show that the lower part of the Drum Tower was built of green bricks, which were slightly rudimentary but designed elaborately. In 1900, under the suppression of the invaders, the Qing government was forced to sign the Treaty of Xin-Chou. The walls of the quarter were torn down. Although Tianjin Drum Tower was preserved, it was transformed into an army watchtower and has suffered some damage. Over the next 20 years, the foundations of the Drum Tower gradually crumbled with beams and pillars corroded, turning it into a "dangerous building".

In 1921, the government decided to repair and rebuild Tianjin Drum Tower. The new Tower was slightly different from the original, as the height of the door was raised and the advanced veneer technique was adopted, with "Flemish Garden Wall Bond" becoming the new masonry method for the platform. In order to remind the humiliating history of Tianjin Old City Hall being forced to be demolished by the invaders, the government decided to inlay plaques from the four gatehouses of the Meiji period on the arch of the tower [24].

After 30 years of continued glory, the Drum Tower was demolished in 1952 because of the need for transport links and the weak awareness of the government about cultural heritage conservation. The disappearance of the iconic landmark left Tianjin Old City Hall without an "Aura" [10]. With the progress of social and spiritual civilization, Tianjin Drum Tower was rebuilt in 1998 under the call of "promoting Chinese civilization and inheriting the culture of Tianjin" [25]. The new tower, completed at the end of September 2001, has an increased volume and the partial use of Chinese white jade and green glazed materials, which arouses the public's memory of traditional culture and increases the sense of identity. However, from a critical point of view, the apparently classical and grand Tianjin Drum Tower is an "archaized building" built of modern reinforced concrete structures and technology, and its spatial form differs considerably from the original tower. The authenticity of the new Tianjin Drum Tower is in doubt. (see Fig. 1).

The photo taken in the Qing Dynasty
The photo taken in 1921
The photo taken in 2001

Fig. 1. Photographs of Tianjin Drum tower from different periods

3 A Comparative Study on the Three Spatial Morphological Evolution and Functional Changes

3.1 The Original Spatial Form of Tianjin Old City Hall

During the Hongzhi period of the Ming Dynasty, with the opening of the Grand Canal, Tianjin became an important transport hub, and the prosperity of transport and trade brought a large number of people into the city. Although Tianjin was only an acropolis at the time and did not have independent executive powers, it was comparable in size to a prefecture-level city. Between the sixth and seventh years of the Hongzhi reign, the city developed rapidly with the restoration and expansion of the walls and established Tianjin Drum Tower as the center, which was the symbol of the city. In terms of overall spatial form, the layout of the cross-staggered streets was established and the pattern of geometric symmetry emphasized the order of the space. The overall space is closed and tight, reflecting the military attributes of the acropolis (see Fig. 2).

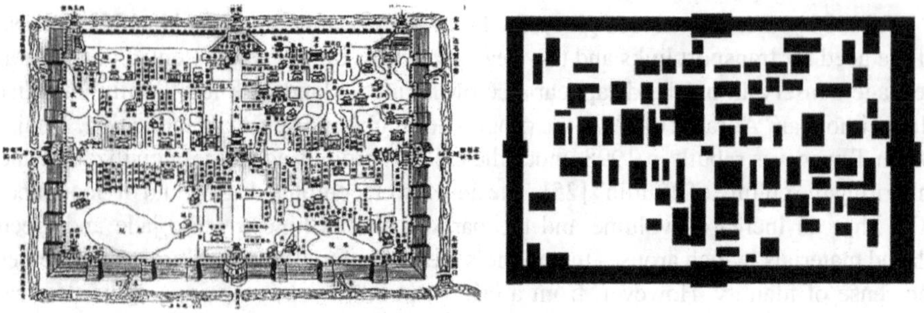

Fig. 2. Map and texture of Tianjin Old City Hall, Daoguang 26 (1846)

As the port trade and commodity distribution functions of the city became increasingly prominent, the original military function of the city had hindered its development. During the Kangxi period, the city began to take on some of the administrative functions, and in the following decades, the city's functions expanded as the official offices such as the Changlu Salt Department and the Office of the Banknote Pass were moved to Tianjin. In the third year of the Yongzheng reign, Tianjin was formally incorporated into the local regime. In terms of spatial form, the quarter center of this period basically follows the spatial pattern of the Ming dynasty, with the four major blocks within the space being more clearly divided and the density of buildings increasing, with traditional courtyards on both sides of the cross streets.

In 1856, Tianjin was forced to open up as a result of the war. The social structure of Tianjin as a colony changed, with some foreigners living in Tianjin Old City Hall and participating in market trade. The emergence of western urban facilities such as commercial companies in the quarter contributed to the development of commerce in Tianjin, but there was no significant change in spatial form, except for the use of western construction methods in the local buildings.

3.2 Three Spatial Morphological Changes in Tianjin Old City Hall

The first dramatic change of spatial form in Tianjin Old City Hall occurred in 1900 when invaders tore down the walls and invaded the Old Town, destroying a large number of historic buildings. In terms of spatial form, the walls surrounding the quarter were demolished and replaced with roads that could be used by the army. The cross-shaped streets in the area were widened and extended on both sides to create several branch roads that intertwined and formed a clear structure (see Fig. 3).

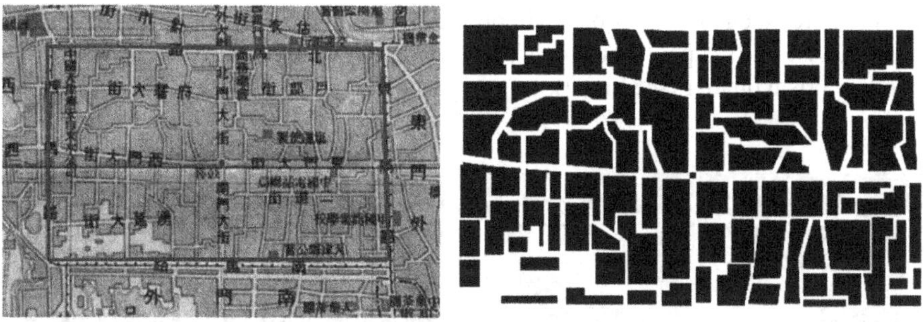

Fig. 3. Map and texture of Tianjin Old City Hall, Guangxu 28 (1902)

The second dramatic change in the spatial pattern of the quarter occurred in the 1930s, when it was turned into a rented area and its administrative functions ceased, limiting its economic development and gradually decaying. During the Republican period, the quarter had lost much of its former glory, with wealthy merchants moving out and becoming a slum area of Tianjin, with a large number of shops being converted to residential buildings in poor condition. The "disorderliness" is a distinctive feature of the spatial form in this period. On the basis of the original road grid, residents have created their own narrow and winding paths according to their own commuting needs, breaking the original order of space and fragmenting the texture, but also making the spatial experience more diverse and intriguing (see Fig. 4).

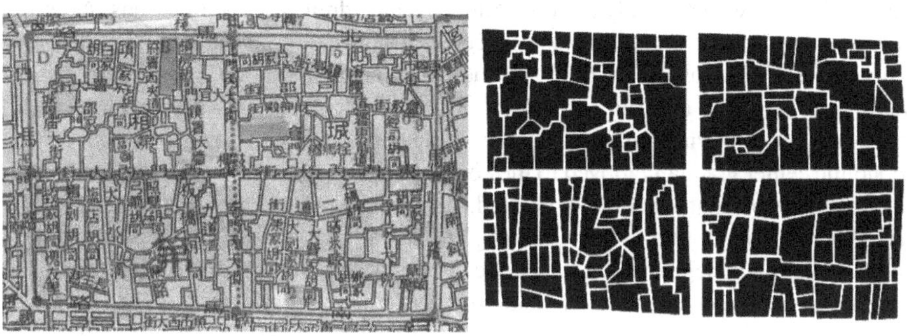

Fig. 4. Map and texture of Tianjin Old City Hall in 1946

The third spatial change of the quarter is the most subversive one occurring in the 21st century. In 2003, developers intervened in the development of the Old Town Hall with the aim of "reviving history". However, the original spatial texture of the quarter was completely destroyed in order to compress the renovation schedule and maximize commercial profits. The quarter was given new spatial functions and texture by the developer. In terms of spatial form, the overall spatial road network is clear and the highways cut the space into 17 blocks, divided into internal and external levels, controlling the building density and height. New functions such as cultural tourism, entertainment, health care, finance, and commercial complex have appeared in the quarter, complemented by infrastructures such as fire stations, schools, hospitals, green spaces, and public squares. Under the use of "scalpel" by capital, Tianjin Old City Hall has been transformed into a modern urban quarter (see Fig. 5).

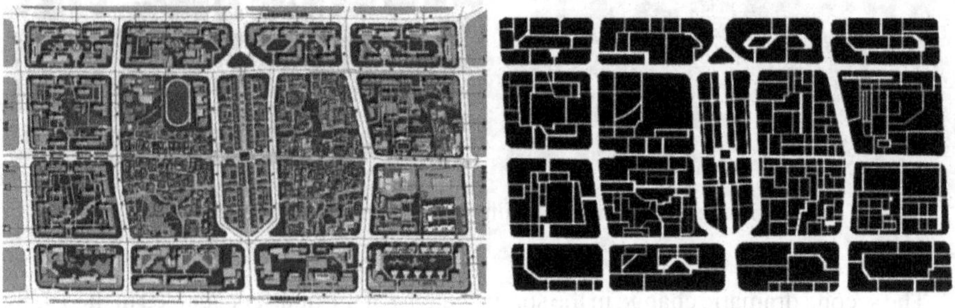

Fig. 5. Map and texture of Tianjin Old City Hall in 2003

3.3 Comparative Analysis of Three Spatial Redesign and Reconstruction

Looking back at the evolution history, Tianjin Old City Hall has experienced three spatial morphological changes and functional adjustments (see Fig. 6), which were dominated by different power leaders. The closed cross-symmetrical spatial form of the Tianjin Acropolis was motivated by the government to show the deterrent power and orderliness of the city, which mainly assumed military and administrative functions. After the invasion, Tianjin Old City Hall was reduced to a semi-colony, with administrative and military functions was replaced by commercial functions, the walls were demolished, roads were widened and forced to open. The overall spatial axis network was clear, reflecting the Western invaders' ambition to develop trade and conquer space. As the economic center gradually moved to the concession area, the quarter became a city with a spatial network that was clearly defined. As the economic center moved towards the rented areas, Tianjin Old City Hall changed from a "rich quarter" to a "poor quarter" and was gradually neglected by the public. The new roads and buildings created by the inhabitants were characterized by randomness, the internal structure of the space was disordered, and it almost became a single residential area, with the reconstruction of spatial forms following the will of the inhabitants themselves. After entering the consumer society, the spatial rights were controlled by capitalists, the original texture was erased from the site, and the planners designed the spatial forms and functions "from top to bottom" according to the modern urban concept, with commerce and tourism becoming the core development orientation of the quarte (see Fig. 7).

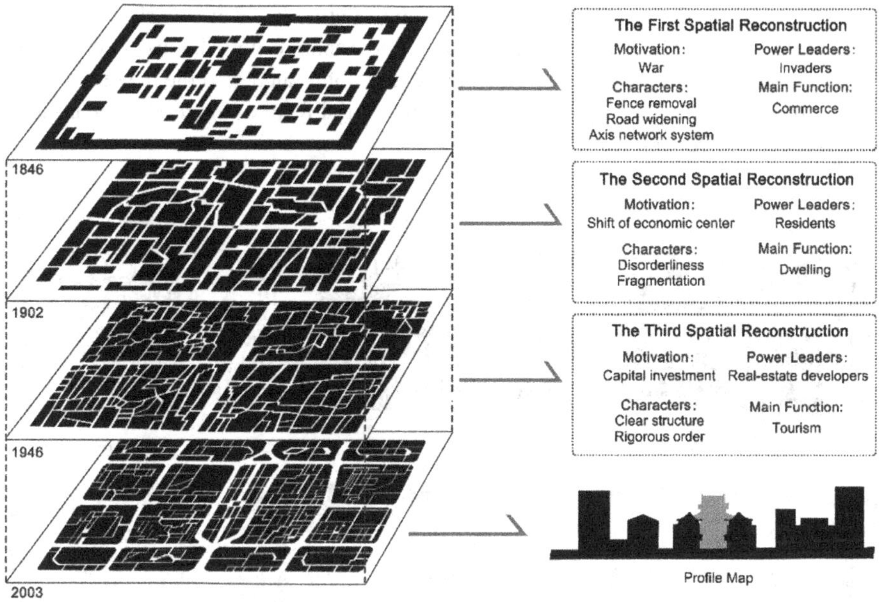

Fig. 6. Comparative diagram of the three spatial reconstruction

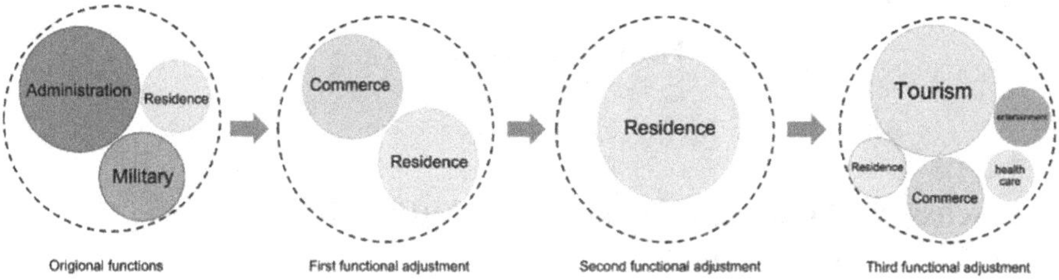

Fig. 7. Spatial functional evolution

The authors superimpose maps of Tianjin Old City Hall from different periods separately. The prominent feature of the first spatial physical form evolution is the increase in density. According to calculations, the proportion of derived space in the map exceeds 50%, and the reconstruction has generated a large amount of architectural space. The proportion of derived space in the second spatial morphological evolution decreases significantly, and the changes are reflected in two points: firstly, the spatial density further increases and the originally unused sites in the space are further developed and built, and the spatial architectural density tends to be saturated; secondly, the spatial texture is fragmented, with the new paths in the space dividing the space and the internal structure becoming more complex. The new horizontal and vertical roads within the quarter are the most visible in the third spatial superimposed map, where the derived spaces occur in each area averagely, with a clear axial network and an orderly system. The new horizontal and vertical roads within the quarter are the most conspicuous in the third spatial reconstruction superimposed map, with a clear axial network and an orderly system. The derived space averagely occurs in each area. The new spatial subdivisions are created by the wide roads, the winding paths in the quarter are obliterated, and the new network of internal roads is clearly organized, typical of the spatial form of the modern man-made "pre-planning" model (see Fig. 8).

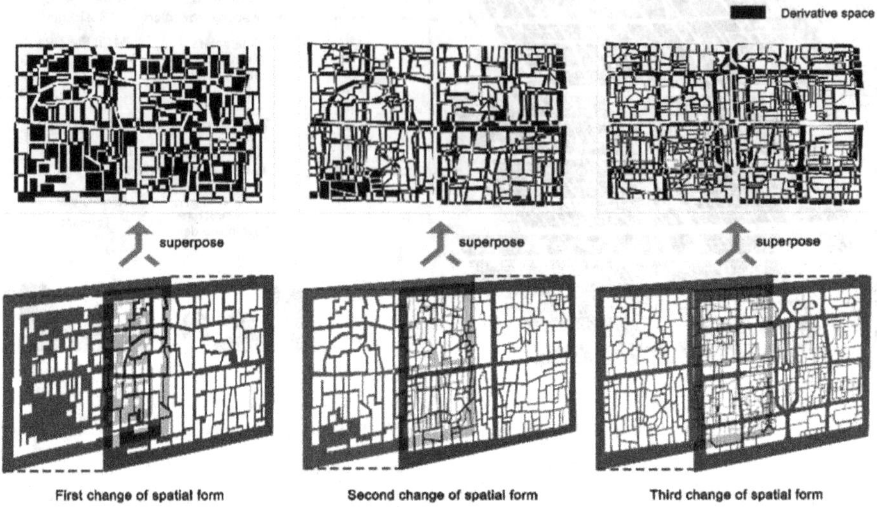

Fig. 8. Map superposition

4 Discussion About the Dilemma of Authenticity Under Multi-cultural Context

The multiculturalism of Tianjin Old City Hall is influenced by the capitalist markets and cultural imperialism, placed in the context of modernity's drive for universalization and global convergence. This process is discussed in the categories of cultural imperialism commonly, Westernization or Europeanisation, in which cultural and commercial companies played an important role by connecting the local culture to global cultural forms which they previously re-appropriated from the West [26]. As Adams writes, by applying global logic to the local level and bringing local culture to the global level, the cultural and commercial companies create a powerful center-marginal dynamic, similar to cultural imperialism's forced placement of culture in a hierarchy of prestige, where each field structure is increasingly influenced by the next higher level structure, leading to a growing homogeneity between local fields rather than being organized, with cultural heritage fields revealing a different dynamic [27].

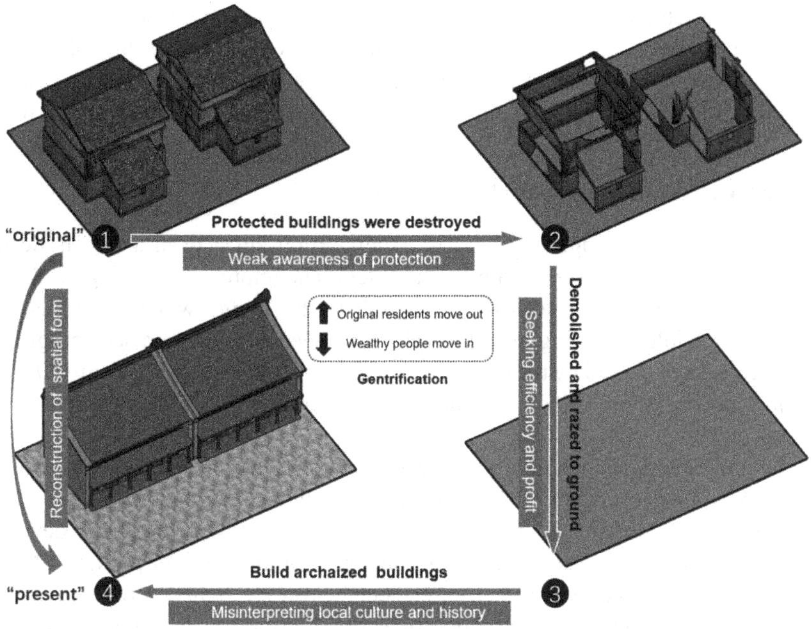

Fig. 9. The process of Tianjin Old City Hall redesign and reconstruction

The decline of Tianjin Old City Hall embodies a model of cultural imperialist globalization that emphasizes the imposition by powerful countries of their own cultural forms on weaker countries, leading to the decline of local cultures characterized by cultural homogenization [28] (see Fig. 9). Cultural heritage represents a global value and its conservation and reuse represent a "universalization of particularism" [29]. The process increases the importance of the region as a "producer" of heritage discourse, reflecting the significance of local culture [30].

4.1 The Capitalization of Spatial Protection

Before the third renovation of Tianjin Old City Hall, the government, in collaboration with heritage conservation units, conducted a detailed survey of the historical buildings in the quarter, recording a total of 34 heritage buildings, including the state-level protected Guangdong Hall built in the 33rd year of the Qing Dynasty, the municipal-level protected temple built in the first year of the Ming dynasty, and 32 district-level protected buildings (Yang Family Courtyard, Xu Family Courtyard, etc.) and working with The development concept of "Bypassing Heritage" was established with developers to ensure that the redesign and reconstruction would not damage the heritage buildings.

However, in the actual development process, the real estate developers only treated the historic building conservation agreement as a negligible process, and in order to shorten the construction period and save money, they adopted a "bulldozer-style" development method, and the protected buildings were damaged or even demolished, which has triggered strong protests from cultural preservation experts. Some of the damaged buildings were restored at a later stage, but a great number of demolished courtyards and houses were lost forever from the history of Tianjin Old City Hall. The loss of historical scenes, with the establishment of high-rise buildings and archaized shops, has made the preserved historic buildings seem out of place and become an "anomaly" in the space.

4.2 The Gentrification of Spatial Development

In the prevailing business logic of developers, "demolition and reconstruction" is the most effective way to solve urban environmental problems and improve the "living condition", a logic derived from Octavio Paz's unique capitalist view of time, which states that "time is linear, irreversible, and progressive" [31]. The linear view of time sees progress as "the replacement of the old by the new" [31]. In the view of developers, Tianjin Old City Hall is just an "outdated" village, and their maintenance and conservation will only add to the cost.

In the third spatial reconstruction project of Tianjin Old City Hall, the original residents do not have any rights. According to the author's interview survey, the original residents of the quarter approved the demolition initially, because the developer promised to change the "dirty and messy" living environment, and promised to give economic compensation. However, the residents' property rights were not respected after the demolition, and the resettlement fees could not cover the rapidly increasing housing prices, forcing a large number of residents to move out of the quarter or choose to rent apartments to maintain their lives. After the original residents were "evicted", high-rise townhouses and villas were built in the planned residential areas. Under the operation and speculation of "cultural symbols of the Old City", the housing price of the quarter increased several times, and numerous rich people moved in and became the living area of the upper class.

4.3 The Superficiality of Spatial Design

In the latest design scheme of Tianjin Old City Hall, a great number of "collage" design methods are used, and a large number of modern elements are adopted while reviving the traditional style, but the relationship is not properly handled, resulting in the construction of a large variety of archaized buildings in a "disparate" style, which is not related to the regional culture. The design team of the developer has irresponsibly copied the traditional architectural "template" while dramatically interspersing modern commercial buildings, not only failing to respect the authenticity of the site, but also destroying the integrity of the space. Tourists from other places have become the main body of the renovated quarter, building the identity of the "other", while residents seldom come. During the author's interview, many citizens expressed their regret for the development of Tianjin Old City Hall, lamenting that the once most familiar old street had become a stranger, and the "real antiques" in the quarter were abandoned and demolished, while the newly built "fake antiques" were widely publicized. The superficially strong atmosphere of the quarter cannot hide the "vacuum" of history and culture behind it. The design has lost the most valuable "localness" of the space, reducing it to an "empty shell" with no appearance.

5 Conclusion

In the history of Tianjin Old City Hall, monarchs, invaders, and capitalist developers have led three separate spatial reconstructions, and the function has evolved from military administration to commercial tourism. Under the impact of multiple cultures, the original fabric of the space was erased from the site and transformed into an "archaized commercial street" designed by planners according to modern urban concepts. The original residents were forced to move out and the "Old City" was constructed by the developers as a "cultural symbol" to attract tourists. The principles of "wholeness", "authenticity" and "liveliness" in the development of the historic quarter are ignored. The author summarizes the dilemma of authenticity in the Chinese historic quarter under the multi-cultural context: capitalization, gentrification, and superficiality.

In fact, the *Nairobi Recommendation Concerning the Safeguarding and Contemporary Role of Historic Areas* has proposed principles for the conservation and reuse of historic districts [32]. The "one-size-fits-all" approach to the redesign and reconstruction of historic quarters in China has damaged the environmental composition of historic heritage for human beings and their identity. The principle of authenticity has been completely misinterpreted.

Local additions and changes made to the historic quarter by the original residents of the quarter based on real-life needs are the only criteria that are consistent with the historical evolution of the quarter. The 2014 edition of *the Operational Guidelines for the Implementation of the World Heritage Convention* also stipulates the principle that "authenticity and integrity are both the standards for evaluating the value of heritage" [33]. The current redesign of the Chinese quarter is oriented towards the performance of tourism development, which has artificially led to the separation of the "material" and "spiritual" aspects of the real-life world, neglecting the attributes of life beyond the commercial function of the quarter, and weakening the "authenticity" of the living scene.

Jane Jacobs argues that "diversity is the nature of the city" [34]. *The Nara Authenticity Document* also argues that "heritage projects must be considered and judged in the context of their cultural relevance, out of respect for all cultures", and proposes a heritage landscape conservation strategy of cultural diversity [35]. In the actual situation in China, the redesign of historic quarters should focus on the diversity and local culture, but it does not mean that the redesign of historic districts can put in some elements that are contrary to the authenticity, but should use the strategy of "inherited innovation", while following the cultural and spatial atmosphere of the site, to enhance some incongruous elements of the site. At the same time, the environmental enhancement of the quarters should focus on the development process of the humanities.

Acknowledgements. This work was supported by Tianjin Postgraduate Research Innovation Project (No. 2021YJSB011).

References

1. Trilling, L.: Sincerity and Authenticity. Harvard University Press, Cambridge (2009)
2. Reisinger, Y., Steiner, C.J.: Reconceptualizing object authenticity. Ann. Tour. Res. **33**(1), 65–86 (2006)
3. MacCannell, D.: Staged authenticity: arrangements of social space in tourist settings. Am. J. Sociol. **79**(3), 589–603 (1973)
4. Berger, D.J.: The challenge of integrating Maasai tradition with tourism. People and tourism in fragile environments, pp. 175–198 (1996)
5. Boorstin, D.J.: The Image: A Guide to Pseudo-events in America. Vintage, New York (1992)
6. Cohen, E.: Authenticity and commoditization in tourism. Ann. Tour. Res. **15**(3), 371–386 (1988)
7. Greenwood, D.J.: Culture by the Pound: An Anthropological Perspective on Tourism as Cultural Commoditization. University of Pennsylvania Press, Pennsylvania (2012)
8. MacCannell, D.: The Tourist: A New Theory of the Leisure Class. Univ of California Press, California (2013)
9. Taylor, J.P.: Authenticity and sincerity in tourism. Ann. Tour. Res. **28**(1), 7–26 (2001)
10. Benjamin, W.: The Work of Art in the Age of Mechanical Reproduction, 3rd edn. Routledge, London (2011)
11. Bruner, E.M.: The Maasai and the Lion King: Authenticity, nationalism, and globalization in African tourism. Am. Ethnol. **28**(4), 881–908 (2001)
12. Zukin, S.: Naked City: The Death and Life of Authentic Urban Places. Oxford University Press, Oxford (2009)
13. Salah Ouf, A.M.: Authenticity and the sense of place in urban design. J. Urban Des. **6**(1), 73–86 (2001)
14. Jive'n, G., Larkham, P.J.: Sense of place, authenticity and character: a commentary. J. Urban Design **8**(1), 67–81 (2003)
15. Pottie-Sherman, Y., Hiebert, D.: Authenticity with a bang: exploring suburban culture and migration through the new phenomenon of the Richmond night market. Urban Stud. **52**(3), 538–554 (2015)
16. Wesener, A.: 'This place feels authentic': exploring experiences of authenticity of place in relation to the urban built environment in the Jewellery Quarter. Birmingham. J. Urban Des. **21**(1), 67–83 (2016)
17. Wesener, A.: Adopting 'things of the little': Intangible cultural heritage and experiential authenticity of place in the Jewellery Quarter. Birmingham. Int. J. Heritage Stud. **23**(2), 141–155 (2017)
18. De, Naeyer. A., Arroyo, S.P., Blanco, J.R.: Krakow charter 2000: principles for conservation and restoration of built heritage. Bureau Krakow (2000)
19. Jamal, T., Hill, S.: Developing a framework for indicators of authenticity: the place and space of cultural and heritage tourism. Asia Pacific J. Tourism Res. **9**(4), 353–372 (2004)
20. Xie, Q.: Renovation of Tianjin old City Hall. Tianjin University (2007)
21. Wang, Y.: Research and exploration on renewal and reconstruction of Tianjin old City Hall. Tianjin University (2007)
22. Hou, T.Y.: Study on the landscape of Tianjin Old City Hall from the perspective of literature. Tianjin University (2019)
23. CPPCC.: Tianjin collection of cultural and historical materials. Tianjin People's Publishing House, Tianjin (1981). (in Chinese)
24. Jia, C.H., Chen, B.L.: The old stories of Tianjin Old City Hall. Tianjin Ancient Books Publishing House, Tianjin (2004).(in Chinese)

25. Luc, G.: China's provinces in transition: Tianjin. CreateSpace Independent Publishing Platform, South Carolina (2012)
26. Clark, K.: Moscow, the Fourth Rome: Stalinism, Cosmopolitanism, and the Evolution of Soviet Culture, 1931–1941. Harvard University Press, Cambridge (2011)
27. Adams, L.L.: Globalization, universalism, and cultural form. Comp. Stud. Soc. Hist. **50**(3), 614–640 (2008)
28. Crane, D.: Culture and globalization. Theoretical models and emerging trends. In global culture. Media, arts, policy, and globalization. Routledge, London (2002)
29. Robertson, R.: Globalization: Social Theory and Global Culture. Sage, London (1992)
30. Pieterse, N.: Globalization and culture: Global mélange. Rowman & Littlefiled, Lanham (2019)
31. Heynen, H.: Architecture and Modernity: A Critique. MIT Press, Cambridge (2000)
32. UNESCO: Recommendation concerning the safeguarding and contemporary role of historic areas. UNESCO, Nairobi (1976)
33. UNESCO World Heritage Centre.: Operational guidelines for the implementation of the world heritage convention. UNESCO World Heritage Centre, Paris (2014)
34. Jacobs, J.: The Death and Life of Great American Cities. Vintage, New York (2016)
35. Stovel, H.: Origins and influence of the Nara document on authenticity. APT Bull. **39**(2–3), 9–17 (2008)

Strategy and Practice for the Design-Driven Local Rural Revitalization

Lyu Ji(✉)

Tongji University, Shanghai 200092, People's Republic of China
jilyu@foxmail.com

Abstract. Taking rural revitalization as the background and context, this paper explores the possibilities and specific ways of design intervening in rural problems and driving rural innovation and change with the help of design theory and case studies, which illustrates the leading and constructive role of design in solving issues in local contexts such as rural revitalization, as well as the powerful ability to drive innovation. The article first expounds on rural revitalization in the local context, and points out the essence of the current local rural problems and the direction of the rejuvenation and development of local villages by combing the historical changes of Chinese rural areas. Subsequently, the article introduces and expounds two important design theory concepts: "Four Orders of Design" and "Active Design", based on these two design concepts, the article further elaborates the specific ways of design intervening and driving rural revitalization through the description of some cases, and specifically introduces and analyzes the "Design Harvest" project, which validates and illuminates the driving role that design can play in the face of challenges in the local context.

Keywords: Design-driven · Rural revitalization · Four Orders of Design · Active design · Design harvest

1 Introduction

This study attempts to take China's local rural revitalization as the context and entry point, with the help of the more classic and cutting-edge theoretical concepts in the design discourse system such as the Four Orders of Design and Design Activism, to explore the possible ways for design to actively intervene in local rural problems and drive local rural revitalization, and introduces the case of design-driven rural revitalization project in Shanghai - "Design Harvest". China is a country with thousands of years of agricultural civilization history, China's social and cultural origins and deeply rooted in the countryside, in the early 20th century China has a group of scholars and practitioners committed to the reconstruction and rejuvenation of the local countryside, and a hundred years later today the rural revitalization strategy has risen to the Chinese official national development strategy. Like the rest of the world, China's countryside, which has developed over the millennia, was hit hard by urbanization at the end of the last century, the deterioration of the rural environment, the loss of young workers, and

P.-L. P. Rau (Ed.): HCII 2022, LNCS 13314, pp. 360–370, 2022.
https://doi.org/10.1007/978-3-031-06053-3_25

the growing gap between urban and rural areas bring China's countryside once again entered a state of decline. The essence of local rural problems is the problem of mutual prosperity and sustainable coordinated development of urban and rural areas, and in the face of policy opportunities for rural revitalization, design may be able to play a leading, coordinating and promoting role in solving local rural problems.

2 Rural Revitalization in Local Context

The rural issue is a global issue as well as a regional one, and calling it a global issue is intended to show that rural issues are a universal problem that occurs in different corners of the world in all parts of the world, but that countries or regions that have experienced or are undergoing industrialization and urbanization have faced or are facing the challenge of change such as rural decay and rural revitalization. Calling it a regional issue also means that rural development is not only a global and universal issue and challenge, but also has a problem Quite regional and unique. Each country or region, based on its own historical and cultural background and economic and social development, will experience the huge impact of the wave of urbanization, and will produce rural problems based on its own context That is, the rural problem in the local context.

The word "village" (乡村, xiangcun) in Chinese is composed of the Chinese characters "xiang" (乡) and "cun" (村), the interpretation of "xiang" in Cihai is the grass-roots administrative region of rural China, generally referring to areas outside the city, and the interpretation of "cun" in Cihai is the basic unit of rural communities, so the word "village" in the Chinese context refers to rural areas outside of urban areas. China is a big agricultural country with a thousand years of farming civilization, Chinese civilization is a representative agricultural civilization, and China's ideological culture and social and economic system all originated and been established And deeply rooted in the countryside, it can be said that Chinese society is vernacular [1]. If we look at the evolution and development of China's rural areas from the perspective of history, it may be roughly divided into the following stages. Before the modern Western powers to open China with guns, Chinese society has maintained a stable self-sufficient small-scale peasant economy for a long time, and China's traditional countryside has maintained a super-stable state. It was not until after the First Opium War that the ultra-stable situation in China's traditional countryside began to be slowly broken and disintegrated, and China's countryside really entered a state of decline for the first time since then. The outside world's thinking, different cultures, and unstable situation prompted a group of people of insight at that time to have a deep reflection on the future and destiny of the Chinese nation, which was reflected in the Republic of China period with Liang Shuming, Yan Yangchu, Tao Xingzhi, Lu Zuofu, Chen Hansheng, and Fei Xiaotong And a group of scholars and practitioners dedicated to the research, construction and rejuvenation of China's rural areas have taken action, including the famous "Hebei Dingxian Experiment", "Shandong Zouping Experiment", "Chongqing Beibei Experiment", "Nanjing Xiaozhuang Rural Normal School" and *Peasant Life in China—A Field Study of Country Life in the Yangtze Valley*, *From the Soil—The Foundations of Chinese Society*, *Rural Construction Theory*, *China's Rural Studies* and other works. These actions dedicated to rural rejuvenation can be collectively referred to as the "rural construction movement", and the "rural construction movement" in the Republic of China period can be said to be the second historical stage experienced by the revival and development of China's rural areas, and the rural construction movement brought to the Chinese countryside a hope for change at that time, but the turbulent situation and the general environment make it difficult for these influential regional experiments to shake the overall pattern of China's rural areas in the end. After the founding of New China in 1949, land reform and socialist transformation in the vast rural areas were carried out nationwide China's urban-rural dual social system also took shape during this period, and the complete institutional transformation provided a policy environment for revitalization in China's rural areas, but then came the "Great Leap Forward" and the " People's communization movement" undermined the further emancipation and development of rural productive forces, and it was not until the establishment of the "household contract responsibility system" in 1982 that China's rural areas ushered in a real leap-forward development. Since the 1990s, with the intensification of urbanization, China's rural areas have once again been wrapped up in a new wave, and the rapid pace of urbanization has led to the third recession crisis in China's rural areas. In the context of the long-term urban-rural dual system, a large number of resources to the one-way tilt of the city to further expand the existing gap between urban and rural areas, the increasingly intensifying urban-rural contradictions make people further think about the future direction of China's rural areas, Represented by Wen Tiejun, Chinese scholars put forward the famous "three rural problems", that is, the agriculture, the rural area and the farmer, pointing out the key essence of the future development of China's rural areas. After entering the 21st century, China began to focus on solving rural development problems from the institutional and policy levels, and successively put forward a series of strategic measures such as "socialist new rural construction" and "increasing the overall planning of urban and rural development", and in 2017 The "Rural Revitalization Strategy" was officially proposed, and the "Rural Revitalization Strategy" rose to an important development strategy at the national level in China, which means that China's rural areas have begun to enter the fourth stage of historical development and ushered in a period of opportunity.

By combing the historical context of China's rural development, it can be found that local rural society and local rural culture are the essential characteristics of local villages, and they are also the root veins of local villages. Every crisis of the decline of the local countryside means the disintegration and rupture of the local rural society and local rural culture, and the deep contradiction behind the appearance of this crisis is the contradiction between the city and the countryside, and between people and the land. For a long time, the imbalance between urban and rural development in China is difficult to fundamentally improve, the integration and integrated development of urban and rural areas is difficult to effectively promote, and the dual structure of urban and rural areas is difficult to effectively break the situation, which is the dilemma that local villages have been facing in the past and at present, and it is also the focus and difficulty of rural revitalization in the local context. Therefore, the essence of the local rural problem is actually the problem of mutual prosperity and sustainable coordinated development of urban and rural areas, and the establishment of balanced, coordinated and sustainable urban-rural relations and human-land relations is the key to achieving rural rejuvenation and prosperity The mutual infusion of resources between urban and rural areas and the circulation of production factors are the basis for achieving mutual prosperity and sustainable and coordinated development between urban and rural areas. China's policy bias and industrial division of labor in the past period of time have aggravated the imbalance in the ownership and distribution of resources that already existed between urban and rural areas, hindered the flow of production factors between urban and rural areas, making it difficult for cities to effectively promote rural upgrading, and it is difficult for rural areas to attract resources to return from the city, and it is impossible to establish a benign interaction and cycle between urban and rural areas, and the countryside has always been in a weak position in this process. It is necessary to improve the current problem of resource ownership and distribution and the inequality of production factors between urban and rural areas, promote the interaction and integration of urban and rural areas, and realize localization The revitalization and development of rural areas, the excavation, reorganization and output of resources in rural areas, the injection of external resources into rural areas, and the diversion of resources between urban and rural areas will be the key. This process involves multiple stakeholders such as government agencies, urban and rural residents, enterprise organizations, and non-governmental organizations, and different stakeholders have different interest demands and contradictions between each other, balance different interest demands, ease and resolve contradictions, and guide and coordinate different stakeholders to work together, fully excavate and exert the value of rural stocks and create new value for rural areas through collaborative co-creation, so that rural areas can be transformed from the end of development to the front end and source of innovation, so as to create a harmonious and emerging urban-rural relationship, social relationship, and the relationship between people and land will be the top priority in promoting the interaction and integration of urban and rural development and ultimately realizing the revitalization of local rural areas and the common sustainable development of urban and rural areas.

3 Four Orders of Design and Active Design

Design is a creative behavioral activity, design discipline is the study and practice of creative thinking discipline, design is the use of creative thinking to solve problems, but also the process of improving, creating and giving meaning and value to things. The concept of design thinking was proposed in the late 1980s and was developed in the 1990s by the practice and enrichment of Professor David Kelley and others in IDEO and Stanford University. Design thinking has become an important design theory that is widely used and accepted. At the same time that design thinking was proposed, Professor Richard Buchanan proposed an important theoretical concept called the "Four Orders of Design", which he had in mind In his article Wicked Problems in Design Thinking in 1992, it was mentioned, "We may be able to see how design has widely influenced people's contemporary lives from the following four aspects… The first is symbol and visual communication design… The second is the design of things… The third is the design of organized services and event planning… The fourth aspect involves the design of complex systems or living, working, playing and learning environments" [2]. Professor Richard Buchanan's "Four Orders of Design" divides the areas involved in design problems into four aspects: the communication of symbols, the construction of things, the interaction of behaviors, and the integration of ideas, and the design objects of each aspect Symbols such as words and graphics, tangible objects, activities, services and processes, systems, environments, organizations, ideas and values, respectively, design thinking plays the role of invention, judgment, decision and evaluation in these four aspects.

The theory of the "Four Orders of Design" outlines a clear blueprint for us to intervene in, influence and change all aspects of our human society, and from this theory we can find the way design looks at and solves problems from different perspectives and the way of constructing meaning Through these four dimensions, a huge system of order has been constructed. In the face of increasingly complex problems and challenges today and in the future, design faces many more uncertain factors in solving them, and the problem ontology is often not a physical problem in the traditional sense, such as the design of a symbol or object, but rather a complex thing, state, or process involving multiple factors, such as behaviors, systems, services, and environments. With the help of the "four orders of design" theory, design can start from a more holistic perspective, systematically and comprehensively examine the problem itself and the context in which the problem is located, and at the same time, when specifically considering the solution to the problem, it is also We have clarified multiple sub-perspectives of thinking that allow us to create and give richer meaning to design objects.

The role of design is changing, not only in the horizontal dimension, but also in the vertical dimension. Professor Lou Yongqi believes that design thinking can enter almost any field to drive innovation, but compared with the previous role of passive service provision, design needs to be more actively involved in the solution of these problems, that is, "Active Design" [3]. In the past, design was always in the position of being needed, and Professor Fang Xiaofeng believed that "in the social division of labor and cooperation system, designers live in the downstream of the industrial chain, resulting in a loss of initiative" [4]. The transformation and improvement of the vertical role and status of design requires us to re-examine the positioning of design, current and future design researchers and practitioners should turn the tide, enhance their own initiative, take the initiative to break into the solution of more complex social problems, design can not only be used as a tool and means to solve problems, but also should become an active discovery of problems, definition of problems, integration of resources, Propose solutions, empower enablers, and drive innovation leaders. According to and combined with the "four orders of design" theory, active design facing the complex challenges of the present and the future should take the initiative to identify problems and be more active in the solution of problems Think about different levels of design objects including symbols, artifacts, behaviors and events, systems and environments, proactively explore the rich potential value behind problems and design objects, and propose solutions to problems that can bring different meanings to different stakeholders.

4 Interface and Touchpoint: Specific Ways to Drive Rural Revitalization

Given that local rural areas need to rely on the transformation from the end of development to the front end and source of innovation to achieve revitalization, design may be able to bring impetus to the mining and reorganization of rural resources and the full drainage and interaction of urban and rural elements, The best evidence is the practical action case of design intervention in rural revitalization that is being carried out or has been carried out in China. Previous practices and reflections on the relationship between rural and urban-rural areas in the domestic design community have focused more on the planning, renewal and transformation of the physical and material contents of the landscape, architecture, space and environment in rural areas. By conducting literature searches on CNKI with "countryside" and "design" as the keywords of the juxtaposed themes, it can be found that the top ten subject distribution areas involved in the search results are rural tourism (11.52%), rural revitalization (9.51%), and rural landscape (8.39%)), Beautiful Countryside (6.19%), Planning and Design (5.48%), Beautiful Rural Construction (4.56%), Landscape Design (4.24%), Rural Revitalization Strategy (4. 04%), landscape planning and design (3.51%), rural landscape planning (3.46%), and rural design practices with landscape planning and spatial transformation as the purpose and orientation are still the more mainstream design intervention rural development models in China. In many domestic design practices around rural areas, the traditional mainstream model of single design intervention from the level of rural spatial planning has been broken, and the more well-known projects include the "Bishan Plan" jointly initiated by Ou Ning and Zuo Jing, the "Xucun Plan" initiated by Qu Yan, and the "New Channel" project initiated by Hunan University, and Sichuan Academy of Fine Arts explored design intervention in rural poverty alleviation and design-driven rural revitalization projects. In these practical projects where design intervenes in the countryside, practitioners go beyond the traditional mainstream model of simply aiming at the transformation of the rural environment, but use art and design as a booster to innovate rural production and lifestyle, create new models and mechanisms, and promote the revitalization and development of local villages. Ou Ning in *A Case Study on the Bishan Commune: The possibility of Utopian Practices* introduced the original intention, background, operation process and content of the "Bishan Plan" project, as well as the author's experience and reflections on the project, the author hopes to build a rural community in Bishan that "transcends the traditional concept of property rights and promotes true sharing and sharing", the author tries to start from the restoration of rural public life, mobilize and connect villagers, and promote them to become the real subject of rural construction[5]. Qu Yan in the article *Back to the Traditional Art Promotes Village Rejuvenation and "Xucun Plan*" introduced the "Rural Restoration Plan" carried out by the author in Xucun, Shanxi, the author "tried to use the theory of 'art to promote village rejuvenation and art to restore the countryside', and implemented a series of restoration and regeneration plans in Xucun", and summarized the generalizable models and experiences from it, "which can truly condense the concept of 'rural restoration' into a complex of efficient rural rejuvenation" [6]. Guo Yinman and Ji Tie in *Soctal Transformation and Design Participation in Rural Culture Construction* putted forward the strategy of design participation in rural cultural construction, including "the design transformation with community as the basic research unit, the system theory with understanding the countryside as the premise of construction, the interdisciplinary collaboration with the goal of rural co-construction, the construction of the 'local knowledge' platform with empowerment as the foundation, and the use of new technologies oriented towards the future", and introduces the achievements and experience of Hunan University in the "New Channel" project [7]. Duan Shengfeng, Jiang Jinchen and Pi Yongsheng in *One More than Taobao: Design the Practice and Research of the Rural Supply and Marketing Mode* [8], and Pi Yongsheng, Duan Shengfeng, and Zhang Tiantian in *What Do Rural Factories Produce? Research on Value Promotion of "Handicraft + Agricultural Products" Driven by Design* [9] respectively introduced and elaborated on the practical achievements of the Sichuan Academy of Fine Arts in designing and intervening in the rural supply and marketing system to enhance the value of agricultural products, as well as design-driven traditional handicrafts and agricultural products to enhance the value and empower commodity conversion and rural industrial development.

The exploration and practice of rural revitalization in the domestic design community confirms the possibility, reality and uniqueness of rural rejuvenation and development through design intervention and drive, highlights the advantages of design in leading rural revitalization, and further promotes rural revitalization in a wider and wider scope for future exploration and design The development and in-depth support provide strong peer support and evidence. Judging from the above cases, these practitioners of design intervention in rural revitalization do not stick to the previous changes from a single dimension such as space and environment to the countryside, but reconstruct the value of the rural content from a multi-dimensional perspective with the help of design Whether it is the symbols, visual elements, products of the countryside, or the activities and events of the countryside, or even the behavior of the villagers and the system of the countryside, these different levels of rural content involving different orders have been incorporated into the design consideration object by practitioners in the above cases, and have become the interface and contact point for design intervention and driving rural revitalization. With the help of the "Four Orders of Design" theory proposed by Professor Richard Buchanan described above, we can clearly identify and sort out the specific entry points of design in influencing rural development and driving rural innovation and change, these different order dimensions The transformation of rural content reflects the design in inheriting rural culture, excavating rural values, empowering rural stakeholders, and giving new meaning to rural content On a unique role.

5 Design Harvest: A New Attempt of Urban-Rural Interaction Driven by Design

Design thinking can comprehensively and actively intervene in the solution of rural problems, and support and drive the rejuvenation and development of rural areas through the design of different specific objects. The "Design Harvest" project may be a good example of design-driven rural revitalization, such an urban-rural interaction research project has been a research process for 14 years since its launch in 2007, and the project is an innovation and entrepreneurship platform in the field of urban-rural interaction It was initiated and led by Professor Lou Yongqi. The "Design Harvest 1.0" project conducts design research in Xianqiao Village, Shuxin Town, Chongming Island, Shanghai, hoping to start from design thinking, explore the potential of traditional rural production and lifestyle, and promote urban-rural exchanges and sustainable development Through the experimental work of Xianqiao Village, the project hopes to create a "prototype" of research and practice to discuss the future vision of urban and rural development. Under the leadership of Professor Lou Yongqi, based on an acupuncture-style strategy proposed by him, the "Design Harvest" project has been officially implemented and implemented since 2010, during which a series of research and practical activities including space transformation, theme workshops, artists stationed in village projects, and digital platform construction have been carried out and organized to establish a way to explore and solve rural problems in China. And the idea and program to implement the prototype platform. As the attempt and effort of Professor Lou Yongqi and his team around urban-rural interaction, the "Design Harvest" project is a new active exploration and practice of design thinking and "active design" theory to intervene in and drive rural revitalization and urban-rural interaction He has also made great contributions to academic fields such as rural development issues in China and sustainable environment, and the team was born in 2013 In 2006, he published the book *DESIGN HARVESTS, an acupunctural design approach towards sustainability* [10], which introduced and elaborated in detail the thoughts and views of Professor Lou Yongqi, the initiator of the "Design Harvest" project, on design transformation, rural issues, urban-rural relations, and design intervention in urban-rural interaction in China, as well as the origin, background, method, and exploration process of the "Design Harvest" project. Implementation content and phased results.

The "Design Harvest" project began with Professor Lou Yongqi's in-depth thinking on the relationship between city and countryside. Professor Lou Yongqi believes that the city and the countryside under the traditional Chinese culture is an interactive yin and yang balance relationship, the development problems of urban and rural areas need to rely on the combination of urban and rural complementarity to solve, if the city and the countryside can be regarded as an organic whole, through the design to promote urban and rural interaction, then the respective problems of urban and rural areas may be able to become each other's solution. Based on such a reflection on the relationship between urban and rural areas, for the "Design Harvest" project, Professor Lou Yongqi believes that it provides us with a new possibility, which may be design as a new tool to connect the city and the countryside, guide the urban and rural areas to produce new ways of interaction, realize the mutual injection of resources between the city and the countryside, and at the same time design can fully develop the multiple values behind the countryside. Bring momentum to the development of rural economy [11, 12].

Since its inception, the "Design Harvest" program has conducted more than 20 research projects and workshops, attracting more than 1,000 young people and more than 500 students Non-arts people have been involved in the Design Harvest community-supported agriculture project as well as artist-based projects. The "Design Harvest" project also remodeled three vacant houses as homestay space for the local area and remodeled six agricultural greenhouses to carry out a series of workshops and activities with team members A space for stakeholders such as rural residents to discuss ideas and solutions, has gradually become a small and interconnected rural innovation center. Through its own incubation and cooperation with other brands and organizations, the "Design Harvest" project team has initiated a number of sub-projects, including design homestays, rural creative activities, ecological experience farms, creative agricultural products, natural creative classes, artist residency programs, etc. And thus gave birth to and established a new model of rural economic development. In 2019, Xianqiao Village on Chongming Island in Shanghai was rated as a national rural tourism key village by the Ministry of Culture and Tourism.

At present, the "Design Harvest" project team is committed to developing an urban-rural interaction research and practice project called "Design Harvest 2.0" in the field of urban-rural interaction, which includes "a scale of 3,000 acres of land, crowdfunding and crowd-creation of a village, thousands of ideas, hundreds of companies, and thousands of jobs." How China's rural areas have changed from a 'consumer terminal' to a 'source of innovation' and become a strong economic and innovation engine for China's future development [13]. In November 2019, Professor Lou Yongqi led the launch of the "Zhangyan Harvest - Future Rural Life Festival", on the basis of "Design Harvest 1.0", and proposed a new paradigm of rural revitalization with "demand upgrading, economic cycle, community thinking, and platform logic" as the main features for Zhangyan Village, Chonggu Town, Qingpu District, Shanghai [14]" Design Harvest 2.0 - "Zhangyan Harvest" project thus kicked off. In April 2020, Zhangyan Village was selected as the third batch of rural revitalization demonstration village construction list in Shanghai. At the "Zhangyan Harvest, Yangtze River Delta Chuangcheng Network - 2020 Urban-Rural Co-creation Forum" held in November 2020, Professor Lou Yongqi proposed, "In the future, the countryside should bring together a group of the most imaginative young people and collaborate with local communities to reshape rural life, production methods and values."Every inch of Shanghai's rural land should be a 'test field', and Shanghai's countryside should become a new source of urban innovation in Shanghai, and a 'low-density innovation engine' for Shanghai's global science and technology innovation center. In the future, Zhangyan Village will gather a group of start-ups focusing on future science and technology agriculture and scientific and technological and creative enterprises in rural areas, and superimpose a high-attached industrial cluster on the 'socialist circular economy agriculture base', thus becoming a test field for the future economy" [15].

The experiment of the "Design Harvest" project more completely reflects the value of design in driving the revitalization of local villages, on the one hand, design is no longer simply from the perspective of things to the countryside, but is based on the transformation of the different order content that drives the countryside The design not only beautifies and creates the rural environment and products, but also excavates the new value behind the rural content, creates and gives new meaning to the original countryside, thus driving the upgrading and development of the rural industry, and also attracting the attention from the city, establishing a new way of urban-rural interaction; on the other hand, the designer and designer play an important role in this project, from the passive recipient of the previous problem, Becoming the initiator of the project, the proposer of the problem, the definer and the leader of the change, the designer can take the initiative in the process of empowering the commoners of rural interests Understand and connect with needs, and even propose and create new needs, bringing innovation drivers to the countryside from the source. As Professor Lou Yongqi said, "The essence of 'Design Harvest' is an entrepreneurial project, committed to opening up a business model with self-hematopoietic function; it is also a platform to gather more people to display their talents and contribute wisdom on this platform to promote rural revitalization and social innovation" [16].

6 Conclusion

The conclusion of this paper is that based on the theory of "Four Orders of Design" and "Active Design", design can play a more leading and constructive role in solving problems in the local context of China, and design thinking has a strong driving force to drive innovation. In the process of design-driven revitalization of local rural areas, we have seen two major order systems, one is a rural stakeholder system composed of different social roles such as designers, citizens, villagers, governments, enterprises, etc., and the other is a larger complex system composed of rural things, space, environment, culture, and society Actively intervene and influence different specific elements in complex systems, and through the co-creation and transformation of these complex system elements, drive innovative changes in rural areas, while designers can promote the transformation of rural systems Actively dock different social roles in the countryside, connect and unite rural stakeholders, play the role of communication bridge, drive stakeholders to carry out rural co-governance and innovation, actively guide the flow of resources, and seek the establishment of rural communities and urban-rural communities.

Acknowledgements. This research supported by the Foundational Research Funds for the Central Universities in China (kx0140020210219).

References

1. Xiaotong, F.: From the Soil—The Foundations of Chinese Society. Shanghai People's Publishing House, Shanghai (2019)
2. Buchanan, R.: Wicked problems in design thinking. Des. Issues **08**(02), 5–21 (1992)
3. Yongqi, L.: Design Activism in an Era of Transformation. Zhuangshi, vol. 07. pp. 17–19, Tsinghua University, Beijing (2015)
4. Xiaofeng, F.: On Design Activism. Zhuangshi, vol. 07, pp. 12–16. Tsinghua University, Beijing (2015)
5. Ning, O.: A case study on the Bishan commune: the possibility of utopian practices. New Arch. **01,** 17–22. Huazhong University of Science and Technology, Wuhan (2015)
6. Yan, Q.: Back to the traditional art promotes village rejuvenation and Xucun plan. Arch. J. **12**, 22–26. The Architectural Society of China, Beijing (2013)
7. Yinman, G., Tie, J.: Social Transformation and Design Participation in Rural Cultural Construction. Zhaungshi, vol. 04, pp. 39–43, Tsinghua University, Beijing (2018)
8. Shengfeng, D., Jinchen, J., Yongsheng, P.: One More than Taobao: Design the Practice and Research of the Rural Supply and Marketing Mode. Zhaungshi, vol. 04, pp. 28–33, Tsing-hua University, Beijing (2018).
9. Yongsheng, P., Shengfeng, D., Tiantian, Z.: O What Do Rural Factories Produce? Research on Value Promotion of Handicraft + Agricultural Products Driven by Design. Zhaungshi, vol. 08, pp. 130–131. Tsinghua University, Beijing (2020)
10. Yongqi, L., Valsecchi, F., Diaz, C.: Design Harvests: An Acupunctural Design Approach Towards Sustainability. Master Urban Futures, Gothenburg (2013)
11. Renpan, P., Wu, A.: Design Harvest in Chongming. Mingrifengshang, vol. 10, pp.66–87. Nanjing Federation of literary and artistic circles, Nanjing (2012)
12. Chao, T.: Design and Harvest and Distant Places: An Interview with Lou Yongqi, Dean of College of Design and Innovation Tongji, vol. 03, pp. 18–20. Oriental Publishing Center, Shanghai (2015)

13. Zixuan, T.: Stimulating New Impetus with Design Thinking——Visiting Lou Yongqi, Dean of College of Design and Innovation, Tongji University, vol. 07, pp. 59–61, Oriental Publishing Center, Shanghai (2019)
14. Zhangyan, Y.:| Design Harvest 2.0 is coming!. https://mp.weixin.qq.com/s/NI0Pz-Vu-_Zo8UGBxPoP4Q. Accessed 17 June 2020
15. Forum Review | Zhangyan Harvest, Yangtze River Delta Chuangcheng Network-2020 Urban-Rural Co-creation Forum. https://mp.weixin.qq.com/s/OAvEid48IasGajMFGtHrYQ. Accessed 28 Nov 2020
16. Yongqi, L.: Design-driven urban-rural interaction: An Exploration of Design Harvest. People's Daily, 17–06–2018

Smart City Constructions in China; Digital Reform in Zhejiang Province: The Case of Wuzhen

Ziyang Li[1], Hui Yu[2(✉)], and Xuefeng Zhang[2]

[1] China Academy of Industrial Internet, Beijing 100102, China
[2] People's Government of Wuzhen Township, Tongxiang 314501, China
yuhui7red@outlook.com

Abstract. With the development of new information and communication technologies, the pace of smart city construction has accelerated. This study investigated the case of Wuzhen's smart city construction (hereinafter Smart Wuzhen Construction) to analyze the smart city construction of small-sized cities. Zhejiang Province, where Wuzhen is located, is vigorously conducting digital reforms. Wuzhen's smart city construction is also an epitome of Zhejiang's digital reform. This paper introduces the background and the four domains of Smart Wuzhen Construction. Then, we analyze the console of Smart Wuzhen Construction (i.e., Smart Wuzhen Platform) with its basic functions and application scenarios. The results of the case study showed that Smart Wuzhen Construction follows the idea of top-down design and bottom-up construction and exploits the online and offline advantages. Wuzhen has taken the very first step in smart city construction and digital reform, providing good guidance for smart city construction.

Keywords: Smart city · Digital reform · Wuzhen · Smart Wuzhen construction

1 Introduction

Fast development information technologies and digitalization contribute to the surge in smart city construction. The recent decades have witnessed the birth and development of many smart cities. There is a "smart city mania" around the world. It is estimated that the market size of global smart cities was valued at USD 98.15 billion in 2020 [1], and that of China's smart cities reached USD 26.6 billion, which is the second-largest after that of the United States. Deloitte argued that, of the 1000 smart city projects that are currently being built worldwide, China is home to half of them [2]. By 2020, more than 700 cities in China were planning and constructing smart cities. China's experience in smart city constructions has garnered much attention. Among them, big cities such as Beijing, Shanghai, and Shenzhen are the most notable; however, only a few studies have investigated small-sized cities such as Wuzhen.

Wuzhen is a historic scenic town that belongs to Tongxiang City, Zhejiang Province, China. Zhejiang announced its digital reform plan (*The Plan of Zhejiang Province's Digital Reform* [3]) in 2021 and vigorously promoted local digital transformation and

P.-L. P. Rau (Ed.): HCII 2022, LNCS 13314, pp. 371–382, 2022.
https://doi.org/10.1007/978-3-031-06053-3_26

modernization development. With Wuzhen being the basic administrative unit of Zhejiang,[1] its smart city construction is a microcosm of Zhejiang's digital reform. It also has unique township characteristics.

In this paper, we introduce the case of Wuzhen smart city construction. First, we review the related studies on smart cities and the development of smart cities in China. The history and present status of Wuzhen are illustrated. Second, Wuzhen's smart city construction (hereinafter Smart Wuzhen Construction) is analyzed and introduced. Then, the benefits and challenges of Smart Wuzhen construction are discussed. Finally, we present the insights generated from the case study.

2 Literature Review

2.1 Smart City

There is no universally acknowledged definition of smart cities. In general, a smart city can be described as a technologically modern area that utilizes human and technological capital to enhance its livability, workability, prosperity, and sustainability at multiple levels (e.g., social, economic, and governance). In the compound term "smart city," the term "smart" is interchangeable with the term "intelligent" or "digital," which emphasizes the utilization of new generation information and communication technologies (ICTs) [4, 5], and the term "city" refers to an urban area where humans settle and where there is a high population density and decent infrastructure rather than the city regime itself. As national definitions of urbanization differ substantially, there is no global standard for the classification of cities or urban areas [6]. The concept of a smart city could encompass the smart metropolis, smart town, or even smart suburbs.

Smart city construction is a multidimensional, systematic, and expensive project; thus, various stakeholders are needed such as governments, companies, technology vendors, and research institutes. Many studies have been conducted on this subject. These studies can be classified into three aspects:

(1) Methodological aspect: Some studies have proposed the concepts and frameworks of smart city construction from a methodological aspect [7–9]. Chourabi et al. (2012) determined that eight crucial factors, namely, management and organization, technology, governance, policy context, people and communities, economy, built infrastructure, and natural environment, form the basis of a smart city framework [10].
(2) Technological aspect: Some studies have analyzed the technological path and infrastructure of smart cities from a technical perspective [9, 11]. ICT is perceived as a driver of smart city initiatives [12]. New ICTs such as the Internet of Things (IoT) [13], blockchain [14], and digital twin [15] have brought new opportunities and scenarios to smart city construction.

[1] The names of different levels of administrative divisions vary for each country. China has three levels (i.e., province, county, and town) or four levels (i.e., province, city, county, and town) of administrative divisions. A town is China's basic administrative unit.

(3) Case study aspect: Some studies have introduced the practical path of smart cities from the perspective of case-study analysis, such as the cases of Dubai [16], Barcelona [17], Saint Petersburg [18], Shenzhen [19], and New York [20]. The aforementioned cities mainly focus on international metropolises, which are large and wealthy cities with many industrial and economic activities. Given that "one size does not fit all," the cases of metropolises can hardly satisfy the needs of most ordinary urban areas. In addition, cities in different countries show strong national characteristics in regard to smart city construction. For example, they might differ in definitions and standards because of regional interests and abilities [21].

2.2 Smart City Constructions in China

In recent years, smart city constructions have been surging in China. In 2012, the Ministry of Housing and Urban-Rural Development of the People's Republic of China (MOHURD) released the *Interim Measures of National Pilot Smart Cities*. It regards smart city construction as an important measure for achieving innovation-driven development, new-type urbanization, and moderately prosperous society building [22]. The scope of "national pilot smart cities" includes cities, districts, and towns. To date, 290 national pilot smart cities have been announced (e.g., Dongcheng District in Beijing, Tangshan in Hebei Province, and Changle in Fujian Province). These cities would receive financial support and reviews from MOHURD. In 2014, China's eight ministries (e.g., the National Development and Reform Commission, Ministry of Industry and Information Technology of the People's Republic of China) jointly released the *Guidance on Promoting the Healthy Development of Smart Cities*, which was the first national guidance for smart city construction. It defines a smart city as a new idea and a new model of smart urban planning, construction, management, and service through the use of new generation ICTs (e.g., IoT, cloud computing, big data, and spatial geographic information integration). It emphasizes the acceleration of the integration of industrialization, informatization, urbanization, and agricultural modernization, thus enhancing the ability of urban sustainable development [23].

Driven by factors such as rapid urbanization and government investments, cities in China are actively implementing smart city construction. It is estimated that the market value of China's smart cities would grow from USD 30.4 billion in 2018 to USD 59.9 billion by 2023, at a compound annual growth rate of 14.5% [24]. As a latecomer, China has been catching up with the leading regions, such as Europe, North America, Japan, and South Korea, and has dominated them in the number of smart cities [2].

2.3 Wuzhen

Wuzhen is located in the north of Zhejiang Province, China, and is a typical ancient water town in the south of the Yangtze River. With an ancient canal that runs through numerous riverside buildings, Wuzhen is nicknamed the "Last Riverside Town in China" and the "Venice of the East" [25, 26]. Moreover, Wuzhen integrates ancient and modern elements simultaneously. On the one hand, it was built 1300 years ago and has a civilization history of more than 7000 years. On the other hand, it has been the permanent site of the annual World Internet Conference (WIC) since 2014 [27]; thereafter, the Internet industry has flourished. To date, nearly 800 Internet projects have been established (e.g., Wuzhen Internet Hospital, Wuzhen Integrated Circuit Public Service Platform, and Wuzhen Baidu Brain Innovation Center) and many Internet industry platforms have been built (e.g., Virtual Industry Park, Wuzhen Design Park, and World Internet Industrial Park) [25]. All of these have provided favorable conditions for Smart Wuzhen Construction.

3 Smart Wuzhen Construction

In this study, we interviewed 20 staff members involved in Smart Wuzhen Construction. Each staff member was interviewed for approximately 1.5 h. Among them, there were ten civil servants, eight system developers, and two product managers. We analyzed Smart Wuzhen Construction from a neutral perspective.

3.1 Zhejiang's Digital Reform

In 2021, Zhejiang released *The Plan of Zhejiang Province's Digital Reform* [3], which was the first province-level digital reform plan in China. Zhejiang's digital reform emphasizes the overall use of digital technology, digital thinking, and digital cognition; it puts digitalization, integration, and modernization through all aspects and the entire process of economic, political, cultural, social, and ecological civilization construction. Zhejiang selected and announced two batches ($N_{\text{first batch}} = 25$, $N_{\text{second batch}} = 30$) of the "best applications" for digital reform [28, 29]. For example, the application "Zhejiang Takeaway Food Online" has functional modules for ensuring food safety, protecting the rights of customers and delivery men, strengthening traffic management, etc., thereby promoting a healthier online catering industry. These applications were from five domains, namely, the overall intelligent governance, digital government, digital economy, digital society, and digital rule of law of the Party and administrative agencies. Zhejiang works hard for better quality, higher efficiency, and more robust drivers of economic growth through digital reform.

Digital reforms help empower urban governance and make cities smarter. Smart Wuzhen Construction is an important measure for implementing the requirements of Zhejiang's digital reform and is also a starting point for Wuzhen's digital reform. Smart Wuzhen Construction empowers this ancient town through digitalization and helps modernize Wuzhen's system and capacity for governance and enhance people's well-being.

3.2 Three-Year Plan for Smart Wuzhen Construction

Since the WIC was permanently held in Wuzhen in 2014, the Internet-based life experience and good network infrastructure have continued to enhance the well-being of Wuzhen residents. To take advantage of the huge dividends brought by the WIC, the Wuzhen government released the *Three-Year Plan for Smart Wuzhen Construction* (hereinafter the three-year plan) in 2019. The three-year plan aims to make Wuzhen a world-class tourist destination and a national model for smart city construction.

Smart Wuzhen Construction has the following four domains (see Fig. 1):

Smart Brain refers to building an efficient and orderly smart system, including the building of the information infrastructure (e.g., optical fiber network, IoT equipment, and data pool) and the operating platform (i.e., Smart Wuzhen Platform; details are given in Sect. 3.3). Smart Brain is the central hub of Smart Wuzhen Construction.

Smart Government emphasizes the informatization upgrading of government affairs. The existing information systems of various government departments are integrated and managed as a whole, through which information sharing, business collaboration, and telecommuting can be realized.

Smart Governance focuses on improving governance services from the dimensions of smart transportation, smart water conservancy, smart energy conservation, smart fire-fighting, etc. With smart water conservancy as an example, deploying water-level sensing equipment, correlating weather warning information, and applying advanced technologies (e.g., situation analysis and artificial intelligence) will enable the water conservancy systems to realize advanced warning and automatic execution.

Smart People's Well-Being focuses on the improvement of people's livelihood and well-being. For residents, a smart and livable community would be created by integrating medical services, school education, elderly care services, safety protection, etc. For tourists, a unified tourism service platform would be built by integrating food services, accommodations, transportation, tours, and others.

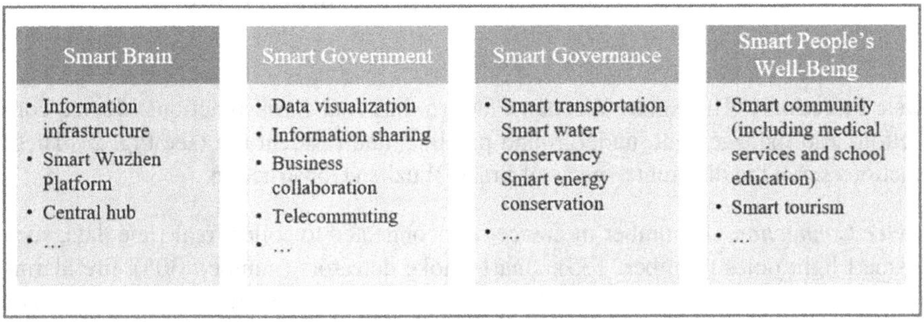

Fig. 1. Four domains of Smart Wuzhen construction

3.3 Smart Wuzhen Platform

Overview. The Smart Wuzhen Platform is the core component of Smart Brain and is the console of Smart Wuzhen Construction. It was designed to provide convenient government services, efficient urban governance, comfortable lives for residents, scientific system structures, advanced communication networks, and controllable information security. The development of the Smart Wuzhen Platform enables the vision of Smart Brain, Smart Government, Smart Governance, and Smart People's Well-Beings to be realized.

Specifically, the Smart Wuzhen Platform is a system that combines an online platform and offline forces. In terms of the online part, with the help of technologies such as IoT, digital twin, situation awareness, geographic information system, and city information model, the governance elements (i.e., people, things, and events) can be collected and presented. For instance, a three-dimensional (3D) digital twin map of Wuzhen was drawn as the background of the interface interaction (see Fig. 2). In terms of the offline part, the pattern of the "online command plus offline response" and "government force plus social force" was formed. For instance, when an online requirement is released (e.g., time, locations, and events), the corresponding offline forces are informed to help solve the problems on time. The offline forces include civil servants and social volunteers.

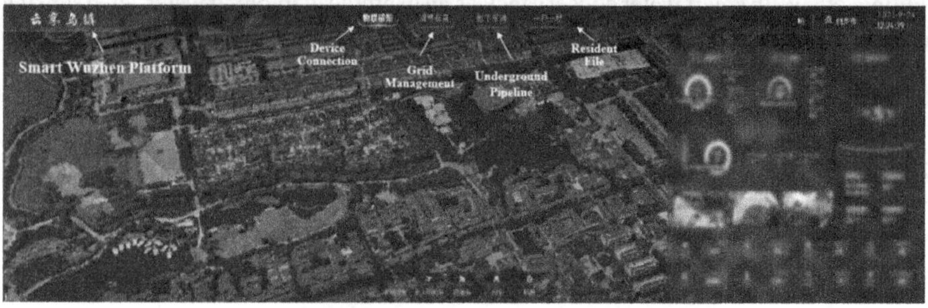

Fig. 2. An example of the front page (some information was blurred)

Basic Functions. The Smart Wuzhen Platform has four basic functions: device connection, grid management, underground pipeline, and resident file (see Fig. 2). These functions serve the different aspects of Smart Wuzhen Construction.

Device Connection. A number of devices are connected to collect real-time data, such as smart light poles (number: 135), smart smoke detectors (number: 305), fire alarms (number: 2300), smart sluices (number: 141), and drones (real-time connection). The information about the connected device and the information collected by the device can be recorded, presented, and retrieved. For instance, the status information, flight files, and inspection data of the drone are shown in Fig. 3.

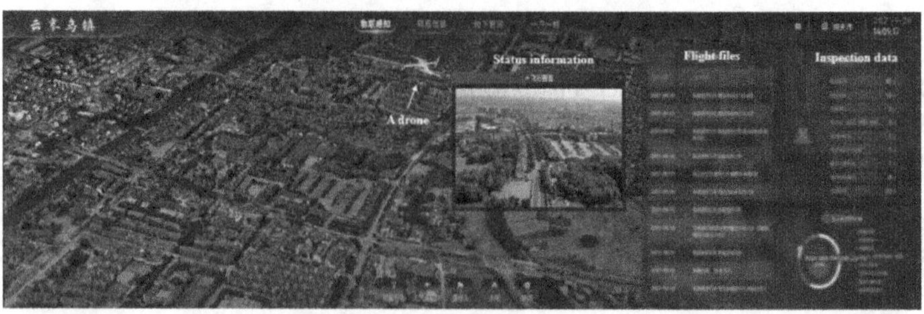

Fig. 3. An example of the device connection part

Grid Management. Grid management is an administrative management method in China. City/town/village management areas can be divided into grids according to certain standards. Wuzhen is divided into 108 grids with 108 grid leaders, 220 grid staff members, and 4016 volunteers. They are responsible for collecting the number of local population and households; reporting potential safety hazards and illegal incidents; and helping vulnerable groups in their grid.

The grid division, grid staff information, and grid information can be clearly displayed on the Smart Wuzhen Platform (see Fig. 4). In addition, unresolvable incidents reported by the grid staff members are allocated to the corresponding law-enforcing departments. This promotes and supervises multi-departmental collaboration, thus increasing governance efficiency. In 2021, the grid staff members reported 12,797 pieces of information, all of which were successfully solved.

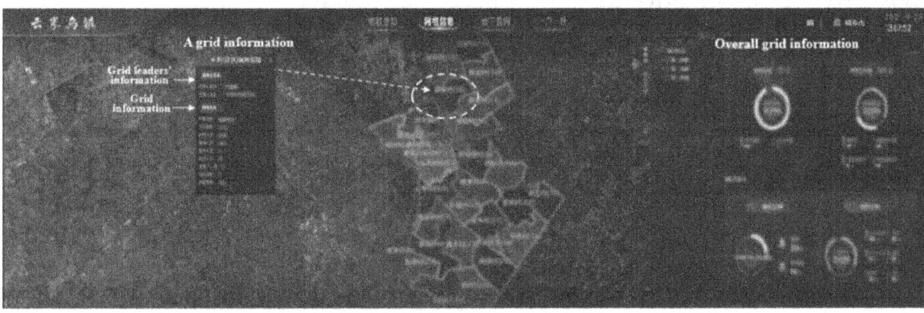

Fig. 4. An example of the grid management function

Underground Pipeline. The Smart Wuzhen Platform integrates the data of multiple underground pipelines, such as electricity, water, and gas, to realize 3D visualization. At present, the total length of the water supply and drainage pipelines in Wuzhen is 1049 km and the total number of pipe points exceeds 50,000. Information on water pipelines (including the supply and drainage pipelines) in four streets is shown on the platform. For instance, the length, quantity, and diameter of the water pipeline in Huanhe Street are shown in Fig. 5. More underground pipelines are being connected. With the visualization of the underground pipelines, construction teams could preview building construction, thus empowering future planning and construction in Wuzhen.

Fig. 5. An example of the underground pipeline function

Resident File. The demographic data and resident information of Wuzhen are integrated into the Smart Wuzhen Platform. There are more than 86,000 people in Wuzhen, and the ratio of men to women is approximately 1:1. The rural population accounts for 47%, whereas the urban population accounts for 53%. Moreover, building information modeling technologies were introduced into the Smart Wuzhen Platform to improve the interactive accuracy. The platform took the buildings on Longyuan Road as a pilot and built around 20,000 resident files (e.g., addresses, households, and residents). When a specific building on Longyuan Road is clicked, the corresponding resident files will pop out. Certainly, high-level management authorities are required to check the resident files.

Application Scenarios. The three-year plan proposed the idea of top-down design and bottom-up construction for Smart Wuzhen Construction. Smart Wuzhen Construction is constructed using the top-level design to expand various bottom-up application scenarios. Two typical scenarios were introduced in this study:

Smart Enterprise Safety Check. There are 494 manufacturing enterprises in Wuzhen. It is a time-consuming task for government departments (e.g., emergency, fire protection, environmental protection, market supervision, and economic development) to conduct production safety checks on all these enterprises. For example, it took around two months for the emergency department to conduct a full-range check of the enterprises. Untimely checks or inspections may result in serious accidents. On the other hand, enterprises had to spend a great deal of energy to respond to various checks.

To solve the above problems, the developers of the Smart Wuzhen Platform added an enterprise safety check scenario to it (see Fig. 6). Enterprises are required to upload operational procedures to the platform. In addition, the platform can access warehouse cameras, smoke detectors, and other IoT sensing devices, to realize real-time monitoring and early warning. The emergency department formulated a standardized guidebook for safety checks and promoted cross-departmental collaborative checks. For example, when the staff members of the environmental protection department carry out safety checks on an enterprise, they can use the guidebook to check the items of all the other departments. All the information about safety checks (e.g., risk level, hidden risks, the location and descriptions of the risks, and photos of risks) will be uploaded to and synchronized in the platform, thus improving the efficiency of safety checks and ensuring production safety.

Fig. 6. An example of smart enterprise safety check

Smart Street Management. The superposition of scenic spots and living areas puts forward higher requirements for governance in Wuzhen. The government needs to guarantee life convenience and landscape beautification at the same time. The Smart Wuzhen Platform took one street as a pilot and used modern technologies to realize automatic and smart street management. Empowered by artificial intelligence, edge computing, and image recognition technologies, the Smart Wuzhen Platform can identify uncivilized and bad behaviors (e.g., going/driving through a red light, illegal parking, and fights) and report them to nearby grid staff members or volunteers for proper action. If the problems cannot be solved, they would be distributed to law-enforcement departments, such as traffic police and public security. The problem-solving process is tracked and supervised by the platform.

4 Discussion

Wuzhen has taken the first step in the smart city construction and digital transformation of the township. At the end of 2020, there were more than 21,000 towns in China. Wuzhen is not one of the most economically developed towns, although it is one of the first towns to start smart city construction. In the context of Zhejiang's digital reform, Wuzhen's smart city construction has strong support and huge potential. Following the idea of top-down design and bottom-up construction, Smart Wuzhen Construction moved successfully in these years. In terms of the top-down design, the Wuzhen government's top-level design pointed out the right direction and provided strong support for Smart Wuzhen Construction. The Wuzhen government (1) introduced the three-year plan and proceeded with it step by step; (2) coordinated multi-party resources for digital transformation and infrastructure constructions; (3) established a joint venture company (Zhejiang Zhizhi Yun Technology Co., Ltd.) with a state-owned enterprise; the company was in charge of the development of the Smart Wuzhen Platform to ensure the government's control of the platform; and (4) connected the systems of multiple departments to the platform, thus breaking the "information isolated islands" between departments.

In terms of the bottom-up construction, Smart Wuzhen Construction was carried out according to existing conditions, actual needs, and application scenarios: (1) existing digital infrastructure was used to build the four basic functions of the Smart Wuzhen Platform; (2) application scenarios were derived according to the needs of the people and the problems faced in governance work; (3) the online platform (i.e., the Smart Wuzhen Platform) and the offline forces (e.g., civil servants, grid leaders, grid staff members, and social volunteers) were fully used.

Wuzhen provided a sample or guidance for the construction of smart scenic cities. Wuzhen has approximately 110 km^2 and a total population of 8,6000. In 2019, more than 9 million tourists came to Wuzhen; despite being affected by the COVID-19 pandemic, Wuzhen received over 3 million tourists, generating nearly 795 million yuan in revenue in 2020. Faced with the number of tourists 50 times more than that of the local residents, the local government has the difficult task of balancing tourism services and residents' lives. At the same time, the image of a beautiful, healthy, and culturally rich riverside town needs to be maintained for Wuzhen [30]. Smart Wuzhen Construction has improved the overall governance services through digital transformation. Combining online and offline forces, Smart Wuzhen Construction has explored various application scenarios (e.g., smart street management), thus increasing the efficiency of problem solving and service responses.

Like many other smart city constructions, the construction in Wuzhen faces several challenges. First, collaboration across departments is challenging sometimes [17]. There is a need for a clear definition of the roles and responsibilities of multiple departments. To the best of our knowledge, Wuzhen is working on relevant management methods and manuals. Cross-regional, cross-departmental, and cross-business functions and scenarios need to be effectively built and explored. Second, considering and meeting diverse needs are challenging [10]. The needs of the government, residents, tourists, and enterprises are diverse, irregular, and sometimes conflicting. Multi-party needs should be considered as a whole without bias. Third, data security is always a primary concern. The pros and cons of data collection and usage are like two sides of the same coin. While the scope of access and application is expanded, it is necessary to pay more attention to the accuracy, integrity, and security of the data.

5 Conclusion

Digital reform and transformation would not wait until you are ready. In this study, we analyzed Wuzhen's digital reform and smart city construction to provide insights for small-sized and scenic cities in their governance. (1) Smart city construction should adapt to local conditions and follow the ideas of top-down design and bottom-up construction. Wuzhen introduced the three-year plan and coordinated multi-party resources. (2) Smart city construction needs to take government, governance, and people's well-being as a whole. The four domains of Smart Wuzhen Construction, namely, Smart Brain, Smart Government, Smart Governance, and Smart People's Well-Being, were considered and constructed together. (3) Smart city construction is accomplished using online and offline forces. The Smart Wuzhen Platform is the console of Smart Wuzhen Construction. The basic functions and application scenarios combine the online and offline advantages.

Acknowledgement. Thanks to Zhejiang Zhizhi Yun Technology Co., Ltd. for their supports in this study.

References

1. Smart Cities Market Size & Share Report, 2021–2028. https://www.grandviewre-search.com/industry-analysis/smart-cities-market
2. Deloitte China: Super Smart City - Happier Society with Higher Quality. https://www2.deloitte.com/cn/en/pages/public-sector/articles/super-smart-city.html
3. Digital Reform in Zhejiang Province. http://fzggw.zj.gov.cn/col/col1229534816/index.html
4. Wolfram, M.: Deconstructing smart cities: an intertextual reading of concepts and practices for integrated urban and ICT development. In: Schrenk, M., Popovich, V.V., Zeile, P., Elisei, P. (eds.) Proceedings of the REAL CORP 2012, pp. 171–181. Schwechat (2012)
5. Angelidou, M.: Smart city policies: a spatial approach. Cities **41**, S3–S11 (2014)

6. Dijkstra, L., et al.: Applying the Degree of Urbanisation to the globe: a new harmonised definition reveals a different picture of global urbanisation. J. Urban Econ. 103312 (2020)
7. Duan, W., Nasiri, R., Karamizadeh, S.: Smart city concepts and dimensions. In: Proceedings of the 2019 7th International Conference on Information Technology: IoT and Smart City, pp. 488–492 (2019)
8. Eremia, M., Toma, L., Sanduleac, M.: The smart city concept in the 21st century. Procedia Eng. **181**, 12–19 (2017)
9. Lu, H.-P., Chen, C.-S., Yu, H.: Technology roadmap for building a smart city: an exploring study on methodology. Future Gen. Comput. Syst. **97**, 727–742 (2019)
10. Chourabi, H., et al.: Understanding smart cities: An integrative framework. In: 2012 45th Hawaii International Conference on System Sciences, pp. 2289–2297. IEEE (2012)
11. Park, E., Del Pobil, A.P., Kwon, S.J.: The role of Internet of Things (IoT) in smart cities: technology roadmap-oriented approaches. Sustainability **10**, 1388 (2018)
12. Mohanty, S.P., Choppali, U., Kougianos, E.: Everything you wanted to know about smart cities: the internet of things is the backbone. IEEE Consum. Electron. Mag. **5**, 60–70 (2016)
13. Sharma, M., Joshi, S., Kannan, D., Govindan, K., Singh, R., Purohit, H.C.: Internet of Things (IoT) adoption barriers of smart cities' waste management: an Indian context. J. Clean. Product. **270**, 122047 (2020)
14. Biswas, K., Muthukkumarasamy, V.: Securing smart cities using blockchain technology. In: 2016 IEEE 18th International Conference on High Performance Computing and Communications; IEEE 14th International Conference on Smart City; IEEE 2nd International Conference on Data Science and Systems (HPCC/SmartCity/DSS), pp. 1392–1393. IEEE (2016)
15. Farsi, M., Daneshkhah, A., Hosseinian-Far, A., Jahankhani, H.: Digital Twin Technologies and Smart Cities. Springer (2020)
16. Breslow, H.: The smart city and the containment of informality: the case of Dubai. Urban Stud. **58**, 471–486 (2021)
17. Bakıcı, T., Almirall, E., Wareham, J.: A smart city initiative: the case of Barcelona. J. knowl. Econ. **4**, 135–148 (2013)
18. Vidiasova, L., Cronemberger, F.: Discrepancies in perceptions of smart city initiatives in Saint Petersburg. Russ. Sustain. Cities Soc. **59**, 102158 (2020)
19. Hu, R.: The state of smart cities in China: the case of Shenzhen. Energies **12**, 4375 (2019)
20. Shah, J., Kothari, J., Doshi, N.: A survey of smart city infrastructure via case study on New York. Procedia Comput. Sci. **160**, 702–705 (2019)
21. Lai, C.S., et al.: A review of technical standards for smart cities. Clean Technol. **2**, 290–310 (2020)
22. Ministry of Housing and Urban-Rural Development of the People's Republic of China: In-terim Measures of National Pilot Smart Cities. http://www.mo-hurd.gov.cn/gongkai/fdzdgknr/tzgg/201212/20121204_212182.html
23. National Development and Reform Commission, Ministry of Industry and Information Technology of the People's Republic of China, Ministry of Science and Technology of the People's Republic of China, Ministry of Public Security of the People's Republic of China, Ministry of Finance of the People's Republic of China, Ministry of Land and Resources of the People's Republic of China, Ministry of Housing and Urban-Rural Development, Ministry of Transport of the People's Republic of China: Guidance on Promoting the Healthy Development of Smart Cities. http://www.cac.gov.cn/2014-08/27/c_1112850680.htm
24. China Smart Cities Market by ICT Components. https://secure.livechatinc.com/
25. About Wuzhen. http://www.wuzhenwic.org/2020-10/15/c_547687.htm
26. Wuzhen. https://en.wikipedia.org/w/index.php?title=Wuzhen&oldid=979461973
27. Overview of World Internet Conference. http://www.wuzhenwic.org/index.html
28. Zhejiang Issues First List of Best Applications for Digital Reform. https://www.zj.gov.cn/art/2021/11/3/art_1568565_59132153.html

29. The second batch of best applications for digital reform announced. https://www.zj.gov.cn/art/2021/12/24/art_1568565_59176796.html
30. Wuzhen tourism official website. http://en.wuzhen.com.cn/

Factors Affecting Users' Loyalty to Earthquake Early Warning Technology - An Example of Earthquake Early Warning App

Lili Liu, Aile Wang, Yimin Chen, Dongdong Guo, and Hao Tan(✉)

School of Design, Hunan University - Hunan University, Yuelushan, Changsha 410082, Hunan, People's Republic of China
htan@hnu.edu.cn

Abstract. This research has conducted an investigation of users' loyalty to earthquake early warning technology with the purpose of describing how different factors affect users' loyalty. This research is aimed at establishing a human-computer model of users' loyalty aforementioned with the example of an application (hereinafter referred to as APP) named "Earthquake Early Warning". Respondents (n = 332) were required to assess their loyalty to the APP in the research. Their answers which shall be analyzed are related to social stimuli, perceived usefulness, users' satisfaction and frequency of use so as to make sure influences of these factors on loyalty of respondents. The result has shown that influences of these factors on users' loyalty are various. The research suggests that social stimuli positively affect perceived usefulness which positively affects satisfaction and loyalty, and satisfaction and frequency of use positively affect loyalty. This investigation has emphasized the significance of taking into consideration different factors of users' loyalty in terms of earthquake early warning technology. Hence, this research has put forward a framework to assist relevant staff to enhance users' loyalty to earthquake early warning technology in different aspects and help users take right responses to a coming earthquake as soon as possible in order to maximize the effect of earthquake early warning technology and minimize casualties and economic losses.

Keywords: Loyalty · Perceived usefulness · Social stimulation · Satisfaction · Frequency of use · Earthquake early warning app

1 Introduction

Earthquakes are caused by movements within the Earth's crust and uppermost mantle. They range from events too weak to be detectable except by sensitive instrumentation, to sudden and violent events lasting many minutes which have caused some of the greatest disasters in human history. Earthquakes are a natural phenomenon in which the Earth's crust rapidly releases energy after a long period of gravitational action and produces seismic waves during the period. At present, there are two seismic belts around the

P.-L. P. Rau (Ed.): HCII 2022, LNCS 13314, pp. 383–403, 2022.
https://doi.org/10.1007/978-3-031-06053-3_27

world, namely the Circum-Pacific Seismic Belt and the Mediterranean-Himalayan Seismic Belt. Earthquakes have the following characteristics: high frequency, wide range, high intensity, shallow source and obvious regional differences and so on, which determine the severity and extensiveness of earthquakes. As many as 1.2 million people have died from earthquakes in the world since the 20th century, of which nearly 600,000 are in China, accounting for about a half of the casualties. In China, deaths caused by various natural disasters have been about 550,000, while deaths caused by earthquakes have been about 280,000 since the founding of the People's Republic of China.

When an earthquake occurs, the rapid assessment of its impact is essential for timely and appropriate emergency operations, such as securing people and crucial infrastructures exposed to serious damage [1]. Earthquake Early Warning (EEW) systems are timidly becoming operational in some areas of some seismic countries [2]. Earthquake early warning can be used to detect earthquakes and provide advance notices of strong shaking, enabling people to take responses in advance, which not only facilitates timely maintenance of infrastructure, but also reduces casualties. While EEW technology has matured, questions about who sends alerts and who is responsible for errors or omissions of detection limit the speed at which EEW can be widely open to the public. In addition, high costs of implementation and operation are an obstacle to the roll-out of EEW systems in both underdeveloped and developing countries. In parallel to EEW systems run by government agencies at the national level, the last decade has witnessed the development of unofficial platforms providing fast earthquake alerts at the global level. This was possibly thanks to smartphone technology and to the crowdsourcing model, with people making their smartphones available in order to receive a useful service in return [3]. In recent years, with the rapid development of the field related to smartphones, many things that could only be done on computers before can now be finished by mobile smartphones. The fully developed hardware configuration of smartphones plus the maturity and openness of operating systems have made it possible to use accelerometers in mobile phones to monitor seismic waves. According to a study by Becker Julia S., Potter Sally H. and Vinnell Lauren J., it is said that respondents preferred to receive earthquake warnings on their phones and be informed what responses to take [3].

Customer loyalty is considered to lead to repeated purchases, positive attitudes, intentions of continuing the affiliation and intentions of positive recommendations [4–8]. Based on the research aforementioned, it is certain that the public have a preference for earthquake early warning systems. This preference reinforces users' intention to continue using the Earthquake Early Warning APP. In addition, a large number of studies have investigated public perceptual satisfaction of the APP, but might lack investigations of the customer loyalty of the public for the APP, and did not make effective use of resources of the masses, which might undermine the competitiveness of the APP [9]. It is known that customer loyalty has three functions from a lot of literature: firstly, to motivate users to continue using the APP [10]; secondly, to be used as basic information to provide a reference for the design and construction of the APP [11–14]; thirdly, to improve users' satisfaction through design and construction [15]. At the same time, although the public are not so clear about the customer loyalty of the Earthquake Early Warning APP, there is evidence indicating that the public's understanding of related knowledge has a positive impact on promoting customer loyalty [16]. Customer loyalty is the basis for the updating and iteration of the APP. To enhance its customer loyalty is to improve the quality of system services of the APP and provide a foundation for improving future strategies [17]. When users of the APP use it, relevant information may crowd in. And the more frequently users use it, the more information they receive. It is unknown that whether this will affect the customer loyalty. Users' feedback on the usefulness and other functions may be mixed with praises and criticism according to users' experience and other reasons. Besides, the frequency of use affects how well users understand the APP, and therefore impacts the overall customer loyalty [18].

Few scholars focused on the customer loyalty to study which factors are the driving factors, and even fewer scholars used frequency and other factors to explain the influence of users' loyalty. The main purpose of this research is to construct and verify a conceptual framework with the Howard-Sheth Model and Technology Acceptance Model (TAM) as the theoretical basis combined with previous research. We try to explore the correlation among the determinants of users' loyalty of the Earthquake Early Warning APP, and study the complex relationships between four factors namely social stimuli, perceived usefulness, frequency of use, satisfaction and the customer loyalty with the methods of literature reviews and mathematical statistics with the purpose of conducting research related to the APP and provide theoretical guidance and data support for relevant enterprises to make operational adjustments.

In this study, we take the Earthquake Early Warning APP developed by the Institute of Care-Life (hereinafter referred to as ICL) as the research case. The APP applies the system of earthquake early warning technology developed by ICL which was established after the Wenchuan earthquake in 2008. Committed to research of earthquake early warning technology, ICL has used information and other resources of Wenchuan earthquake and the aftershocks, and initially mastered the core technology of earthquake early warning and rapid reporting of seismic intensity. And these technologies have been integrated into the system integrated with software and hardware it has developed as independent intellectual property rights of ICL. The system has passed the appraisal of scientific and technological achievements organized by the Department of Science and Technology affiliated with Sichuan Province in Beijing on September 2nd, 2012. At that time, the review experts believed that the system was advanced nationwide, and some technologies of it were leading and advanced ones at home and abroad. This is the first system of earthquake early warning technology in China that has passed the provincial appraisal of scientific and technological achievements. At present, the "System of Earthquake Early Warning Technology of ICL" is mainly used in the aftershock areas of the Wenchuan earthquake and the junction of Sichuan and Yunnan Province. In addition, the system has been preliminarily applied to some projects such as the construction of urban systems of earthquake early warning in Chengdu, the capital city of Sichuan Province and the City of Chuzhou in Anhui Province.

At present, there are more than ten types of software related to earthquake early warning in smartphones in China, but except the Earthquake Early Warning App of ICL, most of the other applications are not quite professional, and they obtain information of earthquake early warning through their connection to some official platforms on phones, which might cause some problems such as belated warnings and other errors. However, the App of ICL features a greater promotion, a wider range of application and a larger number of users. Before an earthquake really occurs, the APP will issue an alarm a few seconds ahead of its occurrence when the triggering conditions are reached. After earthquakes, we can upload the feedback of risk avoidance and other collected data related to the earthquakes and risks on the uploading page in order to launch accurate rescues. Meanwhile, we can learn about some knowledge of earthquakes, sounds of early warnings, and cases of earthquake early warnings on the science-popularized page of the APP. The ICL and the Department of Emergency Management (the former department of earthquake prevention and disaster reduction) jointly built a mainland network of earthquake early warning which extends to 31 provinces and municipalities in China, covering 90% of the population (about 660 million people) in China's seismic areas. Since 2011, the system has continuously warned of all destructive earthquakes (as of September 2019, a total of 53 times) within the network such as 7-magnitude earthquake in Lushan County, 6.5 earthquake in Ludian County, 7-magnitude earthquake in Jiuzhaigou Vally Scenic and Historic Interest Area, and 6-magnitude earthquake in Yibin City. Users have taken appropriate measures to avoid risks and reduce casualties and secondary disasters after receiving the early warnings.

Therefore, we take the earthquake early warning APP developed by the ICL as an example to study factors affecting the users' loyalty to earthquake early warning technology.

The rest of this article is as follows: the second part introduces the theoretical background and research hypotheses; the third part shows the research methodology, which is used to validate the proposed model and test hypotheses; and the next section displays the results of the study after analyzing relevant data. Eventually, this paper concludes with a discussion of the significance, and limitations of our study, and recommendations for future research.

2 Theoretical Background and Research Hypotheses

2.1 Background of Research

Although the importance of the customer loyalty has been recognized and there has been lots of research about it, there is still a lack of research on the customer loyalty of applications of disaster early warning. Since earthquake early warning systems are typically designed from technical perspectives, the benefits in this study could be driven from the Technology Acceptance Model (TAM model) used for understanding the adoption of technology-based initiatives [19]. Literature of safety-critical systems has acknowledged the importance of usefulness, with some theoretical and empirical studies on the usefulness of safety-critical systems [20]. The usage conditions of applications of disaster early warning are different from those of normal applications used on a daily basis [21], and at the same time, applications of disaster early warning may be used less frequently, with only a minority of people downloading smartphone applications for emergency responses (16%) [22]. What's more, when using those applications for emergency responses, users may be in a high-risk environment [23].Therefore, in the context of applications related to disaster early warning, it is necessary to develop related models of the customer loyalty and conduct empirical verifications to explore the relationship between customer loyalty and willingness of continuous use as well as the four factors affecting the customer loyalty.

Users' satisfaction and perceived usefulness of the system have been extensively studied as determinants of users' loyalty in the literature on the factors influencing users' loyalty [24]. Similarly, users' frequency of use and social stimuli are key factors in understanding the customer loyalty to earthquake early warning applications in the field of earthquake early warning [25].

After reviewing the relevant literature, it is found that few studies explored the impacts of social stimuli, perceived usefulness, satisfaction, and frequency of use on users' loyalty of the APP. In addition, previous studies have not centered on the complex interrelationships among these variables to conduct any investigation. Thus, this study will address these research gaps.

2.2 Conceptual Framework

Perceived usefulness is an important factor in measuring users' perceptions. Davis [26] defines perceptual usefulness as "the degree to which a person believes that using a particular system will improve his or her job performance". In general, we define users' satisfaction as an emotional condition to comprehensively evaluate all aspects of consumers' relationships. Customer loyalty is considered to lead to repeated purchases, positive attitudes, intentions of continuing the affiliation and intentions of positive recommendations [4–8]. It can be understood from the perspective of users' behaviors and attitudes. Research on users' loyalty can help measure users' willingness to continue using the APP. Since the models discussed are relatively sophisticated, we have also introduced the Howard-Sheth Model to help construct the theoretical models. Because reactions of social media and the public have a greater impact on self-perception responses in the case of disasters, the social stimuli at the time of early warning are considered as the input of the model.

2.3 Research Hypotheses

Figure 1 shows the model of users' loyalty to the APP. Attributes including social stimuli, frequency of use, perceived usefulness, and satisfaction are treated as independent variables, and users' loyalty is deemed as the dependent variable. The framework is based on the Howard-Sheth Model which includes three steps: inputting variables → intermediate architecture → outputting variables.

H1: social stimuli have a direct positive influence on perceived usefulness on earthquake early warning APP. Some studies have identified usefulness as a determinant that influences users' intention to continue use of the APP. For example, the study of consumers' engagement on applications of mobile phones conducted by Tarute and other researchers [27] has demonstrated that a positive view of usability promotes better engagement, which in turn increases willingness to continue use of applications. Similarly, research on hotel-booking apps by Ozturk et al. [28] also illustrates that improving usefulness will enhance users' perception of value, which in turn has a positive impact on the willingness to continue using the applications. Users' willingness to continue use of

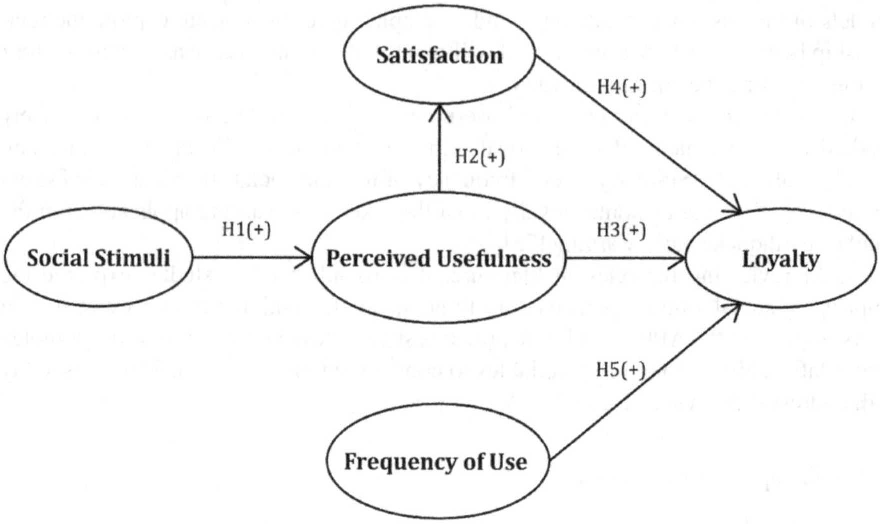

Fig. 1. Proposed Conceptual Model.

applications depends on their satisfaction with the usage and their perceived usefulness of continuous use of them [29].

From the above discussion, it is assumed that perceived usefulness directly affects users' satisfaction and loyalty, as shown below.

H2: Perceived usefulness has a direct positive influence on satisfaction on earthquake early warning APP.

H3: Perceived usefulness has a direct positive influence on loyalty on earthquake early warning APP.

Users' satisfaction plays a crucial role in the relationship between perceived value and the customer loyalty [30]. Many previous studies have identified the relationship between customer satisfaction and the customer loyalty in different contexts [31–34].

Therefore, it is assumed that satisfaction directly affects users' loyalty, as shown below.

H4: satisfaction has a direct positive influence on users' loyalty on earthquake early warning APP.

In the context of applications related to disaster early warning, we have considered the frequency of use as an important factor. Therefore, it is proposed that the frequency of use directly affects users' loyalty, as shown below.

H5: frequency of use has a direct positive influence on users' loyalty on earthquake early warning APP.

3 Research Methodology

3.1 Survey Design

Data for this study were collected from a structured, self-administered questionnaire based on a previously validated methodology was used to assess demographic characteristics, perceptions and users' satisfaction of the earthquake early warning app.

The questionnaire was designed in three sections:

The first section included two questions. The first question elicited information on user's experience of the earthquake. The second question elicited information on the usage frequency of the earthquake early warning app.

Based on our previous investigation of the factors affecting the adoption of the earthquake early warning app and a careful review of the existing literature [25] on adoption and frequency of use of the earthquake early warning app, we divide the key explanatory variables used in our final models to explain the variation in the frequency of use of the earthquake early warning app into four main groups. The key attributes of the four groups of individuals who have heard about the earthquake early warning app but never used it (non-users), those who used it before but do not plan to use it anymore(zero-frequency users), those who install the app but not constant concern notice (infrequent users), and those who install the app and often concern notice (more frequent users). Using this screening question, we screened people who had used the earthquake warning APP, using only survey data from people who had used the earthquake warning APP. An explanation of earthquake warning APP with examples was included at the first section of the questionnaire to make sure that the respondents have a clear idea of earthquake warning APP.

We adapted the measurement projects of relevant studies related to early warning in the human factors engineering literature [25]. All of the items (36) used a 5-point Likert scale ranging from 'strongly disagree' (1) to 'strongly agree' (5).

The third section of the questionnaire sought to determine the information regarding demographics including gender, age and region.

The questionnaire was anonymous.

3.2 Data Collection

Data were collected from November 2021 to December 2021, using online methods.

Through the online survey, 524 samples were obtained, of which 481 were valid, as 43 questionnaires were discarded as participants need not less than 30 s to complete the questionnaire. In the meantime, people who have not used the app were screened out. Accordingly, a total of 332 questionnaires were used for data analysis. Gender distribution was fairly uniform (156 participants were male, 176 female participants). Regarding the overall perceived satisfaction of all participants with the application, they were asked the same questions, namely their current opinions of the application.

3.3 Data Analysis

Due to the complexity of the proposed model, this study uses both the TAM and the Howard-Sheth Model as well as the correlation analysis and stepwise regression method to verify the hypotheses mentioned before.

Accordingly, SPSSAU was used to analyze the data.

The instrument's "Reliability" was established through Analysis of Cronbach's reliability and the instrument's "Validity" was established through KMO test and Bartlett Spherical Test. [35].

4 Results

Through the questionnaire, we collected 332 valid respondents as a sample (Table 1).

4.1 Reliability and Validity Analysis

Table 1. Cronbach's reliability analysis

Number of items	Sample size	Cronbach alpha coefficient
12	332	0.856

As can be seen from the above table: the reliability coefficient value is 0.856, which is greater than 0.8, thus indicating that the study data are of high reliability quality and can be used for further analysis (Table 2).

Table 2. KMO and Bartlett's test

KMO value		0.901
Bartlett sphericity test	Approximate cardinality	1291.410
	df	66
	p value	0.000

The validity was verified using KMO and Bartlett's test, as seen in the table above: the KMO value is 0.901, the KMO value is greater than 0.8, and the study data is very suitable for extracting information (a good validity from the side response).

4.2 Profile of Respondents

The results of this study followed a step-by-step procedure for data analysis. The descriptive analysis provided demographic information of respondents.

Table 3. Profile of respondents (n = 332).

Name	Option	Frequency	Percentage (%)	Cumulative percentage (%)
Gender	Male	156	46.99	46.99
	Female	176	53.01	100.00
Age range	20 years old and below	40	12.05	12.05
	20–30	117	35.24	47.29
	31–40	113	34.04	81.33
	41–50	48	14.46	95.78
	50 years old and above	14	4.22	100.00
Any earthquake experience	Yes	231	69.58	69.58
	No	101	30.42	100.00
Total		332	100.0	100.0

Table 3 presents the demographic information of the respondents in terms of gender, age, and whether they have experienced earthquakes or not. There were slightly more female respondents than male, 53.01%, compared to 46.99% male respondents. In terms of age, the sample had a relatively high proportion of "20–30" respondents, with 35.24%. The proportion of the 31–40 sample was 34.04%.

In addition to the demographic information, the study also asked the respondents if they had ever experienced an earthquake. From the above table, the highest percentage of "experienced an earthquake" was 69.58%. The percentage of those who had not experienced an earthquake was 30.42%.

4.3 Evaluation of Path Relationship

The path relationship is reviewed by the stepwise regression method. First of all, the R Square(R^2) of the model fitting condition is analyzed, and then the VIF value could be analyzed (to determine multicollinearity); secondly, the significance of X is analyzed, and if it is significant, it indicates that X has an influence on Y, and then the concrete direction of the influence shall be analyzed [35].

4.4 Hypothesis 1: Social Stimuli Positively Influences Perceived Usefulness

A stepwise regression method was used to test the hypothesis that the higher the social stimulus, the higher the perceived usefulness of the earthquake warning app. Perceived usefulness is the outcome variable and social stimulus is the predictor variable.

Perceived usefulness was assessed by 3 items: I think the earthquake warning app is an effective warning tool; I would find the frequency of warning messages in the earthquake warning app appropriate; and I think the alerts in the earthquake warning app are useful.

Social stimulation was assessed by 2 items: other people's reactions to earthquake warnings influenced my reactions; social media influenced my reactions to earthquake warnings (Table 4).

Table 4. Results of stepwise regression analysis (n = 332) for hypothesis 1

	Unstandardized coefficient		Standardized coefficient	t	p	VIF	R^2	AdjustedR^2	F
	B	Standard error	Beta						
Constant	3.089	0.123	-	25.037	0.000**	-			
Social stimuli	0.114	0.033	0.189	3.493	0.001**	1.000	0.036	0.033	F (1,330)=12.199,p=0.001

Dependent variable: perceived usefulness

D-W value: 1.708

* p<0.05 ** p<0.01

Social stimuli were used as independent variables, while perceived usefulness was used as dependent variable for stepwise regression analysis, and after automatic identification of the model, a total of 1 item of social stimuli was finally left in the model, and the model formula was: perceived usefulness = 3.089 + 0.114*social stimuli, with an R-squared value of 0.036, implying that social stimuli could explain 3.6% of the cause of change in perceived usefulness. Moreover, the model passed the F-test ($F = 12.199$, $p = 0.001 < 0.05$), indicating that the model is valid. In addition, the test for multiple cointegrations of the model found that all the VIF values in the model were less than 5, implying that there was no cointegration problem; and the D-W value was around the number 2, thus indicating that there was no autocorrelation in the model, and there was no correlation between the sample data, and the model was better. The final specific analysis shows that.

The value of the regression coefficient for social stimuli is 0.114 ($t = 3.493$, $p = 0.001 < 0.01$), implying that social stimuli can have a significant positive relationship with perceived usefulness.

Summarizing the analysis, it can be seen that: social stimuli can have a significant positive influence relationship on perceived usefulness.

4.5 Hypothesis 2: Perceived Usefulness Positively Influences Satisfaction

Stepwise regression was used to test the hypothesis that the higher the perceived usefulness of the earthquake warning app, the higher the user satisfaction. Satisfaction is the outcome variable and perceived usefulness is the predictor variable.

Satisfaction is assessed by 2 items: the information I receive from the earthquake warning app increases my sense of urgency; and installing the earthquake warning app makes me feel safer (Table 5).

Table 5. Results of stepwise regression analysis (n = 332) for hypothesis 2

	Unstandardized coefficient		Standardized coefficient	t	p	VIF	R^2	AdjustedR^2	F
	B	Standard error	Beta						
Constant	1.226	0.244	-	5.029	0.000**	-			
Perceived usefulness	0.722	0.069	0.501	10.526	0.000**	1.000	0.251	0.249	F (1,330)=110.807,p=0.000

Dependent variable: satisfaction

D-W value: 2.071

* p<0.05 ** p<0.01

Perceived usefulness was used as the independent variable, while satisfaction was used as the dependent variable for stepwise regression analysis, and after automatic identification of the model, a total of one term of perceived usefulness was finally left in the model, and the model formula was: satisfaction = 1.226 + 0.722*perceived usefulness, with an R-squared value of 0.251, implying that perceived usefulness could explain 25.1% of the causes of change in satisfaction. Moreover, the model passed the F-test (F = 110.807, p = 0.000 < 0.05), indicating that the model is valid. In addition, the test for multiple cointegrations of the model found that all the VIF values in the model were less than 5, implying that there was no cointegration problem; and the D-W value was around the number 2, thus indicating that there was no autocorrelation in the model, and there was no correlation between the sample data, and the model was better. The final specific analysis shows that.

The regression coefficient value of perceived usefulness is 0.722 (t = 10.526, p = 0.000 < 0.01), which means that perceived usefulness has a significant positive relationship with satisfaction.

Summarizing the analysis, it is clear that perceived usefulness will have a significant positive influence relationship on satisfaction.

4.6 Hypothesis 3: Perceived Usefulness Positively Influences Loyalty

Stepwise regression was used to test the hypothesis that the higher the perceived usefulness of the earthquake warning app, the higher the loyalty of users. Loyalty is the outcome variable and perceived usefulness is the predictor variable.

Loyalty was assessed by five items: I like the earthquake warning app; I would take the alerts from the earthquake warning app seriously; I tend to use the earthquake warning app; the earthquake warning app was developed by the Chengdu High-Tech Institute of Disaster Reduction, and I would like to learn more about the earthquake warning program provided by the institute; I would change my plan if I received an alert from the earthquake warning app (Table 6).

Table 6. Results of stepwise regression analysis (n = 332) for hypothesis 3

	Unstandardized coefficient		Standardized coefficient	t	p	VIF	R^2	AdjustedR^2	F
	B	Standard error	Beta						
Constant	0.878	0.172	-	5.104	0.000**	-			
Perceived usefulness	0.819	0.048	0.682	16.944	0.000**	1.000	0.465	0.464	F (1,330)=287.088,p=0.000

Dependent variable: loyalty

D-W value: 1.818

* p<0.05 ** p<0.01

Perceived usefulness was used as the independent variable, while loyalty was used as the dependent variable for stepwise regression analysis, and after automatic identification of the model, a total of one item of perceived usefulness was finally left in the model, and the model formula was: loyalty = 0.878 + 0.819*perceived usefulness with an R-squared value of 0.465, which means that perceived usefulness can explain 46.5% of the reasons for the change in loyalty. Moreover, the model passed the F-test ($F = 287.088$, $p = 0.000 < 0.05$), indicating that the model is valid. In addition, the test for multiple cointegrations of the model found that all the VIF values in the model were less than 5, implying that there was no cointegration problem; and the D-W value was around the number 2, thus indicating that there was no autocorrelation in the model, and there was no correlation between the sample data, and the model was better. The final specific analysis shows that. The regression coefficient value of perceived usefulness is 0.819 ($t = 16.944$, $p = 0.000 < 0.01$), which means that perceived usefulness will have a significant positive relationship with loyalty.

Summarizing the analysis, it is clear that perceived usefulness can have a significant positive influence relationship on loyalty.

4.7 Hypothesis 4: Satisfaction Positively Influences Loyalty

Stepwise regression was used to test the hypothesis that the higher the user's satisfaction with the earthquake warning app, the higher the user's loyalty. Loyalty is the outcome variable and satisfaction is the predictor variable (Table 7).

Table 7. Results of stepwise regression analysis (n = 332) for hypothesis 4

	Unstandardized coefficient		Standardized coefficient	t	p	VIF	R^2	AdjustedR^2	F
	B	Standard error	Beta						
Constant	1.636	0.131	-	12.517	0.000**	-	0.455	0.453	F (1,330)=275.279,p=0.000
Satisfaction	0.563	0.034	0.674	16.592	0.000**	1.000			

Dependent variable: loyalty

D-W value: 1.920

* p<0.05 ** p<0.01

Satisfaction was used as the independent variable, while loyalty was used as the dependent variable for stepwise regression analysis, and after automatic identification of the model, a total of 1 item of satisfaction was finally left in the model, and the model formula was: loyalty = 1.636 + 0.563*satisfaction, with an R-squared value of 0.455, which means that satisfaction can explain 45.5% of the reasons for the change in loyalty. Moreover, the model passed the F-test ($F = 275.279$, $p = 0.000 < 0.05$), indicating that the model is valid. In addition, the test for multiple cointegrations of the model found that all the VIF values in the model were less than 5, implying that there was no cointegration problem; and the D-W value was around the number 2, thus indicating that there was no autocorrelation in the model, and there was no correlation between the sample data, and the model was better. The final specific analysis shows that.

The value of regression coefficient of satisfaction is 0.563 ($t = 16.592$, $p = 0.000 < 0.01$), which means that satisfaction will have a significant positive influence relationship on loyalty.

Summarizing the analysis, it can be seen that: satisfaction will have a significant positive influence relationship on loyalty.

4.8 Hypothesis 5: Frequency of Use Positively Influences Loyalty

Stepwise regression was used to test the hypothesis that the more frequently users use the earthquake warning app, the more loyal users will be. Loyalty is the outcome variable and frequency of use is the predictor variable (Table 8).

Table 8. Results of stepwise regression analysis (n = 332) for hypothesis 5

	Unstandardized coefficient		Standardized coefficient	t	p	VIF	R^2	AdjustedR^2	F
	B	Standard error	Beta						
Constant	3.531	0.108	-	32.674	0.000**	-	0.014	0.011	F (1,330)=4.700,p=0.031
Frequency of use	0.110	0.051	0.119	2.168	0.031*	1.000			

Dependent variable: loyalty

D-W value: 1.905

* p<0.05 ** p<0.01

Using frequency of use as the independent variable and loyalty as the dependent variable for stepwise regression analysis, after automatic identification of the model, a total of 1 term of frequency of use was finally left in the model, and the model formula was: loyalty = 3.531 + 0.110*frequency of use, with an R-squared value of 0.014, implying that frequency of use could explain 1.4% of the reasons for the change in loyalty. Moreover, the model passed the F-test ($F = 4.700$, $p = 0.031 < 0.05$), indicating that the model is valid. In addition, the test for multiple cointegrations of the model found that all the VIF values in the model were less than 5, implying that there was no cointegration problem; and the D-W value was around the number 2, thus indicating that there was no autocorrelation in the model, and there was no correlation between the sample data, and the model was better. The final specific analysis shows that.

The regression coefficient value of frequency of use is 0.110 ($t = 2.168$, $p = 0.031 < 0.05$), which means that frequency of use has a significant positive relationship with loyalty.

Summarizing the analysis, it can be seen that: frequency of use will have a significant positive influence relationship on loyalty.

5 Discussion

5.1 Theoretical Implications

This study explored the determinants of loyalty to the Earthquake Early Warning APP, which has not been adequately studied in the related literature. The relational model was examined by data obtained from a questionnaire for the APP. A conceptual framework representing direct and indirect relationships between five constructs namely social stimulation, perceived usefulness, users' satisfaction, frequency of use, and users' loyalty was validated. The framework helps to understand the formation of user loyalty to the earthquake warning app under the influence of safety and technology-related factors. It is important to explore the factors that influence the customer loyalty of applications of earthquake early warning, especially in China, where these applications are considered to be a powerful tool in the current earthquake early warning system that enables people to avoid disasters.

Three factors, including perceived usefulness, frequency of use, and satisfaction, have a direct impact on the loyalty of earthquake warning app users. In addition, the results of the study also showed that users' perceived usefulness of the earthquake warning app was higher if they were more influenced by others or social media. For example, users can browse information about the earthquake warning app from social media. In this study, perceived usefulness is an important factor that influences users' loyalty. In addition, the perceived usefulness of the earthquake warning app may satisfy users. In fact, the perceived usefulness of the earthquake warning app, such as sending effective warning messages and having the right frequency of warnings, contributed to the satisfaction of the riders, which in turn made them willing to continue using the earthquake warning app, rate the earthquake warning app positively, or recommend the earthquake warning app to their friends. Overall, this study still emphasized the importance of effective warnings. In addition to factors related to frequency of use and social stimulation (Tables 9, 10, 11, 12 and 13).

Table 9. Pearson correlation between Social stimuli and Perceived usefulness

	Perceived usefulness
Social stimuli	0.189**

$* p < 0.05$ $** p < 0.01$

Table 10. Pearson correlation between Perceived usefulness and Satisfaction

	Satisfaction
Perceived usefulness	0.501**

$* p < 0.05$ $** p < 0.01$

Table 11. Pearson correlation between Frequency of use and Loyalty

	Loyalty
Frequency of use	0.119*

$* p < 0.05$ $** p < 0.01$

Table 12. Pearson correlation between Satisfaction and Loyalty

	Loyalty
Satisfaction	0.674**

$* p < 0.05$ $** p < 0.01$

Table 13. Pearson correlation between Perceived usefulness and Loyalty

	Loyalty
Perceived usefulness	0.682**

* $p < 0.05$ ** $p < 0.01$

Based on the results of the correlation analysis, perceived usefulness was found to have the highest impact on users' loyalty (correlation coefficient of 0.682). Consistent with previous research in the field of disaster apps, this study affirms app dependability as a usability factor in the disaster apps' context.

This is followed by satisfaction (correlation coefficient of 0.674), while frequency of use has the least effect on loyalty (correlation coefficient of 0.119).

It is undeniable that people will be loyal to an earthquake warning app if they are satisfied with it. More importantly, the findings suggest that satisfaction plays a mediating role in the relationship between the two factors mentioned above, including perceived usefulness and loyalty. This study provides preliminary insight into the indirect relationships among these constructs and provides a basis for understanding the complex formation of loyalty to the earthquake warning app. Since perceived usefulness has a direct effect on satisfaction, perceived usefulness needs to be increased in order to improve users' loyalty.

5.2 Practical Significance (Recommendations Based on Theoretical Suggestions)

From the perspective of practice, the study has proposed and verified the determinants of improving the users' loyalty to the Earthquake Early Warning APP, including three positive and direct factors namely perceived usefulness, satisfaction and frequency of use, and a positive and indirect factor--social stimulation. Therefore, it is recommended that the ICL focuses on these four aspects to improve the use of the APP.

According to the study [24], there are three factors having the greatest impact on users' perceived usefulness: whether the Earthquake Early Warning APP is effective; whether its early warning information frequency is appropriate; and whether the reminder is useful. Therefore, it is suggested that developers always monitor the service status of the APP to ensure timely updates and maintenance. In addition, it is recommended that developers conduct multiple tests before the APP is listed into market to improve the accuracy of earthquake early warning, and study how to keep the information frequency within an appropriate range. Our research points out that perceived usefulness positively affects the customer loyalty, so it is recommended that developers focus on improving perceived usefulness.

At a time when the Earthquake Early Warning System is gradually becoming more widely used, if developers hope to attract more users to use the APP, they should also focus on other aspects in addition to improving the quality of service. The study has pointed out that social stimuli positively affect perceived usefulness, which shows that the perceived usefulness is correspondingly increased when responses to earthquake early warning of other people or social media affect users' responses. Therefore, it is also a sound strategy to increase the positive publicity of the earthquake early warning APP in the aspect of social media, and at the same time, it is advisable to organize the promotion of the APP on a community basis and hold practice or exercises for disaster prevention and mitigation [37, 38].

Our research points out that to increase users' loyalty to the APP, it is also necessary to improve users' satisfaction. Some studies [24] show that two factors have the greatest positive impact on users' satisfaction: whether the information received from the APP increases users' sense of urgency and whether the installation of it on smartphones will make users feel safer. Therefore, it is recommended that developers carefully consider the content of early warning information, and the information should increase users' sense of urgency. At the same time, after users install the APP, there shall be an appropriate reminder to make them feel that they are protected by the APP with a great sense of safety [39]. Finally, our research points out that to increase users' loyalty to the APP, it is also a necessity to increase the users' frequency of use. The higher the frequency of use is, the more information users will receive, and their understanding of the APP will be much deeper. How to increase the frequency of use of users is also a significant issue that developers need to consider.

The earthquake early warning system can quickly assess seismic elements and issue early warnings to the seismic areas to avoid casualties and property losses. The main significance of earthquake early warning is to provide more time for people to avoid danger. After earthquakes, the average time for a house to go from the start of shaking to collapse is about 12 s. With the early warning system, the time for early warning has risen, and the time for judgment and decision is reduced, while the time of risk avoidance is greatly increased.

Although the time for early warning of earthquakes is short, the accuracy rate is high, and China has begun to attach importance to the role of earthquake early warning systems in earthquake prevention and disaster reduction. If an early warning is issued a few seconds before an earthquake, theoretically, people can also do a lot of things to help themselves, and make different countermeasures according to different conditions of local situations. However, the success or failure of earthquake early warning is largely reflected in the speed and attitude of the public towards it. At present, the masses in China are not vigilant enough for the information of the earthquake early warning system, and after the earthquake early warning APP issues an early warning, users fail to save themselves immediately, which wastes valuable time for early warning. According to previous studies, the public has satisfaction and expectations for earthquake early warning systems. However, after reviewing relevant literature, it is found that this study explores for the first time the interrelationship among the determinants of the customer loyalty to the earthquake early warning APP, and the complex relationship between two factors including perceived usefulness, frequency of use and customer loyalty. The study has shown that the following five aspects determine users' loyalty: whether users like the APP; whether they will take its alarm seriously; whether they want to learn about its developer; whether they will change their plans because of alarms released by the APP; whether they tend to use the APP. We hope to find out factors that increase users' loyalty to earthquake early warning technology, and then improve the APP so as to enhance the public's trust in the APP, encourage them to open permissions in their smartphones to the APP, and promote their beliefs in information related to earthquake early warning of the APP. Meanwhile, we also hope that the public's vigilance to information related to earthquake early warning of the APP could be enhanced by increasing the perceived value of the APP so that they pay attention to the information in a timely manner and make responses as soon as possible, and that the early warning function of the APP could be improved to ensure that the public receives the information in a timely manner.

In line with the 17 Sustainable Development Goals proposed by the United Nations, the eleventh goal of which is to build inclusive, safe, sustainable cities and residence areas that have the capacity of resisting disasters, and significantly increase the number of integrated policies and plans adopted and implemented to build inclusive, resource-efficient and resilient cities and human residence areas which can mitigate and adapt to climate change and have the capacity of resisting against disasters by 2020, and establish and implement comprehensive management of disasters and risks at all levels in accordance with the *Sendai Framework for Disaster Risk Reduction from 2015 to 2030* [40]. Earthquakes always cause casualties and economic losses, and thus earthquake early warning technology came into being. The link between people and technology is also very vital, and if we can better respond to it when receiving earthquake early warning, then the work of earthquake prevention and disaster relief will also be more effective.

6 Conclusion

The investigation showed that different factors such as social stimuli, perceived usefulness, frequency of use, and satisfaction affect users' loyalty to earthquake early warning technology. This study also shows that users' loyalty to earthquake warning technology depends on a variety of factors, some of which can be expected and considered at the initial stages of designs. Taking into consideration the users' loyalty that affects the earthquake early warning technologies is one way to guide design decisions toward more effective solutions.

This study aims at exploring how factors such as social stimuli, perceived usefulness, frequency of use, and satisfaction affect users' loyalty to earthquake early warning technologies. As a result, models originally designed to assess the tendency of customer loyalty have also proven to be an effective tool. Factors that are easy to consider, such as social stimuli, perceived usefulness, frequency of use, and satisfaction, can provide insight into creating earthquake early warning technologies with high loyalty.

However, the research results and framework advanced herein are just the initial efforts towards this end, and its insights shall be used to guide further investigations.

Limitations

The results of this study are mainly from online surveys, and there is a lack of offline experimental data. Besides, some of the theoretical models referenced in this study are applicable to commercial scenarios, but the earthquake early warning application selected in this study are not conventional and commercial ones and the use scenarios of it are different. Hence, this causes certain limitations.

Due to the particularity of earthquake early warning technology, the dimensional measurement of various factors affecting users' loyalty in this study draws on conventional applications and thus has certain limitations.

Recommendations for Future Research
The methodology adopted by this study is effective in generating understanding or insights into HCI literature and practice. Therefore, the first recommendation for future research is to conduct research on users' loyalty to earthquake early warning technology with the ways of online and offline, using other related applications as examples. Additionally, generally there is a lack of information on earthquake early warning in the HCI literature, which shall be should be given more considerations. Finally, more efforts should be put into creating tools to assist in the development of earthquake early warning systems with high loyalty and to bridge the gap between research and practice on users' loyalty to the technology.

References

1. Colombelli, S., Carotenuto, F., Elia, L., Zollo, A.: Design and implementation of a mobile device app for network-based earthquake early warning systems (EEWSs): application to the PRESTo EEWS in southern Italy. Nat. Hazard. **20**(4), 921–931 (2020). https://doi.org/10.5194/nhess-20-921-2020
2. Cremen, G., Galasso, C.: Earthquake early warning: recent advances and perspectives. Earth Sci. Rev. **205**, 103184 (2020). https://doi.org/10.1016/j.earscirev.2020.103184
3. Finazzi, F.: The earthquake network project: a platform for earthquake early warning, rapid impact assessment, and search and rescue Front. Earth Sci. **8** (2020).https://doi.org/10.3389/feart.2020.00243
4. Jinkai, L.: Discussion and solutions of two main Problems restricting the development of earthquake early warning technology in China. South China Earthq. **37**(03), 90–97 (2017)
5. Oliver, R.L.: Whence consumer loyalty? J. Mark. **63**, 33 (1999). https://doi.org/10.2307/1252099
6. Zeithaml, V.A., Berry, L.L., Parasuraman, A.: The behavioral consequences of service quality. J. Mark. **60**(2), 31 (1996). https://doi.org/10.2307/1251929
7. Bowen, J.T., Chen, S.: The relationship between customer loyalty and customer satisfaction. Int. J. Contemp. Hosp. Manag. **13**(5), 213–217 (2001). https://doi.org/10.1108/09596110110395893
8. Zins, A.H.: Relative attitudes and commitment in customer loyalty models. Int. J. Serv. Ind. Manag. **12**(3), 269–294 (2001). https://doi.org/10.1108/eum0000000005521
9. Davis-Sramek, B., Mentzer, J.T., Stank, T.P.: Creating consumer durable retailer customer loyalty through order fulfillment service operations. J. Oper. Manage. **26**(6), 781–797 (2007).https://doi.org/10.1016/j.jom.2007.07.001
10. Chen, C., Chen, S., Lee, H., Tsai, T.: Exploring destination resources and competitiveness–a comparative analysis of tourists' perceptions and satisfaction toward an island of Taiwan. Ocean Coast. Manag. **119**, 58–67 (2016). https://doi.org/10.1016/j.ocecoaman.2015.09.013
11. Cho, J.: The impact of post-adoption beliefs on the continued use of health apps. Int. J. Med. Inform. **87**, 75–83 (2016). https://doi.org/10.1016/j.ijmedinf.2015.12.016
12. Oravec, G.J., Artino, A.R., Hickey, P.W.: Active-duty physicians' perceptions and satisfaction with humanitarian assistance and disaster relief missions: Implications for the Field. PLoS One **8**(3) (2013). https://doi.org/10.1371/journal.pone.0057814

13. Lee, H.-S., Shepley, M., Huang, C.-S.: Evaluation of off-leash dog parks in Texas and Florida: a study of use patterns, user satisfaction, and perception. Landsc. Urban Plan. **92**(3–4), 314–324 (2009). https://doi.org/10.1016/j.landurbplan.2009.05.015
14. Delpla, I., Legay, C., Proulx, F., Rodriguez, M.J.: Perception of tap water quality: assessment of the factors modifying the links between satisfaction and water consumption behavior. Sci. Total Environ. **722**, 137786 (2020). https://doi.org/10.1016/j.scitotenv.2020.137786
15. Jose, J., Shukili, M.N.A., Jimmy, B.: Public's perception and satisfaction on the roles and services provided by pharmacists – cross sectional survey in Sultanate of Oman. Saudi Pharmaceut. J. **23**(6), 635–641 (2015). https://doi.org/10.1016/j.jsps.2015.02.003
16. Gerstenberg, T., Hofmann, M.: Perception and preference of trees: a psychological contribution to tree species selection in urban areas. Urban Forestr. Urban Greening **15**, 103–111 (2016). https://doi.org/10.1016/j.ufug.2015.12.004
17. Deng, L., Cai, L., Sun, F., Li, G., Che, Y.: Public attitudes towards microplastics: perceptions, behaviors and policy implications. Resour. Conserv. Recycl. **163**, 105096 (2020). https://doi.org/10.1016/j.resconrec.2020.105096
18. Park, J., et al.: Analysis on public perception, user-satisfaction, and publicity for WEEE collecting system in South Korea: a case study for Door-to-Door Service. Resour. Conserv. Recycl. **144**, 90–99 (2019). https://doi.org/10.1016/j.resconrec.2019.01.018
19. Attwood, S., Parke, H., Larsen, J., Morton, K.L.: Using a mobile health application to reduce alcohol consumption: a mixed-methods evaluation of the drinkaware track & calculate units application. BMC Public Health **17**(1) (2017). https://doi.org/10.1186/s12889-017-4358-9
20. Legris, P., Ingham, J., Collerette, P.: Why do people use information technology? A critical review of the technology acceptance model. Informat. Manage. **40**(3), 191–204 (2003). https://doi.org/10.1016/s0378-7206(01)00143-4
21. Kwee-Meier, S.T., Wiessmann, M., Mertens, A.: Integrated Information Visualization and Usability of User Interfaces for Safety-Critical Contexts. Lecture Notes in Computer Science, pp. 71–85 (2017). https://doi.org/10.1007/978-3-319-58475-1_6
22. Tan, M.L., Prasanna, R., Stock, K., Doyle, E.E., Leonard, G., Johnston, D.: Understanding end-users' perspectives: towards developing usability guidelines for disaster apps. Progress Disas. Sci. **7**, 100118 (2020). https://doi.org/10.1016/j.pdisas.2020.100118
23. Reuter, C., Kaufhold, M.-A., Spielhofer, T., Hahne, A.S.: Social media in emergencies. In: Proceedings of the ACM on Human-Computer Interaction, vol. 1(CSCW), pp. 1–19 (2017). https://doi.org/10.1145/3134725
24. Sarshar, P., Nunavath, V., Radianti, J.: On the usability of smartphone apps in emergencies. In: Kurosu, M. (ed.) HCI 2015. LNCS, vol. 9170, pp. 765–774. Springer, Cham (2015). https://doi.org/10.1007/978-3-319-20916-6_70
25. Nguyen-Phuoc, D.Q., Su, D.N., Tran, P.T., Le, D.T., Johnson, L.W.: Factors influencing customer's loyalty towards ride-hailing taxi services – a case study of Vietnam. Transp. Res. Part A: Policy Pract. **134**, 96–112 (2020). https://doi.org/10.1016/j.tra.2020.02.008
26. Kopel, D.E., Sims, V.K., Chin, M.G.: Taking emergency warnings seriously. Proceed. Hum. Fact. Ergonom. Soc. Ann. Meet. **58**(1), 1129–1133 (2014). https://doi.org/10.1177/1541931214581236
27. Davis, F.D.: Perceived usefulness, perceived ease of use, and user acceptance of information technology. MIS Q. **13**(3), 319 (1989). https://doi.org/10.2307/249008
28. Tarute, A., Nikou, S., Gatautis, R.: Mobile application driven consumer engagement. Telematics Inform. **34**(4), 145–156 (2017). https://doi.org/10.1016/j.tele.2017.01.006
29. Ozturk, A.B., Nusair, K., Okumus, F., Hua, N.: The role of utilitarian and hedonic values on users' continued usage intention in a mobile hotel booking environment. Int. J. Hosp. Manag. **57**, 106–115 (2016). https://doi.org/10.1016/j.ijhm.2016.06.007
30. Bhattacherjee, A.: Understanding information systems continuance: an expectation-confirmation model. MIS Q. **25**(3), 351 (2001). https://doi.org/10.2307/3250921

31. Lin, H.-H., Wang, Y.-S.: An examination of the determinants of customer loyalty in mobile commerce contexts. Inform. Manage. **43**(3), 271–282 (2006). https://doi.org/10.1016/j.im.2005.08.001
32. Oliver, R.L.: A cognitive model of the antecedents and consequences of satisfaction decisions. J. Mark. Res. **17**(4), 460 (1980). https://doi.org/10.2307/3150499
33. Cronin, J.J., Taylor, S.A.: Measuring service quality: a reexamination and extension. J. Mark. **56**(3), 55 (1992). https://doi.org/10.2307/1252296
34. Fornell, C.: A national customer satisfaction barometer: the swedish experience. J. Mark. **56**(1), 6 (1992). https://doi.org/10.2307/1252129
35. Hellier, P.K., Geursen, G.M., Carr, R.A., Rickard, J.A.: Customer repurchase intention. Eur. J. Mark. **37**(11/12), 1762–1800 (2003). https://doi.org/10.1108/03090560310495456
36. Eisinga, R., te Grotenhuis, M., Pelzer, B.: The reliability of a two-item scale: Pearson, Cronbach, or Spearman-Brown? Int. J. Public Health **58**(4), 637–642 (2012). https://doi.org/10.1007/s00038-012-0416-3
37. Sun, D.: Selection of the linear regression model according to the parameter estimation. Wuhan Univ. J. Nat. Sci. **5**(4), 400–405 (2000). https://doi.org/10.1007/bf02850764
38. Macherera, M., Chimbari, M.J.: A review of studies on community based early warning systems. Jàmbá: J. Dis. Risk Stud. **8**(1) (2016). https://doi.org/10.4102/jamba.v8i1.206
39. Baudoin, M.-A., Henly-Shepard, S., Fernando, N., Sitati, A., Zommers, Z.: From top-down to "community-centric" approaches to early warning systems: exploring pathways to improve disaster risk reduction through community participation. Int. J. Dis. Risk Sci. **7**(2), 163–174 (2016).https://doi.org/10.1007/s13753-016-0085-6
40. Strahan, E.J.: Enhancing the effectiveness of tobacco package warning labels: a social psychological perspective. Tob. Control **11**(3), 183–190 (2002). https://doi.org/10.1136/tc.11.3.183
41. Sendai Framework for Disaster Risk Reduction 2015–2030. (n.d.). Human Rights Documents Online. https://doi.org/10.1163/2210-7975_hrd-9813-2015016

Research on Ecological Design Strategies of Smart City Refined Governance--Taking Xunsi River as an Example

Yiming Ma, Mengke Lu, and Yangshuo Zheng(✉)

Wuhan University of Technology, 430000, Wuhan, People's Republic of China
925992146@qq.com

Abstract. As a level of smart city construction, ecological environment plays an important role. This article takes the campus river pollution control in the construction of a smart city as an example to study the ecological design strategy. It aims to discover the limitations of current river monitoring and governance methods by analyzing the current situation and governance methods of the Xunsi River, and propose a future smart city river water quality monitoring system, combining blockchain technology with the monitoring system, and using blockchain Technology makes monitoring data open and transparent, and strengthens the supervision of river ecological protection by the government and other relevant departments. At the same time, with the help of data visualization design, people's attention to water resources and environmental protection are enhanced, and people are encouraged to actively participate in the action of protecting rivers, so as to jointly build green and harmonious communities and promote the sustainable development of smart cities in the future.

Keywords: Smart city · Blockchain technology · Water quality monitoring system · Data visualization · Ecological design

1 Design Object

1.1 The Current Situation of Xunsi River

At present, rivers in large and medium cities in my country generally suffer from various degrees of river siltation and black and odorous water quality. Among them, the Xunsi River in Wuhan City is the river that the government currently focuses on. Although the water quality has been improved to a certain extent after many treatments, it still exists Many problems. The Xunsi River is located at the southern end of the urban area of Wuhan, with a total length of 16 km. It flows through the three districts of Jiangxia, Hongshan and Wuchang in Wuhan and joins the Yangtze River. It passes through Hubei University of Technology, Wuchang Shouyi College and other universities. In the 50's, the patrol division river water quality is good, clear and transparent [1]; to the 70's, the water quality began to deteriorate, becoming the largest city of Wuhan sewage in open channels [2]; 1995 years after the patrol division river turned into a smelly river. A large

P.-L. P. Rau (Ed.): HCII 2022, LNCS 13314, pp. 404–416, 2022.
https://doi.org/10.1007/978-3-031-06053-3_28

amount of domestic sewage produced by nearby residents was discharged into the Xunsi River, directly causing river water pollution. As the "school river " of Hubei University of Technology, Xunsi River runs through the entire campus and is closely connected with the daily study and life of teachers and students. The current governance of Xunsi River is a common concern of the government and schools. After several years of remediation, the water quality of Xunsi River still has not reached the standard, which has a greater impact on the health of surrounding residents.

1.2 Governance Approach

Wuhan has recently implemented a strict lake protection system, setting a "high-voltage line" for lake protection, implementing the 20- character policy of "locking the shoreline, comprehensively intercepting pollution, returning the lake to the people, one lake and one scene, connecting the rivers and lakes", and introduced the " More than 20 local regulations on lake protection and management, including the Wuhan Lake Protection Regulations, the Central City Lake Protection Planning, and Wuhan Lake Rehabilitation Management Measures, severely crack down on behaviors that damage the river water ecosystem. As one of the urban rivers in Wuhan, the Xunsi River mainly includes engineering measures, biological measures, and policy support. Among them, policy support is the key to river governance, which is connected with the participation of every citizen. The prevention and control measures for the water pollution of the Xunsi River mainly used techniques such as bottom silt cleaning. In terms of river governance methods, the domestic governance model is mainly government-led, which mainly relies on government power and functions to comprehensively manage the environment of urban rivers. However, the current treatment methods have limitations, such as inadequate implementation by government departments and lack of pertinence in supervision of relevant departments. In many cases, the preliminary supervision is not good, causing the river to be contaminated before treatment, which increases the later treatment of the river. Difficulty of pollution. The pollution of urban rivers has destroyed the ecological environment, increased the risks and difficulties of community environmental management, and hindered the development of smart cities.

2 Design Research

After investigation, it was found that the Xunsi River lacked water quality monitoring and the monitoring was not in place, and the school did not pay enough attention to the water quality protection of the campus river, resulting in serious river water pollution in the past few years and no one to manage it. Through questionnaire surveys, user interviews, etc., the satisfaction of school personnel with the water environment of the campus river was collected. A total of 125 questionnaires were distributed this time to learn about the views of the teachers and students of Hubei University of Technology on the ecological environment of the Xunsi River, including the degree of concern about water pollution and the satisfaction with the water environment of the Xunsi River. There are 63% of people for the current situation of river ecosystem do not understand; in terms of concern about water pollution, 55% of people do not focus on water pollution problem; 47% of people are not satisfied with the current campus river water environment. It can be seen that the school personnel are not very concerned about the environmental protection of the river, and lack of access to relevant information. During the investigation, it was also found that some students lacked environmental awareness and threw the packaging bags beside the river after eating snacks during walking, which further aggravated the deterioration of the ecological environment around the river. In addition, the students' participation in the governance and protection of the Xunsi River is not high, and they do not fully realize the importance of protecting the river. Therefore, in the process of river pollution prevention and control, how to raise people's environmental awareness and drive the public to take the initiative to participate in environmental protection; how to make the results of water quality monitoring data open and transparent to facilitate the supervision of the government and relevant departments are issues that need to be resolved (Fig. 1).

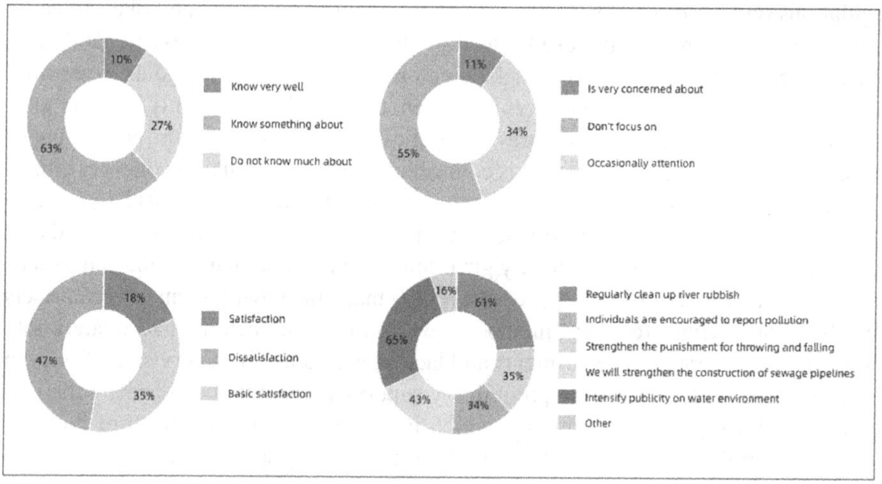

Fig. 1. Questionnaire chart

3 Design Framework

In the early investigation of Xunsi River, we learned the attitudes of teachers and students of Hubei University of Technology towards the pollution and government of Xunsi River, and found the research problems and objectives. Therefore, a new design driven pollution control scheme of Xunsi river is proposed to improve the water quality pollution of Xunsi river. With the successive deepening of research, we begin to conceive the design scheme, reconstruct the system, and combine the water quality monitoring system with blockchain technology. We utilize blockchain technology to visualize and transparent complex water quality monitoring data, so as to realize open and fair intelligent monitoring. In the later stage, with the help of visualized design, the water quality monitoring data of the campus river section will be displayed more intuitively, so that the teachers and students can clearly understand the pollution degree of the river in the recent period. Through these measures, it will make it easier to disseminate environmental protection information, promote mutual supervision of stakeholders in the Xunsi River Basin, and enhance people's awareness and enthusiasm for environmental protection in the meantime. The design framework is shown in the figure below (Fig. 2).

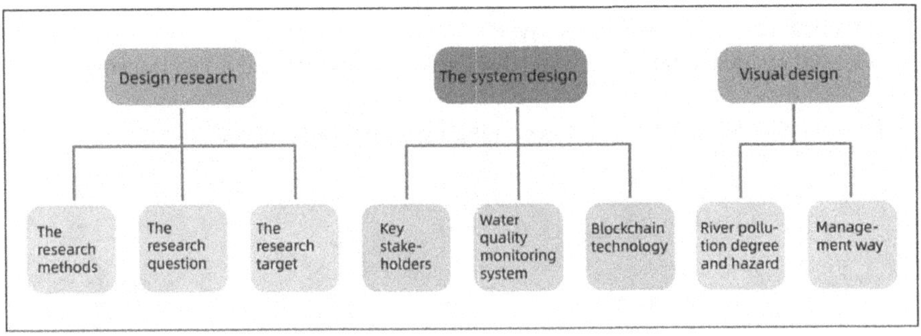

Fig. 2. Design framework diagram

4 System Design Scheme

4.1 Analysis of Main Stakeholders

For the system design, a multi-faceted stakeholder analysis is carried out. The relevant people involved in this system mainly include the government, the Environmental Protection Agency, the Campus Environmental Management Office, faculty, students, and coastal residents. The specific analysis is as follows.

(1) Government: According to the monitoring results of river water quality data, the government arranges relevant departments to supervise the campus rivers, and formulate relevant policies to strengthen the governance of the river water ecological environment, and enhance the people's sense of identity with the water environment.
(2) Environmental Protection Bureau: conduct investigation and supervision of campus environmental quality, regularly send professionals to monitor the water quality of the patrol river, and make water quality reports, and organize personnel to carry out river protection actions. The Environmental Protection Agency can quickly and accurately obtain water quality data through the system, analyze the pollution level of the river, and arrange relevant personnel to treat river pollution in a targeted manner.
(3) Campus Environmental Management Office: Use this system to evaluate water quality indicators, and timely feedback governance status to superiors, and at the same time formulate corresponding river protection measures, work hard to promote environmental protection knowledge, and call on teachers and students to jointly protect the water quality and environment of the Xunsi River.

(4) Faculty: abide by the campus environmental rules and regulations, and actively participate in the inspection activities of the river.
(5) Students: Regulate their own behavior, not littering, and reduce the impact on the ecological environment of the river. Student volunteers can carry out activities such as cleaning up rubbish and waste on both sides of the river, planting trees and grass, organize to pick up rubbish and waste along the river, clean up waste paper, plastic bottles and other rubbish in the green belt on both sides of the river, and take practical actions to protect the river.
(6) Coastal residents: reduce sewage discharge in daily life and avoid littering.

The stakeholder diagram is shown in the figure below (Fig. 3).

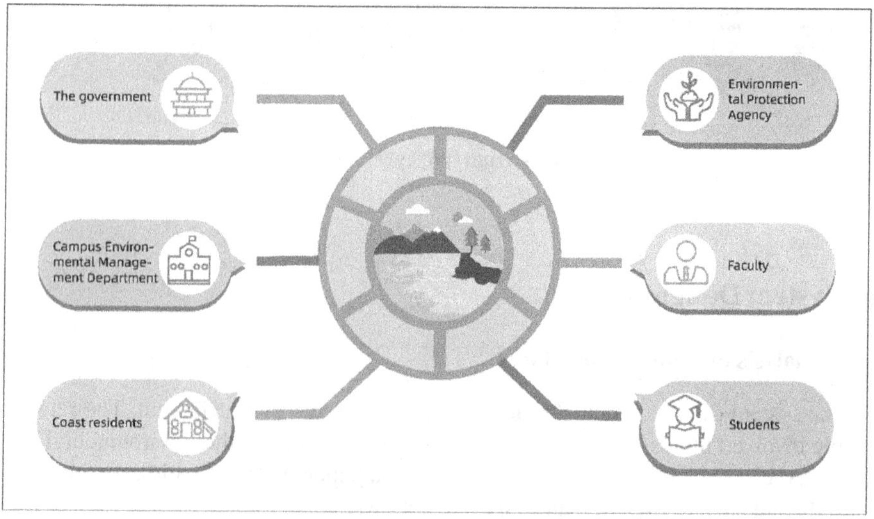

Fig. 3. Stakeholder chart

River pollution control is a long-term process. As far as the situation of river management in Wuhan is concerned, the participation of the general public is required. In the governance of Xunsi River, we should give full play to the role of different groups, let more people actively participate in the action of protecting the river, and build a bridge for the government, environmental protection departments and schools to jointly manage Xunsi River.

4.2 Water Quality Monitoring System

Water quality monitoring, as the name implies, is to monitor and determine the types and concentrations of pollutants in water bodies and their changing trends. It is an important technical means for the process of evaluating water quality and preventing and treating water pollution. The main body of water quality monitoring is mostly surface water and groundwater, in addition, there are some wastewater from production and life. Water quality monitoring data can provide beneficial data and information for environmental management and important data and information for environmental science research [3]. According to the national standards for river water quality, river health can be classified into Class I, Class II, Class III, Class IV, and Class V. The water quality of the Xunsi River meets the Class IV standard. The method of monitoring water quality is to install sensors in different areas of the Xunsi River, set up multiple monitoring points, and conduct regular river water quality monitoring. The current sensors for monitoring river water quality mainly monitor river temperature, dissolved oxygen, pH, chemical oxygen demand, total nitrogen, total phosphorus, conductivity, turbidity, etc. Based on the current river water quality monitoring system, a shared platform for the interconnection of future monitoring data will be established.

Therefore, a new intelligent water quality monitoring system based on the Internet of Things is proposed. The submersible water quality monitoring device is used to detect the water quality of the Xunsi section. The background system can monitor water pollution in real time and realize real-time dynamic monitoring of water quality [4]. The system can detect water temperature, pH value, dissolved oxygen, etc., and has two modes: autonomous detection and manual detection. Monitoring personnel can understand the water quality pollution of Xunsi River in real time through the large-screen data visualization, which is convenient for later targeted management, while improving monitoring efficiency and reducing the work intensity of water quality monitoring personnel (Fig. 4).

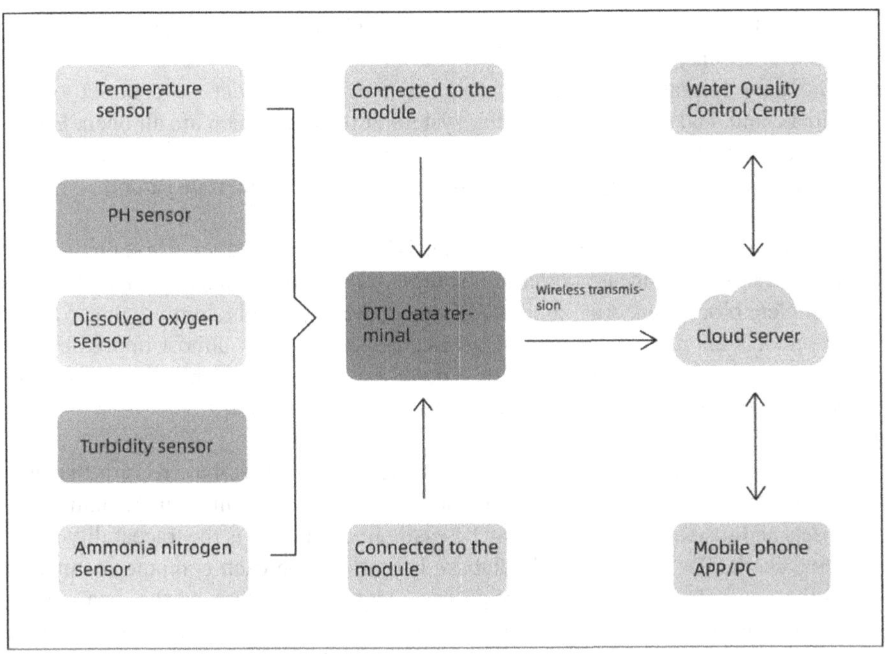

Fig. 4. Water quality monitoring system structure drawing

4.3 Blockchain Technology

Overview of Blockchain Technology

Blockchain is a data structure composed of data blocks in a chronological order in a manner similar to a linked list, and is cryptographically guaranteed to be non-tamperable and non-forgeable distributed decentralized ledger, which can safely store simple, sequential Relational data that can be verified in the system [5]. Blockchain is a new application mode of computer technology such as distributed data storage, point-to-point transmission, consensus mechanism, and encryption algorithm. The future society will pay more attention to the concept of environmental protection, and blockchain technology can play a supporting role. The application of this technology reduces the cost of data management in environmental protection and simplifies the data transmission process, which is of great significance for improving the environment of the future society.

Characteristics of Blockchain Technology

(1) Decentralization
Blockchain does not rely on centralization. Through distributed computing and storage, it realizes the self-verification, transmission and management of each node's information. The decentralized nature of the blockchain can effectively establish an information platform for data sharing, and relevant departments can see the results of monitoring data, which improves the efficiency of environmental supervision.

(2) Open and transparent
The data format, data content, data exchange agreement or contract of the blockchain, and even the underlying system of the blockchain are all open. Everyone can develop applications and query data within the established rules of the system, so the entire system information is highly open and transparent.

(3) Cannot be tampered with
The storage of each node of the blockchain is independent and equal in status, and the consistency of storage is guaranteed by the consensus mechanism. Each node stores complete block data. Any node modifying data needs to obtain more than 51% of the node's approval. This consensus mechanism makes it almost impossible for information to be tampered with [6]. Therefore, the data of the blockchain is stable and reliable, ensuring that the shared data is true and reliable.

(4) Traceability
Blockchain is a decentralized database. The decentralized database records the input and output of each transaction on the blockchain, so that changes in the number of assets and transaction activities can be easily tracked. This is the traceability of the blockchain. The decentralized database is scattered on each computer connected to the network and is not controlled by a centralized server, so the data storage method of the blockchain cannot be tampered with. We can track the data in the blockchain and trust the data. Used in the monitoring system, the monitoring data of water quality in various places can be clearly understood, which is convenient for departmental supervision and management.

Application of Blockchain Technology in Water Quality Monitoring System

This solution uses blockchain technology in the water quality monitoring system, and the entire system is a network service system composed of smart devices.

In this system, by monitoring the content of pollutants in the campus rivers, the data is open, transparent and traceable, and it is convenient for data transmission and sharing. For the government, the ability to understand the data fed back by the monitoring system in time prevents data falsification, which is conducive to the government's supervision of environmental protection departments and further improves the supervision system [7]. In addition, not only the government and the regulatory bureau have data, but with the help of blockchain technology, the school's faculty, staff, students, and citizens can learn about river pollution-related data, which promotes social equity. In terms of social management innovation, relying on the nation's leading digital Wuhan geospatial framework, and on the basis of an information sharing platform, the use of blockchain technology can strengthen and innovate environmental management, promote the construction of urban grids, and establish information that links up and down. Platform, hierarchical and zoning management of the environment, to better promote the construction of ecological civilization in Wuhan. The integrated social management and service digital information system is an important part of strengthening and innovating social management. Through the construction of this system, the existing environmental data is integrated, the environmental management model is planned uniformly, and the water quality monitoring data of urban rivers and lakes can be standardized. Operation to achieve accurate data control. This is conducive to improving the level of social management and service, resolving social conflicts, and promoting the goal of social harmony.

System Structure

The blockchain system is composed of data source layer, node layer, contract layer, application layer and user layer [8], as the picture shows.

(1) Data layer: sensor equipment, data collector.
(2) Node layer: After the sensor device monitors the water body, it will not store the data in a centralized database, but on the blockchain. Each sensor device is a node with data, which can synchronize the monitored data to the distributed ledger and store it. At the same time, the distributed operation mode is used to realize real-time monitoring of river water quality, which improves monitoring efficiency and simplifies data processing procedures.
(3) Contract layer: The smart contract is traceable and irreversible [9], so that the data will not be tampered with, ensuring the safety and reliability of the data in the transmission process. In addition, it provides users with data sharing, replication and synchronization database functions and data exchange functions in the blockchain network service system, making data open and transparent, and anyone can become a recipient of data.
(4) Application layer: mobile WeChat applet, large-screen data visualization.
(5) User layer: including the government, regulatory agencies, water quality monitoring personnel, and the public. The main function is for user authentication, and administrators can be set up in the system to maintain the system (Fig. 5).

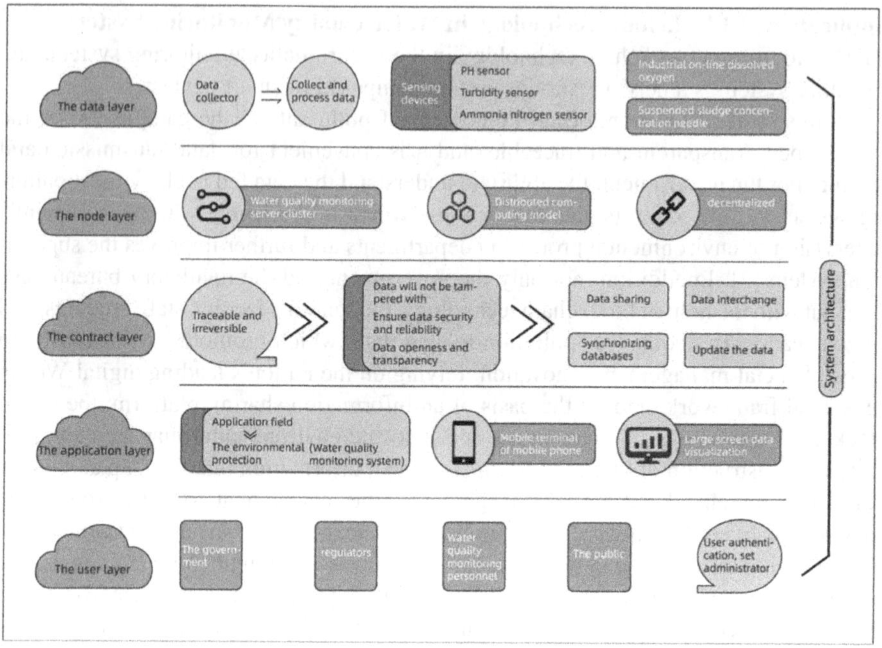

Fig. 5. System architecture diagram

5 Visual Design of Water Quality Monitoring Data

5.1 Purpose and Significance

By regularly monitoring the water quality of Xunsi River, the data results are presented in a visual manner. With the help of this data visualization design expression, popularize the knowledge of river pollution to people, and make the ecological management of rivers receive more attention. People can more clearly recognize the seriousness of urban river pollution and the importance of protecting rivers, and increase their attention to environmental protection. At the same time, it stimulates people's motivation to protect the environment, so that people can actively participate in environmental protection actions, work together to improve the surrounding ecological environment, build a green city in the future, and be a practitioner of environmental protection. The school personnel view the visualization of information on river water quality monitoring and related treatment methods through the mobile phone applet, and intuitively understand the current river pollution situation, prompting teachers and students to pay attention to the ecological management of the river, and improve the awareness of protecting the water environment. Teachers and students work together to create more A beautiful green campus; the government and relevant management departments use the large data visualization screen to observe the changes in the degree of river water pollution, and then conduct targeted treatment of the river, which is conducive to improving work efficiency.

5.2 Visual Presentation

Based on the data results of water quality monitoring, design data visualization. The various indicators of the water quality monitoring of the Tusi River are: temperature, transparency, dissolved oxygen, pH, chemical oxygen demand, total nitrogen, total phosphorus, etc. [10]. The data will change according to the degree of pollution of the river water every period of time, so only selected The most recent monitoring data is presented as a visualization. Through field research, I learned that the environmental engineering teachers and students of Hubei University of Technology have done relevant water quality monitoring reports and obtained some water quality data. According to the various monitoring indicators of water quality, the pollution degree of the river can be judged, and the pollution degree can be divided according to different standards. First, according to the main types of pollutants, river water pollution can be divided into three types: oxygen consumption pollution, eutrophication and heavy metal pollution. Secondly, according to the calculation methods of each pollution index, different types of pollution can be divided into five different grades, namely none or low, mild, moderate, severe and extremely severe. Information visualization in the mobile terminal also mentions the hazards of water pollution and treatment methods. There are two main ways to visualize the display. The first is the mobile terminal of the mobile phone, and the second is the large-screen display. The design renderings are shown in the figure below (Figs. 6, 7, 8, 9 and 10).

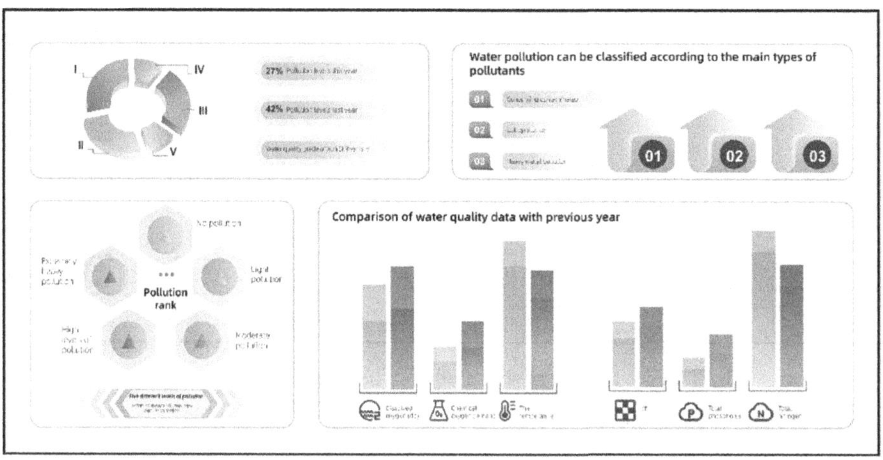

Fig. 6. Visualization of water pollution level (mobile terminal)

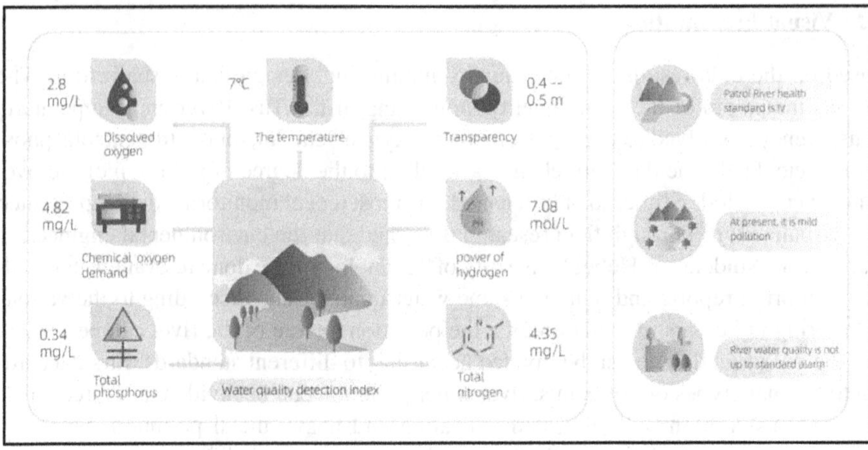

Fig. 7. Visualization of water quality monitoring data (mobile terminal)

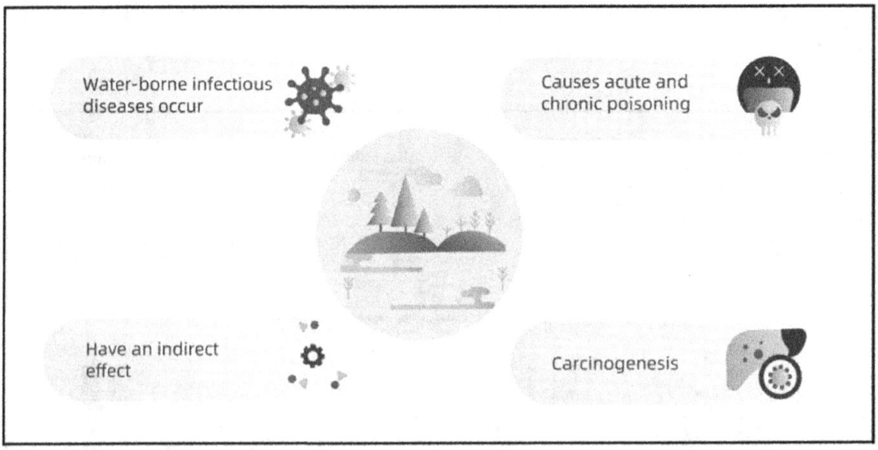

Fig. 8. Visualization of river Pollution hazards (mobile terminal)

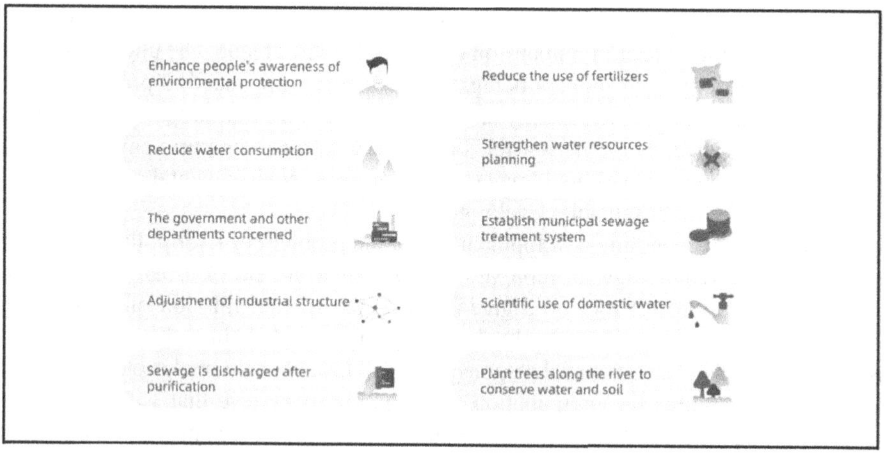

Fig. 9. Visualization of River Pollution Control Methods (mobile terminal)

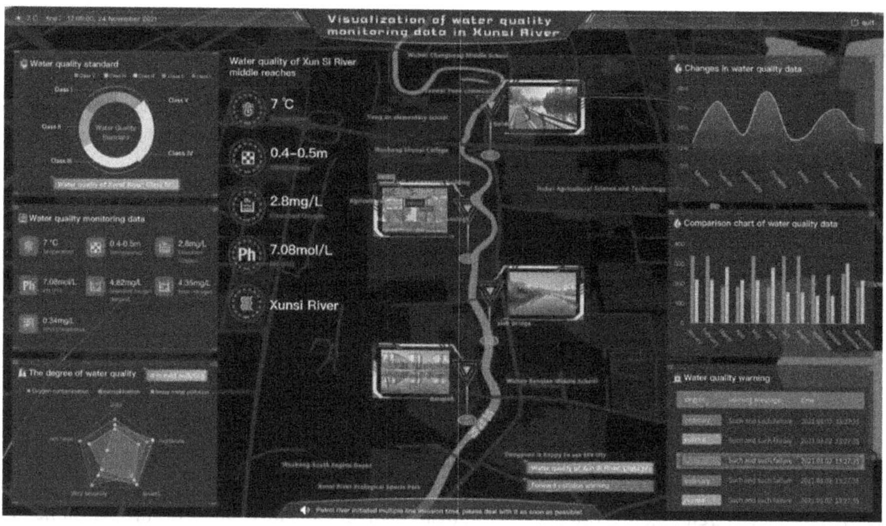

Fig. 10. Large screen visualization of water quality monitoring data

6 Summary Outlook

This paper uses the characteristics of blockchain technology and combines it with the water quality monitoring system to realize the transmission, sharing, and update of water quality data, ensuring the safety and reliability of the data. By disclosing the water quality monitoring data of the campus river, the government can know the pollution level of the river at any time, supervise the relevant management departments to manage it, and various departments can also supervise each other, which improves the transparency of work. At the same time, with the help of data visualization design, people realize the seriousness of current river pollution, enhance people's awareness of protecting the ecological environment of the river, and also let people start to reflect on themselves and think about the impact of humans on the natural environment. The ultimate goal of building a smart city is for human beings to live better. Cities need to provide people with a good quality of life. The quality of life is reflected in the public space environment on which people live. The criterion for judging is whether the natural environment is good or bad.. Therefore, we should pay more attention to environmental protection and adhere to the path of sustainable development.

With the rapid economic development today, the problem of river pollution control is urgent. Using technology to improve the water environment of urban rivers and to promote the rivers to set foot on a green road is the solemn mission of science and technology given by the times. In the future, through blockchain technology, each of us will begin to assume our social responsibilities. The environmental protection of the future society requires the participation of the public. I believe that with the efforts of individuals participating in environmental protection and the support of blockchain technology, people will solve the pollution problem of urban rivers in the future and build a green and harmonious society.

References

1. Han, H., Yan, G., Fan, W.: Planning scheme for comprehensive water environment management in the Xunsi River Basin in Wuhan City. Urban Roads Bridges Flood Control (07), 133–135+157+17 (2021)
2. Zhiqing, Z., Nuoya, Y.: Research on the co-governance strategy of water cities in the Xunsi River area of Wuhan. Urban Archit. **18**(21), 66–68 (2021)
3. Xinpeng, W., Xinggang, F.: Real-time and efficient new water quality monitoring system based on Internet of Things technology. Small Medium-Sized Enterprise Manage. Technol. (Late Issue) **12**, 194–196 (2020)
4. Peng, H., Zhou, X.: Research on a new water quality monitoring system based on the Internet of Things. Equip. Manage. Mainten. **22**, 98–99 (2021)
5. Xin, S., Qingqi, P., Xuefeng, L.: Overview of blockchain technology. J. Network Inf. Secur. **2**(11), 11–20 (2016)
6. Sa, H., Yi, C., Guangcai, F.: Application research on tracking and tracing of ship pollutants based on blockchain technology. China Maritime Aff. **02**, 57–59 (2021)
7. Dingyi, S., Mingming, R., Xinhua, W.: Application of blockchain technology in environmental protection. Sci. Technol. Innov. **22**, 57–58 (2019)
8. Yuntian, Z.: Design of village sewage treatment monitoring system based on blockchain. Electron. Technol. Software Eng. **21**, 159–163 (2021)
9. Hao, Y., Nianzhu, Z., Hang, X.: Research on meteorological data sharing scheme based on blockchain technology. Mod. Agric. Sci. Technol. **11**, 205–207 (2020)
10. Jing, C., Jun, L., Wei, Z.: The change trend and evaluation of the water environment quality of the Tounsi River. In: Proceedings of the Tenth Annual Conference of China Association for Science and Technology (2), pp. 1038–1046 (2008)

Exploring the Role of Design in China's Rural Revitalization Project—The Nice2035 Future Countryside Living Prototyping

Jing Wang and Yongqi Lou(✉)

College of Design and Innovation, Tongji University, Shanghai, China
wangjing7733@tongji.edu.com

Abstract. With China's increasing rate of urbanization, development in rural areas becomes a challenge, creating the need to redesign the relationship between urban and rural areas. The Chinese village ZhangYan is a very fertile area to be innovated and experimented on. In this paper, a pilot project investigating the new role of design(er) in rural development will be presented.

This paper presents the NICE2035 Future Countryside Living Prototyping (NICE2035&FCP), an initiative by the College of Design and Innovation in Tongji University and QingPu (青浦) People's Government (Shanghai) to achieve sustainability transitions in Chinese villages. The project design brought together local stakeholders, both private and public, including local authorities, NGOs, academic centers and third-party investors, through regular seminars and workshops with the aim to co-create. Particularly, this paper focuses on: how some specific social/cultural dimensions of prototyping, namely 'infrastructure' that the expert design favored the coordinated action and building long-term relationships.

The paper contributes to the ongoing discussion about the new strategy and methods in which Chinese rural revitalization can shift away from government support, toward a broader, more open process where smaller, more diverse, participatory initiatives can interact to achieve a larger vision.

Keywords: Design for sustainability (DFS) · Prototype · Infrastructure · Future country living

1 Introduction

The author used worked in the marketing department of a Chinese medicine health club in Shanghai. As a packaging designer, the author engaged in lots of health care projects packaging. Under the spotlight and excessive packaging, many health care programs, claim to cure heavy and dangerous disease (for example, cancer, which has broken my psychological defense. I was confused and began to doubt the value of being a (packaging) designer. In 2017, I quit my job and went to the SustainX Lab (design for sustainable future) for further study. This lab is a social innovation design and research laboratory. I worked as a social work researcher deeply participated in the Chinese rural revitalization project. In these years, the author constantly ask the following question,

P.-L. P. Rau (Ed.): HCII 2022, LNCS 13314, pp. 417–434, 2022.
https://doi.org/10.1007/978-3-031-06053-3_29

how the designer build his own capacity? what is the ontology of design(er)? How the designers change the way they see themselves?

Rural revitalization is put forward by Chinese President Xi Jinping in the report of the 19th National Congress of the Communist Party of China, which has created macro environments for rural development [1]. How to improve rural village vitality, stimulate creativity and enhance local employability are issues in need to deeper research.

This paper reports on a pilot project exploring the rural revitalization strategy. As for Chinese local Village (ZhangYan), the current situation—decaying countryside, backward health care and schools, cannot meet local young people's growth up needs, which lead to the young force leaving. The purpose of NICE2035&FCP is to explore solutions of ZhangYan revitalization, provides an analysis of the participatory future country living [2, 3], in which the local authority collaborates with innovation and entrepreneurship community, integrating the local demands to shape the future country living landscape.

The mainly focus is aimed to contribute to explore the new role of designers played in technological development and environmental ethics [4–6]. Generally, designers team evaluate biodiversity, social, and cultural diversity locally, in order to promote sustainable social actions [7]. Designers is not only to be a creator, but also to be a cultural agent, act as the glue of a multidisciplinary team and create new forms of culture.

1.1 Aim and Scoping Questions

This paper based on the empirical research, NICE2035—ZhangYan pilot project as the context, bring the local practice, contributing to the international social innovation research community. In this paper the following questions were asked: (1) what is the new role the designer played in facilitating social dialogue during the collaborative future-making process? and (2) How some specific socio-cultural and technological dimensions of prototyping, namely 'infrastructure' that the expert designer favored the coordinated action and building long-term relationships?

2 Theoretical Background

2.1 Design for Sustainability (DFS)

In 1987, World Commission on Environment and Development proposed in ***Brundtland Report*** that sustainability aimed to evaluate extensive impact of "technologies" on the economy, environment and society [8]. Obviously, it conveys values that care for natural environment [9], and takes into account an interdependent relationship among human and non-human communities [10].

The discussion of sustainable entry into the **Design Field** focused on the new role of designers, such as victor papanek, in his book *Design for the Real World—Human Ecology and Social Change,* points out the designers' responsibility in terms of social and environmental challenges. He believes that 'design' should explore the middle zone between industrial market logic and socially responsible practice [11]. From then on, our general understanding of 'Design for Sustainability (DFS)' evolved from product design such as, ecological design and green design, into social responsible design [12,

13]. However, critical voices point that the discussion should be focused at new level of the philosophy of what is valuable life [14], how the relations we ought to have with other people in their moral status as human beings [15]. **In particular, Manzini** believes that sustainable design is not about physical products, it is actually a kind of re-shaping of culture and behavior, and designers serve as the main driving force for transformation of society and culture [16]. It reminds us to reflect on ethical relationships between people, especially in the man-made system constructed by technologies [17], discusses a valuable life at a broader philosophical level [14], and how moral humans establish relationships with other humans [15].

2.1.1 What is the Ontological Underpinnings of 'Design'?

In a broad sense, what is design? According to Christopher Alexander, design is to create new patterns of things and behavior [18]. Scientists trying to define existing structures, while designers are always shaping new structural components. Science is analytical, while design is constructive. Herbert Simon synthesizes different disciplines, viewed innovation as a particular type of problem-solving behavior, transforming a given situation into a desirable situation [19].

According to Richard Buchanan, the innate drive of design is to create an desirable future, it has the natural Entrepreneurial framework [20], which analyzes and synthesizes different viewpoints at the intersection of constraint, possibility and contingency to provide solutions to indeterminate problems. However, the problem solving involves not only search for alternatives, but [also] search for the problems themselves.

As the agent of 'design' (designers in their specific context) in the design and social innovation process cannot be studied separately from their contexts, this study adopts a social constructionist perspective, in the sense that it assumes that social interactions construct meaning and understanding to human activity [21] and examines these different realities and phenomena, along with their implications, definitions and experiences [22].

2.2 Prototype

Prototype is at the core of design, as a way to 'fail early and succeed sooner' [23]. The remarkable strength of design practice are visualization techniques that support the rapid iteration of the prototype and testing models in practice [24]. In a sense, prototype is dynamic value relationship, tie together the needs of different stakeholders. Je'gou and Manzini described prototype as a stakeholder system, and the 'infrastructure' is built to serve this stakeholder network, which provides the trust basis for relationship attributes [25]. However, Chantal mouffe take the prototype as the 'agonostic spaces', acted as the vehicles to raise questions, reveal controversies and dilemmas, as well as negotiate consensus [26]. It is a meaning negotiation process including practical meaning, social meaning and Individual meaning [27]. People's understanding of sustainability embedded into the prototype which guides people reflect, debate, express and redefine the values of their daily life [28].

In a sense, prototype is a dynamic value-based cooperative relationship where demands of different stakeholders are bundled together [29], generate innovative forms of expression and expectations of different stakeholders [30], building empathy [31], helped establish a shared mental model and promoting coordination among stakeholders [32]. Donald Norman pointed out that individual designer cannot make meaning of the products they design, they had to socialized it, developing it into interconnected things [33].

However, it's worth noting that, in the prototyping process, the co-creation management strategy is contrary to the traditional project management method. It requires the design manager be able to easily manage the uncertain results (complexity), act as the promoter/facilitator, rather than guiding participants use any predefined thinking or solutions.

2.3 Social/Cultural Dimension—The New Roles of Design(er)

Design used to be thought as a way of giving forms/graphics to objects, but now, is a way of cultivating cultural diversity, and even the approach to understanding the complexity of systems and environments [34]. The mission of designer is enables people recognize their value, push them use their own skills and abilities to achieve their potential [35].

Infrastructure is important in developing and maintaining social potential. The concept of infrastructure was firstly introduced into design field by Susan leigh star and his collaborators in 1996 when they applied concept of information infrastructure into the participatory design (PD) community [36]. Manzini introduced the 5 elements of infrastructure, such as (1) digital platforms which connect decentralized social innovators; the (2) physical space which provides working space for people to communicate, such as conference rooms or coffee shops; (3) logistics services meet organizational needs for mobility of people and things; (4) information services give suggestions on what to do and how to do it; (5) evaluation serves for monitoring activities and results.

In sum, infrastructure is a complex set of tools, including training centers, workshops that brings together the technical and social dimensions of social action. The function of infrastructure is to integrate social resources, and encourage a sharing economy.

3 Research Methods

This study leveraged qualitative research methods to answer the research question. A qualitative research approach enabled us to collect in-depth descriptions—a foundation of qualitative analysis [22]. Further, a qualitative research approach enabled us to gather concrete experiences and perspectives that were detail-rich, as opposed to generalizations [37] or self-identified general strategies. We used an emergent approach, a method in which themes were derived inductively from the data [38]. Qualitative research studies aim for transferability of findings, which involves articulating rich descriptions that support the translation to other contexts [22].

3.1 Date Collection

The author was part of the NICE2035&FCP project and had the chance to gather data from June 2018 to October 2020. The main role of the author in this project was to contribute to the organization of different project sponsors to participate in seminars and explore the knowledge dissemination process during the prototype making. The data was collected in three ways: (1) participatory observation and (2) face-to-face interview with the project sponsors (3) semi-structured conversations with key project stakeholders. The semi-structured conversations were a complements method that enriches research's perspectives, and confirm the authenticity of the information source [39]. The purpose of the interview was to elicit concrete stories of experiences that practitioners engaged during front-end design activities. This paper use the multiple data production and collection method to exploit the synergistic effects of triangulation, the integration of different investigative techniques to reduce the bias of a single observation [40] (Table 1).

Table 1. Overview of types of initiatives and respondents

Initiatives	Type	Respondent	Data	Interview media	Time
Public sector/Yang Pu district government					
Bamboo leaves plaiting art	Project	Respondent A	2019.11.03	Informal interview	1 h28′
Qingpu pyrography	Project	Respondent B	2020.03.02	Voice call	20′30
Mixed vessel	Project	Respondent C	2019.11.04	Informal interview	23′18
Regional industry/investment alliance					
Pole play	Project	Respondent D	2019.11.06	Informal interview	20′30
Slow food international	Organization	Respondent E	2019.11.06	Face-to-face interview	23′18
XPORT	Project	Respondent F	2020.03.02	Voice call	1h
D&I universities/Academia					
Ellen Macarthur foundation	Organization	Respondent G	2019.11.03	Informal interview	1h28'
City eco lab	Exhibition	Respondent H	2018.11.04	Face-to-face interview	20′30
5 Universities alliance exhibition		Respondent I	2019.11.03	Face-to-face interview	1h
ZhangYan harvest forum	Forum	Respondent J	2020.11.02	Voice call	17′30
Civil society/entrepreneur					
Food forest	Project	Respondent K	2020.11.06	Informal interview	17′10
Garbage renovation campaign	Project	Respondent L	2020.11.06	Informal interview	20′10

We piloted the protocol with 12 participants to gain familiarity with the protocol and refine questions as per recommended practice. Most of participants job roles varied; many had senior, lead, or product design, design research, or technology management roles. As such, the respondents broadly represent variation among backgrounds, job roles, and years of design experience.

The practice of contextualizing interview questions in the participants' experiences supports the collection of authentic responses and rich descriptions. The data collected ranging from 20 min to one hour per interview. These were supplemented by notes and images taken during observations at events organized by some of the initiatives as well as various printed materials, such as books and leaflets, provided by the practitioners. Audio-recordings of the interviews were transcribed, verified against the audio recordings for accuracy, and de-identified. Initial analysis was conducted by two members of our research team; each person read the collection of transcripts and documented emergent themes and associated data.

3.2 Data Analysis

Thematic analysis was selected for data analysis, as it adopts a more structured approach which can be used in a variety of epistemological positions which investigate the causes underpinning human action [41]. It is a method that can identify, analyze and report patterns or 'themes' within data, and is widely used in qualitative research [42]. In this study, the data was approach in an inductive manner, entailing that it is presumed that the findings are a result of interactions of the analyst with the data, resulting in the identification of themes, patterns and categories [22]. For purpose of this paper, the author had only focused on relevant themes that have contributed to the development of the sociable designer concept.

SuxtainX lab[1] seminar sharing session as the thematic analysis of the case study.

After the NICE2035&FCP project has finished over 2years, the author organized a seminar and invited the related stakeholders to review and give a reflective analysis about this project. The Online meeting, is selected as a discussion space, the participants (SustainX lab members) including 3 professors—one of them is the initiator of the nice2035 project, 2 postdoctoral students, 6 doctoral candidates, 5 master's candidates. Through the discussion, the observed phenomenon was put into a real-life context. perspective switch between different participants, bringing the external perspective down to the research level [43]. These design experts provided feedback and suggestions based on materials, photographs, project journey map and annotated timeline provided by the authors which help identified the ambiguity between the phenomenon and context.

Reoccurring topics were grouped into broader themes, which resulted in 8 key themes (see Table 2). Themes were identified by finding an action in the data which involved a stakeholder being engaged in the context of project's activities. Literature that was used

[1] **SustainX lab** (Sustainable future design research center) focus on 'Design X agenda' which proposed complex social technology system design, systematic thinking in AI era, and explore the new roles, methods, path, tools of design.Doctoral candidate student Gong yu bei is responsible for operation of these lab (2022.02.11).https://mp.weixin.qq.com/mp/profile_ext?action=home&__biz=MzAwNjgzMjU3OA==&scene=123#wechat_redirect.

in the development of the interview protocol was consulted when refining theme names and definitions. During this process, code definitions were minimally refined to ensure clarity, specificity.

Table 2. Overview of themes pertaining to the new role of the designer

Reoccurring themes pertaining to the new role of the designer		**NICE2035 future countryside living prototyping**		
		Design harvest innovation and entrepreneurship platform	Prototype Seminar	Collaboration curator
Design-enabled infrastructure	①Collective public, social cohesion	✔	✔	✔
	②Expert resources and laboratories	✔		
	③Prototype kit		✔	✔
	④Governance framework		✔	
	⑤Momentary, fluid and short-lived connections			✔
	⑥Social-material relationship assembly			✔
Designer's new role	⑦Deal with uncertainty and complexity		✔	✔
	⑧Embraces vulnerability		✔	✔

4 NICE2035 Future Countryside Prototyping as a Case Study

The project aimed to explore the **urban-rural bridge** [44], attracting the entrepreneur community take root in the Chinese rural countryside. The author chose the NICE2035—ZhangYan pilot prototyping as a case study which has two features: first, participants pluralism, based on the "co-creation" approach, designers, researchers, policy makers, and community partners participated in the design process which was defined as collaborative future-making; second, new forms of organization, such as collaboration curator exhibition.

4.1 Design Harvest Innovation and Entrepreneurship Platform

Infrastructure is a physical form, provide space for people to communicate face-to-face or work together, such as conference rooms or coffee shops. However, it is also intertwined with political and cultural dynamics, with which, individuals and groups are allowed to generate and maintain psychological resources to achieve important goals.

Social Cohesion. Design Harvest is an innovation and entrepreneurship platform, act as an infrastructure which created opportunity to connect with others and maintaining social cohesion. Innovation quadruple helix, such as civil society, universities, public sectors, entrepreneurs has been seen as the regional industries transformation wheels which create a real experimental environment, and reconnect the relationship between policymakers, scientists, engineers and activists. Knowledge innovation community develops a series of projects strengthen the ability to adapt to environmental, and created opportunity to connect with others and maintaining social relationship.

The base of NICE2035 future country living project is **DESIGN HARVEST innovation and entrepreneurship Platform** (http://www.designharvests.com/), an 8 years of rural-urban redesign project which was initiated by the college of design and innovation (Tongji University) and embedded the strategy of 'acupuncture design', exploring the interactive mechanisms between urban and rural [45]. This paper mainly discusses the third pilot project of Stage3 NICE2035—ZhangYan pilot project (Table 3). A brief overview of the NICE2035 project was as follows:

Table 3. The three stages of the Nice 2035 project

Project stage	Major invents	Innovation levels
Stage 1 Strategy exploring and problem framework formulation	Press conference for NICE 2035 Future Life prototype street, a future community oriented to innovation, creativity and Entrepreneurship in 2035 (2018.12)	**Spatio-social innovation level** Build long-term vision and make prototype testing based on real community environments
Stage 2 Agenda and transformation tactics agreed between stakeholders	Announce the NICE CITY as an innovation and research platform for the future city life (2019.07)	**Socio-technical system innovation level** Concept of future digital technology infrastructure; formulation and exploration of transformation path via agendas
Stage 3 Deploy pilot project and put into trial operation	"Zhang Yan Harvest" Future country living festival acting as a prototype for the rural industry revitalization (2019.10)	**Spatio-social innovation level** Speculate the future scenarios, embed knowledge in prototype, implement rapid pilot project

Expert Resources and Laboratories. Set Up Infrastructure Labs. In March 2018, Tongji University College of Design and Innovation established a partnership with Siping sub-district office in Yangpu District, Shanghai to develop "NICE2035: 'Re-imagine the future living'. The aim was to explore innovative approaches to activate urban community. NICE 2035 stands for "Neighborhood of Innovation, Creativity, and

Entrepreneurship toward 2035 [46]. The university brought in its global knowledge community and talents to Siping community to establish labs and start-ups. Lane 1028 of Siping Road was selected as the project location, docking 15 LABs settled on the block. These included the Tongji-Dadawa Sound Lab, Tom's BaoBao Food Lab, NoCC Fashion Lab, Neuni Material Lab, Design Harvests Rural Lab [46], etc. The Lane 1028 of Siping Road—houses a series of innovative education units, prototype stores and co-creation spaces functioning as co-creation hubs where ideas, people, labs, resources, and capital come together.

In 2019.10, NICE2035—ZhangYan pilot project was deployed with the societal embedding process. It created a protective environment and mobilized socio-material things as matters of public things which challenged the current relationship of social practice and society. Projects assembly process outline the commitment to the related stakeholders.

4.2 Prototyping Seminar

Prototype Kit. Prototype kit contains story maps, shared timeline, visualizations tools which share the project assembly process. The prototyping meetings, as an interactive environment, involve the participants, including (1) Expert designers (2) Interdisciplinary researchers team (community cooperation, sociology, economy and cultural geography) (3) Shanghai ChongGu public sectors; (4) CSR social enterprise; (5) environmental protection NGOs (see Fig. 1).

Fig. 1. Prototyping seminar (sketch source: provided by Guo Ling)

In the prototyping seminar, the designer emphasized imaginative space, introduced scenarios and design artifacts and tools. The purpose of expert designers was to make participants awake to sense of their potential. Use their own manner/approach to realized their potential. It was a strategy to set up imaginative places for an open and inclusive participation. Designers used specific design tools (See Fig. 1) such as artifacts, scene sketch, game cards, encouraged participants to engage in future speculative activities. It provided new ways to introduce knowledge into debate, and expert designers facilitating negotiations, helping other participants express their expectations in public.

Picture A shows the scene of the prototype seminar; Picture B is the space planning of activities venue which is made up with the modular containers. Functional partition and unit area are also marked in the planning map; Picture C presents the 3D virtual model scene drawn by Sketchup discuss the possible visiting lines (supporting prototype visualization discussion by spatial modeling). Jointly, they discussed where the project resources should be place into specific area and the in what way should be presented, such as 2D, 3D or audiovisual forms.

Governance Framework. The concept of governance which means steering, guidance and manipulation. It implicit a political process of building consensus, so as to implement a plan. While governance framework maintain long-term relationship that requires specific standards, norms and protocols, and involves transparency and accountability. Entrepreneurship does not enough to support the collaboration framework between the decentralized social innovators. The concept of common mainly refers to shared control which was proposed as a guideline for jointly production. However, there exited a big controversy on how to reach a consensus on 'common' (Table 4).

Table 4. Interview notes excerpts

Respondent H: "12:21 Governance framework, require specific standards, norms and protocols, and involves transparency and accountability [...] 14:11 Expert designers also face challenges if they want to integrate social innovators and maintain long-term relationship [...]"

4.3 Collaboration Curator and the Project Output

Collaboration curator exhibitions attracting public and political attention, and contributing to public reflection and awareness. This renewed interest exhibitions forms have prompted a rethinking of curatorial practice as knowledge making site.

Momentary, Fluid and Short-Lived Connections

Table 5. Interview notes excerpts

Respondent F: "01:11These projects show examples of how casual and momentary encounters are becoming unified action of community building" [...] 13:09 Momentary, fluid, short-lived connections can be as powerful as long-term relationships".

Relational dialogue exhibitions are increasingly referred to as the 'laboratories' which support emerging knowledge process. It engages in "creative performance, using the world to think, affirm and reform the world". This new kind of exhibitions forms prompted collaboration curator practice as a knowledge production site while attracting public attention, and contributing to the self-reflection and daily social life awareness (Table 5).

Innovation activities are usually concentrated in specific urban center, while remote rural areas rarely get the access to resources radiation. In this case, future countryside living prototyping, as a process of resources integration, is a mechanism to stimulate local economy [47]. It transported resources to remote areas and the 'infrastructure' creates the conditions which break the geographical divide and created positive externalities and knowledge spillovers.

On the exhibition opening day, based on the vision of the future countryside industry, happened a series of highly participatory programs which was set up by the modular container. It included 30 international exhibition projects, 30 environmental protection market brands, 10 artists' art works, 10 specific theme workshops, 5 specific talks and the "production-learning-research" of 5 shanghai universities alliance (See Fig. 2). Through experiential participation, audience are encouraged to enter the speculative activities of the future.

Fig. 2. The future urban-rural lifestyle scenario staging by the modular container

From the Fig. 2, we can observe a stakeholder ecosystem. Prototype as a dynamic value-based partnership relationship bundled stakeholder demands and generate innovative expression forms. we can call it as 'new' museum which planned the new ideas in the forms of workshop, forum, market show and exhibition, cultivating a vibrant, creative and collaborative community (See Fig. 3). Stakeholders participate in the ecosystem, acting as agents of these resource (capitals, knowledge, market feedback and brand reputation) [48]. Through this process, invisible values are transformed into explicit, and offer new insights into the potential of the current world. Design thinking is regarded as a strategy to support and stimulate the interaction and negotiation of different stakeholders. They gathered into an energized ecosystem to discuss the preferable future country living.

4.4 Social-Material Relationship Assembly

Table 6. Interview notes excerpts

Respondent G: "03:45 While bottom-up initiatives which are often initiated by marginal actor networks (unstable socio-technical configuration) emerging at the microscopic level, **Art** is a social engagement tool to practice connecting with each other. [...] 13:45 Designing things and assemblies giving the new forms of unstable socio-technical configuration and shaping people's behavior.

The assembly of design things is the assembly of social material relationship and behavior. Cultivated assembly culture need the physical prototype which is a dynamic value-based partnership ties the needs of different stakeholders, and generates innovative forms of expression (See Fig. 3 and Table 6).

Relationship welfare is an open, conversational design process that arises from the interaction between organizations, groups. When stakeholders are brought together to explore alternatives to promote social change and sustainability, it is not a definite design outcome, but a continuous design process that is vague, complementary, and even confrontational. Relationship art is a practical form of social interaction that integrates collaboration, participation, intervention. The practice of relational art provides nodes to reflect the potential of social transmission. In this situation, art is no longer a representative of utopia but an attempt to construct a social environment.

Module Units	Modules Description	Interaction Forms
Workshop 	The workshop as a learning process, Show the fun of fixing things in a relaxed atmosphere, Teaching the repair techniques; It can be observed that the discarded denim clothing can be brought new life with a simple repair process which delivers the social value of recycling;	The "alternative sustainable future" is providing people with an opportunity to learn about the future. Through Hands-on experience method, transform invisible values from invisible to explicit.
Market Show 	The market includes a lot of recycled products renovation projects; It exhibited the fashionable bags made from discarded truck tarps, hangouts from the museum of antiquities, and the embroidery collecting, et.	The market is not only a place for buying and selling, but also a flexible participation structure, which uses product as the medium and excavates a new lifestyle through meaningful dialogue.
Urban-Rural Exhibition 	The future Agricultural Technology Museum displays the frontier of agricultural science, explores the prospect of data technology, risk management in the area of new farmer; The supply chain technology trace the agricultural products information link rom the materials to the customer process;	Through the multimedia method, Envisage the future agricultural infrastructure, explore the application scenarios.
Entrepreneur Forum 	The local sustainability and self-reliance considered as the important factor to rural development. entrepreneurship is seen as great potential to shape local community changes; The entrepreneurs spread their project achievements, which is beneficial to the innovation genes injection in local environment;	A public dialogue that communicates ideas about the future to a wide range of participants in an accessible, meaningful, and influential way.

Fig. 3. The modules description of future country living prototype

5 Reflection and Findings: The Designer's New Role

5.1 A Design-Enabled Infrastructure for Collaboration

Social infrastructure refers to the spaces, facilities, institutions network that create the conditions for social connection. There are so many studies related to infrastructure research while this article mainly discussed a social/culture infrastructure that supports social cohesion. The NICE2035 &FCP project, through a series of visual performances and experiential technologies, supports the public assembly. People encountered with different intentions, creating unforeseen complexity, 'infrastructure' guided them into the direction of inclusive socializing, and achieve deep harmony.

The infrastructure consist of 3 significant design components: (1) Design Harvest, an innovation and entrepreneurship platform, which accommodates spontaneous social initiatives; (2) Design experts and laboratory cluster, with the foresight to apply design thinking into industry transformation programmes; (3) A series of spaces, services and experiences, involved the audience participated and engaged in the new forms of collaboration organization (see Fig. 4).

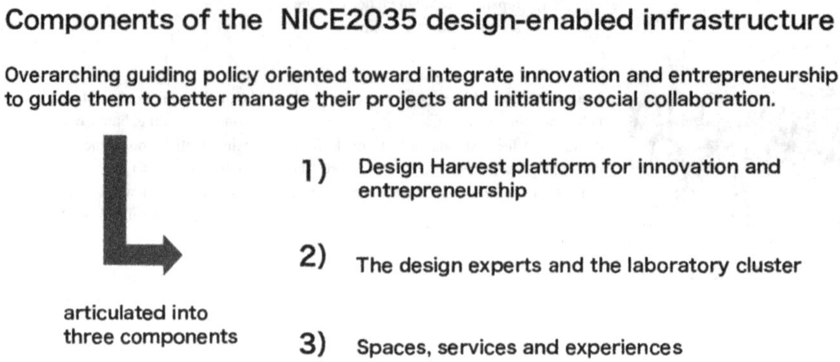

Components of the NICE2035 design-enabled infrastructure
Overarching guiding policy oriented toward integrate innovation and entrepreneurship and to guide them to better manage their projects and initiating social collaboration.
1) Design Harvest platform for innovation and entrepreneurship
2) The design experts and the laboratory cluster
3) Spaces, services and experiences
articulated into three components

Fig. 4. Components of the NICE2035 design-enabled infrastructure for collaboration

All these elements were tied together by a coherent guiding policy, i.e. to integrate spontaneous initiatives forming extensive social collaboration, such as cross-regional integration. These articulated components can be considered as infrastructure, as (a) they extensively spread the expert resources and knowledge resources of University; (b) It opened to broader range of people, both the local public departments, who explore local economic revival, and to third parties like NGO organizations, entrepreneurship communities, and startups, specifically, these new institutions regard the infrastructure as a platform for sustainable learning, to develop its own business models, and service system.

5.2 Design at the Multi-stakeholder Dialogue Level

Deal with Uncertainty and Complexity. How do people think the new role of designer in generating sustainable changes? In this project the author observed that the designer plays the agnosticism role of Prometheus (Οπρομηθέας) [50], accept the pluralistic naturalism, and admit the complexity, uncertainty, antagonist of the world and which was different from the traditional way who used to scaling down phenomena by doing experiments in closed site.

In the NICE 2035—ZhangYan pilot project which was an open-ended architecture where diverse stakeholders participate and innovate together [51]. Planning by projects can be seen as a strategy to combine different kinds of participation [52], which is seen as a new combination of resources thus execute new production function. Stakeholders are the solution providers, jointly exploring solutions based on the same problem situation. There is no "view from everywhere" but many different perspectives can create a mosaic of different micro-narratives.

In the prototyping seminar, the author observed the expert designer adapt to the environment, and construct collective understanding about the preferable future. They investigated the existed power relationship and negotiated expectations between the different stakeholders. Intermediary objects such as sketches and models are usually regarded as "objects to be considered", and as knowledge containers to express intentions.

Embrace Vulnerability. Vulnerability is a complex phenomenon and has strong ethical implications. The purpose of recognize vulnerability is not about trying to be invulnerable, which cannot be achieved. Rather, we should recognize the importance and emphasize its positive potential which strengthens the means we might use to respond to threats and clarify the institutions' responsibility in addressing vulnerability.

An environment that embraces vulnerability is very important. When people show vulnerability to each other, the possibility of a relationship is greatly increased. As designers, and as social work researchers we should empowering the people we're studying the concept of power. Help them understand how social relationships, structures and institutions control and organize their daily lives.

What is more, designers also face challenges such as developing new profile can be identified by other members which means that their various contributions can be identified by external environment.

6 Conclusion and Discussion

6.1 Conclusion

In this paper, a pilot project of social innovation is provided to explain how to gather stakeholders into an energized ecosystem to discuss the preferable future country living. The author focused on respond to the following questions: what is the new role of the designer? Through the case study the author found that the role of designer and the design-enabled infrastructure are completely different concepts.

The author discussed this issue through the prototyping perspective which is a physical carrier, captured the people's vision (Figs. 3 and 4) and shows possible future. From the **cultural dimensions of prototyping, namely 'infrastructure'** which overarching guiding policy oriented toward to guide people better manage their projects and organize social collaboration. Design-enabled infrastructure has been explored from the case study which empowers people to develop projects and fosters a mutually supportive ecosystem.

Undoubtedly, design-enabled infrastructure play the following roles: (1) Ensures the prototype captures the goals and interests of the related stakeholders; (2) Take advantage of expert resources of local universities academia; (3) attracts investment, and help them develop business models; (4) Maintaining the self-sustaining relationship network.

6.2 Discussion

We provide a descriptive presentation of the stakeholder interaction throughout the prototype design process. We find that relational-based economy has a strong correlation with the environment that embraces vulnerability. When people show vulnerability to each other, the possibility of building relationships is greatly increased.

Limitations: This paper does not propose a framework, rather, we provide a description of prototype design process, mainly aimed at enriching the design research community and contribute to the social innovation community. Despite systematic guidelines for collecting and analyzing data, qualitative research is not suitable for generating generalized insights. The case studied in this paper are only suitable for local situations. There are some exceptions that occur, such as the creative and destructive moments. However, the established framework does not allow the identification. Due to the limited length of this article, it is not discussed.

Future Work: In this project, the designer accepted the pluralistic naturalism, and admit the complexity which also defined the value dimension of being designer. It is necessary to define the value dimension of the designer's role, and develop relevant quantitative procedures to study how to maximize the value of each dimension. This is a question that the literature needs to consider in the following research work.

Acknowledgements. This work was supported by the Professor Lou Yong Qi; Professor Cheng Yi Heng; Tektao design director Guo Ling; Publicity and media director Liu Lian Ying (Publicity and Media Promotion Department of D&I); Dr Jiang Ying (Future design and research institute of Tsinghua international innovation center, Shanghai);

Many thanks to Professor Lou for his RRI Scholarship.

Disclosure Statement. No potential conflict of interest was reported by the author(s).

References

1. Cao, Y., Ji, T., Zhong, M.: Design Education for Rural Revitalization (2019)
2. Van Waart, P., Mulder, I., Bont, C.: Participatory Prototyping for Future Cities (2015)
3. Brodersen, C., Dindler, C., Iversen, O.: Staging imaginative places for participatory prototyping. CoDesign **4**, 19–30 (2008)
4. Johnson, J., Immerwahr, J.: First Things First. Public Agenda, New York (1994)
5. Maldonado, T.: Design, Nature, and Revolution. Harper & Row, New York (1972)
6. Meadows, D.H., Meadows, D.L., Randers, J., et al.: The limits to growth. New York **1972**(102), 27 (1972)
7. Sarmento, F., Moura, M.: Material resignification in the Amazon. A way to construct sustainability scenarios. Des. J. Routledge **20**(sup1), S1852–S1868 (2017)
8. Sovacool, B.K., Hess, D.J.: Ordering theories: typologies and conceptual frameworks for sociotechnical change. Soc. Stud. Sci. SAGE Publications Ltd. **47**(5), 703–750 (2017)
9. Martin, A.: Diseñosustentable (2009). Recuperado de. http://foroalfa.org/articulos/diseno-grafico-sustentable
10. Köhler, J., Geels, F.W., Kern, F., et al.: An agenda for sustainability transitions research: state of the art and future directions. Environ. Innov. Soc. Transit. Elsevier **31**, 1–32 (2019)
11. Papanek, V.: Design for the Real World: Human Ecology and Social Change (1985)
12. Oh, S.: From an ecodesign guide to a sustainable design guide: complementing social aspects of sustainable product design guidelines. Arch. Des. Res. **30**(2), 47–64 (2017)
13. Taylor, D.: A brief history of (un) sustainable design. In: The Routledge Handbook of Sustainable Product Design, pp. 11–14. Routledge, London (2017)

14. Taylor, C.: Dilemmas and Connections: Selected Essays. Harvard University Press, Cambridge (2011)
15. Margalit, A.: On Compromise and Rotten Compromises. Princeton University Press, Princeton (2009)
16. Brooks, S.: Design for social innovation: an interview with Ezio Manzini. Shareable (2011)
17. Heidegger, M.: The Question Concerning Technology. Harper & Row, New York (1977)
18. Alexander, C.: Notes on the Synthesis of Form, p. 5. Harvard University Press, Cambridge (1964)
19. Simon, H.A., Barenfeld, M.: Information-processing analysis of perceptual processes in problem solving. Psychol. Rev. Am. Psychol. Assoc. **76**(5), 473 (1969)
20. Buchanan, R.: Leading design: managing the challenge of innovation. In: Unpublished Keynote Presentation at 19th DMI: Academic Design Management Conference, London, UK, pp. 2–4 (2014)
21. Lock, A., Strong, T.: Social Constructionism: Sources and Stirrings in Theory and Practice. Cambridge University Press, Cambridge (2010)
22. Patton, M.Q.: Qualitative Research & Evaluation Methods: Integrating Theory and Practice. Sage Publications, Thousand Oaks (2014)
23. Brown, T., Wyatt, J.: Design thinking for social innovation by. Stanf. Soc. Innov. Rev. **8**, 30–35 (2010)
24. Mulgan, G.: Big Mind: How Collective Intelligence Can Change the World. Big Mind (2018)
25. Jégou, F., Manzini, E.: Collaborative Services – Social Innovation and Design for Sustainability (2008)
26. Mouffe, C.: The Democratic Paradox (2000)
27. Walker, S.: The object of nightingales: design values for a meaningful material culture. Des. Cult. **4**, 149–170 (2012)
28. Stegall, N.: Designing for sustainability: a philosophy for ecologically intentional design. Des. Issues **22**, 56–63 (2006)
29. Holmlid, S.: Participative; co-operative; emancipatory: from participatory design to service design. In: Conference Proceedings ServDes, 2009; DeThinking Service; ReThinking Design; Oslo Norway 24–26 November 2009. Linköping University Electronic Press, no. 059, pp. 105–118 (2012)
30. Sanders, L., Stappers, P.J.: From designing to co-designing to collective dreaming: three slices in time. Interactions **XXI** (2014)
31. Segelström, F., Holmlid, S.: Visualizations as tools for research: service designers on visualizations. Nordes **2009**(3) (2009)
32. Neyer, A.K., Doll, B., Möslein, K.M.: Mission (im) possible?–Prototyping service innovation. Supporting service innovation through knowledge management: practical insights and case studies, pp. 143–164 (2009)
33. Norman, D.A.: Emotional Design: Why We Love (or Hate) Everyday Things. Basic Civitas Books, New York (2004)
34. Buchanan, R.: Branzi's dilemma: design in contemporary culture. Des. Issues JSTOR **14**(1), 3–20 (1998)
35. Manzini, E.: Design research for sustainable social innovation. Des. Res. Now 233–245 (2007). Springer
36. Star, S.L., Ruhleder, K.: Steps toward an ecology of infrastructure: design and access for large information spaces. Inf. Syst. Res. INFORMS **7**(1), 111–134 (1996)
37. Weiss, R.S.: Learning from Strangers: The Art and Method of Qualitative Interview Studies. Simon and Schuster, New York (1995)
38. Boyatzis, R.E.: Transforming Qualitative Information: Thematic Analysis and Code Development. Sage, Thousand Oaks (1998)

39. Myers, M.: Qualitative Research in Business & Management (2008)
40. Tarrow, S., King, G., Keohane, R., et al.: Bridging the quantitative-qualitative divide in political science. Am. Polit. Sci. Rev. **89**, 471 (1995)
41. King, N.: Using templates in the thematic analysis of text. In: Casssell, C., Symon, G. (eds.) Essential Guide to Qualitative Methods in Organizational Research, pp. 256–270. Sage, London (2004)
42. Braun, V., Clarke, V.: Using thematic analysis in psychology. Qual. Res. Psychol. Taylor & Francis **3**(2), 77–101 (2006)
43. Yin, R.: Case Study Research: Design and Methods (2009)
44. Thackara, J.: Bioregioning: pathways to urban-rural reconnection. She Ji: J. Des. Econ. Innov. **5**(1), 15–28 (2019)
45. Valsecchi, F., Yongqi, L., Diaz, C.: Design Harvests. An Acupuncture Design Research Approach Towards Sustainability (2013)
46. Lou, Y., Ma, J.: Growing a community-supported ecosystem of future living: the case of NICE2035 living line. In: Rau, P.-L.P. (ed.) CCD 2018. LNCS, vol. 10912, pp. 320–333. Springer, Cham (2018). https://doi.org/10.1007/978-3-319-92252-2_26
47. Hillgren, P.-A., Seravalli, A., Emilson, A.: Prototyping and infrastructuring in design for social innovation. CoDesign **7**, 169–183 (2011)
48. Hedström, P., Swedberg, R.: An Analytical Approach to Social Theory. Revue Française de Sociologie, p. 40 (1998)
49. Edwards, P.N., Bowker, G.C., Jackson, S.J., et al.: Introduction: an agenda for infrastructure studies. J. Assoc. Inf. Syst. **10**(5), 6 (2009)
50. Latour, B., Hackne, F., Glynne, J., et al.: Proceedings of the 2008 Annual International Conference of the Design History Society. Universal (2008)
51. Murray, R., Caulier-Grice, J., Mulgan, G.: The Open Book of Social Innovation: Ways to Design, Develop and Grow Social Innovations. The Young Foundation & NESTA (2010)
52. Manzini, E., Rizzo, F.: Small projects/large changes: participatory design as an open participated process. CoDesign **7**, 199–215 (2011)

Analysis of Image Perception and Influencing Factors Based on Online Reviews: Take Kaiping Watchtowers and Villages of China as an Example

Xi Xu[1,2] and Hai Lin[3](✉)

[1] Shouzhan New District, Fuzhou University of International Studies and Trade, No. 28 Yuhuan Road, Changle 350202, Fujian, China
[2] Khon Kaen University, 123 Mittraphap Road, Khon Kaen 40002, Thailand
[3] College of Tourism, Huaqiao University, No. 269 Chenghua North Road, Quanzhou 362021, China
hailintourism@163.com

Abstract. With the arrival of the era of big data, text databases provide new ideas for the study of rural tourism destination image perception. The article takes Ctrip.com and other Chinese tourism websites and uses content analysis and grounded theory research methods to analyze the original paper, withdraws high-frequency characteristic words of Kaiping watchtower, explores tourists' overall image perception and emotional evaluation. The results showed that: (1) "watchtower" "Kaiping" and "architecture" are the basic cognition of the tourist image of Kaiping watchtower, the specific cognition of watchtowers can be subdivided into four aspects of architectural image, artistic atmosphere, architectural function and human history; (2) Visitors to the overall image shows the layout of the watchtowers, architectural decoration, the history of overseas Chinese deep into the core circle of divergent characteristics and the tourist environment, local food, Chinese and Western culture as the edge of the distribution characteristics of the circle; (3) Visitors' emotional expression is dominated by positive positive emotions, followed by neutral and least negative; (4) the main factors affecting the expression of tourists' negative emotions are the scenic area management factor, the Chinese historical factor, the architectural property factor and the human environment factor.

Keywords: Kaiping watchtower and villages · Online reviews · Image perception · Content analysis · Grounded theory

1 Introduction

In the era of big data, all kinds of network data are exposed on all major platforms, and a large amount of data, easy accessibility and dissemination power have become the irreplaceable advantages of this kind of data [1, 2]. The technology of the Internet and the use of mobile devices has created lots of UGC data [3], and this has led to

P.-L. P. Rau (Ed.): HCII 2022, LNCS 13314, pp. 435–460, 2022.
https://doi.org/10.1007/978-3-031-06053-3_30

changes in the study of travel, hotels and other related fields [4–6]. More and more tourists use the Internet to plan their travels in advance, and actively record and share their travel experiences in blogs, forums and microblogs after their travels [7, 8], while the emergence of online reviews provides a reference for the development of tourists' travel process [8] and becomes one of the channels for the dissemination of urban and rural images [9]. Its free, open and shared features provide the public with scientific and comprehensive analysis data. In addition, the presence of these reviews on the Internet has a feedback effect on the destination, spreading the awareness of its tourism products very quickly, giving rise to a large number of hot tourist places, but the negative image of the destination will also be highlighted the negative impact. Therefore, it is of practical significance to study and explore the image problems of tourist destinations reflected behind the online texts for the improvement and enhancement of tourist destinations.

The study of tourism destination image began in the 1970s and gradually gained widespread attention. The image of a tourist destination is a concept that represents the personal attitude of the tourist, it refers to the individual's perception, emotion and impression of the tourist destination [10]. From a supply and demand perspective, Michael Grosspietsch distinguishes between the perceptions and impressions that potential and actual travelers generate about a destination and the projected image that the tour operator intends to establish in the minds of potential tourists [11]. In the study of perceptual image, scholars also divide it into the cognitive image and emotional image, considering that cognitive image is mainly based on the tourist's awareness of the attributes of the tourist destination, while the emotional image is a kind of tourist's feelings towards the tourist destination [10]. From before and after the visit perspective, Martin Selby proposes the concept of original and reassessed images as a way to distinguish between the original impressions and perceptions formed before visiting the destination and the attitudes held after visiting the destination [12]. Influence on pre-visit image generation can be categorized as external stimuli and personal factors of the traveler. As far as external stimuli are concerned, visual content is an important aspect, that is a predictor of the destination image, and its attractiveness, uniqueness and structure are the main dimensions that influence the formation of the destination image [13]. The number and variety of information sources are also important external factors influencing the formation of the pre-visit image, but they only contribute to the tourist's perceived image. Studies have shown that word-of-mouth and advertising among information sources are also moderately correlated with tourists' perceived image, tourism brochures also have an impact on the pre-visit image, and the information they provide about the destination has a positive impact on the formation of tourists' pre-visit image [14]. Postcards can also trigger positive feelings about a destination and influence the choice of that destination [15]. In addition, psychological characteristics such as tourists' values, motivation, personality and social characteristics such as age, education level, marital status and nationality are subjective factors that influence the image of pre-visit tourism destinations. The empirical study showed that characteristics such as age and education affect the cognitive image of tourists as well as their emotional image [16], while travel motivation and cultural values significantly affect the emotional image [17]. There are three directions of post-visit image development, namely, tourists' deepened image perception of the destination, no change in their impression of the place, and aversion to the tourist destination. The image of a tourist destination also changes over time, for example, the different needs of tourists in different seasons [18]. Political unrest [19], popular culture [20], historical films [21], media guidance [22], sports activities [23] and major international events [24] can all have varying degrees of impact on tourist destinations. In summary, although many factors influence the perception of the image of a tourist destination, we find that most of them are based on the external macro-environment, information dissemination and personal factors of tourists, and less on how the attributes embedded in the tourist destination itself affect the tourist experience and what kind of perception the tourist has of the image of that tourist destination. Therefore, exploring tourists' perceptions of tourism destinations from the perspective of their attractiveness has implications for industry management and academic research.

This study explores the image cognitive process of Kaiping watchtower, a World Cultural Heritage site, using online text as the data source, a cognitive-emotional model as the basis, and a text mining analysis method and a rooted theory research method. The objectives of the study include: exploring the factors perceived by visitors to the case place in their online reviews and their importance; how these factors are related to each other; a hierarchical analysis of visitors' emotional composition toward the case place; what factors influence visitors' overall perceptions; and what factors influence visitors' expression of negative emotions during their tour. Finally, it is hoped that this will facilitate the study of online big data such as tourist reviews and provide a scientific basis for destination image management and marketing.

2 Research Area and Method

2.1 Overview of the Study Area

Kaiping watchtower, located in Kaiping City under the jurisdiction of Jiangmen City, Guangdong Province, is a special type of Chinese vernacular architecture, and a set of defense, residential and Chinese and Western architectural art in one multi-story tower-style buildings [25]. It features a mix of Chinese and Western dwellings, with a variety of ancient Greek, Roman and Islamic styles. The watchtower has a long history, dating back to the late Ming and early Qing dynasties, when the heyday of more than 3,000, there are more than 1,800 well-preserved, mostly established in the late 19th century and early 20th century. It is a multi-story tower-style country house built by local Chinese who returned from North America, South Asia, Australia and other countries, combining their wisdom and foreign architectural styles, and was built by local Chinese to protect their families from natural disasters and bandits. At the same time, it is the crystallization of the wisdom of overseas Chinese, fully demonstrated the modern Chinese love of the motherland and love their hometown and family of overseas Chinese sentiment. Diaspora culture is an important part of the local tourism industry, and it is highly feasible to tap into Diaspora culture and meet the core pursuit of culture by tourism consumers.

2.2 Research Method

Content Analysis. Content analysis is a prominent method in social science research, which can transform the non-systematic and non-quantitative symbols of this text into systematic quantitative data, and quantitatively analyze these textual data materials [26]. Research with text, photos, films, coordinates and other symbolic content has become a hot spot for tourism management disciplines to study tourism destination image perception research [27]. In this study, ROST CM6 and python web text analysis software are used as research tools, and the formation of custom word lists and word frequency filtering word lists are used as precursors to the precision of word division and word frequency statistics in the Jie-ba module in python. Firstly, the crawler collects the text of related online reviews on famous websites in China and filters the pictures, motion pictures, videos and audio contents on the websites; secondly, the predefined custom word list and filter word list are embedded in python word separation programming, and the high-frequency word statistics are analyzed to explore the basic elements of tourists' cognitive images of destinations in history, humanities, landscape, emotions, etc. Secondly, the semantic network is used again to analyze the relationship network among high-frequency words, to explore the main key nodes and the degree of connection among the elements, and to explore the overall emotional image of tourists towards the destination through the sentiment analysis function, and to provide relevant management suggestions for this study.

Grounded Theory. Grounded theory is a bottom-up approach to theory building first proposed by two scholars, Glaser and Strauss [28]. It emphasizes the search for core concepts that reflect social phenomena based on systematic data collection and then establishes connections between concepts to form theories. Grounded theory method is a dynamic research process, including five stages of generating research design, data collection, data processing and data analysis, and literature comparison [29], in which coding the data level by level is the most important aspect of grounded theory, including three main steps of open coding, axial coding, and selective coding [28]. Coding refers to the constant comparison between events and between events and concepts, which leads to the formation of categories and features and the conceptualization of data. There is still a lack of systematic research on the influencing factors of tourists' image perception, and using the rooting theory research method can extract the concepts affecting tourists' perception from the travelogues, and establish various links between concepts through constant comparison and generalization. The article uses the qualitative research software Nvivo11 to complete the coding process.

2.3 Data Sources

In this paper, Ctrip.com, Ma Hive.com and Where to go.com travel guide travelogue sites to collect "Kaiping watchtowers and Villages" text data as the basic information database. The text screening information was involved in the content of the image evaluation of the research object between 2002 and 2020, and 449 travelogues were finally selected through manual screening, among which the number of Ctrip was 335, Ma Hive was 69, and Where to go was 45. Subsequently, the pre-processing operation was carried out to delete the text with more irrelevant information and repetitive contents, remove the cumbersome contents such as emoticons, letters, garbled codes and advertisements in this paper, convert some traditional Chinese characters into simplified ones, and unify the similar words with the same meaning, and finally save the processed paper as a.txt format file.

3 Destination Image Perception Analysis Based on the Content Analysis Method

3.1 Cognitive Image Analysis

The python program was used to analyze the word frequency statistics of the collected and collated web texts, and some meaningless words were excluded through custom word lists and deactivated word lists, and the top 100 high-frequency words about the image perception of Kaiping watchtowers and villages were extracted from them (see Table 1). From the lexical analysis of these 99 words, a total of 77 nouns, 12 verbs and 10 adjectives are included. The high-frequency vocabulary has more nouns of attraction elements, specifically focusing on architectural landscape, human environment, tourism characteristics, history and culture, etc. Verbs specific to the act of tourism and architectural conservation. The adjectives are mainly positive and express the subjective feelings of tourists about the attraction and its surroundings.

Table 1. High-frequency vocabulary of Kaiping watchtowers and villages tourism image perception

Words	Attribute	Frequency	Words	Attribute	Frequency	Words	Attribute	Frequency
Watchtower	Noun	1706	Bandits	Noun	110	Hotels	Noun	63
Architecture	Noun	803	Styling	Noun	106	Travel	Noun	62
Kaiping	Noun	705	Garden	Noun	98	Hometown	Noun	60
Chikan	Noun	540	Republic of China	Noun	97	Overseas Chinese Township	Noun	59
Zili Village	Noun	416	Movie	Noun	96	Bean curd Corner	Noun	59
Liyuan	Noun	343	"Let the Bullets Fly"	Noun	96	Rome	Noun	58
Overseas Chinese	Noun	325	Countryside	Noun	96	Environment	Noun	57
Culture	Noun	269	Film City	Noun	94	Aliens	Noun	56
China	Noun	264	Reside	Verb	91	Materials	Noun	56
Style	Noun	250	Tourists	Noun	89	Ban li	Noun	56
Village	Noun	228	Weili Xie	Noun	89	Unique	Adjective	56
Villager	Noun	219	Story	Noun	86	Paddy	Noun	56
Maxianglong	Noun	208	Tanjiang River	Noun	85	Intact	Adjective	56
Feature	Noun	182	Structure	Noun	83	Bamboo forest	Noun	54
Villadom	Noun	168	Construct	Verb	82	Western style	Noun	53

(continued)

Table 1. *(continued)*

Words	Attribute	Frequency	Words	Attribute	Frequency	Words	Attribute	Frequency
Mingshi Tower	Noun	165	Kilometers	Noun	82	All concerned	Adjective	53
Scenic spot	Noun	153	South Tower	Noun	80	Fang Runwen	Noun	52
Chinese and Western	Noun	151	Distribute	Verb	79	Village entrance	Noun	52
Arcade	Noun	148	Lingnan	Noun	78	Sturdy	Adjective	52
Ruishi tower	Noun	146	Penthouse	Noun	76	Beautiful	Adjective	51
History	Noun	142	Combination	Verb	76	Build	Verb	50
Heritage	Noun	139	Tickets	Noun	76	Hong Kong	Noun	50
Guangdong	Noun	137	Save	Verb	75	Open up	Verb	49
Art	Noun	135	America	Noun	74	Look around	Verb	49
Master	Noun	134	Decoration	Noun	73	Doorway	Noun	49
Overseas	Adjective	133	Combination Ticket	Noun	72	Cement	Noun	48
Atlantic	Noun	132	Shoot	Verb	71	Concrete	Noun	48
Scenic	Noun	131	Taste	Noun	70	House	Noun	48
Traditional	Adjective	120	Fancy	Adjective	69	Furniture	Noun	47
Region	Noun	120	Defend	Verb	67	Society	Noun	47
Visit	Verb	119	Renowned	Adjective	66	Tangkou Town	Noun	47
Time	Noun	116	Rice in Casserole	Noun	64	Chinese style	Adjective	47
Jinjiangli	Noun	115	Rebar	Noun	64	Embody	Verb	47

The higher the word ranking indicates the higher the awareness and attention of tourists to the imagery element. Through the statistical analysis of high-frequency vocabulary in Table 1, it can be seen that Chikan, Zili Village, Liyuan, Maxianglong, Jinjiangli and other tourist attractions ranked in a higher-order, ranking 4, 5, 6, 14, 33, respectively, indicating that tourists pay more attention to the main attractions of Kaiping towers and villages. The above five tourist attractions are the primary object of perception for tourists visiting Kaiping watchtowers and villages, but also tourists in the case of sufficient time must pass through the place. On the other hand, among the words representing the architectural image of the scenic spot, the words traditional, fancy, renowned, unique and intact are in a higher order of positive adjectives, at 29, 62, 64, 77 and 79 respectively, and there are no derogatory adjectives in the high-frequency words, indicating that tourists are more satisfied with the overall tourism evaluation of the scenic spot and have a more favorable tourism impression. The above five adjectives are to express the architectural features of the towers and the historical survival of the relevant evaluation, showing that tourists visiting the attractions of the architectural decoration preferences. Overseas Chinese, culture, Chinese and Western, overseas, Western and other related to the cultural exchanges and integration of Chinese and Western word frequency order is higher, respectively, ranked 7th, 8th, 18th, 26th, 27th, highlighting the historical characteristics of Kaiping watchtower as a product of the integration of Western and Chinese art and culture. In terms of folk specialties, boiled rice, bean curd corner, eel rice, steamed goose in Chikan, duck congee and dog meat are the local delicacies in Kaiping, which are the must-try foods for visitors to the area as experience seekers. In terms of environmental perception, visitors to the garden, Tanjiang river, paddy, bamboo forests and other elements of the landscape environment show a better emotional evaluation, that these environments and towers buildings with each other, complementing each other, forming its unique quiet environment.

Therefore, the overall perception of visitors to Kaiping watchtowers and villages presents a core circle: the layout of watchtowers - architectural decoration - overseas Chinese history in decreasing order, layer by layer depth of divergent characteristics, and the tourist environment - local food - Chinese and Western culture as the edge of the distribution characteristics of the circle. Watchtower landscape and overseas Chinese history as the main attractions and vistas are the main factor for tourists to generate tourism motivation, with the declaration of World Cultural Heritage and the movie "Let the Bullets Fly" and other television publicity, derived from the tourists Netflix card sites and other tourism behaviors. but another aspect is the exploration of overseas Chinese cultural tourism, roots study tour and other forms of tourism lack due to recognition, so rely on the rich history of overseas Chinese in Kaiping watchtower, which launched rural tourism development and enhancements are promising.

The high-frequency words of Kaiping watchtowers and villages tourism image are visualized in the form of word cloud map (Fig. 1), in which words with higher word frequency are presented in a larger form, while words with lower word frequency are presented in a smaller form.

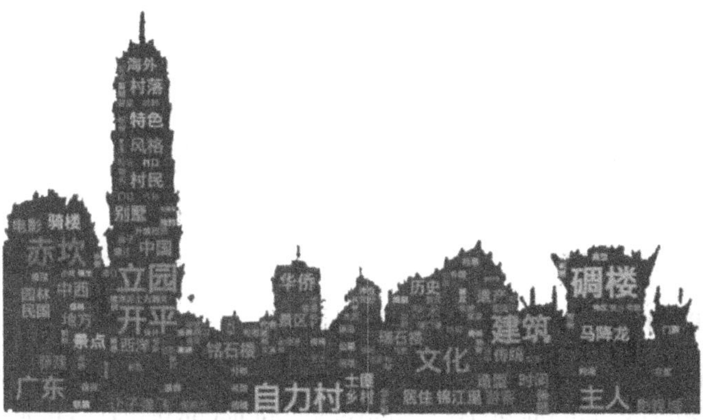

Fig. 1. Word cloud map of high frequency

3.2 Overall Semantic Network Analysis

The semantic network analysis diagram can represent the related connections between elements, and the overall relational network is composed of nodes and connecting lines that indicate semantic connections. It makes up for the fact that high-frequency word analysis can only reflect the characteristics of things presented in that study but not the deeper structural relationships. The semantic network analysis function in ROST cm6 software was used to analyze the visual graphs (Fig. 2). From the diagram, it can be seen that the words "watchtower" and "architecture" form the core nodes of the network relationship. Therefore, the semantic network diagram of the network text forms a double core of "watchtower" and "architecture", with Kaiping, culture, overseas Chinese, Liyuan and Zili Village as the secondary center of the layout, indicating that tourists mainly perceive the architectural and cultural value of Kaiping Watchtower. With a common line to see the connection strength, "watchtower" has a strong common line relationship with Kaiping, architecture, Zili village, overseas Chinese, culture, style and other terms, the connection degree reached 389, 286, 176, 150, 139 and 115 times respectively. The word "architecture" has more common lines with Kaiping, overseas Chinese, culture, style and Chinese and Western, with 174, 133, 101, 143 and 100 times respectively. As can be seen from Fig. 2, visitors to Kaiping watchtower's perception of the image is obvious, superficial summary image, the perception of the historical scene of Kaiping watchtower, the perception of cultural connotations, the perception of the atmosphere of the overseas Chinese community is more superficial.

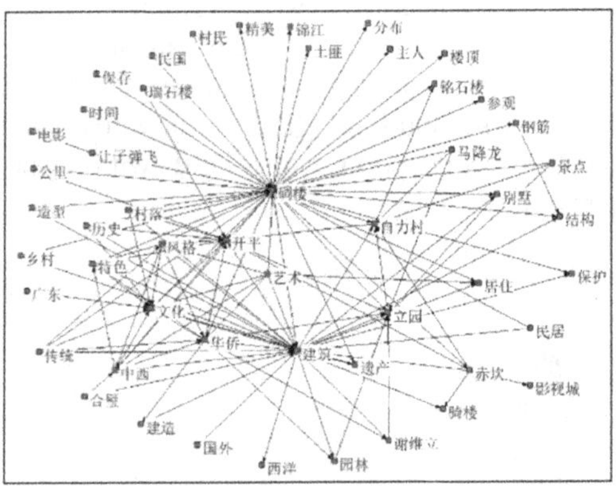

Fig. 2. Semantic network analysis

3.3 Overall Emotional Image Analysis

Emotional imagery of tourist places has received extensive attention from the academic community with the introduction of cognitive-emotional theory. The emotional imagery perception of tourists is an important part of the image perception of the Kaiping watchtower, and the emotional response is based on the further expression of tourists' perception of the object. We use the sentiment analysis module to count the number of statements containing sentiment (see Table 2). Overall, visitors' emotion types were mainly positive emotions, with the number of 1414, accounting for 70.91% of the overall sample size, followed by neutral emotions, with the number of 320, accounting for 16.05% of the overall sample size, and finally, negative emotions, with the number of

260, accounting for 13.04% of the overall sample size. The percentage of highly positive emotions is much higher than highly negative emotions in the emotion type breakdown. From the content of the textual material, the tradition and simplicity of the watchtowers, the simplicity and hospitality of the residents, the grandeur and refinement of the architecture, as well as the quiet, slow pace of life and the tranquil ambiance are important driving factors influencing the positive emotional expression of tourists.

Table 2. Sentiment analysis of visitor review

Emotion category	Proportion (%)	Degree	Proportion (%)
Positive emotion	70.91	General	29.19
		Moderate	19.41
		Height	22.32
Neutral emotion	16.05	/	16.05
Negative emotion	13.04	General	8.68
		Moderate	2.96
		Height	1.40
Total	100	/	100

Rural tourism is the basic need to leave the usual environment for enriching life experiences under modern living conditions, and it is the requirement to pursue a short period of physical and mental freedom and find the true self in the fast-paced oppressive situation of modern life. Under the anti-modernization mentality of consumer groups, tourists are eager to get away from the monotonous and boring workplace. However, because of its unique Chinese and Western cultural characteristics of the "local" to meet the needs of tourists to escape from "reality", Kaiping watchtowers and villages becoming a psychological and spiritual stopping point. As one visitor commented: "Because usually in the city cannot set off fireworks, our family came to play in Chikan specially bought a lot of fireworks to set off, then there are many local people and you look at the fireworks together, this kind of peaceful, calm, restful feeling is so perfect."

4 Analysis of the Factors Affecting Destination Image Based on Grounded Theory

4.1 Factors Affecting Image Perception

According to the step-by-step coding procedure of the grounded theory research method, open coding, axial coding and selective coding were used to analyze the contents of the online text in turn, from which the influential factors affecting tourists' perceptions of the image were extracted.

Primary open coding from conceptualization to categorization. Open coding means that the original textual material is summarized and generalized into a refined connotation, the concept can represent the meaning of the original text to a larger extent, and through the correlation between concepts and concepts and then refine the category. In the coding process, a total of all the contents of the original text were coded and 646 relevant paragraphs of the original text were finally extracted for conceptualization, the conceptualization process and some of the original texts are shown in Table 3, and then the concepts derived from the induction were compared and linked, and finally, 36 initial categories were derived. These 36 primary categories in the overall perception of the number of tourists image in descending order is the fusion of Chinese and foreign art, beautifully decorated and furnished, food customs and traditions, aesthetic representation of architecture, film and television derivative products, excellent architectural craftsmanship, defense against enemies, western art of architecture, history of overseas Chinese struggle, idyllic scenery, family groupthink, Rich interior facilities, explanation by residents, master craftsmanship, quiet scenic atmosphere, advanced construction technology, a wide range of artworks, home country sentiment, unique architectural structure, interior decoration symbolism, folk heroic deeds, watchtower Museum, traditional environmental thinking, Furniture vintage and original, Liyuan studio, Chinese art subjects, artistic effect presentation, Chinese architecture geomantic omen (Feng Shui), farmhouse features, integration of architecture and nature, wonderful layout of appliances, clever architectural formula, architectural trace representation, commercial street district, pattern modernization, highlights of the war. Among them, the number of the top 12 initial categories can cover 54.87% of the total number of factors influencing the perceived image perception of Kaiping watchtowers and villages by tourists.

Table 3. Partial open coding on cognitive images

Number	Part of the original content	Conceptualization	Categorization
1	Kaiping watchtower as the only one in Guangdong Province World Heritage Site, is by no means a vainglorious name, its beauty, from the essence of its innate beauty of tragedy	The tragic beauty of heritage architecture	Aesthetic Representation of Architecture
2	Speaking of director Jiang Wen's "Let the Bullets Fly", I'm sure many people remember it well, as Zhou Yunfa, Ge You and Jiang Wen and many other well-known actors and actresses outstanding performance, the movie attracted audiences from 18 to 80 years old, and created a box office and word-of-mouth double success at the time of the film industry, which known as a miracle. It is also the film, so people know that in Guangdong, there is a unique building called "towers"	The movie "Let the Bullets Fly"	Film and television derivative products

(*continued*)

Table 3. (*continued*)

Number	Part of the original content	Conceptualization	Categorization
3	During the war, the enemy attacked Chikan town and the government troops fled on the wind, leaving only the Stuart-style escorts to hold their position and fight the enemy for seven days and nights, and they heavily defeated the enemy forces. Then the enemy called artillery and other heavy weapons to bombardment, but the bombardment was ineffective because the building was strong. Finally, the enemy put gas bombs into the towers, the seven warriors in the building were killed and thrown into the river. After the war victory, the people of Kaiping held a memorial meeting in Chikan town, a total of more than 30,000 people attended the memorial service, it can be seen that the seven martyrs of the heroic deeds of the people	History of people fighting against enemy forces	Folk heroic deeds
4	These different styles and schools of different religious architectural elements in These different styles of religious architectural elements in Kaiping show great inclusiveness, the convergence of harmonious coexistence, the formation of a new comprehensive and very strong type of architecture, showing a unique artistic charm	The architectural style is highly inclusive	Fusion of Chinese and foreign arts
5	In addition to the charm of the towers' cultural heritage is amazing, the surrounding scenery is also enchanting. The village is very clean and tidy, next to the village are the rice fields, the rice has been harvested, the fields are left half high golden rice stalks, the place is as beautiful as walking into a painting	Beautiful countryside scenery	Idyllic scenery

(*continued*)

Table 3. (*continued*)

Number	Part of the original content	Conceptualization	Categorization
……	……	……	……
643	The floor of the villa is decorated with carefully chosen patterns, such as this place where four red hearts are cleverly linked together to form a circular pattern of unique love, and colored Italian stone mills are set in the center of each hall and room. It is presumed that the owner treated the four wives equally and that his love for them had reached the level of heart-to-heart connection	Decorative expressions of affection	Interior decoration symbolism
644	There is a pavilion in the small garden, the top of which is painted with the Chinese mythological story "Eight Immortals Crossing the Sea". it features a gray mural with bright colors and vivid characters, a golden dragon coiled at the top and a lamp dangling below, just like the pearl it spits out, which is exquisite and admirable	Chinese Mythological Figures	Chinese Art Subjects
645	Walking in the village, each watchtower has a different style of gray carving. Gray carving is a special treatment of lime as the main material, with a batch of knives directly carved and pasted on the wall or under the eaves, after the formation of a variety of dry patterns. Such as landscapes, birds, flowers and figures, with the artistic effect of anaglyph. It is often used in the hall and the decoration of the house	Usage of construction materials	Excellent architectural craftsmanship

(*continued*)

Table 3. (*continued*)

Number	Part of the original content	Conceptualization	Categorization
646	According to legend, at the beginning of the garden, the owner hired a man who is good at Feng Shui, and he pointed out the front door to the Tiger Mountain looks very much like a big green-hair tiger, which destroyed the feng shui here, unfavorable to the development of the Xie family. The feng shui master suggested the owner set up a pair of stone lions at the front gate to deter the green-haired tiger across the street	Architectural design focusing on Feng Shui	Architectural Feng Shui theory
647	Kaiping watchtower walls are thicker and stronger than ordinary homes. Watchtower upper four corners generally built with a prominent overhang of the fully enclosed or semi-enclosed corner fort, corner fort opened forward and downward-firing holes, you can return fire from above the enemy. At the same time, the towers on each floor wall open firing holes, increasing the point of attack of the residents of the building	Architectural features emphasize aggressiveness	Defending against foreign enemies

Create axial coding for organic links between categories. The axial coding process encompasses the organic connections between the vast majority of the textual material by discovering and linking the intrinsic relationships of the various categories. The 36 categories obtained from the above primary open coding were deeply categorized and assigned new genera according to their interrelatedness (see Table 4), resulting in seven main categories: external image, internal image, Chinese and foreign art, defensive function, settlement function, historical plots and humanity and environment. The most significant factor affecting the perceived image of tourists is the perception of Chinese and foreign art, accounting for 20.40%, including the integration of Chinese and foreign art and other 6 initial categories, followed by the perception of the external image of the building, accounting for 18.08%, including the aesthetic representation of the building and other 7 initial categories, while the least is the towers of the settlement function, accounting for 7.26%, including protection against foreign enemies and other 3 initial categories.

Table 4. Three-level coding process of the factors influencing the overall image perception

Open coding	Axial coding	Selective coding
Aesthetic Representation of Architecture (30), Excellent architectural craftsmanship (29), Advanced Construction Technology (18), Unique architectural structure (15), Integration of architecture and nature (10), Clever architectural formula (8), Pattern Modernization (7)	External image (18.08%)	Architectural image perception (35.24%)
Beautifully decorated and furnished (35), Rich interior facilities (20), Master Craftsmanship (19), Interior decoration symbolism (15), Furniture vintage and original (13), Wonderful layout with appliances (9)	Internal image (17.16%)	
Fusion of Chinese and foreign arts (38), Film and television derivative products (29), Western Art of Architecture (25), A wide range of artworks (16), Chinese Art Subjects (12), Artistic effect presentation (12)	Chinese and Foreign Art (20.40%)	Artistic atmosphere perception (20.40%)
defense against enemies (28), Home Country sentiment (16), Highlights of the war (7)	Defensive Functions (7.88%)	Building Function Perception (15.14%)
Family Groupthink (21), Traditional environmental thinking (14), Chinese architecture geomantic omen (Feng Shui) (12)	Settlement function (7.26%)	
History of overseas Chinese struggle (25), Folk heroic deeds (15), Watchtower Museum (15), Liyuan Studio (13), Architectural Trace Representation (8)	Historical plots (11.75%)	Humanity and History Perception (29.22%)
Food Customs and Traditions (32), Idyllic scenery (23), Explanation by residents (20), Quiet scenic atmosphere (19), Farmhouse Features (11), Commercial Street District (8)	Humanity and Environment (17.47%)	

Selective coding that eliminates secondary categories and summarizes core categories. Selective coding is the process of verifying the relationships with other categories in the core category system and adding the categories that are not yet complete and eliminating those that are not relevant [30, 31]. By analyzing the 36 initial categories obtained from primary open coding and the 7 main categories obtained from spindle coding (see Table 4), and at the same time, continuously comparing them with the textual data, we finally summarized the four core categories that affect tourists' perception of

Kaiping towers and villages: architectural image perception, artistic atmosphere perception, building function perception and human and history perception. Among them, the perception factor of architectural image occupies the largest proportion, accounting for 35.24% of the total, and contains two main categories of external image and internal image.

The architectural image of Kaiping towers and villages is one of the first factors that tourists perceive in the travel process, including the external and internal image. What visitors see when they enter this particular non-habitual environment is the overall impression of the watchtower complex, which has typical western modern architectural aesthetic elements, in contrast to the traditional Chinese architectural style. Because the Chinese have lived in the country of residence, absorbing the architectural styles of various countries, it will be designed during the return of drawings, and in the local craftsmen's skill and bold creativity, a good blend of Chinese flavor and the soul of Western-style in the building of the watchtower. In the latter, out of the climbing heart, a variety of strange styles continue to emerge, forming a unique style, rich in the cultural flavor of Chinese and Western architectural complex. out of the heart of climbing, a variety of strange styles continue to appear, forming a unique style, rich in the cultural flavor of Chinese and Western architectures. For example, the coupon arch of ancient Roman style, the colonnade of ancient Greek art, the mountain flower of Baroque style and the dome of Islamic genres. These different styles genres and religious architectural elements in Kaiping watchtowers in harmony, showing the unique artistic charm. Visitors enter the interior of the watchtowers, the most perceived is the layout of the interior furnishings. Overseas Chinese tend to accumulate more wealth than others and therefore pay more attention to living facilities, landscape design and artistic pursuits. From the internal structure of watchtowers, 1 to 5 floors are mainly residential areas, each floor of the window skirt, window lintel, window mountain flowers of different shapes and compositions, the overall shape and detailing is very delicate, with a strong Western architectural style. Each floor has a different line footing and column trim, adding to the effect of the building's facade. The interior arrangement and utensils are in the Chinese traditional Lingnan style. The imitation Roman coupon arch at the top of the 5th floor and the four corners of the chic bracket column instead of the commonly rolled grass bracket foot in other towers, a very aesthetic visual effect, forming a natural transition to the upper part. The 6th floor has columns consisting of columns with coupon arches in the Ionic style. The seventh floor is a platform with corner pavilions with vaulted roofs at the four corners and Baroque-style mountain flowers on both the north and south sides. The three large characters of the Ruishi watchtower in the seventh-floor plaque are engraved, which are the ink of a famous calligrapher in Guangdong at that time. In short, from the floor layout can be seen, the owner of the building in the construction of towers is very concerned about the beauty, refinement and diversity.

The emergence of watchtowers in Kaiping city is a product of the Chinese rural people's initiative to accept the art of Western architecture and fusion with local architectural art. It is a skillful blend of Western art and local architectural art, expressing the traditional Chinese sense of environment and the perfect combination of man and nature. In terms of artistic atmosphere, in addition to the architectural techniques, the architectural styles of western countries are integrated and applied, and the artistic atmosphere is also emphasized in the interior decoration. For example, the towers' indoor floors and staircases are Italian-colored stone, the walls are decorated with ancient Chinese characters and stories as the subject of large murals, reliefs and gilded wood carvings. The relief carving is a historical story about the characters of the Three Kingdoms period in ancient China. The characters are realistic, lifelike, exquisite carving and original composition, and now more than sixty years later, they are still glorious, which is the peak of the skill of skilled craftsmen. Secondly, the art of towers is not only embodied in itself, Chinese director Jiang Wen towers for the second creation, the production of the film "Let the Bullets Fly". The film was loved by the Chinese people, as well as international acclaim, and was considered one of the best Chinese comedies. In the creation process, through the film and television material and the image of the towers fit so that people have a deep impression of Kaiping towers, a move to create a double success at the box office and word of mouth miracle of the film industry. Since then, Kaiping watchtower has become a popular place for tourists to take the perfect Wechat Moments to snap at the internet-famous site. In addition to creating the movie "Let the Bullets Fly", the rural tourist site has also created film and television works such as "The Grandmaster", "Three Family Lane", and "East Mountain Drifting Rain and West Pass Clear".

Kaiping City, the construction of towers with its time-honored historical background. At that time, Kaiping was located at the junction of Xinhui, Xinxing, Enping and Taishan counties, which was an ungoverned area with rampant banditry. During the late Ming and early Qing dynasties, the Qing government implemented a harsh "sea ban" and "boundary relocation" policy to cut off the connection between the people and the Ming government in exile, forcing the coastal residents of Kaiping to move inward for tens of kilometers, resulting in the bankruptcy of a large number of families and the displacement of peasants. In this context, the residents began to move out to Southeast Asia, Europe and other regions to seek a living, after accumulating a certain amount of money abroad would return home to build watchtowers. The defensive nature of the watchtowers was paramount in those days and was an important barrier to protect the personal safety of family members. In order not to continue to be robbed of their belongings by bandits, the Chinese paid particular attention to the defensive function of the buildings when they were built. The walls of the watchtowers reach 30 cm thick and are all pounded with cement. Villagers used iron to make doors and windows, equipped with firearms, gongs and searchlights in the window section, and shooting holes all around the building, which became a public shelter built by villagers to prevent flooding and bandits. In addition, the watchtower building scale is more ambitious than the general, the reason for this is due to the traditional Chinese idea of family group living. A watchtower can accommodate three generations of the family, including servants, housekeepers and other people up to 20 people, enough to maintain long-lasting family living conditions. In terms of the location of the towers, the design of the drawings, and the symbiosis with the environment, the owner also pays attention to how the Feng Shui of the building. Legend has it that when building one of the watchtowers, the owner hired a Feng Shui master to point out that the front door to the tiger mountain like a big green-haired tiger, which disrupts the balance here, and it would lead to unfavorable development for the family, so the master suggested that the owner build a pair of stone lions at the front door to counterbalance it, and after the family's past misfortunes also disappeared.

Watchtowers have a strong rural atmosphere, and the natural environment of the village is beautiful. Ponds, lotus ponds, rice paddies, grass scattered among them, and many towers reflecting each other, forming a quiet and elegant environment, with a unique rhythm of the Lingnan countryside. In the ancient town of Chikan, there are many snack stores. Potted rice, bean curd corner, Magang Setian, etc. are the famous snacks there, and they are also the places that tourists will go to taste when they visit, and these snacks show that the local food customs have the typical Lingnan flavor. In addition to the food and drink specialties, tourists can also enjoy a special service from the residents during the trip, which is interpretation. The scenic interpreter is partly the owner of the towers, especially the older elderly, they will take visitors into the interior of the towers, and introduce to visitors the history of the local overseas Chinese stories, the origin of the towers and the local culture. Moreover, the Kaiping watchtower, as a world cultural heritage, has a strong value of cultural examination, so visitors are also able to deepen their impression of the scenic spot through local museums, libraries and other means.

4.2 Factors Affecting Negative Emotional

Interestingly, we found that there are some negative emotions expressed by visitors to the scenic spot, and these negative emotions tend to affect the visitors' experience. Similarly, we used the grounded theory research method to codify the sentence segments affecting the expression of negative emotions of tourists at three levels to understand the influencing factors behind the coding process and make relevant suggestions for the management improvement of scenic spots.

A total of 258 comments about the original content of perceived negative emotions were searched for in the primary coding process (see Table 5), and 21 primary categories were obtained after comprehension and analysis, which could reflect the connotation of the original text to a larger extent. These 21 primary categories in the number of security tourists negative emotions perceived in order from most to least are: inconvenient transportation, the tragic history of the Chinese diaspora, ticket price confusion, interior decoration equipment idle and abandoned, some towers are not open, sad love stories, secondary charge phenomenon, fewer accommodation services, unable to visit the whole tour, cluttered human environment, the watchtower are poorly restored, lack of signage guidelines, watchtowers homogenization, lack of popularity of scenic spots, poor food environment, watchtower are dilapidated and silent, lack of competitiveness, poor personnel management, uneven distribution of commercial areas, unprofessional interpretation services and bizarre and quirky products. The first seven of these categories can cover 53.10% of the factors influencing tourists' perception of negative emotions in Kaiping watchtowers and villages. Then carry out axial coding, its 21 codes for categorization to give a new class genus, and get the inadequate regulation, inadequate basic services, expatriate history emotional, watchtower architectural features and poor humanity experience of the five main categories (see Table 6). Finally, by continuously comparing the original data, we get the four core categories influencing factors that affect tourists' expression of negative emotions towards Kaiping watchtower: scenic management factor, Diaspora history factor, Building property factor and humanity experience factor. Among them, scenic management factors occupy the largest proportion in influencing the expression of negative emotions.

Table 5. Partial open coding on negative emotion perceptions

Number	Part of the original content	Conceptualization	Categorization
1	Walking along with the X555, after getting off the highway, from Tangkou to Chikan, you can see a variety of towers, a random village to walk into, are such towers building	Various kinds of towers	Watchtower homogenization
2	Jiangmen city is quite suitable for photos tour, the biggest pit should be Kaiping towers, only four towers are available to visit the building, if not on the towers, completely free to buy tickets, the roadside randomly finds an entrance to get in	Part of the towers can not be visited	Some towers are not open
3	We kept thinking on the way: what if we can't get a taxi back…that should tell you how desolate it is along the way. Feels more remote than the village, this is not a former large family, is it just for vacation? It's also too inconvenient!	Desolate and remote along the way	Inconvenient transportation
4	The last attraction is the Maxianglong, which is far from other attractions, so the driver asked us to add money, which is the most uncomfortable part of this tour, after bargaining, gave an extra 50 yuan	Drivers add money on the spot	Poor personnel management
5	I do not like the Kaiping watchtower with not Chinese but also not foreign appearance. Fujian Yongding Hakka Tulou and Sichuan Qiang tower are more suitable for my feelings	Like other cultural heritage more	Lack of competitiveness
……	……	……	……

(*continued*)

Table 5. (*continued*)

Number	Part of the original content	Conceptualization	Categorization
254	And more towers are now empty, standing alone in the dense bamboo forest. The slanting sun reflects the swaying figure of the bamboo forest on the dappled fence as if a vivid ink painting. Inside the wall was empty and overgrown with weeds. The dark black door and narrow windows are closed and rusted. I do not know when the owners of the towers left the fortress-like building, and there is no way to know where they went	No one lives in the towers	The towers are dilapidated and silent
255	Modern tourism development also made some miniature towers placed in the scenic area, but how to look like a tomb, which makes me feel uncomfortable	Miniature towers like graves	Bizarre and quirky products
256	The more thunderous is to see a giant cockroach passing under our table, causing us to lose our voice and scream, and then the cockroach leisurely crawls to the neighboring table, the table of a four or five-year-old girl was shocked to step on, was stopped by her mother, my husband and I suddenly lost appetite, although the psychological preparation of the big stalls, but can not help such a test	Cockroaches crawl on the table	Poor food environment
257	To enter the Ruishi tower, we currently must give the owner a 10 yuan entrance fee, if you want to listen to his explanation, that needs another 10 yuan, and the owner of Mandarin is not very good, those who do not understand Cantonese will find it difficult to accept, it is not recommended	The local accent is too heavy	Unprofessional explanation

(*continued*)

Table 5. *(continued)*

Number	Part of the original content	Conceptualization	Categorization
258	I think you can escape the ticket, as long as you go in the other side of the villager's entrance, or find a villager to take you in and then give him some money that is not as expensive as the ticket 80 yuan, and although the student ticket only costs 40 yuan, I think it's only worth 20 yuan inside	Tickets are too expensive	Ticket price confusion

Table 6. Three-level coding process of negative affective influences

Open coding	Axial coding	Selective coding
Secondary charge phenomenon (15), The watchtower are poorly restored (10), Poor food environment (8), Poor personnel management (6)	Inadequate regulation (15.12%)	Scenic management (44.96%)
Inconvenient transportation (28), Ticket price confusion (19), Fewer accommodation services (15), Lack of signage guidelines (9), Uneven distribution of commercial areas (6)	Inadequate basic services (29.84%)	
The tragic history of the Chinese diaspora (25), Interior decoration equipment idle and abandoned (17), Sad Love Stories (16)	Expatriate history emotional (22.48%)	Diaspora history (22.48%)
Some towers are not open (17), Watchtower homogenization (9), watchtower are dilapidated and silent (7), Lack of competitiveness (7)	Watchtower architectural features (15.51%)	Building property (15.51%)
Unable to visit the whole tour (13), Cluttered human environment (12), Lack of popularity of scenic spots (8), Unprofessional interpretation services (6), Bizarre and quirky products (5)	Poor humanity experience (17.05%)	Humanity environment (17.05%)

Scenic area management mainly refers to the relevant government departments, scenic spot developers and watchtower owners and other stakeholders in the management of the loopholes that exist, which affects the image of tourists on the perception of the scenic area. The influence of scenic management factors on the expression of negative emotions of tourists is mainly manifested in the following points: Firstly, the destination range of service control on the impact of tourists, the light will cause boredom to tourists, the heavy will have an impact on the willingness of tourists to revisit and the dissemination of adverse external rhetoric and affect the status of the image of Kaiping Watchtower in the public vision. For example, one visitor mentioned that: "Jinjiangli, as a tourist attraction, is not friendly to the tourist, there was only one one-way lane when we drove into the place of interest, and there were no signs along the roads in the village to guide us to our destination, except for a parking fee at the intersection. Upon entering the village, there was a wild dog that came out of the village lane and barked at us from time to time. We changed several lanes to avoid that bad dog before approaching the watchtowers, yet we had to pay extra to enter the towers. Later we heard that this attraction is the tourism sector to sell tickets, but the management of the watchtowers is not them, but the owner of the watchtowers." Secondly, the quality of basic tourism services is poor, the industry is still immature resulting in the emergence of tourist dissatisfaction. As one visitor who was eating said: "I was stunned to see a giant cockroach pass under our table and screamed in terror, then the cockroach leisurely crawled to the next table, next to the little girl of four or five years old was shocked to step on, but was stopped by her mother, my husband and I suddenly appetite, although we have prepared in advance for a bad food environment here, we also couldn't withstand such a test."

Kaiping watchtowers and villages are Chinese first world cultural heritage sites with the characteristics of the overseas Chinese community. It is rich in historical traces because of the blood, geographical and business ties between overseas Chinese and their hometowns, including heroic deeds of defending the country against foreign enemies, as well as popular, touching and sad love stories, etc. Some of the visitors have emotional resonance when they experience the living environment of overseas Chinese and learn about the past through interpretation services. As one of the guides explained to us: "After the 1840s, the enemy's invasion plunged the people of the Kaiping area into the miserable plight. The colonists recruited Chinese people in large numbers by various swindles, and thousands of laborers were shipped to the United States and other places....... In the mid-nineteenth century, there were three large waves of labor migration in Kaiping under the deceptive propaganda of rhetoric....... However, the reality was cruel, as some Chinese were suffocated or died of disease in the bottom compartments of ocean liners before they could reach their destinations, and then the dead were thrown directly into the sea. However, even if the Chinese arrived abroad successfully, they were engaged in the dirtiest, most tiring and lowly jobs such as digging mines and building roads." On the other hand, there are also sad emotions that arise from hearing about the past experiences of the owner of the watchtower. For example, there is a tragic love story of a man named Tan Jixing, who was born in 1887: "In the past, Kaiping people have always held the tradition of starting a family before establishing a business. After marrying his wife at the age of 18, Tan Jixing went to Montreal, Canada, with his brother from the same village to engage in the laundry industry, hoping to save enough money to go home and revitalize his family. However, he was unable to save up enough money and spent his whole life in another country, not to mention reuniting with his parents and wife. It was not until he was 73 years old that he went back to see his wife. Two years later, his wife died of illness, and Tan Jixing also died in a foreign country." In Kaiping and Taishan, many women were widowed for life and raised their children and elderly alone.

The unique architectural art of the watchtower is a fusion of cultures from around the world, thus creating an appearance that some visitors consider "not Chinese, and not foreign". The scenic area inside the watchtower and nearby villages watchtower have greater similarities, the scenic area watchtower does not highlight their diversity, visitors perception that looks at the village watchtower and the watchtower in the scenic area is no different, so it is not considered worthwhile to spend money on tickets. Just like the visitor comments: "At first we saw one or two towers and thought we had never seen such a retro style of architecture before. But then we saw a lot of towers in this area felt that they all look the same, think it is not worth the 100-yuan admission fee." There are also tourists who do not have a deep understanding of the local diaspora culture, but only from the external appearance of the buildings for sightseeing. As one visitor said: "The interior of Watchtower does not give me too much feeling, I have been on the way to say with my partner that this is not the appearance of the countryside? Rural children know what these are, right?" There is also that the main building part of watchtowers after years of history, both external walls or internal decoration have different degrees of aging and damage, watchtowers owners or government escrow failed to repair promptly resulting in a decline in the psychological expectations of tourists. Once a visitor mentioned: "In the vicinity of the Zili village and Liyuan there are several watchtowers, but these watchtowers are slightly dilapidated, renovation is not good enough, and I also do not see someone in charge. I don't know if anyone still lives there, but no one should want to live in such a dilapidated place."

In addition to enjoying the architectural features of the towers, visitors will also experience the local human environment, hoping to become a part of the local community. For example, the combination of towers and the natural environment creates a peaceful and calm atmosphere, giving visitors the impression of relaxation and enjoyment. The local scenic area of dense bamboo forests, golden rice paddies, green lotus ponds and the long Tanjiang River into the watchtower buildings, giving us a sense of spatial and temporal dislocation. However, improper product design in the scenic area will destroy this atmosphere. Like a miniature watchtower as the epitome of the scenic area, it is considered that the design is like a tomb, which very much affects the visitor's sense of experience. There are also obstacles in communication with residents due to accents and other reasons. For instance, into the towers inside, the owner of the watchtower asked to explain, and the cost of admission requires an additional charge of 10–20 yuan, due to the relationship between the local accent, in the process of explaining the towers is not so smooth to convey the historical information to visitors. As one consumer reported that: "Ruishi tower not only famous, but also extremely personal, but because the towers owner and the government failed to negotiate, so enter the Ruishi tower must pay a separate fee to the owner, the owner will strongly recommend that tourists listen to him about the Feng Shui of Ruishi tower, of course, this is also charged separately. However, the accent was so heavy that those of us who came from the north didn't understand much.

5 Conclusion and Suggestion

5.1 Conclusion

This paper uses content analysis and grounded theory research method to analyze the visitor's perceived image and emotion analysis of Kaiping Watchtowers and villages and explores the factors influencing the expression of negative emotions of visitors. The main findings of this study are as follows: visitors to Kaiping watchtower's perception of the image is generally intuitive, summary, rough and superficial, the most prominent impression of the watchtowers are "Architecture" "Zili village" "Liyuan" "Overseas Chinese", etc. Visitor comments contain more intellectual descriptions and fewer statements expressing personal feelings. Visitors to Kaiping watchtower tourism perception image can be summarized as the image of the architectural landscape, the image of the spatial environment, the image of basic services, etc., and can be divided into four core categories of architectural image, artistic atmosphere, architectural function and humanistic history. In the tourist's perception of Kaiping watchtower tourism image, mainly positive emotions, followed by intermediate emotions, negative emotions last. The negative emotional expressions mainly include historical nostalgia, product features, transportation facilities, accommodation conditions, ticket prices, tour programs and interpretation services. Therefore, the manager should improve the real problems reflected by tourists to enhance the experience of tourists in the process of Kaiping Watchtower tourism. The article also explores the influencing factors of tourists' negative emotional expressions towards watchtowers through the grounded theory, summarizing 21 initial categories, 5 main categories and 4 core categories. Affecting tourists' negative emotions from high to low in the order of management-history-construction-environment, of which scenic management factors are the most important factors affecting the expression of tourists' negative emotions, concentrated in the supervision is not in place and service is not perfect.

5.2 Management Implication

The online image of Kaiping watchtowers and villages reveals a wide range of meaningful activities, while the characteristic activities are more lacking. The overall activity planning of rural tourism still needs to be improved, and the rural landscape, lifestyle, history and culture need to be expressed creatively. The presentation of the towers cannot remain merely visual, which may lead to aesthetic fatigue, and requires the development of specific, varied and creative destination interaction and experience activities. From a marketing perspective, the destination image is related to destination identity, and a successful rural tourism destination image needs to be maintained through strategic planning of tourism activities and stakeholder relationship management, therefore, corporate marketers need to carefully plan their image so that they can deliver a better experience for tourists and residents.

Explore the cultural and creative products of the diaspora to enrich the form of local tourism. In the context of the cultural and tourism integration era, the tourism process to highlight the cultural features, innovative cultural connotations is an important strategy to enhance tourist attractions. Managers should combine the local overseas Chinese culture, dig deep into the spirit of Chinese overseas Chinese who love to fight, love their families and country, and design it as tourism products so that the integration of intangible culture and tourism is transformed into itemization and industrialization. Such as the establishment of overseas Chinese cultural museums, to provide visitors with more channels and forms of understanding of local culture, the use of digital technology to virtualize the reality of watchtowers, so that the public use multiple channels to learn the history of watchtowers and architectural style in depth and detail. Secondly, there are many folklore festivals in Kaiping, such as lantern dances, dragon boat races, music festivals, etc. Using folklore activities for product innovation, realizing the development of cultural resource products, satisfying tourists' desire to consume local culture, driving the overall development of the tourism industry and promoting local economic development. Finally, we should work to expand the tourism population, create forms of tourism for educational purposes and to find ancestral homelands, and design product development for the descendants of overseas Chinese for educational purposes.

Strengthen tourism infrastructure services and support high-quality development of rural tourism. Negative comments from tourists are focused on transportation, entrance fees, programs, interpretation, accommodation and food, so managers should focus on service improvement in these areas. For example, the design of tour routes to help visitors to explore the target, the design of joint ticket tour bus service to help visitors to quickly tour route connection; Coordination of towers residents entrance fees, to eliminate the phenomenon of secondary charges, to achieve "a joint ticket, tour the whole", to prevent the tourist psychological gap, affecting the tourism experience. Open more access to watchtower tours, so that visitors have more options to visit the different watchtowers; Enhance the service quality of tourist attractions staff, to provide professional interpretation services, so that visitors can more easily feel and understand the story of the towers; The landscaped environment of the scenic area is renovated, the environmental health of the streets in the scenic area is improved, and a street of food and accommodation is planned to meet the basic consumption needs of tourists, such as food, accommodation, travel, entertainment and shopping.

5.3 Limitations

In this paper, only plain text on the well-known Chinese travel websites Ctrip, Ma Hive and GoWhere.com are selected for research and analysis, while there is a lack of research on pictures, videos, audios and other related data, which is a single source of data and has certain shortcomings in diversity. More attention should be paid to multiple sources and multiple data as research tools in future studies, so as to improve the scientific and persuasive power of research findings. In addition, the image perceptions and emotional expressions of tourist destinations identified in this paper through the method of grounded theory are all external cognitive processes expressed by tourists through words, and whether there are implicit cognitive processes and ways of tourists need to be further explored. Finally, because qualitative research relies more on the subjective judgment of the researcher, subsequent studies can use other empirical methods to test and refine the findings.

References

1. Yang, X., Pan, B., Evans, J.A., Lv, B.: Forecasting Chinese tourist volume with search engine data. Tour. Manage. **46**, 386–397 (2015). https://doi.org/10.1016/j.tourman.2014.07.019
2. Li, X., Pan, B., Law, R., Huang, X.: Forecasting tourism demand with composite search index. Tour. Manage. **59**, 57–66 (2017). https://doi.org/10.1016/j.tourman.2016.07.005
3. Mariani, M., Baggio, R., Fuchs, M., Höepken, W.: Business intelligence and big data in hospitality and tourism: a systematic literature review. Int. J. Contemp. Hosp. Manag. **30**, 3514–3554 (2018). https://doi.org/10.1108/ijchm-07-2017-0461
4. Boyd, D., Crawford, K.: Critical question for big data: provocations for a cultural, technological, and scholarly phenomenon. Inf. Commun. Soc. **15**, 662–679 (2012)
5. Hashem, I.A.T., Yaqoob, I., Anuar, N.B., Mokhtar, S., Gani, A., Khan, S.U.: The rise of "big data" on cloud computing: Review and open research issues. Inf. Syst. **47**, 98–115 (2015). https://doi.org/10.1016/j.is.2014.07.006
6. Li, J., Xu, L., Tang, L., Wang, S., Li, L.: Big data in tourism research: a literature review. Tour. Manage. **68**, 301–323 (2018). https://doi.org/10.1016/j.tourman.2018.03.009
7. Chen, G., et al.: Federation in cloud data management: challenges and opportunities. IEEE Trans. Knowl. Data Eng. **26**, 1670–1678 (2014)
8. Chen, G., Wu, S., Zhou, J., Tung, A.K.H.: Automatic itinerary planning for traveling services. IEEE Trans. Knowl. Data Eng. **26**, 514–527 (2014). https://doi.org/10.1109/tkde.2013.46
9. Zhu, Z., Shou, L., Chen, K.: Get into the spirit of a location by mining user-generated travelogues. Neurocomputing **204**, 61–69 (2016). https://doi.org/10.1016/j.neucom.2015.04.129
10. Baloglu, S., McCleary, K.W.: A model of destination image formation. Ann. Tour. Res. **26**, 868–897 (1999)
11. Grosspietsch, M.: Perceived and projected images of Rwanda: visitor and international tour operator perspectives. Tour. Manage. **27**, 225–234 (2006). https://doi.org/10.1016/j.tourman.2004.08.005
12. Selby, M., Morgan, N.J.: Reconstruing place image: a case study of its role in destination market research. Tour. Manage. **17**, 287–294 (1996)
13. MacKay, K.J., Fesenmaier, D.R.: Pictorial element of destination in image formation. Ann. Tour. Res. **24**, 537–565 (1997)
14. Molina, A., Esteban, Á.: Tourism brochures: usefulness and image. Ann. Tour. Res. **33**, 1036–1056 (2006). https://doi.org/10.1016/j.annals.2006.05.003
15. Yüksel, A., Akgül, O.: Postcards as affective image makers: an idle agent in destination marketing. Tour. Manage. **28**, 714–725 (2007). https://doi.org/10.1016/j.tourman.2006.04.026
16. Beerli, A., Martín, J.D.: Tourists' characteristics and the perceived image of tourist destinations: a quantitative analysis—a case study of Lanzarote, Spain. Tour. Manage. **25**, 623–636 (2004). https://doi.org/10.1016/j.tourman.2003.06.004
17. Martín, H.S, del Bosque, I.A.R.: Exploring the cognitive–affective nature of destination image and the role of psychological factors in its formation. Tour. Manage. **29**, 263–277 (2008). https://doi.org/10.1016/j.tourman.2007.03.012
18. Hong-bumm, K.: Perceived attractiveness of Korean destinations. Ann. Tour. Res. **25**, 340–361 (1998)
19. Sönmez, S.F.: Tourism, terrorism, and political instability. Ann. Tour. Res. **25**, 416–447 (1998)
20. Kim, H., Richardson, S.L.: Motion picture impacts on destination images. Ann. Tour. Res. **30**, 216–237 (2003). https://doi.org/10.1016/s0160-7383(02)00062-2
21. Frost, W.: Braveheart-ed Ned Kelly: historic films, heritage tourism and destination image. Tour. Manage. **27**, 247–254 (2006). https://doi.org/10.1016/j.tourman.2004.09.006

22. Mercille, J.: Media effects on image: the Case of Tibet. Ann. Tour. Res. **32**, 1039–1055 (2005). https://doi.org/10.1016/j.annals.2005.02.001
23. Smith, A.: Reimaging the city: the value of sport initiatives. Ann. Tour. Res. **32**, 217–236 (2005)
24. Kim, S.S., Morrsion, A.M.: Change of images of South Korea among foreign tourists after the 2002 FIFA World Cup. Tour. Manage. **26**, 233–247 (2005). https://doi.org/10.1016/j.tourman.2003.11.003
25. Yi, X., Fu, X., Yu, L., Jiang, L.: Authenticity and loyalty at heritage sites: the moderation effect of postmodern authenticity. Tour. Manage. **67**, 411–424 (2018). https://doi.org/10.1016/j.tourman.2018.01.013
26. Camprubí, R., Coromina, L.: Content analysis in tourism research. Tour. Manage. Perspect. **18**, 134–140 (2016). https://doi.org/10.1016/j.tmp.2016.03.002
27. Lian, T., Yu, C.: Representation of online image of tourist destination: a content analysis of Huangshan. Asia Pacific J. Tour. Res. **22**, 1063–1082 (2017). https://doi.org/10.1080/10941665.2017.1368678
28. Glaser, B.G., Strauss, A.L.: The discovery of grounded theory: strategies for qualitative research. Nurs. Res. **17**, 377–380 (1967). https://doi.org/10.2307/2575405
29. Pandit, N.R.: The creation of theory: a recent application of the grounded theory method. Qual. Rep. **2**, 1–15 (1996). https://doi.org/10.46743/2160-3715/1996.2054
30. Strauss, A., Corbin, J.: Grounded Theory Methodology: An Overview. Handbook of qualitative research thousand oaks sage publications (1994)
31. Noble, H., Mitchell, G.: What is grounded theory? Evid. Based Nurs. **19**, 34–35 (2016). https://doi.org/10.1136/eb-2016-102306

Research on the Future Trend of Digital Culture Driving the Development of Regional Culture:

Taking Liaoning National Pattern Database Design as an Example

Lu Zhao and Ruhe Zhang(✉)

Luxun Academy of Fine Arts, Shenyang 110004, Liaoning, People's Republic of China
zhangruhe1984@qq.com

Abstract. Under the concept of Society 5.0, cities strive to give humans a more meaningful way to attract visitors to communicate with each other to reshape their own regional space, and the digital economy has empowered the development and transformation of regional culture in the digital space. The research question of this paper aims to explore the digital cultural information transmission with ethnic patterns in Liaoning region through design practice. The research methods include literature study, case analysis, in-depth interviews, etc. Starting from the research on the relevance of information design, through theoretical analysis of digital cultural information carriers, media, channels, media, etc., focusing on the problems and challenges encountered in practice, and introducing "futuristic" methods through "causal hierarchical analysis". The result of practical research is that the information visualization design of digital culture can drive the revitalization of Liaoning regional culture. In the information transmission problem of different dimensions, the innovative method provided by the causal level analysis can be regarded as a process of "practice" and "speculation". This also provides more possibilities for future researchers and designers to solve similar practical topics.

Keywords: Information design · National culture · Digital culture · Cultural revitalization · Futurology

1 Preface

The Viejo Museum of Panama provides an online archaeological register digital platform where visitors to the website can browse the collections and view the results of current archaeological investigations, helping the data museum find new roles to assume at the level of information transmission and find new audiences. And build the museum website into a new carrier of digital culture, which can carry out more diversified information dissemination and interpretation of museum collections [1].

From a practical point of view, the above case is very important for us to optimize the digital cultural issues for the purpose of optimizing the tangible and intangible cultural heritage of Liaoning, as Schachtner (2013) said: The cultural content and space presented by digital media The best embodiment of interaction is the tourism industry [2]. The

P.-L. P. Rau (Ed.): HCII 2022, LNCS 13314, pp. 461–473, 2022.
https://doi.org/10.1007/978-3-031-06053-3_31

team used innovative thinking to build a database platform with culture as the core, focusing on the information dissemination of Liaoning culture, establishing a unique cultural confidence in the north, and empowering Liaoning's digital culture and tourism. Revitalize the overall development of Liaoning.

From the perspective of theoretical research, Fig. 1 (see Fig. 1) uses CiteSpace to search and count the literature in the fields of "information design" and "visualization". The lines indicate the distribution of keywords that have appeared in the past literature at the same time. We can observe that the current research in related fields focuses on data visualization, database, computer science, etc. Specifically focusing on digital museum collections, a large number of researchers and designers include Manovic [3], Wendhag et al. [4], Serves et al. [5], Shakley [6], Shakley Gretzell and others [7] all study and research in this field. Therefore, the ability to introduce information design to the study of regional culture from the perspective of design theory and practice is a powerful supplement to "visualization" in literature research, and it is also the meaning of research.

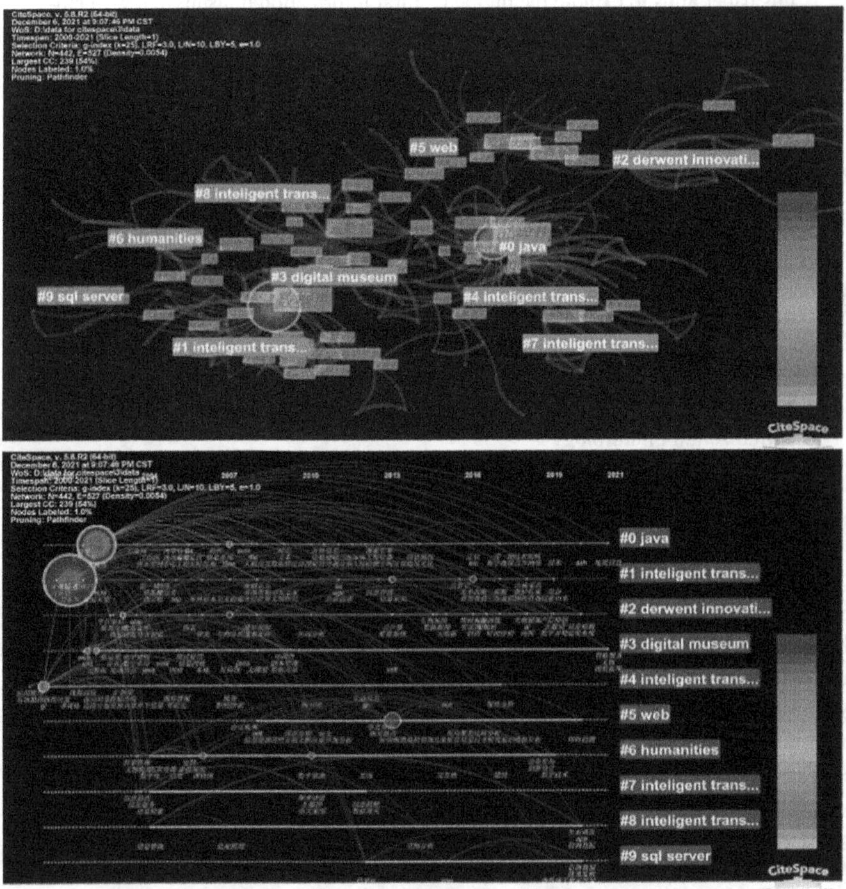

Fig. 1. Literature review about visualization by CiteSpace, 2021

2 Carriers, Channels, Media, and Media of Digital Cultural Information

The value of the research of this subject is to promote the design of the source power from task-driven to problem-driven. In the Liaoning environment, information design empowers the full-dimensional information transmission of national culture in digital media. The concept of "database" is no longer a task of integrating a large collection of "metadata" in the traditional sense. On the contrary, we do not pursue the volume of data, but use innovative ideas to find out our own understanding of the subject.

The "library" in the theme expresses the meaning of "integrating into the library" for each category of design. The digital website in this practice covers the process of data collection, research and analysis, design and implementation of digital content for detailed display, so there is the concept of "database", which is also called "carrier" in semiotics [8].

With the deepening of the research, the team found that the graphics that can represent the national culture of Liaoning are not limited to pattern forms. Many regional cultures such as technical crafts, architectural heritage, and festival folk customs can be transformed into graphics for information transmission. Subject to discussion, the design will be limited to the graphical visualization of a certain ethnic group, which is not conducive to the full display of Liaoning's national culture. So, we redefine the previous "Pattern" and "Form" respectively. "Pattern" represents the substance when the symbolic information including patterns and graphics is transmitted. It has the function of a sensor to allow information to be transmitted in perception, which means "medium".

"Form" is for in-depth study of the delivery method of digital content. Any fragmented data such as primitive graphics, images, sound, and video can be called data. Different types of data will be set by the designer into different acquisition modes, including perception systems such as vision, hearing, smell, touch, etc., and then guide users to understand the transformation of data into information. This is a process of selecting and transmitting "paradigms" for different information, Is also the extended meaning of "form" in "pattern forms". It refers to the transmission path of visual "form" and the path of data to the visual sense organs, which is described as "channel".

The information conveyed by the media will get more people's attention, and at the same time, it will be abstracted as information. Several groups or people report on the same event to form a news event. This is the embodiment of information placed in the society and is called media. This design practice also encourages more people to pay attention to the characteristics of Liaoning's region and national culture, and arouses discussion on the digital platform, forming news attention points. Therefore, the design of this database is a process of researching Liaoning cultural information symbols from "carrier-media-channel-media" to meet the demands of more visitors for "acquisition of cultural information".

3 Problems and Challenges in Practice

Design practice often finds solutions from problems, and each problem is actually a task goal finally achieved by practice. Through research, we have summarized three major issues around this topic: the "pertinence", "boring feeling" and "authenticity" of information.

The first problem is the lack of targeted digital information transmission in the display of regional culture. After decades of digital development, the network has become a huge digital museum, and the digital content carried by the virtual space is endless. The scholar Manovich (Manovich, L) is aware of the next problem: finding the content you want, such as historical and cultural information, is very complicated [3]. Because most visitors or users are not historians or cultural experts, they usually don't know what they can get from digital information.

Apply the first question to this design practice, and the corresponding focus is cultural cognition and topic selection. 1. Cultural cognition, Liaoning culture is rich in material and intangible cultural resources due to its geographical and historical reasons. The minority culture represented by Manchu is even more unique. How to guide users who are not familiar with this field to create faster efficiency in the process of receiving information, remembering information, and transforming knowledge is a challenge. 2. Accurate dissemination, the team needs to select the most representative and influential themes from many Liaoning cultural materials. This is the fundamental solution to the lack of "targeted" cultural information dissemination problem described in the previous article.

The second problem is the visual transmission of boring information. The presentation of most regional and cultural information media is unattractive. This view, called the "passive dimension" [9], further shows that it is difficult for the boring and unfamiliar digital content to generate valuable knowledge to encourage users to remember. Although there are a lot of related research and practice about digital information transmission to regional culture and national culture, most of them focus on digital technology issues such as content websites and mobile terminal information transmission and lack the "technical aesthetics" that juxtaposes information functions and aesthetics discussion.

The practical research of visualization under digital media, which conducts efficient transmission of information on mobile terminals such as mobile phones and tablet computers via the Internet, is not mature enough. We need to think about how to display attractive data and vividly portray cultural data in an environment where "everything is a screen" the story of back. Furthermore, the team needs to think about the intelligent innovation of visual interactive experience, stimulate the core values of cultural interaction, use "deep experience" to link the online participation of creators and visitors, emphasize the concept of "co-creation" [2], and increase information Flowing fun.

The third problem is the humanity of digital information, which is also described as the "fact" deviation control in the content of the communication [10], and cultural information design should not be reduced to an inherent mode. The team also agrees that people are willing to accept more specific forms of information to convey. Of course, this is to put the context in the humanistic information. If you blindly simplify it, you may lose the meaning of creativity.

We also need to be aware of another kind of sound: the more beautiful and richer the image is perceived; the viewer will spend more time and energy trying to interpret its meaning. What needs to be considered in the visualization of Liaoning's national pattern, culture, and history information is also the grasp of the "degree" of facts from the perspective of humanism. In the design process, it is necessary to combine the knowledge and understanding of historical documents, take into account the true reproduction of objective things, have the function of efficient transmission, and take into account the aesthetic experience. Therefore, the visual expression of this topic is neither purely "functionalism" nor purely "crafts and arts" thinking but should be an exploration of "data humanism" under "conceptual thinking".

From a micro perspective, the three issues are the issues that this research should focus on, but at the macro level, they are the challenges faced by information design in the dissemination of digital content. We can use mapping technique (mapping technique, direct expression of data, or use metaphor to refer to the meaning of data) and data focus (data focus, the content presented when data is transformed into information) to "empirically" information design characterized by "technical aesthetics" Inductive research, but more problem-solving ideas come from challenges in practice. The best solution is to experience problems in the process of "discovering".

4 The Determination of Digital Content-Thinking on Question One

"Rare is precious", choosing the cultural heritage on the brink of disappearance among the many Liaoning cultures is the motivation for determining the theme, which is also an attempt to solve the problem of "targeted" information. The team found that there are very few carriers that truly include the traditional culture of Liaoning. They can only start with ancient books, which are important carriers for recording national history and thoughts. They not only condense the essence of traditional national culture, but also can look back on the past, understand customs, and understand culture through ancient books. Many ancient books are a double-edged sword. On the one hand, a large number of text and picture records are indeed the most solid resources for research on this subject; on the other hand, a large variety of ancient books also means that there will be a large number of repetitions and directly lead to lack of the output of "targeted" information.

When describing the "passive dimension", Professor Servez mentioned that one of the factors that produce the sense of boredom is because they are produced in different time and space and seem to have nothing to do with the current "you". The futurist Sohail Inayatullah (2008) put forward the futuristic theory (Futures Thinking) [11] this problem has brought a source of inspiration: "To predict the future is to explore the present, And the past that has an impact on the present". As shown in Fig. 2 (see Fig. 2), according to the "future triangle" model, we can regard "future" as a dynamic point in a time dimension, and "future" can be "now" or eventually "past", consisting of three-time nodes The three different forces are also destined to be inseparable. Therefore, the best way to solve the "targeted" dissemination of information is to infiltrate the historical characteristics of culture and its impact on the present in the focus of the data, to guide visitors to judge the future results of the theme, so that visitors can feel the "pattern"——The media and channels of cultural information are related to oneself.

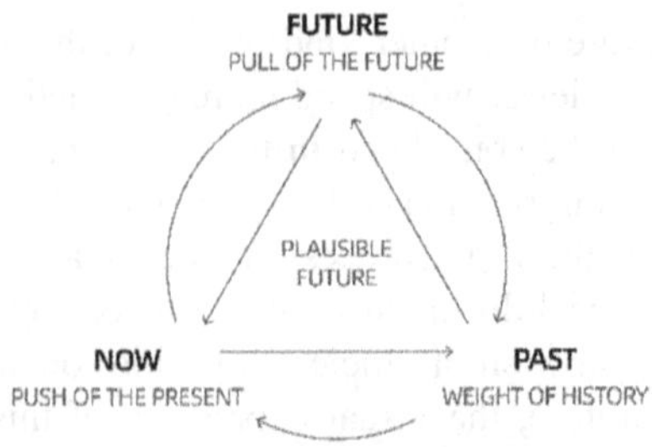

Fig. 2. The futures triangle Sohail Inayatullah, 2008

The ancient book "Shengjing Fu" is used as the main reference material for this subject because of its precious and rich information records of Liaoning history and resources. As an ancient book that is poorly understood by modern people, "Shengjing Fu" recorded a lot of information about Manchu from tribe to society, from emperor to common people, and these "pasts" have a huge impact on the development of Liaoning and even the whole country. The team compared many materials of ancient books and finally determined several themes. Here, three representative themes were found for description:

1. The main body of Shengjing Fu. "Shengjing Fu" is an important ancient book describing the whole picture of Liaoning. Through a comparative study of Manchu and Simplified Chinese, we drew the information map shown in Fig. 3, summarizing the order of Fu, Fu, and Ode, mainly about the tradition of Shengjing, the ancestors of Manchu, Baqi culture, Shengjing history, Liaoning products and other details. The ancient books stimulated the team's interest in studying the related influences on modern society in the past, which are very good design subjects in themselves.

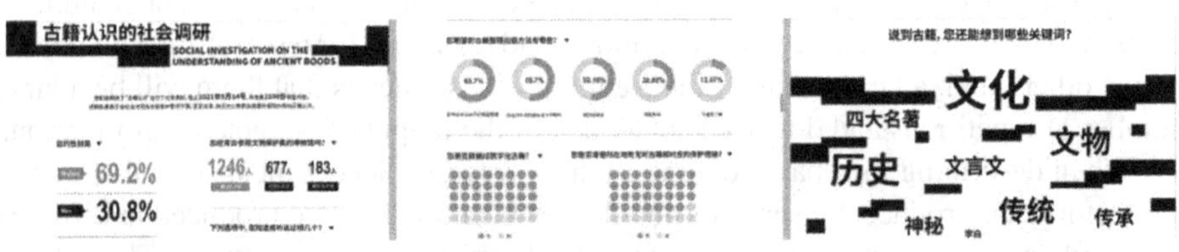

Fig. 3. Survey information map of Ode part of Shengjing Fu Lu zhao, Ruhe Zhang, Yijia Sun, Qianlan Jin, Ming Jin, Xiang Li) 2021

2. Count. Embroidery. Manchu embroidery was included in the second batch of China's national intangible cultural heritage catalog in 2008. As shown in Fig. 4 below, the research team has collected 200 sets of embroidery works through "Shengjing Fu" and documents. Statistics show that 81 sets of works contain 25 animal patterns, 91 sets of works contain 14 kinds of plant patterns, and 28 sets of works contain 8 other patterns. This topic can be explored through process information diagrams and

modern visual language to explore the "modernization" of the history of the "past" as visual knowledge, and to provide a basis for solving the second problem-avoiding "boring" information. Seek the "initiative" of the visitor to read the information.

Fig. 4. Information collection of Manchu patterns in Liaoning (part) Lu Zhao, Ruhe Zhang, Yijia Sun, Siqi Yang, Jialin Dong 2021

3. Square and circular trajectories. The focus of the data is on the design and research of the Manchu cultural relics in Liaoning. There are six world cultural heritages in Liaoning Province, four of which are Manchus, namely Qing Fu Mausoleum, Shenyang Imperial Palace, Qing Zhao Mausoleum and Qing Yong Mausoleum. Although the site has experienced many different degrees of natural disasters or man-made damage, it has fully recorded the splendor of the Manchu culture during its heyday. The information visualization of spatial subjects is faced with problems two and three, namely, avoiding the accumulation of boring information and grasping the degree of "real" reproduction of objective things.

5 Upgrading of the Visualization Paradigm of "strengthening the Future"——Thinking of Question Two and Question Three

The specific visualized execution stage is to speculate on core issues two and three. From an innovative point of view, the team has learned valuable experience in solving problems from futuristic theory, using "Deepening the Future", one of the six major elements of theory, and discussing it through Causal Layered Analysis (CLA) The method of solving "problems two and three", this process is also regarded as the process of upgrading the research in the decision-making stage of the visualization paradigm. What needs to be explained is that futurology is not only a narrowly defined space-time concept of "future", it is also regarded as an intelligent theory that describes problems in all dimensions and proposes solutions. After all, "new" descriptions and solutions are all geared toward "new" The exploration of the future is also an optimization process for explaining and solving current problems in the future. This method of analysis includes four levels: the first is declarative, that is, the future that passes day by day. Describe things or what they might look like from the surface, and usually the solutions are short-term; the second is a deeper level of systemic factors, mainly focusing on the social, economic and political factors; the third level is the world view, To place the problem on a global scale, to stimulate the overall view of the problem, this level is the key level to understand the real or virtual world, which can help people shape the world in cognition; the fourth level is metaphor or myth. It belongs to the exploration level of deep consciousness. Generally speaking, the first and second levels are easy to see, while the third and fourth levels are more extensive but deep. The last two core questions have been sorted out and answered, so as to facilitate the exploration of solutions in design practice.

In response to problem two-the problem of dull information, after brainstorming, the team design department put forward suggestions to solve the problem from four levels. On the first level, the objectively stated problem is the abstraction of national cultural data and lack of image and graphic expression. The solution is to increase the design of visual elements, including graphics, colors, etc. At the second level, the team tries to find out the reason for the abstraction of the information. Corresponding to social relations, is this because people themselves feel boring to the abstract quantification of raw data? Corresponding to the economic relationship, the conversion of abstract data into visual graphics requires higher technology or cost? Systematic decomposition of problems and solutions is to make the entire system more efficient and agile to intervene in the core problems, to ensure that the decomposed sub-problems can be closely connected. The final method proposed is to increase the narrative logic and narrative power of data and transform the "passive acceptance of knowledge" into "active acquisition of content" through design innovation. On the third level, from the perspective of the world, the team found that people are full of "knowledge" strangeness to regional ethnic culture, and the distance of information on the Internet. The digital content at this stage, as the medium of information symbols, seems to be at the highest level of cognition, while the visitor, as the receiver of information, is the lowest level of cognitive behavior, so only the transformation and design of graphics and the system are emphasized. The construction of a modernized digital platform is useless. The solution is to shift the focus of data through a mapping method, weaken the concept of "knowledge" with a more vivid visual expression, and relieve the interviewer's sense of oppression of cultural information. Visualization method to further solve.

At the mythological level, the deeper level of the problem is that "the focus of data is the content that the information wants to convey to the visitor, but it is not necessarily the easiest content for the visitor to understand." In fact, this part is to think in reverse. "If Information is unwilling or difficult to be understood by others, what will happen?" At this stage, there is often no direct method. We need to create a new story to change the way of thinking, create a new paradigm for the future optimization of the problem, and increase new understanding. The causal hierarchical analysis process for question two is shown in Fig. 5 (see Fig. 5) below.

Problem 2	The Content Of Information Dissemination Is Boring	
Causal Layered Analysis Level	Questions	Strategies
Litany	Cultural data is abstract, lacks image and graphic expression	To add visual elements such as graphics and colors
Systemic Causes	Unfamiliar with abstract perception, higher technology is needed to guide the transmission of cultural information	To increase narrative logic and motivation. To change "passive" to "active"
Worldview	The sense of strangeness and distance of "knowledge"	Mapping data focus with meta-phor to weaken the oppression of "knowledge"
Myth & Metaphor	The information itself does not want to be understood	To create new paradigms, new stories and new cognition

Fig. 5. Problem 2 description based on causal layered analysis level Lu Zhao, Ruhe Zhang 2021

For question three, the team tried to "strengthen the future" to propose the "degree" of the authenticity restoration of Liaoning "pattern" data.

At the declarative level, the problem can be described as "the information in the database is difficult to balance the transmission function of the information and the aesthetic experience of restoring authenticity". The solution is to ensure functionality and increase aesthetics.

At the systemic level, the question should be viewed from the dimensions of the "database" carrier, channel and media of Liaoning national culture. Do visitors recognize the metaphorical meaning of information in the mapping? Should the function of information be put in the first place to meet the needs of visitors? The implementation method is to think about the essence of information transmission from the perspective of "people-oriented". Taking "Shengjing Fu" as an example, the team used the emperors who established the core political status in Shengjing (now Shenyang) as the prototype to visualize the design, but its past experience The narrative expression is based on font typesetting as much as possible, with a small amount of graphic design, and more is to import the data "original" content of ancient books into the data platform to reduce the occurrence of "excessive" design and facilitate more people to read the information (see Fig. 6).

Fig. 6. Display of <Sheng Jing Fu> on the data platform (part) Lu Zhao, Ruhe Zhang, Yijia Sun, Qianlan Jin, Ming Jin, Xiang Li) 2021

In the world view stage, the focus of the problem is that the context problem determines the information design as a measure of technical aesthetics. Specifically, the information of historical and cultural events needs to consider background factors such as time stage, origin area, participants, etc., that is, starting from the three factors of "person, time, and space" of narrative logic, comprehensively considering the priority of function and aesthetics relation. Figure 7 shows the work "Square and circular trajectories". Although the work uses architecture as the core for a visual narrative, the innovative ideas skip the discussion of "authenticity" restoration but cross the "time" factor from the "space" factor to establish the Liaoning Manchu the evolution of the "people" of the architectural heritage, and then effectively visualize the spatial database, restoring the changes and hidden narrative clues of different buildings in the special time and space. This design method does not entangle the problem of "degree", but visually analyze the data from the context, which is invisibly related to the function and aesthetic essence of the data "pattern".

Fig. 7. Display of <The tangible cultural heritage of Manchou architecture> on the data platform (part) Lu Zhao, Ruhe Zhang, Yijia Sun, Lu Liu, Ruhe Zhang 2021

In the stage of myth and metaphor, the team simulated the most extreme situation: If there is only textual expression, how will the information be presented? This is a pseudo-scientific idea of reverse deduction. Through this method, the situation is pushed to the most extreme result, and then corrected back. This can solve problems such as "Which one to choose from this two" and "how much". problem. Figure 8 shows the visualization of "Numerical Embroidery" through the flow chart paradigm. When real graphics are used to map Manchu pattern data, from the very beginning to the concrete graphics, the graphics are gradually "subtracted" and observed by more interviewees. Give feedback and stop the abstraction and simplification work at the node where the interviewee thinks the recognition rate is the highest. This can effectively help visitors perceive what the data should have, bring it into the real past time and space, and experience the narrative field of the information.

As Yin Yandi said: The highest state of cultural aesthetics is "harmony" with culture, and the result of harmony is the convergence based on the common human emotions [12]. When the design achieves resonance between information transmission and emotional cognition, it is the best explanation for the problem of "degree". The causal hierarchical analysis process for question three is shown in Fig. 8 below (see Fig. 8) (Fig. 9).

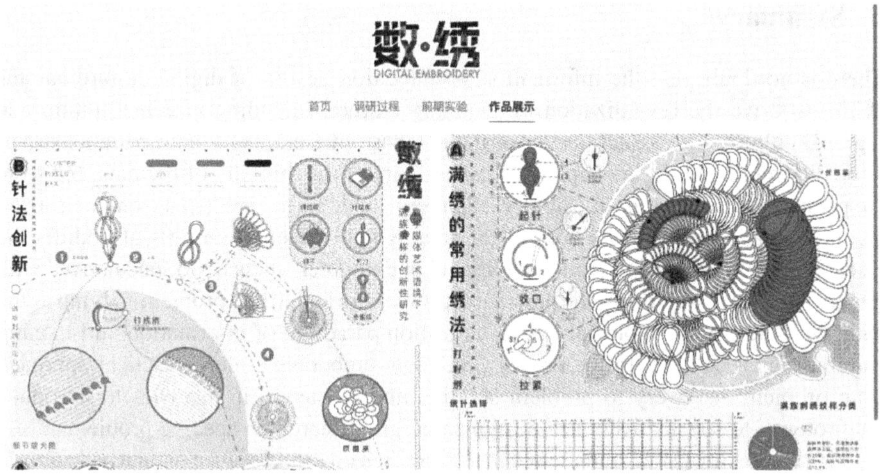

Fig. 8. Display of <Digital Embroidery> on the data platform (part) Lu Zhao, Ruhe Zhang, Yijia Sun, Siqi Yang, Jialin Dong 2021

Problem 3	"Degree" Of Information "Authenticity" Restoration	
Causal Layered Analysis Level	Questions	Strategies
Litany	Difficult to balance the "degree" of function and aesthetics	To ensure function and Then increase Aesthetics
Systemic Causes	Does the metaphor of information carrier, channel and media correspond to the interviewer's cognition	To Think about the essence of information transmission from the perspective of "humanism"
Worldview	The context of information determines the standard of technical aesthetics	To consider the three factors of "person, time and space"
Myth & Metaphor	What happens if there is only text	To add detailed design from extreme nodes

Fig. 9. Problem 3 description based on causal layered analysis level Lu Zhao, Ruhe Zhang 2021

It needs to be explained that there is no right or wrong in the four dimensions of "strengthening the future". Futurology is a multi-dimensional prediction of the description and solution of the problem. In actual use, it is more appropriate to choose a certain dimension to solve the problem according to the specific problem. This also reflects the rationality and comprehensiveness of the introduction of futurology on the subject. In the practice of this topic, the "strengthening" level selected in the second question is the third-dimensional worldview dimension, that is, the "knowledge" attribute of the database is weakened with a vivid graphic scheme; and the third question is for different topics corresponding to different dimensions. This also reflects the diversity and flexibility of this research method.

6 Summary

There is no doubt that the information visualization design of digital culture has the ability to drive the revitalization of Liaoning culture, including national culture and regional culture. The visual design of the database of Liaoning ethnic patterns strives to be different from the concept of "database" under the thinking of big data, but from the perspective of innovation, "library", "pattern" and "form" are taken from the carrier, medium, channel and media concept of data symbols. Definition, this also shifts the research path of the design from "empirical" in computer science to "speculative" with humanism. The beginning of the practice is problem-oriented and problem-solving as the path, with the goal of exploring the visualization paradigm of information on Liaoning cultural digital content. In the process, the team embodies a more practical approach from problem discovery to problem solving, and in theory, it also tries to introduce "futurology" to speculatively and design paradigm research on specific problems.

Myra Shackley (1997) mentioned in the research on the relevance of data and cultural tourism: digital culture as a content of tourism, the core of which is whether information can be effectively transmitted and pointed out that it is "effective" It is the double meaning of "meaningful" and "interesting" [13]. Therefore, the challenge of the team in the practice of this subject is also the trade-off relationship between the function of information design and the aesthetics. In the process of "empirical" and "speculative", we conducted different specific analyses on different topics, and tried to use "enhance the future". Innovative way of thinking to solve this problem.

The research on this subject is sustainable, and the innovation of Liaoning national culture in design is not overnight. In the future, on the existing basis, the team will introduce innovative concepts from the user's interactive behavior of digital information and digital collections (NFT) with national cultural characteristics, and implement the cross-border integration of technology and art into specific practices., And strive to transform Liaoning's national "pattern database" into a multi-dimensional platform for Liaoning's digital culture, combining specific policies and pragmatic design to empower Liaoning's revitalization and development in the fields of digital economy, digital tourism, and digital culture.

References

1. Boyd, D.: Taken Out of Context: American Teen Sociality in Networked Publics. Diss. D. Phil. Berkeley: University of California (2008)
2. Schachtner, C.: Digital media evoking interactive games in virtual space. Subjectivity **6**(1), 33–54 (2013). https://doi.org/10.1057/sub.2012.27
3. Manovich, L.: Cultural Data. Museum and Archive on the Move, 259–276 (2017). https://doi.org/10.1515/9783110529630-017
4. Windhager, F., Federico, P., Mayr, E.,Smuc, M.: A Review of Information Visualization Approaches and Interfaces to Digital Cultural Heritage Collections, pp. 74–81 (2016)
5. Services, C., Development, E., Change, C., Use, L., Safety, P., Trust, P.: How the Arts and Cultural Tourism Spur Economic Development (2013)
6. Shackley, M., Shackley, M.: Sustainable Tourism Saving Cultural Information : The Potential Role of Digital Databases in Developing Cultural Tourism, pp. 244–249, November 2014. https://doi.org/10.1080/09669589708667289

7. Gretzel, U., Koo, C., Sigala, M., Xiang, Z.: Special issue on smart tourism: convergence of information technologies, experiences, and theories. Electron. Mark. **25**(3), 175–177 (2015). https://doi.org/10.1007/s12525-015-0194-x
8. Yiheng, Z.: "Media" and "media": a Semiotic discrimination. Contempor. Literary Circ. **5** (2012)
9. Binkhorst, E., Dekker, T.D.: Agenda for co-creation tourism experience research. J. Hosp. Leis. Mark. **18**(2–3), 311–327 (2009). https://doi.org/10.1080/19368620802594193
10. Richards, G.: Recipes for sustainable creative tourism. In: Proceedings of the Third Business Management International Conference, Pattaya, Thailand, 5–6 November 2015
11. Inayatullah, S.: Six pillars: futures thinking for transforming. Foresight **10**(1), 4–21 (2008). https://doi.org/10.1108/14636680810855991
12. Yandi, Y.: Aesthetic Interpretation of Cultural Tourism (Master's thesis, Shandong Normal University) (2010)
13. Shackley, M.: Saving cultural information: The potential role of digital databases in developing cultural tourism. J. Sustain. Tour. **5**(3), 244–249 (1997). https://doi.org/10.1080/09669589708667289

Reconstruction Strategy of Traditional Village Architecture Based on System Theory

Li Zheng(✉) and Xiaolan Huang

South China University of Technology, Guangzhou 510641, China
lizheng@scut.edu.cn

Abstract. Guangzhou Puxin Village is a typical traditional village on the fringe of Guangdong.Its traditional village architecture has distinctive Lingnan characteristics and has important research value. However, with the rapid change of society and the rapid advancement of urbanization, the structure and functional space of traditional village buildings in Puxin Village can no longer meet the needs of The Times, and a large number of village buildings are facing the dilemma of idle, collapse or even disappearance all the year round. This dilemma is accompanied by the destruction of the fabric of traditional villages and the loss of cultural heritage. Starting from the protection and activation of traditional village buildings in Puxin Village, Huangpu District, Guangzhou, this article will use the system theory to analyze the hierarchical relationship of "element-structure-relation-environment" in the protection and activation of traditional village buildings, discuss the systematic characteristics of traditional village buildings in Puxin Village, Guangzhou, and discover, diagnose, qualitatively identify its system problems, and confirm Revamp the target and propose a design strategy for protection and activation. It is hoped to provide guidance for the protection and activation of surrounding traditional village buildings and add samples for the protection and activation of surrounding traditional village buildings.

Keywords: System theory · Traditional village architecture · System theory

1 Overview of Puxin Village, Guangzhou

1.1 A Subsection Sample

Puxin Village is located in the northeast of Longhu Street, Jiulong Town, Huang-pu District, the eastern suburbs of Guangzhou, Guangdong Province. It is adjacent to Yingxia Village to the southeast, Folong Village of Jiufo Street to the north, Hetangxia Village to the southwest, and Fuhe Town, Zengcheng to the east. The location of the village is combined with the mountain topography, and together with the fields and transportation in the settlement, it shows the ideal relationship of "near fields, near mountains, and near traffic", reflecting the inter-connected and interdependent relationship between the village and the geographical environment. Today, Puxin Village basically retains the "field-village-hill" spatial pattern, forming an overall style pattern built on hills and rich in layers (see Fig. 1).

P.-L. P. Rau (Ed.): HCII 2022, LNCS 13314, pp. 474–484, 2022.
https://doi.org/10.1007/978-3-031-06053-3_32

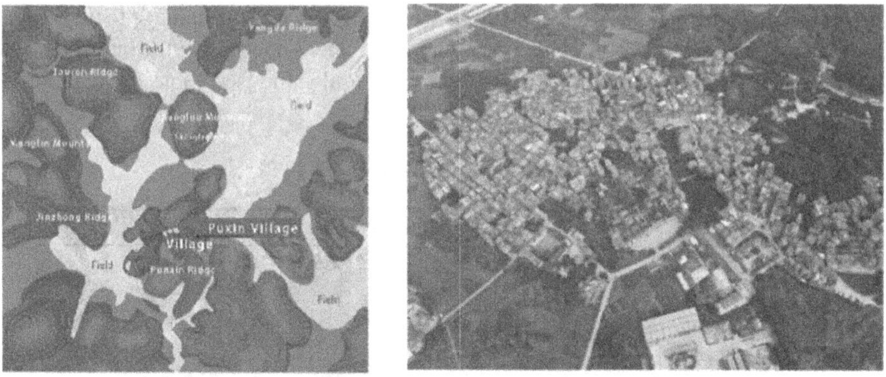

Fig. 1. Left: Landscape pattern map during the period of 1955; Right: Aerial view of the status (Source: from the project team)

1.2 The Current Situation of Traditional Village Buildings in Puxin Village

With the changes of the times, the old houses that have been built for a long time can no longer meet the growing residential needs of residents, which has caused part of the population in the village to move to the city and part of the population to the new village. On the other hand, the property rights of traditional dwellings in Puxin Village are complex. They are usually old ancestral houses, and descendants have separated and moved out of the old houses. The village is gradually becoming hollow, uninhabited and used, and because the old house that has been in disrepair requires maintenance and repair costs much higher than the new building, it also makes future generations neglect the maintenance of the old house, so that the old village of Puxin Village Decline further(see Fig. 2).

Fig. 2. Current state of some buildings in Puxin Village

As Guangzhou has a subtropical monsoon climate, with long rainy seasons, frequent typhoons, and hollowing, traditional buildings are left unattended for a long time and are easily damaged in the natural environment. This has caused many traditional buildings to be damaged in varying degrees due to disrepair over the years, posing safety hazards. For example, brick walls have cracks and collapses, serious wall foundation moss and other problems, and wooden structures have problems such as decay and fracture, and serious damage. The building has even collapsed partially or completely, becoming ruins. In addition, the villagers' ignorance of traditional building repairs and renovation methods led to wrong repairs or renovations, which aggravated the damage to traditional buildings and repeated cycles, which could neither restore nor protect the buildings, but also destroy the history of traditional buildings Cultural value (see Table 1 and Table 2).

Table 1. Damage of building structure

Type	Concrete example		
Wall	 Wall cracking	 The wall collapsed	 Moss on wall base is serious
Beam	 Wooden beam damage	 Pillar broken	 Beam column collapsed

Table 2. Damage to the exterior of a building

Type	Concrete example		
Facade	 Metope damaged	 Mismatch between old and new	 Pipeline crossing
Decoration	 The mural is mottled and faded	 Sculpture is damaged	 Doors and Windows broken
Roof	 The roof is damaged	 The roof collapsed	

2 Perspective of Research on Protection and Revitalization System of Traditional Village Buildings

2.1 A. Understanding of the Systematic Research on the Protection and Activation of Traditional Village Buildings in Puxin Village, Guangzhou

The protection and activation of traditional village buildings in Puxin Village, Guangzhou is an integrated design, which requires systematic consideration of architectural technical hardware, architectural design prototypes, and architectural grammar, which will eventually be compounded in the era transformation of traditional village buildings [1]. The protection and revitalization of traditional village buildings in Puxin Village is a system with regional, cultural characteristics and models, and its value should be evaluated using system theory. When constructing the traditional village building system of Puxin Village, it should first be refined into the four levels of element, level, structure, and environment. Then, each level should be analyzed in a simple way, and the problems should be found, diagnosed, and qualitatively established. Goals, and finally put forward a solution strategy. The protection and activation of the traditional village buildings in Puxin Village can be achieved by integrating system elements, optimizing the system structure, caring for the system and the environment, while enhancing the multi-level correlation between the traditional village building system, and realizing the protection of the traditional village buildings in Puxin Village. And activation.

The traditional village building system of Puxin Village in Guangzhou is integrated. If the various elements in the system are confused, the quality of protection and activation of traditional villages will be reduced and the goal of protection and activation will not be achieved. Therefore, it is necessary to effectively coordinate the traditional village protection and activation system from the perspective of system theory, and finally achieve the purpose of protecting and activating traditional village buildings.

2.2 Analysis on the Protection and Activation System of Traditional Village Buildings in Puxin Village, Guangzhou

System Element Analysis. There are many types of system elements involved in the protection and activation of the traditional village building system of Puxin Village in Guangzhou, which can be divided into tangible elements and intangible elements.

Among them, the tangible elements include the volume, materials, components, functions, etc. of the building. Nowadays, Puxin Village is traditional Most of these elements in the village buildings no longer meet the needs of modern use. In response to this situation, the following methods can be used to reproduce and reuse: maintain the original traditional village architectural features and inherit its original craftsmanship; incorporate new materials and new technologies to break through the traditional villages The limitations of the building itself in terms of function and structure; appropriately change the function and purpose of the original building to inject new vitality into it.

The intangible elements include design strategy elements, design techniques elements, laws and regulations elements, etc., which provide basic guidance for specific protection and activation design. The elements are interrelated and inseparable, and have an impact on the protection and revitalization of traditional village buildings in different aspects that cannot be ignored.

System Element Analysis. For the traditional villages of Puxin Village in Guangzhou, the architectural system has obvious hierarchical characteristics, and its systems and elements have relativity. The traditional village building system of Puxin Village is divided layer by layer, and each layer can be further subdivided into different systems, which can be protected and activated step by step, and the layers are interconnected, interacted, and influenced each other.

For the protection and activation of the village buildings in Puxin Village, Guangzhou, the four aspects of grasping elements, intervening structure, sorting out functions, and adapting to the environment can be used to enhance the correlation between the multiple levels of the system, and then realize the reproduction and reuse of the system [2].

System Structure Analysis. The analysis of the architectural system structure of the traditional village of Puxin Village in Guangzhou not only needs to grasp the concrete architectural appearance, but also to understand the Lingnan regional culture and social culture of the traditional village buildings in Puxin Village, Guangzhou. To grasp the concrete architectural appearance, it is necessary to find out the structure of each layer of the original traditional village building, and figure out the points that need to be corrected, and then modify it and graft it with the new structure. In the meantime, it is necessary to analyze and process the surrounding environment so that the new structure can be combined with the new structure. Adapt to the village environment.

System Environment Analysis. Traditional village architecture in Puxin Village, Guangzhou The traditional village architecture system environment includes physical and non-material environments, and these environments continue to change and develop.

Among them, the physical environment refers to the objective environment that actually exists in the protection and activation system, including the original site of the building and the traditional village environment, and the intangible environment mainly refers to the human environment of Puxin Village. The environment and the traditional village building system are interconnected and restricted, and the continuous dynamic communication affects the strategic choice and function conversion of the protection and activation of the traditional village buildings in Puxin Village, Guangzhou.

3 The Reconstruction Strategy of Traditional Village Buildings Based on System Theory

3.1 Village Buildings in Puxin Village, Guangzhou

To grasp the problems of traditional village architecture in Puxin Village, Guangzhou, it is necessary to give full play to the emergence of the system and to fully understand the contradictions of the system. In the protection and revitalization of the traditional village buildings in Puxin Village, Guangzhou, there are two main contradictions: one is the conflict between tradition and modernity, the old traditional village buildings are gradually aging due to the passage of time, and the increasing living needs of residents in Puxin Village Not suitable. The second is the contradiction between closed and open.

The traditional houses in Puxin Village are three houses with two corridors. The space is relatively closed to the outside. Each building is an independent small space. With the change of lifestyle and social form, the villagers need to communicate with the outside world. Increasingly, outsiders explore the interior more and more intensely, and the small independent space makes the connection between the buildings lacking. These two contradictions also caused the hollowing problem of the traditional village buildings in Puxin Village, Guangzhou. The buildings were damaged and collapsed without care, and the overall style of the village was eventually destroyed.

In the protection and renovation of the traditional village buildings in Puxin Village, Guangzhou, attention should be paid to the problems brought by these two contradictions to the design, follow the system coordination of architecture and humanity society, respect the coordination of man and land and the integration of the environment, and give full play to the traditional villages of Puxin Village. The characteristics and advantages of architecture make it "live".

3.2 Integration of System Elements

To upgrade the building system of the traditional village of Puxin Village in Guangzhou as a whole, integrating the system elements is the first step. First of all, it is necessary to find out the "integration factor" of the system elements. It is the core that integrates the various subsystems and can enhance the integrity of the various subsystems and elements.

The traditional village buildings in Puxin Village, Guangzhou are mostly three houses with two corridors. This form is one of the most representative traditional residential forms in Lingnan. Its distinctive architectural form is determined by the regional culture of Lingnan and reflects the local culture. The connotation of culture and homestay, so the "integration factor" in this system is the folk culture of the village (see Fig. 3). For the protection and activation of the relatively complete preservation of traditional village buildings, integrate its structure, space, modeling, materials, environment, technology, equipment, functions and other elements, and optimize the structure of the original building based on the original building structure. Carry out activation design. In the

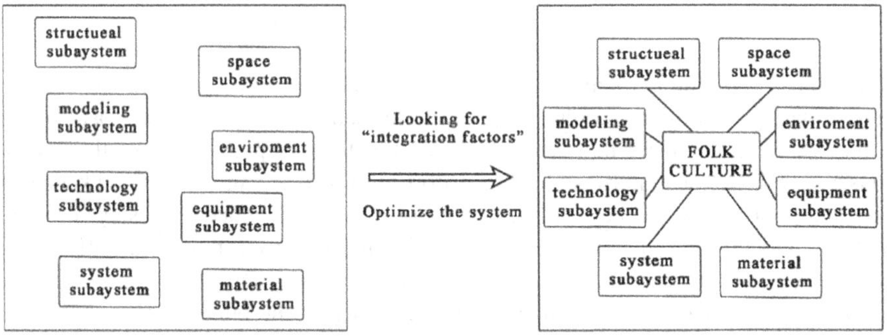

Fig. 3. Mechanism diagram of the "integration factor" of traditional village buildings in Puxin Village, Guangzhou

design, the original expression of living habits in Puxin Village is retained, and the original way of life is continued, without destroying the original form of the building, so that it can be integrated with the texture and culture of the village.

3.3 Optimization of System Structure

After the system is formed, the various subsystems need to be connected by path nodes. The public space serves as a place for gathering information and providing communication in the village, and is the link between the villages. In the protection and revitalization of traditional village buildings in Puxin Village, the reconstructed buildings and group relationships should reflect the traditional architectural style of the villages on the fringe of Guangfu, reflect the cultural characteristics of the traditional villages of Puxin Village, and be able to intervene in the original village structural system and social system After sorting out the original building use, inherit and reshape the space of the building, increase the utilization rate of the building, or make use of it, or change the use to fill the missing functions, so that it can intervene in the lives of the villagers. In the process of reconstruction, the quality of life of the villagers has been improved(see Table 3).

Table 3. Optimization strategy of system structure

Building type	Approach	Use
Buildings of high historical value	Restore traditional style	Open to visit
Other well-preserved buildings with traditional features	Restore lifestyle	Visit, experience and use
To preserve other buildings with average and poor traditional features	To preserve other buildings with average and poor traditional features	Experience a home stay or public space

For buildings with high historical value, such as the Puxin Tang's Ancestral Hall, Economic Hall and Dawang Hall in Puxin Village, the traditional style and appearance of the building should be restored and authenticity should be restored during the renovation. Visit to improve the utilization rate of the building. Under the principle of not compromising the authenticity of historical features, the transformation of some traditional village buildings should consider the influence of traditional atmosphere and traditional methods in the new era in terms of functional replacement. Well-preserved houses, consider restoring lifestyles for visitors to experience and use; if you keep ordinary and poor buildings, they will be transformed into experience homestays or public spaces based on their specific locations, while preserving the traditional atmosphere of the building, combined with Puxin The relationship between people and land in the village is to optimize the original structure and space of the building to make it more in line with the needs of modern use, so that the idle and dilapidated old houses are transformed into exhibition places, commercial places, new public spaces, etc., which can gather information and communicate with people. New place.

3.4 Caring for the System and the Environment

The system is inseparable from the environment, so the coordination between the system and the environment is the key to caring for the system. The protection and activation of traditional village buildings in Puxin Village, Guangzhou and the care of the environment can be related to its material, space, environment and other subsystems. The reconstructed buildings should be coordinated with the surrounding buildings and the environment, and should not have a negative impact on the village texture and architectural cultural heritage.

In the process of transformation design and construction, the use of local traditional materials is encouraged. In addition, considering the needs of functional changes, new materials can be used appropriately. While forming a contrast between the new and the old, attention should be paid to the harmony of the architectural color and the village to integrate it with the original building (see Fig. 4).

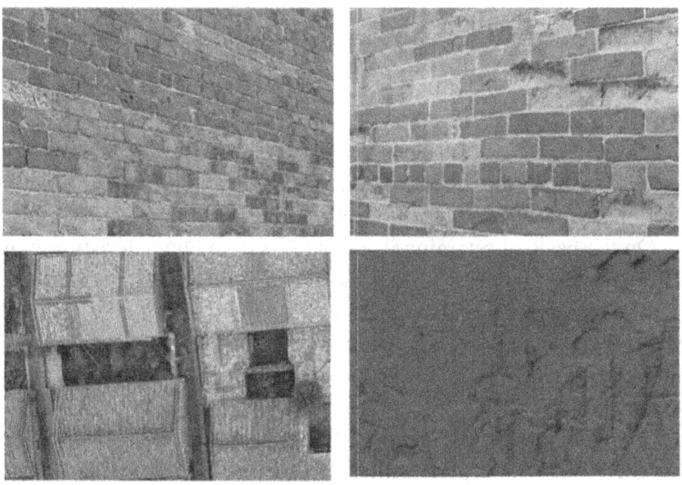

Fig. 4. Building materials and architectural colors in Puxin Village

At the same time, the plan layout and spatial structure characteristics of the original traditional village buildings should be followed, and the basic shape of three rooms and two corridors should be maintained, and the building entrances should be unified on both sides. Keep the original width of the traditional streets, try not to make horizontal expansion, and maintain the current height of the building unchanged (see Fig. 5). When revitalizing a part of the poorly preserved building, consider opening part of the indoor space to blur it with the outdoor space, breaking the boundary between indoor and outdoor, so that the space and the environment blend together, and the connection between the building and the surrounding environment is improved.

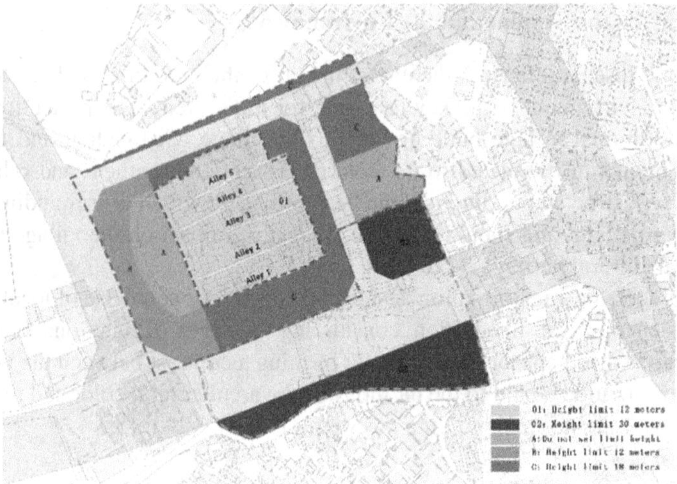

Fig. 5. Planning of building streets and building height control in Puxin Village

4 Conclusion

In response to the rapid changes in urbanization, the scientific method of system theory was combined with the culture of traditional village architecture in Puxin Village, Guangzhou. On the basis of retaining its original system characteristics, grasp the deep structure and complex functions of the traditional village buildings in Puxin Village, Guangzhou in a hierarchical and targeted manner, and apply new technologies, new materials and new concepts to Guangzhou on this basis In the protection of the traditional buildings of Puxin Village, the space is renewed and revitalized, so as to realize the transformation of the times.

Compared with the original village and the conventional village building reconstruction method, the system theory activation and reconstruction method is more closely related to folk culture. The interconnection of structures makes the village more vigorous and at the same time more coordinated with the village environment (see Table 4). Such a transformation method can improve the utilization rate of village buildings and increase the vitality of the village, while retaining and inheriting the cultural connotation of the traditional village and making it truly alive.

Applying the scientific method of system theory to the traditional village buildings of Puxin Village can not only help it be revitalized and transformed scientifically, but also provide a model for the development of surrounding traditional villages.

Table 4. Comparative analysis on the reconstruction of village buildings

	Village in its original state	Renovation of conventional village buildings	System village building renovation
System elements	Vacant buildings or repairs by villagers as needed	Reconstruction centered on meeting modern needs, resulting in cultural loss	Focus on folk culture
System structure	The structure is independent, and it is only used for home sacrifices	Focusing on the individual building, the renovation only meets the needs of the individual without changing its original state of independence	Village nodes are connected in series, open to the outside world, and intervene in the lives of villagers
System and environment	The texture of the village is destroyed	The individual buildings were considered closely during the renovation, which resulted in incompatible with the texture of the village	System transformation is coordinated with the environment

References

1. Bechman, L.R.: Integrated architecture-system elements of architecture, Liang Duolin, translated. Mechanical Industry Press, Beijing (2005)
2. Wang, S., Zhao, Y., Fu, X.: A systematic analysis of the adaptability of contemporary regional architecture. Urban Architecture 20–24 (2017)
3. Che, R., Wang, S.: Integration, Optimization, and Care——Research on Fujian Earth Building Reconstruction Strategy Based on System Theory, Urban Architecture (2020)
4. Zheng, L.: Research on the History of Urban Construction and Development in Shantou in Modern Times. South China University of Technology (2018)
5. Chai, Y.: Research on industrial building design strategy based on system theory. Wuhan University of Technology (2016)
6. Yang, W.: Research on the design of rural architecture renovation aimed at the revitalization of the sightseeing-experience rural villages—Taking the renovation design of Huizhou Xinlou Village as an example. Beijing University of Architecture and Architecture (2019)
7. Zheng, L., Huang, X.: Reconstruction Design of Urban Buildings in Historical Environment. In: 2020 International Conference on Intelligent Transportation, Big Data & Smart City (ICITBS), Vientiane, Laos, pp. 323–326. IEEE (2020)
8. Peng, J.: Research on the Revitalization and Utilization of Historic Hakka Residential Buildings in Huizhou—Take Crane Lake as an example. South China University of Technology (2018)
9. Zheng, L., Lin, S.: The reuse, reconstruction and renaissance of the sotto arcade in Shantou. In: 2018 3rd SSR International Conference on Social Sciences and Information(SSR-SSI 2018), November 28–30,2018 ,Nagoya ,Japan, advances in Social and Behavioral Sciences, vol. 25, p. 61(2018)

10. Li, H.: Study on the shape of three rooms and two corridors of residential houses in Guangfu Area. South China University of Technology (2018)
11. Wen, R.D.: Promoting activation with protection and promoting protection with activation -- Reflections on the protection and activation of Guangzhou historical and cultural blocks. Shandong Youth, pp. 141–142(2017)
12. Li, Z., Qinyu, L.: An Analysis of Historical Urban Area's Renovation in Shantou. In: 2019 International Conference on Smart Grid and Electrical Automation (ICSGEA), Xiangtan, China, pp. 408–412. IEEE (2019)
13. Zheng, C.: Research on rural Traditional building Reconstruction oriented by spatial publicity. Xiamen University (2017)
14. Zhang, X., Xu, X.: Discussion on renewal and spatial optimization of existing rural buildings: a case study of Government building upgrading and Renovation in Datian Town, Wuyi County, Zhejiang Province. Urban and Rural Construction, pp. 25–27 (2019)
15. Zheng, L., Wang, J.: A case study on landscape design of campus in university of technology. In: 2020 5th International Conference on Smart Grid and Electrical Automation (ICSGEA), Zhangjiajie, China, pp. 547–550. IEEE (2020)
16. Tian, J.: Classification protection and Renovation of residential buildings in Traditional Villages -- A case study of Guobi Village, Qinshui County, Shanxi Province, Beijing Jiaotong University (2017)
17. Lin, W.H.: Research on protection, activation and renewal strategy of hollow traditional villages in Guangzhou suburbs, Guangdong: South China University of Technology (2019)
18. Li, Z., Xinlu, Z.: Study on reviving on village though renovation of building-base on the project about Xiaoshan Village. In: 2020 5th International Conference on Smart Grid and Electrical Automation (ICSGEA), Zhangjiajie, China, pp. 623–626. IEEE (2020)

Cross-Cultural Design in Intelligent Environments

Empathy and Symbiosis: Design Preferable Future AI Product and Service

Chiju Chao and Zhiyong Fu[✉]

Department of Information Art and Design, Tsinghua University, Beijing 100084, China
zjr21@mails.tsinghua.edu.cn, fuzhiyong@tsinghua.edu.cn

Abstract. Design theory is evolving with rapidly changing societies and accelerating technologies. In the past, the design concept of "starting from the problem" was challenging to face the ever-changing design challenges, so the concept of "starting from the future" in design combined with futurology is being valued. At the same time, the relationship between products and people in the future will change from a tool related to a collaborative relationship, and human-machine symbiosis will become a future trend. In human-machine symbiosis collaboration, empathy experience plays an important role, and human-machine empathy can help people trust products more and influence decision-making.

We hope to help designers find the most suitable future products and services with a new design concept. Therefore, this paper will describe new design theories and design tools and rethink the issue of human-machine symbiosis and empathy from a future perspective. We analyze the empathy and symbiosis relationship and create empathy and symbiosis tools according to the characteristics of three different degrees of empathy and symbiosis. The tool has undergone two user tests and has received good feedback, and the tests also point us in the direction of future improvement.

Keywords: Design tool · Human-machine symbiosis · Empathy · Design future

1 Introduction

1.1 The Evolution of HCI Triggered by Technology

From the 1970s to the 1980s, with the accumulation of academic research, human-machine interface design expanded from theory and practice. Human-machine interface design began to pay more attention to the theoretical guidance of cognitive psychology, sociology, and other humanities knowledge disciplines. As a result, human-computer interaction, a new field that studies the feedback interaction between machines and humans, is gradually formed.

In just a few decades, human-computer interaction has developed rapidly from the early mouse, keyboard, button interaction, to graphical interface (GUI) interaction, gesture and voice interaction, and finally to multi-channel, multimedia interaction led by artificial intelligence technology. Human-computer interaction has shown a new state with the development of artificial intelligence technology. Human-computer interaction

P.-L. P. Rau (Ed.): HCII 2022, LNCS 13314, pp. 487–500, 2022.
https://doi.org/10.1007/978-3-031-06053-3_33

is not just to set up interactive functions to interact with people, but to start a direct dialogue with products, that is, "interactions with increasing autonomy and sensitivity" [21]. The interaction between humans and AI has also been explored at different stages, from substitution (AI replaces humans) to augmentation (humans and AI reinforce each other), and now to combination (AI and humans are dynamically combined as an integrated unit) [8]. Such evolution has led to new discussions on the relationship between human and machine.

1.2 Design Theory Changes from Complex Social Issues

With the outbreak of COVID-19 in 2020, the behaviour and ethical relationship between people have undergone unpredictable changes. In the past, designers mainly designed from the perspective of "object-based" and "problem-based". Various design tools have been developed to help people understand existing problems and emanate ideas from various perspectives [20]. However, when society undergoes drastic changes, such a design method is challenging to respond to and predict quickly. At the same time, the development of technology has accelerated, many products have been born with the idea of solving challenges through breakthrough technologies [1]. However, thinking about design goals from unknown future technical factors often leads to the wrong results for designers.

Especially with the arrival of the AI era, there is new thinking on the relationship between people and technology. Following the Three Laws of Robotics, experts and scholars have also proposed AI ethics to deal with new ethical issues. Various reasons have prompted design researchers and practitioners to rethink new design perspectives that combine future technology, society, and culture, bringing about design processes and methods changes.

1.3 Revolution in Design Method

Therefore, we began to consider how designers can change the traditional design theory and use new ideas to deal with increasingly complex design issues. We no longer start from "solving problems" but focus on how to design with "people-oriented", "society-centered", and "starting from the future". Many design methods, such as critical design [4], speculative design [18], design fiction [9], etc., have been proposed to guide different design trends and directions.

This article hopes to help designers start from the human perspective, combine the concepts of human-machine symbiosis and human-machine empathy, and use methods such as speculative thinking, design fiction, and design foresight. The goal is to explore how to design the human-machine relationship for future scenarios to achieve the harmonious goal of empathizing with people and coexisting with nature.

2 From Interpersonal to Human-Machine Society

2.1 Empathy in Interpersonal Society

Empathy was proposed by Rogers, the founder of humanism, and refers to the ability to experience the inner world of others. Empathy is also the first step in design thinking [10].

Generally, through observation, interview, interaction and other methods [23], designers can think about users' feelings with empathy and carry out design.

In traditional design methods, many design tools assist designers in empathy. For example, PERSONA helps designers analyze users in all aspects, and the user journey map analyzes the user's experience when completing a task. These tools help designers to empathize with people in existing scenarios. With the evolution of design theory, empathy cannot be limited to the above concepts. Empathy needs to include insight and speculation, digging out people's essential appeals, and exploring people's signs of future lifestyles.

2.2 Human-Machine Symbiosis in Human-Machine Society

In the natural world, two different organisms live together in an intimate cooperative way, called symbiosis. The relationship between humans and robots has gradually developed from a tool relationship to a symbiotic relationship.

J. C. R. Licklider first proposed the concept of human-computer symbiosis. He hypothesized that computers cooperate with humans to create symbiotic relationships by performing tasks. He distinguishes symbiotic systems from semi-automated systems. Machines in semi-automated systems are still used as single-threaded tools. In symbiotic systems, computers cooperate with humans to make decisions and control complex situations without relying on predetermined programs [14]. He also specifically pointed out that human-machine symbiosis is different from "machine-augmented humans". Symbiotic computers need to exhibit human-like characteristics in interpersonal teams [3]. In the era of artificial intelligence, "human-machine symbiosis" means that humans and artificial intelligence "humanoids" form a symbiotic social relationship [19].

2.3 Human-Engaged Computing

In 2013, Professor Ren Xiangshi from the Kochi University of Technology in Japan proposed the concept of Human-Engaged Computing (HEC) [16]. HEC consists of three parts: human participation, computer participation and human-computer-organic interaction. Human- computer cooperation emphasizes the high-quality and equal interaction between humans and computers. Humans benefit from the services of computers and contribute their unique soft capabilities such as empathy, morality, creativity, etc., and grow their capabilities in interaction. Computers increase productivity, solve problems, and unlock human potential while accomplishing tasks [15]. HEC is a concept that emphasizes neither technology nor business guidance but guidance through people, society and values.

The HEC concept points a clear direction for human-machine symbiosis design. Based on HEC, we try to get out of the technology-driven future scene design and move towards the future scene design of humanistic thinking. We try to develop a new way of thinking, which aims to help designers design current products by exploring future ways to adapt to the humanized product innovation process.

3 Empathy and Symbiosis

3.1 Empathy Experience in Human-Machine Society

Artificial intelligence aims to make machines more and more like humans. Humans are emotionally and intellectually driven, and empathy exists everywhere in a symbiotic society. Facing an increasingly human-like artificial intelligence, experts in the computer field can now quantify human emotions through facial recognition, speech recognition, and bioelectrical signals. Experts began to simulate human emotions through algorithms, which gave birth to the research field of "Artificial Empathy" [24]. Research shows that artificial intelligence which can empathize with people is more likeable and trustworthy than artificial intelligence without empathy [2].

However, does AI possess real emotions? Artificial intelligence allows machines to use algorithms to understand human emotions and respond appropriately, enabling empathy between humans and machines [6, 11]. In other words, artificial emotion is not so much the simulation of human emotional experience inside the robot. Instead, it stimulates the innate empathy ability of human beings and makes the human user attribute a specific experience state to the machine with emotion. Therefore, when discussing the human-machine empathy experience from the design perspective, we still have to return to the "human" itself.

3.2 Human-Machine Empathy and Symbiosis

As mentioned earlier, human-machine symbiosis is different from "machine-augmented humans" and "automated systems" [14]. It is a symbiotic social relationship between humans and "humanoids" [12], with the characteristics of teamwork and specific social interaction Attributes. Therefore, when discussing human-machine symbiosis, we regard intelligence as a cooperative object and discuss its empathy and symbiotic relationship with humans.

Human-machine empathy is an important factor in human-machine symbiosis. Human-machine empathy often has a positive impact on human-machine symbiosis. Studies have shown that human-machine empathy improves teamwork in emotional interaction and affects the quality of decision-making [6]. However, the human-machine symbiotic relationship is not necessarily accompanied by human-machine empathy. In some human-machine symbiotic relationships, humans do not necessarily need emotional communication with AI to collaborate.

As shown in Fig. 1, if we analyze the human-machine symbiosis relationship from weak to strong, then the relationship between human-machine empathy and symbiosis is proportional—the more robust the human-machine symbiotic relationship, the stronger the empathy ability that can be carried. Only weak human-machine empathy can occur in the weak human-machine symbiotic relationship. Conversely, if man and machine produce a strong empathy experience, it must be a robust symbiotic relationship.

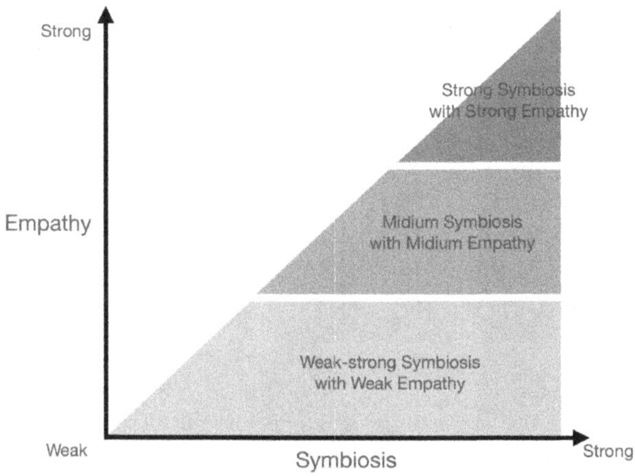

Fig. 1. The relationship of symbiosis and empathy between human and machine

4 Three Human-Machine Symbiotic Relationships from a Design Perspective

When designing future-oriented intelligent products and services, the core is to understand the ideal role of human beings in the relationship between humans and machines [17]. Find the optimal human-machine symbiosis relationship under the user's worldview, and define the human- machine empathy experience based on this. It is essential to involve humans in appropriate tasks according to task characteristics and environment [7]. We propose three symbiotic relationships based on the proportion, intensity, and importance of human and AI participation in the design process. It should be noted that these three relationships are defined by comparing the proportions and roles played by humans and artificial intelligence in the design process. We delineated weak, medium, and strong intervals and gradually obtained a clearer vision of the future by using the "approximation method" between the three intervals.

People have different opinions on product development with the participation of artificial intelligence technology, and there is particular theoretical support behind it. However, most of them discuss human and artificial intelligence as opposites. Designers should use their creativity and emotions to intervene in the relationship between artificial intelligence and people and create new possibilities (Fig. 2).

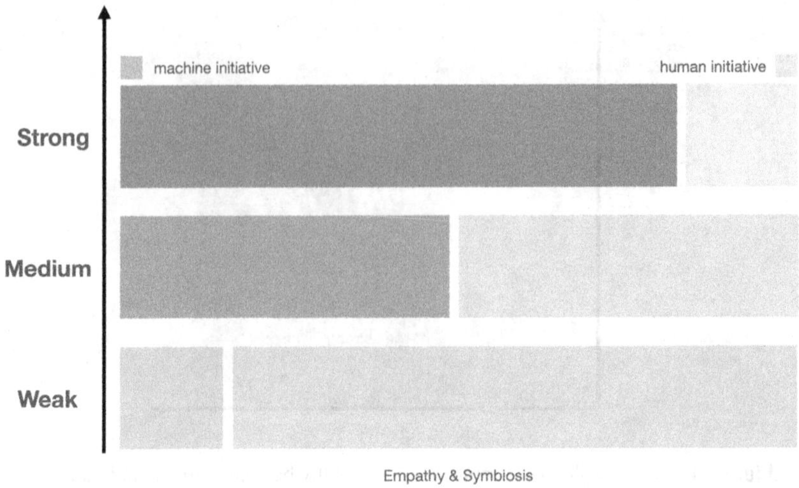

Fig. 2. Three levels of empathy and symbiosis

4.1 Weak Interaction

In weak artificial intelligence, AI is mainly based on automated computing. The sense of participation in human-machine collaboration is weak, and human-machine symbiosis mainly relies on the human initiative for control. In this phase, human-machine empathy is weak, as the researchers preset feedback on the user's language, emotions, and behaviour. In this relationship, the symbiotic relationship between humans and machines has the following characteristics: 1. All situations and corresponding feedback content must be preset in advance; 2. The machine needs to be constantly adjusted by humans to adapt to new challenges.

For example, Huawei smart home provides several preset scenes: movie viewing mode, festival mode, and dining mode. Users can choose different scenes to switch. At the same time, the intelligent home engine obtains multiple conditions such as season, time, and current indoor light to create a healthy lighting environment for users intelligently. When users go out and leave home, the intelligent home system will act as a "housekeeper" and protect home safety through camera monitoring, gas management, flooding alarms, etc. [13]. This human-machine symbiotic relationship requires users to preset in advance, and artificial intelligence makes fine adjustments according to environmental changes in the preset scene. The operation of the whole system mainly depends on people's active command and control.

4.2 Medium Interaction

There is a specific cooperative relationship between man and machine in the middle relationship. AI can actively perceive the user's state for feedback, and AI has the learning ability to improve continuously. Artificial intelligence has the ability of artificial empathy and can understand the user's psychological state and give feedback through calculation methods. At this stage, the human-computer empathy symbiosis relationship has the following characteristics: 1. Can understand the human situation (facial recognition, emotion analysis, body language, voice patterns); 2. Can give corresponding feedback according to human changes; 3. Continuity /Persistent experience; 4. People and machines will continue to improve.

Smart speakers, for example, need to understand human communication and semantic understanding when designing and developing. At the same time, in human use, the smart speaker will continue to learn, better understand the user's dialogue habits, and give personalized feedback. Through emotional feedback, artificial intelligence can give users an emotional empathy experience. In a medium-penetration relationship, AI and humans benefit and progress simultaneously. People benefit from the convenience provided by artificial intelligence solutions. At the same time, artificial intelligence collects data about interactions when people use it, and by using these data to learn, the whole system becomes more effective [5].

4.3 Strong Interaction

In a strong relationship, AI occupies a dominant position, and people only need to maintain the AI system. Computers actively make judgments and decisions while completing their daily work. AI at this stage can simulate a more realistic human-machine empathy experience. The human-computer empathy relationship at this stage has the following characteristics: 1. AI can make decisions and responses independently; 2. Data can be freely mobilized for further processing; 3. Autonomous perception and automatic execution. 4. It can completely simulate artificial emotions, giving people an authentic empathy experience.

Strong symbiotic relationships are currently only found in conceptual designs and sci-fi works for technical reasons. For example, JARVIS in "Iron Man", TARS in "Interstellar", MOSS in "The Wandering Earth". These AI products can execute human commands well, and they also have autonomous authority to act according to their judgment of the situation. At the same time, they interact emotionally with humans as an assistant and as a reliable companion of human beings. In a strong symbiotic relationship, intelligent products and services can have a human-machine empathy experience, helping users better accept this symbiotic relationship.

There is no "best answer" in the symbiotic relationship of the above three dimensions. Different symbiotic relationships apply to different types of activities or needs. Even under the same activities, humans and machines will have different needs for collaboration based on different values and cultural backgrounds. We help designers find the optimal and ideal roles in human-machine systems in different scenarios. We create some new design thinking methods to help designers design the relationship between future products and people from a future perspective.

5 Design Tool for Human-Machine Empathy and Symbiosis

5.1 Limitations of the Original Design Theory

In the Ideate and Prototype stages of design thinking, designers often use existing knowledge to create design solutions. However, AI is widely regarded as difficult to sketch and prototype [22]. It is difficult for UX designers with non-technical backgrounds to imagine and build prototypes containing AI technology systems during the design process. Even designing some simple AI applications can generate design reasoning errors. These mistakes create user experience problems and sometimes even cause serious ethical issues or lead to social-level consequences.

In the face of increasingly complex future problems, design challenges often fail, in part because of a lack of imagination. The lack of imagination is because the old design concept is still used to combine the problem itself and solve it from the perspective of demand, technology, and market. This way of thinking cannot keep up with the rapid social change and technological factors, and it also ignores people's vision for the future [1].

Therefore, we try to develop new design concepts and methods that combine future thinking. Help designers predict future visions from a human perspective. Overcome practical problems such as technical limitations and correctly guide desirable future products.

5.2 The Concept of Our Design Tool

Possession

Possession works by assuming the future, imagining a future solution based on a specific value, and then returning the real solution to find a way to achieve it in the present. The Possession Method divides the creative stage into four steps:1. decomposing the problem. 2.setting the future world view. 3.envisioning the intelligent assistant to solve the problem. 4.returning to reality to give an achievable solution.

This method emphasizes solving problems through a humanoid and attaching human characteristics and solutions to specific design product to imagine future products. Possession can help designers search for broader ideas with fewer constraints and then realize the ideas through existing technical conditions (Fig. 3).

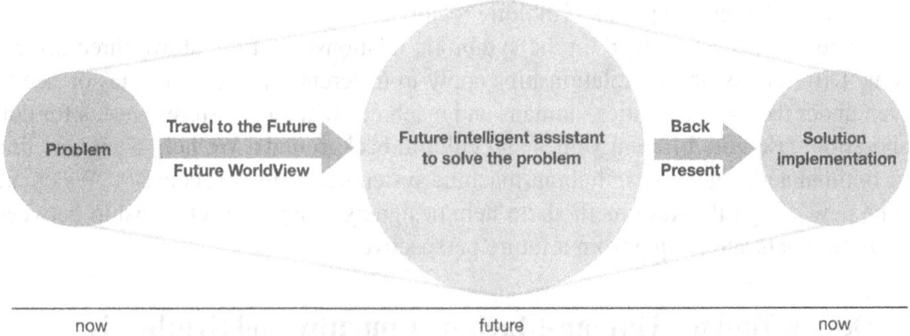

Fig. 3. The concept of possession

Approximation

The symbiotic relationship between humans and machines will also be different based on different scenarios and different users. However, when we design brainstorming directly on the problem, the thinking process often starts from a specific point, and the current environment easily constrains the thinking.

To help designers find the best human-machine relationship, we introduce the concept of approximation. Based on the concept of the approximation method, we first set three interval states of weak, medium and strong to help designers expand the scope of thinking from a point to an interval. After analyzing the symbiotic relationship between humans and machines in these three intervals, choose a more desirable target interval to continue subdividing. Through several iterations, the optimal solution is gradually approached (Fig. 4).

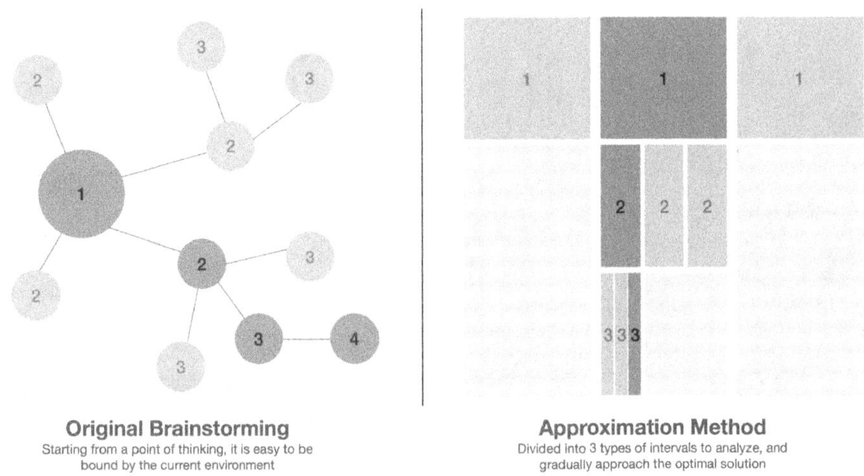

Original Brainstorming
Starting from a point of thinking, it is easy to be bound by the current environment
Approximation Method
Divided into 3 types of intervals to analyze, and gradually approach the optimal solution

Fig. 4. The concept of approximation

5.3 Empathy and Symbiosis Tool

The Empathy Symbiosis tool is divided into 4 main components:

1. Problem setting: Transform and decompose design problems through HMW (How Might We? method). The HMW method helps designers quickly define problems through simple narrative sentences;
2. Definition of worldview: According to the set question, collect various observations about this question in life. Discuss this issue from social, economic, historical, technological and other perspectives, and define at least two worldviews based on the characteristics of target users;
3. Future intelligent assistant: Imagine how the future intelligent assistant will solve problems through empathy and symbiosis with people under this world view. In

this part, we will start from the weak, medium and strong human-machine empathy and symbiotic relationship, and use the sentence form of What if to propose future solutions;

4. Modern products: Pull back from the future smart assistant solution to the present, and find the solution corresponding to the current product solution. This step requires the user to view from a macro perspective and to deeply understand the user's personal point of view. Through the approximation method, the product solution that meets the expectations is found and further realized (Fig. 5).

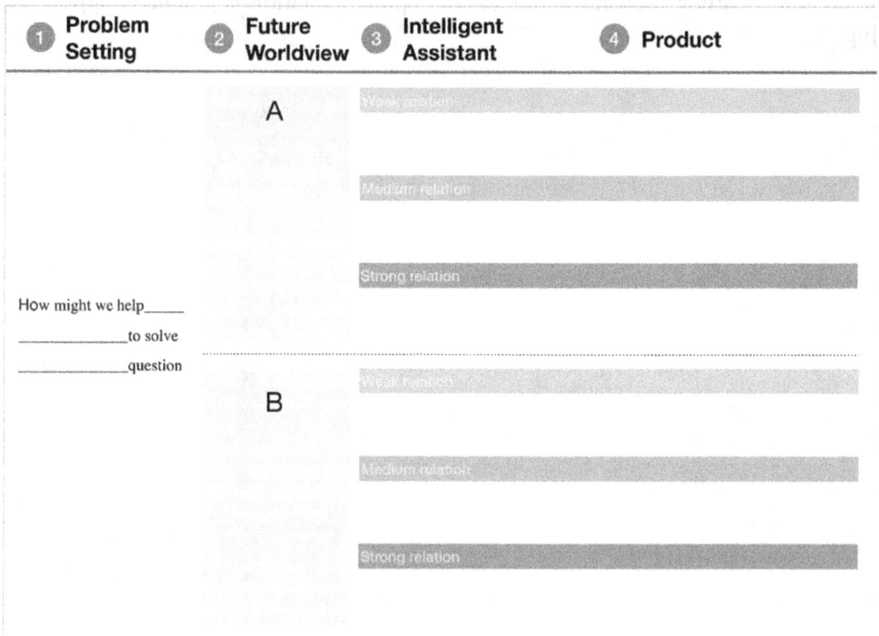

Fig. 5. Empathy and symbiosis tool

6 The Use of Empathy and Symbiosis tool

We put the empathy and symbiosis tool into use in two courses to advance the process of student ideation. The tool is scheduled for the fourth week of the course. Before using the tool, students need to understand the basic design theory, research the target problem, and conduct interviews with users. The tool is mainly used for ideation in the course, helping students create products and services from problems they already understand. The total number of participants in the course is about 21 people, a total of 6 groups. Most of the students are design students (Fig. 6).

Fig. 6. The use of empathy and symbiosis tool

After the two courses, the teachers and teaching assistants of the course commented on the students' final assignments: "Compared with the past assignments, the students' final designs are more futuristic and speculative", "I feel that the students' creativity has been inspired", "The final design of some groups feels unrealistic and too sci-fi". In general, the instructors are satisfied with the design results produced by using the tool. They believe that the tool has helped students to inspire ideas from different perspectives, but they are also worried that the tool will lead to unreliable design solutions.

Also, we distributed questionnaires to each student to understand the actual use of the symbiotic tool. The questionnaire data is as follows. It is gratifying that students are willing to use the tool again for design activities (4.75 points). They have a greater sense of recognition that the tool can help develop ideas and stimulate creativity (4 points, 4.25 points). The disadvantage is that the students think that there is still a gap between the use of the tool and the actual practice (2.75 points) (Table 1).

Table 1. The questionnaire feedback

Question	Score 1Totally disagree - 5Totally agree
I would love to use the tool again	4.75
Using tools produces unexpected design results	4
This tool can help develop ideas	4.25
There is a gap between the use of the tool and the actual practice	2.75

We conducted interviews with some tool users in response to the above ratings. First, the students agreed on the concept of symbiotic tools. Almost all of them are the first attempts to design with a futuristic vision. The students thought: "This method can spread more ideas and more future product forms", "This tool can help to sort out the thinking process and guide the thinking divergence step by step", "The steps are clear and reasonable, and the design elements are clearly arranged. According to this process, you can Achieving design goals very well", "It can help to find possible solutions, and it can also help to sort out the time point", "Opening up ideas from the perspective of the future is a different way of thinking about product design".

However, the disadvantages of this tool are also apparent. First, it is difficult for students who do not understand futurology to establish a future worldview. 4 students mentioned that they could not find the direction for their insight into the future worldview; 3 students said that they did not know the definition of worldview; 3 students said that they tended to forget to combine with the worldview in the follow-up design thinking. Second, some students think that when thinking about the future human-computer empathy and symbiosis, they are easily affected by the current accurate technology, and it is still difficult to open their creativity. They thought that perhaps other better categories of empathic symbiotic relationships could be found to stimulate thinking.

7 Discussion and Future Work

The empathy and symbiosis tool is mainly designed and used for the products and services of the future human-machine society. Judging from the students' completion, we are pretty satisfied with the tool as a whole. During the course, students generated a lot of unexpected design ideas through this tool and completed the prototype design of design concepts.

In the process of use, we also found the follow-up improvement direction. First, symbiotic tools require thinking in conjunction with future insights. In the next practice, we will increase the use of 1–2 step futurology tools to help students better establish a future world view so that students can design and think about future products and services based on a well-founded future world view. Second, we will continue to look for more appropriate human-machine empathy and symbiosis classification. This paper distinguishes between weak, medium and strong levels and lists the corresponding characteristics. We believe that this classification is easy to understand and more in line with the technical characteristics of human-machine symbiosis. In future work, maybe we will try to distinguish from social roles, interaction patterns, etc., or try to distinguish from empathy. To this end, we will conduct more explorations on the theme of future human-machine empathy and symbiosis to find more possibilities.

In addition, this study has only been tested in college teaching and research, and its application population and application scenarios are limited. It is hoped that we can combine more practical projects to test and expand to different groups of people and different industries in future research.

8 Conclusion

In this paper, we design "Empathy and Symbiosis Tool" to help designers design products and services for future human-machine symbiosis.

We first describe the future change from interpersonal society to human-machine society. We have sorted out the future human-computer symbiosis relationship through extensive literature research and discussed human-computer empathy. After that, we combined the technical principles and the characteristics of empathy and symbiosis and divided the symbiotic empathy relationship into three categories: strong, medium and weak for discussion. Based on these three types of relationships, we combine the concepts of possession and approximation to generate a tool for empathy and symbiosis and put this tool into teaching use.

Empathy and symbiosis tools can help designers reverse the current products from the perspective of the future human-machine society. It can help students transcend the limitations of past object-based design thinking and search for broader ideas with fewer constraints. It helps designers use the future as a clue to find more breakthrough intelligent product and service ideas from the perspective of human values.

Acknowledgments. We gratefully acknowledge Qing.X(Department of Information Art and Design, Tsinghua University, Beijing China) and Yuyao.Z(Ant Group CO., Ltd. Zhejiang China). Thanks to them for the preliminary arrangement of the basic theoretical data, and the design and production of the Empathy and Symbiosis tools.

References

1. Angheloiu, C., Sheldrick, L., Tennant, M.: Future tense: exploring dissonance in young people's images of the future through design futures methods. Futures **117**, 102527 (2020)
2. Brave, S., Nass, C., Hutchinson, K.: Computers that care:investigating the effects of orientation of emotion exhibited by anembodied computer agent. Int. J. Hum.-Comput. Stud. **62**(2), 161–217 (2005)
3. Chakraborti, T., Kambhampati, S., Scheutz, M., Zhang, Y.: AI challenges in human-robot cognitive teaming. arXiv preprint arXiv:1707.04775 (2017)
4. Critical design WikiPedia. https://en.wikipedia.org/wiki/Critical_design. Accessed 14 Jan 2022
5. Cho, J., Rader, E.: The role of conversational grounding in supporting symbiosis between people and digital assistants. In: Proceedings of the ACM on Human-Computer Interaction, vol. 4, no. CSCW1, pp. 1–28 (2020)
6. Dalvandi, B.: A Model of Empathy for Artificial Agent Teamwork. Doctoral dissertation, University of Northern British Columbia (2013)
7. Davenport, T.H., Kirby, J.: Just how smart are smart machines? MIT Sloan Manag. Rev. **57**(3), 20–25 (2016)
8. Dellermann, D., Ebel, P., Söllner, M., Leimeister, J.M.: Hybrid intelligence. Bus. Inf. Syst. Eng. **61**, 637–643 (2019). https://doi.org/10.1007/s12599-019-00595-2
9. Design Fiction WikiPedia. https://en.wikipedia.org/wiki/Design_fiction. Accessed 14 Jan 2022
10. Design school, Stanford University: Design thinking bookleg. shttps://dschool.stanford.edu/resources/design-thinking-bootleg/. Accessed 14 Jan 2022
11. Empathy: The Killer App for AI. https://insights.sap.com/empathy-affective-computing-ai/. Accessed 14 Jan 2022
12. Guangyun, C.: From a man-machine relationship to inter human relations: definition and strategy of artificial intelligence. Journal of Dialectics of Nature 41(1) (SerialNo.245), 9–14 (2019)
13. Huawei wholehome Intelligent. https://consumer.huawei.com/cn/wholehome/wholehome/intelligent-scenes/. Accessed 14 Jan 2022
14. Licklider, J.C.R.: Man-computer symbiosis. IRE Trans. Hum. Fact. Electron. 4–11(1960)
15. Markoff, J.: Machines of Loving Grace: The Quest for Common Ground Between Humans and Robots. Ecco Books, New York (2015)
16. Ren, X.: Rethinking the relationship between humans and computers. Computer **49**(8), 104–108 (2016)

17. Revisiting the Human-Machine Symbiosis https://cra.org/crn/2016/04/revisiting-human-machine-symbiosis/, last accessed 2022/01/14
18. Speculative design WikiPedia. https://en.wikipedia.org/wiki/Speculative_design. Accessed 14 Jan 2022
19. Shuheng, H., Yugiong, X.: The complexity of AI moral judgment and its solution—from the perspective of man—computer symbiosis. J. Jiangsu Univ. (Soc. Sci. Ed.) **22**(4), 16–28 (2020)
20. Theodore, L.: Creativity: a framework for the design/problem solving discourse in technology education. J. Technol. Educ. **17**(1), 35–52 (2006)
21. Wallach, W., Allen, C.: Moral Machines: Teaching Robots Right From Wrong. Oxford University Press, Oxford (2008)
22. Yang, Q., Steinfeld, A., Rosé, C., Zimmerman, J.: Re-examining whether, why, and how human-AI interaction is uniquely difficult to design. In: Proceedings of the 2020 Chi Conference on Human Factors in Computing Systems, pp. 1–13. Hawai'i (2020)
23. Zhang, Z., Yongyan, G.: Empathy—first step of design thinking. Design 54–55 (2015)
24. Zhiqiang, Y., Jinlong, S., Yanjie, S.: From human empathy to artificial empathy. J. Psychol. Sci. **42**(2), 299–306 (2019)

Smart Home Service Experience Strategic Foresight Using the Social Network Analysis and Future Triangle

Yu Cheng and Sanghun Sul(✉)

Sungkyunkwan University, Suwon 16419, South Korea
sanghunsul@skku.edu

Abstract. With smart homes' development and market expansion, we must explore the smart home service experience with a long-term perspective with future thinking. First, this study reviewed the literature of smart home service experience, future thinking, and foresight. Then, data about smart home experience were collected from a Chinese social media, Weibo, and the weak signals of future smart home service experience were explored by conducting the social media analysis. The weak signals were analysed according to three dimensions of future triangle to predict the alternative futures of smart home service experience. Finally, four strategies were proposed for future smart home service experience from two aspects: functional and emotional experiences. First, system-connection experience must be improved, and incompatibility problems between different brands or platform products must be resolved through the means such as technology and communication protocols. Second, the device-usage experience must be enhanced, and the automation degree of smart home products must be improved using algorithms. Furthermore, enhanced privacy experience, user data security and social equality must be improved, protected, promoted, respectively. Finally, value-perception experience should be improved, the problems of energy saving and environmental protection for smart homes must be addressed, and user value-perception experience of ecological sustainability must be encouraged. In conclusion, we can use future thinking to develop smart homes service experience with a long-term perspective and enhance social equality and environmental sustainability.

Keywords: Smart home · Future thinking · Service experience · Social network analysis · Future triangle

1 Introduction

With the development and market expansion of smart homes, smart home technology has rapidly evolved into a mainstream market and has attained the user segmentation stage [20]. The trend of turning products and services into smart industries contributes to the global smart home market. Smart homes are emerging as common homes and becoming a part of the lives of people [19]. The global

P.-L. P. Rau (Ed.): HCII 2022, LNCS 13314, pp. 501–518, 2022.
https://doi.org/10.1007/978-3-031-06053-3_34

market for smart homes is expected to reach $138.9 billion by 2026 from $84.5 billion in 2021, with a forecasted growth rate of 10.4%, showing rapid growth in the future.

Changing lifestyles affect the future society to a certain degree. Technology changes all the aspects of human lives and provides convenience. Simultaneously, human activities increasingly affect the planet at all levels to a greater extent than natural processes. The Earth is now in the Anthropocene, where human activities have become a major geological force [7]. The great challenge being faced during the Anthropocene is how to move towards a sustainable future [25]. In 2015, the United Nations proposed goals for sustainable development; these goals provide a blueprint for a better future [3]. In a rapidly evolving technological environment, visions of future changes become new opportunities. Understanding and applying the theories and methods of future studies can allow people and groups to predict the alternative future effectively [8]. Future thinking holds important implications for future generations and societal development.

The effects of smart homes on the future society and environment must be understood. In the future, the service experience strategy of smart homes should consider the future generations, future societies, and future environments. We must explore the smart home service experiences with a long-term vision and estimate whether stakeholders' demands for future smart home service experience are beneficial for future generations through future thinking and related foresight tools. By exploring the weak signals of smart home prospective service experience requirements, we can anticipate the alternative future and thus help us attain a preferred future.

In previous studies, some scholars have predicted the future of TV experience through the 'innovation foresight' approach [9]. There are also studies on designing intelligent objects for the next generation from the perspective of user experience and interaction design [28]. However, the literature on the smart home service experience from future thinking is still scarce. In addition, previous studies' research methods have mainly been selected from a few samples for interviews, workshops, and case studies. The lack of exploration of large samples' data may bias the predicted results.

In this study, we combined the social network analysis and future triangle tool to predict the future smart home service experience strategy. Social media stores the opinions and social opinions of many smart home stakeholders such as smart home users, technical experts, technophiles, media news, smart home brand, and manufacturers about the smart home experience. Researchers can obtain many weak signals associated with future development from social media data by analyzing data related to smart home experience through social network analysis methods. These weak signals are then analysed using the future triangle tool to predict alternative futures of smart home service experience and foresee the future development strategy of smart home service experience.

In the rest of the paper. Section 2 reviews the literature on smart home service experience, future thinking, and foresight methods. Section 3 describes the process of obtaining the weak signals about smart home service experience on

Chinese social media Weibo by conducting a social network analysis. Section 4 presents alternative future prediction and proposes future strategies for smart home service experience by employing the future triangle tool. Section 5 concludes this study and provides the limitations of this study and scope for future research.

2 Related Works

2.1 Smart Home Service Experience

Table 1. Literature on the dimensions of service experience.

Authors	Service experience dimensions	Service sector
Leonard L. Berry, Eileen A. Wall, and Lewis P. Carbone (2006)	Technical performance of the service, Tangibles associated with the services, Behavior and appearance of services providers	Service marketing
Sara Sandstrom, Bo Edvardsson, Per Kristensson, and Peter Magnusson (2008)	Total functional, Emotional value	Technology-based services
Anu Helkkula (2010)	Phenomenological service experience, Process-based service experience, Outcome-based service experience	Literature review (conceptual)
Elina Jaakkola, Anu Helkkula, Leena Aarikka-Stenroos (2015)	Control dimensions, Factual dimension, Spatial dimension, Temporal dimension, Organization dimension, Locus dimension	Literature review (conceptual)
Hyo-Jin Kang, Gyu Hyun Kwon, Bora Kim, Eunohk Park (2017)	Physical: (1) equipment, (2) space, (3) ambience, (4) design Social: (1) in-service relationship, (2) non-commercial relationship	Smart home
Lijun Han (2020)	Usability, Emotional experience, User value	Livestreaming service

Smart homes are houses that provide customised services to users through smart integrated technology [20]. Technology is the foundation of smart homes, and service is their purpose. Smart homes collect information from the surrounding environment by employing sensors and smart devices and provide residents with services such as management, monitoring, support, and response with the aid of various home smart devices [2]. Smart homes are advantageous in supporting residents to improve their quality of life, assisting them in health management, and helping special populations to live independently. Additionally, smart homes are beneficial for promoting environmental sustainability [22]. Some scholars stated that smart homes are equipped with multiple devices, which co-operate as a homogeneous system to monitor electronic equipment and promote efficient energy management and sustainability. Smart homes present numerous economic, social, health-related, emotional, sustainable, and security benefits that have critical implications for users and societies.

In smart homes, service experience constitutes an essential user satisfaction indicator. Many scholars have studied service experience, but limited literature is available on smart homes or smart products service experience. Through a detailed literature review, some scholars classified service experience into phenomenological, process-based, and outcome-based service experiences [14]. Some studies have indicated that the technical performance of services, tangible materials associated with services, and the behaviour and appearance of service providers influence the rational and emotional perception of customer towards the services [4]. Most studies have reported that service experience can be interpreted as a combination of sensible or functional and affective or emotional customer responses or assessments [16,24]. Some studies have emphasised the impacts of interactions among service providers, customers, smart technologies, services, and delivery channels on experience for smart services [23]. Some studies distinguish the service experience from physical and social aspects; the physical element includes equipment, space, ambiance, and design; the social part has nurturing and non-commercial relationships [17]. In addition, some studies have classified experience from three aspects: usability, emotional experience, and user value [13] (Table 1). This study defined smart home service experience as functional experience as well as emotional experience. Functional experience includes device usage, system-connectivity, and spatial experiences. Emotional experience comprises privacy, ambiance, and value perception.

2.2 Future Thinking and Foresight

Future Thinking. Future research applies scientific theories and methods to explore and predict trends, movements, and prospects and respond to future developmental changes, planning, management, strategies, and various decision-making services. Future research is the search of weak future signals, which are analysed to predict the future. The exact future cannot be predicted, but alternative futures can and should be predicted. A fundamental task of future research is to identify and examine alternative futures by parsing various weak signals, thereby assisting individuals or groups in developing, implementing, and re-imagining the organisational preferred futures [8]. Future thinking can help create highly effective strategies, enhance organisation information, and create the preferred future [15]. Designing futures implies that future thinking generates design ideas and suggestions that guide the present and lead to new products or services. In the initial design stage, design environments and objects must be explored to obtain predictions and solve problems.

Applying Social Network Analysis Method for Foresight. Social network analysis can identify trends in social perceptions of an event in social media. The social network analysis methodology was proposed by Harrison White of Harvard University in the 1960s [26]. His research combines the formal techniques of social network analysis with some essential sociological concepts to study interpersonal relationships in sociology. The current research on social network analysis is not limited to studying interpersonal relationships. Many studies analyze the relationship between the content posted by users in social networks by collecting data in social media such as Twitter, Facebook, and Weibo. Terms for social media analysis are nodes, links, centrality, etc. In social media, Twitter, Facebook, Weibo, nodes represent the user name or a word posted by the user in the collected data, links represent the relationship between two nodes, and the centrality is used to describe the importance of a node in the entire network. Commonly used methods for measuring centrality include degree centrality, closeness centrality, betweenness centrality, etc. Degree centrality represents the sum of the links between a node and other nodes. The greater the degree of centrality, the more connections the word represented by this node has with other words in the network. Checking the degree can confirm the most critical words in the collected data. Researchers can analyze the public's social perception of certain events in social media through social network analysis methods. Compared to experiments and questionnaires, public insights in social media are thoughts that people spontaneously and naturally say and more realistically represent trends in social insights. Another advantage of social media is that it stores a large amount of data containing a variety of stakeholders, including product users, technical experts, technophiles, media news, and industry. Through social network analysis, researchers can study the most critical speeches or words in social media from various stakeholders of an event or product to obtain their social views and trends on this event.

Different fields have different applications by using social network analysis. In the future strategic research field, social media network analysis is one of the ways to predict future trends. Some organisations and government departments are aware of the benefits of social media as an information source and a tool for acquiring social feedback and identifying future trends [12]. Some research indicates the advantage of social network data analyses or foresight programs only require a short time, allowing foresight practitioners to obtain valuable insights with a small investment of resources. Some scholars have explored weak signals by conducting the social network analysis to anticipate research aspects. Kayser and Bierwisch used the social network analysis to predict the public perceptions of quantified self [18]. Pang and Kim used the social network analysis method to collect online content generated by futurists and foresight practitioners [21]. Also, scholars employed social media to identify weak signals of emergency events to detect dissemination event sources and report strategy foresight [1]. And some studies also explore the strategic foresight of health policy by social network analysis method [27]. Social network analyses are reliable for future weak signal prediction.

Future Triangle and Alternative Futures. The Future Triangle is a commonly used tool for predicting future trends. Inayatullah proposed six pillars of the future; the first pillar is mapping, where the past, present, and future are depicted, and by describing time, we can obtain a clear picture of event causes and trends [15]. The future triangle is a tool for the mapping pillar and reflects the current view of the future through three dimensions. Three dimensions are: pull of the future, push of the present, and weight of the history. Pull of the future refers to people's imagining of the future. The push of the future relates to some influencing factors that have a driving force for the future. Such as what kind of future does the trend of population aging push us into? What impact will medical advances and increased life expectancy have on the future? Finally, the weight of the future refers to the obstacles where people want to carry out reforms. Through the combination of three dimensions of pull, push, and weight, the future triangle model provides various images of the future. The future triangle provides various images of the future, but the following five archetypes can summarise them: evolution and progress, collapse, Gaia, globalism, and back to the future [15]. Evolution and progress refer to technology and belief in rationality. Collapse refers to the deterioration of the world in terms of inequity, climate disasters, and human beings reaching their limits. Gaia refers to development of technology and culture has reached a balance. Globalism focuses on how economies and cultures can move closer together. Back to the future is the possibility of returning to a past, where hierarchies were more apparent and technology was less destructive. Alternative futures may be similar to these five archetypes. Some scholars use the future triangle to analyze social worker organizations' plausible future [10] and the roles of alternative climate change models [6]. By analyzing the three dimensions of the future triangle, we can predict alternative futures to inform future strategies.

Combining Social Network Analysis and Future Triangle Tool to Predict the Future. Social network analysis and future triangle are commonly used methods for predicting the future, but they have their strengths and limitations. In previous studies, the ways to obtain information about the three dimensions of the future triangle are generally workshops and brainstorming. These methods have two weaknesses; one is that workshop and brainstorming are highly dependent on the experience of researchers and have limitations on accuracy, and the other is that both workshop and brainstorming methods cannot make predictions based on large amounts of data. Through web crawler technology, social network analysis can analyze many social media data. Furthermore, important social speeches in the network can be determined quantitatively with the social network analysis method, filling the limitations of workshop and brainstorming methods. Social network analysis can be used with future triangle tools for future foresight to gain broad insights for future service experience strategy forecasting.

3 Methodology

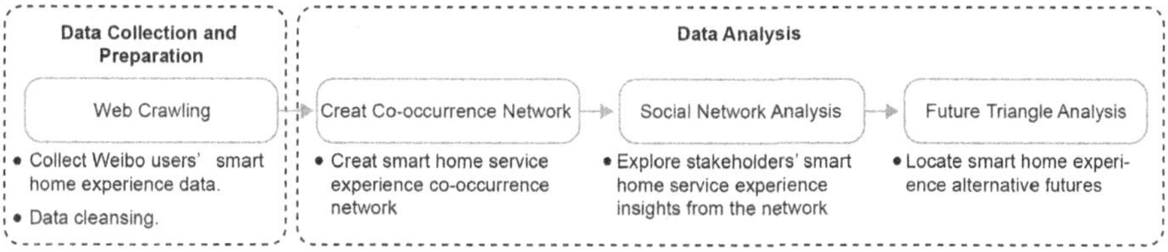

Fig. 1. The framework of the research methodology

This study used the social network analysis and future triangle tool to predict the alternative futures of the prospective service experience of smart homes in China and propose smart home future service experience strategies. The analysis data collected from a Chinese social media, Weibo. The primary methodological process was divided into data collection, preparation, and analysis. In the data collection phase, Weibo user data were collected through a crawler program (Fig. 1). In the data preparation phase, the collected data concerning advertising and irrelevant data were manually cleaned up. In the data analysis phase, the Weibo text was divided into words by using the word segmentation technique in the natural language processing, and then, the co-occurrence network was created. Subsequently, the centrality of the co-occurrence network was analysed using the social network analysis to explore the essential experiences of Weibo smart home stakeholders in the network. Finally, the weak signals of service experience explored in the network were analysed on the basis of the three dimensions in the future triangle; foresight the alternative futures of smart home service experiences.

3.1 Data Collection and Preparation

Social media store many social views of users and stakeholders; these views are rich data sources for studying the social sectors of smart home service experience. Weibo is one of the most dominant social media platforms in China, and Weibo users can share text, images, and videos to express their opinions. First, executive a Python crawler program to crawl the Weibo text, collect data from 1 January 2021 to 1 December 2021, crawling keywords is "smart home experience" (Table 2). We acquired 2421 posts, the information in the dataset was the user ids, user nicknames, Weibo text, Weibo URLs, topics, number of comments, number of likes, post time, and style of the obtained data. Table 3 presents the type of the fetched data.

Table 2. Key parameters of the dataset.

1	Search for	#smart home experience
2	Period	From 1 January, 2021 to 1 December, 2021
3	Number of Weibo post	2421
4	Number of deleted Weibo post (data cleansing)	135
5	Number of analysis Weibo post	2286

Table 3. Overview on basic functionalities of Weibo.

Functionalities	Description
User ID	ID set by Weibo for registered users
User Nickname	Nickname set by Weibo user
Weibo Post	Texts and paragraphs posted by Weibo users representing their thoughts
Weibo URL	Weibo post's web address
Topics	User tagged topics
Number of comments	Number of messages for this Weibo post
Number of likes	Number of views that agree with this Weibo post
Number of repost	The number of reposts of this Weibo post
Post time	The time the user posted this Weibo post
Style of the obtain data	Text, picture or video

Because the obtained dataset comprised invalid data to promote products, we manually separated the data from the repeated ads. The number of Weibo posts obtained after data cleansing was 2286. Weibo texts are presented in the form of paragraphs, and words need to be extracted through word segmentation technology. Then social network analysis can be used to determine central words in the network. Finally, we can understand the critical experience of smart home stakeholders in Weibo. In the next step, we perform word segmentation technical analysis, extract words in the text, create the co-occurrence network, and perform social network analysis.

3.2 Data Analysis

Word Segmentation and Co-occurrence Network Construction. For the following social network analysis, we first construct the co-occurrence network. The first step of creating an occurrence network is using the natural language word segmentation technique to extract keywords from the original Weibo text. Next, the necessary vocabulary is initially selected according to the principles of high noun orientation. Finally, construct a co-occurrence network with the words that have semantic relationships. The specific process is shown below.

1. A word frequency table was obtained using the python 'Jieba' Chinese word sorting library for word segmentation, which comprised 19129 words.
2. The words in the frequency table were further fine grained to make the result highly noun oriented. Finally, 446 words were selected.
3. Using the Weibo text as the analysis unit, the co-occurrence relationship between the words that appear in 1 Weibo text and simultaneously exist in the 446 words was considered.

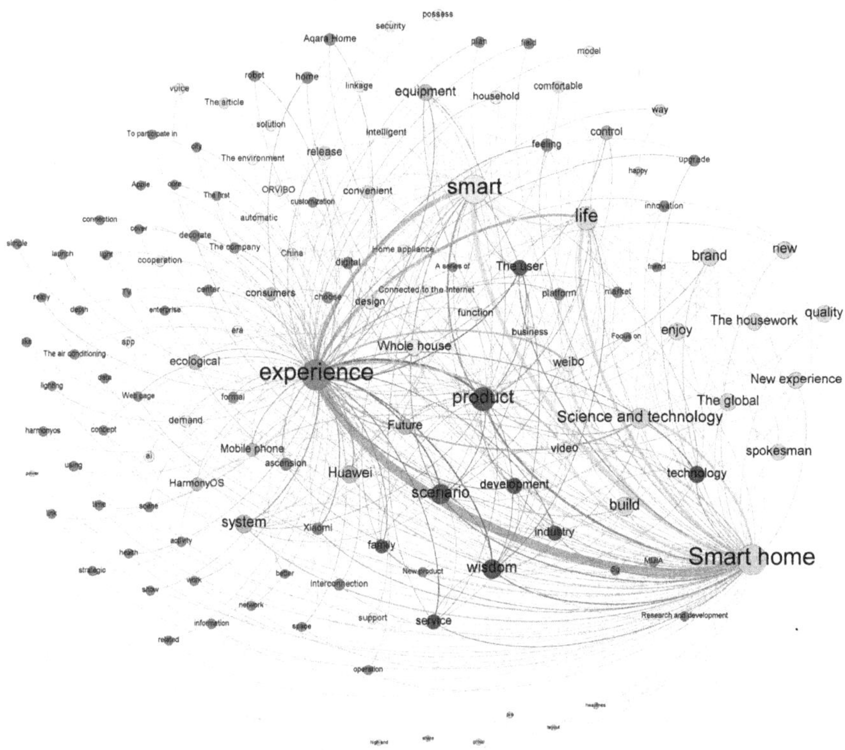

Fig. 2. Smart home service experience network

The co-occurrence network constructed in the previous step was visualised using Gephi software to obtain a network with 134 nodes and 498 edges (Fig. 2). The vocabulary of the co-occurrence network reflected information relevance [11]. By constructing a co-occurrence network, we organize the Weibo data into a network with intrinsic semantic connections, which provides conditions for the following social network analysis. In the next step, we conduct the social network centrality analysis, find the most critical keywords in the network, and explore essential smart home experiences among Weibo users.

Table 4. The top 30 nodes with the highest degree.

Nodes	Degree	Nodes	Degree
Smart home	133	Quality	12
Experience	122	Equipment	11
Smart	76	New experience	11
Product	38	Spokesman	11
Life	36	The housework	11
Science and technology	22	Whole house	10
Scenario	20	Technology	10
Wisdom	18	Weibo	9
Build	17	The user	9
System	16	Future	9
Brand	14	Development	9
Huawei	13	Video	8
The global	13	Industry	8
New	13	Service	7
Enjoy	13	Ecological	7

Social Network Analysis. In this phase, we investigated the co-occurrence network by performing the centrality analysis in social networks analysis method. Centrality is an essential metric in social network analysis; each node represents a keyword, the node centrality defines the importance of a node in the network. In Fig. 2, each node represents a keyword, there are a total of 134 nodes, meaning 134 keywords in the Weibo data we collected. We perform a centrality analysis in social network analysis to determine which words are essential in 134 keywords. Degree centrality is a metric used to assess centrality in the social network and indicates that the more node connections are, the higher its centrality is. This metric can be used to evaluate node relevance or structural importance in the network [5]. In Fig. 2, looking at the links of a word can determine the degree centrality of the word. We represent the word with a higher degree of centrality with a larger circle. The larger the circle, the more critical the keyword is in the network. In Fig. 2, you can know that essential keywords in the network are "experience," "smart home," "smart," "product," "life," etc. To show the specific value of the keyword degree centrality, we made the 30 keywords with the highest degree centrality value in Fig. 2 into Table 4. The Nodes in Table 4 represent the top 30 most important keywords in the network, and the degree means the importance of each keyword. The higher the degree, the more critical the keyword. As shown in Table 4, the most important keyword in the network is "smart home," followed is "experience," and the third is "smart." The data we collect is Weibo posts containing "smart home experience," all texts must include these three words. Therefore, we start the analysis with "product," ranked fourth in Table 4. We look for posts that contain "product" from Weibo to explore user insights about product. And so on, analyze the Nodes in Table 4. By analyzing the original Weibo texts of the most important words in the networks, we can understand the most critical opinions in the smart home experience network.

The examples of social network analysis results are presented in Table 5. The analysis results are enormous, so we selected six examples in Table 5. The data include various stakeholders' opinions on smart homes, including smart home users, technical experts, technophiles, media news, and smart home brands. The experience insights derived from the data include both positive and negative parts. Positive experience includes the terms such as good product connection speed and device usage experience, the freshness of product interaction, the smart homes make life convenient, and a better sense of belonging. Negative insights include sensing error, privacy concerns, and cross-brand product incompatibility. Subsequently, we classify the insights of Weibo data from the perspective of service experience. The service experience of functions includes device usage, system-connectivity, and spatial experiences, and the service experience of emotions comprises privacy, ambiance, and value perception experiences. In the next stage, we used the service experience insight results as weak signals, combined them with future triangle tools, explored the alternative futures of smart home service experience, and suggested future service strategies.

4 Smart Home Service Experience Strategic Foresight

4.1 The "Future Triangle:" Smart Home Service Experience

In this phase, we summarised and classified the weak signals investigated in the previous step and used the future triangle tool to determine foresight and form a future visions. First, we placed the scenario in the future five years from now, that is, 2026. Then, the weak signals were classified into three dimensions of the future triangle. Pull of the future refers to the vision related to the future smart home service experience. Push of the present is the trend influencing future smart home experience development. Weight of the history is the service experience pain point that has already appeared in smart homes. The following can describe the three dimensions of the future triangle of smart home service experience (Fig. 3).

Pull of the Future. In the pull of the future, visions or conditions that pull the smart home towards the future were mainly explored. First, for emotional experience, smart homes carry the community dream of a better life. Second, from the perspective of considering the entire Earth and society, smart homes also carry the beautiful vision of realising a low-consumption, eco-friendly lifestyle. Finally, the development of local storage technology and other technologies helps solve user privacy and security problems, enhance the emotional experience of users of privacy and security experience, and promote the development of human rights and equality in the society. For functional experience, technology development

Table 5. Service experience insights from the Weibo dataset (excerpts).

Weibo ID	Stakeholders	Weibo Post	Insights	Service Experience
1738082612	Smart Home User	The sweeping robot must manually replace the water tank and wash the mop by hand every day. Sometimes it feels like this is not smart, and it is no different from the traditional mop sweeping. Another pain point is that sometimes the sweeping robot does not switch between different working modes when encountering floor materials such as carpets or malfunctions	The product requires manual operation and is not automated	Device usage experience & Privacy experience
7709744108	Technical Expert	Be sure to choose one intelligent home brand. Different brands are incompatible and require a lot of APP control, which will be very troublesome	Different brands are not compatible	System connectivity experience
3638428821	Technophiles	I hope to unlock more application scenarios, better integrate intelligent products into the smart home system	Rich application scenario requirements	Spatial experience
5263400066	Smart Home User	Completely Smart Home Room #What is the experience of living in a room without privacy#	Users feel no privacy in the smart home	Privacy experience
7711743787	Media News	Family life will not only become more convenient, safer, and smarter. Enhance expectations for the ideal home environment, have a better sense of belonging, and better enjoy the comfortable atmosphere at home	News reports that smart home users feel a convenient life and a better sense of belonging	Ambiance experience
7382457154	Smart Home Brand	Incorporating green concepts into product development, energy-saving products such as LED light sources, water-saving valves, high-efficiency faucets, and water-saving toilets reflect the brand's pursuit of sustainable development	The brand pursues sustainable development	Value perception experience

and protocol compatibility cause the vision of free connectivity between various systems and platforms to accelerate. Compatibility between different platforms will promote the development of smart homes from a current situation dominated by one smart product to an intelligent scene connected by multiple products in the future, enhancing the overall user experience of smart homes. In addition, the pursuit of rich application scenarios by users can bring technology

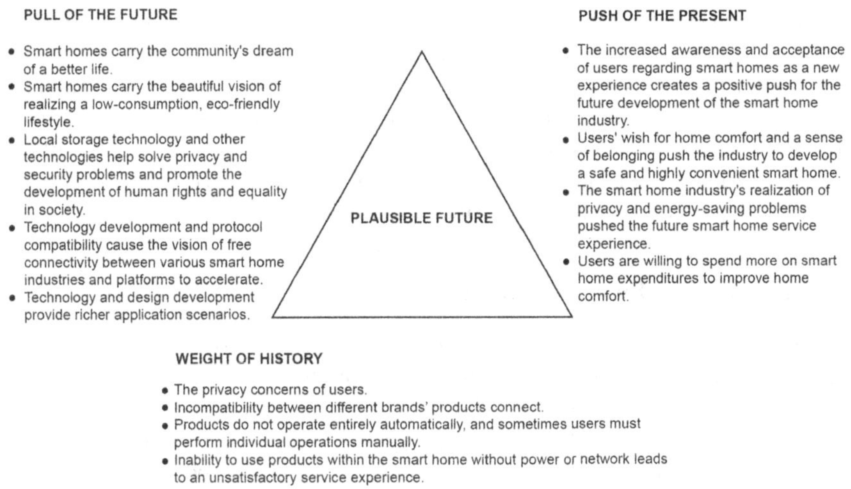

PULL OF THE FUTURE
• Smart homes carry the community's dream of a better life.
• Smart homes carry the beautiful vision of realizing a low-consumption, eco-friendly lifestyle.
• Local storage technology and other technologies help solve privacy and security problems and promote the development of human rights and equality in society.
• Technology development and protocol compatibility cause the vision of free connectivity between various smart home industries and platforms to accelerate.
• Technology and design development provide richer application scenarios.
PLAUSIBLE FUTURE
PUSH OF THE PRESENT
• The increased awareness and acceptance of users regarding smart homes as a new experience creates a positive push for the future development of the smart home industry.
• Users' wish for home comfort and a sense of belonging push the industry to develop a safe and highly convenient smart home.
• The smart home industry's realization of privacy and energy-saving problems pushed the future smart home service experience.
• Users are willing to spend more on smart home expenditures to improve home comfort.
WEIGHT OF HISTORY
• The privacy concerns of users.
• Incompatibility between different brands' products connect.
• Products do not operate entirely automatically, and sometimes users must perform individual operations manually.
• Inability to use products within the smart home without power or network leads to an unsatisfactory service experience.

Fig. 3. The "Future Triangle:" smart home service experience

and design industries efforts together. The pull of the future promotes smart homes towards a happy, sustainable, secure, fair, convenient, and prosperous future service experience.

Push of the Present. In the push of the present, factors or trends that derive the future direction of smart homes are determined. For emotional experience, the increased awareness and acceptance of users regarding smart homes as a new experience creates a positive push for the future development of the smart home industry. Additionally, the pursuit of users for home comfort and their sense of belonging drive the industry to work together to develop safe and highly convenient smart homes. For functional experience, the industry has realised the need to address the privacy and energy-saving problems of smart homes through technology upgrades, which has provided a push to the future smart home service experience. Overall, user experience and satisfaction with the current stage of smart homes, their sense of expectation, and the industry emphasis on privacy and energy-saving problems drive the future service experience of smart homes.

Weight of the History. In the weight of the history, problems or situations that prevent or hinder the future smart home service experience are determined. For emotional experience, the concerns of users about privacy affect smart homes. For functional experience, incompatibility between the products of different brands, for example, due to different systems, the intelligent speaker of brand A cannot control the intelligent fan of brand B block the user experience of smart homes. Then, some products do not operate completely automatically, and users are required to manually perform individual operations. Finally, inability to use products within the smart home in the absence of power or network leads to unsatisfactory service experience. Overall, the functional pain points and privacy concerns hinder the future development of smart homes.

Through the analysis of three dimensions, the future elements of the smart home experience have been clearly seen. The main role of the future triangle tool is to combine the analysis of the three dimensions of the future into different alternative future scenarios. Next, alternative future scenarios will be proposed by combining elements within the three dimensions.

4.2 Alternative Future of Smart Home Service Experience

Inayatullah suggested that the future can be mapped through the three dimensions of the future triangle with today's view of the future [15]. Although many alternative futures are available, the following five archetypes are regarded as the future scenarios: "evolution and progress," "collapse," "Gaia," globalism, and "back to the future." Based on the analysis of the three dimensions of the future triangle, we estimated three alternative futures of smart home service experience to be "evolution and progress," "collapse," and "Gaia." The evolution and progress scenario is to help the future smart home realize the change in service experience through technological progress, design concepts, and cooperation between industries. Currently, the main limitation emerges from the product inability between different brands and systems to achieve technical and protocol compatibility. We should focus on solving integration system construction through technology and new, industrial agreements. In the future, we will achieve compatibility with different brand products in a smart home scene and realise the vision of rich scene-based experience. In addition, the sustainable concept of ensuring user privacy and security through technological updates and achieving high efficiency and energy saving will be investigated and developed. Overall, through technological advancement and industrial co-operation, the future smart homes can overcome the current limitations of service experience and meet the expectations of people in terms of functional and emotional experiences. The evolution and progress scenario is the most likely alternative future for the future service experience of smart homes.

The next scenario for the future of smart homes is "collapse." People think that smart homes cannot live because of an enormous privacy crisis, technological crisis, or environmental crisis. Collapse is the least favourable alternative future of smart home service experience, and we must prevent it by developing policies and strategies.

Finally, the smart home scenario moves towards the "Gaia" future. Gaia refers to that our world requires a partnership between men and women, between human and nature, and between culture and technology. Smart home future experience may present a perfect combination of culture and technology. People experience a sense of belonging and happiness in smart homes. Smart homes provide energy saving and environmentally sustainable development. Technology and nature attain a balance.

4.3 Future Smart Home Service Experience Strategies

By analyzing alternative futures, we can determine what futures we do not want to face and what we look forward to developing strategic plans to move closer to the preferable futures we want to go. In the future smart home service experience, the user must be considered, along with service experience beneficial to future generations, society, and future environment. To get closer to the preferable future smart home, we summarize the future service experience strategies from two aspects of functional experience and emotional experience.

Functional Experience. To provide a satisfactory smart homes service experience to the future generation, we need to solve the following problems of functional experience. First, for the scenario-based vision of smart homes moving towards whole house interconnection, the products of different brands and platforms must overcome the problem of connection incompatibility among them through technologies or communication protocols. To prevent the situation when users purchasing different brands need to download different settings and operations, the situation of different products cannot interconnect, and smart scenes cannot form. We need to solve the compatibility problem to move towards the whole house interconnection scenario and enhance the system connectivity experience. Second, the current products in smart homes present disadvantages, such as the lack of complete automation. In the future, smart home products can strengthen algorithms to predict user requirements and improve user equipment experience.

Emotional Experience. To fulfil people's sense of belonging at a home and vision of a better life, in the future emotional experience of smart homes, the privacy protection experience and sustainable value perception experience of users of smart homes must be strengthened. First, people's sense of belonging to a smart home is an emotional experience based on a safe and private home environment. In the future, smart homes must ensure user data security in terms of technology, regulations, and policies and enhance user privacy and security experience. Second, an energy-saving, sustainable smart home ecological environment must be created. Stakeholders have a strong sense of identity with the sustainable brand and concept of smart homes. These ideas to promote social equity and sustainability are obligations to the future ecology of the planet.

5 Conclusions

In the Anthropocene, human behaviour and activities have profoundly affected the environment and society. To understand whether the people demand for future smart home service experience benefits the future generations, we must combine future thinking and explore future smart homes with a long-term perspective. This study first reviewed the smart home service experience, future thinking, and foresight-related literature. Then, the data on smart home experience were collected on the Chinese social media, Weibo, and the insights and requirements of the society and smart home stakeholders about the smart home service experience were explored by conducting the social network analysis. Subsequently, the insight results were analysed according to the future triangle, and three alternative futures were predicted for future smart home service experience. Finally, four suggestions are provided for future smart home service experience strategies from two aspects: functional and emotional experience.

According to the data analysis results collected from the Weibo platform, one of the three alternative futures can be obtained for smart home service experience in the next five years from. These futures are "evolution and progress," "collapse," and "Gaia." The evolution and progress scenario refer to the future smart home service experience attained through technological advancement and industrial cooperation; this future can emerge from a single, smart product experience to a whole-house innovative experience and meet people's expectations of functional and emotional experiences. The collapse scenario indicates that because of serious privacy, technological, or environmental problems, people can assume that smart homes are unreliable or provide negative experience, and smart homes may be abandoned. The Gaia scenario indicates that the future experience of smart homes may present a perfect combination of culture and technology. People experience a sense of belonging and happiness in a smart home, and the struggle from all walks of life is balanced. And smart homes, which provide energy conservation and environmental sustainability, can be achieved. We can improve the future smart home strategy from functional and emotional experience strategies. For functional experience strategies, the incompatibility between different brands and platform products must be solved through technology or communication protocols and smart homes must be promoted to achieve a true full house interconnection. Strengthening algorithms and other methods improve the automation degree of smart home products and enhance the experience of device use. For emotional experience, in future smart homes, privacy and safety experience must be improved, and social justice must be promoted. In addition, we must pay attention to value-perception experience as well as the energy conservation and environmental protection of smart homes and promote the sustainable environmental development. People's sense of belonging and better life in smart homes can be improved by enhancing service experience. Using social network analysis and future triangle tools, we can design service experiences from next generation's perspectives and design future service experiences to benefit future society and the planet.

In theory, service experience is divided into functional and emotional experiences. We combined smart home characteristics and revealed researches that smart home functional experience is divided into device-usage, system-connection, and spatial experiences. Emotional experience involves three parts: privacy, atmosphere, and value-perception experiences. In practice, we conducted the future triangle tool combined with the social network analysis for foresight. For future exploration, the social network analysis can more rigorously analyse a broader range of data than qualitative methods, such as interviews and brainstorming. This method can be used as an auxiliary means of qualitative studies.

This study also has several limitations that must be noted. First, the data source of this study is the Chinese social media, Weibo, and most of its users are from China, analysis in other regions requires the execution of different datasets. It is difficult for researchers to confirm social media users' real identity and age. Generally speaking, the people who use social media are mainly young and middle-aged people who use smartphones, and there may be a lack of data on the elderly. The data collected contains only 11 months of information, and all analyses and assumptions apply only to the range of intercepted data. Second, we must realise that the opinions posted on social media should be viewed dialectically, irrespective of whether the information comes from experts, brands, or users. Finally, the social network analysis of the original Weibo text and the construction of future triangle may be affected by the subjective judgment of researchers. In the future, we will improve the insights of future service experience and explore how to apply the results of insights to the future service experience design. Enhancing the happiness of future generations, promoting the equitable development of the society, and the sustainable development of the earth's environment are the common goals of designing future services for smart homes.

References

1. Amanatidou, E., Butter, M., Carabias, V., Könnölä, T., Leis, M., Saritas, O., Schaper-Rinkel, P., van Rij, V.: On concepts and methods in horizon scanning: Lessons from initiating policy dialogues on emerging issues. Sci. Publ. Pol. **39**(2), 208–221 (2012)
2. Balta-Ozkan, N., Boteler, B., Amerighi, O.: European smart home market development: public views on technical and economic aspects across the united kingdom, germany and italy. Energy Res. Soc. Sci. **3**, 65–77 (2014)
3. Ban, K.M.: Sustainable development goals (2016)
4. Berry, L.L., Wall, E.A., Carbone, L.P.: Service clues and customer assessment of the service experience: lessons from marketing. Acad. Manag. Perspect. **20**(2), 43–57 (2006)
5. Camacho, D., Panizo-LLedot, Á., Bello-Orgaz, G., Gonzalez-Pardo, A., Cambria, E.: The four dimensions of social network analysis: an overview of research methods, applications, and software tools. Inf. Fus. **63**, 88–120 (2020)
6. Conroy, M.J., Runge, M.C., Nichols, J.D., Stodola, K.W., Cooper, R.J.: Conservation in the face of climate change: the roles of alternative models, monitoring, and adaptation in confronting and reducing uncertainty. Biol. Cons. **144**(4), 1204–1213 (2011)
7. Crutzen, P.J.: The "Anthropocene". In: Ehlers, E., Krafft, T. (eds.) Earth System Science in the Anthropocene, pp. 13–18. Springer, Heidelberg (2006). https://doi.org/10.1007/3-540-26590-2_3
8. Dator, Jim: What Futures Studies Is, and Is Not. In: Jim Dator: A Noticer in Time. AS, vol. 5, pp. 3–5. Springer, Cham (2019). https://doi.org/10.1007/978-3-030-17387-6_1

9. De Moor, K., Saritas, O., Schuurman, D., Claeys, L., De Marez, L.: Towards innovation foresight: Two empirical case studies on future tv experiences for/by users. Futures **59**, 39–49 (2014)
10. Fan, G., Khng, J.N.W.: The futures of the Singapore association of social workers: an analysis using CLA and the "Futures Triangle". Foresight **16**(4), 329–343 (2014)
11. Feicheng, M., Yating, L.: Utilising social network analysis to study the characteristics and functions of the co-occurrence network of online tags. Online Inf. Rev. **38**(2), 232–247 (2014)
12. Grubmüller, V., Götsch, K., Krieger, B.: Social media analytics for future oriented policy making. Eur. J. Fut. Res. **1**(1), 1–9 (2013). https://doi.org/10.1007/s40309-013-0020-7
13. Han, Lijun: User experience: the motivation and promotion of livestreaming innovation in Chinese marketing. In: Rau, Pei-Luen Patrick. (ed.) User experience: The motivation and promotion of livestreaming innovation in chinese marketing. LNCS, vol. 12772, pp. 344–361. Springer, Cham (2021). https://doi.org/10.1007/978-3-030-77077-8_27
14. Helkkula, A.: Characterising the concept of service experience. J. Serv. Manage. **22**(3), 367–389 (2011)
15. Inayatullah, S.: Six pillars: futures thinking for transforming. Foresight **10**(1), 4–21 (2008)
16. Jaakkola, E., Helkkula, A., Aarikka-Stenroos, L.: Service experience co-creation: conceptualization, implications, and future research directions. J. Serv. Manage. **26**(2), 182–205 (2015)
17. Kang, H.J., Kwon, G.H., Kim, B., Park, E.: A framework for smart servicescape: a case of smart home service experience. In: IASDR 2017 (International Association of Societies of Design Research), pp. 1665–1677 (2017)
18. Kayser, V., Bierwisch, A.: Using twitter for foresight: an opportunity? Futures **84**, 50–63 (2016)
19. Khedekar, D.C., Truco, A.C., Oteyza, D.A., Huertas, G.F.: Home automation-a fast-expanding market. Thunderbird Int. Bus. Rev. **59**(1), 79–91 (2017)
20. Marikyan, D., Papagiannidis, S., Alamanos, E.: A systematic review of the smart home literature: a user perspective. Technol. Forecast. Soc. Chang. **138**, 139–154 (2019)
21. Pang, A.S.K.: Social scanning: improving futures through web 2.0; or, finally a use for twitter. Futures **42**(10), 1222–1230 (2010)
22. Reinisch, C., Kofler, M., Iglesias, F., Kastner, W.: Thinkhome energy efficiency in future smart homes. EURASIP J. Embed. Syst. **2011**, 1–18 (2011)
23. Roy, S.K., Balaji, M., Sadeque, S., Nguyen, B., Melewar, T.: Constituents and consequences of smart customer experience in retailing. Technol. Forecast. Soc. Chang. **124**, 257–270 (2017)
24. Sandström, S., Edvardsson, B., Kristensson, P., Magnusson, P.: Value in use through service experience. Manag. Serv. Qual. Int. J. **18**(2), 112–126 (2008)
25. Schellnhuber, H.J.: 'Earth system' analysis and the second Copernican revolution. Nature **402**(6761), C19–C23 (1999)
26. Scott, J., Carrington, P.J.: The SAGE Handbook of Social Network Analysis. SAGE Publications, London (2011)
27. Uhl, A., Kolleck, N., Schiebel, E.: Twitter data analysis as contribution to strategic foresight-the case of the EU research project "foresight and modelling for European health policy and regulations" (fresher). Eur. J. Fut. Res. **5**(1), 1–16 (2017)
28. Wu, Y., Pillan, M.: From respect to change user behaviour. Research on how to design a next generation of smart home objects from user experience and interaction design. Des. J. **20**(sup1), S3884–S3898 (2017)

Media Intelligent Content Production in the AI Horizon

Hanfu He(✉), Fang You, and Yu Wang

College of Desgin and Innovation, TongJi University, Shanghai, China
myside1919@163.com

Abstract. With the advent of the era of artificial intelligence (AI), all walks of life are facing the subversion and reconstruction from characterization to the core, and the media industry that is highly cohesive with the society is naturally no exception.In the past 10 years, the media has emphasized the intelligent intelligence system of artificial intelligence—improved the communication effectiveness of content by increasing immersion and "presence" experience, reformed the content production system, and designed a new mechanism that meets the new media content production standards. [Objective] This paper studies the two aspects of content production mechanism and mode of production, fmethod] through literature analysis, deep observation of specific practice cases, and experimental analysis, [conclusion] proposes an effective content production mechanism, and proves that with the latest VR/AR (Visual Reality/Augmented Reality) information presentation technology, media can produce content products with immersive and better experience.This article conducted in-depth research on the two professional media, participated in the content production process of VR and AR according to the research requirements, and successfully presented the content works.

Keywords: Central Kitchen · AI · VR · Intelligent content production · AR

1 The Content Production Mechanism Adapted to Intelligent Media

1.1 Design the Integration and Innovation of the Media Content Production Mechanism

In the era of traditional media, the news reporting editing process basically follow the live interview, rear editing, instant release, and audience feedback, plus professional news institutions verification procedures [1], formed the main closed-loop of news content production, many media in the closed-loop mode according to their own characteristics, such as multimedia field linkage, set up a hotline to strengthen the communication between the media and the audience.

Therefore, it is necessary to explain the traditional media in the beginning of the study. In the field of media research, we call the media with one-way communication and slow communication speed "traditional media". Such media include newspapers, magazines,

P.-L. P. Rau (Ed.): HCII 2022, LNCS 13314, pp. 519–534, 2022.
https://doi.org/10.1007/978-3-031-06053-3_35

radio and television, etc. The production and distribution of traditional media content is relatively fixed - different newspaper pages and TV channels, broadcast content is closely related to the subject matter. New media is a concept relative to traditional media. This concept is dynamic and constantly changing, extending from the technological base of Internet technology. According to Media research institutions in the United States, the foundation of new media comes from computer, communication and digital technology, which realizes interaction with terminal devices such as computers and smart phones through communication carriers such as the Internet. Compared with traditional media, the communication of new media is two-way or even multi-directional, which enables more people to have the right to speak. The audience can choose the channel of experience, from passive acceptance to active experience. New media will also spread faster, depending on the development of Internet technology.

However, with the rise of new media, in the context of media convergence, the traditional news content production mechanism and new media are more and more prominent. The "4A" feature (Anytime/Anywhere/Anyone/Anyway) required for new media is unattainable by traditional media using the past production mechanism.

Effectiveness for a Given Period of Time. In the content production process of traditional media, the audience has received the reporter writing, editing rear processing, reviewer review, inspector details, then through the leadership after printing factory or TV-radio recording, some major emergencies, in order to strive for the best time of reporting, television and other media choose to work in the way of life. Live streaming has become a standard match for many emerging media organizations or platforms and reflects the advantages of more convenience, efficiency, and low cost.

Scene. Compared with the traditional media, the new generation of content presentation methods represented by virtual reality (VR) and augmented reality (AR) technology provides the audience with a sense of immersion and presence that the traditional media does not have. With the empowerment of 5G technology, the hybrid spatial information presentation technology integrating virtual and reality can also be recorded on the news scene, such as text, pictures, and short videos in the past, producing immersive content works in a short time. That is to say, the reconstruction and restoration of scenes will become one of the core elements of the future media content ecology.

In some scholars, including big data, social media, mobile, sensor, and positioning system, five elements is an important part of the "scene" and call it "five force", think people's life experience is changing with five kinds of force, and then change the rules of the game of this era [2].

Interaction. Traditional news content is rarely considered interactive. As mentioned above, some TV stations and radio stations have set up hotlines with hotlines or by answering questions online to achieve limited interaction with the audience.

With the support of new media technology, the interaction between audiences and content producers can be achieved all-weather, whole-process, and across time and space. From the message after the content, the barrage of video flow, to the new interaction methods between time and space in the virtual space, the audience experience will also force the media to constantly improve their intelligence level, and find a content production mechanism in line with this new communication law (Table 1).

Table 1. The main application of intelligent media production (drawn by the author)

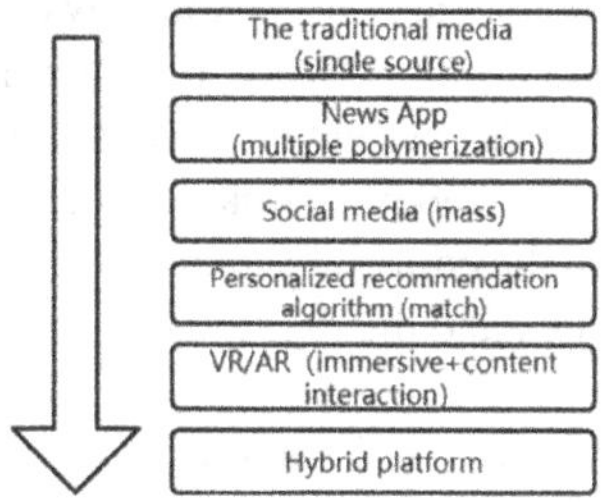

1.2 Design Practice of the "Central Kitchen" Mode Under the Media Fusion Framework

In recent years, with the increasing transformation pressure of traditional media, the concepts such as "financial media" and "media integration" have frequently become the hot spots of public opinion. In 1983, Itcher.Soller.Poole, the Professor of the Massachusetts Institute of Technology(MIT) put forward the concept of "Media Convergence". In his book Free Science and Technology, he proposed "The Convergence of Modes", pointing out The Convergence trend of various media towards functional integration. His definition of media integration is that various media show the development trend of multi-functional integration. "A single medium, whether it be telephone lines, cable or radio waves, will carry services that used to require multiple media to carry." At the same time, it used to rely only on "services provided by a single media, such as newspapers, radio, etc., which can now be supplied through diversified media." [3]. Poole believes that the past "one-to-one relationship between the medium and the services it provides is being eroded" [4].

At present, the definition of financial media is "the new media forms of—media, content and complementary different media forms from the broad integration of radio, television, and newspapers [5], based on the systematic integration from content, publicity, and other functions" [6].

This initial attempt was made by the BBC, by reorganizing the "Super editorial" [7], integrating television, radio, and network, replacing the original BBC programming and multimedia journalism, the original BBC Radio, television, and network [8]. The original system of the content chief of each department is replaced with the role of "editor in chief". The new "editor in chief" will be rotated by the editor in chief of each department, and each content production department will be merged and reorganized according to production factors. In terms of the specific tasks of journalists and editors, different from the previous way of division by the line, the "super editorial department" adopts the "all-media matrix" mode of various types of work for production [9].

This is the prototype of the "Central Kitchen" content production system design concept. In recent years, mainstream media groups in China have also tried to design and build a "Central Kitchen" for content production. To research group familiar with Guangzhou daily, for example, in 2014, as one of the earliest media, Guangzhou daily in the attempt of the original editorial department, on the basis of the "central editorial department", the original editorial center, all media news center, digital news laboratory, audio and video department and ocean network, the intention of the newspaper and new media port (Weibo WeChat and App client) release together, change the original content production department "independent" situation. In the design of the administrative structure, the former director of the editorial center served as the executive director of the Editorial Department of the CPC, and the digital news laboratory and other departments served as the deputy director.

Through practice, Guangzhou Daily's practice has been widely recognized by the industry. Later, Guangzhou Daily completed the construction of the "Central Kitchen" content production system on the basis of the "Central Editorial Department", followed the concept of "one collection, multiple generation, and multiple communication", and processed news content products in different processing ways to meet the needs of different ports.

The purpose of the "Central Kitchen" design is to achieve diversified production and processing, multi-channel release, combined with big data and cloud computing technology, and provide personalized content supply services for different audiences. In this system, each port can also order the "Central Kitchen" according to its own actual needs, and the "Central Kitchen" allocates the human and technical resources needed to produce content products that meet the needs.

With the practical cases of Guangzhou Daily, we can see that the operation mechanism of the "Central Kitchen" is carried out at three levels.

Content Layer. Relative to the traditional content production mode in the past, "Central Kitchen" will be all editorial staff to redefine—command personnel, information collection personnel, information processing, and processing personnel and technical production personnel, etc., after the command personnel preliminary planning topic selection, through professional staff collection processing, through the division of labor cooperation to complete the established tasks.

Technical Layer. Guangzhou Daily set up the new media technology support center with the original technology department as the core and cooperated with the content production team of the "Central Kitchen" to produce content products that meet the timeliness, visualization, immersion, and communication power. In 2020, In the production of the traditional essence "Cantonese opera" content product "VR takes you Explore Before and Behind the scenes of Cantonese opera", The reporter entered the backstage dressing room and the rehearsal room respectively, The stage and in the audience were filmed, The technical team assisted reporters with panoramic shooting equipment, Take the dressing room in the performance backstage as an example, In a 360° VR lens, The dressing room in the horizon becomes a virtual reality space, In addition to the actors who answered questions from reporters, Viewers can also focus to the other actors, You can even listen close to the discussion between the actors, Actively select the focused content, This is an experience never had in traditional content works (Fig. 1).

Fig. 1. "VR takes You to Explore the Front and Behind the scenes of Cantonese Opera"

Hardware Layer. As an important carrier to run the "Central Kitchen", the financial media command center of Guangzhou Daily is established in the largest office space of the headquarters editorial building of Guangzhou Daily, with a construction area of 2,800 m^2, It is the largest editorial and editing command center in China. The integrated media editorial command platform in the center realizes the integrated large screen, "cloud desktop" display, and "three screens": the integrated large screen adopts ultra-high HD DLP display technology with a display area of 64 square meters, the "cloud desktop" display in the editorial hall connects the central server through the small box and interactive sharing; At the same time, the media editorial system can realize the integrated news production of reporter handheld writing and port release, and the whole process communication effect can be presented on the integrated comprehensive large screen [10] (Fig. 2).

Fig. 2. Guangzhou daily AI media editorial center live scene

2 Practice of Content Production with VR Technology

In the media that has adopted the "Central Kitchen" mechanism design, on the basis of this mechanism, it has innovated the specific way of content production and proposed to improve the experience of receiving information with better immersion. The most representative one is the content production model based on VR technology. This section, through specific cases, presents the main characteristics of the content production mode based on VR technology and conducts specific analysis and comparison with the two main production pathways.

2.1 Main Features of VR News Content

In the media that has adopted the "central kitchen" mechanism design, on the basis of this mechanism, it has innovated the specific way of content production and proposed to improve the experience of receiving information with better immersion. The most representative one is the content production model based on VR technology.

Virtual Reality (also referred to as VR) is also known as artificial environment in the field of professional research. It is characterized by creating a virtual simulation visual environment for users to "immerse" in virtual scenes reconstructed with the computer through visual, auditory, and even touch. Some scholars have summarized the content dissemination of VR as immersion (Immersion), interaction (Interaction), and imagination (Imagination) [11].

In 2010, Nonny de la Pena, a researcher from the University of Southern California Annenberg School of Communication and Journalism at the University of Southern California, first proposed the idea of using VR technology for news content production [12], and regarded it as "a way of news production that enables the audience to obtain a first-person perspective experience of stories or scenes in the news"[13].

Thus, the concept of "VR news" emerged.

Compared with the production of traditional news content, the news reports produced by VR technology provide panoramic news scene presentation, strengthening the audience's audio-visual perception experience. The transmission of content is transmitted one way from a two-dimensional perspective to the audience's multi-item perception of news and information. The audience has also changed from the recipient of content in traditional news communication programs to a common participant of content.

The research group integrated the practice of media using VR technology in content production. Compared with the narrative mode of traditional news content, VR news has two main characteristics:

The Empowering Audience Actively Chooses. Compared with the traditional news content, the biggest difference between the audience in the viewing experience is that the VR news gives the audience a greater active choice. In traditional news reports, both the text and video, the audience understand the context of news events from the perspective of reporters and form their first impression. The reporter's perspective takes a single lens as a unit, and the combination of content units guides the audience to gradually narrative from shallow to deep.

In VR news, the biggest feature is the panoramic perspective, which almost will hardly leave the dead Angle of sight to the audience, to create a virtual sense of "reality", so as to achieve the immersive effect. 360 The panoramic news content from the ° perspective allows the audience to independently choose any horizon in the VR scene in the viewing process. At the same time, the audience can also interact with the characters in the VR to make themselves part of the news story through the interaction.

Seek Precise Content Details. In traditional news images, what journalists should have to pay great attention to is the details within the focus range, because this already covers all the horizon viewing possibilities of the audience.

VR has a panoramic view, the processing of scene details can have a great impact on the audience experience. When shooting the VR panoramic view, the news film team needs to observe and divide all the surrounding scenes and the details included.

Analysis, make a good plan in advance. These details include sound, touch, light, etc., as well as human expression control and the true presentation of objects in the scene.

2.2 Design of the Two Main VR Products

For the media, there are currently two major VR news content production models. One is to capture the whole scene image in a 360° panoramic shot and generate content works after post-editing and modification. The other is to make it in 3D modeling and then be generated by the post-adding effect. To facilitate research, the research team selected the same theme—in the centenary of the founding of the Communist Party of China to produce works related to the theme.

Panning. The team chose a memorial hall of the Communist Party of China that just opened in June as the content to complete a high-definition 360° panoramic camera and supporting operating software. Compared to traditional cameras, when shooting with VR using a panoramic camera, the photographer needs to keep the appropriate distance from the subject, aiming to avoid a "line-of-sight coverage" of the subject during imaging. Between the two scenes shot, the linked narrative logic can be completed through the hot spots added in the later stage, which has the function of guiding the audience to go deep into the scene.

In practice, the panoramic image splicing operation platform used by the group has either Premiere or Kolor AutoPano Giga. After the shooting, a good transmission effect was achieved (Fig. 3).

3D Modeling. The team used 3D modeling to make the same content as the theme of the narrative of the Red Army's Long March. This production mode requires content producers to have a certain spatial imagination ability while referring to real history.

In the initial stage of production, the research team completed the primary model by hand drawing and logic drawing, and then the program operator models the output according to the scene diagram. Later, the output primary model is superimposed based on the storyline advance and rendered in real-time.

Fig. 3. Panoramic shooting of the memorial hall of the First Congress of the Communist Party of China.

At this time, the content producer enters the scene with the programmer for logical testing of the content. Based on platforms like Unity3D and unreal, modifications were made to the story framework provided by the authors.

In this 3D modeled image, the team took pre-designed story script as the main narrative line, superimposed characters and related historical information in the scene, by rendering reconstruction virtual scene and finally the people and things in the scene embedded into the story script. The audience is immersed in VR in an artificially outlined narrative scene.

The scenes made through 3D basically restore the historical images, but the disadvantage is that there are still defects in the design of the characters, especially the human body coordination, which is still significantly different from the real people.

3 Impact of AR Technology on Content Production

Like VR, the purpose of AR technology is to better connect the information between reality and virtual space, but it is more optimized than VR technology in terms of physical space digitization. The production practice case of AR content selected in this paper has the characteristics of full-scene space presentation, strong comprehension ability, and immersive rendering. At the same time, this chapter discusses the production process of AR news content with experiments.

3.1 Overview and Development Status of AR Technology

AR started late compared to VR technology. However, because it can seamlessly connect virtual information with the real world through system design, it has attracted much attention in the industry and gained rapid development momentum in recent years. The general definition of AR technology in the industry is that, with the help of computer technology, 3D scene models, pictures, voice, and video information is presented in the real physical world, giving people an immersive deep experience.AR has the characteristics of tracking registration, virtual and real integration, and human-computer interaction [14]. In the relevant research of AR, in addition to visual and auditory perception, there can also be real-time interaction with virtual information placed in the objective physical world through gestures and face recognition. For intelligent content producers, in the existence of VR, the emergence of AR provides a new content production mode [15].

It is reported that AR technology has been applied with—mobile phones, head displays or glasses, and other wearable devices in many fields, which are effectively integrated with AR technology. At present, the main application areas of AR technology cover live TV, private sports customization, health care, and tourism guide. The examples in this article also include adding deep social interaction through bullet screen mapping (Table 2).

Table 2. AR technology application case (drawn by the author)

Apply styles	Application scenarios
Wear-type AR head display	Highlight the interior object details
Overlay the computer information in real space	New broadcast room
Overlay the scanned, translated text on the real-world text	Portable translation
Virtual private education/health assistant, the body function indicators of reality in a specific area	Private Sports Customization/Health Assistant
Virtual guidance/introduction information is superimposed on the real scene, and visitors complete the interactive task at the interface	Travel/Navigation

In content production, the first attempt to use AR technology was the American Esquire magazine. From 2010 to 2012, several major mainstream American media, such as the New York Times, USA Today, The Wall Street Journal, and the Los Angeles Times, began to expand the scope of AR technology in content creation, and many TV stations set up professional AR sets to broadcast non-political programs such as sports competitions.

In 2017, the content design team from the New York Times teamed up with the famous technology company IBM to launch the first AR deep experience application, APP, Outthink Hidden, aiming to show the true story of three African-American female mathematicians during the 1960s space race through the "AR+content" style. Their breakthrough calculations of space orbit contributed greatly to astronaut John Glenn successfully biting Earth. While achieving their own value, the three scientists did not forget to spread their scientific knowledge to more people, such as a heroine named Dorothy Vaughan, who not only taught themselves IBM's first large computer programming language but also actively taught others what they have learned. Readers can choose the narrative lines and angles from them to experience the story content in depth.

Sai Sebastian Tomich, senior vice president of Advertising and Innovation at the New York Times, said, "While developing experiential storytelling, we have been waiting for the perfect opportunity to take advantage of Fake Love's rich talent and creativity. We can't just develop the Times' first AR experience because we have a way to do that. We need the right partners and the right story. When we talk to IBM about Hidden People, we recognize that this is an opportunity for users to experience the film and the outstanding women they show."

Also in 2017, the Washington Post outlined the global innovative architecture with AR technology. Through the client downloaded on iOS, readers can experience the superposition of objective reality and virtual information without leaving home, and can more intuitively understand the conception and connotation of architectural design. Architect Philip Kennicott believes that AR technology effectively brings building closer to readers and "makes the content look more enjoyable" (Fig. 4).

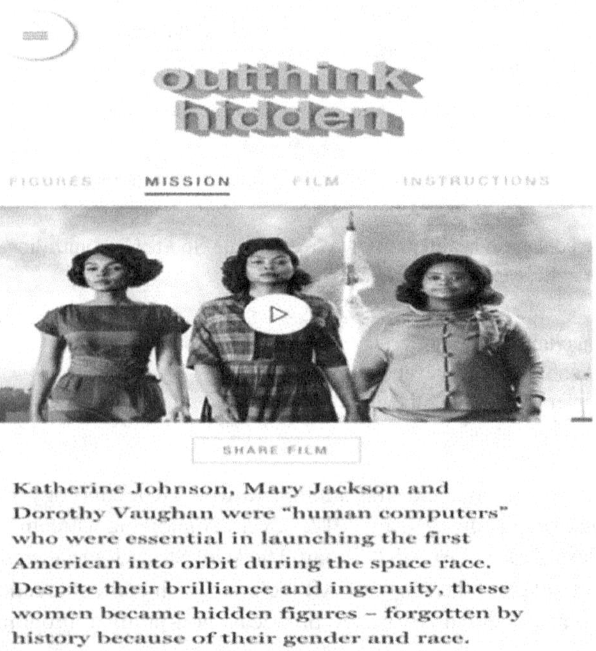

Fig. 4. The hidden people interface

In China, Chengdu Business Daily, the first company to use AR technology, and its AR photo social platform has received praise from its release. But at the time, the app was mainly about the addition of the later image, and the impact on the content itself was very limited.

3.2 Content Design Based on AR Technology

Compared with the content narrative supported by VR, which puts the immersion in the first place, the content creation based on AR also emphasizes the influence of interaction while emphasizing the immersion in the content narrative.

As the application of Internet technology becomes more and more extensive, new media technology represented by VR/AR integrates Cross-cultural factors into communication. Simple information is replaced by multi-culture, which enables users to get different information experience when interacting with media.

For creators of new media, the key to Cross-cultural design is to integrate themselves into the "Target Culture". This also means that in the content production process of new media, there is a higher requirement for authors to be "on site". The author's on-site experience can be transmitted to users through immersive audio-visual technology. Such immersion not only comes from the interpretation of information, but also from the cultural experience.

This kind of immersive cultural experience is the main way of Cross-cultural design of media. This requires the author to communicate closely with the subject in the process of making content, and understand their cultural and educational background. This new type of media product will endow the audience with the values of Cross-cultural experience.

Generally speaking, the "interactivity" of the content refers to the cycle process that "occurs between more than two subjects, the subject has a certain activity, and each other can listen to, communicate, and complete the thinking". Through this interpretation, we can roughly understand the three stages of interactive narrative in AR content production: the first stage, the user will show the willingness to interact and input relevant information; the second stage, the computer identifies, analyzes, and processes the information in the virtual world; the third stage, in the third stage, the processed information is fed back to the user from the virtual world.

The concept of "the fourth wall" in the traditional narrative theory refers to an invisible "wall", which is virtually separated from content producers and users, virtual and reality. The VR technology described above solves the problem of "making users present" through immersion, but the boundary separating virtual and reality is very obvious. AR completely broke the wall completely, enabling users to realize two-way communication with content producers in a new space integrating reality and virtual.

Therefore, the content narrative design using AR technology must take into account the following elements: 1. the superposition effect of virtual and real integration, the interface into the real physical environment; 2,3 D image, visual immersion; 3, real-time interaction, which is an important feature in AR narrative, users interact with the virtual space through the superimposed virtual interface, and then get a good immersive experience.

In conclusion, in addition to the immersive experience, real-time interaction is an important feature of AR content. When users experience AR content,—can choose the Angle and distance of viewing the content independently, because the content presented by AR is based on the real scene. Therefore, if users want to ensure the option to experience the whole content scene, designers need to do more preparations.—This is not rendering for a single scene, but scene presentation based on high-precision maps and real-time modeling.

3.3 Real-Time Rendering of the Full-Scene Space Comprehension Capability Enables Content Production

Currently, the common technical support for designing AR content is Unity3D. This is a set of content design engines configured with level editors covering graphics, sound, and scene physical features, using computer languages such as JavaScript as the basis of script design, enabling designers to achieve the production design of AR content without having to understand the complex underlying computational editing techniques. Unity3D with cross-platform features supports mainstream application platforms, including PC, Linux, Web, IOS, and Android. The AR content production design case introduced in this article will also be launched with Unity3D as the main design platform.

The case is a "Shanghai Bund" AR smart city work produced by a technology company. For AR works, model construction is the top priority. The preprocessed topographic map was imported into 3DMax to generate the initial landmark model and building elevation maps, and then to build the scene and the building model therein by texture mapping. In this process, the model can be simplified with the model and the scene structure optimized by removing the nonvisible buildings, compression, and reducing the number of maps.

In terms of interaction design, the already constructed scenes are imported into the Unity3D, and the interactive scripts are written using JavaScript, etc., to establish the virtual and real interaction between the user and the target scene at one time.This part of the interaction design task mainly consists of three parts: scene roaming, scene interaction, and information interaction (Fig. 5).

Fig. 5. "Shanghai Bund" AR city intelligent image interface

Based on it, users can view the information that the designer has been superimposed on the relevant buildings through the mobile phone interface, including the location and function of the building, as well as the historical connotation. When using it, the user can complete the interaction between the user and the superimposed virtual information through the touch screen and select the dialog box of interest to watch the scene introduction information and video.

At present, because the local points required by the system are just rolled out stage, the system only deals with the integration of virtual and real space in specific scenes, and the design of content focuses more on guidance and introduction of scenic spots, the social function is limited to users to add "barrage" to the architectural graphics. Other content products of the interface, such as robots, brocade carp, and other images can not realize the interaction between people.

The overall production of the system content can be divided into two stages, first, the construction of the scene model, based on the scene modeling software 3DMAX for the corresponding scene terrain, environment, and representative building modeling; then write the interactive script to connect the original static content model and Unity3D, so that the whole system can have real-time interaction capability.

In the next future design, the content producer will further optimize and upgrade the content experience in four aspects: 1. Free content editing rights, users can design and edit information and upload specific scenes; 2, strong environmental understanding ability, can automatically identify animals and plants, text, characters and buildings and other target content; 3, combined with POI (Point of Interest) full-scene space calculation, can recommend appropriate content for users; 4, immersive real-time rendering, high-precision modeling, and avatar integration.

4 Summary and Outlook

4.1 Positive Factors and Challenges Posed by the "Central Kitchen" System Design

The intelligent production of media content is the trend of The Times. "Central Kitchen", as the central mechanism of concentrating various intelligent software and hardware and human resources in the future media, promotes the integration of a variety of new technologies, including the application of VR/AR technology in the presentation of news content, and is an innovation in the systematic design. For content production, the positive factor of "central kitchen" is mainly manifested in:

Instantaneity. The emergence of the "central kitchen" mechanism further promotes the development of media operation and management to the direction of "flat". Many intermediate links are canceled and replaced by simple, efficient, and unified content management and school examination mechanism. At the same time, the use of professional reporter content production advantages and the "central kitchen" information integration attributes, to effectively solve the problem of content supply to the main ports. For media such as radio and television, the central kitchen is still significant. This is mainly reflected in the overall layout of live news. In addition to the whole point of news, it can be broadcast through the port or platform at any time, improving the immediacy of the news.

Stereo Perception. The innovation of the "central kitchen" for the design of the content production mechanism is also reflected in helping the media to achieve the "three-dimensional live broadcast". Research group in-depth study of Guangzhou daily, for example, for the same subject of news content, "central kitchen" can choose multiple ports multiple platforms live—live interview, platform, port video, and H5 content products to expand the influence in WeChat circle of friends, constantly guide the traffic into the live port. This way of operation greatly makes up for the original existing defects of various ports. For example, in the on-site interview, you can let the audience interact with the reporter in front in a timely manner.

Audience-Centered. The interactive experience of the audience is a significant advantage of the new media over the traditional media. Take Guangzhou Daily as an example. During the live broadcast of the first site of the First Congress of the Communist Party of China, audiences can not only watch the live content through their mobile phone or iPad but also watch the reporter from other perspectives through contact points. Reporters entering the pavilion also took 360° panoramic images with a panoramic camera device, and the audience could even conduct immersive views through the head display.

In the process of watching, the audience can also put forward different content needs to the front reporters at any time through barrage, message or voice interaction at any time, and can also interact with the reporter in front kindly and talk about their feelings. In this process, the core production authority of news content has shifted from journalists to the audience.

Of course, the challenges faced by the "Central Kitchen" cannot be ignored, which is mainly reflected in the invisible homogenization rate of the unified initial processing content. At the same time, the new content operation mechanism represented by the "Central Kitchen" on the role of the traditional reporter cannot be ignored.

Content Homogenization. For the subsystems within the media, there is also competition in addition to cooperation. And the emergence of the "Central Kitchen" will virtually eliminate the invisible competition within the media. The same editing team or even the same editor handles the same material manually, and the probability of content homogenization is significantly increased.

Lack of Design Planning. Considering the reality of China's media ecology, traditional media in a low tide need an immediate systematic mechanism design. The emergence of the "Central Kitchen" has attracted many media to embrace the—from the central government to provinces and cities, and then to counties and townships, many media regard the "Central Kitchen" as a "good way" to transform, regardless of their actual situation. Some experts believe that the "central kitchen" should bring the media community a "concept", that is, the integration of multi-department and multi-level staffing and institutional innovation, to find the "Central Kitchen" design path suitable to their own situation.

4.2 Problems Encountered in Content Production Design Based on VR/AR Technology

This paper introduces the current situation of media use of VR/AR technology for content production, as well as the positive impact of the technology on—space sense, physical presence, and stronger immersive and interactive experience on content production and user experience. However, in a specific practice, this group also found that using VR/AR for content design needs to ensure the user experience and pay attention to avoid or optimize through the design:

The Audience Is "out of focus". Different from the traditional content production mode, VR/AR represented by the spatial content production process, production structure fundamental changes—audience to virtual or immersive, achieve the "present" effect, the role of reporter guide focus is weakened, spatial content production gives the audience greater autonomy and choice, they can complete the different clues to the same news event, leave a different impression and draw different conclusions—process, the audience focus is gradually spreading.

Therefore, post-processing is particularly important based on content production with VR/AR technology. The team's post-editors have to sort out several main clues in the many news clues in the scene and edit them along with the narrative logic they want to express. In the multiple clue selection, the audience is guided to continue to explore with the main narrative chain through the design such as content, sound interaction, and augmented reality, especially while disrupting the audience experience without interruption. Remind the audience to find the focus in the immersive scene, which is a big problem facing intelligent content production.

Content Themes Are Limited. From the current media practice of VR/AR technology, this technology favors the choice of content themes: ① sudden in-depth investigation of major news events and events; ② meets the audience curiosity about occasions and environment, such as deep-sea, space, polar, desert, etc.; ③ tourism and sports competitions.

According to the research group, similar scenic spots, scientific curiosity and in-depth reporting may be the topics that can simultaneously meet the actual situation of public opinion publicity and the law of spatial content dissemination. At the same time, considering the viewing experience, VR / AR indoor shooting is better than outdoor.

The subjects generally avoided by the industry in practice include: (1) too bloody and cruel scene; (2) easy to induce the theme of the audience too much pain, thriller, and other subjective feelings, because this emotion is easily amplified under the intervention of VR technology, coupled with the sense of substitution, which is not suitable for all audiences to watch.

References

1. Han X., Benjamin, L.: Data News Editor. China Publishing (05) (2016)
2. Scober, R., Isrel, S.: The Coming Scene Era. Beijing United Publishing Company, Beijing (2014)
3. Penlan: The "Broken Wall" and Reconstruction of the Digital Age News Ecology. Modern Publishing (05) (2021)
4. Jenkins, H.: Convergence Culture. Newyork University Press, New York (2006)
5. Kun, Q.: Research on the Development Requirements of Rong Media Era. Technology Outlook (24) (2015)
6. Bao, X.: Practice and Thinking on the Reengineering of News Editorial Process under the Background of Rong Media. China Radio Tel. J. (02) (2017)
7. Yang, J.: How did BBC achieve a strategic transformation from traditional media to omnimedia? http://www.xmtnews.com/p/2121
8. Liao, J., Fang, Q., Liang, C.: Guangzhou Daily integrated communication force for three years of national local Party newspapers NO.1, Guangzhou Daily (0731, Version A5) (2019)
9. Immersive Journalism: Immersive Virtual Reality for the First-Person Experience of News. Elsevier Journal (2010)
10. Zhao, H.: Shanghai Jiao Tong University-School of Cultural and Creative Industry, University of USC; the 3rd Shanghai Jiao Tong University—ICA International New Media Forum (10) (2016)
11. de la Peña, N., et al.:Immersive Journalism: Immersive Virtual Reality for the First-Person Experience of News. Presence (4) (2010)
12. Hu, T., Zhang, Q., Shen, Y., Dong, H.: Augmented reality technology review. Comput. Knowl. Technol. (03) (2017)
13. Wu, F., Zhang, L.: Augmented reality principles and its application in TV. P41–43. TV Technology (02), (2013)
14. Zhang, Y., Wang, Y.: Research and Implementation of interactive 3D ebooks based on AR. P60–63. Journal of Qiqihar University (Natural Science Edition) (02) (2016)
15. Liu, H., Wang, X., Wang, L.:Virtual campus model construction and optimization. P1–3, Electronic Technology (11) (2010)

Attention Distribution and Decision-Making in the Process of Robot's Appearance Design and Selection

Nicholas Hong Li Khoo[1], Fan Li[2(✉)], Chun-Hsien Chen[1], Yisi Liu[3], Fitri Trapsilawati[4], and Olga Sourina[5]

[1] School of Mechanical and Aerospace Engineering, Nanyang Technological University, Singapore, Singapore

[2] Department of Aeronautical and Aviation Engineering, The Hong Kong Polytechnic, University, Hung Hom, Hongkong
fan-5.li@polyu.edu.hk

[3] Centre of Excellence in Maritime Safety (CEMS), Singapore Polytechnic, Singapore, Singapore

[4] Universitas Gadjah Mada, Yogyakarta, Indonesia

[5] Fraunhofer Singapore, Nanyang Technological University, Singapore, Singapore

Abstract. Humanoid robots gaining popularity in the service industry all over the world. When designing humanoid robots, product designers put additional thought into the aesthetic design to avoid the complications that arise from the "uncanny valley". It has long been found that genders, personalities, and cultural upbringings may affect individual ratings on the appearance of humanoid robots. To better aid and hasten the appearance design and selection process, this report explores the use of Electroencephalography (EEG) and vision tracking devices to evaluate preferences based on "aesthetic" criteria of robot designs. Based on the analysis, it was found that individuals, regardless of the three traits, paid more attention to their top choices during the selection. In rating the robots' appearance, it was also found that Eastern students rated a significantly higher score of "intelligence" than Western students. However, both eastern and western students have a similar choice of their favorite robots.

Keywords: Electroencephalography · Eye-tracking · Robots appearance design · Preference

1 Introduction

Recently, the service industry has seen an increase in the adoption of robots, such as robots for elderly people, robots for children, and robots for patients [1, 2]. For example, Pepper Parlour Café adopted robots for taking customer orders and cleaning up. With the increase in the adoption of robots in service industries, their design has been increasingly important, as service industries are normally customer-centered markets. Unlike industrial robots, which are created for the sole purpose of performing repetitive

P.-L. P. Rau (Ed.): HCII 2022, LNCS 13314, pp. 535–544, 2022.
https://doi.org/10.1007/978-3-031-06053-3_36

processes, requiring less focus on their aesthetic design, the service robots design is much more complicated due to its requirements for human enjoyment [3].

According to the uncanny valley of the humanoid robot [4], a robot with a bad social design may be off-putting instead of engaging. Hence, a number of studies have been conducted to test the human perception of the appearance design of service robots. It has been found that both physical aesthetic features and emotional preference features are important influencing factors of human perception of service robots [5]. In addition, to maximize user experience in human-robot interactions, designers should try to match the appearance with communication [2]. Beyond the physical design of a robot's appearance, an individual's personality, cultural difference, and gender contribute to the difference in perception of robots [6]. A study recruited subjects from China, Korea, and Germany to investigate their response to robots appearance. The study found that subjects from low-context cultures showed less engagement to the less sociable robots [7]. The gender effects on the perception of users of robots appearance are significant, too. Males seem to have a relatively more positive attitude toward robots in healthcare than females. Normally, the response to robots' appearance, such as task engagements and attitudes can be assessed [7]. The subjective questionnaire, such as quality of service can be used, too. Nevertheless, limited studies investigated the visual attention distribution and decision processing during the evaluation of robots appearance. In this study, a novel method based on electroencephalography (EEG) and eye-tracking devices has been adopted for understanding the evaluation process. It is expected the novel approach can assist companies to design and develop an objective approach to assess the response of consumers to service robots [4]. These psychophysiological data generated from consumers can be transformed into meaningful design recommendations and deliver more tailored, customer-centric services robots.

The objectives of this project are to evaluate the effect of different cultural backgrounds (Eastern vs. Western) on an individual's selection of humanoid service robot design. The organization of this study is as follows: Sect. 2 reviews the effects of cultural differences on users' perception of service robots. Section 3 lays out the methodologies and tools utilized in the experiment and the recorded variables. Section 4 elaborates on the key findings, experimental limitations and the proposed design for a humanoid robot to be adopted in the service industry. Section 5 delivers the conclusion of the study and recommendations for future research.

2 Literature Review

2.1 Cultural Differences Bias

Different cultures have led to different traditions for robots. The positive attitude towards robots in Eastern culture, especially the Japanese, is largely based on the image conveyed by popular media such as movies and Anime cartoons [8]. On the other hand, attitudes toward the Western culture are less positive because of the destructive and hostile robots portrayed in movies such as "Terminator Genisys" or "The Matrix".

The Western world believes that there should be a separation between nature and culture, to organize the world in an orderly and precise fashion. There is no place for hybridization in such classifications [9]. In Japan, all intermediary beings are part of the big picture. As shown in Fig. 1, the Japanese make no distinction between them and try to create links to form a continuous network of beings [6].

The Western world views robots as a step backward on a social level and that it creates paranoia of replacing people. The Japanese choose to adopt a different belief by viewing robots as a means of turning away from the digital virtual world to more human-like objects, thus facilitating contact in the physical world again [6].

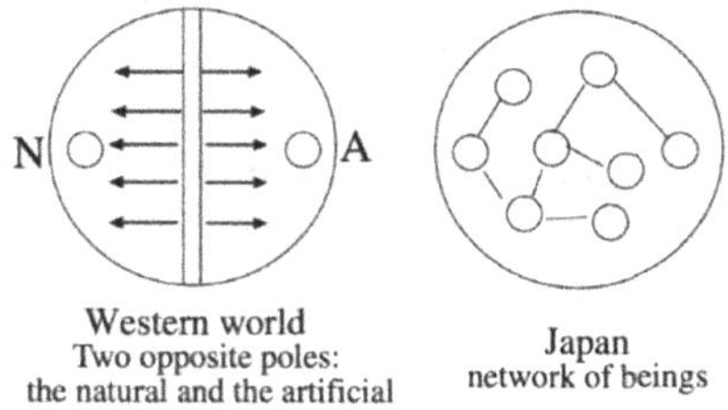

Fig. 1. Distinguishing vs Linking Beings [6]

2.2 Gender Bias

Existing research has illustrated that the simple gendering of robots through manipulation of their voice and name can affect an individuals' behavior towards it. However, this is also dependent on other factors such as the evaluator's gender [10].

The preference of robots by either gender is a key study in HRI and determines the amount of service received by the robot. Nomura et al. mentioned in their research that females have more negative feelings towards the interaction with robots compared to males [10]. This can be supported by an experiment conducted by Kuo et al., where humans interacted with a robot in a healthcare environment. It was found that females were less receptive to the usefulness of the robot and the possibility of using it in the future [11].

Eyssel and Hegel investigated the effects of facial cue manipulation and how it relates to human gender stereotypes for traits and tasks [12]. By altering simple facial features such as adding short hair (male robot) or long hair (female robot), they revealed that male robots were perceived as being more masculine than female robots, and stereotypically male tasks were perceived as more suitable for male robots.

2.3 Myers-Briggs Type Indicator (MBTI)

A personality is defined as the combination of qualities or characteristics that form an individual's distinctive character, usually evolved from biological or environmental factors. Individuals with different personalities behave differently and this influences their economic choices [13] such as willingness to pay for a product as well as career choices [14]. Personalities are also capable of influencing an individual's perception of an object, which generally involves complex psychological mechanisms and processes in the perceiver.

To help psychologists better understand the different personality types, one popular "sorter" is the Myers-Briggs Type Indicator (MBTI), devised by Isabel Briggs Myer and her mother, Katharine Briggs. The theory of MBTI comes from Swiss psychiatrist, Carl G. Jung, who observed that people engaged in one of two mental functions: perceiving or judging. Today, the two main applications of MBTI are to identify basic preferences of each of the four dichotomies specified in Jung's theory and identify the 16 distinctive personality types that result from the interactions among the preferences [14].

Based on Myers Briggs theory, there are four preference types [15]: Sensing (S) and Intuition (N) determines if the individual pays more attention to the information derived from their five senses (Sensing) or to the patterns in the information in which they receive (Intuition). Individuals with "S" traits tend to be practical while those with "N" traits exhibit traits similar to that of a Visionary [15].

3 Methodology

To test the effects of robots appearance on the perception of consumers, five steps, including robots' appearance design, area of interest (AOI) generation, user experiments, data collection, and data analytics have been conducted, as shown in Fig. 2.

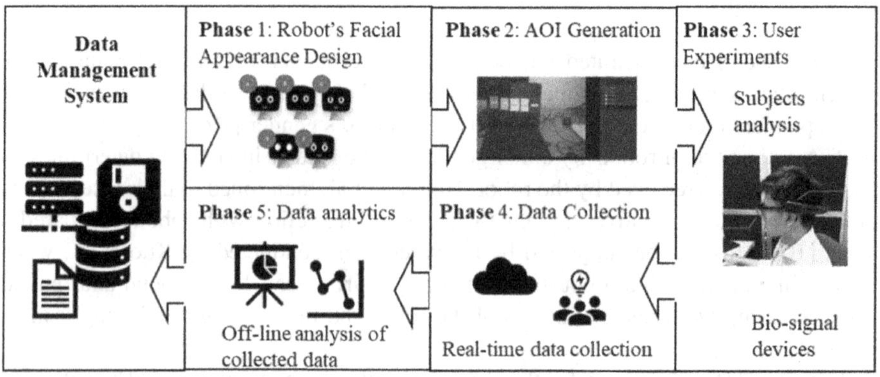

Fig. 2. A general framework work of the study

3.1 Robots Facial Appearance Design

Several preliminary studies have been conducted, it was identified that human perception of service robots is largely influenced by the upper body appearance. This comes as no surprise as humans commonly form impressions of others' faces and also tend to do so with artificial agents. With past research having a strong focus on robots' upper body appearance, especially their facial appearance, the experiment conducted focuses on the robots' facial features. In this study, participants are shown 5 controlled robot images, namely baseline, no mouth, eyelids, no eyes, and eyebrows, as shown in Fig. 3. The images differ by one feature from the base image (Image A) to increase the difficulty of robot design selection.

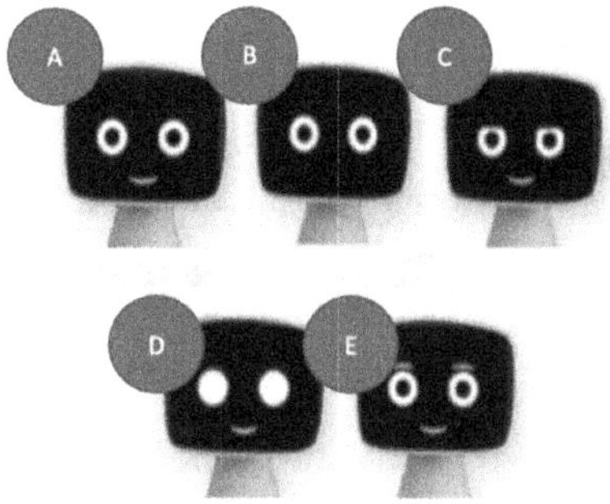

Fig. 3. Robot images

3.2 AOI Generation

This study focuses on figuring out the visual distribution and the perception of users in evaluating the appearance of robots. Hence, all the five robots are presented to subjects on one page. To investigate the visual distribution, which is represented by fixation number and fixation duration, each face of the robot is selected as one AOI. Five rectangles of the same size are designed. The rectangle can cover the robot face with a 1mm allowance on both length and width.

3.3 User Experiments

The study has been approved by the Institutional Review Board of NTU (IRB-2019-02-032). 30 participants (17 Females and 13 Males) between the age of 21–24 years were recruited for the experiment. Of the 17 females, 11 originated from the Eastern world (nations in Asia including the Middle East) while 6 originated from the Western world (North and South America, Europe, Australia, and New Zealand). Of the 13 males, 8 originated from the Eastern world and 5 originated from the Western world.

The device to be used in the experiment is the EMOTIV EPOC+. The device is equipped with 14 channels with a sample rate of 2048. The eye tracker used in the experiment is the Tobii Pro Glasses 2, which has a one-point calibration procedure for easy setup.

The entire experiment includes 3 stages, as shown in Fig. 4. In the first stage, participants are briefed on the flow as well as objectives of the experiment to give them a better understanding of how the recorded data is relevant to the study. In the second stage, both EEG and Eye Tracker are calibrated for every new participant to minimize discrepancy in data. To ensure accuracy in data recorded, a 100% fit rating has to be detected by the device before proceeding with the experiment. To calibrate the eye tracker, participants are positioned at a comfortable distance away from the computer screen (50cm). The eye-tracker captures the calibration spots on the screen before commencing the actual experiment. In the last stage, the images of robot faces are shown to participants, and questionnaires are designed to evaluate their responses.

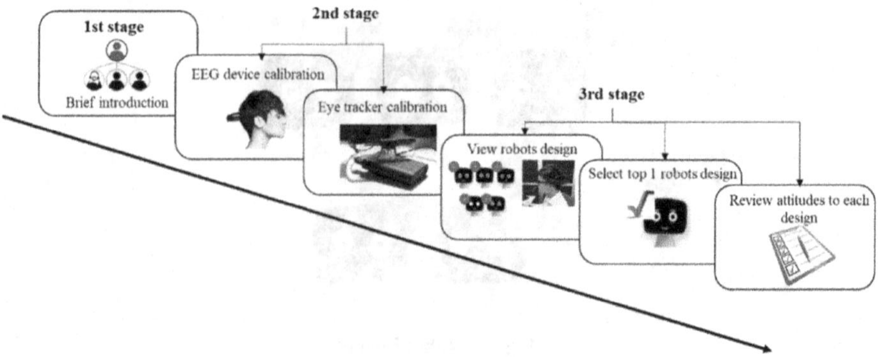

Fig. 4. The process of user experiments

3.4 Data Collection

Two types of data were collected, namely subjective report data via questionnaire and objective biosignals via Emotive and Tobii glass. The subjective responses to the robots appearance were collected after user experiments with personal metric ratings, likability, friendliness, intelligence, valence, arousal, and dominance. The personal metric ratings are derived from standardized models. This experiment uses Arousal, Dominance, and Valence as evaluation metrics, proposed by Russel and Mehrabian [16]. Likability, smartness, and friendliness are subsets for Human-Robot Interaction (HRI) [17]. Raw EEG data and eye-tracking data were collected during the user experiments. The EEG device is capable of recording the EEG signals at 120 Hz. The Tobii glass has a sampling rate of 100 Hz.

3.5 Data Analytics

Figure 5. shows the process of data analysis. Emotions values, namely positive and negative were obtained via EEG data analytics. To evaluate the raw EEG data, an EEG Subject-independent Processor developed by Fraunhofer Singapore was used. The EEG Subject-independent Processor is a stand-alone off-line application that uses advanced transfer learning algorithms to recognize different physiological signals from raw EEG data [18, 19]. The software is able to recognize the mental states of a subject without the need for any calibration. This is achieved through the use of an existing database consisting of EEG data with labels from other subjects. The window is sliding over the raw EEG data with 1-s step. The first sample is extracted from 0–4 s on the raw data, and the second example is extracted from 1–5 s on the raw data. The process repeats until the window reaches the end of the whole signal. Positive emotion is indicated with a "1" and negative emotion is represented with a "0". The extracted emotions are then labeled with "P" for positive and "N" for negative.

The Time To First Fixation (TTFF), fixation durations, and fixation counts were obtained from eye-tracking data. The I-VT method [20] was applied in the raw eye-tracking data to extract the fixations based on gaze velocity. According to the fixation position and AOI position, the TTFF, fixation durations, and fixation counts were calculated for each AOI. Analysis of variance (ANOVA) was carried out to determine if there is a correlation between the individual's top choice and their vision tracking data. Biserial Correlation was used to analyze all the collected data.

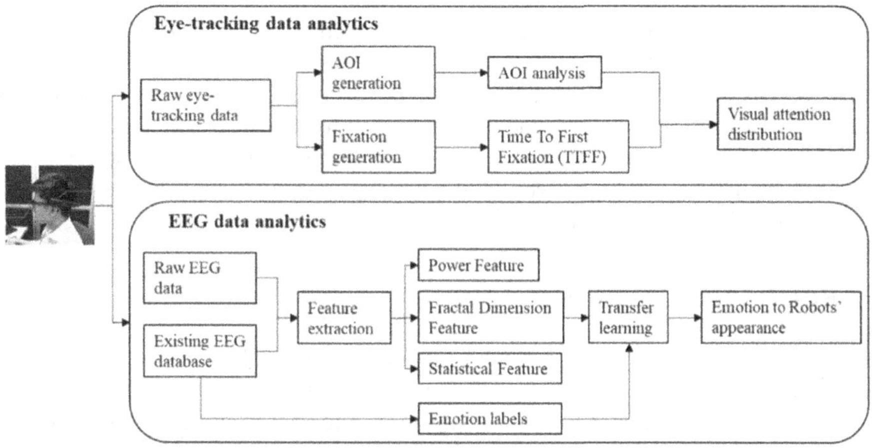

Fig. 5. EEG and Eye movement-based method for appearance evaluation

4 Results and Discussion

The responses gathered from participants were first analyzed using Biserial correlation analysis. The analysis is used to determine if there is any correlation between the likability, friendliness, intelligence, valence, arousal, and dominance of the robot and gender, culture, and personality of the respondent. A p-value below 0.05 indicates that the two variables are correlated.

Based on the data analysis, the following conclusions can be derived:

- Individuals' gender is correlated with the perceived intelligence, valence, and dominance of a robot.
- Individuals' culture is correlated with the perceived friendliness and dominance of a robot.
- Individuals' personality is correlated with the perceived intelligence and valence of a robot.

ANOVA was conducted to test the effects of gender, culture, and personality on users' perceptions of the humanoid robot design. The ANOVA results showed that gender and culture have significant effects on users' perception of the intelligence of the robot design. Specifically, males felt the Tapia is intelligent while females felt it was normal. Though the effects of personality on user's perception are not significant, the interaction effects between personality and gender were significant (intelligence $F_{(1,26)} = 7.35$, $p < 0.05$; valence: $F_{(1,26)} = 5.92$, $p < 0.05$; arousal: $F_{(1,26)} = 10.233$, $p < 0.05$).

The participants' most liked and disliked robot designs were identified based on the questionnaire and matched with their "TTFF", "Fixation Durations" and "Visit Counts".

Analysis of variance (ANOVA) was carried out to determine if there is a correlation between the individual's top choice and their vision tracking data. For Time To First Fixation (TTFF), $F_{(1,26)} = 0.56$, $p = 0.07$. For Fixation Duration, $F_{(1,26)} = 10.18$, $p < 0.05$. For visit counts, $F_{(1,26)} = 1.38$, $p = 0.2$. Based on the results gathered, only "Fixation Duration" has a *p*-value less than 0.05. As a result, it can be concluded that participants tend to spend more time fixated on their top choice of robot design.

Biserial Correlation was used to analyze the EEG-based emotion data set and it was shown that emotions recorded were not consistent with their choices. However, this could be attributed to the noise in emotion data.

5 Results and Discussion

After an arduous product design process, product designers have to decide on which product is best to launch to market. As the service industry sees a rise in the adoption of robots to replace manual labor, robotic companies struggle to design a suitable robot that avoids the effects of the "Uncanny Valley". When it comes to the design of robots. which require social interaction with humans, the design process becomes increasingly complex as it requires the consideration of representation, anthropomorphism, and task orientation, depending on the service context. The report covered several important attributes to be examined in robot design such as its perceived friendliness and intelligence. It also explored how one's gender, personality, and cultural difference influences their perception of a product. In the case of the robot design study, results showed that gender and culture are closely correlated to users' perception of intelligence. The interaction effects between personality and gender were also significant. In addition, it was also observed that the amount of time spent looking at a particular design further confirms the participants' choice of the preferred design. For EEG metrics, although no significant findings were derived, proper calibration using IADS will bring about new findings in the field of product design selection. The combination of both EEG and vision-tracking devices, would ultimately accelerate the product design selection process and ease the mental workload of product designers.

6 Appendix D – Computer Experiment Questionnaire

6.1 Test Scenario

Group Images.
Pick your 1st, 2nd, and 3rd choice of design out of the whole set. Please give a brief explanation as to why those three were your preferred design.

Individual Images.
Utilizing the 9-Point Hedonic Scale:

1. Likability is closely related to a positive emotion. Rate the likability of the robot image that you have just seen.
2. Friendliness is an important factor to be considered for robots employed in the service industry due to its interaction with humans. Rate the friendliness of the robot image that you have just seen.
3. Smartness determines how useful the robot is perceived to be and gives consumers the confidence to approach the robots for assistance. Rate the smartness of the robot image that you have just seen.
4. Valence is defined as the feeling of pleasure derived from the robot. Rate the valence level.
5. Arousal is the level of attention drawn by the robot. Rate the arousal level.
7. Dominance is defined as an overwhelming feeling induced by the robot. Rate the dominance level.

Acknowledgment. Thanks for all the subjects that participated in the user experiments.

References

1. Walters, M.L., Koay, K.L., Syrdal, D.S., Dautenhahn, K., Te Boekhorst, R.: Preferences and perceptions of robot appearance and embodiment in human-robot interaction trials. Procs of New Frontiers in Human-Robot Interaction (2009)
2. Klüber, K., Onnasch, L.: Appearance is not everything-preferred feature combinations for care robots. Comput. Hum. Behav. **128**, 107128 (2022)
3. Pokojski, J.: Evaluation of humanoid robot design based on global eye-tracking metrics. in transdisciplinary engineering for complex socio-technical systems–real-life applications. In: Proceedings of the 27th ISTE International Conference on Transdisciplinary Engineering, July 1–July 10, 2020. IOS Press (2020)
4. Mori, M., MacDorman, K.F., Kageki, N.: The uncanny valley [from the field]. IEEE Robot. Autom. Mag. **19**(2), 98–100 (2012)
5. Gan, Y., et al.: Integrating aesthetic and emotional preferences in social robot design: an affective design approach with Kansei engineering and deep convolutional generative adversarial network. Int. J. Ind. Ergon. **83**, 103128 (2021)
6. Kaplan, F.: Who is afraid of the humanoid? Investigating cultural differences in the acceptance of robots. Int. J. Humanoid Rob. **1**(03), 465–480 (2004)
7. Li, D., Rau, P.-L., Li, Y.: A cross-cultural study: effect of robot appearance and task. Int. J. Soc. Robot. **2**(2), 175–186 (2010)
8. Bartneck, C., Hu, J.: Rapid prototyping for interactive robots (2004)
9. Latour, B.: We Have Never Been Modern. Harvard University Press, Cambridge (2012)
10. Nomura, T.: Robots and gender. Gender and the Genome **1**(1), 18–25 (2017)
11. Kuo, I.H., et al.: Age and gender factors in user acceptance of healthcare robots. In: RO-MAN 2009-The 18th IEEE International Symposium on Robot and Human Interactive Communication. IEEE (2009)
12. Eyssel, F., Hegel, F.: (s) he's got the look: Gender stereotyping of robots 1. J. Appl. Soc. Psychol. **42**(9), 2213–2230 (2012)
13. Boyce, C., Czajkowski, M., Hanley, N.: Personality and economic choices. J. Environ. Econ. Manag. **94**, 82–100 (2019)

14. Varvel, T., S.G. Adams, and S.J. Pridie. A study of the effect of the Myers-Briggs Type Indicator on team effectiveness. In: Proceedings of the 2003 ASEE Annual Conference and Exposition, Session (2003)
15. Quenk, N.L.: Essentials of Myers-Briggs type indicator assessment. Wiley, New York (2009)
16. Russell, J.A.: Affective space is bipolar. J. Pers. Soc. Psychol. **37**(3), 345 (1979)
17. Bartneck, C., Kulić, D., Croft, E., Zoghbi, S.: Measurement instruments for the anthropomorphism, animacy, likeability, perceived intelligence, and perceived safety of robots. Int. J. Soc. Robot. **1**(1), 71–81 (2009)
18. Liu, Y., et al.: Human factors evaluation of ATC operational procedures in relation to use of 3D display. In: Stanton, N. (ed.) AHFE 2019. AISC, vol. 964, pp. 715–726. Springer, Cham (2020). https://doi.org/10.1007/978-3-030-20503-4_64
19. Liu, Y., et al.: Detection of humanoid robot design preferences using EEG and eye tracker. In: 2019 International Conference on Cyberworlds (CW). IEEE (2019)
20. Li, F., Chen, C.-H., Xu, G., Khoo, L.-P.: Hierarchical eye-tracking data analytics for human fatigue detection at a traffic control center. IEEE Trans. Hum.-Mach. Syst. **50**(5), 465–474 (2020)

Multitasking with Intelligent Assistant: Effects of Task Relevance and Interruption Mode

Na Liu(✉) and Quanlin Pu

School of Economics and Management, Beijing University of Posts and Telecommunications, Beijing, China
{liuna18,ql2018}@bupt.edu.cn

Abstract. In order to better understand the user's multitasking behavior, this study takes service-oriented intelligent assistants as the research object. It conducted a 2 × 2 within-subject experiment to explore effects of task relevance (task-related vs. task-independent) and interruption mode (internal interruption vs. external interruption) on individuals' task performance and subjective feelings (cognitive load, needs gratification, flow). Obtained data were analyzed by repeated measures ANOVA. The results indicate that multitasking interruption has negative effects on task performance and cognitive load, but has positive effects on needs gratification. Additionally, when performing related multitasking, the internal interruption results in higher needs gratification and flow than external interruption. These findings provide insights into the design and optimization of intelligent assistants in real life.

Keywords: Smart assistant · Multitasking · Task relevance · Interruption mode

1 Introduction

As a common task situation in daily life, multitasking is typically characterized by individuals performing or switching between two or more tasks at the same time [1]. It includes multiple types with varying lengths of time spans. In different multitasking scenarios, user needs, behaviors, human-computer interaction experiences, and task performance are different [2, 3].

Task relevance refers to the extent to which tasks achieve related or similar goals [4]. Based on the resource theory of information processing, some researchers argue that humans have a limited cognitive capacity for information, and when two concurrent tasks compete for limited cognitive resources, people may experience cognitive overload and task performance may be reduced [5, 6]. Multiple resource theory (MRT) states that humans have several separate pools of cognitive resources, so that individuals can use these resources to perform tasks simultaneously [7]. When the content of tasks is related, they can create synergy with each other, thereby facilitating task performance and improving task performance [8].

Interruptions occur when the users decide to stop their current activities and move to perform a different task [9]. Internal interruptions are determined by people's self-willingness, while external interruptions are triggered by external environmental [10]·

P.-L. P. Rau (Ed.): HCII 2022, LNCS 13314, pp. 545–554, 2022.
https://doi.org/10.1007/978-3-031-06053-3_37

Some studies show that external interruptions are somewhat nested, when people are interrupted by one thing they do not immediately return to their original task [11]. While internally interrupted work takes longer to resume and may be more disruptive [12]. Self-regulation theory (SRC) states that when unable to immerse themselves in task performance, individuals will self-regulate their behaviors to restore the balance between task demands and skills [11]. Later research find that people are more inclined to multitask when they are in a negative state, such as feeling frustrated, stressed or mentally exhausted [13]. Although multitasking interruptions have a negative impact on task performance, they can help individuals relax and relieve stress [14].

In summary, the present study aims to design a multitasking scenario in which university students interact with a service-oriented intelligent assistant, to investigate the effects of task relevance and interruption mode on users' cognitive load, need gratification, flow and task performance.

2 Method

2.1 Participants

Thirty participants were recruited to participate in the experiment (15 males and 15 females, 18–25 years old). All the participants were with normal or corrected visual acuity and had English proficiency at cet-6 level. Additionally, in terms of a priori knowledge, all participants had experience with multitasking behaviors in their daily lives (mean normalized multitasking proficiency of 0.59 as measured by the MMT-R scale [15, 16]) and all had experience with intelligent assistants.

2.2 Design

This experiment adopted a 2 × 2 within-subject design. The independent variables were task relevance (task-related vs. task-independent) and interruption mode (internal interruption vs. external interruption). Participants were randomly assigned to different English reading topics and completed four sets of control variable experiments formed by different combinations of task relevance and task interruption mode, and one set of experiments in which no interaction with the intelligent assistant occurred as a control group. The dependent variables were task performance (percentage of correct English reading completed) and subjective feelings (cognitive load, needs gratification, flow).

Cognitive load was measured by the NASA-TLX, which includes six dimensions, each rated on a scale from 0 to 100 [17]. The scale for needs gratification was adapted from Jeong et al. [18, 19], and flow was adapted from the widely used flow scale [20], using a seven-point Likert scale for each statement ("1" = "strongly disagree", "7" = "strongly agree"). All the measurement items used here have been widely used and validated in prior studies.

2.3 Procedure

The experiment was completed offline in a one-to-one session. Each participant was equipped with one Bluetooth headset and one tablet computer. The Bluetooth headset was connected to the experiment computer and transmits the voice of the voice assistant. The participant used the tablet (iPad Air3) to complete the English reading and post-experiment subjective evaluation. The voice assistant was achieved with the read-aloud plug-in in the experiment computer, which simulates the voice interaction between the participant and the intelligent assistant.

Each participant completed five sessions in sequence under the guidance (Table 1). Each group of participants had different voice interactions with the intelligent assistant. Completing a word query that affected the comprehension of the English reading content was a relevant task, and completing an interfering email check and reply was an irrelevant task. The participant initiated the query command was an internal interruption, and the participant responded to the interaction initiated by the voice assistant was an external interruption.

The voice of the intelligent assistant is female. All instructions are based on secondary tasks. In internal interruption experiments, the intelligent assistant responds directly to queries about the meaning of words or whether an email has been received. During external interruption experiments, the intelligent assistant prompts "Have you encountered any problems" or "You have received an email ".

Table 1. Experimental tasks

Items	Main task	Interactive tasks
Control group	Complete 1 cet-4 English reading	No interaction with intelligent assistants
Experiment group: Task-related - Internal interruption		The participant initiates a query request to the intelligent assistant at any time and completes at least 2 queries for the blue marked words
Experiment group: Task-independent - Internal interruption		The participant initiates an email query request to the intelligent assistant at any time to check the unread email status of the experimental mailbox and completes at least 2 queries
Experiment group: Task-related - External interruption		Every 4min the intelligent assistant prompts if help is needed, and the participant responds by completing a blue marked word search

(*continued*)

Table 1. (*continued*)

Items	Main task	Interactive tasks
Experiment group: Task-independent - External interrupts		Every 4min the intelligent assistant will indicate the receipt of emails. If it indicates the receipt of new emails it will give feedback on the content of the emails, and the participant will complete the email collection by responding

Analysis of Variance (ANOVA) was used to analyze the effects of task relevance and interruption mode on task performance and subjective perceptions. Bonferroni was used for difference comparisons. Effect sizes were assessed by the $\eta^2{}_p$. All data were analyzed using SPSS 26.0 software and the significance level was set at 0.05.

3 Results

3.1 Task Performance

According to the results of the analysis (Fig. 1), there was a significant effect of whether to perform multiple tasks on correct task completion (F (1, 29) = 15.09, $p < 0.01$, $\eta^2{}_p$ = 0.34). Furthermore, there was no significant effect of task relevance, interruption mode on correct task completion (Fig. 2) and no significant effect of the interactions on correct task completion (F (1, 29) = 1.54, p = 0.23, $\eta^2{}_p$ = 0.05). Post-hoc tests showed that the control group, which did not perform multiple tasks, had a higher rate of correct task completion compared to the experimental group (t (29) = 3.88, $p < 0.01$).

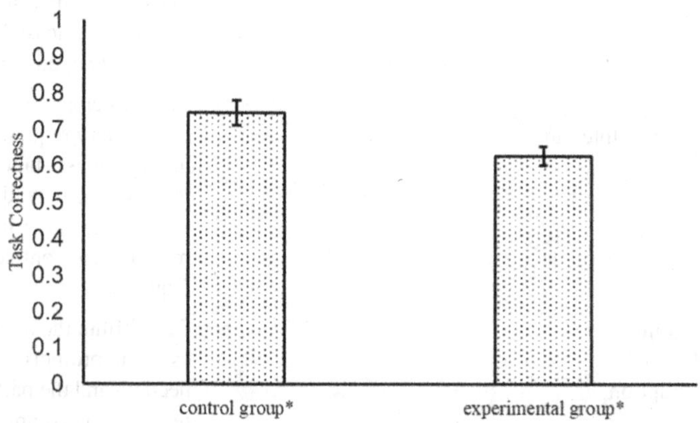

Fig. 1. Effects of multiple tasks performing on task correctness (error line is ± 1 standard error)

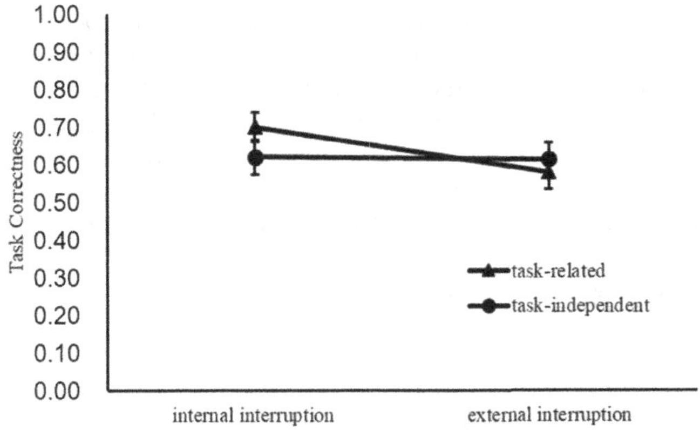

Fig. 2. Effects of task relevance and interruption mode on task correctness (error line is ± 1 standard error)

3.2 Subjective Feelings

Figure 3 presents the cognitive load of users with different task relevance and interruptions. The analysis showed that whether multitasking was performed had a significant effect on cognitive load (F (1, 29) = 16.78, $p < 0.0001$, $\eta^2_p = 0.37$) (Fig. 4). However, the main effects of task relevance and interruption mode on cognitive load were not significant, and the interactions had no significant effect on cognitive load (F (1, 29) = 0.28, $p = 0.60$, $\eta^2_p = 0.01$). Post-hoc tests showed that the control group that did not perform the multitask had lower cognitive load compared to the experimental group (t (29) = 4.10, $p < 0.0001$).

For need satisfaction, the presence or absence of multitasking had a significant effect on subjective perceived need satisfaction (F (1, 29) = 4.45, $p < 0.05$, $\eta^2_p = 0.13$). Although the main effects of task relevance and interruption mode on need satisfaction were not significant (Fig. 5), the interactions had a significant effect on need satisfaction (F (1, 29) = 6.64, $p < 0.05$, $\eta^2_p = 0.19$) (Fig. 6). Post hoc tests showed that the control group that did not multitask had lower need satisfaction compared to the experimental group (t (29) = 2.11, $p < 0.05$). While for the main effect of task relevance, there was no significant difference in needs gratification between relevant and irrelevant multitasking (t (29) = 0.02, $p = 0.99$). For the main effect of interruption mode, there was also no significant difference in needs gratification between internal and external interruptions as well, (t (29) = 0.99, $p = 0.33$). Further simple effects analysis revealed that, in the case of performing related multitask, needs gratification was significantly higher for internal interrupts ($M = 4.49$, $SD = 0.88$) than for external interrupts ($M = 4.13$, $SD = 1.11$, t (29) = 2.29, $p < 0.05$).

For flow, there was no significant effect of whether perform multiple tasks (F (1, 29) = 2.40, $p = 0.13$, $\eta^2_p = 0.08$). While the main effects of task relevance and interruption mode on flow were not significant (Fig. 5), the interaction effects of both were borderline significant (F (1, 29) = 4.18, $p = 0.05$, $\eta^2_p = 0.13$) (Fig. 6). Post hoc tests showed that for the main effect of task relevance on flow, there was no significant difference between relevant and irrelevant multitasking (t (29) = 1.95, $p = 0.06$). For the main effect of interruption mode on flow, there was also no significant difference between internal and external interruptions, (t (29) = 1.10, $p = 0.28$). Further simple effects analysis revealed that, in the case of performing the relevant multitask, the flow of internal interrupts (M = 4.66, SD = 0.75) was significantly higher than that of external interrupts (M = 4.33, SD = 0.85, t (29) = 2.11, $p < 0.05$). In the case of internal interruptions, the flow level for performing relevant multitasking (M = 4.66, SD = 0.75) was significantly higher than for performing irrelevant multitasking (M = 4.28, SD = 0.76, t (29) = 2.65, $p < 0.05$). Overall, in the multitasking experimental setting, the execution of relevant multitasking with internal interruptions performed best in terms of flow.

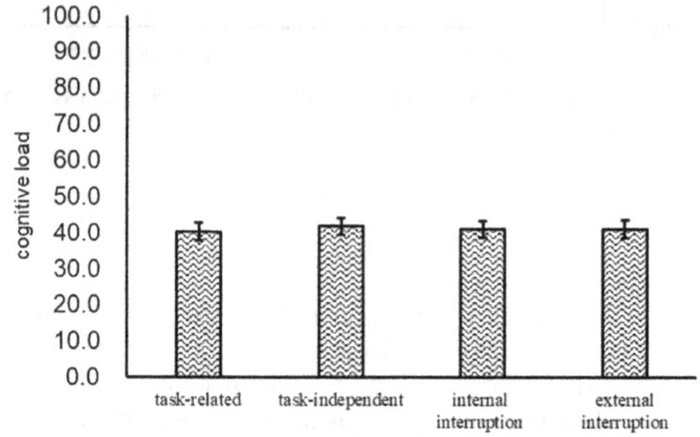

Fig. 3. Effects of task relevance and interruption mode on cognitive load (error line is ± 1 standard error)

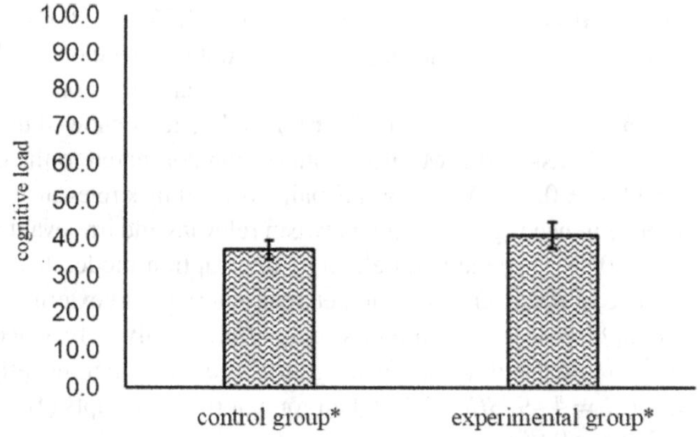

Fig. 4. Effects of multiple tasks performing on cognitive load (error line is ±1 standard error)

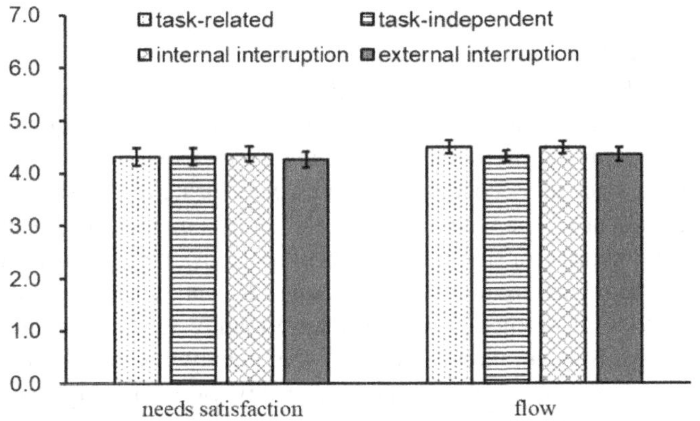

Fig. 5. Effects of task relevance and interruption mode on needs gratification and flow (error line is ±1 standard error)

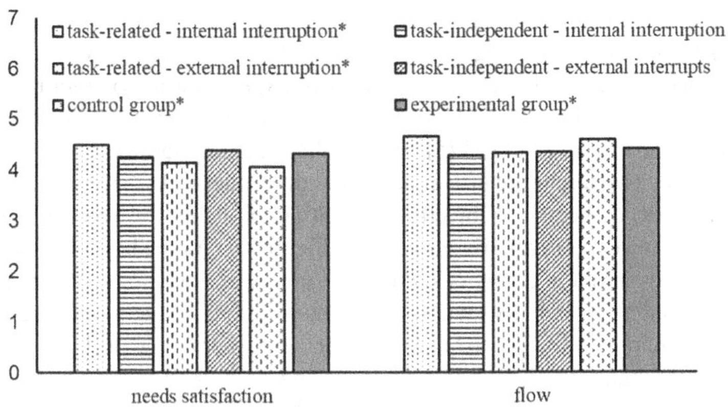

Fig. 6. Interaction effects of task relevance and interruption mode on needs gratification and flow (error line is ±1 standard error)

4 Discussion

The experiment results suggest that multitasking impairs task performance and increases cognitive load and need satisfaction. This result is in line with many previous studies, such as Kirschner and Karpinski [21] who found that Facebook users had lower task performance in relevant research activities compared to non-users, and Jacobsen and Forste [22] who assessed college students' media use behavior on their academic performance, they obtained similar results. This study suggests that multitasking in learning situations, whether performing related or independent tasks, has a negative impact on task performance, which supported by some scholars who think "once students use smart devices during their studies, their academic performance decreases".

However, the main effect of task relevance on both objective performance and subjective perceptions was not significant in this experiment. It is inconsistent with previous experiments by Hembrooke [23] et al. in which they found that for students of similar levels, groups dealing with relevant multitasking outperformed groups dealing with irrelevant multitasking. The non-significant main effect between the two levels of task relevance may be since the secondary task completed during multitasking was less difficult than the main task. The secondary task did not take up much cognitive resources, which in turn did not have a significant effect on objective performance. Additionally, in previous studies related to multitasking, Zhang [24] and others found that, in work-related multitasking, instrumental demands were mainly satisfied, whereas in media multitasking interaction, emotional demands were mainly satisfied. Based on this, the main and related tasks taken in this experiment satisfy users' instrumental needs, while the unrelated tasks satisfy users' affective needs. Although the sources of the needs satisfied are different, they both have a positive impact on users' needs satisfaction. As the main task itself have a high satisfaction of the participants' overall needs (normalized mean value of need satisfaction for the control group >0.7), the needs for emotional experience, social interaction and self-identity arising outside the main task were low, and the impact caused by dealing with related and unrelated multitasks was not significant. Similarly, for flow, the user's high level of experience in completing the entire task, which measures the level of concentration and engagement with the task during the task. Wang et al.'s study [25] showed that, learning tasks are inherently more immersive as they require more task engagement than other tasks. The participant effect on objective performance and subjective perception, probably for internal and external interruptions in the experiment triggered less difficulty in multitasking. The information brought about by partial interruptions to multitasking was likely to be completed by the participant through parallel tasks without task interruptions, reducing the cognitive cost due to task switching, affecting the user's subjective perception as well.

The interaction effects of task relevance and interruption mode on need satisfaction and flow were significant. Flow Theory and Self-regulation Theory [26] suggest that self-interruption occurs when individuals are unable to achieve a state of flow through the ongoing task. Whereas internal drivers of multitasking behavior are mainly due to the generation of psychological, emotional or social demands [27]. Based on Motivated Cognition Theory (MCT), internal interruptions are individuals themselves in a position where needs gratification and higher levels of flow occur. Therefore, internal interruptions lead to higher needs gratification and flow.

In summary, future research could be investigated in the following ways. First, the range of participants could be increased to expand the experimental coverage group. Previous multitasking studies have shown that there are differences in multitasking ability and cognitive load among participants of different ages [28, 29]. Multitasking performance and perceived levels also vary according to individual multitasking ability and individual characteristics [30]. The results lacked significant differences in terms of need gratification and flow, as the participants' perceptions of flow and task satisfaction fluctuated less under different experimental settings. Secondly, secondary tasks with quantifiable task difficulty can be used to balance the difficulty and time spent on the primary and secondary tasks. And the impact of differences in secondary task difficulty on the users' experience could be explored. In this study, the secondary tasks were set at a relatively low level of difficulty and occurred for a shorter period than the main task, making the differences in participants' subjective feelings with respect to different task relevance and task interruption modes relatively small.

Acknowledgements. This work was supported by grants from Natural Science Foundation of China (Project No. 71901033) and Beijing Natural Science Foundation (Project No. 9204029).

References

1. Lui, K.F.H., Wong, A.C.N.: Does media multitasking always hurt? A positive correlation between multitasking and multisensory integration[J]. Psychon. Bull. Rev. **19**(4), 647–653 (2012)
2. Jeong, S.H., Hwang, Y.: Media multitasking effects on cognitive vs. attitudinal outcomes: a meta-analysis. Hum. Commun. Res. **42**(4), 599–618 (2016)
3. Mark, G., Iqbal, S., Czerwinski, M., et al.: Focused, aroused, but so distractible: temporal perspectives on multitasking and communications. In: Proceedings of the 18th ACM Conference on Computer Supported Cooperative Work & Social Computing, pp. 903–916 (2015)
4. Wang, Z., Irwin, M., Cooper, C., et al.: Multidimensions of media multitasking and adaptive media selection. Hum. Commun. Res. **41**(1), 102–127 (2015)
5. Lang, A.: The limited capacity model of mediated message processing. J. Commun. **50**(1), 46–70 (2000)
6. Basil, M.D.: Multiple resource theory I: application to television viewing. Commun. Res. **21**(2), 177–207 (1994)
7. Wickens, C.D.: Multiple resources and performance prediction. Theor. Issues Ergon. Sci. **3**(2), 159–177 (2002)
8. Moreno, R., Mayer, R.E.: Cognitive principles of multimedia learning: the role of modality and contiguity. J. Educ. Psychol. **91**(2), 358–368 (1999)
9. Mark, G.: Multitasking in the digital age. Synthesis Lect. Hum.-Centered Inf. **8**(3), 1–113 (2015)
10. Miyata, Y., Norman, D.A.: Psychological issues in support of multiple activities. In: User Centered System Design: New Perspectives on Human-Computer Interaction, pp. 265–284 (1986)
11. Carver, C.S., Scheier, M.F.: Action, affect, multitasking, and layers of control. In: Psychology of Self-regulation: Cognitive, Affective and Motivational Processes, pp. 109–126 (2009)
12. Mark, G., Gonzalez, V.M., Harris, J.: No task left behind? Examining the nature of fragmented work. In: Proceedings of the SIGCHI Conference on Human Factors in Computing Systems, pp. 321–330 (2005)
13. Adler, R.F., Benbunan-Fich, R.: Self-interruptions in discretionary multitasking. Comput. Hum. Behav. **29**(4), 1441–1449 (2013)
14. Wang, Z., Tchernev, J.M.: The, "myth" of media multitasking: reciprocal dynamics of media multitasking, personal needs, and gratifications. J. Commun. **62**(3), 493–513 (2012)
15. Lopez, R.B., Heatherton, T.F., Wagner, D.D.: Media multitasking is associated with higher risk for obesity and increased responsiveness to rewarding food stimuli. Brain Imaging Behav. **14**(4), 1050–1061 (2020)
16. Lopez, R.B., Salinger, J.M., Heatherton, T.F., et al.: Media multitasking is associated with altered processing of incidental, irrelevant cues during person perception. BMC Psychol. **6**(1), 1–7 (2018)

17. Hart, S.G., Staveland, L.E.: Development of NASA-TLX (Task Load Index): results of empirical and theoretical research. In: Advances in Psychology, vol. 52, 139–183. North-Holland (1988)
18. Leung, A., Sheng, Y., Cruickshank, H.: The security challenges for mobile ubiquitous services. Inf. Secur. Tech. Rep. **12**(3), 162–171 (2007)
19. Jeong, S.H., Fishbein, M.: Predictors of multitasking with media: media factors and audience factors. Media Psychol. **10**(3), 364–384 (2007)
20. Csikszentmihalyi, M., Csikzentmihaly, M.: Flow: the Psychology of Optimal Experience. Harper & Row, New York (1990)
21. Kirschner, P.A., Karpinski, A.C.: Facebook® and academic performance. Comput. Hum. Behav. **26**(6), 1237–1245 (2010)
22. Jacobsen, W.C., Forste, R.: The wired generation: Academic and social outcomes of electronic media use among university students. Cyberpsychol. Behav. Soc. Netw. **14**(5), 275–280 (2011)
23. Hembrooke, H., Gay, G.: The laptop and the lecture: the effects of multitasking in learning environments. J. Comput. High. Educ. **15**(1), 46–64 (2003)
24. Zhang, W., Zhang, L.: Explicating multitasking with computers: gratifications and situations. Comput. Hum. Behav. **28**(5), 1883–1891 (2012)
25. Wang, S., Wang, T., Chen, N., et al.: The preconditions and event-related potentials correlates of flow experience in an educational context. Learn. Motiv. **72**, 101678 (2020)
26. Deng, L.: Laptops and mobile phones at self-study time: examining the mechanism behind interruption and multitasking. Australas. J. Educ. Technol. **36**(1), 55–67 (2020)
27. Cardoso-Leite, P., Kludt, R., Vignola, G., et al.: Technology consumption and cognitive control: contrasting action video game experience with media multitasking. Atten. Percept. Psychophys. **78**(1), 218–241 (2016)
28. Guimond, A., Braun, C.M.J., Rouleau, I., et al.: Remembering the past and foreseeing the future while dealing with the present: a comparison of young adult and elderly cohorts on a multitask simulation of occupational activities. Exp. Aging Res. **32**(3), 363–380 (2006)
29. Todorov, I., Del Missier, F., Mäntylä, T.: Age-related differences in multiple task monitoring. PLoS ONE **9**(9), e107619 (2014)
30. Dönmez, O., Akbulut, Y.: Timing and relevance of secondary tasks impact multitasking performance. Comput. Educ. **161**, 104078 (2021)

The Effect of Human-Robot Extroversion Matching on Individual Work Performance

Yang Liu, Zainur Akbar, and Na Chen(✉)

Beijing University of Chemical Technology, Beijing 100055, China
2017050132@mail.buct.edu.cn, chenn4@163.com

Abstract. Extroversion is one of the important anthropomorphic characteristics of partner robot. This study aims to explore the relationship among human-robot extroversion matching, robot acceptance and individual work performance, and to further explore the mediating effect of robot acceptance and the moderating effect of human extroversion.

This research adopts the method of questionnaire survey, including independent variables: human-robot extroversion (two levels: extroversion and introversion) and human-robot extroversion matching (two levels: homogeneous and heterogeneous), dependent variable: respondents' self-assessed work performance, mediating variable: robot acceptance, and moderating variable: human's extroversion. Each respondent was asked to rate their self-extroversion, their robot acceptance and own work performance when working with extroverted and introverted partner robot in turn. A total of 152 valid questionnaires were recovered.

Data analysis results show that human-robot extroversion matching has a significant impact on respondents' work performance. When human-robot extroversion is homogeneous, respondents' work performance is higher. In addition, respondents' acceptance of robots is a complete mediating variable between human-robot extroversion matching and work performance, and human extroversion is a moderating variable between human-robot extroversion matching and robot acceptance. The effect of human-robot extroversion matching on robot acceptance is more significant when the human personality is extroverted.

This study suggests that in the organizational design of human-robot collaboration teams, the homogeneity of individual characteristics of human-robot team members and the level of human acceptance of robot anthropomorphism should be fully considered.

Keywords: Partner robot · Human-robot extroversion matching · Robot acceptance · Human-robot collaboration team

1 Introduction

Robot not only undertakes the tasks of traditional manual labor, but its functions are also increasingly enriched. For example, in children's English learning, it helps improve children's reading and thinking skills (Mazzoni and Benvenuti 2015), helps humans make daily movement plans (Obo et al. 2015), and acts as a learning partner for humans

P.-L. P. Rau (Ed.): HCII 2022, LNCS 13314, pp. 555–570, 2022.
https://doi.org/10.1007/978-3-031-06053-3_38

providing motivation and better learning experience (Lu et al. 2018), etc. This kind of robot can become a partner in close contact with humans and plays an important role in human-robot collaboration. For example, older adults prefer to be accompanied by a companion robot compared to walking alone (Karunarathne et al. 2019). Human-robot collaboration team is one of the future development directions of human-robot interaction research (Baker et al. 2018; De Visser et al. 2020), but at present, more in-depth and systematic research is still needed on how partner robot affects individual performance.

Robot anthropomorphism means that robot has the same or similar characteristics as human, such as appearance, emotion, cognition, etc. (Duffy 2003). One of the important differences between partner robot and traditional robot is whether they have anthropomorphic features. Robot with anthropomorphic features is more acceptable in human-robot collaboration. For example, robot with human features in the team is more popular with members than abstract robot, and can express their responses to people better (Fraune 2020). In the tourism industry, tourists are also more inclined to interact with robots with anthropomorphic features such as anthropomorphic appearance, voice and emotion (Christou et al. 2020). Most of the existing research focuses on the impact of robot appearance on human behavior and how to design appearance to improve their anthropomorphism. For example, the appearance of a robot affects human perception and expectations of it (Haring et al. 2013; Tung 2016), and robot with anthropomorphic appearance can significantly facilitate human-robot collaboration (Kwak 2014). However, there are also studies that suggest that the first impression of a robot based on its appearance alone does not indicate how people feel about it during the entire interaction process, and the impression during the process is more important (Paetzel-Prüsmann et al. 2021). In addition to appearance, the scope of robot anthropomorphism also includes behavioral aspects such as action, ability, and autonomy (Murphy et al. 2017), as well as psychological aspects such as emotion and personality (Christou et al. 2020) and cognitive aspects such as memory (Murphy et al. 2019).

However, there is no simple positive correlation between the level of anthropomorphism of robot and the impact on human's cognition and behavior. For example, the "uncanny valley" theory describes this phenomenon (Brenton et al. 2005). Roesler et al. (2021) pointed out that when the anthropomorphic factor of robot is at a low level, it does not have a significant impact on human behavior and performance. And even at a high level, its impact is more complex and largely depends on the moderating effect of certain factors. And excessive anthropomorphism is more likely to make people feel uneasy during interactions (Bartneck et al. 2010). Therefore, when designing a robot, it is necessary to carefully consider its anthropomorphic factors to avoid falling into the "uncanny valley" trap, so it is necessary to accurately measure these anthropomorphic characteristics. To this end, Spatol et al. (2021) proposed a scale for evaluating four anthropomorphic characteristics of robot (sociability, agency, vitality, and distraction).

Robot's personality is one of its important anthropomorphic characteristics, which will have a positive impact on the user's response and acceptance in human-robot interaction. For example, it can improve the acceptance of users by affecting their perception of roles (Tay et al. 2014). In addition, there are also studies discussing the different effects of different personality traits of robot on people. For example, human responds more positively to interactions with extroverted robot than introverted robot, especially those who are extroverted (Robert et al. 2020). Robot with higher neuroticism and conscientiousness can reduce human's abnormal perception during interactions (Paetzel-Prüsmann et al. 2021).

Extroversion is one of the important dimensions of the Big Five, and it is often discussed by scholars in robot anthropomorphism and human-robot interaction. For example, Santamaria and Nathan-Roberts (2017) found that 26% of the studies used extroversion to represent personality when summarizing the measurement methods of human's and robot's personality in human-robot interaction. Similar to human, extroverted robot is lively, cheerful, and good at communication while introverted robot is quieter, more attentive, and good at analyzing and thinking (Niculescu et al. 2010). However, the current research on robot extroversion has opposite conclusions. Some studies have shown that the extroversion of robot will affect the quality of human behavior and human-robot interaction, and human react more positively in the interaction with extroverted robot, and their performance level is higher (Robert et al. 2020), but there are also studies that suggest that extroverted robot brings fewer positive effects than introverted robot (Esterwood and Robert 2020) does. Therefore, discussing the personality of human or robot alone may have greater limitations, and the results of the interaction between the two should be considered.

According to the related research results of human teamwork, the personality homogeneity of team members can affect individual performance to a certain extent (Van et al. 2001; Lu 2021). In the human-robot collaborative team, there are also different matching results between the personalities of human and robot, which is also one of the important factors affecting the performance of the human-robot collaborative team (Robert et al. 2020). However, there are some contradictions in the conclusions of different studies on this aspect. For example, although humans are more active, they still maintain a certain social distance from robot with homogeneous personalities, and social distance is an important factor affecting the results of human-robot interaction (Walters et al. 2005). In addition, the influence of personality homogeneity and heterogeneity on human is still unclear. Studies have shown that when interacting with robot with the same personality, human responds well (Robert 2018), and prefers to interact with the robot (Jung et al. 2012; Aly and Tapus 2013). However, other studies suggest that humans are more prone to interact with robot with heterogeneous personalities (Lee et al. 2006; Bernier and Scassellati 2010). Some studies have also pointed out that when both humans and robot are extroverted, humans have the strongest sense of participation in the interaction, while when they are both introverted, human have the lowest sense of participation (Salam et al. 2016). This complex paradox may be closely related to experimental scenarios and tasks. For example, Joosse et al. (2013) found that when the robot needs to actively interact with human, the homogeneity of the human-robot personality will have a more positive effect. On the contrary, when the robot only needs to work quietly, the performance of the heterogenous human-robot personality will be higher. All this shows that different work situations will lead to changes in the influence of human-robot personality matching. Therefore, the purpose of this study is to discuss the influence of the homogeneity of human and robot personality on individual work performance in human-robot collaborative teams, and to use questionnaires to eliminate the specificity of scenarios and tasks.

In human-robot collaborative team research, scholars also focus on team members' acceptance of robot and their impact on human-robot team behavior and performance (Wu et al. 2014; Li and Wang 2021). For example, Kory-Westlund and Breazeal (2019) assessed children's perception and acceptance of social robots in a child-human-robot interaction study. De Graaf and Allouch (2013) proposed several dimensions to evaluate robot acceptance, such as usefulness, adaptability, and sociality, which are helpful for the design of the robot acceptance questionnaire in our experiment. Beer et al. (2014) found that robot acceptance can significantly affect human's behavior.

The robot acceptance is affected by many factors. The characteristics of the robot itself, such as visual image, anthropomorphism, auditory characteristics, tactile characteristics, behavioral and action characteristics, will affect the acceptance of humans to varying extents (Xu and Yu 2019). Among them, human-robot personality is the more important factor. For example, some scholars have pointed out that human personality is one of the predictors of robot acceptance (Rossi et al. 2020; Esterwood et al. 2021). Vuchkov and Nikov (2020) believe that in the Big Five, human openness and agreeableness are positively correlated with robot acceptance, neuroticism has a significant negative impact while extroversion and conscientiousness have no significant effect on robot acceptance. Brandon (2012) discussed the impact of human-robot personality and personality matching on robot acceptance, in which extroverted robot is more acceptable to humans (Arora et al. 2021), but personality matching has not reached a clear conclusion. There are also studies that show that humans are more receptive to robot when their personalities are homogeneous (Esterwood et al. 2021). In addition, the higher the social presence of robot, the higher robot acceptance (Heerink et al. 2008). Humans' gender, age, and culture all have impacts on robot acceptance (Xu and Yu 2019), and education and work experience also play a role (Heerink 2011). However, there are also studies that suggest that robot acceptance has no relationship with people's gender and education level, but is only related to factors such as age, emotion, and familiarity with robot (Bishop et al. 2019), some of which will be studied as control variables in this paper.

Based on current research, we found that robot anthropomorphism, especially in terms of personality, has a significant impact on human-robot collaborative team performance, but there are some differences and contradictions in the conclusions of different studies. In addition, most studies have not discussed the mechanism that affects individual work performance. Therefore, the method of this study tries to eliminate the interference of uncertain factors such as work tasks and situations, and uses questionnaires to explore whether the homogeneity of human-robot extroversion in human-robot collaborative team will affect individual work performance, and try to verify whether there is a mediating role for robot acceptance in this process, and also discuss the influence of some control variables. The research results are of great significance for optimizing the robot characteristics and human-robot collaboration team design, and improving the work performance of the human-robot team.

2 Hypotheses

In a human-robot collaboration team, the extroversion of human or robot will affect individual work performance, and similar to the interaction between people in life, the homogeneity of the two (that is, extroversion matching) is likely to have a significant effect. When the human-robot extroversion is homogeneous, humans may feel more relaxed and close to the robot, and work performance is improved; while when the human-robot extroversion is heterogeneous, human may feel abnormal and nervous, which will lead to a decrease in work performance. Therefore, hypothesis 1 is proposed.

H1: In a human-robot collaboration team, human-robot extroversion matching affects individual work performance. When human-robot extroversion is homogeneous, individual work performance is higher.

Although there are many studies discussing the impact of human-robot personality matching on individual work performance, there is no further research on its mechanism. Therefore, human-robot extroversion matching may not directly affect individual work performance, but is achieved through some intermediate psychological or cognitive factors, such as robot acceptance, so hypothesis 2 is proposed.

H2: In human-robot collaboration teams, robot acceptance is a mediating variable between human-robot extroversion matching and individual work performance.

Since humans actively choose the partner robot, human-robot collaboration also takes human behavior and performance as the main research object. Therefore, when human's extroversion is different, the impact of human-robot extroversion matching on robot acceptance and individual work performance may also change, so hypothesis 3 is proposed.

H3: In human-robot teams, human's extroversion is the moderator between human-robot extroversion fit and robot acceptance (Fig. 1).

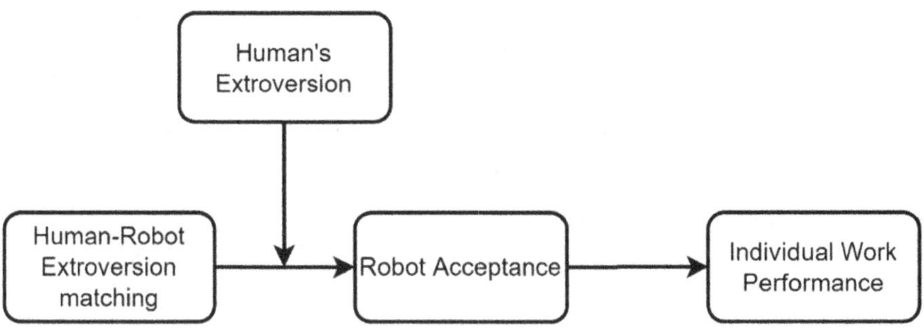

Fig. 1. Research model

3 Experimental Design

3.1 Respondents

In this study, questionnaires were distributed through the online questionnaire system, and a total of 250 questionnaires were returned. 152 valid questionnaires were finally obtained by deleting the questionnaires whose filling time was less than 30 s or had missing options, and all the questionnaires whose answers were at the highest or lowest level.

Including 74 males (48.68%) and 78 females (51.32%), the proportions are basically the same. 18 respondents were under 20 years old (11.84%), 115 respondents were between 21 and 30 years old (75.66%), and the rest of the respondents were over 31 years old (12.50%). Most of the respondents have a bachelor's degree or above (90.79%), of which 19 respondents have a graduate degree or above. 120 respondents had a working experience of less than 1 year(78.95%), 17 respondents had 1–3 years of work experience (11.18%), and the rest had more than three years of work experience (9.87%). Among the respondents, 92 had no or little understanding of the companion robot (60.52%), while the rest of the respondents had a certain understanding (39.48%). 72 respondents thought they were extroverted (47.4%), and the remaining 120 people thought they were introverted (52.6%). See Table 1 for details.

Table 1. Basic information of respondents

Measure	Item	Frequency	Percentage (%)
Total		152	
Gender	Male	74	48.68
	Female	78	51.32
Age	Below 20	18	11.84
	21–30	115	75.66
	31–40	12	7.89
	Over 41	7	4.61
Education	Under senior middle school	4	2.63
	Junior college	10	6.58
	Undergraduate	119	78.29
	Over postgraduate	19	12.50
Working experience	Below 1 year	120	78.95
	1–3 years	17	11.18
	3–5 years	2	1.32
	Over 6 years	13	8.55
Robot knowledge	Never known	18	11.84
	Less known	74	48.68
	General known	50	32.89
	More known	10	6.59
	Very much known	0	0.00
Extroversion	Extroverted	72	47.37
	Introverted	80	52.63

3.2 Variables

The independent variable of this study is human-robot extroversion matching, which is derived from the extroversion of man and robot, with two levels of homogeneity and heterogeneity. The dependent variable is individual work performance, human extroversion is the moderator variable, robot acceptance is the mediator variable, and the control variables are gender, age, education, work experience and robot knowledge whose impact will also be analyzed separately in the study.

3.3 Questionnaire Design

The questionnaire consists of three parts: basic information of respondents, robot acceptance and individual work performance self-evaluation.

Among them, the basic information part includes respondents' gender, age, education, work experience, knowledge of partner robots, personal extroversion, etc. The robot knowledge degree adopts the Likert 5-point scale (1 = never known, 5 = very much known), and the respondents also need to self-evaluate extroversion (two levels: extroversion or introversion).

The robot acceptance part adopts the leader subordinate acceptance scale (Wang and Niu 2004). In order to make the problem content more consistent with this study, the "supervisor" in the original scale is replaced by "robot". The scale contains four questions: "I like the social attributes of the robot very much", "it is meaningful to work with the robot", "I am willing to learn the usage of the robot" and "I like working with the robot" using Likert 5-point scale, 1 = strongly disagree, 5 = strongly agree.

The self-evaluation part of individual work performance adopts the employee basic work performance scale (Tsui et al. 1997). The original scale includes two sub dimensions: task performance and peripheral performance. The peripheral performance is generally evaluated by the comparison between the superior and the overall average level. This evaluation method is not applicable to this study. Therefore, only the task performance dimension is adopted, with a total of 5 questions, involving the evaluation of three aspects: quantity, quality and efficiency: "the increase in the quantity of my work results", "The improvement range of my work quality", "the improvement range of my work efficiency", "the range of my work quality standard higher than the original work quality standard" and "the range of my work quality higher than the specified quality level" using Likert 5-point scale, 1 = no improvement, 5 = very much improvement.

4 Data Analysis

The data analysis of this study includes four steps: the validity of the questionnaire, the impact of human-robot extroversion matching on individual work performance, the mediating role of robot acceptance, the regulating role of human extroversion, and the results of other variables.

4.1 Validity of Questionnaire

According to Cronbach alpha Test and KMO sampling appropriateness test results, 152 valid questionnaires of robot acceptance and individual work performance scale's Cronbach alpha and KMO values are all greater than 0.8 (all $p < .001$), indicating that the questionnaire has certain reliability and validity and can be analyzed in the next step (Table 2).

Table 2. Reliability and validity test of questionnaire

	Robot acceptance				Individual work performance			
	Number of items	Cronbach's alpha	KMO	p	Number of items	Cronbach's alpha	KMO	p
To extroverted robot	4	.855	.822	<.001	5	.866	.855	<.001
To introverted robot	4	.877	.837	<.001	5	.909	.887	<.001

4.2 Influence of Human-Robot Extroversion Matching on Robot Acceptance and Work Performance

The results of one-way ANOVA are shown in Table 3, and human-robot extroversion matching has a significant impact on individual work performance ($F = 4.427$, $p = .036$). After the post-test, compared with the heterogeneous human-robot extroversion, when the human-robot extroversion is homogeneous, the individual work performance (homogeneous: mean = 18.68, SD = 3.81; heterogeneous: mean = 17.81, SD = 4.00) are significantly higher. Therefore, hypothesis 1 is verified.

Table 3. One-way ANOVA of human-robot extroversion matching's impact on individual work performance

Variables	F	p
Gender	1.574	.211
Age	.088	.767
Education	16.072	<.001
Work experience	4.725	.031
Robot knowledge	7.559	.006
Human-robot extroversion matching	4.427	.036

4.3 Mediating Role of Robot Acceptance

Human-robot extroversion matching in model 1 and model 2 significantly affected robot acceptance (Model 1: $F = 9.608$, $p = .016$) and individual work performance (Model 2: $F = 10.546$, $p = .036$), respectively. In model 3, after human-robot extroversion matching and robot acceptance are put into the model at the same time, human-robot extroversion matching has no significant impact on individual work performance, while robot acceptance has a significant impact on individual work performance (Model 3: $F = 28.123$, $p < .001$), indicating that robot acceptance is a completemediating variable between human-robot extroversion matching and individual work performance, Therefore, hypothesis 2 is verified (Table 4).

Table 4. Regression analysis of mediating effect of robot acceptance

Variables	Model 1	Model 2	Model 3
	Robot acceptance	Individual work performance	Individual work performance
Human-robot extroversion matching	.057*	.043*	.017
Robot acceptance	–	–	.460**
Gender	−.032	−.027	−.013
Age	−.010	−.007	−.003
Education	.116**	.093	.039
Work experience	−.026	−.036	−.024
Robot knowledge	.104*	.116**	.068
R^2	.163	.176	.400
Adjusted R^2	.146	.159	.385
F	9.608	10.546	28.132

* indicates the significance level is 0.05.
** indicates the significance level is 0.01.

4.4 The Moderating Effect of Human Extroversion

Taking human-robot extroversion matching and human's extroversion as a fixed factor, and robot acceptance as a dependent variable, a one-way ANOVA was performed, and the covariates were kept unchanged, and the results are shown in Table 5. The interaction term of the two has a significant impact on robot acceptance ($F = 5.005$, $p = .026$), indicating that human extroversion has a moderating effect between human-robot extroversion matching and robot acceptance.

The post-test results showed that when the human extroversion is extroverted, human-robot extroversion matching had a significant impact on robot acceptance (homogeneous: mean = 14.61, SD = 3.41; heterogeneous: mean = 12.83, SD = 3.71; $p = .003$). When humans ware introverted, human-robot extroversion matching had no significant effect on robot acceptance (homogeneous: mean = 14.88, SD = 3.47; heterogeneous: mean = 14.75, SD = 3.21; $p = .813$).

Table 5. One-way analysis of variance on the moderating effect of human extroversion

Variables	F	p
Human-robot extroversion matching	6.634	.010
Human's extroversion	5.402	.021
Human-robot extroversion matching * Human's extroversion	5.005	.026

4.5 Other Variable Analysis Results

From the multivariate analysis of variance, it can be concluded that gender and age have no significant effects on robot acceptance and individual work performance (all $p > .05$), while education and robot familiarity have significant effects on robot acceptance and work performance. Work experience only had a significant effect on individual work performance (all $p < .05$).

The specific post-tests are shown in Table 6 and Table 7. First, the robot acceptance and individual work performance of respondents with education below high school and junior college were significantly lower than those of other respondents (all $p < .05$; below high school: mean = 7.75; junior college: mean = 11.25; undergraduate: mean = 16.63; postgraduate or above: mean = 15.21), and there was no significant difference between respondents with undergraduate and postgraduate education. Individual work performance also showed the same difference (all $p < .05$; below high school: mean = 11.75; junior college: mean = 14.80; undergraduate: mean = 18.54, graduate and above: mean = 19.55).

Second, for work experience, we found that respondents with 3–5 years of work experience had significantly lower individual work performance than other respondent groups. The individual work performance of respondents with more than 6 years of work experience was significantly lower than that of respondents with less than 3 years of work experience, but significantly higher than that of respondents with 3–5 years of work experience (all $p < .05$; less than 1 years: mean = 18.68; 1–3 years: mean = 18.18; 3–5 years: mean = 10.75; more than 6 years: mean = 15.42), there were no significant differences among other groups of respondents.

Table 6. Post-test of the effect of education on robot acceptance and individual work performance

Dependent variable	Education		Mean difference	t	p
Robot acceptance	Under senior middle school	Junior college	−3.500	−2.568	.011
		Undergraduate	−6.876	−5.872	<.001
		Over postgraduate	−7.461	−5.884	<.001
	Junior college	Undergraduate	−3.376	−4.448	<.001
		Over postgraduate	−3.961	−4.401	<.001
	Undergraduate	Over postgraduate	−.584	−1.026	.305
Individual work performance	Under senior middle school	Junior college	−3.050	−1.996	.047
		Undergraduate	−6.792	−5.173	<.001
		Over postgraduate	−7.803	−5.491	<.001
	junior college	Undergraduate	−3.742	−4.402	<.001
		Over postgraduate	−4.753	−4.711	<.001
	Undergraduate	Over postgraduate	−1.011	−1.585	.114

Table 7. Post-test of the effect of work experience on individual work performance

Dependent variable	Work experience		Mean difference	t	p
Individual work performance	Below 1 year	1–3 years	.507	0.741	.460
		3–5 years	7.933	4.213	<.001
		Over 6 years	3.260	4.228	<.001
	1–3 years	3–5 years	7.426	3.760	<.001
		Over 6 years	2.753	2.829	.005
	3–5 years	Over 6 years	−4.673	−2.330	.021

According to the analysis results in Table 3, it can be concluded that the respondents' knowledge of robots has a significant positive impact on robot acceptance and individual work performance (all $p < .05$), but after testing, it does not have any mediating or moderating effect. However, this shows that people's knowledge of robots can be enhanced through in-depth learning to improve the acceptance of robots and individual work performance in human-robot collaborative teams.

After the above tests, the three hypotheses proposed in this study have been verified. First, human-robot extroversion matching affects individual work performance. When human-robot extroversion is homogeneous, individual work performance is higher. Second, robot acceptance is a mediating variable between human-robot extroversion matching and individual work performance. Finally, human's extroversion is a moderator between human-robot extroversion matching and robot acceptance.

5 Discussion

When discussing the influence of personality factors in human-robot collaboration teams, most studies only discuss one of the human and robot (Vuchkov and Nikov 2020), and some studies have proved that the personality matching of team members also has an impact on work performance (Robert et al. 2020), but none of these studies explored the impact mechanism. Therefore, this study further explores its impact mechanism on the basis of verifying the impact of human-robot extroversion matching on work performance, as well as the differences in individual performance of human-robot collaboration teams under different extroversion homogeneity.

The results of the questionnaire survey show that the human-robot extroversion matching has a significant impact on individual work performance in the human-robot collaboration team, and work performance is higher when human and partner-robot extroversion are homogeneous (hypothesis 1), which is also consistent with Robert (2018), Jung et al (2012), Aly and Tapus (2013) and Esterwood et al. (2021) have basically the same conclusions. When human-robot extroversion is homogenous, people seem to be interacting with a partner who has the same personality, it is easier to communicate and reach consistent conclusions, so the performance will be higher; when interacting with partners with mutually exclusive extroversion, certain difficulties may arise in the communication, and people may psychologically reject robot partners and interfere with work performance.

Hypothesis 2 and 3 of this study were both validated, indicating that human-robot extroversion matching affects individual work performance through robot acceptance and is mediated by human extroversion. When people are extroverted, the effect of human-robot extroversion homogeneity on the acceptance of robots is significant, but when people are introverted, there is no significant effect, which indicates that the influence of human-robot extroversion homogeneity is mainly reflected in the group of extroverted users, while the robot acceptance of introverted users is hardly affected by the homogeneity of extroversion, which was not found in studies such as Brandon (2012), Arora et al. (2021) and Esterwood et al. (2021). This may be because humans play a major role in human-robot collaboration, and extroverted users are keen to communicate. Therefore, working with robot with homogeneity of extroversion will improve the enthusiasm and efficiency of communication, while interacting with robots with heterogeneity of extroversion, communication barriers are more likely to occur, which in turn affects robot acceptance and work efficiency.

In addition, the results of the study also showed that gender and age had no significant effect on robot acceptance and individual work performance, but educational background and robot knowledge had a significant effect. The conclusions of previous studies are also inconsistent. For example, Xu and Yu (2019) believe that robot acceptance is affected by gender, age, and culture, and Heerink (2011) believes that education and work experience also have a significant impact on robot acceptance. On the other hand, Bishop et al. (2019) argue that robot acceptance is only related to factors such as age, emotion, and robot knowledge.

Respondents in this study are mainly between 21–30 years old, with less than 1 year of work experience, their acceptance and recognition of robots may be different from other groups. This study is a preliminary study, so a more convenient questionnaire survey method is used, but this method has its inherent limitations. For specific work tasks, objective behavior data is used to reflect robot acceptance and work performance, or objective assessment by third-party experts is conducted to more accurately explore the relationship between variables to obtain more effective and extensive research conclusions.

6 Conclusion

In the near future, robots will be more common in our life, and the significance of their existence is not only to complete physical activities mechanically. There will be a wider demand for partner robots, which communicate with people and assist in affairs like partners. Therefore, how robots affect the work performance of individuals in human-robot collaboration team needs further research and discovery. We found that robots with anthropomorphic characteristics have better performance in human-robot cooperation. We chose extroversion as the main feature of the study, focusing on the impact of human-robot extroversion matching on individual work performance. In addition, we also attempt to explore the mediating role of robot acceptance between human-robot extroversion matching and individual work performance, as well as the moderating role of human's extroversion. A total of 152 valid questionnaires were collected and the results of data analysis show that when the extroversion of human and robot is homogeneous, the work performance of respondents is higher. In addition, robot acceptance plays a complete mediating role between human-robot extroversion matching and individual work performance, and human's extroversion plays a moderating role between human-robot extroversion matching and robot acceptance.

In addition, we also conclude that gender and age have no significant impact on robot acceptance and individual work performance, while education and robot knowledge have a significant impact on robot acceptance and individual work performance, and work experience has a significant impact on individual work performance.

Therefore, this study suggests that when selecting partner robots to assist in office, we should pay more attention to the matching between robots and our own characteristics, and try to choose robots with the same or similar characteristics. In the organization design of human-robot collaboration work team, we should consider the matching degree of human and robot characteristics and human acceptance of robot, so as to achieve better team work performance. Robot acceptance can be achieved through more frequent communication, or multiple collaboration and cooperation. In addition, we also need to consider the educational background, work experience and robot knowledge of the members of the human-robot collaboration team.

The research results help relevant researchers better understand the needs of people in the organization for robot partners, provide ideas for the design of robot products, especially in personality characteristics such as extroversion, and provide a reference for improving the performance of human-robot collaboration team.

Acknowledgements. This study was funded by a Ministry of Education of Humanities and Social Science project 19YJC840002, a National Natural Science Foundation of China 71942005 and a Beijing Social Science Fund 17SRC021.

References

Mazzoni, E., Benvenuti, M.: A robot-partner for preschool children learning English using socio-cognitive conflict. J. Educ. Technol. Soc. **18**(4), 474–485 (2015)

Obo, T., Loo, C.K., Kubota, N.: Imitation learning for daily exercise support with robot partner. In: Proceedings of 24th ACM/IEEE International Symposium on Robot and Human Interactive Communication, pp. 752–757. IEEE (2015)

Lu, Y., Chen, C., Chen, P., Chen, X., Zhuang, Z.: Smart learning partner: an interactive robot for education. In Proceedings of International Conference on Artificial Intelligence in Education, pp. 447–451. Springer, Cham (2018). https://doi.org/10.1007/978-3-319-93846-2_84

Karunarathne, D., Morales, Y., Nomura, T., Kanda, T., Ishiguro, H.: Will older adults accept a humanoid robot as a walking partner? Int. J. Soc. Robot. **11**(2), 343–358 (2019)

Baker, A.L., Phillips, E.K., Ullman, D., Keebler, J.R.: Toward an understanding of trust repair in human-robot interaction: current research and future directions. Trans. Interact. Intell. Syst. (TiiS) **8**(4), 1–30 (2018)

De Visser, E.J., et al.: Towards a theory of longitudinal trust calibration in human-robot teams. Int. J. Soc. Robot. **12**(2), 459–478 (2020)

Duffy, B.R.: Anthropomorphism and the social robot. Robot. Auton. Syst. **42**(3–4), 177–190 (2003)

Fraune, M.R.: Our robots, our team: robot anthropomorphism moderates group effects in human–robot teams. Front. Psychol. **11**, 1275 (2020)

Christou, P., Simillidou, A., Stylianou, M.C.: Tourists' perceptions regarding the use of anthropomorphic robots in tourism and hospitality. Int. J. Contemp. Hosp. Manag. **32**, 3665–3683 (2020)

Haring, K.S., Watanabe, K., Mougenot, C.: The influence of robot appearance on assessment. In: Proceedings of 8th ACM/IEEE International Conference on Human-Robot Interaction (HRI), pp. 131–132. IEEE (2013)

Tung, F.W.: Child perception of humanoid robot appearance and behavior. Int. J. Hum.-Comput. Interact. **32**(6), 493–502 (2016)

Kwak, S.S.: The impact of the robot appearance types on social interaction with a robot and service evaluation of a robot. Arch. Des. Res. **27**(2), 81–93 (2014)

Paetzel-Prüsmann, M., Perugia, G., Castellano, G.: The Influence of robot personality on the development of uncanny feelings. Comput. Hum. Behav. **120**, 106756 (2021)

Murphy, J., Gretzel, U., Hofacker, C.: Service robots in hospitality and tourism: investigating anthropomorphism. In: Proceedings of 15th APacCHRIE Conference, vol. 31 (2017)

Murphy, J., Gretzel, U., Pesonen, J.: Marketing robot services in hospitality and tourism: the role of anthropomorphism. J. Travel Tour. Mark. **36**(7), 784–795 (2019)

Brenton, H., Gillies, M., Ballin, D., Chatting, D.: The uncanny valley: does it exist? In: Proceedings of Conference of Human Computer Interaction, Workshop on Human Animated Character Interaction. Citeseer (2005)

Roesler, E., Manzey, D., Onnasch, L.: A meta-analysis on the effectiveness of anthropomorphism in human-robot interaction. Sci. Robot. **6**(58), eabj5425 (2021)
Bartneck, C., Bleeker, T., Bun, J., Fens, P., Riet, L.: The influence of robot anthropomorphism on the feelings of embarrassment when interacting with robots. Paladyn **1**(2), 109–115 (2010)
Spatola, N., Kühnlenz, B., Cheng, G.: Perception and evaluation in human–robot interaction: the human-robot interaction evaluation scale (HRIES)-a multicomponent approach of anthropomorphism. Int. J. Soc. Robot. **13**, 1517–1539 (2021)
Tay, B., Jung, Y., Park, T.: When stereotypes meet robots: the double-edge sword of robot gender and personality in human–robot interaction. Comput. Hum. Behav. **38**, 75–84 (2014)
Robert, L., Alahmad, R., Esterwood, C., Kim, S., You, S., Zhang, Q.: A Review of Personality in Human–Robot Interactions. Available at SSRN 3528496 (2020)
Santamaria, T., Nathan-Roberts, D.: Personality measurement and design in human-robot interaction: a systematic and critical review. In: Proceedings of the Human Factors and Ergonomics Society Annual Meeting, vol. 61, no. 1, pp. 853–857 (2017)
Niculescu, A., van Dijk, B., Nijholt, A., Limbu, D.K., See, S.L., Wong, A.H.Y.: Socializing with Olivia, the youngest robot receptionist outside the lab. In: Ge, S.S., Li, H., Cabibihan, JJ., Tan, Y.K. (eds.) Social Robotics. ICSR 2010. Lecture Notes in Computer Science, vol. 6414. Springer, Heidelberg (2010). https://doi.org/10.1007/978-3-642-17248-9_6
Esterwood, C., Robert, L.P.: Personality in healthcare human robot interaction (H-HRI): a literature review and brief critique. In: Proceedings of the 8th International Conference on Human-Agent Interaction, pp. 87–95 (2020)
Van Vianen, A.E., De Dreu, C.K.: Personality in teams: its relationship to social cohesion, task cohesion, and team performance. Eur. J. Work Organ. Psychol. **10**(2), 97–120 (2001)
Lu, X.: Heterogeneity vs Homogeneity: Which is Compatible with Team Agency vs Communion? (Doctoral dissertation, University of Illinois at Chicago) (2021)
Walters, M.L., et al.: The influence of subjects' personality traits on personal spatial zones in a human-robot interaction experiment. In: Proceedings of Roman 2005 IEEE International Workshop on Robot and Human Interactive Communication, pp. 347–352. IEEE (2005)
Robert, L.: Personality in the human robot interaction literature: a review and brief critique. In: The Proceedings of the 24th Americas Conference on Information Systems, pp. 16–18 (2018)
Jung, S., Lim, H.T., Kwak, S., Biocca, F.: Personality and facial expressions in human-robot interaction. In: Proceedings of 2012 7th ACM/IEEE International Conference on Human-Robot Interaction (HRI), pp. 161–162. IEEE (2012)
Aly, A., Tapus, A.: A model for synthesizing a combined verbal and nonverbal behavior based on personality traits in human-robot interaction. In: Proceedings of 2013 8th ACM/IEEE International Conference on Human-Robot Interaction (HRI), pp. 325–332. IEEE (2013)
Lee, K.M., Peng, W., Jin, S.A., Yan, C.: Can robots manifest personality? An empirical test of personality recognition, social responses, and social presence in human–robot interaction. J. Commun. **56**(4), 754–772 (2006)
Bernier, E.P., Scassellati, B.: The similarity-attraction effect in human-robot interaction. In: Proceedings of 2010 IEEE 9th International Conference on Development and Learning, pp. 286–290. IEEE (2010)
Salam, H., Celiktutan, O., Hupont, I., Gunes, H., Chetouani, M.: Fully automatic analysis of engagement and its relationship to personality in human-robot interactions. IEEE Access **5**, 705–772 (2016)
Joosse, M., Lohse, M., Pérez, J.G., Evers, V.: What you do is who you are: the role of task context in perceived social robot personality. In: Proceedings of 2013 IEEE International Conference on Robotics and Automation, pp. 2134–2139. IEEE (2013)
Wu, Y.H., Wrobel, J., Cornuet, M., Kerhervé, H., Damnée, S., Rigaud, A.S.: Acceptance of an assistive robot in older adults: a mixed-method study of human–robot interaction over a 1-month period in the Living Lab setting. Clin. Interv. Aging **9**, 801 (2014)

Li, Y., Wang, C.: Effect of customer's perception on service robot acceptance. Int. J. Consum. Stud. (2021)

Kory-Westlund, J.M., Breazeal, C.: Assessing children's perceptions and acceptance of a social robot. In: Proceedings of the 18th ACM International Conference on Interaction Design and Children, pp. 38–50. ACM (2019)

De Graaf, M.M., Allouch, S.B.: Exploring influencing variables for the acceptance of social robots. Robot. Auton. Syst. **61**(12), 1476–1486 (2013)

Beer, J.M., Fisk, A.D., Rogers, W.A.: Toward a framework for levels of robot autonomy in human-robot interaction. J. Hum.-Robot Interact. **3**(2), 74 (2014)

Rossi, S., et al.: The role of personality factors and empathy in the acceptance and performance of a social robot for psychometric evaluations. Robotics **9**(2), 39 (2020)

Esterwood, C., Essenmacher, K., Yang, H., Zeng, F., Robert, L.P.: A meta-analysis of human personality and robot acceptance in human-robot interaction. In: Proceedings of the 2021a CHI Conference on Human Factors in Computing Systems, pp. 1–18 (2021a)

Vuchkov, B., Nikov, V.: Effect of personality on robot acceptance (2020)

Brandon, M.: Effect personality matching on robot acceptance: effect of robot-user personality matching on the acceptance of domestic assistant robots for elderly (Master's thesis, University of Twente) (2012)

Arora, A.S., Fleming, M., Arora, A., Taras, V., Xu, J.: Finding "H" in HRI: examining human personality traits, robotic anthropomorphism, and robot likeability in human-robot interaction. Int. J. Intell. Inf. Technol. (IJIIT) **17**(1), 19–38 (2021)

Esterwood, C., Essenmacher, K., Yang, H., Zeng, F., Robert, L.P.: Birds of a feather flock together: but do humans and robots? A meta-analysis of human and robot personality matching. In: Proceedings of 2021b 30th IEEE International Conference on Robot & Human Interactive Communication (RO-MAN), pp. 343–348. IEEE (2020)

Heerink, M., Kröse, B., Evers, V., Wielinga, B.: The influence of social presence on acceptance of a companion robot by older people (2008)

Xu, L., Yu, F.: Factors that influence robot acceptance. Chin. Sci. Bull. **65**(6), 496–510 (2019)

Heerink, M.: Exploring the influence of age, gender, education and computer experience on robot acceptance by older adults. In: Proceedings of 2011 6th ACM/IEEE International Conference on Human-Robot Interaction (HRI), pp. 147–148. IEEE (2011)

Bishop, L., van Maris, A., Dogramadzi, S., Zook, N.: Social robots: the influence of human and robot characteristics on acceptance. Paladyn, J. Behav. Robot. **10**(1), 346–358 (2019)

Wang, H., Niu, X.Y.: Multidimensional structure of leader subordinate exchange and its impact on job performance and situational performance. Acta Psychol. Sin. **36**(2), 179–185 (2004)

Tsui, A.S., Pearce, J.L., Porter, L.W., Tripoli, A.M.: Alternative approaches to the employee-organization relationship: does investment in employees pay off? Acad. Manag. J. **40**(5), 1089–1121 (1997)

Learning-Based Visual Acuity Test System with Pepper Robot for User Behavior Research

Shih-Huan Tseng(✉) and Pei-Yuan Sun

National Kaohsiung University of Science and Technology, Kaohsiung 824005, Taiwan
shtseng@nkust.edu.tw

Abstract. Hand pose estimation based on deep learning is widely used in Human-Computer Interaction (HCI) field. This paper combines state-of-the-art hand pose estimation to build a gesture recognition model based on Long Short-Term Memory (LSTM) for a visual acuity test system with the Pepper robot. The size of the optotype is updated according to the distance between a user and the robot and displayed on the table. Experimental results show that the system is robust for users to perform well with different fingers. In the future, the HRI system is good to design a questionnaire to investigate users' preferences which include acceptances, a distance of visual acuity test, sit or stand, number of fingers.

Keywords: Gesture recognition · Deep learning · Human-robot interaction

1 Introduction

In recent years, the rapid development of deep learning has brought about the maturity of computer vision technology, such as human and hand pose estimation. Pose estimation has always been an active research direction in the field of Human-Computer Interaction (HCI) and is widely used in virtual reality, sign language recognition, smart home systems, robot control, etc., replacing the previous keyboard and mouse input allows users to operate and use more intuitively.

This paper's motivation is to develop a visual acuity test System with the Pepper robot to investigate users' preferences. The objectives of this paper are the following:

- Combining with MediaPipe hands [1], we build a gesture recognition model based on Long Short-Term Memory (LSTM)
- Develop a distance-dependent visual acuity test system with the Pepper robot.

The visual acuity test system architecture for gesture recognition is mainly divided into two parts. The first is to use the MediaPipe hands to capture the sequential hand feature points from the image of Pepper, and then use the Long Short-Term Memory

This research was supported by the Ministry of Science and Technology of Taiwan, under the grant numbers MOST 107-2923-S-002-001-MY3.

P.-L. P. Rau (Ed.): HCII 2022, LNCS 13314, pp. 571–582, 2022.
https://doi.org/10.1007/978-3-031-06053-3_39

(LSTM) model to identify them. The time-series hand feature points derive four directions: up, down, left, and right. Then, the distance data of the subject is obtained from the distance sensor on the robot. According to the distance between the subject and the robot, the size of the optotype is updated and displayed on the tablet on the chest of the Pepper robot.

2 Related Works

2.1 Gesture Recognition

In the field of gesture recognition, it can be mainly divided into two categories: static gesture recognition and dynamic gesture recognition [2], as shown in Fig. 1. Static gestures are mainly classified by hand shape and bending angle, while dynamic gestures change continuously over time. Therefore, when performing dynamic gesture recognition, not only hand shape and bending angle, but also reference its position and direction, etc.

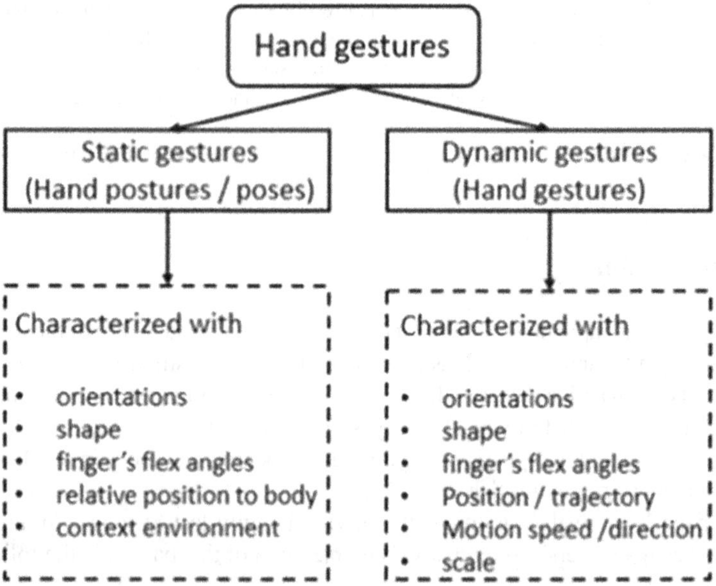

Fig. 1. Gesture recognition types [2]

Early gesture recognition methods, William T. Freeman et al. [3] used the direction histogram for gesture recognition and the research of Xiaoyan Wang et al. [4], they used the Hidden Markov Model (HMM) for dynamic gesture recognition. Recently, in machine learning and deep learning methods, such as the research of Cem Keskin et al. [5] and Gongfa Li et al. [6], the former uses Support Vector Machine (SVM) to train deep images for gesture recognition, and the latter uses Support Vector Machine (SVM) to train deep images for gesture recognition. Convolution Neural Network (CNN) processes two-dimensional image features to reduce the number of parameters to be trained for gesture recognition.

2.2 Gesture Recognition for Human-Robot Interaction

Brock et al. [7] propose a system for close non-verbal communication with the desktop robot Haru using gesture-interactive poses, a machine learning architecture for real-time gesture recognition was trained using Leap Motion, and a novel gesture understanding system was implemented. About 29 gesture interaction poses are designed to interact with the robot. As long as the robot recognizes the relevant gestures, it will interact with the human (as shown in Fig. 2).

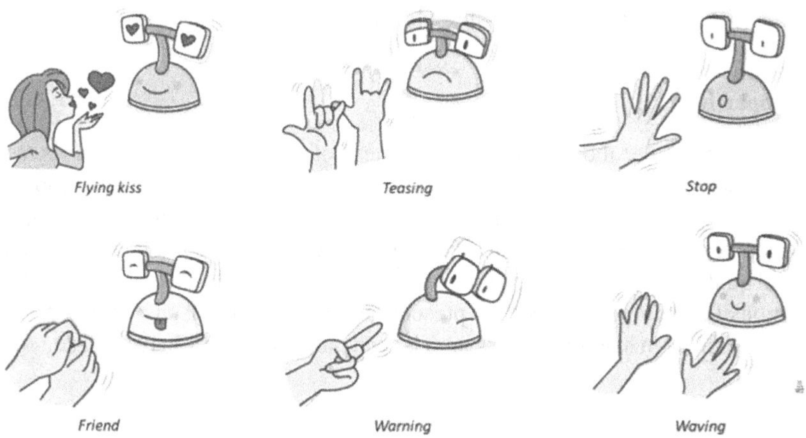

Fig. 2. Gesture interaction with Haru robot [7]

Wang Ke et al. [8] used the Hidden Markov Model (HMM) and Support Vector Machine (SVM) to implement a real-time gesture recognition based on service robots. In this study, the authors divided them into two tasks, mainly the classification of static gestures and the recognition of dynamic trajectories. In recent years, due to the prosperity of deep learning (Deep Neural Network), in the research topics of robotics and gesture recognition, there are also quite a lot of studies to replace traditional algorithms with neural networks. Among them, the research of Giovanna Castellano et al. [9] is to recognize the waving gesture in the interaction with the Pepper robot. There are three main steps in the architecture of the research, the tracking of the region of interest (ROI) of the hand, the feature segmentation of the ROI of the hand, and the gesture recognition of waving. The author first uses the HandTrack [10], a convolutional neural network (Convolutional Neural Network, CNN) method to obtain the ROI of the hand in each frame, and then subtract and segment it from the background. After preprocessing, the features of the hand can be extracted. Figure, and then the feature map is classified and identified by the CNN model built by the author as shown in Fig. 3.

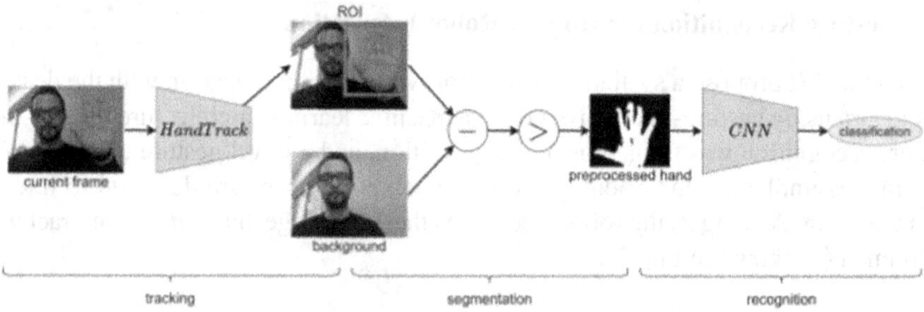

Fig. 3. System flow of gesture recognition [10]

2.3 Pepper Robot

In recent years, under the vigorous development of the field of robotics, robots with different functions have been developed one after another, such as the Pepper robot used in this paper, as shown in Fig. 4(a), a social robot developed by SoftBank Group [11], its development purpose, Therefore, human beings can improve interpersonal relationships and quality of life. The creator hopes that independent developers can create new applications for the Pepper robot. At present, the Pepper robot is also used on various occasions, such as in shopping malls, hotels, and education on [12, 13] and so on.

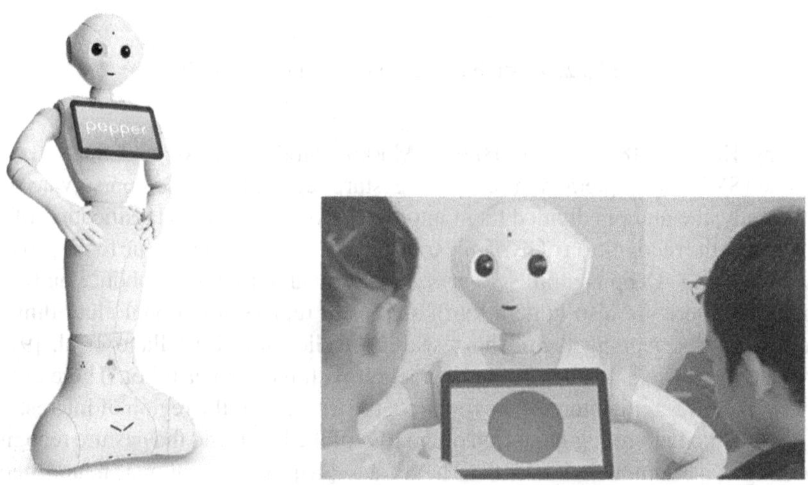

(a) (b)

Fig. 4. (a) Pepper robot (b) child education [12]

According to the above literature review, this research hopes that gesture recognition and deep learning can be applied to the field of robotics, which can combine accuracy and automation at the same time, so that this research can be applied to relevant visual acuity testing units such as medical institutions and major campuses, and effectively enhance its convenience and ease some of the human burdens.

3 Visual Acuity Test System with Pepper Robot

The distance of the user is obtained by the sonar sensor of the Pepper robot. The optotype is modified by the distance conversion formula (as shown in Fig. 5), and the optotype is displayed on the tablet on the chest of the Pepper robot for the user to answer, the robot will identify the direction of the user's gesture, and determine whether it matches the direction of the optotype. After a few mistakes, the robot will tell the user's vision.

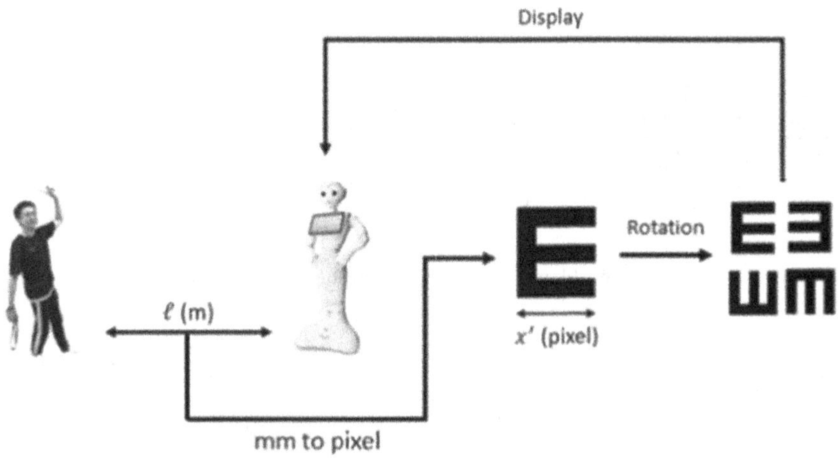

Fig. 5. Schematic diagram of the optotype size conversion according to the distance

3.1 Dynamic Gesture Recognition

Using the Pepper robot visual sensor to obtain images, track the hand features through MediaPipe, and then use the temporal features in the gestures as input, after training the long short-term memory network model, classify the four directions of up, down, left, and right. The detailed process is shown in Fig. 6.

MediaPipe is a multi-frame machine learning model published and open-sourced by Google research in 2019. This paper refers to Hand Tracking [1] in MediaPipe, extracts the features of the image, and its output value is 21 hand nodes of x, y, z, as shown in Fig. 7(a). By extracting the hand features in the 320 * 240 image, 21 hand node positions of x, y, and z can be obtained, as shown in Fig. 7(b). Among them, we do not consider them part of the z-axis, leaving only x and y with a total of 42 hand points. After preprocessing, the range of x is 0 to 320, and the range of y is 0 to 240.

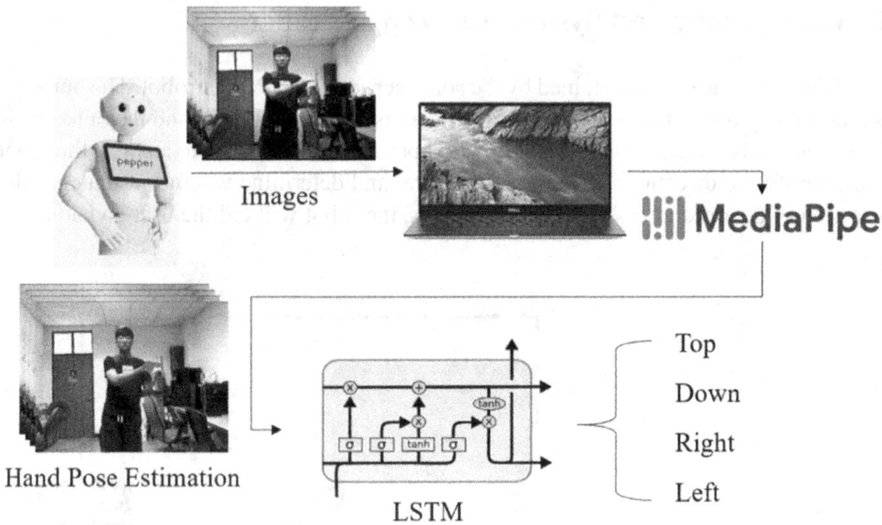

Fig. 6. Flowchart of dynamic gesture recognition

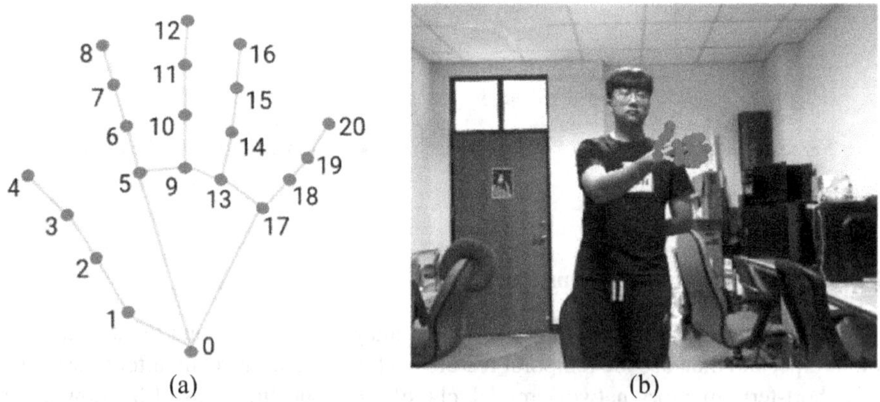

Fig. 7. (a) Hand nodes [1] (b) feature extraction of a hand

Take 42 nodes as input and feed them into a Long Short-Term Memory (LSTM) [14] model for training. The model consists of two layers of LSTM layers, then in the Multilayer Perceptron (MLP) part, including a fully connected layer (Fully connected layer) and an output layer, and finally outputs four categories (up, down, left, and right). The model architecture is shown in Fig. 8.

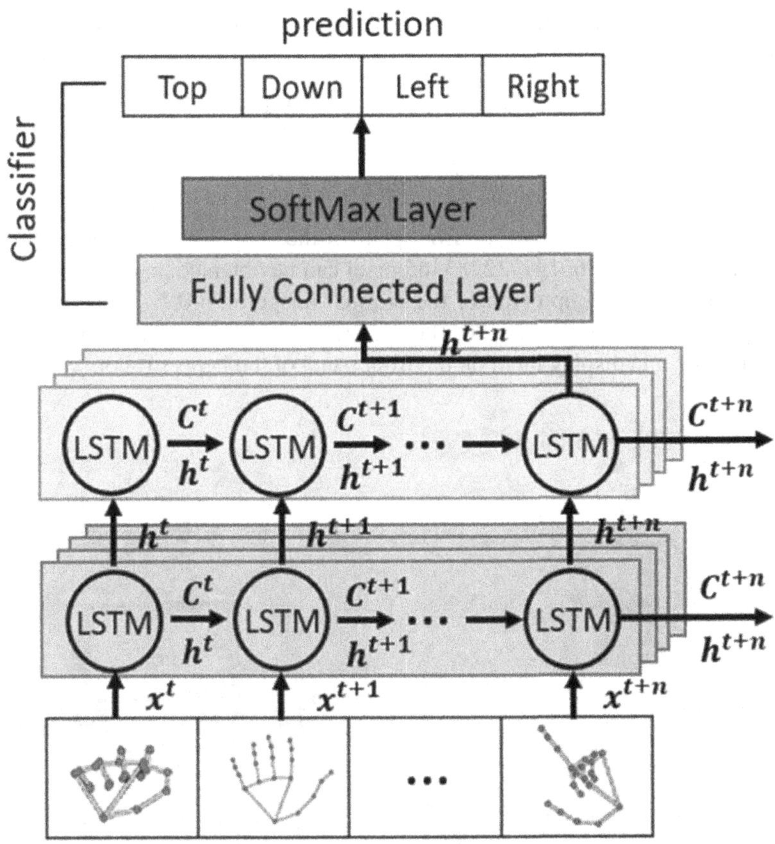

Fig. 8. LSTM gesture recognition model architecture

3.2 Optotype Distance Conversion

Develop a visual acuity test system on the Peeper robot, with the distance sensor on the robot (as shown in Fig. 9(a)), and convert the size of the optotype to the tablet of the Pepper robot after the distance conversion (as shown in Fig. 9(b)).

The optotype size formula calculates the optotype size according x to the inspection distance ℓ obtained by the Pepper robot. The original formula is defined as follows:

$$VA = \frac{1}{12\,tan^{-1}\frac{x(mm)}{1000*\ell(m)}} \tag{1}$$

When we obtain the visual acuity VA and the inspection distance ℓ to calculate the optotype size x, then rewrite formula (1) as follows:

$$x(mm) = tan\frac{1}{12*VA}*1000*\ell \tag{2}$$

Convert from millimeters to inches by formula (3) and from inches to pixels by formula (4).

$$x(mm) = y(inch) * 25.4 \quad (3)$$

$$y(inch) = p(pixel)/PPI \quad (4)$$

The Pixels Per Inch (PPI) of the front plate of the Pepper robot is about 149. After calculation, 1 mm = 5.866141732283465 pixel can be obtained, and it is converted to the size of the E-shaped optotype of the original image of 400 * 400 pixel, and then randomly rotate its optotypes at 0, 90, 180, and 270° to obtain four different orientations of the optotypes and display them on the front panel of the Pepper robot.

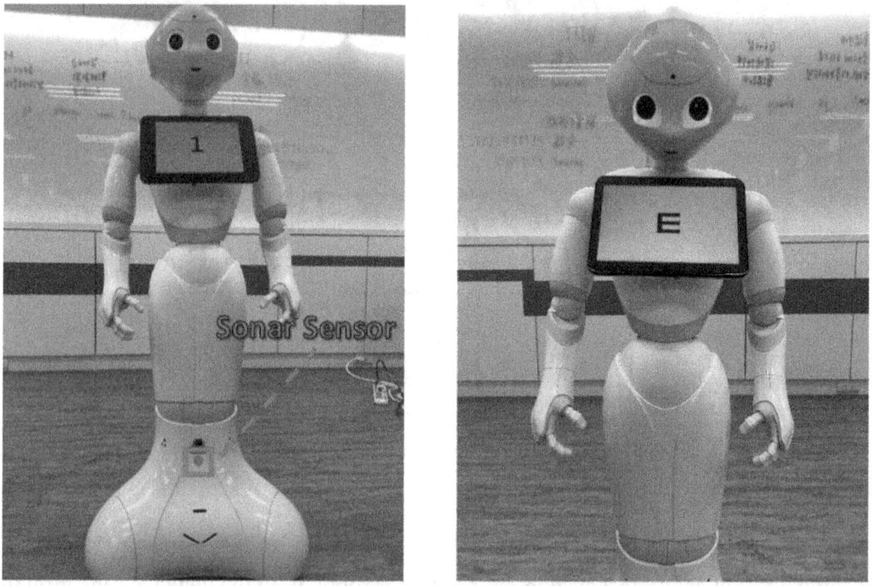

(a) (b)

Fig. 9. (a) Sonar sensor (b) optotype is displayed on a tablet

4 Experiments and Results

4.1 Dataset

The dataset collected videos of four people from the laboratory pointing to the up, down, left, and right directions during the simulated experiments. Collect 300 videos in each of the four directions, for a total of 4,800 videos. The video scenes included standing and sitting; in the gesture part, subjects pointed to different directions with one finger, two fingers, and five fingers.

The dataset is affected by external factors, such as clothes, light, and white walls. After data preprocessing, there are 823 records in the upper category, 762 records in the lower category, 917 records in the left category, and 712 records in the right category, and the total remaining data is 3,214 records, as shown in Table 1.

Table 1. The numbers of train data after preprocessing

Users	Down	Left	Right	Top	Total
1	207	255	226	228	916
2	204	293	240	162	899
3	212	198	139	167	716
4	107	139	171	266	683
Total	730	885	776	823	3,214

4.2 Experimental Results

Figure 10 illustrates the parameters setting of LSTM model implementation. The input features are 42 and 10. Because the dynamic gestures are time-series data, a complete gesture in the actual process can take about 20 frames as units on Timesteps. The first two layers of LSTM are 128 units and 64 units, and dropout is added in the middle to avoid the overfitting. A fully connected layer is connected to the third layer while last layer is the output layer whose activation function is SoftMax, and outputs the final four categories (up, down, left and right).

The first experiment is designed to compare the loss values on training, confusion matrices on testing with different feature points of a hand. The second one shows the evaluations of models.

Total 42 feature points of a hand are not easily extracted when users use one or two fingers. Therefore, we use 42 and 10 (significant feature points) as input the train the LSTM model with 128 and 64 neurons. Figure 11(a) illustrates the training process with 42 features as input. After 50 iterations of the training and validation data for the loss function changes, the number of parameters is 139,172. Although the results oscillate a bit, it still converges stably. Figure 11(b) illustrates the training process with 10 features as input. After 50 iterations of the training and validation data, the loss functions of the training and verification data are also slightly fitted. Although the number of parameters is 122,788 slightly reduced, it can be explained that only the main features are used for training, and they are less affected by other features.

Figure 12 shows the confusion matrix of LSTM model classification on testing data. The horizontal axis is prediction, the vertical axis is the ground truth. Figure 12(a) illustrates a few wrong classifications in the right category and the top category using 42 feature points. Figure 12(b) shows more wrong classifications on the top category using 10 feature points. The reason may be that the model is more complex, and the learning effect is not better by using fewer features points.

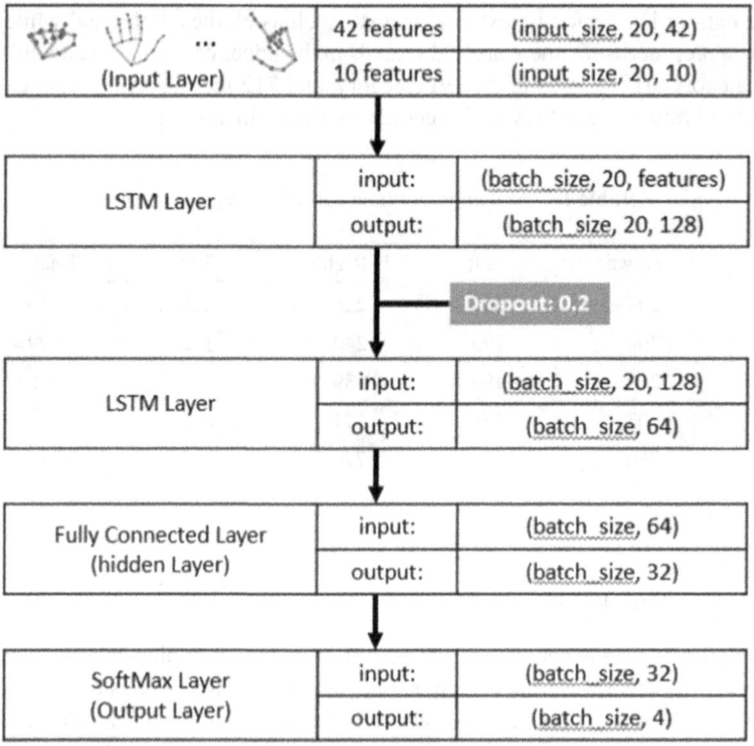

Fig. 10. Parameters setting of LSTM model

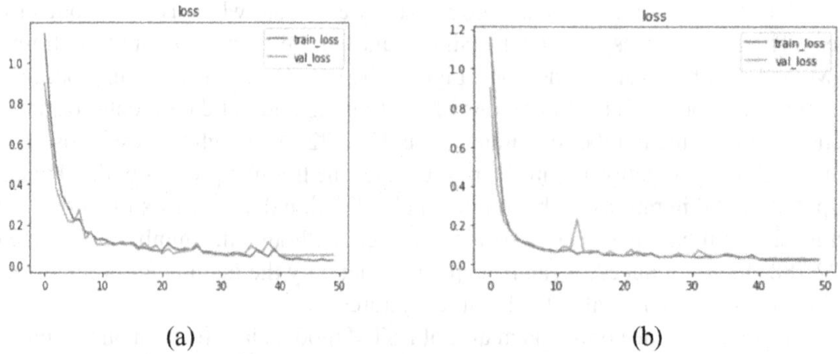

Fig. 11. Change in loss function value of LSTM model with 128 and 64 neurons (a) 42 feature points (b) 10 significant feature points

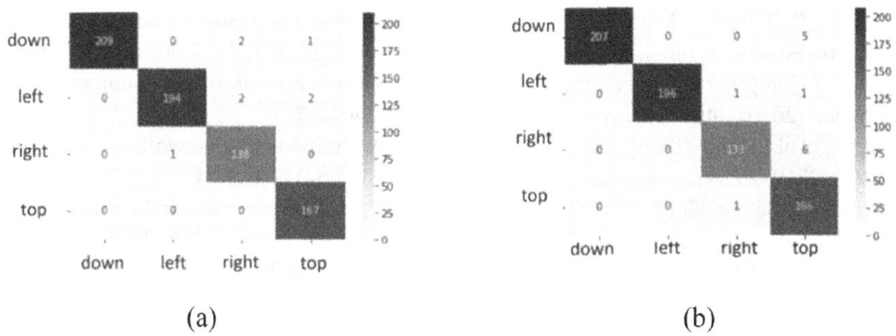

Fig. 12. Confusion matrix of LSTM (a) 42 feature points (b) 10 significant feature points

Table 2 shows the evaluations of models including precision, recall, accuracy, and Time. It reveals the model's robustness, performing well with fewer features points.

Table 2. Model evaluation

Model	Precision (Avg.)	Recall (Avg.)	Accuracy	Time(s)
LSTM-42	0.99	0.99	0.995	0.2283
LSTM-10	0.98	0.98	0.993	0.2238

5 Conclusion

This paper developed a learning-based visual acuity test system with Pepper robot. System features are that combines with MediaPipe hands to build a gesture recognition model based on Long Short-Term Memory (LSTM) and the optotype is modified by the distance conversion formula. The experimental results show the recognition model is robust for users to perform well with different fingers. The system is good for user behavior research in the future to investigate users' preferences which include acceptances, a distance of visual acuity test, sit or stand, number of fingers.

References

1. Zhang, F., et al.: Mediapipe hands: on-device real-time hand tracking. arXiv preprint arXiv: 2006.10214 (2020)
2. Pisharady, P.K., Saerbeck, M.: Recent methods and databases in vision-based hand gesture recognition: a review. Comput. Vis. Image Underst. **141**, 152–165 (2015)
3. Freeman, W.T., Roth, M.: Orientation histograms for hand gesture recognition. In: International Workshop on Automatic Face and Gesture Recognition, Zurich, Switzerland, vol. 12, pp. 296–301 (1995)
4. Wang, X., Xia, M., Cai, H., Gao, Y., Cattani, C.: Hidden-Markov-models-based dynamic hand gesture recognition. Math. Probl. Eng. **2012**, 1–11 (2012)

5. Keskin, C., Kıraç, F., Kara, Y.E., Akarun, L.: Real time hand pose estimation using depth sensors. In: Fossati, A., Gall, J., Grabner, H., Ren, X., Konolige, K. (eds.) Consumer Depth Cameras for Computer Vision. Advances in Computer Vision and Pattern Recognition. Springer, London (2013). https://doi.org/10.1007/978-1-4471-4640-7_7
6. Li, G., et al.: Hand gesture recognition based on convolution neural network. Clust. Comput. **22**(2), 2719–2729 (2017). https://doi.org/10.1007/s10586-017-1435-x
7. Brock, H., Sabanovic, S., Nakamura, K., Gomez, R.: Robust real-time hand gestural recognition for non-verbal communication with tabletop robot haru. In: 2020 29th IEEE International Conference on Robot and Human Interactive Communication (RO-MAN), pp. 891–898. IEEE (2020)
8. Ke, W., Li, W., Ruifeng, L., Lijun, Z.: Real-time hand gesture recognition for service robot. In: 2010 International Conference on Intelligent Computation Technology and Automation, vol. 2, pp. 976–979. IEEE (2010)
9. Castellano, G., Cervelione, A., Cianciotta, M., De Carolis, B., Vessio, G.: Recognizing the waving gesture in the interaction with a social robot. In: 2020 29th IEEE International Conference on Robot and Human Interactive Communication (RO-MAN), pp. 733–738. IEEE (2020)
10. Victor, D.: Handtrack: A library for prototyping real-time hand tracking interfaces using convolutional neural networks. GitHub Repos. **3**, 6 (2017)
11. Pandey, A.K., Gelin, R.: A mass-produced sociable humanoid robot: pepper: the first machine of its kind. IEEE Robot. Autom. Mag. **25**, 40–48 (2018)
12. Tanaka, F., Isshiki, K., Takahashi, F., Uekusa, M., Sei, R., Hayashi, K.: Pepper learns together with children: development of an educational application. Humanoids **2015**, 270–275 (2015)
13. Castellano, G., De Carolis, B., Macchiarulo, N., Rossano, V.: Learning waste recycling by playing with a social robot. In: 2019 IEEE International Conference on Systems, Man and Cybernetics (SMC), pp. 3805–3810. IEEE (2019)
14. Hochreiter, S., Schmidhuber, J.: Long short-term memory. Neural Comput. **9**, 1735–1780 (1997)

Facial Expression Change Recognition on Neutral-Negative Axis Based on Siamese-Structure Deep Neural Network

Junyao Zhang(✉), Kei Shimonishi, Kazuaki Kondo, and Yuichi Nakamura

Kyoto University, Kyoto, Japan
zhang.junyao.65m@st.kyoto-u.ac.jp, shimonishi@i.kyoto-u.ac.jp

Abstract. Facial expressions are very crucial in everyday communication, since a person's internal state of emotion swings can be assessed based on changes in expressions. Because there have been previous studies on positive expressions, and people with diseases are more inclined to show negative expressions, we focused our study on negative expressions. And we provided a new objective measure of facial expression that can be applied to dementia care, rehabilitation support, QOL assessment, etc. We analyzed the process of "change" in facial expressions for obtaining the degree of negative expressions, rather than the extreme facial expressions previously studied in various fields. Unfortunately, since there is no database on expression change picture sequences, we collected a small-scale database on our own in the experiment. We applied Siamese-structure deep neural network for classification of the pictures. The results show that the muscle parts affected by the change of facial expressions from neutral to negative, such as lip corners and forehead, can also be extracted accurately by the network, and a recognition accuracy of over 92% is obtained.

Keywords: Facial expression change · Siamese network · HRQOL

1 Introduction

Face is a mirror of the soul, reading face is a useful and essential to estimate person's internal emotion states. This kind of "reading" is crucial not only in socialization, but also in doctor-patient relationship. For example, dementia becomes one of the main causes of disability in elderly, which has led to verbal communication with them becoming increasingly difficult, and they needed to communicate with more often through non-verbal means. Therefore, automatically detecting human's facial expressions to analyze their inner emotions is desirable for families or caregivers to understand the patients' true feelings in a timely manner.

To trace face and analyze expressions in daily life, our research aim is to construct axes connecting two different expressions in expression space. Through

P.-L. P. Rau (Ed.): HCII 2022, LNCS 13314, pp. 583–598, 2022.
https://doi.org/10.1007/978-3-031-06053-3_40

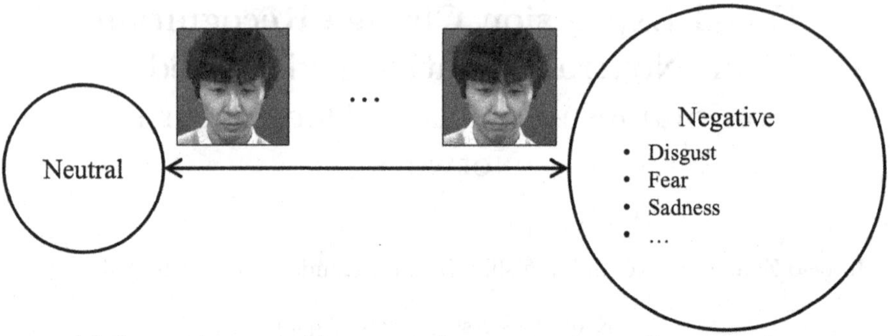

(a) One axis connected from neutral expression to negative expressions.

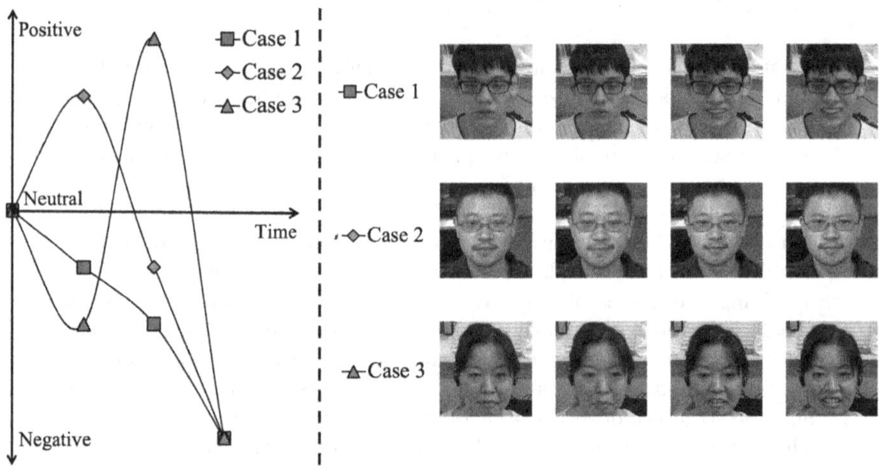

(b) There may be multiple ways to change the expression from neutral to negative.

Fig. 1. Neutral - Negative expression axis.

these axes, we can obtain the intensity of expressions represented by any point in this space. In this paper, we pay special attention to the neutral-negative axis, because patients tend to show negative expressions more often. To find this axis, intermediate expression needs to be recognized because the axis is made up of the points represented by the intermediate expressions. While current facial expression recognition (FER) methods mainly focus on clear expressions, for example, methods that analyzing the movement of facial muscles [1], or extracting features by machine learning [2–4]. To recognize intermediate expressions, we borrow the idea from Kondo et al. [5], which comparison based method can be used to obtain the smiling level by recognizing facial expression changes. And, we extend the application of the network to neutral-negative expression axis.

On this neutral-negative axis (see Fig. 1(a)), we connect the neutral expression and negative expression, and can arrange the facial expression images in order to get different expression intensity. For facial expression changes, there are non-linear transitions, as shown in Fig. 1(b) for Case 2 and Case 3, where the former first goes from neutral expression to positive expression and then drops to negative expression; the latter first drops from neutral expression, followed by a relatively larger expression fluctuation, rising to positive expression, and finally dropping to negative expression again. There are also linear transitions existed as in Case 1, with a gradual decline from neutral expression to negative expression. Although the transition is not always monotonic, we assume that a linear monotonic expression change sequence can be obtained by cutting the non-monotonic sequence.

2 Related Work

This research is closely related to the 3 branches of study; Emotion and expression, Facial action coding system (FACS), and facial expression recognition (FER).

2.1 Emotion and Expression

In 1964, Tomkins and McCarter [6] demonstrated that facial expressions were reliably associated with certain emotional states. When a person perceives certain emotions, such as smiling and frowning, facial muscles will make corresponding movements, these muscles are commonly called muscles of facial expression, their specific location and attachments enable them to produce movements of the face. Based on this, the American psychologist P. Ekman et al. [7] first defined 7 basic emotion expressions, that is anger, disgust, fear, enjoyment, sadness, surprise and contempt.

2.2 Facial Action Coding System

With the development and in-depth study of facial expressions. They proposed the Facial Action Coding System (FACS) [8], which interprets expressions by analyzing the motion features and regions of corresponding facial action units. Facial muscles are like pieces in a jigsaw puzzle, and by moving them to quantitatively analyze the true emotions of the puzzle's owner.

Subsequently, in recent years, Facial action unit (AU) provide information in describing comprehensive facial expression, such as enjoyment is calculated from the combination of AU6 and AU12, separately describes *Cheek Raiser* and *Lip Corner Puller*, correlated to orbicularis oculi and zygomatic major muscle. K. Zhao et al. [9] proposed deep region and multi-label learning (DRML), which is able to identify more specific regions for different AUs than conventional patch-based methods. The important innovation in DRML is the use of a feed-forward function to induce the network to focus on the crucial regions, and better classification accuracy was obtained by constructing relationships between important facial regions and multiple AUs. J. He et al. [10] designed

CNN models to do facial view recognition and AU occurrence recognition, and achieved 97.7% accuracy in 9 facial views classification. In the next year, A. Romero et al. [11] took advantages of the ability of CNN to do large-scale classification, presented HydraNets and AUNets and did detection and classification on 12 different AUs. G. M. Jacob et al. [12] used the now-hot transformer to classify AU, and achieved absolute improvement on BP4D and DISFA datasets, which contain input images and action unit labels.

2.3 Facial Expression Recognition

Recognition for Clear Expressions. To extract suitable and accurate features is crucial for FER research, for features are important basis for classification. And expression feature extraction is mainly based on mathematical models to extract the continuous deformation and the muscle movement of different regions on the face. For example, Gabor wavelet method [13] and Local Binary Pattern (LBP) operator method [14] for single image, and optical flow method [15] for dynamic sequence.

The great achievement of deep learning in the field of image recognition has provided a new idea for FER. Unlike the traditional approach, deep networks can perform FER using an end-to-end approach, the network can then directly output the predicted probability for each sample. In addition to the end-to-end learning approach, another option is to use deep neural networks (especially CNNs) as a feature extraction tool and then apply additional independent classifiers, such as SVM or random forests.

Most applications of deep learning in face expression recognition are based on VGGNet, GoogleNet and ResNet network models, whose core structure is a deep convolutional neural network (DCNN). Dynamic sequence FER adds analysis of temporal and spatial changes in expressions. And most approaches focus on identifying expressions with peak emotional intensity in a sequence, while ignoring frames with low amplitude emotional expression. This causes several frames with obvious expressions can be accurately recognized, but how expressions change in this sequence cannot be gotten. However, expression intensity-invariant networks, such as peak-piloted deep network (PPDN) [16] and deeper cascaded peak-piloted network (DCPN) [17], or Siamese network [5] can identify trends in expression changes. The former by identifying correlations between frames of different intensities in a sequence, and the latter by comparison, which introduced later in detail. 3D CNN proposed by Ji et al. [18] to capture motion information encoded in multiple adjacent frames for action recognition through 3D convolutions make it possible to recognize dynamic expression changes. In order to capture the differences in expressions over time, a model that can do the comparison between two temporally continuous or non-continuous face images is needed.

Recognition for Intermediate Expressions. In contrast to recognition for clear expressions, there are less research on intermediate expression recognition. A. Toisoul et al. [19] have used jointed face alignment networks and emotion classification networks to estimate the emotion categories of faces under naturalistic conditions as well as their continuous values of valence and arousal levels, and have obtained quite good results. Even though the datasets they used, AffectNet, SEWA and AFEW-VA, have lots of ambiguity in the rating of valence and arousal levels, they still give us inspiration to study the trends of expression intensity change.

And our group has developed comparison-based techniques to detect the changes in facial expression [5]. Kondo et al.successfully classified the smile level by applying Siamese-structure neural network on expression change sequences. The network received two preprocessed face images as inputs, and output two feature vectors. Then rather than calculated the distance between vectors in traditional Siamese network, they applied a sequence of fully connected layers to receive them, and output two likelihood values corresponding to ascension and descension labels relative to the degree of smiling. And this network achieved >95% accuracy in recognizing smiling changes under the reasonable attention regions that contributed to the predicted labels, such as mouth, cheeks, and the tail of eyes.

3 Siamese-structure Deep Neural Network

As introduced in Sect. 1, we apply the comparison-based network proposed by Kondo et al. [5] to solve our problem. Because Siamese network is used for measuring the similarity of two things, such as the application in face verification [25], semantic similarity analysis of vocabulary [26], etc., in order to make it can recognize the changes in expression, a image classification network is attached after. Figure 2 shows the structure, two Images I_0 and I_0 with ground truth (abbreviated as G.T.) y_0 and y_1 respectively, were fed into two identical CNNs (here, VGG16 is employed) with the same weight parameters. Following this, the extracted feature vectors were input into two fully connected layers with rectified linear units, finally output the predicted likelihood values $\hat{y}_0$ and $\hat{y}_1$. The ground truth likelihood values (y_0, y_1) can be considered as a two-dimensional one-hot vector, when I_0 show more negative expression, its corresponding element y_0 is set to be 0, the other element y_1 is set to 1, and vice versa. And, we define the predicted labels as follow:

- $\hat{y}_0 > \hat{y}_1$ means I_1 is predicted with more negative expression than I_0;
- conversely, $\hat{y}_0 < \hat{y}_1$ predicts that I_0 displays more negative expression.

For the sample in Fig. 2, $y_0 = 1, y_1 = 0$, because I_0 displayed more negative expression. If the network outputs the label $\hat{y}_0 > \hat{y}_1$, the prediction is correct, and vice versa.

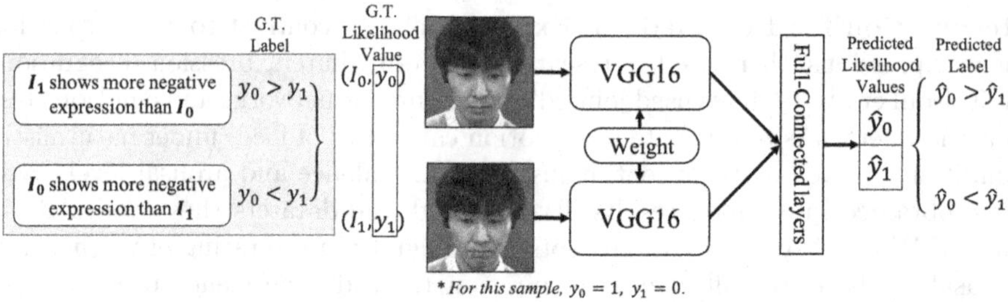

Fig. 2. Siamese-structure deep neural network.

4 Experimental Method and Construction of Data Sets

In the experiment, we invited a total of 11 subjects (male: female = 8: 3). Based on the assumption stated before, we collected the sequence data of facial expression changes by showing the visual stimuli to subjects. 76 groups of image pairs are used as visual stimuli, samples are shown in Fig. 3, and displayed on the liquid crystal display (LCD) monitor (D491UB | DOSHISHA, 4K, 3840 × 2160, 49inches).

(a) Tiny room - messy room.
(b) Normal yogurt - spoiled yogurt.
(c) Dolphins in clean ocean - dirty river.
(d) Cute birds - disgust worm.

Fig. 3. Four pairs of samples from visual stimuli used in the experiment.

Meanwhile, video camera (SONY HDR-CX630) was fixed directly front to recorded subject's facial expressions. During the experiment, subject sit on chair and faced the monitor, after a detailed description of this experiment, one pair of neutral image and negative image would be displayed on the screen for 10 s each in turn after a 3 s-countdown, this procedure is shown as Fig. 4. When the time was up, the next pair would be automatically played until the end of the experiment. The facial expression is expected to be changed from neutral/positive to negative under the influence of images. To prevent the surrounding sounds from interfering with them, a pair of wireless headsets playing white noise was worn.

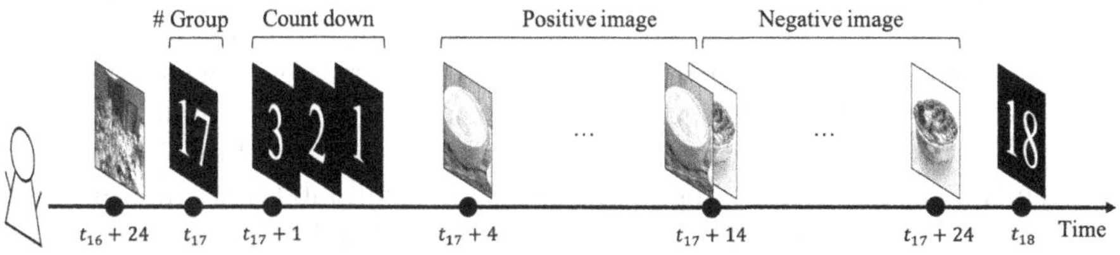

Fig. 4. The procedure of experiment.

We conducted the experiment and collected the dataset. The dataset includes changes in facial expressions from neutral to negative elicited by visual stimuli under laboratory conditions, with a higher level of labeling accuracy.

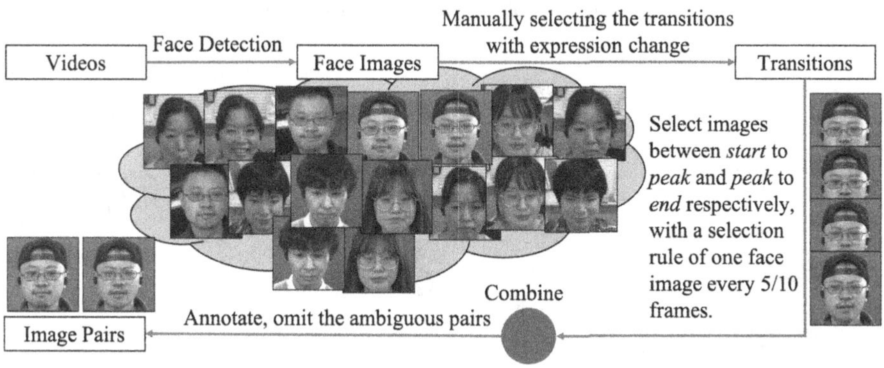

Fig. 5. Preprocessing process.

The original data in dataset are video data, in order to obtain the input required for the deep neural network model, the video data need to be preprocessed as follows (see Fig. 5). Firstly, apply face detection, face alignment and face cutting to get face images. Secondly, manually select expression change sequences of no more than 20 s, and record the start frame (where the expression began), peak frame (where the expression intensity reaches its maximum) and end frame (where the expression ended) of each sequence, the frame rate is 30 frame per second. Thirdly, select 1 frame every 5 or 10 frames in the (start, peak) frame and (peak, end) frame interval respectively, then combine every two frames to get image pairs. After annotating and omitting the ambiguous pairs by human, clear image pairs with obvious difference expressions were finally remained.

Even though we expected expression change to happen when the image change from neutral to negative inside one image pair, when confronting with even the same image, different person will be stimulated with different internal emotions, thus affected in different external expressions. Sometimes we cannot collect expected number of sequences, because of expression change was not observed or appeared several times. The reason for the former one is sometimes emotional intensity is not strong enough to have changes in face visible to the naked eye. For the later one is the presence of intermittent facial expression changes. To illustrate in more detail, in response to a set of stimuli, subjects may exhibit two or more expression changes and there is a certain time interval between two changes. According to the follow-up small interview, this situation is most likely to occur due to the following reason. The first expression change was caused by the subconscious feeling of shock and disgust or displeasure when suddenly facing a negative stimulus on the monitor, while the subsequent expression changes were caused by the internal emotion fluctuation due to thinking. For example, in Fig. 3(c), from dolphins swimming in clean and clear ocean to a child walking in a dirty river polluted by garbage, the subject's first reaction was the disgusting emotion produced by the visual stimulus of clean (blue) to dirty (black) water, but after thinking or associating with the living conditions of the local people, the emotion of sadness would appear.

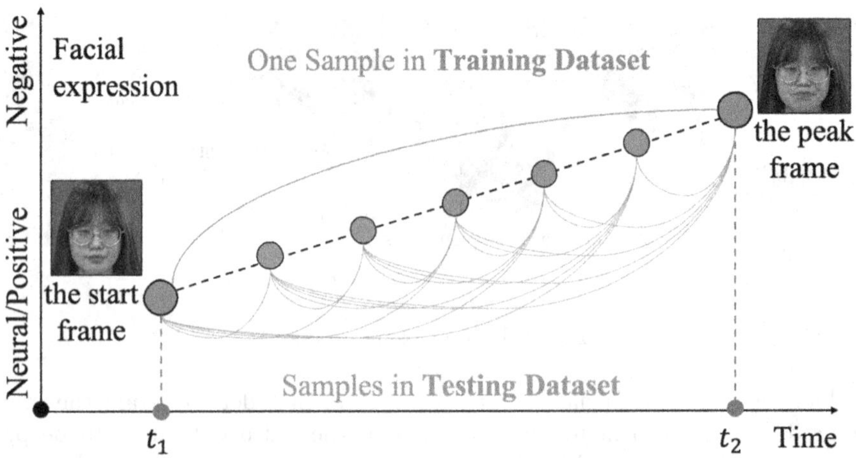

Fig. 6. Training dataset and testing dataset.

For training deep neural network, we need to separate the input image pairs into three parts; training set, validation set and testing set. Training dataset and validation dataset use the (start, peak) and (peak, end) frames in facial expression transitions, the start and peak frame image pair are connected with the orange line in Fig. 6; testing dataset uses the combination of frames inside expression transitions, select one frame every five frames, shown as the blue points in Fig. 6. As a result, we obtained 1360 training samples.

5 Results

15-Folds cross-validator is used in the training process. We obtained the training accuracy on basic data set

$$\frac{\#\text{Correct Classified Samples}}{\#\text{Whole Samples}} = \frac{1263}{1360} = 92.87\%.$$

To validate the region of interest (ROI) of the neural network, we visualize the images on the validation set using the Gradient-weighted class activation mapping (Grad-CAM) to see which pixels at which locations in the image have a strong influence on the output. Grad-CAM calculate the weights through global average of gradients.

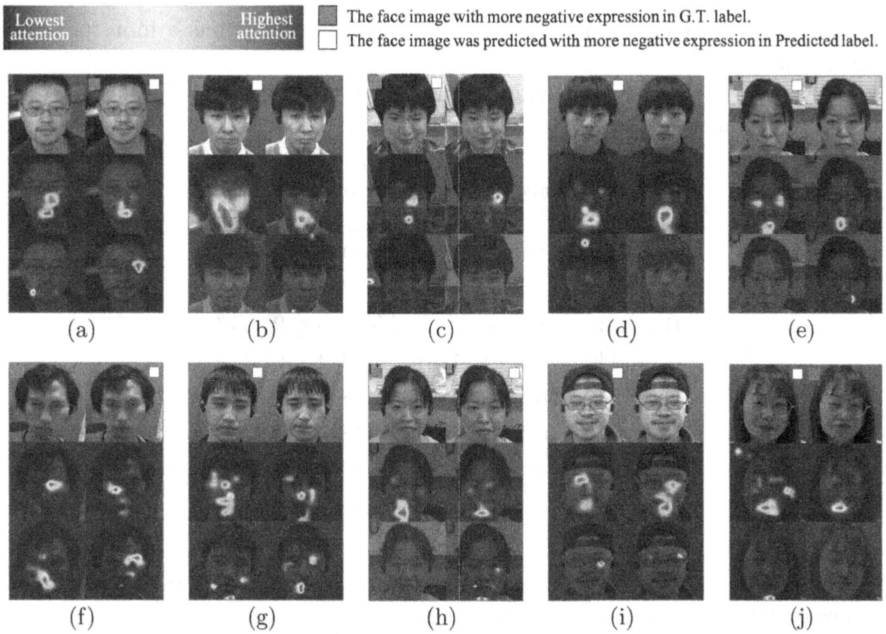

Fig. 7. Recognized samples from training dataset with Grad-CAM. In each sample, the top row displays two input images. The middle and the bottom rows indicate contribution maps corresponding to the predicted label and the discarded label in the estimation, respectively.

Figure 7 shows 10 samples. The upper left of the figure shows the heatmap colorbar, with different colors from left to right meaning from lowest attention to highest attention, used to visualize the importance of the regions on which the network relies in recognition. Two squares in red and white are shown on the upper right, indicating image with more negative expressions in ground truth and prediction, respectively. When the two squares appear on the same image, meaning the more negative one in this pair can be correctly recognized, instead, it is incorrectly recognized. For each sample, the top row shows two images I_0 and I_1 input to the network, and the red and white squares are displayed on the images, the middle row and the bottom row shows the attention regions that contributed to the predicted label and discarded label by contribution maps, respectively. Figure 7(a)∼(e) are correctly recognized samples, from the middle row, attention regions spread of mouth, nose and eyes; from the bottom row, attention to small and meaningless regions such as hair, brow, neck and mouth corners contributed to the discarded label. This results are convincing according to FACS. Figure 7(f)∼(j) are incorrectly recognized samples, which can be classified into two cases. One is two input images with a relatively high degree of similarity, such as Fig. 7(f), as with the middle row, the presence of meaningful ROI contributes to the discarded labels; another is the sample imbalance within the dataset, such as Fig. 7(g)∼(j), although the differences can be accurately identified, it is not possible to determine which one has a more negative expression.

Due to the existence of individual differences, we calculated the classification accuracy for each subject separately, as shown in Table 1.

Table 1. Classification accuracy on each subject.

#Sub	#Sample	Accuracy
A	Fig. 7(a), Fig. 7(i)	311/332 ≈ 93.67%
B	Fig. 7(b)	176/178 ≈ 98.88%
C	Fig. 7(c), Fig. 7(g)	207/224 ≈ 92.41%
D	Fig. 7(d)	52/58 ≈ 89.66%
E	Fig. 7(e), Fig. 7(h)	38/58 ≈ 65.52%
F	Fig. 7(f)	71/80 ≈ 88.75%
G	Fig. 7(j)	153/162 ≈ 94.44%

What causes such low classification accuracy? For subjects E and F, we analyzed them separated as follows:

- E: The change in expression of Subject E was mainly focused on the lip and lip corner, the ambiguous change around lip and samples that facial expression change from positive and negative are less in training set, these two reasons lead to such low classification accuracy, see Fig. 8(a).
- F: Subject F's facial expression is frown and squint, his mouth movement is not obvious. Our training set has more samples of mouth region changes and fewer samples of frowns, and this imbalance of samples might be the cause of low recognition rate, and incorrect region focus, see Fig. 8(b).

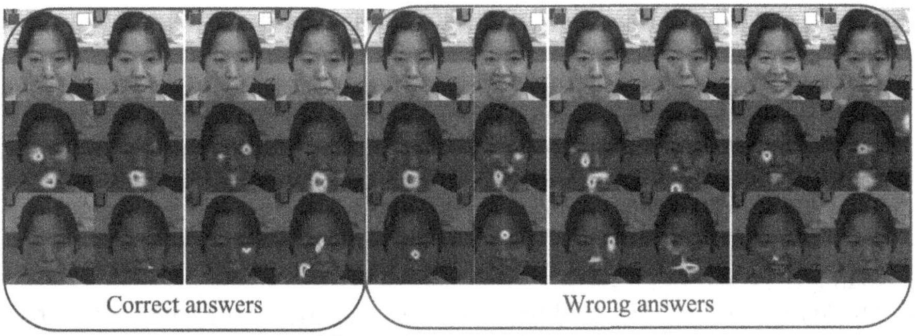

(a) Results from Subject E

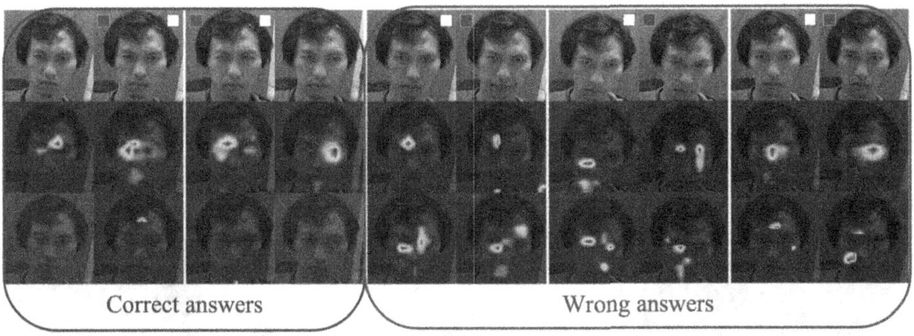

(b) Results from Subject F

Fig. 8. Presentation of the results for subjects E and F with low classification accuracy. Training data and results were visualized using Grad-CAM. The left two samples show the correct answers, the right three samples show the wrong answers.

We test the trained weigh model on the testing dataset, Fig. 9 shows one correct classification case, where whole image pairs in this sequence are correctly classified. and Fig. 10 shows two wrong cases, where some image pairs in the sequence are incorrectly classified.

Take Fig. 9 as an example, we will give a description. This figure can be divided into three parts:

- The left image shows one pair of images ((start, peak) frames) in the training set;
- The middle image shows the confidence map generated by temporal alignment of image pairs in one transition from testing set. The horizontal axis from left to right and the vertical axis from top to bottom both represent all frames arranged in chronological order within an expression transition interval. Each dot represents the recognition result obtained after testing the corresponding two frames on the horizontal and vertical axes through the network. Where (1) blue dot means the correctly recognized image pair, no matter it is in the upper or lower part of the diagonal, which means the predicted label is the same as the ground truth label; (2) red dot means the incorrectly recognized

image pair, which means the predicted label is opposite of the ground truth label.

- For (start, peak) pairs: blue dot means $\hat{y}_0 > \hat{y}_1$ below the diagonal, and $\hat{y}_0 < \hat{y}_1$ above the diagonal; red dot means the opposite;
- For (peak, end) pairs: blue dot means $\hat{y}_0 < \hat{y}_1$ below the diagonal, and $\hat{y}_0 > \hat{y}_1$ above the diagonal; red dot means the opposite.

The shades of red/blue indicate the confidence value, the more red/blue the color, the higher the confidence value; the whiter the color, the lower the confidence value.

– The left image with blue and red rectangles displays some results with Grad-CAM visualization.

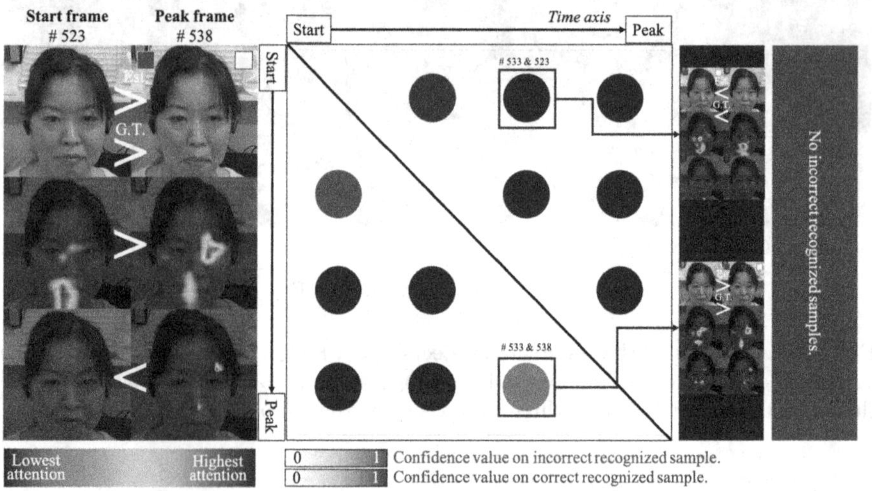

(a) Analysis of the results between frame (523, 538) of Subject E in the testing dataset.

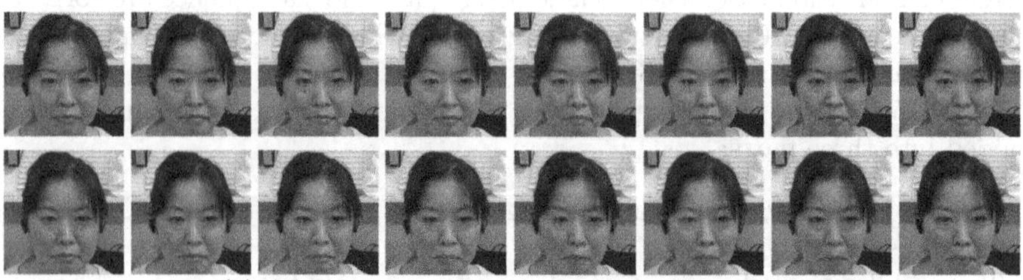

(b) All face images from frame 523 to frame 538.

Fig. 9. Correct classified case.

For the sequence in Fig. 9(b), the expression change from neural (start) to negative (peak). By the fact that the color of all the dots in the confidence map is blue, all pairs of face images obtained at every 5 frames within the sequence can be correctly recognized. Therefore, we can illustrate that the expression within the sequence change linearly, since each face image expressed more negative expression than the previous one.

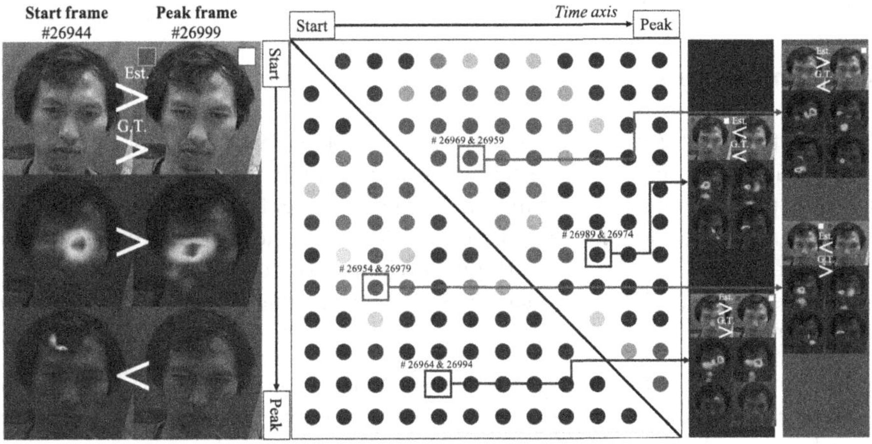

(a) Analysis of the results between frame (26944, 26999) of Subject F in the testing set.

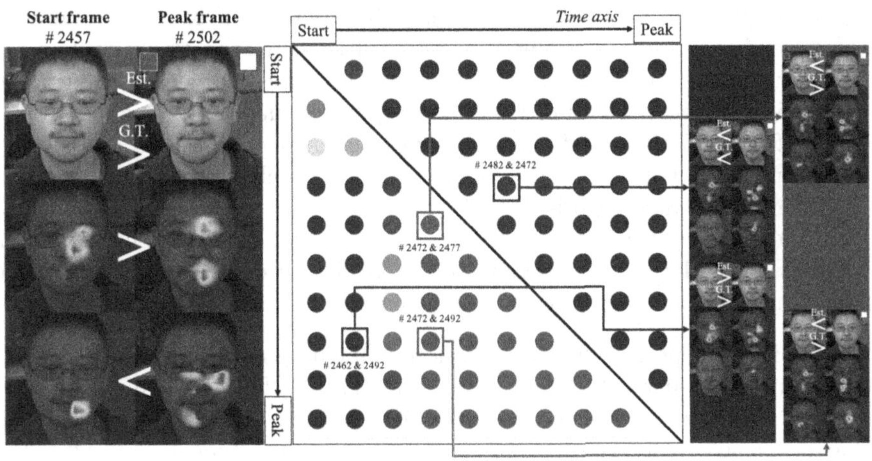

(b) Analysis of the results between frame (2457, 2502) of Subject A in the testing dataset.

Fig. 10. Wrong classified cases with symmetrical misclassification and triangular misclassification.

Figure 10(a) shows the symmetrical misclassification, meaning the wrong answers appears on both sides of the diagonal, the data that fit closely to the diagonal are characterized by a high degree of similarity between the two face images, the reason for this wrong case is probably corresponding to the non-linear transition exists in this sequence. Although we assume the image sequences in our dataset are linear after processing, in Sect. 1, this processing is all based on manual work, and perhaps there are some non-linear changes hidden in these sequences that are not classified by humans. And, Fig. 10(b) shows the triangular misclassification, which means only one side of the data can be classified correctly, while most of the data on the other side of the diagonal cannot be classified correctly, which is probably due to the overfitting.

6 Conclusions

We collected a dataset on expression changes and achieved superior recognition results based on a comparative deep neural network approach on the recognition of expression changes that are on the neutral-negative expression axis. The network used the difference in features at lip corner and forehead of the person in the two images as a key to distinguish whether there is a negative change or not. However, more definite conclusions will be possible when we can take care of three existing problems:

- Inaccurate manual splitting of image sequences. According to visual stimuli, there are non-linear changes in the sequence of expression changes, so it needs to be manually segmented again to cut the non-linear changes into multiple linear changes. However, this manual segmentation will have certain errors.
- The samples in the dataset are unevenly distributed; for example, some subjects tend to make frowns when they are subjected to negative stimuli; some subjects tend to make frowning facial gestures when subjected to negative stimuli, while others tend to make facial gestures such as tugging at the corners of their mouths, and the inconsistent number of frowning and tugging facial pictures will lead to the model's inaccurate classification of a smaller number of sample categories.
- Overfitting is occurred due to the small size of the data set. This issue was addressed by data augmentation, but more data are still needed to achieve more accurate and generalizable conclusions.

Future work will specifically split the more ambiguous classification of negative expressions into clear sub-categories such as disgust, fear, etc., and add positive expressions to explore the variation of expressions on different expression combination axes with the help of Russell's circumplex model [27]. After the implementation into the monitoring device, the patients with dementia will be monitored in real time and suggestions will be given to improve HRQOL in response to their expression changes.

References

1. Ekman, P., Friesen, W., Hager, J.: Facial action coding system (FACS). A human face (2002)
2. Vasudeva, K., Chandran, S.: A comprehensive study on facial expression recognition techniques using convolutional neural network. In: International Conference on Communication and Signal Processing, pp. 1431–1436. IEEE, Chennai, India (2020)

3. Zhang, K., Zhang, Z., Li, Z., Qiao, Y.: Joint face detection and alignment using multitask cascaded convolutional networks. IEEE Signal Process. Lett. **23**(10), 1499–1503 (2016)
4. Zhang, K., Huang, Y., Du, Y., et al.: Facial expression recognition based on deep evolutional spatial-temporal networks. IEEE Trans. Image Process. **26**(9), 4193–4203 (2017)
5. Kondo, K., Nakamura, T., Nakamura, Y., Satoh, S.: Siamese- structure deep neural network recognizing changes in facial expression according to the degree of smiling. In: 25th International Conference on Pattern Recognition (ICPR), pp. 4605–4612. IEEE, Milan, Italy (2021)
6. Tomkins, S.S., McCarter, R.: What and where are the primary affects? some evidence for a theory. Perceptual Motor Skills **18**(1), 119–158 (1964)
7. Ekman, P., Friesen, W.V.: Constants across cultures in the face and emotion. J. Personality Soc. Psychol. **17**(2), 124–129 (1971). https://doi.org/10.1037/h0030377
8. Ekman, P., Friesen, W., Hager, J.: Facial action coding system (FACS). Am. Psychol. Assoc. PsysTests (1978). https://doi.org/10.1037/t27734-000
9. Zhao, K., Chu, W., Zhang, H.: Deep region and multi-label learning for facial action unit detection. In: 2016 IEEE Conference on Computer Vision and Pattern Recognition (CVPR). IEEE, Las Vegas, NV, USA (2016). https://doi.org/10.1109/CVPR.2016.369
10. He, J., Li, D., Yang, B., Cao, S., Sun, B., Yu, L.: Multi view facial action unit detection based on CNN and BLSTM-RNN. In: 2017 12th IEEE International Conference on Automatic Face & Gesture Recognition (FG 2017). IEEE, Washington, DC, USA (2017). https://doi.org/10.1109/FG.2017.108
11. Romero, A., Leon, J., Arbelaez, P.: Multi-view dynamic facial action unit detection. Image Vis. Comput. (2018). https://doi.org/10.1016/j.imavis.2018.09.014
12. Jacob, G.M., Stenger, B.: Facial action unit detection with transformers. In: 2021 IEEE Conference on Computer Vision and Pattern Recognition (CVPR). IEEE, Nashville, TN, USA (2021). https://doi.org/10.1109/CVPR46437.2021.00759
13. Vinay Kumar, B., Shreyas, B.S.: Face recognition using gabor wavelets. In: Fortieth Asilomar Conference on Signals, Systems and Computers. IEEE, Pacific Grove, CA (2007). https://doi.org/10.1109/ACSSC.2006.354817
14. Zhang, G., Huang, X., Li, S.Z., Wang, Y., Wu, X.: Boosting Local Binary Pattern (LBP)-Based Face Recognition. Advances in Biometric Person Authentication. SINOBIOMETRICS 2004. Lecture Notes in Computer Science **3338**, 179–186 (2004)
15. Ranftl, A., Alonso-Fernandez, F., Karlsson, S.: Face tracking using optical flow. In: 2015 International Conference of the Biometrics Special Interest Group (BIOSIG), pp. 1–5. IEEE, Darmstadt, Germany (2015). https://doi.org/10.1109/BIOSIG.2015.7314604
16. Zhao, X., Liang, X., Liu, L., Li, T.: Peak-piloted deep network for facial expression recognition. In: 14th European Conference on Computer Vision (ECCV), pp. 425–442. Amsterdam, The Netherlands (2016)
17. Yu, Z., Liu, Q., Liu, G.: Deeper cascaded peak-piloted network for weak expression recognition. Vis. Comput. **34**(12), 1691–1699 (2017). https://doi.org/10.1007/s00371-017-1443-0
18. Ji, S., Xu, W., Yang, M., Yu, K.: 3D convolutional neural networks for human action recognition. IEEE Trans. Pattern Anal. Mach. Intell. **35**(1), 221–231 (2013)

19. Toisoul, A., Kossaifi, J., Bulat, A., Tzimiropoulos, G., Pantic, M.: Estimation of continuous valence and arousal levels from faces in naturalistic conditions. Nature Mach. Intell. **3**, 42–50 (2021)
20. Ramkumar, G., Logashanmugam, E.: An effectual facial expression recognition using HMM. In: 2016 International Conference on Advanced Communication Control and Computing Technologies (ICACCCT), pp. 12–15. IEEE, Ramanathapuram, India (2016). https://doi.org/10.1109/ICACCCT.2016.7831590
21. Cohen, I., Sebe, N., Gozman, F.G., Cirelo, M.C., Huang, T.S.: Learning Bayesian network classifiers for facial expression recognition both labeled and unlabeled data. In: 2003 IEEE Computer Society Conference on Computer Vision and Pattern Recognition, pp. I-I. IEEE, Madison, WI, USA (2003). https://doi.org/10.1109/CVPR.2003.1211408
22. Khalifa, H., Babiker, B., Goebel, R., Cheng, I.: Facial expression recognition using SVM classification on mic-macro patterns. In: 2017 IEEE International Conference on Image Processing (ICIP), pp. 1757–1761. IEEE, Beijing, China (2017). https://doi.org/10.1109/ICIP.2017.8296583
23. Wang, X.H., Liu, A., Zhang, S.Q.: New facial expression recognition based on FSVM and KNN. Optik **126**(21), 3132–3234 (2015)
24. Li, J., Lam, E.Y.: Facial expression recognition using deep neural networks. In: 2015 IEEE International Conference on Imaging Systems and Techniques (IST), pp. 1–6. IEEE, Macau, China (2015).https://doi.org/10.1109/IST.2015.7294547
25. Nair, V., Hinton, G.E.: Rectified linear units improve restricted Boltzmann machines. In: the 27th International Conference on International Conference on Machine Learning (ICML), pp. 807–814 (2010). https://doi.org/10.5555/3104322.3104425
26. Kenter, T., Borisow, A., Rijke, M.D.: Siamese cbow: optimizing word embeddings for sentence representations. In: the 54th Annual Meeting of the Association for Computational Linguistics, pp. 941–951 (2016). https://doi.org/10.18653/v1/P16-1089
27. Russell, J.A.: A circumplex model of affect. J. Personality Soc. Psychol. **39**(6), 1161–1178 (1980)

Recognition of Weird Tone in Chinese Communication and Improvement of Language Understanding for AI

Ran Zhao and Zhe Chen(✉)

Beijing University of Aeronautics and Astronautics, 37 Xueyuan Road, Beijing 100191, Haidian District, People's Republic of China
zhechen@buaa.edu.cn

Abstract. A weird tone called "yin yang guai qi" has become popular among Chinese youth, especially among Internet surfers. No matter in tone or in emotion, "yin yang guai qi" is very similar to satirical tone, but has its own prosody, phrasing and emotion. Its distinctive linguistic features and unique connotation understanding make it of great significance for research. In this paper, we obtain the audio samples with "yin yang guai qi" tone from some short video websites and reading audio websites. From the acoustic perspective, we judge its existence, and use MLP neural network to simply identify the "yin yang guai qi" tone. Finally, we briefly analyze its application prospect. The results show that the "yin yang guai qi" tone does exist and has very distinct prosodic modulations that can be identified by simple deep learning algorithms. This research focuses on the preliminary exploration of "yin yang guai qi", which has certain reference value in the future research in this field and the application of artificial intelligence.

Keywords: "yin yang guai qi" · MLP algorithm · Identification · AI

1 Introduction

In recent years, a new tone called "yin yang guai qi" has become popular in China. "yin yang guai qi" refers to an eccentric and cold attitude, making sarcastic remarks from the side in a strange tone. This term first appeared in Cao Yu's *Peking Man* -- "Which one of them is trying to please me? Which one of them isn't 'yin yang guai qi' (weird) ?" Through word-for-word translation, "yin yang" means having two different meanings at the same time; "guai qi" refers to a strange and abnormal tone of voice. The core of "yin yang guai qi" is suppression and ridicule. The form of it is not to speak frankly and swear in a roundabout way with sarcasm, anger, and hatred [1]. For example, in a popular TV series recently, there is a line: "If you fail the make-up exam for graduation, you will be a primary school student forever young. Very good." This is a typical "yin yang guai qi literature", which means "If you fail the make-up exam, you'll end up with a despised primary school diploma."

"yin yang guai qi" has become an Internet trend that is hard to stop, gaining popularity on the Internet among young people. The surface reason for this way of speaking

P.-L. P. Rau (Ed.): HCII 2022, LNCS 13314, pp. 599–607, 2022.
https://doi.org/10.1007/978-3-031-06053-3_41

without directly expressing dirty words may be influenced by the increasingly strict Internet blocking system. People can't just say what they want online. Some explicit and vulgar expressions can easily be reported or blocked. At the same time, well-educated youngsters are reluctant to swear too plainly. The euphemistic and more ironic "yin yang guai qi literature" is favored by them. The deeper reason may be that it is a form of young people's rebellion against tradition and authority, catharsis and self-amusement, which is a manifestation of youth subculture in language communication [1].

It is necessary to distinguish some similar concepts. The first is sarcasm. Sarcasm refers to the use of artistic techniques to expose, criticize and attack some mistakes and weaknesses, in order to make people have a more distinct, deep and clear understanding of these mistakes and weaknesses. "yin yang guai qi" can be interpreted as part of satire. It is a lateral sarcasm with ironic connotations. But the emotions expressed are not only sarcasm, but also anger, abuse and so on. Besides, we also need to distinguish between irony. Irony expresses the exact opposite of what is actually meant. In fact, most of the "yin yang guai qi" is an application of irony, such as the example I gave above. But the purpose of "yin yang guai qi" is more to express sarcastic feelings than to speak with irony. For example, there are some "yin yang guai qi" sentences like "hehe" and "Is that all?" Their tone was sardonic, but they didn't express their contrary meaning.

As for the special speaking style of "yin yang guai qi", it has only clearly appeared in China at present. In foreign countries, there are few researches on such intonation, and most scholars' researches focus on sarcasm and irony. In fact, there are three main types of irony expression, which are lexical (for example, the use of exaggerated adjectives and adverbs), non-verbal (for example, facial expressions), and prosodic modulations [2, 3]. Among them, the research on prosodic modulations is more comprehensive and meticulou. Many studies have shown that Support Vector Machine (SVM) is the best and the most commonly used AMLA for sarcasm detection, especially using Twitter samples. Besides, lexical pragmatic frequency and part-of-speech tagging can improve the accuracy of SVM results [4]. There are also some researches on facial expressions (pictures and the like). To identify sarcastic facial expressions, the proposed FSO-based LSTM architecture using the CK + dataset is applied. In addition, The user's mood changes among sarcasm such as rude, polite, furious, and impassive can be identifed with this model [5].

Among the related researches, the research on ironic pronunciation is more extensive. It is proving that in different languages ironic speeches are acoustically differentiated from literal speech, and these modulations display as a cue for the listener to identify these words as irony [3, 6]. In particular, several researches suggest that prosody (intonation, rhythm, phrasing etc.) is an important cue for understanding sarcasm [7]. Concerning, Some important acoustic parameters, such as fundamental frequency (F0), amplitude, speed of speech, sound quality and ultra vowel clarity, are presented of vital importance [2,3,9,10; inter alia]. However, the available data are quite controversial due to differences in research methods, and the specific acoustic parameters that indicate sarcasm cannot be fully determined. For example, some studies show that sarcastic tones are characterized by increased f0 modulations and a global raising of the pitch level and range [10].

The approach to identify "yin yang guai qi" is similar to those above. In this study, we classify and recognize the voice audio of "yin yang guai qi" tone, and analyze its application field. Voiceprint is the acoustic spectrum of the carrier's speech information displayed by the electro-acoustic instrument. It is a biological feature composed of more than 100 characteristic dimensions such as wavelength, frequency and intensity. As the voice print is not as intuitive as the image, it can be drawn and displayed by waveform and spectrogram in practical analysis. In this paper, the characteristics of MEL frequency, MEL cepstrum coefficient MFCC and chroma vector are used to mark the audio, and the deep learning algorithm is used to identify the "yin yang guai qi" tone. The recognition of strange voice has very important application value in life, so we will also make a general analysis and prediction in the second half of the article.

2 Proposed Approach

2.1 Material

The Experimental Group. The experimental group was the audio group with a "yin yang guai qi" tone. In order to make the experimental characteristic and the subsequent identification results more accurate, we set the selection criteria of the experimental group as the audio with a length of about one minute, whose topic contained keywords such as "yin yang guai qi" "yin-yang person". Besides, more than 90% of the audio content used "yin yang guai qi" tone, and most of the hot comments of it were about "yin yang guai qi".

First of all, we chose bilibili website (https://www.bilibili.com/), a short video entertainment platform mainly for young people to create and share videos, as the selection platform for the experimental group samples. The index method of this site was to retrieve the videos containing the search words in the title, so we typed in the search term "yin yang guai qi" to find videos with that word in the title. (Since "yin yang guai qi" is also the group name of a boy band, the search terms were expanded to "yin-yang person", "yin-yang literature" and other related terms.) Since the sample set has subjective and strict screening conditions such as clear pronunciation and almost all lines are in "yin yang guai qi" tone, we adopted manual screening method and selected nearly 20 short videos as experimental samples according to the experimenters and simple interview survey.

Because the small number of samples would lead to the lack of generality of identification results, we chose a life sharing and communication community -- Xiaohongshu APP for secondary sample selection. Xiaohongshu's retrieval algorithm is similar to Bilibili's, so we selected more than 20 short video samples with a length of about one minute using the same selection method. After a simple investigation, these videos had obvious "yin yang guai qi" characteristics. Their sound quality was good and did not affect the judgment of intonation.

Through the two platforms, we screened 41 videos with obvious "yin yang guai qi" features. Since this study is the recognition of "yin yang guai qi" voices, python's audio processing package is used to extract the audio in the 41 videos. We use "yygq - serial number" as the mark of these videos, constituting the experimental group of this experiment.

The Control Group. The control group was the normal tone audio group. The selection criteria of the control group audio was short audio of about one minute in Putonghua with clear pronunciation and no obvious emotions (especially no "yin yang guai qi" tone).

In order to make the recognition result more accurate, we chose the ancient poetry reading as the control sample. Ancient poetry reading was a very standard audio resource with accurate pronunciation, clear pronunciation and dull mood. Choosing reading audio as the control group can clearly show the unique characteristics of "yin yang guai qi" speech. The ancient poetry readers in Ancient Poetry Encyclopedia Website (http://ts300.5156edu.com/) and Good Kids Resource Website (https:// m.ertongzy.com/) are adult male and female, reading with lower or no background music volume. Therefore, the audio in these two websites was selected as the control sample.

The experimenter listened one by one and screened out the audio with slightly high intonation, too long or too short audio time and large background music, and selected 41 ancient poetry reading audio that met the screening conditions. The selected audio lasted about one minute, with clear pronunciation and standard pronunciation. These audio recordings were labeled with "zc-serial number" as the control group of the experiment.

2.2 Procedure

We extracted MFCC and Chroma features from 41 experimental and 41 control audio recordings, and we used a simple deep learning algorithm to recognize the "yin yang guai qi" tone.

Feature Extraction. Feature extraction mainly used Python's Librosa packet. First, we converted all the audio into an array format that can be read and manipulated. Then, we extracted the MFCC and Chroma features of each audio to characterize the audio.

MFCC. It is short for Mel Frequency Cepstrum Coefficient. The Mel Scale is a nonlinear scale based on human auditory perception proposed by Stevens Volkmann in 1937. It is determined by simulating the human ear's perception of speech at different frequencies. Because human beings have different perception abilities for different frequencies of speech. The perception abilities below 1 kHz have a linear relationship with the frequency, while above 1 kHz have a pairwise relationship with the frequency. That is, the higher the frequency, the worse the perception.

The Mel Scale is Expressed by the Following Formula:

$$\mathrm{f_{mel}} = 2595 \times \log 10\,(1 + \mathrm{f}/700) \tag{1}$$

MFCC is a speech signal feature proposed by Mermelstein et al. in 1980 according to human auditory characteristics. By pre-weighting, framing, windowing and so on (Fig. 1) to maximize some information of the speech signal, the extracted characteristic parameters (MFCC) can have good performance. The relationship between MFCC and frequency is nonlinear. With the development of speech signal research,MFCC has proved to be one of the most successful feature description in speech recognition and detection applications [11].

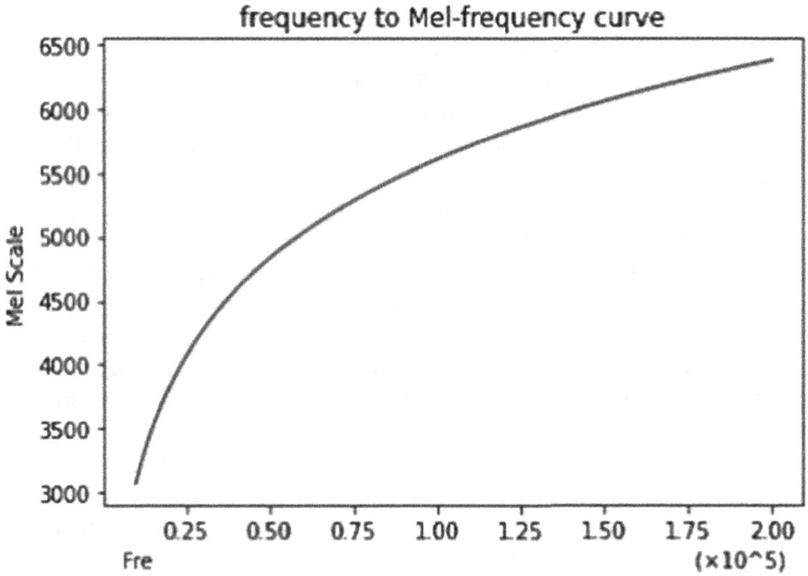

Fig. 1. Frequency converses to Mel frequency

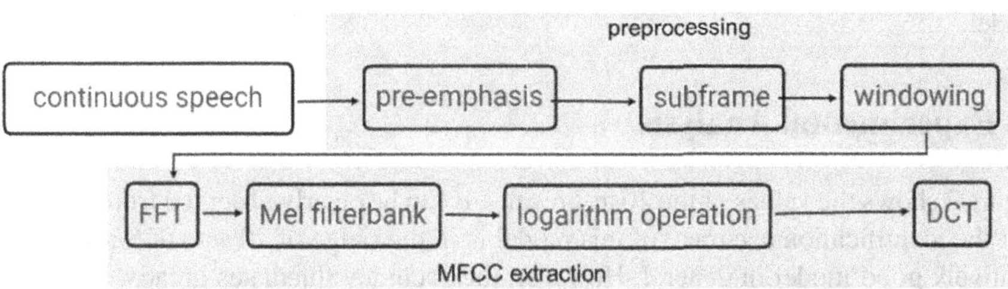

Fig. 2. MFCC Feature Extraction

Chroma. According to the theories of music cognition and psychoacoustics, the perception of tones by human ear is periodic. The two sounds with double sound frequency are similar to human hearing [12]. Based on this, Modern Music Theory defines the octave. In the Twelve-equal Temperament System, the octaves are divided into 12 equal parts according to frequency, and each equal part is called a semitone, which is denoted as C, C#, D, D#, E, F, F#, G, G#, A, A#, B.

The Chroma feature is based on the Twelve-equal Temperament System. The basic principle is that the spectral energy of the original audio signal is quantified into 12 half-order tone classes and the octave is ignored, so that each half-order tone class contains the energy of all octaves of homonyms in that class. So a Chroma feature is usually represented as a 12-dimensional vector, where each vector element corresponds to a semitone. This converts the spectrum of the sound signal into a distribution of its local energy over twelve half-order tones [13].

Chroma feature reduces the interference of noise and non-tonal sound, and has the advantages of good robustness and high discrimination.

Tone Identification. After extracting the speech features, we used the features and a relatively simple deep learning algorithm to identify the "yin yang guai qi" tone. Firstly, all samples were divided into training set and test set in a ratio of 4:1 (Here the samples were randomly assigned in a specified ratio using Python's train_test_split() function). Then, in this study, the MLPClassifier method in Python's sklearn packet was selected. That is, the MLP neural network was used for the identification of the tone.

MultiLayer Perceptron(MLP) is a prefix ANN model, which uses LBFGS or Stochastic Gradient Descent to optimize the logarithm loss function. As a kind of Artificial Neural Network model (ANN), it usually consists of one input layer, one output layer and several hidden layers. The whole process of MLP model construction can be divided into forward propagation and back propagation. Among them, the forward propagation calculates the result and loss value through network structure iteration, and the back propagation is used for parameter optimization to minimize the loss.

In parameter selection, we set alpha = 0.01, batch size = 256, epsilon = 1e-08. We set up a hidden layer with 300 neurons. We chose the learning rate as 'adaptive' and the maximum number of iterations 500.

We use the training set to train the model and the test set to evaluate the accuracy of the model. In order to get a more objective result, we ran the model 20 times. And we recorded the model accuracy each time to observe the accuracy and robustness of the model.

3 Experimental Analysis

Figure 3 shows the values of the 20 test results. It can be clearly observed from the figure that the identification accuracy of this model is in the range of 70% to 95%, which is a relatively good model in general. However, the accuracy fluctuates greatly, sometimes with high accuracy, sometimes with lower accuracy, so the robustness of the model is not good. The mean accuracy is 83.83%. So judging from the mean value, it has certain use value.

Also, it should be noted that we used a very basic ANN model in Python packets, but still got a remarkable result, which shows that the "yin yang guai qi" tone does exist.

However, due to the limitations of the sample, the objectivity of this result is questionable. Even though the number 83.83% is obtained by running 20 times to calculate the mean accuracy of the model, there still exists the limitation of only using 82 samples. So it is difficult to ensure that acceptable results can be obtained after changing the sample set. However, since the focus of this study is not to create a splendid algorithm for the identification of "yin yang guai qi" but only a preliminary attempt, there will be no further discussion on the validity of the algorithm in this report.

To sum up, the result of this study has a good accuracy of 83.83%, but the credibility is quite general.

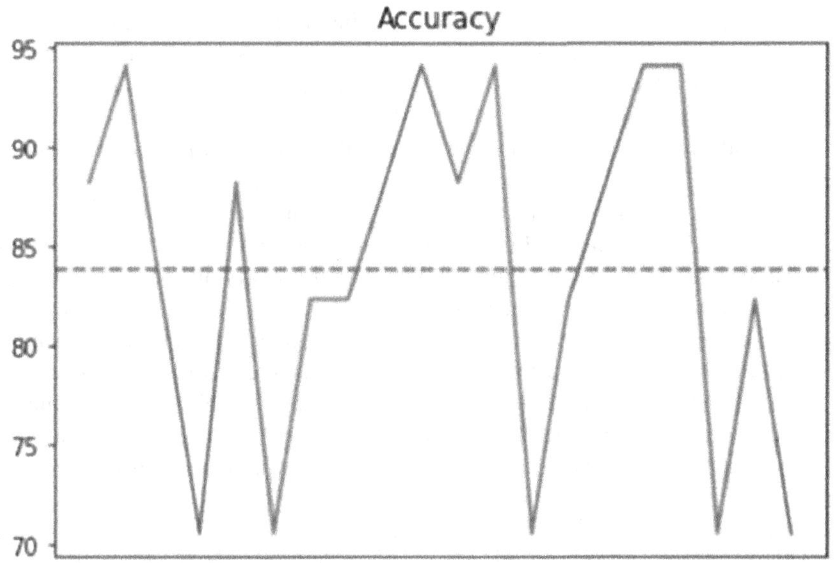

Fig. 3. Accuracy of algorithm

4 General Discussion

4.1 Conclusion

Our study shows that "yin yang guai qi" tone does exist and can be recognized in Chinese. Specifically, according to the identification results of the deep learning algorithm, we can find a significant difference between the "yin yang guai qi" tone and the reading tone. When we compare the differences between the two groups of sounds, it can also be obviously found that the tone of "yin yang guai qi" has obvious characteristics such as inflection and fluctuation of pitch, emphasis on certain words and so on. And this needs to be confirmed by future experiments.

Moreover, the tone of "yin yang guai qi" can be easily identified. Based on the MLP neural network, this study uses Python data package to identify the audio with "yin yang guai qi" voices, and obtains satisfactory results. Of course, it should be admitted that, since the focus of this study is to discover the existence of "yin yang guai qi" and do some preliminary exploration, we did not carry out a complex design for the identification algorithm. Therefore, the following research should focus on the recognition algorithm of this tone.

Thus, we have studied a very interesting tune in Chinese -- "yin yang guai qi", and have carried out a preliminary and simple experiment on it, which is also the value of this paper.

4.2 Application Prospect

Nowadays, the tone of "yin yang guai qi" is used frequently in China, which is slightly heard by the middle-aged and the elderly, but is prevalent among the younger generation.

It is frequently used when teasing friends, arguing with each other and surfing the Internet. This kind of ironic tone may exist in other countries, but we haven't seen any articles discussing it yet. In a word, the discussion of "yin yang guai qi" is of great significance and has a wide application prospect.

First of all, in this period of booming artificial intelligence, people have frequent interactions with artificial intelligence robots and intelligent voice assistants. However, the wrong understanding of the meaning of the "yin yang guai qi" sentences may lead to a lot of misunderstandings and inconvenient situations. For example, when a person says "you're right" in a "yin yang guai qi" tone, what it really means is "I don't agree with you, but I'm not going to argue with you. Say what you like." But the AI will most likely misinterpret it as "He confirms my opinion." Especially in special applications, such as artificial intelligence customer service, where its interaction with people is very important, misinterpretation of the conversation can have troublesome consequences. Therefore, the identification and recognition of "yin yang guai qi" intonation can be applied to the AI, so that the AI can better understand what humans want to say, and make it easier for people to use them.

Further, we can improve the speech system of artificial intelligence based on this, adding "yin yang guai qi" tones to make the speech of artificial intelligence more anthropomorphic and interesting. Compared with text, voice is very convenient. For example, when using navigation driving, people hope that the navigation voice will broadcast the driving route, instead of reading text themselves. We want to hear something close to a human voice, rather than an overtly blunt synthetic one. At present, the speech system of artificial intelligence has made great progress. Based on this, adding a "yin yang guai qi" tone is a meaningful move to make AI more anthropomorphic, making it more comfortable and even fun to listen to. For example, applying this tone to some toys is quite a good choice.

4.3 Limitations and Future Work

The overall research procedure of this article is complete, but somewhat rough. So there are some limitations that needs to be improved.

First of all, this study selected some "yin yang guai qi" videos and poetry reading as the experimental group and the control group. The number of samples is small, which does not have strong objectivity. And the samples were not very rigorously processed. Moreover, compared with normal communication in daily life, poetry reading is too standard, whether in pronunciation or emotion, which may have a certain influence on the experimental results. Therefore, there should be some improvement in sample selection, and field experiments can be added to enhance experimental accuracy.

Second, the algorithm chosen in this paper is very simple, which is not very practical and can only be used as a preliminary judgment. Therefore, the future research can focus on improving the algorithm. Thirdly, the research on "yin yang guai qi" can be further studied. For example, we can further analyze and explore this tone and try to develop some applications. Finally, as mentioned above, "yin yang guai qi" may not only appear in China, but also have the same or similar tone in other countries. More exploration can be made in this aspect.

To sum up, this paper has achieved a preliminary exploration of "yin yang guai qi", and found that "yin yang guai qi" does exist and has made a preliminary identification of it. In fact, as a new trend of tone, there is no accepted accurate definition of "yin yang guai qi". Although this paper starts from the intonation aspect of "yin yang guai qi", it may not only be a tone, but also represent some very rich emotions. And we are surprised to see that "yin yang guai qi" is evolving into a cultural form, as opposed to ironic tones (or moods) and so on, which are very similar to it. One of the most striking evidence of this is the creation of special "yin yang guai qi" phrases, such as "Is that all?", "Oh No, Oh No." etc. This is a very interesting phenomenon. So, what does "yin yang guai qi" represent on earth? And what more abundant and meaningful application value it has? It is worth discussing.

References

1. Chen, S., Zhi, X.: What's the meme that's trending all over the Internet about 'yin yang guai qi' literature. Cultural Ind. Rev. 3308 (2021)
2. Attardo, S., Eisterhold, J., Hay, J., Poggi, I.: Multimodal markers of irony and sarcasm. Humor: Int. J. Humor Res. **16**(2), 243–260 (2003)
3. Bryant, G., Fox Tree, J.: Recognizing verbal irony in spontaneous speech. Metaphor. Symb. **17**(2), 99–117 (2002)
4. Sarsam, S.M., Al-Samarraie, H., Alzahrani, A.I., Wright, B.: Sarcasm detection using machine learning algorithms in Twitter: a systematic review. Int. J. Mark. Res. **62**(5), 578–598 (2020)
5. Karthik, E., Sethukarasi, T.: Sarcastic user behavior classification and prediction from social media data using firebug swarm optimization-based long short-term memory. J. Supercomput. **78**(4), 5333–5357 (2021)
6. Capelli, C.A., Nakagawa, N., Madden, C.M.: How children understand sarcasm: the role of context and intonation. Child Dev. (61), 1824–1841 (1990)
7. Cheang, H.S., Pell, M.D.: The sound of sarcasm. Speech Commun. **50**(5), 366–381 (2008)
8. Cutler, A.: On saying what you mean without meaning what you say. In: LaGaly, M.W., Fox, R.A., Bruck, A. (Eds.) Chicago Linguistic Society, Chicago, pp. 117–127 (1974)
9. Cutler, A.: Beyond parsing and lexical look-up: an enriched description of auditory sentence comprehension. New approaches to language mechanisms: A collection of psycholinguistic studies, pp. 133–149 (1976)
10. Loevenbruck, H., Jannet, M.B., d'Imperio, M., Spini, M., ChampagneLavau, M.: Prosodic cues of sarcastic speech in French: slower, higher, wider. In: Interspeech 2013 - 14th Annual Conference of the International Speech Communication Association, Lyon, France, August 2013
11. Wang, X.G., Zhu, J.W., Zhang, A.X.: Identification method of voice print identity based on MFCC feature. Comput. Sci. **48**(12), 343–348 (2021)
12. Emilia, G., Perfecto, H.: The song remains the same: identifying versions of the same piece using tonal descriptors. 180–185 (2006)
13. Zhang, X., Li, N.Z., Li, W.: Robustness verification of Chroma feature. Comput. Sci. **41**(S1), 24–28 (2014)

Author Index

Printed in the United States
by Baker & Taylor Publisher Services